RF

IVOR
The Story of an Achievement

By the same author:

THEATRE ROYAL DRURY LANE

HAYMARKET: THEATRE OF PERFECTION

GAIETY: THEATRE OF ENCHANTMENT

THE MELODIES LINGER ON: THE STORY OF MUSIC HALL

CARRIAGES AT ELEVEN

TWENTY SHILLINGS IN THE POUND

AN INDISCREET GUIDE TO THEATRELAND

GHOSTS AND GREASEPAINT

Sketch of Ivor made from life by K. Guthrie

Frontispiece

IVOR

by

W. MACQUEEN-POPE

The Story of an Achievement

A BIOGRAPHY OF IVOR NOVELLO

W. H. ALLEN
LONDON
1951

Made and printed in Great Britain by
The Alcuin Press, Welwyn Garden City
for the publishers
Messrs. W. H. Allen & Co. Ltd., 43 Essex St.
London

To That Vast Multitude of People
who found Joy and Pleasure in the Plays,
the Acting, the Music and the Personality of
IVOR NOVELLO
who, whether he knew them personally or not,
he always regarded as
His Best Friends.

ACKNOWLEDGMENTS

My Most Grateful Thanks are due, for their great aid in enabling me to compile this book, to Sir Edward Marsh, Constance Collier, Lily Elsie, Jean Webster Brough, Lady Juliet Duff, Mary Ellis, Henry Kendall, Keneth Kent, Dorothea Sims, Tom Arnold, Douglas Moodie, Leslie Cahn-Rein, Gordon Duttson, Victor Boggetti and many other friends—to Olive Gilbert and The Rev. Meredith Davies and especially to my old and valued colleague and friend, Frederick W. Allen, who has been tireless in assisting. I wish to pay tribute to them all for their willing and unselfish help.

CONTENTS

CHAPTER		PAGE
	Apology for Intrusion	13
One	ENTRANCE	29
Two	THE PUPIL'S PROGRESS	46
Three	GROWING PAINS	64
Four	THE GOLDEN KEY	81
Five	MINSTREL BOY	99
Six	THE STAGE DOOR OPENS	116
Seven	THE BOYS COME HOME	133
Eight	PEACE, FILMS, AND GREASEPAINT	150
Nine	PILGRIM'S PROGRESS	167
Ten	HOW NOW—A RAT?	184
Eleven	ALMOST AT THE TOP	200
Twelve	FILM SUCCESSES: BUT BACK TO THE THEATRE	217
Thirteen	STORM, STRESS—AND AMERICA!	235
Fourteen	HOLLYWOOD HEARTACHE	253
Fifteen	THE GREAT YEARS BEGIN	270
Sixteen	STAGE, FILMS AND DOMESTIC STORMS	286
Seventeen	ON WINGS OF SONG	305
Eighteen	KING IVOR OF OLD DRURY	324
Nineteen	A FAMOUS VICTORY	343
Twenty	THE HAT TRICK	360
Twenty-one	THE DANCING YEARS—AND WHAT THEY LED TO	380
Twenty-two	RETROSPECT—BEFORE THE STORM BREAKS	397
Twenty-three	TRIAL AND ERROR	415
Twenty-four	INTO THE DEPTHS	432

(*continued over*)

CONTENTS

CHAPTER		PAGE
Twenty-five	UP TO THE HEIGHTS	448
Twenty-six	TOWARDS THE END	465
Twenty-seven	LAST ACT	482
Twenty-eight	DE MORTUIS . . .	495
Twenty-nine	PÈRSONAL TRIBUTE—AND ASSESSMENT	509
Thirty	EXIT	528
	INDEX OF NAMES	533
	INDEX OF PLAYS, FILMS AND SONGS	545

ILLUSTRATIONS

FACING PAGE

Frontispiece: sketch of Ivor made from life by K. Guthrie

Family group—Mother, baby Ivor and grandfather 32

Ivor, a few weeks old; Ivor and his mother 33

Early picture of " Mam "; Ivor aged about twenty 48

Ivor bids farewell to " Mam " at Croydon aerodrome; Ivor with his parents 49

Ivor in his twenties; Ivor and Robert Andrews 80

Five pages of snapshots from Ivor's private album 81, 96, 97, 128, 129

Ivor in the R.N.A.S., during World War I 144

Ivor's career as an airman 145

Studies of Ivor over thirty years 176

Bea Lillie, Anthony Eden and Ivor aboard the " Queen Elizabeth "; picnic party including Lily Elsie and Viola Tree; portrait of D. W. Griffith, inscribed " to Ivor Novello." 177

With Olive Gilbert in *Perchance to Dream*; Ivor as a girl in amateur theatricals; with Diana Wynyard in a war-front performance of *Love from a Stranger* 192

Crowds at the stage door, Queen's Theatre; Ivor in his dressing-room; with Lady Kelly and the Marchioness of Headfort at a literary luncheon 193

Ivor in *Symphony in Two Flats*; Edna Best, Robert Andrews, Zena Dare and Fay Compton in Ivor's dressing-room at the Globe Theatre 224

Studies of Ivor, Dorothy Dickson and Walter Crisham from *Careless Rapture* 225

Three studies of Ivor, with Isabel Jeans and Vivien Leigh, from *Happy Hypocrite* 240

With Thea Holme in *Flies in the Sun*; film role in *Bonnie Prince Charlie*; with Lily Elsie in *The Truth Game* 241

Party at Ivor's Jamaican house; with Fred Allen at " Redroofs "; Robert Andrews, Ivor, Lord Beaverbrook and Beatrice Lillie in Jamaica 272

Ivor and Fay Compton in scenes from *Proscenium* 273

(continued over)

ILLUSTRATIONS

Two studies of Ivor in *Perchance to Dream*; Ivor and Vanessa Lee after her success on the first night of *King's Rhapsody* 288

Ivor in the title role of *Henry V;* with Roma Beaumont in *The Dancing Years*; Ivor with Madge Titheradge in *Deburau*; Ivor in *The Firebrand* 289

The Rose Ballet from *Careless Rapture* 320

Ivor in *Careless Rapture*, *Old Heidelberg* and *The White Rose* 321

Ivor in *The Dancing Years*; a scene from the play 336

A scene and two studies from *King's Rhapsody* 337

Stage set for *Glamorous Night* 368

Original Manuscript of " My Heart Belongs to You " 369

Twelve views of interiors at " Redroofs " and at Ivor's Aldwych flat 384, 385, 416, 417

Original manuscript of " I Can Give You the Starlight " 432

View of " Redroofs "; the last snapshot, taken the day before Ivor's death 433

Exit 434

Photos supplied by: Foulsham & Bamfield; Keystone Press; Humphrey and Vera Joel; Alexander Bender; Central Press; Angus McBean; Stage Photo Co.; J. Beagles; Sasha; Dorothy Wilding; W. Gordon Davis; Landseer of London; Gerald Murison; Paul Tanqueray.

Apology for Intrusion

WHEN I was meditating how to begin this book, the way was shown to me by a woman on a 'bus. I was not, at that time, altogether sure that I should undertake the task, for much of the ground I must traverse had already been covered by somebody else. As a rule, I take quick decisions, but this time I was hesitant. My friends, my publisher and my wife were all pressing me to do it. Still I was undecided. Then, in the oddest manner, guidance came. . . .

My wife and I were going out to lunch one Sunday, as we always do in these days of shortage. We caught the 'bus, as usual, which takes us to the hospitable country pub where we have lunched for a good many years now. We have no car in these hard times, but the 'bus serves perfectly. Across the gangway a man and women were sitting—ordinary middle-class folk like ourselves. My mind was full of the problem of this book, but the lady in question had a rather loud and clear voice and one could not help overhearing the conversation. She and her friend—it emerged that the gentleman was not her husband—were discussing books. She liked biographies, she said. It interested her to read about famous people, about extraordinary characters, eccentric or celebrated. " I wonder," she said, " if there are people to-day who are as great characters, whose stories are as interesting, as some of those of the old days? " That, for me, was enough. I knew then I must write the book—for the subject of it is as great as anyone who ever trod the stage of this kingdom, be they who they may. In a flash my mind was made up. And then, by the strangest of coincidences, came complete confirmation. No answer came to the lady's query about the great ones. But, after a slight pause, she supplied it herself, for the next remark she made was " Did you go to Ivor Novello's funeral service? " So far as I was concerned, nothing more was needed. Of course, I must write the book. Here obviously was one of the many people who wanted to know all about Ivor Novello. She talked on. She had not been to the service herself but had heard it on the radio and she was particularly pleased with the way Lyn Harding had read the Lesson. She remembered him in his acting days, she said. The conversation flowed on. Both had seen *King's Rhapsody* The man had seen the understudy play, but the lady had seen Ivor—that was what she called him—on the very night before he was taken ill and went away to have an operation. She remembered how long he was away. She was full of delight about the Dares, Zena and Phyllis. Both she and her companion had thoroughly enjoyed themselves. . . .

My doubts about writing the book were not only resolved, but I knew also that the tentative title I had in mind was the right one. That good lady, a middle-aged, middle-class woman, had never spoken to Ivor Novello, she had seen him only on the stage, but she went to all his plays—not once but several times—and she called him Ivor. Of course she did. So did everyone. It was not possible to call him anything else. Ivor, then, was the only possible title for this book. If the volume should chance to meet the eye of my unknown inspirer, perhaps she will remember the journey to that little Hertfordshire hotel, on the verge of the woodlands, one Sunday morning in April, 1951, and recall what she said. I hereby tender to her my sincere thanks. . . .

But before I begin to relate the story of Ivor, a word of explanation is necessary. It is not my habit, when writing my books, to allow myself to intrude upon them. Nobody cares about me; I am a person of no importance. The subject about which I write, the people I describe—they alone are important. The tale is what matters, not the teller thereof. There is one book which I doubt I shall ever write, although one of my publishers has included it in the contract which exists between us. That book is my own autobiography. I don't believe in them. You can never really tell the truth about yourself, because you don't know it. It is much better to leave it to somebody else. And nobody else would ever trouble to write a book about me. To reach such eminence, I should have to commit some very considerable crime, for I can visualize no other way of attaining notoriety. And I am not in the least criminal minded. So I shall continue to write about other people and other things, of theatres, plays and players, of social conditions in this country of ours, which I know and love—and all the time shall continue to keep myself well out of sight. As it is, I get what is known to-day as " fan mail." To the writers of these letters—they must like my books, or they would not write—I am most grateful. In one such letter, the other day, a man wrote, "I like your books much better than the autobiographies of some actors and actresses which I have read. They are so busy telling us about the peers and the royal personages whom they have met. I do not want to know about that—I want to know what they, themselves, were like." I heartily agree with that view. And recently, when I had delivered a lecture, a gentleman quite unknown to me got up and said that what he liked best about all my books was that I never appeared in them! I could not agree more.

But that is why I write this foreword of apology. For, to do this book at all properly—and I have not the gift to do the subject full justice, I fear—I must myself make fleeting appearances. You see, I knew Ivor so well and so long. We worked so closely together. I had assisted in my little way at his greatest triumphs. I stood by and did my bit in his times of stress, especially in the time of his greatest need and dire difficulty. I must tell you what I know of him at first hand, as seen through my own eyes, in dressing rooms, in theatres in London and the provinces, on stages, at first nights and last nights, at rehearsals and in all the glorious excitement and throbbing anxiety of dress rehearsals—almost always in the Theatre.

For the Theatre was Ivor's life. To him it was the only reality he knew. All else was illusion—that busy workaday life of the streets, the mundane things touched him not at all. Actually his life held two great realities—the Theatre and his audience—and, to him, they were both the same thing. How he knew them and how he loved them both! No one in the Theatre was more audience-conscious than Ivor. I say that with the authority of one who has worked with all the great people of the Theatre for the past fifty years and more. Many of them understood their public and knew how to handle them—but none had that same complete absorption in them or the complete understanding of them that Ivor had. It was one of the main factors in making him what we call "No. 1 Box Office." For, at the time of his death, and for many years before, that was what he was. There was no one in our Theatre who could draw the public as could Ivor. To say he did it without effort is wrong. It was not only his handsome face, his wonderful charm—those were the apparent things, but they were the lesser reasons. It was his great capacity for taking pains to please, his complete understanding of what audiences wanted—what, indeed, the majority of the British people wanted—and his uncanny ability to give it to them, not now and again but almost always. He was able to do this because he had never lost touch with them. He himself, when young, sat in theatres and adored what he saw. He never forgot any of it. He always recalled the things which had thrilled him in the days when he was on the audience side of the footlights. He was a most observant man, he knew the value of detail. So many people, when they become important, leave the details to others—Ivor never did. He had that in common with other great people I have known. When he became a composer and, later, when he became an actor, he always regarded his days as looker-on as his formative period. He was, to the end, sitting out there with an audience; one of them, feeling and experiencing all they felt. He never for one moment under-estimated public taste. And he knew, for he was in many ways a shrewd judge of public taste—a much better judge of taste than of people—that there are certain things, to which they always respond. No matter how the way of life may change, those fundamental things never alter. He knew them, and in all of his plays, straight or musical, he capitalized them. And they never failed his audience—or him.

He had his roots in that generation of our people who lived before World War the First. He knew the Theatre of those days—and he knew its players. It was that Theatre, and those people and their methods which he esteemed and which he adopted as his own. The stars of his youth were the stars of his life and if he could get them into his plays with him, then he knew real happiness. How he adored Lily Elsie—and how right he was to do so—and how proud he was when she became his leading lady and saved his show. How he worshipped Lilian Braithwaite—and how he loved to write parts for her—and how superbly well he did it. How happy he was when he had his beloved Zena Dare with him in a show. His cup of happiness brimmed over when both Zena and Phyllis Dare were with him in *King's Rhapsody*. His admiration for the players of that generation in which the actor-managers were in power was immense. And, naturally, he admired most those players who had grown up beside him and whose roots and early training were, like his, embedded in that great age of Quality. Fay Compton, Gladys Cooper, Edna Best, Marie Lohr, Viola Tree, Billie Burke, Gertie Millar, Madge Titheradge, Marie Tempest, Julia Neilson—many, many more—he would go starry-eyed about them. They stood for what he regarded as perfection. And there was perhaps a special adoration for Constance Collier.

The respect which he showed to the grand old men of his profession would be an object lesson to the young players of to-day. He treated them with veneration. To him Cyril Maude was Royalty of the Theatre and he behaved accordingly. He never tired of hearing about them. He would ask me questions and listen by the hour. We travelled up to Leeds together when *Crest of the Wave* opened there from Drury Lane, and all the way he questioned me and listened to my stories of Yesterday. I am difficult to stop when I start to become reminiscent. Sometimes I fear I may bore people. But not Ivor. To him, it was manna from Heaven. One story was not finished when we arrived at Leeds. Directly he saw me after the show at night, he demanded the completion—and got it.

I recall pleasing him vastly on one occasion. I told him I had known only two people who had the supreme gift of living in the past but being acutely aware of the present—Sir Herbert Tree and himself. I have never seen him more delighted. And it was true of Ivor Novello. That was how he lived. Tree had said, " The whole duty of the Theatre is illusion." Ivor lived up to that maxim. But neither he nor Tree ever forgot the people to whom they purveyed that illusion, and, of the two, Ivor had the keenest and closest perception. When he had reached the highest pinnacle of fame he never lost the common touch. He did not know what it was to be aloof. He remained always a man of the British middle class—and there is nothing better than that in the world. He was not of that somewhat hazy and remote stratum—if it ever really existed—which used to be known as the " upper middle class." He was just, in himself, middle class. That was his sphere and there he remained. He met the mighty ones on equal terms, but he still remained one of the people.

On one occasion, during rehearsals of *Crest of the Wave*, I watched the ballet rehearsing. They were using the Adelphi Theatre because the stage at Drury Lane was needed for scenic rehearsals. It was not far from production date. The Adelphi was being repainted, and tempers, usually a bit uncertain at the near-production period, were not improved by the overpowering smell of paint. The gentleman who was in charge of the choreography (he has now attained eminence) was not at that time as experienced as he is now. Ivor had chosen him because he always wanted to help youth. But the choreographer had not really got in his mind what he wanted to do, and the girls knew it. They were cross, uncertain and tired. They were snappy and inclined to answer back. And there were some caustic exchanges and not a little temperament. " Now, duckies," pleaded the ballet master, " don't create. Be good girls, duckies, don't create." I went back and told Ivor. He loved it. " That's my language," he said, " don't create! That's the right way to speak." But he knew what to do. He got things happy and smooth in no time. The young gentleman retired and the one and only Sokolova came in. What was " created " was beauty. But it became a little catch-phrase between us. Whenever we saw trouble looming, we would whisper, one to the other, " Now, duckie, don't create ! "

How Ivor adored beauty. To him it meant everything. Sokolova showed him what she wanted. There was a mazurka to be danced. Everyone was on the stage at Drury Lane and Lydia Sokolova " walked " that dance to show them what she wanted. I say she walked it. It was pure poetry of movement. Ivor was in the stalls, and when she finished she turned to face him. But he was not there—he was on his way up to the stage. He stood in front of her and before the assembled company he said, " At last—an ambition realized. I have seen Sokolova dance to my music. I did not know before what I had achieved." " I only walked it, Ivor," said Sokolova. " You were my poor music, expressed as I should have liked to have written it," he said, kissing her hand. He meant it, too. That was the sort of thing Ivor did, quite naturally. He was just expressing the audience's point of view, which was also and always his. Eventually the mazurka was danced magnificently by Dorothy Dickson and Walter Crisham.

Ivor never left his public behind him. When he was right at the top, they were there, too. For nobody was ever less of a snob. He never condemned anything on the score that it was " common." He did not know what was meant by that. A thing might be in bad taste, certainly, but that did not imply it was "common." His only standard was quality; he would have nothing which, in achievement or texture, was second rate. Nor had he any time for sophistication. His was not the world of white ties, boiled shirts and exotic gowns. Mink was beautiful, but he did not rank the wearer one jot higher than the lady in the apron who carried the shopping basket. That was the secret of his appeal. He was even more popular in the pit, gallery and upper circle than in the stalls, dress circle and boxes. The former were, basically, his people: he understood them; they understood him.

He had never grown up. He was always about seventeen, possessing the enthusiasm of youth and the belief in to-morrow. He believed in creating illusion, in shutting out the grey, worrying world, and taking people into the Land of Make Believe where he showed them life as they would like it to be. He believed in romance because he was a true Romantic. He believed in sentiment though not in sentimentality. Very, very seldom did his plays end in conventional happiness. But always, at the end, there was hope, there was memory, there was to-morrow. He paid tribute to life by allowing lovers to be parted; but then, the lights dimmed on their sorrow, a blue haze of hope filled the stage and there—in a vision, a vision which had its reality in the hearts of the star-crossed couple—those lovers came together, in a self-made world of romance, clasped in each other's arms, dancing, dancing to the sweep of strings and the throb of violins, secure in the knowledge that their love was their own and enduring. And the audience went mad with delight and left the theatre, moist-eyed but happy. For of all things he hated unhappiness. He hated to feel it himself and to see it in others. He never denied tragedy, he never shut his eyes to sorrow, but he regarded it as something to fight and conquer—and that he always managed to do.

He wanted to see smiles: not forced smiles, but the smiles which came from happy hearts. And he saw to it that he was surrounded by happiness. He radiated it. He made happiness for those who worked with him, those who were near him. He made happiness for the uncountable myriads who saw his plays and heard his music. He could not bear suffering, he could not bear pain. Mercifully, he knew little of either. The end came in time. And that end, sudden and tragic as it was, averted a tragedy worse than his death. He might have lingered, unable to work and, therefore, unable to live. Instead he went out on the crest of his own wave.

He had his limitations, but in the main he was aware of them. He had his faults and he was aware of some. He had an immense sense of gratitude, but he never at any time took his success for granted. He had to earn it and worked hard to the very end. He left absolutely nothing to chance. He never said, "That will be good enough. They will take that from me." It had to be his best. Nor did he ever become bitter. When he was plunged down from the heights into the very depths of what, to a lesser spirit, might have been degradation and ruin, though it left its mark, it didn't leave him one whit the harder or with a trace of bitterness towards anyone. And believe me, there was good cause. I mean when he served that harsh sentence which was pronounced against him. He took it in his stride. He, who led a life remote from reality, faced the most sordid experience that the world can offer and came through unscathed. I was with him through all that. I know all about it and I shall tell of it in the right place. It might have been his end; it might have altered everything. If it had an effect—and it did undoubtedly—it only served to mellow his kindliness to others, to get a deeper note into his music and his work. When it was over, he never mentioned it again. Nor did any of us. It robbed him of what he might have attained, for his name should have had the addition of three letters. If any man in the Theatre deserved that, Ivor did. But it never robbed him of the kingdom where he reigned and which he loved most—the kingdom in the hearts of his admirers.

He stood up to that test because there were two Ivor Novellos. At least, there were two men in that one person. There was David Ivor Davies, the dark-eyed handsome youth from Wales, and there was Ivor Novello, whom the public knew and adored and whom David Ivor Davies created. That creation was one of his major successes. So complete did it become that it was almost impossible to say where one finished and the other began, but I was always conscious of the two and knew and admired them both. For each had something which the other lacked. It was Ivor Novello who trod the stage, who evoked the gasps of admiration, who could charm a bird off a bough, whose smile was like a sunrise and whose tact and courtesy was that of a prince. It was Ivor Novello who made the world around him gay and who became so entirely a part of the fabric of our Theatre. But it was David Ivor Davies who always told Ivor Novello what to do, who was his guide and friend, who kept him true to himself and to the people whom he loved and who loved him, who kept the slightest semblance of conceit or snobbery not merely at arm's length but quite out of mind. And it was David Ivor Davies, too, who had the really great gift—the gift that will live—for David Ivor Davies wrote the music.

In Ivor, Wales was deeply embedded. Not so much in Ivor Novello, who was or could be international, but in the boy from Cardiff with the Welsh name. The Welshman—with the good yeoman stock from the very land of his fathers—that stock which had farmed, worked and sung as Welshmen can—always triumphed over that somewhat exotic creation Ivor Novello. It was not from his mother alone that he derived that gift of melody, that flair for audience control. It went further back, as will be shown later. Do not, for one moment, imagine that I belittle his mother's great gifts or the talent she passed on to her son. Ivor was born into a world of music, but music was also in his blood and his bones. Heredity is the strongest force in the world whatever the scoffers may say.

Ivor was the perfect son. " Mam "—as he and most people who knew her well called her—was at times something of a handful. She was a genius and geniuses are tricky folk with whom to deal. But he adored her and he understood her. There is nothing to add to that. At times he even had to put the curb on her and know that he was doing so. He did it with the velvet glove. But he did it, nevertheless. He only loved her the more, for all her peculiarities. He understood. What he felt about her he expressed, very beautifully, in a broadcast programme not very long before he died. And he showed the great love he had for his father, too. No son in this world had ever more cause to be prouder of his parents than David Ivor Davies.

Yet, what he did, what he achieved, he did by himself. He had no money behind him. He had no great influence in the Theatre. His mother, famous as she was in her own sphere, fought against his desire to be of the Theatre; to her his music was all. In the main, she was right, for it is his music which will live. But that music became immortal because it had behind it the sounding board of the Theatre—the best in the world. And that vast success in the Theatre was Ivor's own creation.

Ivor Novello, who was actually born on January 15th, 1927, when David Ivor Davies took that name by deed poll, might have been a cosmopolitan and international figure. Indeed, he was. But it was David Ivor Davies who kept him purely British, who saw to it that the melodies which poured in an unbroken, flowing stream, were of this soil and untouched by transatlantic rhythm or negroid dissonance. Vienna might be there; but it was the Vienna which we had, in our national way, made our own. Fundamentally, his music was purely British. And so was he. He was thrilled by Hollywood, and he managed to thrill Hollywood too. But none of that ever touched him. He remained just the same in Hollywood as he was in London, never becoming infected by his surroundings. He could have lived there all his life and there would have been no trace of American accent. That good Welsh blood was too strong for that. He was too decided a personality. He became the friend of the stars and they adored him. But perhaps it was what they could do rather than what they were themselves which attracted him the most. He never forgot those who showed him kindness when he first arrived there, a rather lonely young exile. And of them all he placed Garbo in a class apart. That she wanted to be alone was nothing to him . . . for it was something which he understood in her but could not bear in himself.

Ivor never wanted to be alone. He hated it. He must be surrounded, there must be perpetual coming and going; his dressing-room, the sanctuary of so many, was more like Waterloo Station on a Bank Holiday than the dressing-room of a star. Only between the matinée and the evening show, when he had his sleep—and he had that daily—did a notice go up on the door: " Do Not Disturb." Otherwise everyone walked in and out. It was the same at his flat; the same at " Redroofs," his country house. There he would go for week-ends, but there was always company. Not that the company was idle; there was never a moment to be wasted, there was never a moment when that creative mind could lie fallow. It might be that they were all commanded to paint pictures—and he could paint with no small talent. It might be music, or it might be cards—

he adored Canasta most of all. But there must always be mass activity, something doing. Yet, in the midst, he would steal away for maybe an hour, and return with no explanation. That grew more frequent in his last days. There was no explanation: he just went—he came back. And the party went on.

His car was always full of people, and he seldom, if ever, travelled alone. When *King's Rhapsody* went to Manchester for its pre-London try-out, it was the hottest day of the hottest summer for years. Ivor could have gone in comfort in his Rolls. Did he do so? No. He went by train, a crowded, sweaty, steaming train which was like a furnace. Why? Because everyone else was there—there was a crowd. They could talk about the show; they could talk Theatre. When he got his estate in Jamaica and went there for his rare holidays, to bask in the sun he adored, to bathe in the sea—swimming was the only exercise he cared about and of sport he knew nothing and cared less—did he seek the tropical solitude to let inspiration break into his mind? Not a bit. He went with a mob of friends and never let them out of his sight. He could not be alone. But Garbo was a goddess to him. It was her Art he worshipped. To him, she was near perfection in the world of the screen. And perfection was something he idolized. He felt the same for Flagstadt in music and opera. Both these great people, the film star and operatic diva, returned his admiration. It was like calling to like. Flagstadt would sing to him and his friends, at his flat on the roof of the Strand Theatre, little concerts which kings could not buy.

But he remained British to the core. He admired the American musical shows and thought *Oklahoma* a joy, but he never bent the knee nor varied from his own truly home-made technique. He, and he alone, stood rocklike against the flowing tide of American musicals sweeping over this country and towered above it. Americans did not understand his shows or what he was driving at, although he understood theirs. A great friend of mine, a most distinguished American lady, who possesses both riches and good taste, went to see *King's Rhapsody*. I asked her what she thought. "I admire your Ivor Novello," she said, "he's great. He's unique. But don't let him bring it to Broadway. It's just hokum." A very erudite and cultured man of my acquaintance, who is a keen student of the Theatre, but who had never seen an Ivor musical play before, went to see it, too. I had expressed no opinion about the show at all as I wanted his plain reaction. The day after his visit he came to my office. He looked at me curiously. "That's a wonderful production," he said. "What scenery, what dresses, what talent! This Ivor Novello is an amazing man. But it only makes me realize that I'll never understand you British. Back home that show wouldn't run a week."

Ivor had successes in New York with his straight plays, but none of his musical plays had ever gone there, on stage or screen. He was planning to take *King's Rhapsody* there after its London run. I never stopped trying to dissuade him, but I don't think I should have succeeded. As it is, I am glad he never went. He was for us; he stood four square for what we British liked and understood. The American mind is different. Though it thinks it is quicker, it is not. It has little time for Ruritania or the love affairs of kings and queens; it is robustly Republican and still rates all kings on the level of poor old George III, who was not even sane all the time. Not that Ivor wrote many Ruritanian shows, although the critics are firmly convinced that he did. He wrote only two, *Glamorous Night* and *King's Rhapsody*—admittedly, two of the best. *Careless Rapture* was about London and China, *Crest of the Wave* about impoverished noblemen, ancestral homes and Hollywood, *The Dancing Years* was Vienna pure and simple, *Arc de Triomphe* was Paris, *Perchance to Dream* came down the English years from Regency times to to-day. Yet the idea persists that his shows were Ruritanian. He even guyed it himself in the only musical comedy—as such—he ever wrote and composed. That was *Gay's the Word*, written for Cicely Courtneidge, for whose consummate art he had the greatest affection and regard. She, too, had her roots in the great days of his youth. So he wrote a British musical comedy without a trace of Americanism in word or music, and scored a vast triumph.

He went to the first night of *Gay's the Word* when he should have been in bed. He had a temperature, but who could deny him? He wanted to see one of his own first nights from the front, never having seen one of his own musicals under such conditions; he was always either in them or engaged in another. He had not seen a first night of his own since 1933—and that was *Fresh Fields*—eighteen years before. In the afternoon he rang me up, for it had been my job for many, many years to look after his publicity. "Popie," he said, "don't think I'm being shee-shee. It's not that; but be a good boy and keep the reporters and cameramen away from me to-night. Really, I don't feel like it." I promised and I kept my word. At the performance he coughed badly all the time.

It was an easy job to get publicity for Ivor, because he was always news, but the true publicity man must know the difference between good and bad publicity. For, despite Barnum's dictum, all publicity is not good. In those matters, Ivor always did as he was told. Only twice did he go against me—and both times he found he was wrong—and said so. I did not want him to go at all to that first night but I had not the heart to dissuade him. I am so glad now I never tried. He saw his final triumph. He saw what he had made, a real British show, acclaimed to the echo and he saw Cicely Courtneidge make the success of her life—which contains so many successes. She would be the first to give him credit.

Ivor had that gift which of all others only George Edwardes had equally: the gift of making shows to fit the people and not fitting people into shows, of giving them parts which were like their skins and never showed a wrinkle, and of giving them just those things to do in which they most excelled—and leaving out the rest. Ivor knew all about that. He knew all about construction and timing. Those are the fundamentals of success in the Theatre. He never let a mood run for a fraction of a second too long, knowing just when to break the tension, a fragment of time before the audience was aware of it. . . .

But I set out to apologize for my own intrusion and I must go back to that theme, or this book will never take form and shape. Let me say my little piece and then get back into the shadows where I belong, only appearing when absolutely necessary.

What I hope to achieve is not a life story of Ivor Novello. That has already been written with Ivor's own approval. I do not propose to spend too much time on his youthful days for so much has already been said about them. Most people, too, know about his education. How Ivor loved Oxford and how he would light up at the memory of that choir at Magdalen in which he sang! Oxford to him was the ideal place: there the present and past walked hand in hand. Nor shall I worry much about his film career. It was never really a great part of him, more of a lane through which he wandered and from which he learnt. What I really want to tell you about is Ivor and the Theatre. The two things were one and the same. He lived for and by the Theatre: to him it was the only real world. He always wanted to be of it. He always wanted to act. Indeed, he had always, at the back of his own mind, a greater admiration for Ivor the actor than Ivor the composer. Well, there was room for both.

I knew him well. I held him in the greatest admiration, affection and respect, and I am sure he had much the same feeling for me. We were friends. But I was never of the Inner Court, as it were. I did not want to be. I did not fit in. To Ivor I was just part of his life in the Theatre and he was that to me. I did not go to the parties, nor down to "Redroofs" to stay. If I went to the flat in Aldwych, it was to talk business and discuss plans. I had my own life, my own wife and family, even to grandchildren; my own interests; my own business to run. Where Ivor and I met was on the common ground of the Theatre, which was the great thing in both our lives. That was our bond and it was an unbreakable one. So I shall not tell you of that social life of his, a very small and circumscribed one. He never went into " Society " as do so many theatrical people to-day, for he did not like it and was more at home with folk of his own origin. He never sought the company of titled folk, nor craved the high seats at public functions. He had his own circle, his own Court who were faithful servants of King Ivor, and it sufficed him. And I don't think he ever had a more faithful servant than I, although I usually stood a bit outside. I was the man who had to look on, appraise and value. I was the man who had to tell the world. So I, in turn, had to know my man and all about him. And I believe I did. I propose to deal mainly with his achievement in the Theatre—and that was his real life. I shall bring him into it in 1915, when things were pretty fluid, when old orders were going and standards falling beneath the shocks of war.

I shall show his entrance through that breach he made in the wall by his song " Keep the Home Fires Burning." That was his first real step. That was what made his name known. I shall then show his fight—for fight it was—to climb that greasy pole of theatreland and show also the background against which he climbed, that changing tapestry of the Theatre which altered its ways from 1915 to 1918 and onwards and became so mean and thin during the inter-war years, but into which he went, always with his ideal before him that Only The Best Would Do. Charles Morton, who had the same motto, created a very British institution called Music Hall. And Ivor adored Music Hall; it was unsophisticated and down-to-earth, as he was himself. What had been the Music Hall public became his public too, because he gave them British fare, and the best only. He himself was as efficient as Music Hall and that was very efficient indeed.

I shall show him always climbing against the backcloth of plays and the people, always giving value instead of mediocrity, never believing anything would " do " unless it passed his acid test, and that was his own memory of an audience and what he himself liked. I shall try to show his keen watching of himself, his own self-appraisement and how he anticipated, with forethought, the passing of his own youth. That wonderful profile had its drawbacks as well as its advantages. And I shall take him to my beloved Theatre Royal, Drury Lane, where our lives did truly mix and join (I won't use the word " career " in my case), and where I did my little, humble share of placing the crown on his head which he wore so fittingly and becomingly. And from there we shall proceed through the rest of his Theatre saga.

I shall not only tell of his virtues but of his faults. You must allow the shadows to bring up the highlights. I hope to show you what sort of a man this was, how he worked and laid bare his secrets, the secrets of his success and his failure—for there was failure, too. All through his last and greatest years, we went together. During that time he had only two flops and one was not his own fault. The other was, but it was so well-intentioned that it hardly matters. He let his heart rule his head, he let his overwhelming love for the Theatre run away with him and he had not his usual people around him. But it matters little for it is hardly remembered at all.

If you want to read about this man who did so much for our Theatre, who did so much for us all, who brought joy to so many and sorrow to nobody, whose only real enemy was himself, then read on. I shall tell all I know, though others will speak with me as I shall call witnesses to bear out what I say. But you will have to see it through my eyes, and, believe me, they are experienced eyes which have seen much and have observed many people. They are pretty good eyes, both in vision and, although I say it, in judgment. I don't even wear glasses yet, and over sixty summers lie behind me. . . .

I will do my best for this is a book which I want to write about a man whose passing has left a gap in my life that cannot be filled, and a gap in our Theatre that will not be filled, either, these many years. I shall start him off with " Keep the Home Fires Burning." I shall walk by his side from there onwards and I shall be there when he makes his exit and I hope you will be with me too. And again that first great song will be his passing knell.

I call this book " Ivor: A Story of Achievement." I do not think it could be called anything else. It is my tribute to a man who enriched our race. He was always Ivor to me. Let him always be Ivor to you. That is what he would have liked above all things. It was, also, not the least part of his achievement.

CHAPTER ONE

ENTRANCE

ON January 15th, 1893, a male child was born to Mr. and Mrs. David Davies, of Cardiff. To be precise, at "Llwyn-yr-Eos," 95 Cowbridge Road. The Welsh name, in English, meant "Grove of Nightingales" and was not only prophetic but entirely appropriate even at that time. For Mrs. Davies was much better known as Madame Clara Novello Davies, a great figure in Welsh music and the outstanding teacher of singing in The Land of Song. The father, a good-looking, up-standing man, collected rates and was a valued employee of the Cardiff municipality. He and his wife were opposites and therefore an ideally married couple. He had everyday common sense and business ability, to which was added a very keen and distinct sense of humour. These things he passed on to his son. Madame Novello was the very epitome of an "artiste." She was, indeed, a genius, and she not only had tremendous musical knowledge and the power to impart it, but she had tempera-ment, very strongly marked temperament, such as one would expect from a woman whose passion was music and song. But she had something more, something which seldom goes hand in hand with artistic temperament: she had tenacity and deter-mination. She could—she did—steer a course and never be deflected from it. If she made up her mind to achieve some-thing, achieve it she did, no matter what lay between her and the end she decided to reach. That ability, too, was passed on to her son—this newly-born child who arrived, opportunely or inopportunely, when she was at her busiest with singing lessons. But he was not allowed to interrupt them unduly, for she was working with pupils up to an hour or two before the child's birth, and was back at her task with a minimum of delay.

Even at his first entrance into the world, Ivor had something unusual. He was remarkably well endowed in the matter of a nose, a feature which is not as a rule very marked in infants on their arrival in this world. But he had a nose which was notice-able. Some people hold that big noses are the hall-mark of greatness, and instance Julius Caesar, the Duke of Wellington and many more. The argument cannot be pursued here, for this baby proceeded to grow into his nose, as it were, and it soon got into proportion. But there, at birth, was a signal of the greatness to come for those who believe in the significance of physical attributes.

He was born into a world of music, but it was not that alone, of his mother's musical gifts, which was the real well-spring of what this child was to achieve. His love of beauty and his understanding and natural expression of native cadence were not simply brought about by a mother steeped in music and a childhood spent amidst song. They derived from something much deeper. They were rooted in the soil of Wales itself, in the valleys of Glamorgan, in one particular vale at the foot of the mountains which is called Tonyrefail. And they had found expression before in one William Ifan (or, in English, Evans), who was a preacher of the Gospel, and Ivor's great-great-grandfather. That, in Wales, means much. For when inspired Welsh expounders of the Gospel preach, their sermons are songs. And such a one was William Ifan. He was known as Y Gloch Arian—the Silver Bell—for that is what his voice was like. He had mighty music in it and in his soul, and his fame spread beyond the Principality, as did that of his descendant, reaching London itself. In the year 1831, he himself came to Town. He preached to the Welsh people of London, to a Welsh Methodist congregation who worshipped in Denmark Street, Soho. He made a tremendous impression. Much later that congregation joined with another and worshipped at the Welsh Chapel in Charing Cross Road and there the worship goes on to-day. And the great-great-grandson, who had become Ivor Novello, registered his greatest success, as actor-composer-author at the Palace Theatre, a stone's throw from and in sight of that very chapel. And the man who preached there at the time of this success, the Welsh pastor, the Rev. E. Gwyn Evans, B.A., was to conduct Ivor Novello's funeral service and speak a tribute to him which for beauty and matter, voice and diction, was in true descent from Y Gloch Arian. Thus did the wheel come full circle.

These Welsh preachers are remarkable men. You will find one or more in the tree of most Welsh families. That grand actor, Lyn Harding, who at eighty-three set an example of how such things should be done, when he read the Second Lesson at the memorial service to his countryman, friend and brother-actor Ivor Novello at St. Martin-in-the-Fields on March 29th, 1951, had a grandfather who was also a preacher of the Gospel and a man of parts. When he first saw a railway train pull into a station, he fell upon his knees and besought God to hurry up, or Man would get there first! Lyn Harding comes of the soil of Wales and is one of the best actors our land has produced. He had known Novello's parents, had known Novello as a child and in manhood, and had played in Novello's first success at the Theatre Royal, Drury Lane. He was sadly proud to assist at his memorial service. When I asked him to officiate, he wrote of Ivor: " In spite of his great success he remained as I had always known him, simple and kindly. Prosperity had not changed him and I had known him since he was a baby in his perambulator. Before he was born I had known his parents." And there was Lyn Harding to assist at the passing, as solid, true, strong and inspiring as one of his own Welsh mountains.

It was a strange childhood Ivor spent, in and out of his perambulator. He went as a baby with his mother to her concerts all over Wales, with the nurse Jane Thomas in attendance. And when he was only six months old, his mother had to leave him, for she went to Chicago with her Welsh Ladies' Choir, to sing at the wonderful World's Fair of 1893. There was much heart-burning over leaving the infant; but art had to triumph over mother-love and national pride had to have its way. Madame Clara Novello Davies went to Chicago, and she and her Welsh girls triumphed over all other competitors. When, later, she returned to Cardiff vast crowds cheered her, the Mayor and Corporation bid her welcome, the only dissentient voice being that of the infant David Ivor Davies, who clung to his nurse and howled. . . .

All the world of music came to visit his mother and, as he grew up, that small Welsh boy saw all the great ones and heard them sing. He absorbed music through every pore of his body and it was already in his soul. He was a page at the wedding of Clara Butt and Kennerly Rumford. Lyn Harding reports him as extremely shy, quiet and not given to romping like other lads of his age. Nor did he have any desire to go in for sport. That never interested Ivor at any time. Rather was his observant little mind storing up impressions. Music was singing in him, finding expression on the piano, to say nothing of his voice. When only three years old, he sang before a private audience of stars, and he sang well. All his mother's great friends loved and encouraged him. His mother used to go to London to give lessons and as often as possible little Ivor would go with her. He began to go to the theatres, too. He saw the plays and stars of those days, and he never forgot what he saw. Like most children, he had a toy theatre, but to him it was no toy—it was real. Already the Land of Illusion which is the Theatre had claimed him. He entered for eisteddfods and won first prizes. There was no doubt at all about his career. And he also wrote verse, getting it published in the local papers.

He was never really in touch with the workaday world. He lived in an atmosphere of music and among people whose business it was to exercise their gifts and talents for the pleasure of others. Naturally, it seemed to him the only life there was. Anyway, it was his always, right up to the end.

He adored acting, he adored singing. Mrs. Suzanne McCrory, his old schoolmistress, still alive and very active, remembers teaching him his first song at school. The school was in Cathedral Road, Cardiff. Mrs. McCrory was very young then and it was her first job. Confronted with a long table at which were seated twenty children, she was told to " take " them. She herself had reached the advanced age of seventeen. But she " took " those children. She taught them and after their fashion they learnt. And she certainly learnt from them, as do most teachers worth their salt. This is her own description of one of those children, sent to me just after the news of his death had shocked the world: " A dear little boy, with beautiful skin, liquid brown eyes and a very happy disposition—add long eyelashes and imagine how difficult it was not to spoil him." He was David Ivor Davies; and Ivor Novello had all those same attributes up to the end.

Among the things Ivor learnt from his youthful teacher was a ballad, which he sang at the end-of-term concert. He did it "with actions" and in costume. It was, maybe, his first "production number." It was one of those ballads of sentiment so popular then and its title was " Tatters." Perhaps some readers will remember it. I do myself, for I too sang it as a child. Ivor and I had that in common; we both sang as children

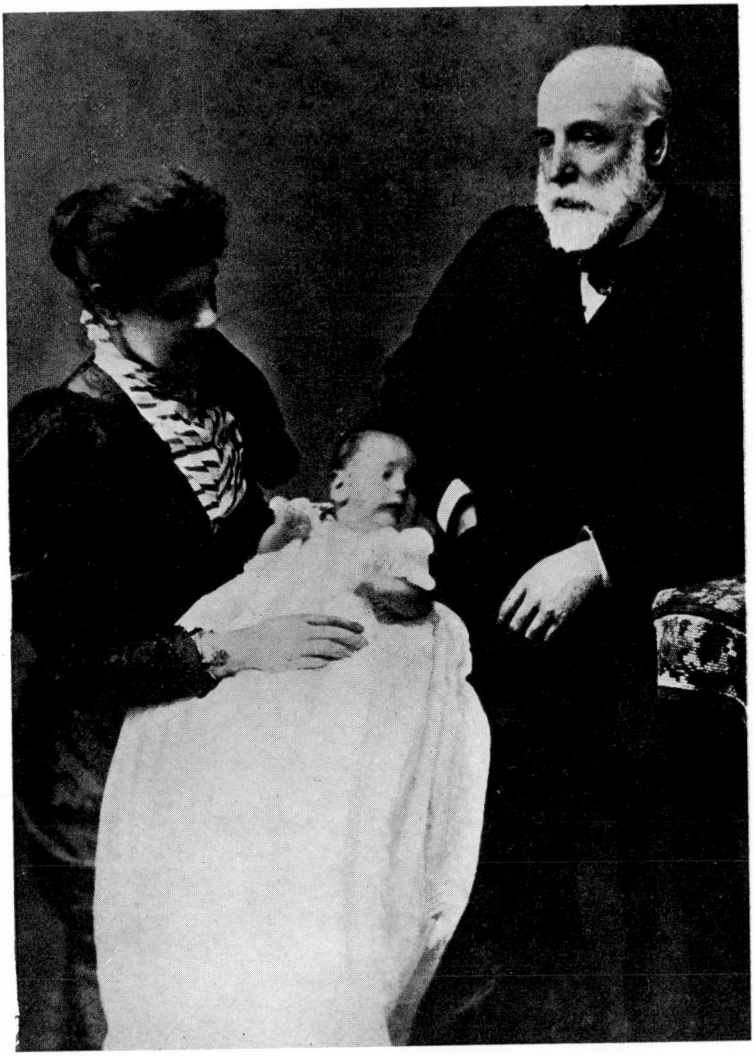

A unique family group: Mother, baby Ivor and grandfather

No actor was more photographed than Ivor. He first posed for his picture at the age of a few weeks. It was taken by a local Cardiff photographer

Three unique pictures of Ivor and his mother; among the earliest ever taken

and when our voices broke—that was the end of personal song. That ballad was " sure-fire " then. It began :

" Tatters, with his little broom
Stands amid the crowd
In the gaslight, in the gloom
Where the strife is loud "

It went on to recount the doings of this unfortunate, ragged little crossing sweeper—a " profession " which has vanished to-day but was much in evidence then—the refrain ending, I think, with the words :

" Ah, little Tatters
In the city square
Fortune little matters
If Love is there."

An admirable sentiment and one which, as rendered by Master David Ivor Davies in his sweet voice, his tatters and even his little broom, brought the house down. Mrs. McCrory reports that everyone cried, including Ivor. It was a triumphant success. The dear lady assures me that she can see and hear it now. I am sure she can. Many years afterwards she got into touch with him and asked him if he remembered. He did, and he spoke the truth. There was little which Ivor Novello forgot. And he was delighted to hear from her and wrote her a charming letter. She says she " is proud to think she had helped very early in his life (he was only six) to create—no, not a matinée idol, I don't like that term, he was so much more." That, of course, was before his eisteddfod successes, which came much later.

Song went on, all day and well into the night, all round him. He heard little else but music. It seemed that everyone in Wales who sang—and who did not?—and who wanted singing lessons, came to Madame Clara Novello Davies for tuition. They came from all classes; she knew no social distinctions, only the levelling gift of song. Out on the lawn of the house she had a marquee and there she taught the miners who came straight from the pits for singing lessons, their faces still black, their clothes dripping coal dust. They had to get a lesson between their shifts, before their rest. Miner or millionaire, it mattered little to Madame Clara, but she drew the line at coal dust in the house. Those men were taught in the tent, but they learned just the same.

There was Ellen, too—Ellen Tushingham, now a married

woman of ripe years, living in Chester. She joined the Davies staff when Master David was six—just when he was singing "Tatters." She helped to look after him until he went to Magdalen College School, Oxford. He won a scholarship which enabled him to do that and Madame Clara sent Ellen a telegram, which she kept and treasured, to announce the news. Years afterwards she showed Madame Clara that wire and the great lady was so pleased that she asked if she might have it. And Ellen gave it to her.

Ellen worked at Llwyn-yr-Eos for twelve years. Even when she married she stayed on and she was working there when her son was born. That baby delighted little Ivor. He was already showing the acting urge. Ellen says that "he was always full of acting. As a small boy he used to dress up in his mother's dresses and sometimes drive us nearly desperate. After he had the dresses on, he would leave them on the floor in a heap." But his natural childish love for dressing up was not confined to that. When Ellen's little son was born, Master David Ivor Davies regarded the child as a godsend. When the poor little thing was a month old, young Ivor seized upon it, would carry it away to the music room, dress it up and act dramas with it in his arms. Ellen says that he had a wig which he put on its head—where the wig came from or how it fitted is not known—so perhaps that little infant, all unknown to itself, played many parts, quite unconscious that it was doing so. It must have been a very good-natured baby. But there was the acting urge, there was the creative force, and there also was the dawn of authorship in young David Ivor. That is very often how authors start, putting words and actions to their games as they play them, dramatizing their play, as it were. My young grandson does it, and I did it as a child. It led Ivor to great heights; it led me into writing books—may a better fate than mine befall my grandson! But there was, in young David Davies, the budding actor and the budding author. The music had already blossomed. Mastery of the piano was as easy to him as being able to speak. He would sit at the lessons which his mother gave and often astound both pupil and teacher by creeping to the piano and playing a passage which had proved an insurmountable hurdle to the eager but clumsy learner.

Ivor and his piano were always one. It was his natural method of expression. Had he chosen the career of solo pianist he would have been in the very top rank. But in that art, as in others, he would not endure the slightest imperfection, as the following story shows. It was during the run of *Perchance to Dream* and I was, as I was so very often, in his dressing-room, chatting to him, giving him the " inside dope " which my Fleet Street contacts enabled me to pick up, for so often I know the news which does not get into print and which is always so much more important and interesting than that which does, and Ivor adored to hear it. We talked of future plays. With *Perchance to Dream* in the full flood of its success, he was not thinking of anything new at that moment, but in the recesses of his mind something always lurked, ready to be pulled out and given life. I made a suggestion, the idea of which had been given me by my friend Anna Instone, a lady of charm, beauty, and great musical knowledge. I asked " Why don't you write a musical play about Chopin, Ivor? You could play it magnificently and what a Georges Sand Olive Gilbert would make." He was making-up at the time. He stopped and looked at me. His mind was working like lightning, as it always did when such a thing was in question. His eyes were alight. Then a cloud came into them. " No, I can't do that," he said. " No, I should love it. It's a beautiful idea. But I should have to play the piano a lot in it." " Well," I countered, " what's the matter with that? You are always playing the piano in your plays." " Ah, yes, Popie," he answered, " but not as Chopin. Chopin was a magnificent pianist—or so I have always understood. I'm a good pianist too, but not so good as all that. Do you know what stopped me from being absolutely first class? This . . ." (and he extended the little finger of his left hand) " . . . there's a slight stiffness there which just holds me back from the perfection I should need as Chopin. What a pity! I almost wish you'd never thought of it. But my thanks, all the same." And that smile went with his words. Nobody but Ivor knew about that tiny drawback, if drawback it were. Nobody else had ever noticed it. But he knew, and he was convinced he would not be as good as his ideal would demand. So he never wrote the play about Chopin, or played it either. Yet he loved to play the piano in public and in his plays, and his public could never have enough of it. He knew that, as a story to be told later will prove. But it goes to show the standard he set himself, always. . . .

That vision of himself in his mother's dresses conjures up pictures. He must have been a real rival to the great Edward Kynaston, the most famous player of women's parts before women were allowed to act. It has been recorded that when, as often happened, Kynaston appeared in dual roles in Restoration plays, he was the prettiest girl on the stage when dressed as such, and when in male attire, the handsomest man, too. Ivor would have been as successful had he lived then.

Ellen Tushingham, who recalls these memories of youth, is another of his childhood companions who mourned his death. In her letter to Fred Allen, Ivor's most faithful friend and man of business, she says, " I did not write to Mr. Ivor. We thought a lot about him here in my home and a week never passed without his name being mentioned. I feel very proud to think that he has been to my little home to see me. Mr. Ivor and Mr. Lloyd Williams called one Sunday in 1941. He had been acting in Southport."

That was a red-letter day never to be forgotten in that Chester home. Here was the little boy grown into a great man but not forgetting. Had Ellen Tushingham grown into a celebrity too, he might not have troubled to go at all. But she was still Ellen, she was one of his people, those people with whom he always remained. And she mourns him. Friends of hers, to whom she had doubtless told much about Ivor, came to London and saw *King's Rhapsody*. They told her all about it. She was going to make the pilgrimage too. Then, sick with bronchitis, she heard the news on the radio. She wrote her letter to Fred Allen and she sent a message to Lloyd Williams, whom she did not know had already passed on. Fred Allen, like the good, faithful, understanding soul he is, answered her and sent her a photo of Ivor. She wrote again: " I am writing to thank you very much for your letter and Mr. Ivor's photo. Although I have a few of Mr. Ivor's photos I shall treasure this one very much. Knowing you are very busy at the moment I am very grateful to you for sending it to me. I would have liked to have been at St. Martin's for the memorial service but London is rather far this cold weather. We heard it very plain on the wireless. My husband and I were listening and two of my sisters that used to be with Madame Davies at Sutherland Avenue came to visit us for the day so we all heard it together. It was lovely, but it made us feel very sad. You will miss Mr.

Ivor very much after being with him for many years. . . ." And she sent a little tribute, which a friend of hers (who never knew Ivor) had written and of which she says, " I think the words are lovely." Here are the words, which come from one of the public, that unseen public which adored Ivor and of whom he was always so conscious and in such close touch. . . .

TO IVOR—FAREWELL

Farewell, O King of song and laughter
You leave with us a choice bouquet
Whose fragrance reaches towards the morrow
And fills the heart from day to day.

You never knew the downward journey
Of a star when on the wane
For you left us all too early
On the very crest of fame.

We are grateful for your passing
Through a world of care and strain
Grateful for the sweet mimosa
Glistening through the showers of rain.

G. R.

I include that anonymous tribute not because it has any claim to be great poetry or inspired verse, but because it is inspired all the same—with that genuine gratitude felt by multitudes for the pleasure which Ivor gave them. It is just the sort of thing which would have pleased Ivor. So it goes into this record of him. G. R., totally unknown to me as a person, has put into words what millions of people who did not know Ivor either, felt when he left the world, and what they will go on feeling, too.

It is the tritest of clichés that no man is a hero to his valet. But Ivor Novello disproved that. He was a hero to his valet—his dresser—Bill Wright, who nearly collapsed at his funeral service. He was a hero to his faithful chauffeur of thirty years' service, Arthur Morgan, who did indeed faint at the crematorium. He was a hero to that old servant-nurse Ellen and to many, many more of such humble people. For he was one of those rare men who never commanded service, never made demands upon his staff, but who got the utmost from them without any request because they loved to be with him. They all felt the same. Winnie Newman, who was the manageress of his last companies, once thanked me for an article I had written about him. " I wish you had said more," she remarked. " I wish you had been able to say what working for him meant to me. Once, before I was with him, I used to get up and dread the day. I never wanted to go to work, was unhappy all the while I was there and longed for the time to come to knock off. But now—how different! To work with the Guv'nor is sheer joy. I don't dread coming to work, what I dread is going home." And that spirit was with all those whose privilege it was to work with him. It was his charm that did it. It was a natural charm, quite innate and it entailed no effort. It was—just there.

In my time I have known many, many famous people who were celebrated for their charm, but in the vast majority of cases that charm was a gift, like an acquired talent—if the simile which sounds paradoxical may be allowed. They had the charm but it was not a permanent thing; they turned it on and off, like the electric light. That was not the case with Ivor. With him the charm was permanent. He could no more have shed it, or put it out, than he could have removed a hand, an arm or a leg. It was just a fixture, as much a part of him as the very breath he drew. He was, of course, aware of it—how could he help be otherwise?—but he did not have to do anything about it. It was the very foundation of the essential Ivor. You might say that it might have become wearisome, like perpetual sunlight. But it did not. It would have done had it been in the least degree mechanical. But he could not help it. He was born with it and it remained. It had the most amazing effects. It soothed everyone. Somebody might have a tremendous grievance and determine to lay it before Ivor. They might arrive at the dressing-room—which was the Novello Exchange —full of thunderous fulmination and breathing fire and slaughter, prepared to be bombastic and stress their case. The moment, however, they were in his presence, all that faded. The charm got them. The smile which was part of it got them too. They became reasonable at once. It was indeed a magical thing, quite irresistible. Perhaps there might be dissension, due to rehearsal troubles. A little group would bicker in a corner; tempers would be frayed and voices be raised and everyone would begin to speak at once. Swiftly, and almost silently, Ivor would appear. At once the charm which he radiated like an aura worked its effect. Quietness reigned, voices were lowered. A short discussion, smiles answering his smiles, and there was peace again. And Ivor would return, also smiling.

It seems a pity that he never had a chance of trying that charm on the hard cases who shelter behind the Iron Curtain. It is possible that he would have succeeded where ambassadors failed. He might have silenced Hitler; but he could not have borne to have been in the same room as that thing of blatant, strident horror. That was something ugly, and Ivor did not like ugly things. Mussolini he could have tackled. He would have understood the underlying showmanship, the theatricality of it all, the illusion which the little bullfrog had wrapped round himself by pageantry and symbolism. But not the frenzy of Adolf. It was hard to say " No " to Ivor. That was something he himself always found difficulty in saying. He made the same difficulty for others. Only once did his charm not only fail to protect him but actually harm him. But that, too, is for later.

His schoolmistress's story proves that he always had that gift, that it was nothing acquired, for Mrs. McCrory fell for his charm when he was a tiny boy of six. So did Ellen, his mother's maid. So did they all. The great ones who came to see his famous mother, the finest musicians and singers of the day—the little Ivor charmed them all. It was out of that charm that David Ivor Davies created Ivor Novello—the Ivor Novello whom the public loved and knew was the son of that charm.

Life went on in Cardiff. He scored his local successes, his Welsh eisteddfod successses. Clara Butt was his friend, so was the great Patti. When he got a gramophone he began to listen to the recorded voices of people from afar who had not come into his ken. Always he remembered and always he learnt from what he heard. He forgot nothing. Meanwhile, the fame of his mother's teaching spread to London, and she went up there from Cardiff to hold classes. She lived first of all at 143 Sutherland Avenue, Maida Vale. The 'phone number was 1032 Paddington and the telegraphic address was " Semibreve, London "—music even got into that. Sometimes Ivor went with her on these trips. That meant visits to the theatre, and those visits to the London shows were, to him, visits to Paradise. There he saw, in their prime, many of the wonderful people who were to become in later days his close friends. And as he, in his youth, had been their admirer so they, in their maturity, became his admirers in turn.

He left the Cardiff School and went to another in Gloucester. It meant leaving home, but that did him good. The temporary parting only tightened the link between himself and his beloved " Mam " or " Mamsie," and also the link, as strong though less outwardly demonstrative, with his father. It did the young David Ivor good to be in other surroundings, to meet other people, to take their measure whilst they took his. And always there was the joy of school theatricals, and always he sang, for he was now a very remarkable boy soprano. Gloucester was to do much for him, as here he studied music under the then Doctor Brewer of Gloucester, who became Sir Herbert Brewer.

He had also begun to fall in love. There were nice little schoolgirls to whose charms this handsome, romantic little boy fell a victim. Those childish, transient love affairs do not go deep but are never forgotten. Ivor always remembered the names of his innocent little *inamoratas*. I remember once, while he was rehearsing for *Henry V*, taking along that renowned film critic Miss Dilys Powell. Miss Powell, at that time working on the theatrical side of her paper, wanted to interview Ivor, and as it was my job to get him publicity, I was delighted. It is my custom in such matters to make things as easy as possible. I always meet the interviewer, take him or her along, do the introducing, stand by and give a helping hand throughout. Sometimes—though never with Ivor—there are matters which it would be premature to disclose, matters best left alone (the whole art of publicity is timing, though that seems to be lost sight of nowadays) and the publicity man who knows his job will manage to intervene, head off an awkward question, and lead the conversation along safer paths. Miss Powell had never met Ivor, nor had he met her. The rehearsal was at Covent Garden Opera House, where the full company was at work on the eve of Agincourt scene, for Drury Lane's stage was having scenery set up. So there I took Miss Powell. Very often, interviewers meeting a star they do not know are very much on the defensive for they have the idea, common to all Fleet Street folk, that the star may try and " put something over " on them. No need to worry about Ivor in that respect, but Miss Powell was not to know that. When we got there,

Ivor was actually rehearsing. We sat in a corner and talked and then, when he had finished, he saw me and came over. I introduced " Miss Dilys Powell of *The Sunday Times*." The smile was, of course, on Ivor's face, but at the word Dilys, it took on another quality and a far-away look came into his eye. " Dilys," he breathed. " Dilys—that was the name of my first sweetheart. A lovely name." From then on, the interview went swimmingly . . . and a most valuable piece of space in a most valuable paper resulted.

I did not forget that meeting. I do not believe Miss Powell, now one of the best and most followed film critics, has forgotten it either. Later I asked Ivor about that Dilys. It was quite true. He told me the little girl's name, her appearance and all about her. I have forgotten the name now, but Ivor had not. One does not forget the names of one's childhood's beloved. I never had much to remember in that respect, being a very possessive sort of man, for my first real sweetheart is still with me to-day. But Ivor had many: there was a Winnie and a Dorothy and several more besides that Dilys. And he had special cause to remember the Dorothy because she was his co-star in his first really important production, a school performance of *The School for Scandal* in which he, at the mature age of ten, played Sir Peter Teazle and little Dorothy was Lady Teazle. It was, of course, a success. . . .

Like most small boys, he was not concerned at this time about his future. Already the world of Illusion had him in its grip. He could not conceive an existence without music and all that went with it, acting being well in the running but perhaps, at that time, second to singing. His mother never considered anything else but music for him, either. But his father, who in that family was the link with real life, the sound keeper of sanity in a little self-contained world intoxicated with music, envisaged a commercial career of steady keel, of sound foundation, safe if not exciting. But Mam had other views. She wanted him to have a musical education of the very best kind. She wanted him to go to Magdalen College School, Oxford, and, if possible, to sing in the choir there—the most celebrated choir in the world. A handful of boys were in that choir: no more than sixteen in number. Her ambition was that Ivor should be one of them, for it was a key which would open almost every door in the musical world, a stepping stone to musical fortune. It was very largely a question of ways and means. The profession of singing teaching was one which varied in remuneration. There were good times and bad. Mr. Davies himself was not the recipient of a large salary, and his wife had recently incurred much expense by the setting up of the Sutherland Avenue establishment where on certain days of the week she taught her London pupils. She was doing well, but the connection must needs grow to meet the heavy rent, the upkeep, the expenses of travel and living in London. Unfortunately, at no time in her long life did Mam even faintly understand the value of money. But she did know—and probably Davies *père* made it plain—that they could not afford the fees at Oxford. However, there were scholarships, and she had made up her mind that Ivor's future lay entirely in music.

Even then, Ivor had his own views. At no time, despite his deep and abiding love for his mother—and there was never a better son in the world than David Ivor Davies—at no time was he as much under his mother's domination as some people would have us believe. When he died, a journalist did what is known as a " profile " of Ivor for one of the more—shall we say—" popular " Sunday papers, whose readers are not of the more cultured classes, but who were, nonetheless, mostly Ivor's fans. The writer suggested that all his life long Ivor had a Mother-complex and that was the reason for his great friendship, admiration and understanding of certain actresses for whom he continually wrote parts and with whom he always associated. Despite the fact that he came to see me and got information, he insisted that all this arose from his adoration of his mother. He said Ivor was always, even after her death, the adoring son of his mother, no matter what lovely girl he clasped in his arms when on the stage. He said Ivor was always terrified of those beautiful creatures.

Well, well, it just goes to show how much better he appeared to know Ivor than we who worked with him. I don't know that he ever really and truly watched Ivor at work let alone knew him well, if at all. None of us ever saw the terror. I never saw Ivor afraid of anything, bombs included, let alone women. Twice in a lifetime, went on the writer of the profile, Ivor had really tried to make serious love to women, but it had frightened the life out of him. Twice? As for the fear I should like the testimony of the women about it. I think—in fact, I know—

the journalist would be proved hopelessly wrong. I know quite a lot about Ivor and I know all about that. I shall tell much that I know in this book, but it has never been my belief that it is necessary to tell the world about the private love affairs, the innermost feelings of people in Ivor's position. That is their own affair. Their work, their life behind the footlights, their life in connection with these things—yes. But even the greatest artiste has the right to some privacy. Public service, the giving of delight to millions, is poorly rewarded if the secrets of the heart are to be laid bare. When, through divorce or other court proceedings, they themselves lay bare their hearts that is another matter. When, by some terrible scandal, the curtains are rent and the secrets tumble out, it cannot be helped. Tell the public all they want to know about their idol, as far as it is their direct concern. But grant him the same privilege of private life as they themselves desire and guard so jealously. I have always disbelieved in the modern tendency to destroy illusion, to drag people whose life is behind the footlights away from that barrier which makes them people apart. The Theatre is Illusion, and, when it goes, it is no longer Theatre; the star is no longer somebody who is different, but just an ordinary person like everyone else—sometimes, alas! very ordinary indeed when out of his or her true sphere. I dislike intensely the familiar way in which the British Broadcasting Corporation calls everyone by their Christian names after thirty seconds' microphone acquaintance. It is a thing which belittles everyone; it is destructive of quality and distinction. That is not snobbish. It is just a retention of old-fashioned courtesy and respect. It so happens that Ivor was one of the few people who could stand up to that because he was Ivor to everyone, and nobody thought of presuming upon it. But there are very few Ivors about. The habit, in the main, is transatlantic in origin. It began about the same time as the general use of the words "Show Business." Ivor survived with dignity intact because he was never in "Show Business." He was always a member of the Theatrical Profession. So, in his humble way, is his present biographer—which is yet another link between us.

But that Sunday scribe also said that right up to her death his mother dominated him . . . that he danced attendance upon her to the exclusion of everyone else. He added that when she occupied a box at Drury Lane he filled it with flowers. So he did. He was the ideal son and he adored his mother. But he was never dominated by her. If you have the patience to read this book, that will be amply proved. You will see how, so far from controlling him, he had to control her, and succeeded, at times, in so doing. He was perhaps firmer and sterner with her than with anyone else. This was because he loved and respected her. I have already said that he had his roots in a past generation, a generation different from that of to-day, a generation which did not treat its mothers with offhand familiarity but which really believed that parents were entitled not only to love but to respect. Of course Ivor loved his mother; most people do. The journalist suggested he was telling the world why Ivor did not marry. Maybe he believed he was; it is not for me to impeach his probity and I would not presume to do so, but I tell him he was wrong.

He then went on to say that after the death of his mother Ivor sought the company of "older actresses with ample bosoms and singing voices which reminded him of her. These older mature motherly women—never the young lovelies who teemed in his shows, unless he admired them for their art alone—were the women with whom he made friends." Again, well, well! Let us, in fairness to the man who is dead examine the facts. Ivor had many women friends who were actresses and whom he admired greatly. Do they fit into this motherly, broad-bosomed portrait so deftly drawn? Would you apply that description to dear Zena Dare, whom he loved to have in his shows? To lovely Lily Elsie, to Cicely Courtneidge, Billie Burke, Dorothy Dickson, Beatrice Lillie, Roma Beaumont, Fay Compton, Edna Best, Mary Ellis, Viola Tree, or to stately Lilian Braithwaite, to Greta Garbo, Ruth Chatterton, Phyllis Monkman, Norma Shearer, Lynn Fontanne, Heather Thatcher—to mention only a few—all of whom were his dear friends and for most of whom he wrote parts? Olive Gilbert and Flagstadt might qualify on chest measurement, but they are *prima donnae*. Olive, it is true, did look after his creature comforts for a long time. But she did that whilst Mam was still alive—just as all those friendships were in existence and operative in Mam's lifetime, too. Ivor adored these women not because of their development of bust or their motherliness, but because of what they could do, because of their artistry—the main attraction for him—as well as their common calling with him. Most of them were not singers, either. Dear old Minnie Rayner looked most like his mother, but that was not the basis of her attraction for him. She was, he considered, his mascot. I write at length because those words in that Sunday paper were read by tens of thousands. Though my words may be read by only a few thousands, I like to get things right. So did Ivor.

To go back to the story, Ivor got things right so far as Oxford was concerned. In 1903, when he was ten years old, he won a scholarship for Magdalen College School. Now, indeed, the doors were opening.

CHAPTER TWO

THE PUPIL'S PROGRESS

IVOR loved Magdalen College School. He was in the seventh heaven when singing in the choir and he adored the surroundings. Oxford appealed to him: its beauty, its romance, its whispers of Yesterday. All these things became part of him. He was just the ordinary schoolboy, not too fond of work, perhaps, but living every moment when he sang. He always enjoyed his holidays like any other boy and, at times, if his mother had a tour of the country with her Royal Welsh Ladies' Choir, Ivor went too and played the accompaniments. He even deputized for singers on occasions and his pure, soprano voice more than filled the breach.

His letters to his mother give the true picture of the lad as he was then. Here is one. It is not dated (at no time in his life had he much cognizance of such things as dates):

"My Own Angel Darling Mamsie,

It will be lovely if I may come. I don't know if Bob will let me as it is so near the end of the Chapel Services. You see, my pet, they finish on the 22nd, but I don't come home until the 28th. But we may as well have a good try, don't you think so? It would be terrible to miss such an important affair. Yes, darling, the white waistcoat is here in splendid condition, the grey gloves (I think they would be best for an At Home) I left them at Cardiff because I said that if I brought them back I should lose them. No, my pet, I have not any patent boots but they would be just the right thing for an At Home. If you wish to get them my size is 6 (!!!!!) Also, my darling, I have a white bow tie here, or two if one isn't enough. Brigger spoke to me last night and said he was rather doubtful if Bob would let me come, but I think Bob would quite think me deserving of a rest after singing so many solos; for instance I sang 'As Pants the Hart' (Spohr); he said it was absolutely perfect, so I think I have a good chance.

Did Auntie Jennie get her letter? Do you think she will answer me? I should love it. Will Lily, Lady Something or Other be coming to the At Home and Marie? Tell her when she comes or if she has come that I am *longing* to see her. Good-bye now, my darling, all my love to you, Auntie Jennie, Marie and Dad, Ellen Lizzie, Aimee and Mrs. Stead.

Ivor."

The punctuation has been added in most cases, for Ivor had a habit of ignoring most things except commas. The promised At Home seems to have been an enticing affair and it is not known if Ivor succeeded in getting there or even if he obtained the patent boots. " Bob " is of course Dr. Roberts but " Brigger " is veiled in the mists.

And here is another which is also illuminating. It does bear a date, May 27th, but no year.

" Darling Pet Mamsie,

It was lovely to have your letter this morning. Yes, I have my suit and am wearing it now; it is absolutely ripping. Darling, I had a good look for my overcoat and found someone else was wearing it, so Duckie there is no need to get a new one, is there? Oh, my pet, I am longing for the 20th. Don't you think, darling, you could persuade Aunt Jeannie to come up for the Concert? I should love her to and I am sure she would enjoy herself so much—and Bob says I sing 'With Verdure Clad' delightfully. Darling, how did the Amateur Concert go off? I hope the influenza did not pass off. How did Ethel play and did she get encored? I should love to have been there.

Dad must come up, he would look so handsome in a nice evening dress. He has not answered my postcard yet, besides I want him to meet Mac. Darling, I have been feeling awfully well just lately; it must have been the Port Wine, I came back rolling (Ha! Ha! Ha!).

Did you manage to get home with your ample fortune? I got home easily in time for lock-up and the Cabby was quite contented with his three bob. How is Miss Clifford? Is she 'Your Ladyship' yet? I am longing to see her again. Darling, you must ask her to send me a photo of herself; signed it would be ripping. How is Lily, Lady Elliot? I should like to see her and Lady Mostyn's niece and Lydia, Jessie, Jennie, Adeline, Cora and Florrie and Miss Abbott and Mrs. Abbott. See, I remember them all.

Darling, I must go now. Give my best love to all. All love to Auntie Jeannie and to you My Darling X X 10000000 XX.

Ivor."

That is a typical boy's letter. The touch about the lost overcoat which another boy had appropriated is delightful and also the cabby's satisfaction with his fare. One is relieved to know that the suit was ripping and would like to discover who was the Miss Clifford, the possession of whose autographed photo would have produced the same state of excellence. Could it have been Camille Clifford, the " Gibson Girl " ? What does he mean by saying that he hopes the influenza did not pass off? But from that boyish letter one phrase always remained with Ivor—the word " Duckie." Everyone he liked was " Duckie " to him—even I have been " Duckie."

Of all the letters to his Mam from Magdalen School, the following is perhaps the best. Again there is no date, not a suggestion of it, and the writing, although that of a boy obviously in a hurry, does already begin to take the shape of the fluid hand of more mature years.

" My Darling Mam,

I am singing two very big solos on Sunday night next. You must—Dr. Roberts says you can—come up in the organ pew with him. He is awfully pleased with me. I have sung two solos and one verse part 'As Pants the Hart' (Spohr), 'Lord God of Heaven and Earth' (Spohr's 'Last Judgment') and a verse from Garret.

I want some grub badly—will you send me a big hamper with plenty of fruit and sweets, chocolate, cakes, shortbread biscuits, potted meats and jams.

Goodbye,
Beauty,
Popsy,
Darling,
Love,
Ivor."

That, I think, reveals Ivor the boy. There is the pride in the music and the boyish desire to explain it to his mother by telling her, in case she did not know them, the composers' names. And then, on top of the ecstasy of the religious melody, that cry from the heart for food, real boy's food in a hamper. There is nothing of the pampered darling and mother's boy about that—he wants grub badly—and he might even have thought that his recital of his musical prowess would result in a bigger supply of grub than usual. These letters, indeed, give a very clear

At right : A very early picture of Ivor's adored "Mam"

Below : A composite picture of Ivor taken when he was aged about 20

At left : Ivor bids Mam farewell at Croydon aerodrome

At right : Ivor with father and mother on holiday

Ivor with his parents

picture of young David Ivor Davies, scholar and choirboy at Magdalen College School, Oxford. Of course Dr. Roberts would have welcomed such a landmark in music to a seat in the organ pew. But to Ivor she was not a celebrity—she was Mam. So he was proud to think she could have the chance—and through him, too. But nowhere is there the slightest trace of conceit or " side." And boys can have plenty of both. Neither David Ivor Davies nor Ivor Novello ever knew what it meant. The only feeling is one of successful achievement. That, too, always remained.

One thing certainly emerges from these letters. Even at that early age (he was between ten and twelve when he wrote them) he possessed a boundless enthusiasm for music and singing. He wants to know about the girl who played the piano: did she get an encore? He wants to know how a concert went: was it a success? He is full of the fact that his singing is giving satisfaction and tells of the music he has mastered. He is already submerged in his work. There is no mention of anything else; nothing of the school life around him, except the reference to the unnamed boy who appropriated the overcoat, and no mention of sport or any other boyish hobby. It is music, it is achievement, even then. So it was always. Here, indeed, the boy was father to the man.

It is no use speculating now as to whether a rather wider scope might not have given him a broader outlook later in life and consequently more breadth and depth to his work. He was not like that. In many ways, his mind was one track: it went along the road it saw and did not deviate. Yet that one-track mind did not, as it does so often, bring the slightest touch of selfishness and self-seeking. Ivor was a clear case of environment. That atmosphere which had always surrounded him, that music which had entered the portals of his new-born ears and had seeped right into him, possessed him completely. In *Brave New World*, Huxley drew a picture of rows and rows of new-born babies (actually I think they had been produced by artificial insemination), lying there with gramophones pouring forth salient facts into their subconscious minds so as to prepare them for what they were to do later. His mother's ceaseless music did that for Ivor. He never visualized any other life at all. He never wanted it. And in those letters, apart from his tutor, the only people he mentions are his folks at home and his mother's friends. There is the passing reference to one "Mac." He is not identifiable now. But there is no talk of the other boys and their doings together, nothing of lessons, nothing but music. Certainly he shows his pride in what he has done, but he does not boast about it. And boys are often given to boasting. He seems grateful. That persisted all his life.

But there is something else in those letters, too, which showed the shape of things to come. That is, for a boy of his years, their remarkable fluency. There is nothing of the short, staccato sentences of most boys' letters, a terseness brought about by lack of power of expression and the ordinary self-conscious repression of youth. Those letters flowed. It is like hearing him talk. There was already the sign of the author-to-be in those screeds, for the form of his dialogue in his plays—allowing for maturity—was much the same. It may not have been great dialogue, but it was always bright, amusing and, above all things, natural. He never struck wrong notes there. And that is forecast in the letters from young David Ivor which I have quoted.

Life at Magdalen College was a delight to Ivor because of the choir. He never retained any memories of what he actually did in school. The knowledge acquired there was of no use to him and, even then, he was probably aware of it. I have asked him about such things but there was nothing left in his mind, except the hope that he had not been too stuck-up over his singing. That was a needless fear. He never remembered at what lessons he got good marks, or what he found easy. Probably his very quick, receptive mind absorbed what they told him, got him by at examinations, and was then forgotten as being useless. He does not appear to have been either in trouble with his form masters, or to have caused any. He was never any trouble to anybody all his life. In all probability he never opposed them—just gave them that smile and put up a moderate show. I have vivid memories of my own schooldays and my dislike—indeed, my horror—of all forms of mathematics, which culminated in a complete refusal to learn algebra. I just went on strike. I downed pens and stuck it out. I won, too. They gave me up as a bad job and taught me history instead which I absorbed with great joy. Music stood in that stead for Ivor.

But Ivor's luck was that he always had the music. He was really a tremendous success. He was much talked about and people crowded to hear that pure, clear voice go soaring into the air and away up to the ancient roof of the church, true as a silver bell. Those solos of his were looked forward to eagerly, as the letters show, and his cup of happiness was full.

This, of course, could not last. A boy's voice must break, though Ivor's held on for a long time. But the end came and came at the wrong moment, as it always does. He was to sing " O, For the Wings of a Dove " on a very special occasion. He did that and gave a very beautiful rendering indeed. Praise was showered upon him. He had put every ounce of himself into that solo and had gone to bed in a happy and excited frame of mind, flushed with his triumph. In the morning he could not speak. He thought he had a chill, that perhaps he was really ill. But it was not that—the voice that had entranced the congregation the night before had gone. The penalty of approaching manhood was paid. Ivor could not believe it, but realization came. At first he was in despair for the light had gone out of his life. But he was only sixteen and youth soon recovers. It was the end of Oxford for him, but there was still his music, his piano, and, away down at the bottom of his mind, that creative desire to act, which always surged up when he went to the theatre. And so, after the first awful pangs of disappointment, he accepted what had to be.

He was already writing songs and little musical compositions. He was learning—had learnt—harmony, counterpoint and all the other necessary things in the equipment of a musician. A commercial career was suggested by prudent Mr. Davies, Senior, but met with little encouragement from David Ivor Davies, Junior. He would go on with music. He would play the piano, accompany, work with his mother, compose, and—now, another ambition was in his mind—he would be a conductor. He never had that ambition dear to so many small boys down the years, of conducting a tram or a 'bus. With Ivor it was to be an orchestra—of course.

He went on composing, trying his hand at one-act plays. The buds were beginning to swell on the tree of his talent. He sent his compositions to publishers, and at length the famous firm of Boosey published one, called " Spring of the Year." This was heaven to the lad and to his mother. Here was a fresh beginning, a door opening to the great world of song. And the song was sung in public, at no less a place than the Royal Albert Hall. Ivor accompanied the singer at the piano, in the glory of an Eton suit. But it was not the beginning of his years of triumphs. It was not the story a publicity man would delight to chronicle, of how a vast audience rose and cheered the youthful composer and acclaimed a coming genius. There was remarkably little applause, only the merest ripple of politeness. In short, it was a flop.

The young composer, however, was not defeated. He had indomitable Welsh blood. Ivor Novello was not yet born. It was David Ivor Davies who took this blow on the point of his chin, shook his head, and went on for more. He kept on writing, and he kept on sending in songs and music to the publishers. And, occasionally, there was a publication. Then, in 1910, he scored a bull's-eye. His song " The Little Damosel " was a nice little hit. And, by poetic justice, it scored its first success at its initial performance—at the Albert Hall! Thus was defeat avenged, thus was the slate rubbed clean. The song went well. Sopranos sang it all over the place. Madame Galli-Curci herself, that amazing vocalist, sang it. This was Fame, this was a real beginning! Imagine the pride of Madame Clara —the beloved Mam—who was now on the summit herself.

She found time in her extraordinarily busy life to do a lot of works at the National Sunday League Concerts. Those concerts and that movement did a tremendous amount of good, not only by providing first-class entertainment on Sunday afternoons and evenings in what was then a dull, soul-destroying desert of a Sunday in London, but much else for the good of the public. The public then was a much harder working one than now. Hours were much longer and the days of leisure offered little chance of relaxation except when the public-houses were open. But in spite of the bitterest opposition from churches, chapels, and a large section of public opinion, not to mention the licensed victuallers, a man called Morrell fought for brighter Sundays—and won. His work was carried on with great energy and unstinted labour and self-sacrifice by Henry Mills, who became the moving spirit of the National Sunday League, aided by a band of devoted and public-spirited men and women, who gave their services and won the day. They got museums opened, they arranged railway excursions at fantastically low prices to all sorts of places hitherto out of reach of the poorer classes of London. For they were working people themselves. It became possible to go to Matlock and back, on a special train with a restaurant car, for as little as 4*s.* (it may even have been 3*s.* 6*d.*), to such places as that lovely spot, Rye, in Sussex, an almost unattainable place then, in the days when few people owned a car. But it was brought into everyone's reach on a Sunday by the special train of the National Sunday League. There were hundreds of excursions each week, all perfectly organized, with complete freedom for the excursionists. All they had to do was take their tickets from the League and catch the right trains. No questions were asked, no membership insisted on, no means test of any sort enforced. The National Sunday League—the N.S.L.—was at the service of the public.

Their concerts were really magnificent. They had them all over the place, every Sunday afternoon and evening. Legally there had to be free admission. So there was—for about a dozen seats in the galleries. That satisfied the law. For the rest the prices were "popular"—very "popular." So were the programmes. There was no insistence on sacred music. Every type of song, composition and attraction was offered: vocalists, entertainers (but not red-nosed comedians in costume), reciters, glees, part-songs, cantatas, brass bands, military bands, orchestras, and, later, dance bands too. To carry the war into the enemy's country, they hired music halls in which to hold their shows. The warmth and popularity of those places brought their own following, as opposed to the dull coldness of ordinary halls. There was comfort, light and warmth and the right atmosphere. All the suburban music halls had their Sunday League shows, and so had many in the West End. The Alhambra was a most popular venue. It has gone now, that famous hall, and become a vast cinema. But the N.S.L. made history there, and one particular piece of history concerns this story.

The National Sunday League became very powerful. Indeed, when the London Palladium itself was being erected a guarantee from the N.S.L. for rent for Sunday concerts helped the finances very much. They had the Queen's Hall, too, on Sundays, where more classical concerts were held. For instance, on Sunday, December 20th, 1896, Handel's *Messiah* was given there, with F. R. Kinkee at the organ and Henry Lewis as principal violin—names with which to reckon then. There was a choir and orchestra of 400, under the direction of Dr. Churchill Sibley. The soloists were Barton McGocklin, Watkin Mills, Ethel Inverni and Medora Henson, all front-rank names in the world of concert and oratoria. And taken at a venture from many old programmes (the price for which was 2*d.* and which gave the words of all the songs) there is one for the Alhambra on April 28th, 1901, with the band of the Grenadier Guards, Jessie Kosminski, Maud Santley, Whitworth Mitton, Ethel March (violin) and no less a person than the great Lewis Waller himself giving recitals and bringing down the house. The programme included Gounod, Liszt, Sullivan, Hubay, Wagner, Haydn, all on the lighter side. Wagner provided *Die Walküre* if that can be described as light. But it was all popular. Lewis Waller gave " The Clamperdown " (and how he could recite it) and Thackeray's " The Cane Bottom Chair " (by special desire). And, of course, before he was allowed to leave he had to do " Once more into the breach " as well. The Sunday League gave young artistes a chance: they discovered talent. One young tenor who owed them much was the famous John McCormack. But he was one of many. The orchestras were of unvarying excellence, like Norfolk Megone's famous " Meistersingers." And you saw all the stars at the Sunday League shows, amongst them Madame Clara Novello Davies.

You could join this most deserving movement, which had been established in 1855, for 6*d.* (or upwards, the brochures said) and be a full member for 1*s.*; or, if you wanted a copy of the League's own journal, *The Free Sunday Advocate*, then your yearly subscription was 2*s.* But you did not have to be a member to go to the shows. Its avowed and published aim was " The opening of Museums, Art Galleries and Libraries on Sunday afternoons; maintaining the ' Sunday evenings for the People '; Sunday excursions; Sunday bands in the Parks and generally to promote intellectual and Elevating Recreation on that day. " It attained and maintained those highly desirable objects. For years its president was Sir William Treloar, J.P., one of the best and most charitable Lord Mayors who ever served the City of London. He did so much good with so little ostentation—like the League itself.

Space has been devoted to this very short and totally inadequate outline of a very great movement because of the opportunity it gave to Ivor Novello. Like so much that was of value to this realm, and which made life so pleasant here, it suffered a severe blow during World War I, from which it never entirely recovered, although it went on with its work unsparingly under very altered conditions of life and outlook. To-day many people may not have heard of it at all. But it did magnificent service during the First World War. It had a War Loan Savings Association for its members—for anyone who liked to take advantage of it. It boosted this by means of shows and the audiences were invited to subscribe.

One such show was held one evening at the Globe Theatre in Shaftesbury Avenue. It was during a period of air raids when theatres closed at night, playing matinées only, except on two evenings a week. The owner of the theatre was dubious about lending it. Not that he had anything against the N.S.L., but he thought the thing might be a flop. But he was persuaded by Alderman T. F. Bryen, J.P., a stalwart of the League, and by myself. The function was held. It was a bill packed with stars, including George Robey and Sir Harry Lauder. The owner made so little of the likely result that he offered to subscribe pound for pound the amount the League succeeded in getting underwritten as it were. He smiled rather broadly as he did so.

Though the performance was held on a rather foggy night, the theatre was packed. It took more than a thought of air raids to keep the public away from the amazing bill offered. In the vestibule there was the Grenadiers Band; on the stage turn followed turn. Then came Sir Harry's appeal. The First Loan had just been launched. He carried with him a " contents bill " of the *Evening News*—there were still such things as contents bills then—announcing that an old lady in Cardiff had taken up the loan to the extent of £2,000,000. He used his oratory. And then the public went to the officials and subscribed. It was a very broadly smiling Alderman Bryen who called on the theatre owner the next morning to announce the result and remind him of his kind promise to double it. The amount subscribed was £32,000, all in small sums. The theatre man was nonplussed. He begged pardon. Naturally he could not keep that rash promise but very nobly he put up £5,000. And he was Sir Alfred Butt, Bt. That just goes to show the power of the League. And Madame Clara helped in all that the National Sunday League did and was herself with her choir always a great draw.

From Oxford, Ivor went back to Cardiff, to 11 Cathedral Road. Of course the house was filled with music, with pupils in almost endless stream, coming to his mother for their lessons. She now taught regularly in Cardiff, Bristol and London. Her energy was boundless. Her London studio was at Chatham House, George Street, Hanover Square, above the offices of a celebrated firm—Concert Direction Daniel Mayer. Olga Lynn and Eduard de Reszke had studios in the same building. Mam had distinguished neighbours. In the Daniel Mayer offices was a young man who worked there, named Frederick W. Allen, who became friendly with Madame Novello Davies. She liked him and there was an arrangement between them whereby he looked after her accounts—a pretty difficult job because she was never a business-minded nor orderly woman. But Fred Allen coped and could get her to see reason, could make her keep track with income and expenditure when everyone else failed. That association became lifelong. Right up to her death, it was Fred Allen who was the trusted keeper of the purse and all that went with it, and who performed the same duty for Ivor as well. All Ivor's business and finances went through Fred Allen's capable and supremely efficient hands. He was the confidant, the advisor, the curber of artistic exuberance and consequent extravagance, and the counsellor of caution and wisdom. Never have two gifted people had a more devoted, loyal or faithful servant. He knew all the secrets but never breathed them. He saw to it that the money was properly spent, profitably and safely invested and must have saved Ivor some thousands of pounds by his calm and judicious judgment. It was, of course, part-time employment at first—but it grew into lifelong association and comradeship. The association, so far as Ivor was concerned, started soon after he came away from Magdalen.

There was the boy, in Cardiff, writing his music, earning a trickle of royalties. He wanted to do more, he wanted to earn more; he was champing at the bit. He would go with his mother to London and Bristol. They always tried and, usually, they succeeded in spending the week-ends at Cardiff, because father was still employed by the Corporation and there was not a sufficient income to enable him to give up his job, even if he had wanted to.

The year was 1909. The Edwardian era was rushing towards its end. King Edward VII died in 1910 but things did not change until the First World War. Ivor the youth was indeed living in great days, days of opulence, of wealth and might, when the British Empire really existed and when to be a Briton meant safety all the world over. The Briton—only then he was usually called an Englishman—was still " Milor " to the benighted foreigners. It was a time of leisure and grace, of peace and security. But, already, there was the threat of world disturbance, already the might of Britain was being challenged by the growing and surging strength of the German Empire. An arms race was on, and the traditional supremacy of the seas, which was Britain's own, was being disputed by Germany. Our Two-Power standard was attacked. Battleship was built against battleship, the Dreadnought being Britain's answer to the German gauntlet. There was no grumbling then at the expense of armament. It was not rearmament, for our Navy was always kept superior to those of Powers likely to come against us. But the usually lethargic public had been annoyed by the upstart Germans. And when the Dreadnought was evolved, they wanted it in quantity. The Government had decided to go slowly, but the public thought otherwise. A slogan arose, growing and growing in thunder as it swept the country. It was the voice of Britain speaking, and when that voice does speak, it does so very clearly and with great point. " We want Eight—We won't Wait," said that voice. It chanted it in the street, it wrote it on walls and pavements, it featured it in the Press. And the eight Dreadnoughts were duly forthcoming. The expense was considered colossal. In relation to modern spending, it was chicken feed. Anyway, the British public were going to keep the Seas and put the upstart Kaiser —popularly referred to as " Bill "—in his place. What the men and women then would have said to the appointment of an American Admiral in supreme command of the British Fleet beggars description. Heads would certainly have fallen. There was considerable bother when, during the Boxer Rising in China, a German General, Graf von Waldensee, was allowed to take over the supreme command of the somewhat scratch force of various nationalities interested in China which was to suppress the rebellion. But they guessed and guessed rightly that the bulk of the fighting would be done by British arms and that those men of the Navy and Army would do as they thought fit. It proved to be so.

The nation trusted King Edward, who was called the Peacemaker. He was, indeed, the most astute and accomplished statesman in the whole realm. He himself had always taken a very poor view of William Hohenzollern, despite their kinship. King Edward dismissed the Kaiser as being " no gentleman," which put him right outside the pale of decent English people. Although good King Edward had plenty of German blood in his own veins and a somewhat Teutonic accent of voice, he was English of the English in outlook, manner of life and heart. He was able to do a most amazing thing. He brought France and England—hereditary enemies for nearly one thousand years and on the verge of war only a short while previously—into alliance. It was not called an alliance; it was an Entente. It was the Entente Cordiale. It worked from the start, because he created it. Englishmen and Frenchmen—the most insular race on the one side and the most purely nationalistic on the other—really became friends and almost blood brothers. Agincourt, Crécy, Poictiers, Waterloo and even Trafalgar were put out of mind, and the bogy of Bonaparte buried. The British and the French knew that this getting together was to stop the Kaiser and they revelled in that. The link was firmly forged by King Edward and it is improbable that anyone else in the world could have done it. And when the test came, a very few years later, the chain held. . . .

Under King Edward life became expansive. The nation began to spend the wealth it had gathered under Queen Victoria. Life became brighter, conventions looser, everything was more free and easy under this most democratic king—but a king who never allowed a liberty or suffered any abatement of dignity, even when patted on the back by his subjects as he led in his Derby winners and though referred to by everyone as " Teddie." He did not mind that, for he was every inch a king. Had not his august and most regally aloof mother, Queen Victoria herself, been really touched when, in the loyal enthusiasm of her Diamond Jubilee Day, a working man in a cap had shouted " Go it, old gal! " . . .

Britain was rich, Britain was colourful, Britain was British and had a standard of living far above that of any other nation in the world. Its money was honoured at the highest rate of exchange all the world over. Wise and careful legislation was wiping out the plague spots of grim poverty which the Industrial Revolution had caused. No wildly expensive schemes were embarked upon, care and caution were observed, and the maximum amount of good was being achieved with the minimum amount of trouble and waste. Life was very good indeed. London was a gay city, ablaze with flowers in summer, bright with lights in winter. It made its own entertainment and exported it to America. It imported musical romance from Vienna and transformed it. It spoke its own language in its own way.

It was a time of private enterprise and low taxation, of really big business honestly done. Britain's goods sold in every market because they were British and Best. Mass production was in the womb of the future, though the internal combustion engine was already beginning to shake the old foundations of civilization. Men were beginning to fly—a Frenchman had flown the Channel. But that did not frighten anyone, even when the *Dail Mail* ran the headlines " England No Longer An Island." Nobody cared. Life moved in waltz time, the nights were gay—and so were the days.

The Gaiety Girls brought beauty to the Strand and to life in general. Sparkling, delightful Gertie Millar, with George Grossmith, Edmund Payne and Connie Ediss formed a team for ever unsurpassed and in 1909 at the Gaiety itself the play was *Our Miss Gibbs*. Daly's glowed with romance and throbbed to the strings of violins and on the stage that woman of real glamour and beauty wedded to talent and charm—Lily Elsie—was finishing the phenomenal run in *The Merry Widow* and embarking on *The Dollar Princess*. The actor-manager, under whom our Theatre shone the brightest, was in command. Tree was at His Majesty's, Alexander at St. James's. Giants like Wyndham, Lewis Waller, Seymour Hicks, Charles Hawtrey, H. B. Irving, Cyril Maude, John Hare strode the stage. Ellen Terry, Irene Vanbrugh, Violet Vanbrugh, Ellis Jeffreys, Mary Moore, Lena Ashwell, Marie Tempest, Constance Collier, Winifred Emery, Julia Neilson, Mrs. Pat Campbell—those were some of the actresses! Men like George Edwardes, Frank Curzon, Robert Courtneidge and Charles Frohman were the outstanding managers. That was theatrical London when Ivor really began to be absorbed by it. Many of its great ones later became his friends. Carriages and cars brought perfectly dressed men and women to the stalls, dress circle and boxes, people put on their best clothes to sit in the upper circle, and the patrons of the pit and gallery queued for hours to see their favourites. In those incredible days the Theatre was the only place and thing for which one queued.

That was the sort of Theatre into which the being of Ivor Novello penetrated and took root. Those were the standards his young eyes saw and those were the standards which he himself adopted. It was a time when only the best was good enough—that was his own standard all his life. He himself was the last of the true actor-managers, he was the last link with those days of theatrical glory and he was the last to carry on its atmosphere and its methods. For although he kept abreast with modernity, he kept that old standard and basic idea. His huge successes at Drury Lane were Drury Lane dramas romanticized and set to music, and played with modern speed. But they had all the structure of the past, and all the formulae which had suited that famous house. 1909 at Drury Lane happened to be the year of *The Whip*, its record-breaking melodrama. *King's Rhapsody* was in the very best tradition of Daly's, but even stronger in story and treatment. *Gay's the Word* would have given George Edwardes cause for pride at the Gaiety. Ivor never forgot the quality he drank in when seeing all those shows of the earlier 1900s. He kept the tradition of our Theatre bright and shining and our Theatre has the finest tradition in the world.

Life outside the Theatre, then, did not bother Ivor much. But he was a great concert-goer. He saw and heard the great ones: Pachmann, Kubelik, Paderewski. He fell under the rising spell of Elgar and all his life he worshipped *The Dream of Gerontius*. He knew well Sir Landon Ronald, who was perhaps the best conductor of Elgar's music. It was during his youth too that Wagner's music had become really popular here.

Opera was to Ivor much more of the world of the Theatre than of Music. That was how he saw it. He heard Melba, Tetrazzini, Caruso, Plançon, de Reszke, Kirkby Lunn, Calvé, Clara Butt—he met most of them, too—and all his life he knew he was moving towards opera. It was in his stars, it was in his ambition. He never spoke about it much, but as one watched his work, as one examined the plays which he wrote, its progress was steady. Often, in those productions, there would be plays within plays, and those inset plays were operas. There was one in *Glamorous Night* and in *The Dancing Years*. There is a scene at the opera in *King's Rhapsody*, while in *Arc de Triomphe* there is a scene from a Grand Opera about St. Joan. That was his first step into the music of opera, his first venture just across the threshold, and it showed what might have been and what was surely to come. He would admit that one of his ambitions was to conduct his own opera at the Royal Opera House, Covent Garden. And I have no doubt that he saw it very clearly in his mind's eye. There is also very little doubt that the opera would have been about St. Joan, a figure towards whom Ivor was irresistibly attracted. It is certain that he would, before long, have laid aside his acting, in which he had got as high as he could, and have contented himself with composition. The music of this land has lost a lot through his death. He might have written his own libretto, certainly he would have devised the story, or he might have collaborated with Christopher Hassall—who knew and understood him so well and who admired him so much—whose lyrics Ivor set to perfection. But he would have given us an opera, and more than one. They might not have been of the highest level of Grand Opera, but they would have been popular successes. Ivor Novello is about the only composer this country ever had who could have made opera pay.

Ivor rode in hansoms, in four-wheelers, in horse trams, in electric trams, in horse buses, motor buses, carriages and pairs, taxis and motors. He saw balloons and the coming of the aeroplane. He loved leisurely movement but he adored to fly himself. He was of the transition period but he saw the real beginning of it. He knew the Edwardian days; he had lived and been born under Victoria, before whom his mother had appeared and whose compliments and praise she had received. Ivor never forgot that—he used it later in one of his shows—but it got cut out because of time. He knew life in this land before 1914. Those who did not, never knew the real England. But Ivor Novello did, and remained part of it, always.

He was a great reader of novels. His early favourites in that respect were Seton Merriman, Stanley Weyman and, above all, Anthony Hope. He himself was a subject of Ruritania, and he kept that delectable country alive, and on the map. The classics did not hold him, but Shakespeare's word music did so always . . . and the plays were to him always something to venerate—and one day perhaps to attempt, though within his limitations. He only did that once, however.

He loved the life of his youth and he never outgrew it. For he was one of the fortunate people who never wholly grew up. He said to me not once, but many a time, " If only I could have achieved all I have done now and known and experienced what I know now—in 1914. That would have been the time to die." But by mercy, he was allowed to live on and brighten the darker, greyer years. . . .

And now, in that year 1909 when he really began life, what was he doing? He was not yet embarked on a career; rather was he feeling his way. And although, obviously, the path he must tread was music, with his own mental reservation for the Theatre too, he did what his mother was doing. He began to teach music. He became a teacher of the piano. He gave lessons at 11 Cathedral Road to pupils when his mother was absent in London and elsewhere. He was a good teacher, too, and had quite a little clientele. But the business side of it worried him; he knew nothing about that and he was only a boy. So he took a very wise step, once again following his mother's example. He turned to Fred Allen for help and guidance. His mother broached the matter to Mr. Allen and told Ivor it would be all right, so on April 10th, 1909, David Ivor Davies wrote this letter to the man who was to be his right hand in such matters all through his life:

" Dear Mr. Allen,

Mother has told me you are going to be kind enough to look after my lucrative business! Will you be satisfied with 5 per cent. (whatever that may mean) ? I can see you increasing your income by at least three-half-pence a year! I am enclosing a list of pupils, number of lessons and the times they come.

Yours,

Ivor Novello Davies."

There were nine pupils. Perhaps one should say there were ten, for Ivor writes against one name " . . . had four lessons but apparently has stopped altogether." One wonders, why? A Novello failure? She must indeed have been hard to please, or perhaps he was too exacting and she not really musical and impervious to charm. They all came on Wednesdays, Fridays and Saturdays. They were all young ladies, though it is significant that the lady who came no more after her four lessons was the only married woman of the lot. . . .

Anyway, that was the beginning of Ivor Novello, teacher of the pianoforte. What luck those girls had! What would not tens of thousands of modern misses have paid for the chance? Mr. Allen's 5 per cent. would have paid surtax. . . .

CHAPTER THREE

GROWING PAINS

THAT pianoforte professorship did not last for long. It was too binding for impetuous youth, and it was not remunerative. Fred Allen has forgotten actually what figures it produced—they were very small—and as regards his 5 per cent. he neither collected it nor even asked for it. What he did, he did as a friend, and, characteristically, he says there was little enough to do.

Ivor was composing all the time. Most of his efforts were just things which he sent to publishers and which were returned with all possible speed. He managed to achieve one or two minor successes, but nothing which made any impact. But he worked on. Sometimes he would be disheartened and wonder if it was any good at all, and then his mother would tell him he was lazy. The truth was that the urge to act was really beginning to be felt. He was spending most of his time in London now, at his mother's flat in Bond Street. He went to every kind of show, from Grand Opera to Music Hall. He drank in all that he saw and heard. Usually he sat in the pit or the gallery, but it did not matter to him. To be in a theatre—that was all that mattered. Once there, the surroundings did not exist; there was just himself and the play, and, of course, the wonderful people in the play whom he was privileged to see. He was lucky for he was seeing the English Theatre at its very best. He was also seeing the English musical stage at its very best. It was the musical plays he liked the most, as was natural for a youth of his upbringing. To him they were realities, for he was the perfect playgoer.

Night after night he worshipped at the shrine, worshipping two goddesses in particular—Lily Elsie at Daly's and Gertie Millar at the Gaiety and, later, at the Adelphi. He watched the musical shows, he watched the perfection of the productions of the great George Edwardes, and to him that was the way things should be done. He was right and that lesson always remained with him.

George Edwardes tolerated only the very best—and would sacrifice anything to achieve it. He scrapped the second act of *The Country Girl* a couple of days before production and the new scene was only being delivered at the theatre when the first act was actually in progress on the opening night. There was a terrible wait, a very prolonged interval, but eventual triumph. Edwardes had been right. The Guv'nor, as Edwardes was called, believed in every detail being correct. He would have no square pegs in round holes. He believed in girls, he believed in femininity, but he never just allowed the girls to parade their beauty and femininity without a proper background. There must be no raw edges. And girls who showed an ability to dance were sent to the best teachers, at the Guv'nor's expense. Girls who showed signs of possessing a voice went, also at his expense, to the best singing teachers, and many of them were sent to Madame Novello Davies. Ivor saw the wonderful creatures in his mother's studio, and marvelled at them. The girls who worked for George Edwardes understood what that meant and knew what was required of them. You never saw them untidy, frowsy or looking anything but their best. No matter how early the appointment at the Hanover Square studio, those girls were on parade—spick, span, smart and shimmering with attraction. They were of Daly's—or they were Gaiety Girls. In those days, that meant a whole lot.

Ivor perhaps preferred Daly's to any other theatre and its offerings were his favourites. He was born a Romantic and Daly's dealt in Romance. The Gaiety was, naturally, gay and sparkling; it was champagne. Daly's glowed like a chalice of burgundy; it was velvety with Romance. The theatre itself was quiet, subdued and had no glaring lights or striking colours. Beautiful polished wood reflected the shaded lamps and soft tones set off the rich dresses of its patrons. The brilliance was there, but it came from the stage, and that is where it should come from. There was no chromium, no forced air of carnival, no bars obtruding themselves on the public notice as soon as they entered the doors. No band played in the vestibule, no garish notices proclaimed the marvels to come or drew attention to shows under the same management elsewhere. No showcases displayed goods or advertisements; that sort of thing was considered vulgar. People went to Daly's knowing they would see Quality. For Daly's and the Gaiety sold branded goods and their quality seldom varied. Some brands sold better than others but even a failure—and there were failures—was an error of judgment rather than an error of taste. The audiences went there, not because they had been lured in by publicity and advertisement, but because they wanted to. They went there because it was Daly's, or the Gaiety, and because they knew what to expect from George Edwardes. They were not bored, blasé audiences, saturated with amusement; they were much simpler, unsophisticated folk, who were just as interested in the slender, sentimental or romantic stories of the musical shows they saw as they were entranced by the music.

You may say how much easier it must have been to entertain them as compared with to-day. You would be wrong. For those audiences were much more critical than modern crowds. They saw a standard which was reached by human exertion at its topmost bent. They heard singers who could sing and be audible, with diction which made every word of the song distinct. They heard actors whose lightest whisper reached the back wall. Above all they saw people who relied on their own efforts and personality to please their public, who were not boosted to mechanical fame by means of film or radio, but who did what they did, achieved that hold on audience affection which stood the test of time, by their own personal efforts.

Of course, they had something in their favour—they had the right setting. The audience entered a theatre and entered another world, leaving the ordinary everyday life behind them. They did not just " go to a show "—they went to the Theatre and all that it meant. They were transported the moment they took their seats, for theatres then looked like theatres and not like severe modern drill halls or converted cinemas. There was plush, there was gilt, there was old gold and vieu rose, there was cream and deep crimson. And, above all, there were footlights. When the magical moment came, and the house lights—never blatant—dimmed down and the golden glow of the footlights lit the rich act-drop, the velvet tabs, and when the orchestra played the opening bars and that curtain swished up, showing the first scene, that was magic! The people they had come to see were magic people, who had no real existence but who lived in that remote, desirable romantic land, shut off from ordinary mortals by the glow of those barriers to reality, those guardians of Illusion, the footlights.

Far too often the footlights themselves have gone to-day and there is no barrier between actor and audience. There is, instead, that familiarity and intimacy which may make for a sort of friendliness—very questionable—but which destroys romance and destroys stage personality. And, above all, destroys Illusion. But when Ivor was a young playgoer, the footlights were there. He knew their value and he kept that golden Theatre of his youth always with him. He was always behind the footlights himself. Approachable as he was, easy mannered as he was, the footlights always glowed. . . . And that he was right he proved time and again.

He was absorbing his knowledge when he sat in front at Daly's or at the Gaiety. But, as I have said, Daly's lured him most. He saw its first nights, when the line of carriages reached from its portals right across Leicester Square to Piccadilly Circus and beyond. He knew the eager buzz of anticipation in the pit. He saw the dress suits and diamonds in the upper circle, worn by people who could not pass Edwardes's social standard for the stalls but who were grateful to be in the upper circle, so long as they were in Daly's. He knew the excitement of the " gods " perched in that high and not over-comfortable gallery, with everyone packed closely together, hanging over the rails, staring down at that big square of light whereon the players they adored moved, acted and sang. . . . He was a real, genuine member of the audience—that audience which George Edwardes always watched so carefully, for he knew all about what was happening on the stage. They were great days and nights and Ivor absorbed them. In after years he was the only man to create an atmosphere such as that, and he was able to do so because he knew how he had felt. Indeed he was conscious of its exciting tingle always—and so he did his best to preserve that atmosphere. And he rarely failed to do so. For when he was about—when he wrote a show and played in it—it was always Theatre first, that true Theatre of plush and velvet, of Romance and Illusion and, above all, of the magic lure of the footlights. . . .

And those people whom he saw, in those now seemingly distant days of 1909, 1910, 1911, 1912 and 1913? Were they really so wonderful? Were they really so great? Were they really so magic as the oldsters would have us believe? Ivor thought so, and, naturally, I think so, for I am of that generation. How can it be tested? Is it possible to test it at all? It is and it has been done. It is trite to say that the actor's art is ephemeral, that it passes with his generation. In the main, that is true enough. But does that mean that when the star has had his or her day, the magic goes? Time is a great testing acid. It sorts out the dross from the true metal. And I was the humble means of such a test being applied. I wrote a book about the Gaiety and my friend Christina Foyle, a pillar of literature, a great bookseller and a most astute woman of business, was so good as to give one of her literary luncheons in honour of the book and its humble scribe, who became guest of honour and had the awe-inspiring task of making the speech.

All the great ones of the Gaiety were invited—from the beginning to the end. There was a direct link with the first night of the first Gaiety in the person of Joe Farren Soutar, son of peerless Nellie Farren herself, and also son of Robert Soutar, her husband, who had been the stage manager on that amazing night. There was dear Sylvia Grey, the matchless dancer of Victorian days, who held London in the palm of her hand. They were all there: sweet Ellaline Terriss, Ethel Sydney, Grace Palotta, who sang " Oh, Listen to the Band," adorable and lovely Lily Elsie, Hilda Jacobson, Phyllis Dare, who shines as brightly to-day, right down to the later stars, like Mai Bacon, strikingly handsome Ruby Miller, Madge Elliott and Cyril Ritchard, Richard Hearn and, of course, Leslie Henson. Vivian Ellis was there as a composer and—so was Ivor Novello. And the two great Gaiety peeresses were there too: graceful, handsome and distinguished Rosie Boote, the Marchioness of Headfort, looking no different from the day when she sang " Maisie " and the boys said " Whoops," and, seated by my side, Gertie Millar, the Countess of Dudley to the world, but always Gertie Millar to us Gaiety people.

Sir Gerald Kelly, President of the Royal Academy, was in the chair, and as he called upon those people, those wonderful people, to rise in response to their names, it did one's heart good to hear the enthusiasm of the cheers which greeted them. Here was no polite applause—here was the kind of welcome they used to receive on those first nights which they had adorned, but with a deeper ring in it because some of them had not been seen by their admirers for all too many years. That reunion touched the heart, eyes were moist all round as they gazed on those true artistes. Men blew their noses and cheered, women cried out their names, handkerchiefs fluttered and people stood up to acclaim them. Age had not withered them, custom had not staled them: they were fresh and bright in the public's fond remembrance. Yet some of them had not appeared for thirty years, some for forty—some had never been seen at all by the younger people present. But they all knew them, they all acclaimed them. In their homes were picture postcards of these people, photographs, old programmes, treasured because of them.

I wonder if thirty years from now such a gathering of artistes could be convened who would have the same hold, the same effect, on their public? I don't think so. Because most of the favourites of to-day are either voices over the air or figures on a screen. They have not the personal touch, the personal appeal. They work through machinery for the greater part and they are not saturated in that preservative of Romance—the gleam of the footlights—the remoteness of the Theatre. These people did what they did themselves; no microphones; no help but what they found in the mystery of their calling; no power save that tremendous force which was their own personal art.

That Gaiety lunch was not only a most emotional and unforgettable experience; it was also a lesson in Theatre. I made my speech. I threw away all the notes I had prepared and spoke from the heart on the inspiration of the minute. There was enough to inspire me anyway. The finest tribute I had came from Ivor, the next evening, in his dressing-room at the Palace Theatre. He looked at me in quite a new manner, as if he had not really seen me before. His eyes glowed. He told me how he had enjoyed every moment of it. And then he said "You know, Popie, you carried me away. I sat there listening and I lost myself. I could not make it out. I said to myself, don't be silly, it's only old Popie talking—you know him—but, you know, it was not. It was those wonderful times come back, and I realized I was of them. And you were of them, and you brought them back to me and made me proud to think those days were my days—the days from which I learned, the days which I still try to keep alive. Thank you, Popie." "But, Ivor," I said, "you do keep them alive. Your shows are just those shows, allowing for it being 1950—and you are the man who keeps that standard in the Theatre."

And it was true. I was very grateful for what he said about my little effort, but then he had never heard me before, and he had forgotten that I am an old actor who knows the tricks and who does a whole lot of lecturing to all sorts of audiences. He had forgotten that I am still, thank God, what Seymour Hicks used to call " an old faker "—able to bring up the little knacks of the stage and who thinks that a speech should be not only spoken, but acted too. But that is by the way. What matters is that the days of Ivor's youth, which was my youth too, had shown themselves as days which stood the test of time, and the people who made those days and nights of the Theatre really great were just as great as ever and had never lost that public whom they served so well. The audiences still remembered. And one of Ivor's great secrets was that he never forgot those days when he was in the audience watching those people. He remembered all he saw, and, more important, what he felt.

At that time Ivor was still writing ballads, and often getting them sung. He was in competition with many other young composers. Nevertheless he held his own. He also heard his music played by a full orchestra, at no less a place than the Crystal Palace, and sung by no less a person than Ada Crossley. He had made a new setting of " Oh God Our Help in Ages Past." It may surprise the countless admirers of his later years to discover that he wrote quite a lot of religious music.

So far, Ivor's outlook had been bounded not only by this country, and by one or two parts of it at that, but in 1912 he was to cross the seas, making a trip to Canada. The opportunity came out of the blue and was mixed up with an attempt to transport the Festival of Empire, which had been held at the Crystal Palace, to the Dominions and even to the United States. Ivor had written some music for it. There was a pageant with exhibits all over the great glass house, a tour on a kind of semi-switchback scenic railway through a potted and very theatrical-looking version of that " far-flung " territory—rather tawdry in sunshine and rather depressing in rain—and a real pageant, very well done indeed, in the big arena of the grounds. It is difficult to recall all the details now, but there come visions of strangely attired people wandering about, from blue-clad Ancient Britons to extremely savage and rather self-conscious representatives of the lesser breeds just within the law. It is probable that most of the performers were enthusiastic amateurs, which would account for their rather ubiquitous appearances and their retention of costume and make-up. The " pro " of that period would have gone into hiding and kept out of sight of the general—and paying—public. I also remember innumerable stalls devoted to the sale and advertisement of a well-known brand of boot polish. But no memory of the music remains at all.

When it was all over, Ivor went to Canada. He saw the great cities, saw and met new sorts of people, absorbed new ideas, witnessed new ways of life and new trains of thought, and he had the exciting and supreme experience of his first sight of New York. That city is an amazing experience when first glimpsed. London does not come up to it in that respect. London does not do that, but, more homely, much more friendly and with the confident poise of centuries, it can capture, fascinate and hold in a manner New York cannot achieve, once the first immense impression is over. Even in these days, when almost everyone is familiar with its appearance and its life—according to the cinema—it is queer how foreign it seems despite the similarity in language. To Ivor it was sheer excitement. He saw all the sights, he saw all the big shows, he saw all the great stars, he made friends everywhere—he always had that gift—and at a party he met a handsome, very handsome, striking and dark lady who was to play a considerable part in his life. Her name was—and is—Constance Collier, one of the finest actresses and arresting personalities of our Theatre. He also saw, on the stage this time, a very lovely person indeed named Billie Burke. He was to meet them both again—many times.

This trip inspired him. He wrote music all the while, in between his playgoing and opera visits and his social round. It was during this period and largely during his stay in New York with its tremendously bracing and stimulating effect that he completed—in fact wrote and composed most of—his first full-length musical play which he called *The Fickle Jade*. It was his first-born. He had the highest hopes of it. He played its music over to all who would listen and he got general praise. But it was to be his first lesson of the heartbreak of Theatre-land. Nobody in managerial circles would look at it. It was universally turned down. Ivor Novello was being created as that play was being made, but David Ivor Davies took the defeat, the series of defeats, with pride and philosophy. In his mind he begged to differ. He believed it was good. But, if they did not want it—all right. Like the villain of old melodrama he probably registered in his mind that " A Time Will Come " . . . and sure enough, it did. *The Fickle Jade*, as such, never saw the footlights; so far as fortune was concerned, she lived up to her name. But that music was played—for Ivor used many numbers from it in his big and very successful musical plays in later years—and had the satisfaction of hearing them applauded to the echo. It just goes to show what name and fame will do.

He returned home, braced and invigorated, his eyes full of remembrance of new marvels, his mind a mass of new impressions and the richer by many friendships, most of which were to last for life. Ivor seldom broke a friendship, and nobody ever wanted to break with him. The change in his routine however was, as usual, the forerunner of other changes in his way of life and surroundings. It often happens that way. He had a new energy . . . the creative force was growing. His mother observed and commented. He felt his luck was in.

When he arrived in London, he found a new home. Mam had moved into another flat in Hanover Square, which in those days was a wonderful place, a place where very high-class commercial people, expensive costumiers, exclusive tobacconists with distinguished clientele and the like rubbed shoulders with " The Best People." Commercialism was marching on, but the old manner of life was still active and undismayed. It was 1913, and young Ivor was still struggling to break into the realm of the Theatre as a composer, but with the idea of acting growing stronger and stronger in his head and his desire. Mam was teaching ceaselessly, though not receiving anything like the financial reward she should have reaped. She was still struggling to pay for the dilapidations due from her at the end of her tenancy of her school of voice production at 143 Sutherland Avenue. She was liable for the rent of her studio at Chatham House, and for an expensive service flat in nearby Hanover Square, and was finally persuaded that she should find a less expensive residence and studio combined.

Let us look back for a moment. Life was changing, life was altering. In 1910 King Edward VII had died and King George V had ascended the throne. With the passing of the Peacemaker the German menace was growing stronger. But the general public did not yet take it seriously. Although the man who gave it its name was dead, the Edwardian Era was still in full flood. The word Zeppelin was in many mouths. England already had some "flying machines" in its armed forces. They were controlled by the Royal Engineers, who, in 1911, formed a special unit called the Air Battalion Royal Engineers. They had at least one airship—rather small—and an aeroplane. The airship was called "Baby"—very suitably—and had first got into the air in 1909. The war of the air, foretold by H. G. Wells, was as yet something rather fantastic in most people's minds. The mere security of the times seemed to make such as flight without visible means of support, as it were, just a new idea of Science. Very nice for fun, but not to be taken seriously.

The Kaiser had even come over for King Edward's funeral. He rode in the procession on King George's right hand, wearing the uniform of a British field-marshal, his baton in his right hand whilst his crippled left hand held the reins of his white or dappled charger—the exact colour is dim at this stretch of time. He had surveyed the crowds over his aggressive upturned moustache much as he had done when he rode behind the gun carriage which bore his grandmother Victoria, but it seemed to the watching people there was more of threat in the eagle-like glances this time. He went to the Guildhall to a City luncheon with the Lord Mayor. London turned out to see. He drove between lines of people five or six deep who watched him go by in silence. Save for little groups of his own subjects scattered here and there, who shouted loudly, there was no cheering—and London crowds love to cheer. They seemed to be taking his measure. And he in turn was taking theirs. A few years later, the great majority of those men—they were mostly men, who watched him, city clerks, shopkeepers and assistants and the like—were to meet his conscript legions face to face. The professional soldier was to meet the amateur, and it was well for his peace of mind that day that he could not foresee the result. It is unlikely that he dreamed that these bowler-hatted or straw-hatted men—99 per cent. of whom had never handled a rifle, except at a fair shooting-range—would bring his Empire and his dream of world conquest crashing and doom him to exile in Holland . . . all his blood and iron liquidated by plain, ordinary British tenacity.

In 1910 the motor-car became almost as frequent on the road as horse-drawn vehicles. Indeed, the pace was quickening. And in 1910 a gentleman called J. C. T. Moore-Brabazon (afterwards Lord Brabazon of Tara) was issued with Certificate No. 1 of the Royal Aero Club. He actually flew eighteen miles in just over half an hour, the longest flight on a British machine ever taken up to then. Even he was not even dreaming of the giant Brabazon so familiar to-day. Dr. Crippen was arrested by means of the new-fangled wireless telegraphy. And Florence Nightingale died . . . new things coming in, old landmarks, persons and materials, departing.

In 1911 the Duke of Windsor was formally invested as Prince of Wales at Carnarvon Castle. That probably moved Ivor's imagination, for this was real Welsh history repeating itself after six hundred years. King George V was crowned and held his Durbar in India later. The first air mail was inaugurated to celebrate the Coronation. Burgess swam the Channel.

Then came 1912, the year in which Ivor went to Canada. Winston Churchill was very much in the news as a result of the amazing " siege " in Sidney Street, Stepney, which he attended in a tall hat and fur-collared overcoat. The whole country and the whole world was stirred by the heroism and death of Captain Scott and his companions. The almost legendary General Booth, creator of the Salvation Army, passed to rest. Alexandra Rose Day was inaugurated—and the terrible disaster of the *Titanic* occurred. There was another double shipwreck, too, nearer home and not so tragic. Both Boat Race crews were swamped during the struggle between Putney and Mortlake.

This year was as memorable for me as for Ivor. For I was then well established in the West End of Theatreland. I was working for Sir George Dance, not then knighted, who was the mighty power behind all the thrones. He had the money—real solid money—and ready cash was not too plentiful in the Profession then. Above all, the year 1912 is memorable to me as the year in which I was married, and, contrary to many rules of my profession and more contrary to the general custom of to-day, I still have the same wife and thank God for her. Whilst Ivor was composing his first operetta, I was working fourteen to sixteen hours a day in Leicester Square. Mr. Dance had a motto. Unlike that of the celebrated " Peter Doody " in *The Arcadians* it was not " Always Merry and Bright." It was of a different nature. We had it framed, in large black type on a white card, in every room at our head office at 48 Leicester Square. It said: "Do It Yesterday."

Dance backed George Edwardes and, consequently, I was always popping into Daly's and the Gaiety—of which Dance was chairman—making friends and admiring the great ones from afar, as became my rather humble status. But many friendships began then which have endured and which were only ended by death, friendships with W. H. (" Bill ") Berry, Joe Coyne, Tom Walls and many more. Humble homage was paid to Gertie Millar and Lily Elsie; it was a privilege to be spoken to by them. I knew all the lesser girls and boys. Sometimes I would take a note—usually a cheque—to George Edwardes from George Dance. It was always the rule to deliver it personally. " The Guv'nor " would open it, glance at it, and say to me in that odd, rather petulant, drawl of his, " Ah, from Mr. Dance eh? Very good. D'you want a receipt? " I would assure him there was no need. Then, if my luck was in, he would say " How are you getting on, eh? Being a good boy? " I would assure him I was. And then, perhaps, he would say " I wonder if you'd do something for me. Mr. Dance won't mind. . . ." And he would give me a job. It would mean I could spend the rest of the day at a rehearsal at Daly's or the Gaiety. Not even Dance could object to my doing a job for " the Guv'nor." My alibi was secure. And I think the Guv'nor knew it was what I wanted for he found me quite a lot of jobs—and, really, they took very little time . . . if you hurried. But, of course, you did not hurry in those days—or in those circumstances.

Another man I met there was W. J. Scott, who was secretary to J. A. E. Malone, Edwardes's right-hand man. Time was to make " Scotty " my own secretary, a job he did well and faithfully for very many years; I mourn him still. Malone, a violent-tempered man, was always polite to me. There was Dance's—G. D., as we called him—money behind me. There was George Slater, too, the ace of Edwardes's touring managers, a man devoted to polysyllabic words who became my life-long friend, and Seymour Hicks, also popping in and out. There was Charlie Brown of the Gaiety, still the same as ever and, although resident in New York, as English as that Charterhouse where he was educated.

But a great memory of mine which goes back to that year is that I very nearly did not get married at all. We worked all the hours that the good God sent and a few that Mr. Dance found lying about and threw in as extras. As the date fixed grew nearer, all hope of getting away faded, but, just in the nick of time, Dance decided he was going away himself so I could take my holiday at once. I did not dare tell him I was going to be wed. He disapproved of such habits in his staff. He said it made them lazy. I kept my guilty secret for months but it was discovered. He was bitter, he was sarcastic. I trembled as I saw dismissal draw near. Instead of that he gave me £100—a fortune then. . . . 1912 was Annus Mirabilis for me.

And so it was for Ivor. Indeed, miracles were happening all round. British boxing went to the canvas when Bombardier Wells fell before Carpentier in 1913: a Frenchman was boxing champion! Entente Cordiale or not, it took some swallowing, but perhaps the visit of the French President patched things up. King George visited Berlin, a year later . . . well! The First International Air Race was held at Hendon and Graham White won it. But a Frenchman called Pegoud managed to loop the loop in the air and to fly upside down. Wonder crowded on wonder. The year ended with ragtime sweeping all before it, with the old barriers going down as the world rushed to the furnace of war which was to melt but never properly reshape it—certainly never in its old form.

Those years thus summarized were the melting pot also for Ivor. They were wonderful years, those last breathless periods of the Old World and they were firmly planted in Ivor's mind. For they were the last of that old England into which he had been born, and the quality which graced them remained within him. The figure the public knew as Ivor Novello was emerging clearly, but it was, as always, David Ivor Davies who pulled the strings. He went to Canada and America in 1912 and returned in the autumn of 1913. The trip was made possible largely by the good offices of Mr. Forbes Dennis, a friend of the family who was, with his wife (Phyllis Bottome) a lifelong friend of Ivor's also.

As I said before, Ivor found a new home. His mother had given up the flat in Hanover Square but had taken another. It was, to Ivor, the ideal spot. It was actually on the roof of a theatre. Could anything be more desirable? That theatre was the Strand Theatre, which had been opened as the Waldorf, had become for a short time the F. C. Whitney Theatre, and then took on its present and most suitable title—the Strand. This, of course, was sheer delight. For the Theatre had now got Ivor right in its spell. No longer was he considering the concert world, the world in which he might work only as composer; he wanted something in which he could express that creative desire now so urgent in him. He wanted to be part and parcel of that truly magic world behind the truly magic barrier of those footlights he loved, a world at which he had gazed in London, into which he had penetrated in New York. He wanted to be of the Theatre—and here was his beloved Mam with a home attached to one! With what excitement must he have ascended that narrow staircase and entered that tiny, awkward, seemingly insecure lift for the first time! Those who knew him can imagine the joy with which he took that ascent and then stepped out into what was to be his home and workshop for so many years. He wanted the Theatre, and here he was living and perfectly at home on top of one. It was symbolic, had he known it. For he was to live there until he, as actor-manager-author-composer, was to be truly at the top of the Theatre of his time. Thirty-eight years he lived there—years of work, of endeavour, of ambition, realization, great triumph and bitter despair and distress, and, then, more success and greater triumph. No thought crossed his mind that autumn day when he first entered the door of No. 11 Aldwych that he was entering the place where the rest of his life would be spent—and that he was entering the place where he would die. . . .

What was going on in the London Theatre in the year 1913? Tree staged the mighty spectacle of his—*Joseph and His Brethren* at His Majesty's with George Relph, then a young actor, in the title role. He contented himself, in the traditionally greedy manner of the wicked actor-managers with the tiny part of Jacob. Gertie Millar adorned *The Marriage Market* at Daly's, with W. H. Berry and G. P. Huntley, while Ina Claire came from America to shine in *The Girl from Utah* at the Adelphi with Joe Coyne and Edmund Payne—his last part. Henry Ainley was scoring an acting triumph at the Kingsway Theatre in *The Great Adventure* with Wish Wynne—from the music halls—as leading lady. *Within the Law* was at the Haymarket, *Oh I Say* with James Welch at the Criterion. There was musical comedy: *The Pearl Girl* at the Shaftesbury, with Harry Welchman, Iris Hoey and a young actress destined to play the last star role Ivor ever wrote, Cicely Courtneidge. Just around the corner from the flat, at Drury Lane itself, was *Sealed Orders* a gigantic melodrama with a scene on a battleship, a wonderful safe robbery, a realistic representation of the Chelsea Flower Show, and a mystery airship brought down into the sea. There had been a " mystery airship " reported over England at night for some time past and " The Lane " was nothing if not topical. And in that same show they reproduced a famous hoax on a battleship by a gang of undergraduates which had made the whole nation laugh.

Across the way from the flat, at the Gaiety, was *The Girl on the Film*—not a very great success—and at the Apollo Charles Hawtrey was giving one of his finest performances in *General John Regan*. Marie Tempest was at the Playhouse in *Mary Goes First* and later Cyril Maude came back with *The Headmaster*. At the Duke of York's was a play destined to strike a note with Ivor—*The Yellow Jacket*. *The Ever Open Door* was at the Aldwych, and Sir Johnston Forbes-Robertson had said farewell at Drury Lane in the spring (but Ivor had seen him and had therefore seen the finest *Hamlet* our stage had owned since Betterton). A clever American actor named Hale Hamilton was at the Queen's Theatre in a play called *Get Rich Quick Wallingford*. *Hullo Tango* was packing the London Hippodrome. Before the autumn drama referred to above at Drury Lane there was that amazing season of opera and ballet, which included *Ivan the Terrible* and the terrific impact of Chaliapine. Sir George Alexander had revived *The Second Mrs. Tanqueray* at St. James's, with himself and Mrs. Patrick Campbell in their original parts. Rosalie Toller, a very pretty girl and a good actress, was the Ellean. *Strife* had been revived at the Comedy. Arthur Bourchier was in the height of his managerial career at the Garrick. He was, later, to move in underneath Ivor at the Strand. But a play at the Garrick was *Who's the Lady?* which gave Fay Compton a chance which she took. The Strand Theatre itself was not so prosperous then as now and had changes of attraction and several periods of closure. Two of the plays, however, were *The Barrier*, in which Matheson Lang starred (it ran for eighty-one performances), and *The Son and Heir* with Ethel Irving, a wonderful actress.

Ivor had not yet broken into the Theatre, although he had had a try. He had written in to the management of Daly's Theatre asking for an audition for the chorus. Anxiously he awaited the reply, but it never came. He was very upset about this. He made inquiries and discovered that he had been sent a card but, according to Daly's, had failed to attend. He made further inquiries at home. His mother owned up. She had got hold of that card and suppressed it. She wanted him to keep to his music. And maybe she was right in keeping him out of the chorus. Despite his lack of voice, his looks would have got him in. He might have toured around the country and lost opportunities. On the other hand he might have gained valuable stage experience much earlier than he did. He always inclined to that view. There was a good deal to be said for it. But, when it came to the Theatre, it really did seem as if Ivor was what was called "a natural." True, he was not a good actor at first, but it was always there and his improvement was steady with almost every part he played. His last was easily his best. He was still learning.

Touring was the finest school. The lucky youngsters then played in a different sized theatre every week, to different mentalities. They learnt how to expand and contract, how to attack, how to make their points tell, their voices carry. For they had to speak up then. If they failed to do so, the audience did it for them. It was a magnificent apprenticeship. There were, of course, theatres in every town, the number being governed by the size of the city. There were theatres in every suburb.

The cinema was, of course, still in its infancy, though it was becoming very popular indeed. In empty and converted shops you saw the show for a few coppers and got cups of tea and a biscuit to lure you in. Safety precautions were primitive, so it is amazing that fires were so few. A pianist sat at a piano and played music suitable to the scene being shown, and the story was, of course, silent but illuminated by captions, which were brief but amazingly to the point. The men who wrote them knew the value of dramatic brevity. Who does not remember "Came the dawn . . ."? It spoke volumes. And already some of the smaller suburban theatres, like the Parkhurst in Holloway, had been captured. Picture palaces were springing up everywhere, offering tip-up seats and plush upholstery, but still the converted shops hung on in the poorer districts.

The background of plays given is, of course, by no means complete. It is an outline to show what the Theatre was like. All the great names of the late Victorian and Edwardian Era were in active participation. That magnificent couple Julia Neilson and Fred Terry, and people like Martin Harvey and Matheson Lang took the West End to the provinces, as did Oscar Asche and Lily Brayton, between London seasons. Benson and Ben Greet gave them Shakespeare and trained the younger generation. Miss Horniman was doing wonderful work at the Gaiety, Manchester. And the Music Hall was alive and very much kicking: revue was seeping in but Music Hall was still there, with its great individualists. But revue captured the Hippodrome, the Alhambra, the Oxford and the London Pavilion, as well as the Empire. The London Opera House had a huge revue called *Come Over Here*. The Palladium varied between revue and " production "—and variety. The Coliseum kept on its majestic respectability of the very musical music hall. The Palace was just preparing to go over to revue as well. The world was beginning to change and the Theatre was mirroring the change. Meanwhile, Ivor Novello was not yet in the Theatre, but he was living on top of one.

Two camera studies of Ivor during his twenties

Ivor with his friend, Robert Andrews, in their early manhood

These snaps Ivor had captioned as follows : 1 Pompeii, 1911 ; 2 Walter Creighton and Self ; 3 Friedie and Self ; 4 Cliff, Mam, Mabel and Self ; 5 Jeanne Eagels and Self ; 6 Clifton Webb, Jeanne and Self

CHAPTER FOUR

THE GOLDEN KEY

WHEN that year of Fate—1914—dawned, Ivor and his mother were installed comfortably and permanently at No. 11 Aldwych, at least as far as anything could be permanent, for his mother had a perfect passion for taking flats, houses and studios all over the place with a view to enrolling more and more pupils. But, for the moment, 11 Aldwych was "Home." It was made more homelike when Ivor's father retired from his municipal job in Cardiff and came to live with the rest of them in London. Much less is heard of Mr. Davies than of his more ebullient and forceful wife, for it is commonly believed that Ivor owed almost everything to his mother. So much so that the figure of the father is entirely overshadowed. Indeed, hardly anyone of the vast Novello public knew anything about him at all, and cared less.

Yet there was as much of his father in Ivor as there was of his mother. From her side of the family came the music, it is true, and that was a tremendous gift, but nearly all the rest, including the good looks, was from the paternal side. David Davies was a very handsome man, sanguine of hue. He did not pass his complexion to his son, but he did pass on the gift of luxuriant, shining hair and the distinction of feature. Ivor was a more finely chiselled version of his father, and when he played the older part of the two he undertook in *Proscenium* he looked very much like his father. Whenever he got the chance, Ivor delighted in playing two parts in the same play. But, then, he was two men himself and it was a form of self-expression.

David Davies had immense charm—natural and inherent charm—and he passed that on to his son, as well as his sense of humour. He was an easy going man and was also very lazy—and the first to admit it. Yet he lived quite happily with the continual and unceasing activity and bustle of his wife all round him and also the immense effort that his son was making too. But that lazy streak of his father's was in Ivor, as well, although he conquered it by the urge of his creative ability. He always wanted to be lazy, but he never found the time. This laziness expressed itself in other ways, however, and chiefly in his intense abhorrence of having to carry anything, even for the shortest distance. He hated it, and he would avoid it if possible.

Jean Webster Brough tells of an incident when on tour with *The Rat*. It was lovely weather, and Flamborough Head was within easy reach. A picnic was devised and the whole company went and spent a delightful day in the open air, all bringing contributions to the open-air meal. When the day was over and everyone was busy packing up, Ivor was missing. They could not find him at all. They were anxious, they called, they searched, but there was no Ivor. Time pressed and they went back to the theatre, wondering what had happened, for nobody had seen him go. But he was found in his dressing-room, making-up and talking gaily as to what a nice day it had been. " Ivor, where did you get to? " demanded Jean Webster Brough. " You gave us a fright. We searched high and low and feared you had fallen over the cliff. Why did you vanish like that? " " Duckie, I'm so ashamed," said Ivor, " I slipped away because I was afraid somebody might ask me to carry something." He had had his contribution sent out from the shop where he bought it and had been able to arrive with empty hands. But he knew what might happen on the return journey.

And in Hollywood, stopping with Gladys Cooper, he was seen, to everyone's astonishment, to carry a tea tray into the room, for there was a servant crisis. He carried that tray for his adored Gladys. But he took care it was the only thing he did carry, and only once. In all the parts he wrote for himself, there was an absolute minimum of what are known as " hand props." He hated them.

In his youth Ivor's father had been something of an athlete, and he had hoped his son might be one, too. But Ivor had not the slightest interest in games. At "Redroofs," when guests played tennis, Mr. Davies would look on with the greatest interest but always with the secret regret that he never saw his son playing—and winning. It was his laziness expressing itself through Ivor in that way. Once, indeed, when young and on tour, Ivor made an effort to play golf. It seemed the thing to do. All actors played golf and he felt a bit out of it. So one morning he acquired some clubs and set off for the links. His close friends marvelled. But it did not last the week. To begin with there was a lot of walking and physical effort; and, secondly, there was the haunting dread of having, perhaps, to carry his own clubs, even for the shortest time. So golf was given up and not grieved over at all. David Davies must have been a bit bewildered at times by all that went on around him. It was a life of which he was not part at all, but he accepted it. When "Redroofs" was bought, that was where he liked to be; he loved the country and he loved gardens, and there was cricket on the green at Littlewick.

Another gift he gave Ivor was his business sense. Ivor always had that, or, rather, David Ivor Davies had, inherited from David Davies, rate collector. For the father was a sane man and pretty shrewd one, if occasionally given to Welsh temperament. He loved and admired his son—and his son loved and admired him, more maybe in maturer years than in youth, when the more energetic and masterful mother and her music were swaying him and calling to him always. Madame Novello Davies forced him on to compose when his father's easier and leisurely manner was upon him. Maybe that was what he wanted. She never for a moment let him believe that he would not be a vast success. He had always been that, but thanks to his own efforts. That charm which came naturally to him, as it did to his father, that wonderful boy's voice which made him so notable when so young—those were his keys to success. But it was his mother made him turn those keys by her force of character and her continual urging, though she never opened a door for him: he always did that himself.

People would often say, when they knew him well enough, that his complete lack of conceit amazed them. Ivor would smile and say " Well, you know, it is not a virtue. It just happened I was always so much the centre of my own little world, always so much in the limelight and always getting away with it, that it just never occurred to me that there was anything to be conceited about. It just came naturally." That was true, in part. But his equilibrium and his deep and abiding sense of gratitude for his great success came from the steadier if less talented blood of his father. And as the years grew, Ivor knew it more and more. He adored Mam always and he admired that tremendous capacity of hers, that driving force which had made her so celebrated as a teacher of singing, which swept the choirs she trained and conducted into the winning place in international competitions and royal palaces, making her the recipient of royal congratulations. He had that tenacity himself, but he never had that unbridled enthusiasm which leapt at obstacles without ever calculating what was on the other side, which would enter into commitments without counting the cost, which always possessed his mother, up to her dying day. For she died almost in harness, as he did himself. He was an ideal son, and an understanding son. Nothing was too good for Mam so long as it was within reason. He gave her wonderful gifts—her box at his shows was always a bower of blossom. He would give her special bows and single her out for homage in front of applauding multitudes, all of which was perfectly sincere and heartfelt. They were both emotional. He wanted her always to have the best, to have every comfort money could buy, but he often called a halt to recklessness and wild extravagance. There were battles-royal between them with much upbraiding from her—but Ivor always won, making her see reason—for the moment—until she dashed off on another track. That was accomplished by the mental balance and the business sense he inherited from his father.

Throughout his life, through all his successes, in all his big earnings Ivor was seldom extravagant. He rarely wasted money, let alone squandered it. He kept a tight hold on it and used wisdom in investing it. Instances of his tussles with his mother and of his own financial flair will recur as the story proceeds. Sometimes he would pay considerable sums of money to gratify a wish of hers, but always he told her what the cost was, and he never did it unless he believed it was really going to succeed and give her pride. Very, very often he saved her from quite considerable disasters by that common sense and firmness which his father had bequeathed to him. She was always doing things which caused him embarrassment and inconvenience. He would put the matter straight, sometimes by rather drastic methods, sometimes by firm reasoning and, sometimes, if they were small matters, by exercise of much patient tact. He was never under her thumb from the time when he began to grow up—although, like his mother, he never completely grew up for there was always a child in his heart. But he knew quite well, and saw quite clearly that his mother had always remained a child, with all a child's enthusiasms, recklessness and lack of thought. His method of handling her was more that of an understanding but not too indulgent father. He let her have her own way until she got out of hand, and then she was checked.

Madame Clara Novello Davies was an amazing person, and not the least amazing thing about her was her immense energy and complete tirelessness. Ivor, like his father, had an aversion to physical energy and a great love of lying in bed. Getting up early was a horror to him. Not so with Mam: she was always up with the lark. Constance Collier, that great actress who was a close friend of Ivor's, who collaborated with him in his first two plays, and who taught him much of what acting and the Theatre meant, remembers Mam's early rising habits only too well.

To Mam, of course, life held only one thing—teaching singing. Music was created for that purpose. Not one second of the day must be lost; every moment must be used to instruct someone in the Art. It did not matter much to her if she got paid or not; she must give someone a singing lesson. Very often when Constance Collier was a guest in the house, she would be aroused by Mam at the (to Constance Collier) utterly impossible hour of seven a.m. She was made to open her eyes and wake up. There was Mam by the bedside. It was seven; it was time someone had a singing lesson. Nobody but Constance Collier was available, so it had to be her. It mattered not that Constance Collier had no vocal ambitions. She had been at the Gaiety, true, but at that time she was a great leading lady and a famous tragedienne. She had given our stage unforgettable pictures at His Majesty's Theatre, then the most famous playhouse in Europe, if not the world, as leading lady to Sir Herbert Tree. She had played, for and with him: Pallas Athena in *Ulysses*, Roma in *The Eternal City*, Mistress Ford in *The Merry Wives of Windsor*, Olivia in *Twelfth Night* and Viola too. She had been truly wonderful as Nancy in *Oliver Twist*, she had been Poppoea in *Nero*, Ethel Newcombe in *Colonel Newcombe* and Cleopatra in *Antony and Cleopatra*—the only actress who ever played the part as it was meant to be played and looked it at the same time—and she had done much else. Her musical comedy career was well behind her, not to be resumed. But Mam, nevertheless, decided on singing lessons, so Constance Collier, refusing to get up, would lie back on her pillows and sing scales under the constant instruction of Mam until that human dynamo charged with song and instruction decided the lesson was over—to Constance Collier's huge relief. And Ivor, safe in bed in his own room with his head tucked well down, would hear the singing (which awakened him) and roar with laughter until he fell asleep again.

He loathed getting up early. He loved to lie in bed when awake and conduct his business from there. I remember when a lady journalist was commissioned by a woman's magazine to write a kind of life story of Ivor. I took her round to see him in his dressing-room, got him to agree, and fixed up a number of interviews. When the question of the time of the interviews arose, Ivor flashed a smile at her. " I am afraid it will have to be early, very early," he said. The girl's face fell a little. " Really early, you know," said Ivor, " so that we have plenty of time. Would eleven o'clock be a bit soon for you?" The girl gasped her relief and agreed with delight. " I hope you won't mind my being in bed and in my pyjamas? " said Ivor apologetically, " I shan't be up, you see." Did she mind ? Not in the least. How many girls would have given their heads for such a sight, such a heart-quickening experience? His tens of thousands of fans would have swooned with delight.

It was strange what power he had over his fans, and what queer things they said and did. It was after a performance of his first play *The Rat* that perhaps the strangest tribute from a fan was paid to him. Coming out of the stage door, he faced the mass of girls and began signing autographs. One girl gazed at him with rapturous adoration as he signed. He smiled at her. " Did you enjoy the play? " he asked. " Oh, Mr. Novello," she spluttered, " you were marvellous. You looked so lovely when you spat! " Ivor always remembered that tribute. As his fame and popularity grew, so the fans increased. Yet some of them who waited for him could never have seen him previously. Well do I remember a visit to Southsea where he opened the try-out week of his play *Comedienne*, with Lilian Braithwaite as the star. The dress rehearsal was, of course, on the Sunday night. I decided therefore to make a long week-end of it—I have never been able, by reasons of my calling, to take proper holidays—so I took my wife and daughter down to the Queen's Hotel and managed to get the best suite of rooms. I am a poor man but I believe in having comfort and the best when you can get it, even at my own expense, and all my family have a weakness for a private bathroom in hotels. I took them down on the Thursday and came up to town the next day, returning at night. The manager asked to see me and was full of apologies. He was in a difficulty, he said. The suite we had was usually in the occupation of a gentleman who actually lived there. He had gone away for a holiday which enabled us to have the rooms, but was now returning unexpectedly. Would we mind, therefore, vacating them? We minded very much indeed and I made a lot of difficulty. Eventually he found us another suite, not nearly so good but with a bathroom, and under great protest we moved. That was on the Saturday. On the Sunday morning, my daughter and I, walking outside the hotel, saw Lloyd Williams, Ivor's devoted and amazing secretary, looking out of the windows which had been ours. A great light shone. Ivor was the " permanent resident " for whom we had been evicted! The stupid manager had not realized that I was of the entourage. Of course we would have turned out for Ivor—who would not?—and done so without protest and trouble.

The manager's stupidity rankled. But I was to be revenged and upon Ivor, who did not at that time know he was the cuckoo in our nest. I went down to the theatre early on the Sunday evening by taxi, and outside the door stood a boy in his teens, complete with autograph book. He sensed me as being of the Theatre and joy and hope lit up his face. He came forward and proffered the book. " Mr. Ivor Novello," he said, " will you please sign my book? " I signed " Ivor Novello " and went through the stage door. I don't resemble Ivor in the slightest degree, and at that time I had not undergone the severe slimming effect caused by my pet—and only—physical complaint. I weighed about seventeen stone! So much for fan worship. I doubt if the lad waited for Ivor at all. Afterwards I told Ivor and also told him it served him right for turning us out. And Lilian Braithwaite said she had always noticed the resemblance and set people on to solicit my autograph. . . .

But all that was years after 1914, when Ivor was a handsome youth, his feet not yet on the stage and himself not yet of the Theatre. Indeed, Ivor Novello as the public knew him was still a rather shy and retiring youth, with a wonderful smile and a charm which disarmed all around him.

There is one other fact to establish before this career of his moves on. I have alluded already to the mistaken journalist who wrote of the mother domination and the fear of women which he alleged Ivor felt. Let me state once and for all that this is quite absurd. There were indeed women in Ivor's life—"women," observe, not "woman." He had what he called his "romps." Those who remember *Glamorous Night* may remember how he used that phrase therein. Ivor Novello had his romps in life, like the vast majority of young men. Nobody is going to give names, but they were there, very definitely there. He did not marry, true, but remained a bachelor. He was not singular in that. But he had a bride, all the same—a most exacting bride—and she was the Theatre. . . .

The year 1914 progressed. It was, throughout, a year of unrest, of menace. Lord Northcliffe, that genius of the newspaper world, easily the greatest man Fleet Street ever contained, had not ceased to proclaim the increasing threat from German violence and the Kaiser's hunger for world domination. The *Daily Mail* was the most popular newspaper and despite the jeers of its competitors, wielded great power. Northcliffe had done his best to awaken public opinion, both in the *Daily Mail*, the *Weekly Dispatch* (as the Sunday stable companion was then called) and his other papers. He had supported Lord Roberts's attempt to form "A Nation of Riflemen" and largely because of Blatchford's serial dealing with the invasion of this country by Germany had put great impetus into the formation and popularity of rifle clubs all over the country. I joined one at Alexandra Palace in 1906—I think the invasion had been timed by Blatchford for 1910—and became a skilled marksman. This came in useful to me and to myriads like me later on.

But there was another cloud upon the immediate horizon which rather obscured the war cloud arising from Prussia. There was threatened civil war in Ireland. Ulster and the South were arrayed against each other. Lord Northcliffe threw himself into that heart and soul, into the cause of Ulster. Men drilled and armies were in course of preparation. Two men destined to play great parts in the history of their country, one a brilliant lawyer and the other a statesman who was to lead his country in her darkest but still most glorious hour through the shadow of terrible defeat to the brightness and brilliance of Victory—these two men were busy in that threatened civil war.

They both had military status: they were Galloper Smith and Galloper Churchill. The Smith was F. E. Smith (Lord Birkenhead), a future Lord Chancellor, and the other was Winston Churchill himself. This threatened war was almost Northcliffe's own private campaign. He went to Ulster and took photos—or his official photographer did—of the Ulstermen drilling. He sent the negatives back to London with the strict instructions to use them " big " in the *Daily Mail* and the *Weekly Dispatch.* The man who picked up the negatives at Euston Station managed to lose them. Nobody dared to telegraph " The Chief "—nobody dared do anything about it. Northcliffe was feared by all. But one man took action—and he was Hannen Swaffer, whom Northcliffe called " The Poet " and whose genius as a journalist he recognized. Swaffer stepped into the breach. He collected all the pictures of Ulstermen drilling which the photo agencies had sent in. He selected those which he thought would resemble those taken under the eye and orders of Lord Northcliffe. And he " ran them big " in the *Weekly Dispatch* and the *Daily Mail.* Everyone sat breathless and terror-stricken to watch the result . . . for Northcliffe could be a ruthless tyrant when the need arose. A telegram came from him and was opened with shaking fingers. It gave high praise and commendation for the excellent use made of his pictures. Nobody ever told him the truth.

Meanwhile war was rushing on the country from outside. In the July the Archduke of Austria, heir to the throne, was assassinated at Sarajevo, a place nobody had ever heard of and few could pronounce, situated, it was said, in a district called Bosnia-Herzegovina, known only to juvenile stamp collectors, the Foreign Office and a few schoolmasters and map-makers. But it was the flash point. Austria sent an ultimatum to Serbia. France, Germany and Russia mobilized, and Britain prepared to do so. Austria invaded Serbia and suffered a severe defeat. The war was on, and at midnight, on August 4th, 1914, Britain was at war for a " scrap of paper "—the treaty which bound this realm to preserve the neutrality of Belgium, which Germany violated at a place called " Vise." . . .

Earl Grey said " The Lamps are going out all over Europe." Indeed they were to go out all over the world. That threatened little war in Ireland was snuffed out and the warring parties came together, with a click which was almost audible, to stand together and face the common foe. So long as it was war it was all right for the Southern Irish, the majority of whom must have itched to be in World War II—and quite a few of them were. Northcliffe turned his attention to the enemies of his country. One day his work will be properly assessed and those who rail against the Press Barons will understand maybe what those men can and did do in times of need.

The whole country was in turmoil. Nothing like this had been known before. But the greatest confusion was in the world of the Theatre, never the most sane or balanced part of the community. After the first shock, war plays, of the most immature and absurd nature, were rushed on. Stars made speeches to encourage recruiting and it began to look like the end for many a rising hope of the Theatre—and indeed it was. This country lost a generation of its best youth, and the Theatre suffered in the same way. But war is a curious thing. To all too many it brings death and destruction; to some few it opens a door and leads to the heights. It was to do that for Ivor Novello. . . .

So far Ivor had made no impact on the Theatre at all. He was still merely one of the audience. On the concert stage he was quite well known and his songs enjoyed some popularity. He spent his life between 11 Aldwych and a little place down at Biggin Hill, a very quiet and peaceful spot then but a centre of battle and glorious victory in World War II. His one play *The Fickle Jade*, of which he had hoped so much, languished in the drawer of his desk.

And now, the whole world was upset. Young men joined up, stupid women with white feathers were already on the prowl. Old men who should have known better were asking " Why aren't you in khaki? " There was such a rush of recruits that they could not be put into uniform, let alone be armed. They marched and drilled in their civilian clothes, though some got dreadful blue overalls served out as a species of uniform. Lord Kitchener, brought back from Dover at the demand of the nation as he was returning to Egypt, was in charge. He had assessed the duration of the war as three years at least, but optimists still spoke of victory before the trees were bare of leaves in winter. The British Navy kept the seas of the world and King George V never spoke a truer word than when he called it the " Sure Shield." Britain stood shoulder to shoulder with its old enemy France and what was left of the Belgian army. Italy was to come in on the same side and Russia was looked upon as a steam roller which by massive weight of numbers would flatten out the Germans. But the steam roller was too slow and out of date to help at all beyond being a diversion. The field-grey hordes spread relentlessly over Flanders and France. The " contemptible British Army "—the finest body of professional soldiers the world ever saw—retreated, fought, maintained itself and won the race for the vital Channel ports. It held on grimly. . . .

Ivor Novello was twenty-one years old, legally a man with a man's responsibilities. There was hardly a question of choice for a young unmarried man in those days. But Ivor had no martial ambitions. He was simply a young Briton whose thoughts had never turned to war. He was not a fighter, not even a sportsman, nor had he ever been a pugnacious boy. He had never looked at real life; the life he knew and believed in was that which he saw through the haze of the footlights. The greatest force he knew was that of music. He had a deep and abiding love of his country, as most young people have and certainly had then. He hated cruelty then, as he always hated it. He hated pain, as he always hated it; he hated to see others suffer as much, if not more, than he hated suffering himself. His father understood what was passing in Ivor's mind. The counsel was to wait and see. They all knew that before long he must join the Forces, and he had already made up his mind what branch he would join. He was young—and modern in the sense of those times. He felt the lure and romance of the Navy and also the lure to be in the forefront of modernity and soar in the air. His friends were joining the Royal Naval Air Service, a nice compromise between the two branches of the Great Adventure. Ivor made up his mind that there was where he would go, when the time came.

Ivor would have been the last to pretend that he was a hero, champing at the bit to enlist and rush to the Front to fight the Huns. He was no coward. I have seen him and been with him during the Second World War when things were pretty warm and he never turned a hair but behaved with exemplary calmness. He was as brave as the next man. In 1914 he knew his turn must come and it was not the fighting that worried him, nor the fear of death. It was the conditions of service, the cramped, disciplined life, utterly different from anything to which he had been used . . . the regimentation, the routine duties, the loss of his music, the stagnation of composing and creation. Life in camp, in barracks, on stations, did not appeal to him at all. If he could have gone into action with no preliminary training, he would probably have welcomed the chance. So he did not make a rush at it. Neither did tens of thousands more, despite the amazing rapidity with which Kitchener raised his first hundred thousand.

So Ivor worked on under the adverse conditions of war. There was music in the war and, true to the British way of life, the music the soldiers sang was not of the rousing, patriotic heroic kind, but the songs of the British Music Hall. They told a certain naughty boy to hold his hand out; they inquired "Who Were You with Last Night?"; and they admitted that all the nice girls loved the sailors. But a journalist in France, during the very early days indeed, who was acting as an "Eye Witness," heard a detachment of British troops come ashore singing a sentimental song, with a good swinging tune, which stated the fact that it was a long, long way to Tipperary, but their hearts were right there. He mentioned that in an article he wired home. Like a flash, "Tipperary" became the second national anthem. It was adopted as the battle hymn of Britain. It was not even a new song. It was some seasons old and it had never really been a big success. It had been acquired from its composer by Bert Feldman, one of the biggest and most enterprising of the music publishers. He was a curious man, with a strange complaining, petulant voice, a ruddy complexion, a big nose, a largish moustache and very bright eyes and—when he liked—a most delightful smile. The moment he saw that story in print he got busy. "Tipperary" was printed by the million copies. It was advertised, it was boomed, and it became the War Song of War Songs—with power still to move the heart of 1914 veterans to-day by the memories and pictures it conjures up. But, had that little body of soldiers not been singing it when they stepped on to the shores of France, nobody might have heard about it any more. It had a good marching tune, as it happened, and despite the fact that its main interest was in Ireland—a country always hostile to England but about which the English always felt sentimental and fond—and they are the same still—it was just the thing. It bade farewell to

Leicester Square and good-bye to Piccadilly. So it echoed the sentiments of the boys in France.

There had been a recruiting song which had a vogue—but not with the soldiers. It was a straightforward recruiting song, which informed the youth of the land that we (presumably the singers and the womenkind) did not want to lose them, but thought they ought to go, because their king and their country both needed them extremely badly. They would be missed, they were assured, but there was a definite promise of a terrific welcome to the heroes on their return home. But the Briton, when forced to fight, never adopts an heroic attitude. He makes the best of it and when a Briton does not like what is going on or is seriously up against it, he either gets sentimental or he makes a joke. Sometimes he does both. So whilst the troops of foreign nations, for whom the British had a quiet contempt, found courage and content in songs glorifying their country, the mad British still sang the songs of that most British of all entertainment media, the Music Hall, but eschewed the patriotism which in peace-time it ladled out and to which, also in peace-time, they responded. They did not mind declaring that there they were, there they were, there they were again, because it enabled them to yell that they were definitely not downhearted. Nothing heroic, thank you! They would pack up their troubles in their old kit bags and smile—but they wouldn't regard themselves as heroes!

Nevertheless, patriotic songs were turned out by the score. It was not natural that Madame Clara should stay out of that. Here was a chance for Ivor to show what he could do, here was his chance to write a national song and win undying fame. She had no doubt at all that he could do it and her ambitions for him were the strongest thing in her life, stronger even than her own ambitions which never ceased until the day of her death. She was the living example of Elgar's "Land of Hope and Glory," always determined that her bounds should be set wider and wider, and that the same thing, only more so, should apply to Ivor. She pestered him, therefore, to write a patriotic song. He protested. It was not his kind of song, and apart from that every single composer in the land was churning them out—and with very little success. She argued and she argued but Ivor remained obdurate. She played her trump card. "Very well, Ivor," she said. "If You won't write one—I will." She did this to drive him on, to make him competitive. She thought he would do one if only to show how much better he could achieve it than she could. But it did not have that immediate result. So she composed her song, and Ivor was treated to the first private performance of it. It scared him, it frightened him . . . it was so bad. In his own words, it was terrible! Later he formed the opinion that she knew it was and only insisted that she would publish it to make him write a song himself.

So he did it. He was determined that Mam should not let the family down with her execrable song. So he went to work. He worked hard, too, there was no sudden inspiration. He hammered on and he wanted to keep away from the idea of his mother's who had called her song " Keep the Flag a 'Flying." He knew that was not the stuff they wanted—and he was right. That " audience mind " of his was working. At last he got a tune he thought would do. Now for the words. There was a friend of the family, an American who had lived in this country practically all her life and who had often wanted him to set to music lyrics which she had written. Her name was Lena Guilbert Ford. Ivor had sometimes written his own words to his own music but nothing seemed to come into his mind this time. So he asked Lena Ford to come round, and played her the tune he had composed. She liked it better than he did. But the more he played it the more unsuitable it seemed. And then, inspiration came: he tried variations, he essayed this and that. At last he shouted " Lena, that tune I played, that's not it. But this is it—listen—how about it? " And he played her his new version. And with his tune he had some of the words—he had the opening phrase—" Keep the Home Fires Burning " and quite a bit of the chorus, which he sang to her. Having played it and sung as much of it as had come into his head, he swung round on the piano stool for her verdict. She was just as excited as he was. " That's it," she cried, " Home Fires—it should be a household word." Ivor agreed and said he believed that the song was likely to be a real hit. He told her to run away and write the lyric, just retaining his opening phrase of " Keep the Home Fires Burning." She dashed off home whilst he played his melody over and over again to himself . . . and then the telephone rang. Lena Guilbert Ford had done the job—and when Ivor heard the last lines:

There's a silver lining
Through each dark cloud shining
Turn the dark clouds inside out
Till the boys come home. . . .

he was convinced that here was something which mattered. He scribbled down the words as fast as he could as she read them to him over the telephone. He dashed to the piano, played his melody, and sang the words. " Keep the Home Fires Burning " was born.

It still had to be launched. Messrs. Boosey's published most of Novello's compositions then, but they refused it. At length Messrs. Ascherberg, Hopwood and Crew accepted it. Still there was no excitement. Ivor, Mam and his father—and maybe Lena Guilbert Ford—were the only people who believed in it. It must have a public performance and one of a popular nature. And that was where the National Sunday League came in. The song was not then called " Keep the Home Fires Burning " but " Till the Boys Come Home." Perhaps that was what kept it back. However, the opportunity Ivor wanted came along. Sybil Vane, a Welsh girl and a pupil of Madame Novello Davies, had an engagement to sing at a National Sunday League Concert at the Alhambra. She elected to sing an operatic aria in the first half and what the B.B.C. are so fond of calling " a group of songs " in the second half. Amongst that group of songs she put " Till the Boys Come Home." There was a tiny programme announcement that it would be accompanied by the composer and that it was the first performance.

The second half of the concert came along and Ivor went on to the stage, shy and shaking with nerves. But he pulled himself together and the song began. Sybil Vane's voice soared out, with excellent diction. Ivor's fingers struck the notes, but some of his attention was on the audience. Sybil Vane sang a verse and chorus, then repeated the chorus. To Ivor it seemed he could hear voices other than hers. She sang the second verse—and again the chorus. This time there was no shadow of doubt. The whole house were singing, and not only singing but marking time with their feet. It was like an army marching. Over and over again they demanded the song; over and over again they sang it—the words were on the programme and the music was easy to learn. At a sign from their conductor's baton, the Guards Band seated on the stage (they had formed the main part of the concert), who had got enthusiastic too, vamped the accompaniment as well. There was the wildest applause and cheers. It seemed as if they would have to go on singing that song for ever. David Davies was standing in the wings and watching his son's triumph. He was weeping for joy. Unfortunately, poor Mam was not there. What a blow for her! She was in bed with a cold. The audience kept on cheering and, what was more important, they kept on singing. And when at last Ivor and his singer got off the stage and rushed home to tell Mam, the audience was hardly listening to what remained of the concert but were humming the tune. They sang it as they came out; they sang it as they went home; and they got the people at home going, too. And so quickly did this amazing song spread that the very next day Ascherbergs were inundated with orders and were reprinting more and more copies as fast as they could.

This was genuine triumph. It had not been gained by carefully built-up publicity with a specialized audience in the exciting and hectic surroundings of a theatrical First Night, with friends in front ready to applaud. It happened in the afternoon, in a music hall, before an audience of ordinary workaday people of the middle and lower middle class: just men and women of all ages in ordinary clothes and mainly on the shabby side, with a large proportion of young couples sitting with hands interlocked—a habit with N.S.L. audiences. But that audience was the one for which Ivor wrote then and always afterwards, and that audience was the first to acclaim him and to remain true always.

You can picture the scene, the vast auditorium of the Alhambra, with its quasi-oriental decorations a little faded, the gold a little tarnished, the blues and greens not so bright as formerly, the atmosphere a bit clouded with smoke and the band in the uniforms seated on the stage as a background to that figure of Sybil Vane and her young, handsome but very diffident accompanist who probably gave that audience a fleeting, sidelong smile at the spatter of polite applause which greeted them. And then—in that music hall where so many great ones had entertained their public, where Leotard had flown through the air with the greatest of ease, where Opera Bouffe had triumphed, where the Can-Can had shocked London and lost the place its licence, where Germans and Frenchmen

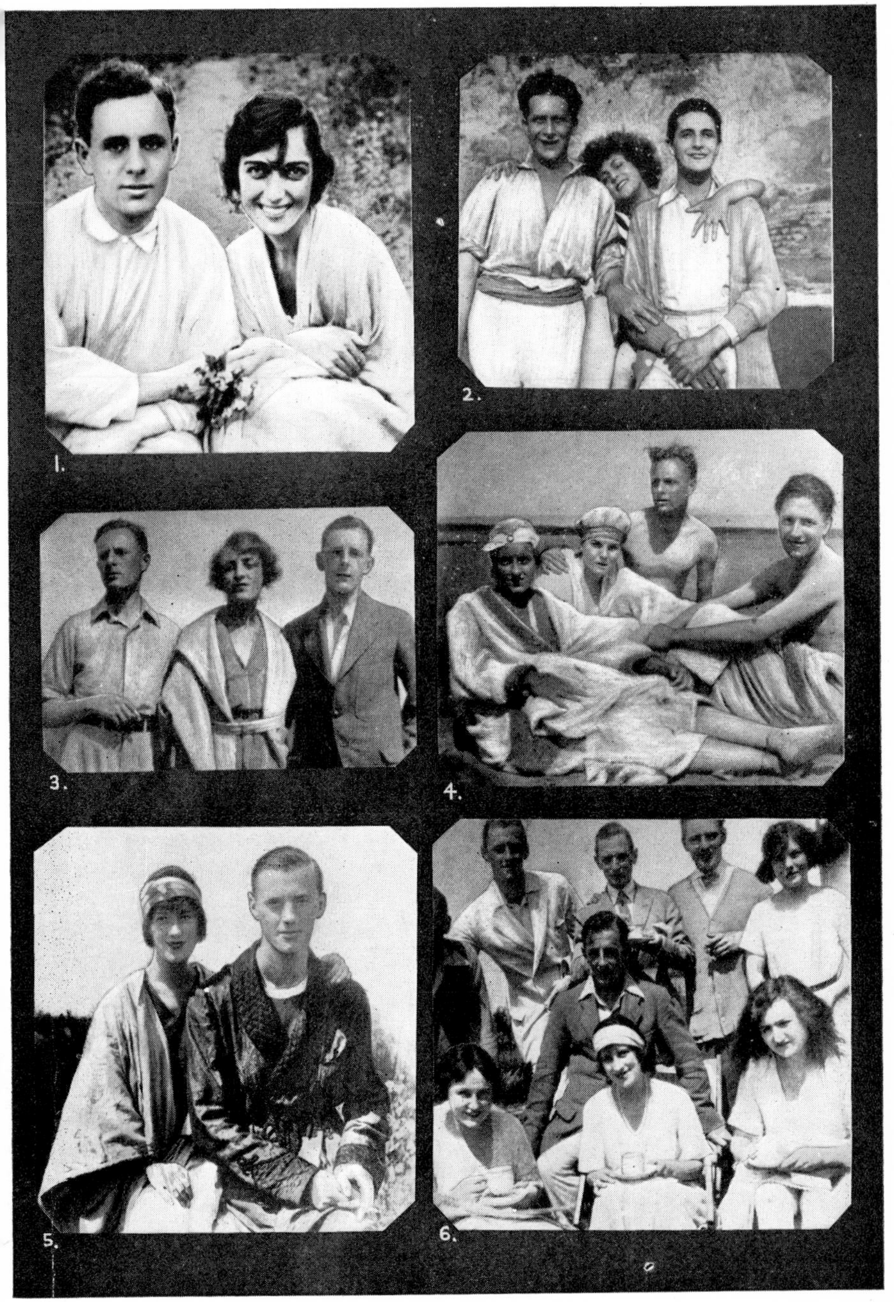

From Ivor's snapshot album. The pictures were captioned in his own writing thus: 1 Bobbie and Laura; 2 Desdemona, Mazza, Taormina; 3 Bobbie, Maidie, Lloydy; 4 Birchington, 1920; 5 Beattie and Bobbie Peel; 6 Fay, Beattie, Glad, Beryl, Bobbie, Frankie, Ronnie, Lloydy

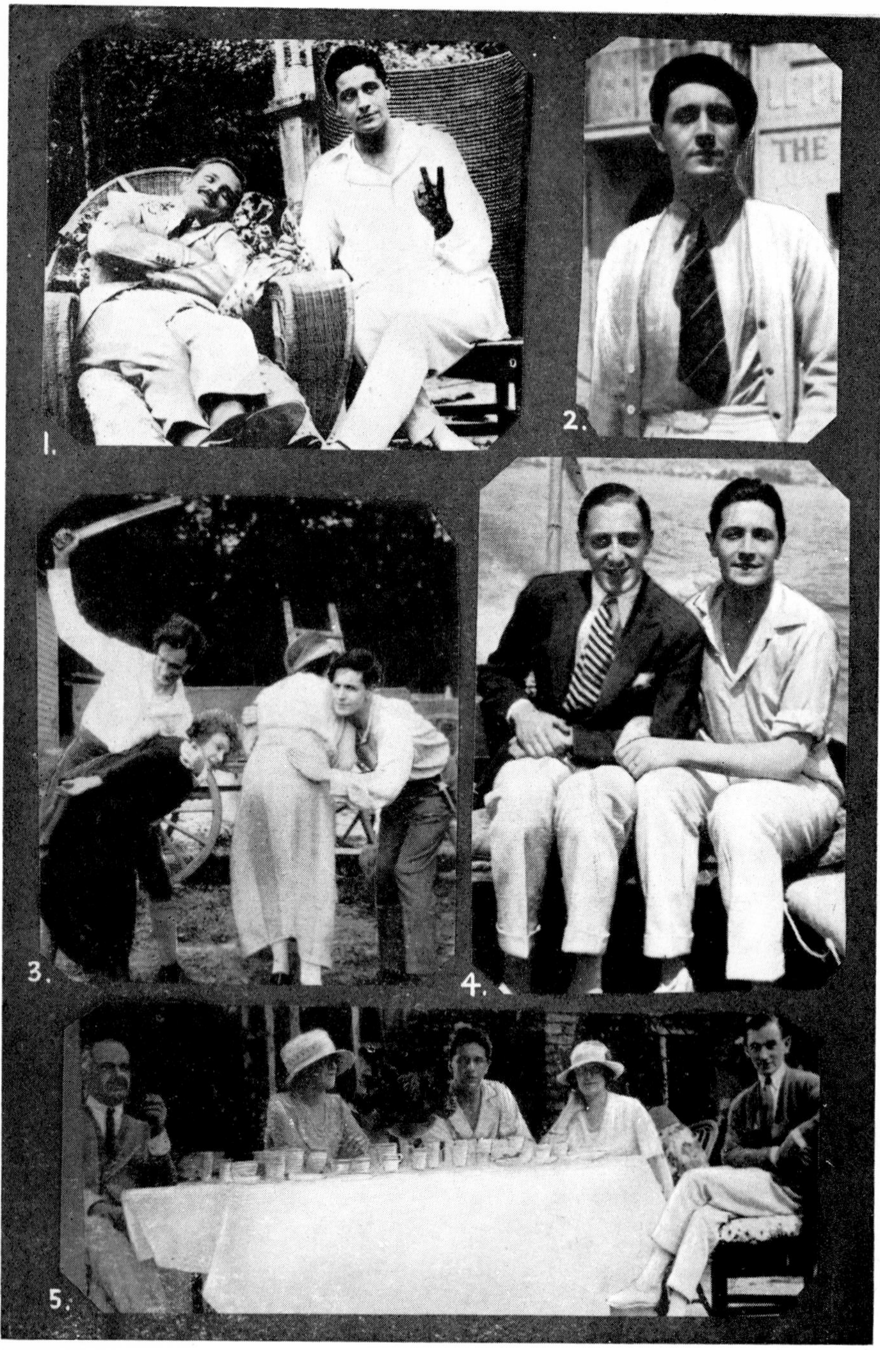

This page from the snapshot album shows Ivor with various friends in the South of France (1, 2, 4 and 5). Snap No. 3 was taken in Long Island in 1919. The gentleman administering corporal punishment is Clifton Webb

had brawled during the Franco-Prussian War, where Charles Morton, who created Music Hall, had been officially dubbed "Father of the Halls," and where later Gracie Fields was to conquer London—a young man who was to become one of the pillars of the British musical stage laid the firm and true foundation of his career before an audience of the sort which remained faithful to him. All that is worth remembering. . . .

Ivor Novello was a success. Ivor Novello was a Name. Ivor Novello was somebody who mattered. He knew that you have to do more than write one song but he knew that he had turned the key in the lock, that a door was opened, and that he was across the threshold in a big way. But he also knew that it was up to him to keep going. He had, in that song, shown his good sense. He had shown that uncanny flair for the pulse beat and trend of thought of the public. In his song there were no appeals to join up, no glorification of flags and battles, no rousing trumpet call to victory or death. Not a bit of it. He appealed not to the warriors, but to the public, that public which had to wait and hope for the end. He knew that the great thing they wanted was Hope and that was what he gave them. Hope was, from then on, the keynote of his effort always. He did it again in the Second World War with the same sentiment differently expressed but with Hope and Certainty of Return which was also in "Home Fires"—and again he scored a triumph. What made the success of "Home Fires" was the first-class yet simple marching tune and the appeal to the ordinary folk at home. It was they who were to do their bit. It was they who were to keep the home fires burning and believe that every cloud had a silver lining, so they were to keep up their hearts and turn those dark clouds inside out—till the boys came home. No question here but that they would—and that was what everyone wanted to think. That bit was Miss Ford's but the idea of the home fires from which it naturally follows was Ivor's own. And whenever he used the formula of that song—not the idea but the formula—of the simple direct appeal to the people, he always won.

"Keep the Home Fires Burning" was something more than a success. Something more than a golden key opening Fortune's door for Ivor. It became a national song. It remains one. During the Second World War, when Ralph Reader and his Gang Show went over to entertain the troops in the early days, the French people insisted on playing that tune when they they appeared, under the impression that it was a National Anthem. And Ralph and the Boys stood stiffly to attention. Ralph and his first lieutenant, William Sutton, were the most amused for they knew and had worked with Ivor. But there it was still, accepted as a British anthem. It is also a classic.

As a result of that Sunday League concert it swept the country and it reached the Front. It went on and on, and when it showed signs of falling off the Americans came into the war and boosted it again. It earned Ivor, in its first flush, the nice fortune of £15,000. It made fortunes for others too, especially for celebrated singers who recorded it. Lena Guilbert Ford, who shared his triumph, had the misfortune to be killed in an air raid. But war made Ivor Novello. That £15,000 was a godsend to Ivor—to the entire Davies family, indeed. But what was more valuable and more important was that Ivor Novello—and his Music—was a success and a big one.

CHAPTER FIVE

MINSTREL BOY

THE year 1914, which was for so many and so much the end of all things—the beginning of the end of the Old Order but not the start of a new one to take its place—was the real beginning of Ivor Novello. He wrote a war song and made himself. It was a completely different war song. Ivor was never a soldier at heart—or in the smallest portion of his heart. He was a civilian and an artist civilian—so he wrote a song for civilians, letting his art serve them. And when that song was first heard, the clouds were indeed dark, the boys were indeed leaving home and there was every need to turn the dark clouds inside out. It was just the kind of song that was wanted for it captured the mood of the times. It is not too much to say that " Keep the Home Fires Burning "—apart from the fame and fortune it brought him—affected Ivor's whole life. He always believed in Luck, he always poured out libations to the goddess of Fortune, he always liked mascots around him. And so into every subsequent score he wrote—he put a few bars of " Keep the Home Fires Burning "—just in case! It never failed him. He was the first man deliberately to write a war song which was not blatantly patriotic. How well he understood the people of this realm.

Things were tightening up as 1914 became 1915—but Ivor worked on. He wrote other songs—he was " news " now—he was interviewed, the royalties rolled in; he was earning what seemed to him amazing money—and it all stemmed from that one song. He followed it up with " The Laddie in Khaki " and " When the Great Day Comes " which were published at once, boosted by the big national newspapers but they never did what " Keep the Home Fires " achieved and they are forgotten now. " Keep the Home Fires " got into pantomime, and in those days the people took their songs from pantomime and not from the cinema so that to have a song featured in pantomime was indeed to have attained the zenith of popularity.

Ivor went over to France, where that great woman and great

actress Lena Ashwell was giving entertainment for the troops with far less fuss and far greater success than ever Ensa attained in the Second World War. At her concerts Ivor played the accompaniment for the artistes who sang his song. It always ended by his accompanying the entire audience as well. For the soldiers liked the song. Not only the British but the Canadians, the New Zealanders, the Australians—all the Empire troops, adopted the song which was just as symbolic for them. And when, at last America entered the war, her troops swelled the chorus. " Keep the Home Fires Burning "—as it was now called—had international appeal.

It is amazing how many old soldiers who heard Ivor accompany that song in France remember it so clearly, and what is more remarkable so many imagine that the occasion on which they heard it was its very first performance! I have received many letters from such men, all full of kindly thoughts and all saying that they well remember the first time Mr. Novello played that tune—it was " Somewhere in France " in 1915 and they were there. Mostly, of course, it was at Rouen, which was Lena Ashwell's headquarters. I always acknowledge those letters, and much as I hate to disillusion the writers I must do so now. One wrote to say he had even kept copies of the leaflets distributed on the occasion, giving the words of the song. And whilst this book was being written came the news that the Middlesex Regiment—the " Diehards "—on vacating the line in Korea to come home and make room for another battalion, came out singing " Keep the Home Fires Burning " —thus bringing it into a third war.

In 1916, Ivor applied for a commission in the Royal Naval Air Service. He became a sub-lieutenant, and was sent to H.M.S. *Crystal Palace*, officially H.M.S. *Victory VI* but only so called in official documents, for his training. He did not like it, for here he was pitchforked into a strange milieu. His life had been bounded by home and the concert stage, and his acquaintances had been people of the world of music and the Theatre. Now he was amongst hordes of hearty young men of all classes and tastes, mostly behaving like schoolboys as the male Briton always does when in the mass. Here was the first taste of naval discipline and although it was but a shadow of the real thing, it was pretty grim for Ivor who had never known any discipline in his life. It is generally considered that undisciplined people are spoilt darlings who are of little use in the world; but like most generalities, this is open to exceptions. Ivor was one of them. He never spoilt himself; not even that instant and vast success he had just attained made him the slightest bit conceited or puffed up. He was surprised at it and he was grateful.

But he did not like H.M.S. *Crystal Palace*. He had to get up at unheard of hours; he had to live in community with others; he had to study at set hours, to be on parade, to answer to his name, to run about, and even to carry things. He had to learn about things for which he had no aptitude and of which he had only the haziest possible understanding. The whole thing revolted him. But he stuck it. Leave was not difficult to obtain and he got his share. He could still go to the Theatre and still get home at week-ends to live at the flat. The contrast between home and Service conditions only made it harder for him. He would frequently scare his mother and father and his friends by declaring that he would desert and never go back. But, of course, he always did go back. He went back to the dreadful servitude which Service conditions impose on artistic and creative minds. He had to do things at a certain time and in a certain way; he had to remember and observe rules and regulations. He had to do the same as everybody else, which he never liked doing. H.M.S. *Crystal Palace* was not the most comfortable of quarters—though infinitely better than many—and Ivor had, all his life, been used to comfort: soft beds with eiderdown quilts, cups of tea on wakening, and so on.

There was, however, one consolation. There was a piano, and there were concerts. They kept him sane and gave him something to look forward to and think about. And despite his hatred of it all, he was a very popular young man with his comrades, especially because of his ability to make those concerts go. In the evenings when the men relaxed and there was a sing-song, Ivor came into his own. Then he was a leader. He might lag behind in the studies, on parade, at drill, at the lectures, but when it came to the concerts, he was chief. He could do what he liked. One of the things he hated was having to wear uniform according to rule and not to " improve it " with things of his own fancy. But when the concerts came, then there was relaxation, then his foot was on his native heath—the piano pedal—and he was happy. Many men who served at the Crystal Palace with him have the clearest memory of him in those days. They remember him as a shy, rather awkward but very good-looking young man, with a touch of sadness in his eyes and face. But he was their great favourite in the evening when he got to the piano stool and took them out of their drab surroundings by his music. Those men are naturally all—shall we say?—middle-aged now, but they remember. Hilton Wadsworth, now an important man in the great firm of Guinness—which is so good for you—recalls many a tale of Ivor in those days. He recalls with the utmost pleasure Ivor's piano playing and how he used to treat them to a composite version of " Keep the Home Fires Burning," " Annie Laurie " and " God Save the King "—all played at the same time and yet all distinct. It always brought down the house. A charming, quiet, unassuming Ulsterman, Mr. Wadsworth served all through World War I with distinction. He takes pride most of all in the possession of a very early pilot's certificate and an acquaintance with Ivor Novello at the Crystal Palace.

Now, indeed, was Ivor, the Minstrel Boy, gone to the wars. If he did not have his father's sword girded on him, and if his wild harp was not slung behind him, at least he had his mother's gift of music, his own success and a piano to work on whenever he could.

From Sydenham Ivor went to Chingford to complete his course, to live and work under active service conditions and to learn to fly. He met many people, and those there in his time all remember him, one especially, Leslie Cahn-Rein, partner in the famous firm of F. C. Rein and Sons, pioneers of deaf-aids and the oldest firm in that business. Leslie Cahn-Rein, who was a captain in the R.N.A.S., has the liveliest recollection of Ivor at Chingford. From his memory he draws very vivid pictures of those days. He recalls wet misty mornings, with the servants shuffling about the Marine Mess making a liquid which they optimistically referred to as coffee and hotting up pat-a-cake biscuits, while, if unobserved, they filled the air with the flavour of shag. Outside, ready for the early morning flyers, a few sleepy eyed " quirks " would parade, many Canadians amongst them.

Ivor had to get up early with the rest and usually experienced difficulty with his white scarf knot, which had to be " centred." He had created a minor sensation when he joined the station, for his uniform was obviously made by a civilian tailor and did not pass muster with the hard-boiled, keen-eyed naval men in charge. His uniform had wrong badges made of the wrong material and he explained them by the fact that he thought they were "original." But he soon fell into line. In less than no time proper Service kit was his wear, although he always tried to embellish it with a scarf of some bright colour not in accordance with regulations. He had at that time an aversion to being photographed—and endured much, for nearly everyone had a camera and wanted to take pictures of the men serving at Chingford. Ivor was always being dragged into groups and disliking it. He would turn his cap the wrong way round, make grimaces and put out his tongue. But he became popular with everyone, for he was good-natured and easygoing and wanted to be friends and make the best of it.

On those early parades for flights he would go up with an instructor at the controls—and be very glad when he was down again. Not that he disliked the flying so much; it was the early hour that he detested. He would go to the sheds with his instructor—sometimes Lt.-Cmdr. Nichol-Mirriam—and then the fun would start. The engines would be started up, and din would fill the air whilst Gerard, and his Marine buglers, in immaculate uniform and bearing themselves as Marines do, provided the background and looked on. Ivor would go whizzing off in a Maurice Longhorn with an instructor at the controls. Circuit and landing, circuit and landing until it was breakfast time. Then it was proper dress for the day and afterwards there were lectures on navigation, engines and the like. It was mostly Greek to Ivor, who could not have cared less.

While at Chingford he was working hard on the score of his first commissioned musical play, *Theodore and Co.*, which was destined for the Gaiety. A new comedian, who had made a tremendous hit in *To-night's the Night*, and whose name is now world-famous as Leslie Henson, was in the cast. Ivor had broken into the Theatre, "Keep the Home Fires Burning" having battered down the walls. He had had one song in *The Bing Boys*, his first real theatrical début, and now came a score for the Gaiety, one of the theatres of his dreams. No wonder his mind was upon that instead of upon such boring and to him incomprehensible matters as aerodynamics and the mysteries of navigation. He was composing a score for a full-sized musical show at his beloved Gaiety, where he had so often worshipped at the shrine of Gertie Millar, George Grossmith, Connie Ediss, Edmund Payne and the rest of that marvellous team. That, to him, was real life; the warlike matters were just to be endured. He did not waste his time at the lectures. He appeared most industrious in the matter of taking notes; but he was not taking notes, he was writing them, working surreptitiously on his score. And sometimes when a pause descended on the lecture room whilst the airmen-to-be concentrated on a knotty problem of dihedral, or whatever the subject was, a faint humming would fill the air. It was Ivor battling with a tune. If reprimanded, he would look very frightened and stammer out that he always hummed when concentrating—a bad habit—he must cure himself. As soon as the instructor's eye was removed, down would go a string of notes. . . .

In the afternoons he had another ordeal, for Exercise for Fitness was the order of the day. This was something which Ivor hated. He had to don shorts and go for cross-country runs—and somehow he did it. He, who hated sports, had to play rugby—and he did it, tackling low and putting up a very good show indeed. With the influx of the Canadians, baseball got into the curriculum. Ivor had to play that too, and Cahn-Rein remembers with joy the sight of Ivor in full baseball kit, who considered it funny and an occasion for clowning. He clowned well, and he made the men roar, but the Canadians took a poor view of it and during the game they were apt to get rough—the slogan being, if you can't get the man, stun him. Soon there were more casualties at baseball than at flying—though Ivor always managed to escape being stunned—so the game was dropped. Nobody was more pleased than Ivor. It was, of course, young David Ivor Davies who played the games; it was his father's old ability latent in him, though perhaps it was Ivor Novello who did the clowning.

But, as at the Crystal Palace, it was in the evenings, when Ivor really came into his own. There was, of course, a piano in the mess and naturally that piano and Ivor Novello were inseparable. Not only would he improvise and play the tunes which he was composing for *Theodore and Co.*, but he played the men anything they wanted, his repertoire ranging from " Mademoiselle from Armentières " to Grand Opera, with a special selection of *La Bohème*, which delighted Ivor, an admirer of the work of Puccini, always much in request. Cahn-Rein remembers that he played it exquisitely, especially Mimi's and Musetta's songs. He would usually round off with " Keep the Home Fires Burning," which the whole mess sang, and then they went to bed.

Leave was fairly easy and Ivor would slip away to town. He had a car, a white Berliet, and Chingford is near to London. Sometimes he would return late and full of inspiration. He would steal into the mess, turn on the lights, and start to work out his tunes on the piano. This late—or early—music, for sometimes he went on to the small hours, was not appreciated by everyone. One objector was a big Yorkshireman who showed his disapproval by coming into the mess carrying a glass of port. Surrounded by some of the other men, summoned by him to see the action, he poured the port into the piano as Ivor was playing it. This resulted in a scrimmage—a free for all—a very popular, if rough pastime in World War I. But Ivor did not stop his composing; he took it as a libation to his muse, and when the scrum was over, he was back on the piano stool.

Sometimes he and his mates would crowd into that white Berliet, a speedy affair, and dash to town with a well-known racing driver at the wheel. On such occasions the journey was done in record time. It was a marvel nobody was killed, but they had a very narrow squeak once, for they found an air raid going on in town. All the lights were out, and in Aldwych they nearly ran over a special constable, almost invisible as he crossed the road. The swerve to avoid him took them sideways on right across the thoroughfare, over the kerb, over the pavement and ended within a couple of inches of a big plate-glass window. Ivor, thrown to the floor, asked rather plaintively, " Where do we go from here? " and supplied the answer by at once taking them all to the flat. But with a less experienced and more nervy driver than Long Thomas at the wheel, they might never have reached it.

They always had to go to the flat first, so that Ivor could see Mam, who took the liveliest interest in his friends and would cross-question them as to what went on at Chingford and try and understand what it was all about. From the flat they went to Romano's, up to the balcony, full of spirits and horseplay. A favourite pastime was putting portions of hors d'oeuvre on the rail and flicking them at the tables below, especially at those at which friends or acquaintances were sitting. That was the sort of life young men in the Royal Naval Air Service lived in the days of the First World War. Ivor was in it, but not perhaps of it, for his mind was always full of his music. But he made himself enormously popular and did all the things he loathed so much without complaint. He and another young sub-lieutenant, Henry Kendall, with yet a third, named Laurence Irving, grandson of the great Sir Henry, son of H. B. Irving, and now a genius at stage design, put on many shows at the station and they were terrific successes.

But eventually the time came for Ivor's great test, his first solo flight. This was an ordeal for every pupil, and must have been a special ordeal for him. He knew very, very little about it —he was not interested—yet it was just something which had to be done.

The day dawned and it was not the best sort of day for such a thing. It was very gusty indeed. Planes then were not the efficient, amazing machines of to-day. It was what was called a " school bus," which looked like a bundle of wood with some rolls of linen wrapped round it, and had an engine which spat out flames better than any dragon in a pantomime ever succeeded in doing. Ivor turned out in his short leather coat and a bright yellow scarf. Nobody who saw the flight will forget it. He had paid little or no attention to his course. He was so backward that the instructors dodged him for they probably knew it was quite hopeless. But a first solo flight he must make—and here it was. Up he went, somehow achieving a series of switchback hops until he got to an altitude of some 500 feet. Then he made a steep " bank " and flew away. The news went round that Ivor was in the air and like lightning everyone came running out. There he was, doing the most remarkable things. People on the ground shivered; they crossed their fingers. They certainly did not expect to see him alive again. For a quarter of an hour he buzzed about, often skimming the roofs of the sheds with engine cut off. Soon it became apparent that he could not get down. Doubtless he had not the slightest idea how to do so. There was panic below. And then he came, diving over the sheds with a swish, and for a moment he seemed to hover. And then—down—down—down to earth with a flop, like a hen settling on a nest . . . it was a crash but a curious one, a sort of pancake landing. Off came the wheels and the undercarriage, and with a bit of crumpling the machine came to rest. There was a rush forward. What had happened to pilot Ivor? Ivor got out of the wreckage showing not the slightest concern and quite unhurt after what might have been a fatal crash. He had to go before his officer for a talk about the flight, an inquest, a kind of pow-wow always held after such affairs. Nobody knows what was said, or what language his chief used to Ivor. He certainly did not get full marks, and he probably heard a good many home truths. But there was general and heartfelt relief at his safety.

Cahn-Rein remembers that although as a flying-man he broke the hearts of the whole station and subjected them to what was then called " vertical draught," he was admired by them all for his guts, his coolness, and the real courage he had displayed. It is bad enough to go up when you know the ropes, but what sort of pluck does it take to do it when you know perfectly well that you do not? But David Ivor Davies did exactly that.

Harry Kendall recalls the Chingford days very clearly. Indeed he has good reason to do so. He is one of Ivor's oldest friends—probably only Sir Edward Marsh and Keneth Kent are senior in this respect. He met Ivor first when he was a very young actor at the Old Vic, in the days of Lilian Bayliss, and was introduced to him by Viola Tree, who also brought Edward Marsh and Ivor together. She was playing at the Old Vic too. The year was 1915. Salaries were small. Shakespeare was played four nights a week and opera on the other two evenings.

Sometimes there were complications. Kendall remembers one being brought about by Viola Tree. She was an amazing person, who had inherited her great father's vagueness. But whereas Sir Herbert Tree had assumed that vagueness, he had imparted it to his daughter in reality. Viola, whom everyone loved, had no idea of time and only the haziest notions, very often, of what was going on. She lived and moved in a world of her own but had moments of that great penetration which her father had also given her. She was playing Viola in *Twelfth Night* one Friday, or, rather, she should have been. It got near to curtain time and she was not in the theatre, nor could she be found. She was not at home, her haunts were combed fruitlessly, and nobody had any idea where she was. Ben Greet, then in charge of the stage, dashed off to find Sybil Thorndike. He insisted she should play Viola. She protested that she had not played it for years. It made no difference to Greet; he had trained her, he knew what she could do. He rushed her to the theatre, he made her dress in Viola's clothes, which were far too large for her, for Viola was very tall, and he pushed her on. Being Sybil Thorndike, she went through that show without missing a word or a syllable and gave an amazing performance. Nothing was heard of Viola Tree. The next evening, Saturday, it was opera. When the *prima donna* of the evening arrived and went to her dressing-room she found it completely occupied by Viola Tree busy dressing for Viola. On being told it was Saturday and opera she resisted strongly. Nothing of the kind: it was Friday and she was going to play Viola. What did they all mean? It took the effort of the entire company and ocular demonstration to convince her. But she was not a bit perturbed.

One evening shortly after, she did get it right and was playing Viola. Henry Kendall was Sebastian. During their scene towards the end of the play he noticed the figure of a young man in the wings, whose handsomeness struck him despite the bowler hat which crowned the head and amazing profile. When he came off, Viola introduced the watcher to him. It was Ivor Novello. When the show was over, the trio adjourned to the adjacent A.B.C. shop and partook of coffee and buns, the staple fare of the Old Vic players then. The two young men took to each other and a friendship sprang up. Ivor mentioned that he was playing at a National Sunday League concert at the Alhambra on the following Sunday and would be very pleased if Mr. Kendall could come. Mr. Kendall went and, of course, heard "Keep the Home Fires," which always had to be sung then.

They met several times and then Henry Kendall joined up. He entered the Honourable Artillery Company as a private. He underwent his training and was on a draft for France. That meant a bit of leave, but the prospect was not alluring. He was walking along Coventry Street, London, between Leicester Square and Piccadilly Circus when he saw a man in the uniform of a naval sub-lieutenant approaching. That, of course, meant a salute and Henry Kendall saluted smartly, the officer returning the salute. To his amazement, the officer was Ivor Novello. It was not possible to stop and speak, discipline in the First World War being very strict on those points, and he passed on. And then something happened. He felt impelled to stop and look in a shop window. There was nothing there to interest him but still he obeyed that tremendously strong instinct. And that pause, that gaze into the shop window—he does not remember at all at what he looked—probably saved his life. As he looked he heard a deep whisper behind him saying " We can't talk here—go to the Kardomah Café and meet me there." " All right," replied Kendall in the same tone, and off he went.

There in the café he and Novello met again. " What are you doing in that make-up? " demanded Ivor. " For the matter of that, what about you? " asked Kendall. " Do you like being a private? " queried Ivor, and the answer was in the negative. Kendall explained that he was proud of being in the H.A.C., that he hoped for a commission some day, but that at the moment he was on a draft for France. " Do you like that? " again asked Ivor and the answer was again a most decided negative. " All right," said Ivor, " give me your number and particulars and leave it to me." Kendall complied, not thinking anything about it, and the two had coffee, a long talk and lots of laughs. A day or two later, when Kendall was just about to leave for France, he received a message asking him to report to the Admiralty. Wondering greatly, he went. There he was informed that he was to be given a commission in the Royal Naval Air Service. He was completely astonished but overpoweringly grateful. He made no demur. He got out of khaki and went into naval blue. Ivor had worked it, by means known only to himself and, possibly, to Sir Edward Marsh. Ivor and Kendall met again at Chingford, both sub-lieutenants now.

Kendall remembers Ivor's second solo flight. Cahn-Rein is of the opinion that Ivor flew once only and then the authorities decided it was enough. Kendall is equally certain he did it twice. He remembers the one he witnessed and shivers at the thought. Once again Ivor got the plane off the ground—goodness knows how—and got the nose of the machine off the ground before the tail became airborne (entirely wrong, of course), skimmed about in the most surprising and frightening manner, and again caused panic over the whole station. Then—he crashed. Everyone held their breath and, as the crash occurred, shouted and rushed forward. An ambulance dashed up and Ivor was removed from the wreckage. He was hurt on this occasion. He had damaged his ankle and he was a bit stunned.

He soon came round, but the ankle was pretty bad and giving him quite a lot of pain. Kendall remained with him when it had been dressed. Suddenly Ivor sat up. " Harry," he said, " what about those tickets we have for the first night at the Haymarket to-night? " " Don't be silly," replied Kendall, " you cannot possibly go. You know that. You must lie still and rest." " Don't be absurd," replied Ivor, " it's a first night. We simply cannot miss it." Kendall argued but it was no use. There was a first night on and Ivor had the tickets. What was a troublesome ankle, what was a bit of shock, compared to that? Furthermore, Ellis Jeffreys was in it—the play was *The Widow's Might* and it simply could not be missed. Out came that white car. They went. . . .

How was it that Henry Kendall's life was saved by that pause to look into the shop window? If he had not done so, if Ivor had not overtaken him and made the appointment at the Kardomah which blossomed into Kendall's commission in the Royal Naval Air Service, Kendall would have gone to France with that draft. And that particular draft was almost completely wiped out in its first action. . . .

But that flight, ending in that nearly fatal crash, was Ivor's last. It was decided that flying was not his line at all, and he could not have agreed more. So they transferred him to the Air Ministry.

Henry Kendall stayed on but remained a friend of Ivor's all his life—one of the oldest and nearest.

Kendall still has his flying log book, which makes fascinating reading to-day. He was a flight sub-lieutenant from August, 1916, to December, 1917, and a flight-lieutenant from January, 1918, to April, 1918. Then he transferred to the Royal Air Force in April, 1918, with the rank of captain. He served at the Crystal Palace, Cranwell, Killingholme, Calshot, Cambridge, Bembridge, Felixstowe and elsewhere—at least, those were his stations. His first time in the air was in October, 1916, with Flt.-Lieut. Irving. They reached an altitude of 1,500 feet and the total time was seven minutes. The remark in the margin is " First time in the air. Liked it awfully." He took partial control, with Flt.-Lieut. Keeble, on December 11th, 1916, and his first time in full control was February 8th, 1917, when he made a good landing. With him was Flt.-Commander Travers. That was Ben Travers, later to become the perfect writer of farces, whose work at the Aldwych for Tom Walls and Ralph Lynn, made theatrical history.

Ben Travers, one of the very nicest men I know, was a very gallant airman when every flight off the ground was a perilous adventure. He, and the rest of them, went up in machines which would fill an airman to-day with terror and dread. Odd-shaped affairs they were, which seemed all tied up with bits of wire and string. But those early airmen like Ben Travers made them fly and did amazing things with them. Travers went up against Zeppelin attacks, sitting on an ordinary egg box, fastened to the aeroplane, with his feet dangling in space, and armed with an ordinary rifle. He did magnificent service and joined up again in World War II. There is no end to the talent of Ben Travers, for he not only wrote very wonderful farces, fitting the cast perfectly, but he knew how to find the odd words so appropriate to the ultra-respectable appearance and precise voice of Robertson Hare, who graduated from small stooge-like parts in the earlier Aldwych farces to stardom on his own, though he himself always denies that he is a star in his own right. And Travers could not only write farces but played in them too. In *Banana Ridge*, which he wrote for Robertson Hare and Alfred Drayton—the team which replaced that of the Aldwych—he played a Malay servant as to the manner born. He had spent many years out there and knew the type exactly. He can—and does—write excellent straight plays, too. And the great love of this real Englishman's heart is cricket. He even wrote a farce about it. But there was precious little real farce in his 1914-18 war service, although his immense sense of humour found many laughs in it. He was one of those who found Ivor such a troublesome pupil, but he understood him.

Henry Kendall avers that he broke so many undercarriages with bad landings—although the log scarcely bears that out he probably knows best—that they transferred him to the flying-boats, where there were no undercarriages to break. He went on active patrol service and had lots of experience. One finds entries like " Sighted enemy submarine—about to drop bombs when it dived leaving no trace " and he saw no more of it. That gave more pleasure to the Germans in the sub than to him. He lived the sort of dangerous life, facing death all the time, that all young men in the Service endured in the First World War, but he says very little about it to-day. There are one or two special thrills recorded in a few words. " Sighted and bombed track of hostile submarine. No definite results observed." But there is a note afterwards: " Since been officially accepted as sunk." And later, in August, 1917: " Sighted and bombed oil patch of enemy submarine. Direct hit. Big spread observed. Forced landing owing to broken petrol pipe. Repaired and resumed patrol." And on August 29th: " Submarine sighted on surface. Bombed. Disturbance of oil observed. Six trawlers guided to vicinity by Very lights. Left them searching for wreckage." Just incidents which were daily and nightly occurrences in the war and the life of the actor-pilot. The log-book closes with the note " Demobbed February, 1919. C'est fini."

Kendall, recalling Ivor at Chingford, says that he never saw any sign of fear or flinching at all. Ivor was never afraid when it came to the point. Nor was he ever afraid of pain, he says. He hated the idea of it, but he stood up to it and took it as it came. On the occasion of that crash, he was terribly shaken; he was indeed within an ace of death. Yet very, very shortly afterwards there was the determination to go to that first night, come what may, M.O.'s orders and Kendall's persuasion notwithstanding. He limped badly and he was in pain, but he went to the theatre. The date was November 15th, 1916. They both enjoyed the play to the full. It ran for 104 performances.

The man who went up in those odd planes and who stood up to that crash was David Ivor Davies and it was his *alter ego*, Ivor Novello, who decided to go to the theatre. For there was no Ivor Novello without the Theatre and it was in the Theatre that Ivor Novello came to full stature and really existed. If that crash had been a fatal one, if Sub.-Lieut. Ivor had been killed, it is, to a lover of the Theatre, dreadful to contemplate what the Theatre of this country would have missed. But the Fates were kind. That sort of death was not in his destiny. He was spared to become King of the Musical Stage. And those experiences of Henry Kendall, the very young actor, at the Old Vic, show that institution as it was when on its way to the great position it holds to-day. Prices were cheap, salaries very small and, as I said earlier, the players found their chief sustenance in buns and coffee at the Aerated Bread Company's depot which was a sort of unofficial green room to the theatre. No dress shirts and backless gowns graced the stalls of the Old Vic in those days, but its audiences were loyal, keen and full throated in applause and approbation, as also in disapproval. Lilian Bayliss was its Queen, and knew how to rule. She built well and the little seedling she planted has produced two magnificent and lasting blossoms, even if they flourish under very different conditions.

And perhaps a further word about Viola Tree, that quite amazing woman. She was a true daughter of her father. He adored her and she adored him. They understood each other completely. Maybe he saw more talent than she really possessed. He gave her chances. And he had his jokes with her too. On one occasion when she was rehearsing Ariel in *The Tempest* and was hovering in mid-air on a wire. Tree suddenly called "Half an hour break"—and left her so suspended. Both of them enjoyed it. He was often chaffed about his determination to make her a star. In *The Spring Chicken* at the Gaiety, George Grossmith joked about it. He sang a song, dressed as Shakespeare, a topical song and poked fun at Tree. The chorus ended:

> "How's your pretty Miss Viola?
> Fair and so beautiful she
> And a very short time
> It will take her to climb
> To the top of the Beerbohm Tree."

Viola, a dear friend of mine, married handsome Alan Parsons, then of the Foreign Office, who left that august calling to become a dramatic critic. He did so with joy. There had been a Minute which had pursued him for many months and the purport of which he never understood. It filled him with dread. It was his Old Man of the Sea. It disturbed his rest at nights. Then came the last day at the Foreign Office. Something had to be done about that Minute before he left. He dealt with it at last. Just before leaving his room for the last time he put the dreadful piece of paper which had caused him so much mental distress on the fire and watched it burn with satisfaction. That Minute was answered at last. . . .

Alan, too, was very fond of Ivor. He was in many ways as erratic as his wife. He had no money sense at all, and the pair of them were nearly always in financial straits. He would never sit in his seat, he would roam about the back of the dress or upper circle and if he could get me to stand, or move about with him, then his sense of happiness was complete. When, after a long time as dramatic critic of the *Daily Sketch* he became dramatic critic of the *Daily Mail* he had more trouble. He had to get his notice in to catch the early editions, and this meant writing it against time and sending it in before the show was over, so that at least something could appear in the very early and provincial editions. Shows then were not over until past eleven. If he was at a show of mine, I always gave him a typed résumé of the plot. Indeed I provided many of the critics with this little aid. Alan would study it, groan and hold his head, and write snatches on little bits of paper held against a wall, or in the lavatory. He would bump his head against fire buckets, and often make quite a disturbance, of which he was never aware, and finally, having dispatched it in bits by relays of boys who waited in the vestibule, he would 'phone a real notice for the late London editions. He died all too soon and all too young. We saw each other daily and I miss him yet. Sometimes, still, at first nights I look round for him when I see something which I know would have amused him. Maybe something of him still lingers in the Theatre, and if so, it is the Duke of York's that he will haunt. . . .

But as to Viola, she was never a first-class actress. She was as erratic on the stage as in real life. She would have flashes of genius and long stretches when she was as raw as an amateur. But always there was the charm and the arresting personality. She could, when she chose, or when the right mood was upon her, cause the heartiest roars of laughter heard in the Theatre of her day; she adored clowning. And at parties she was without equal. She never cared how she looked, but whatever she wore—and she wore some very odd things at times—she always looked distinguished. She carried her height with perfect poise and she had a very good singing voice. She was never the least bit self-conscious: she had her own world. Once, travelling fourth class, she was stopped at the Franco-Italian frontier because she had a lot of bananas and they were dutiable. She returned across the frontier, ate all the bananas and entered the country that wanted to tax her with pride and satisfaction.

One night I remember driving Alan back to their lovely house in Regent's Park. Viola was out. There was no doubt about that, for across the front door in that most select neighbourhood she had written, in big letters and in chalk, " Out. Don't worry, I have fed the cat." A lesser woman would have left a pencilled note in the hall. Not so Viola. Often in fine weather she slept on a mattress on the roof under a stack of chimney pots. She just ignored the smuts. And she introduced Ivor to Sir Edward Marsh and Henry Kendall. Ivor always adored her and if he could give her a part in his shows—which part he wrote for her—his cup of happiness was full. And so was hers. . . .

CHAPTER SIX

THE STAGE DOOR OPENS

IVOR NOVELLO was not allowed to do any more flying. He might aspire to Pegasus if he liked, he might soar on wings of song, but aeroplanes were taboo. The men in charge of Chingford saw to that. Whatever this handsome young man might be, whatever prizes the future might hold in store for him, he was no airman. Chingford trained men to fly, so there was no room there for him.

Sub-Lieut. David Ivor Davies was transferred to the Air Ministry, to do clerical and ordinary Service routine work. He found it insufferably boring, but he did not care. For another door had opened—to him the one of Paradise—the door of the Theatre. He was now inside. He was not on the stage, but he was supplying the music. " Keep the Home Fires Burning " had been the key. In the Theatre success follows success. Until you force yourself upon managerial attention, you may languish unseen and unheard. But they had all heard " Keep the Home Fires Burning "; they could not help it. Even the most exclusive manager in his remotest office could not escape it.

But, as it happened, there was one man in London who had only the haziest notion of what it was all about. He happened to be watching Lily Elsie one night when that wonderful person was appearing at His Majesty's Theatre in *Mavourneen*. It so happened that Ivor was there too, the guest of Viola Tree, daughter of the great Sir Herbert, a giant of the Theatre compared with whom the biggest of them to-day are but pygmies. Viola, close friend of Ivor's, introduced the two members of the audience to each other, mentioning that Ivor was the composer of " Keep the Home Fires Burning." The other man looked blank. But always the pink of politeness he tried to cover up his momentary confusion. Viola spotted it, however, and forced an admission that this amazing man, whose name was Edward Marsh, really did not know what she was talking about. She enjoyed the situation. "But you must know it, " she said, " everyone knows it." And she hummed the tune.

"Oh that!" said Edward Marsh, "Oh, I know that. But I did not know what it was called." Not, perhaps, the best introduction to a young composer whose fame rested at that time on the one single tune. But the composer happened to be Ivor Novello, who was then, as always, without a trace of conceit but with an immense sense of humour. They shook hands—and chatted—and discovered that both shared an overwhelming adoration for Lily Elsie. It was enough. That brief meeting in His Majesty's became a lifelong friendship. Edward Marsh became one of Ivor's inner circle, and the friendship endured from 1915 to 1951—to Novello's death.

Edward Marsh is now Sir Edward Marsh, knighted as a reward for his most distinguished services in the Civil Service. In the First World War he was personal secretary to Winston Churchill. He is a figure of the West End and of the Theatre. His upright, slim figure, his clear-cut features, his prominent eyebrows, his air of distinction—all are known to playgoers and to practically everyone who is anyone in the world of the drama. He is a regular first-nighter; indeed a first night is almost incomplete without him. A man of the utmost culture and taste, of great erudition and knowledge, he has a finely discriminating sense of values and a grand sense of humour. He can tell good tales and tell them well. And underneath the suavity of his manners and breeding is a steely determination to see justice done, to fight for a cause and to overthrow oppression. He is, as Ivor always found, a good man to have on one's side. He has a frankness which is refreshing when an opinion is asked and, although aloof with strangers, is the staunchest of friends. He stands by, no matter what happens. And Ivor was to find that too.

Edward Marsh was one of the very few non-theatrical members of the select band of Old Novellians, which included Keneth Kent, a boyhood friend, Robert Andrews, Henry Kendall, Viola Tree, Constance Collier, Lily Elsie, Zena Dare, Heather Thatcher, Lloyd Williams (his secretary who will figure more hereafter), Lilian Braithwaite, Fay Compton, Oliver Gilbert, Peter Graves, Gwen Floyd, Phyllis Monkman, Gladys Henson, Dorothy Dickson, Clemence Dane, Gladys Cooper, Adrianne Allen, Beatrice Lillie, Christopher Hassall, Barry Sinclair, Noël Coward, and many others who will come into the story. There were others, too, whom he liked to have in his companies, for whom he not only found but made parts, and there were his loyal business associates such as Fred Allen, who, like myself, did not enter into the social life. You can do better for a man if you stand outside the coterie of friends. You retain your perspective, you do not become too close, too absorbed. Therefore, at times, your words carry much more weight. There were also Ivor's American friends from both stage and screen.

But one could not give the names of all his friends, for they were the whole profession. In a calling which is very " personal ", in which the line between success and failure is so finely drawn, and in which everything is reduced to the personal dimension, Ivor had hardly an enemy, and certainly none of note, a thing which can be said of very few men in the Theatre. Many envied him his possessions, his looks, his ability and above all his success, but he envied nobody and made no distinctions. He found his friends and kept his friends not only amongst the stars but amongst all ranks of stage folk. He himself was utterly without envy or any form of jealousy. He did not measure people by their success. If he liked them, he liked them. If he did not—well, they were not there. His pet aversion was a bore. And a bore to him was usually a person who was not interested in the Theatre.

His main regret, in the midst of his success, was probably that our present King and Queen never came to see his shows. There was, late in his life, probably a reason for it, one of those strict rules of royal etiquette which made it impossible. But even before that they did not come, and he was always very sorry. They had no more loyal, admiring or devoted subject than he. The reason for the lack of such royal visits was probably because Their Majesties did not care about the type of shows he did, which is a perfectly good reason indeed. They have to do so many things which they probably do not want to do that it is indeed hard if they cannot please themselves at times and in private. But it was a source of pride to Ivor that King George V used to attend quite regularly, while that most gracious Lady of the Land, Queen Mary, always came to see them, often more than once, and would always receive Ivor and talk to him about them. Princess Margaret came to *King's Rhapsody*, too. Ivor had no politics; he hardly understood what the word meant. But he was an ardent royalist. Had he lived in the seventeenth century, he would have been galloping behind Prince Rupert, and what a Cavalier he would have made.

A true member of the middle class, Ivor had a balanced mind. He hated oppression and he abhorred anything in the nature of sweated labour or injustice. He would overpay rather than underpay although he expected proper service—and saw that he got it. He did not like the type of Socialism which has governed this country since 1945. It hit him hard financially, but that was not his main complaint. He considered it went too fast without counting the cost; he considered it stultified creative ability. He was not class conscious—to him a man was what he made himself—but he did insist that the position should be made and not acquired by law. A working man in overalls, a woman in a coarse apron, carrying a pail, these could be, and were, as much his friends as a gentleman of title in white tie and tails, a woman in the glory of furs and tiara. But they were only his friends if they did their job. Those who did so much and no more, those who watched the clock, who gave nothing but expected overtime for the completion of a ten-minute job, they were not for him. He had not the slightest objection, he said, to a One-Class Country; what he objected to was a No-Class Country. He had made his own way, he had fought for himself. He adored a fighter. It followed therefore that Winston Churchill was to him a demi-god. And he admired Ernest Bevin, too. He appreciated his achievement. But there were others of whom he thought very little, concerning whom he would express his opinion in good set terms, accompanied by a variety of rude noises.

Ivor could be very downright and he possessed a wealth of invective. He was addicted to certain good old Anglo-Saxon words, short, terse but extremely expressive. It was not so much the politics he disliked as the type of men who professed them. He did not go into the subject deeply. He read the papers every day. He would look for theatrical news first and study that carefully. That to him, was the news of the world which mattered. He would look at the headlines and gaze at the pictures. They told him all he wanted to know. The rest he could see for himself. His dislike of certain politicians was based upon the destruction of the world he had known and loved. He held beauty sacred. He was born of a generation which preserved beauty and which venerated the Past. To him it was horror when the great houses of England—as well as of Scotland and Wales—ceased to be what they had been, and either languished in semi-occupation, with ruin before them, or became public institutions. He felt that something was leaving the country in which he had grown up: that wonderful peace, so quiet yet so strong; those lovely parks full of ancient trees, greensward hardly trodden save by deer, great masses of bracken which had been there when the Romans came and in which the birds and the little beasts had their haven, the old lodges and the pillared gates, the outward serenity of the villages clustering near the great house, like little ships in convoy.

To him, achievement was all. He did not, of course, look below the surface, he did not know what kind of places those cottages were to live in. Questions of sanitation and water supply did not enter into it. Here was a setting in which a great epic drama had been enacted, and he did not want to see it change. He was never given to probing deeply, either into people or things. Like Keats he believed that a thing of beauty was a joy for ever and he wanted it preserved on that account. He was, at heart, a fine, old crusted Tory. Changes—yes, but let them be wrought by time.

He treasured relics which had associations. Something which had belonged to a great actor was to him more precious than rubies. When Naomi Jacob gave him a paste star which had been worn by Edmund Kean, his eyes filled with tears. He wore it at once, in *King's Rhapsody*. When Muriel Martin Harvey sent him some belongings of her father, Sir John Martin Harvey, I was there when he unpacked them. There was a dagger which Sir John—" Jack " to the profession in his day—had used as *Richard III*. Ivor handled it as a devout Roman Catholic might have handled the finger bone of a patron saint. I must admit to a twinge of envy myself then, for I feel the same about such things, and those which I possess myself will be mine until I die, no matter what disasters befall. He gave me those Harvey relics to handle—it was in his dressing-room at the Palace—and he smiled to see how I felt about them. That sort of thing was a bond between us. Yet he would not have wasted two minutes in examining the most remarkable scientific machine or glancing at a new mechanical invention. Those things meant nothing. He took progress as he found it. He adored flying—when he was not a pilot—and appreciated air travel. It got him where he wanted to go without delay. He had his Rolls-Royce—by no means a new model—and that he loved too, despite the trouble it was unwittingly to bring upon him. But he did not drive it. His faithful chauffeur, Arthur Morgan, did that. Ivor had not the remotest idea what went on under the bonnet of that car. But he did know what went on in Kean when that star shone on his breast and what motive power moved Martin Harvey when he gripped that dagger. And that made all the difference.

Ivor was a good conversationalist when he chose and could talk on a variety of subjects. Yet he was not a well-read man, nor, of course, highly educated. Latin and Greek meant nothing to him. He read voraciously, but he read novels—modern novels—and an occasional biography, if it happened to be a theatrical one or about somebody he had known or knew. In one of his few letters to me he ended by saying "How I adore your books!" But I doubt if he ever read one of them right through. They are history, of course, though they are Theatre. I always sent him an inscribed copy, and then, when I saw him next he would clasp my hand and say "Popie—your lovely book—oh . . ." and give a look of ecstasy. But I don't believe he read much of them. Not that it matters. They were not novels. Sometimes I would tell him tales out of those very books and then he would listen with real attention and enjoyment, and so I knew. . . .

Sir Edward Marsh constituted himself his mentor in art and pictures. He would take Ivor to picture galleries, to exhibitions of paintings, talk to him about them and encourage him to buy pictures. Ivor did, indeed, buy some. Though he loved the old fashions and clung to melody in music, in Art he was more impressed by the moderns. Not Picasso or the most advanced, but the modern school nevertheless. He had one picture of a cornfield which he esteemed greatly and made it a special bequest in his will. And he himself would have spasms of painting, and for one who had no training, he showed considerable aptitude. He liked painting as a form of self-expression. And the painting he did showed that had his bent lain in that direction he would have accomplished with his brush what he accomplished with his music. As it was, it was only a hobby, taken up and put down.

He admired very greatly and with good reason, the work of that most charming and accomplished woman, Clemence Dane, a very dear friend of his. Her bust of him is a little masterpiece and was one of his most prized possessions. Very fittingly it now stands in Theatre Royal, Drury Lane, to perpetuate his memory there.

Clemence Dane is a remarkable woman. She is a magnificent novelist, writer, story-teller and artist, and a good actress as well as a fine dramatist. Seldom does a person possess so many great gifts. She is a poet of standing too. When in London she lives in a flat overlooking Covent Garden Market, with a fruit and flowers salesman underneath her premises and a busy coffee shop next door. It is as noisy and malodorous a spot as can be found in London. I know because for years my offices were just round the corner. But when you enter her door you are in surroundings which speak only of artistry and from which the cabbage stalks are leagues away. Quite apart from my admiration for the work of this gracious and handsome lady, I have a very soft corner in my heart for "Winifred" (as her intimate friends call her, because her name is Winifred Ashton).

There is a reason for it. She, Basil Dean and I were sitting in Dean's office at Drury Lane Theatre during the Second World War discussing a big production envisaged (the current word of power in Ensa at the moment) as a pageant at the Albert Hall on the subject of Nelson. Miss Dane was saturated in the subject just then, for she was working on a book about Nelson. I am afraid I had other things on my mind. I was waiting for news of supreme importance to me. The telephone rang. I answered it. My wife was calling to tell me that, just fifteen minutes before, our grandson had arrived. And Clemence Dane was the first person to congratulate me on that terrific event. Those are the things one remembers. And marvellous to say, Miss Dane remembers too. Whenever we meet, at first nights and the like she always asks after that boy, although nine years have passed since then and she has never seen him. To me, that matters a lot. Only those who have grandchildren know the thrill of the first one's arrival.

But politics, art and great possession meant little to Sub-Lieut. David Ivor Davies (Ivor Novello) in the year 1916. He had tasted achievement. He was beginning to feel the joy of money which one's efforts have earned. The royalties from

"Keep the Home Fires Burning" were rolling in nicely and represented to him then almost fabulous wealth. He was ostensibly working at the Air Ministry. His body was there but his mind was far away. He himself was through the door of the Theatre—through the Stage Door at last.

When he joined up, his work as a composer naturally suffered. He had so much else to do. Besides he was still that very lazy young man who followed his father in that respect. Sir Edward Marsh says that Davies senior was as handsome and charming a man as he ever saw and quite the laziest. He does not believe that Davies *père* ever did a stroke of work in his life, even when employed amongst the rates of Cardiff. He liked to play games, but that was not work. He could encourage and exhort but he did not see the necessity for doing work when it could be avoided. He was, in this, only preserving the balance of Nature, for his wife, the redoubtable Mam, never stopped working for a moment. True she put far more energy and fuss into the simplest thing than was necessary. She would make mountains of labour for herself and her pupils. There was not room for two such in that not very large space of 11 Aldwych, which at that time contained herself, her husband, a perpetual guest for no ostensible reason, Ivor, and an old friend who was always called "Wam" and who of course was Welsh too. It was as noisy and busy a place as one could wish to find and the decorative scheme matched it, always wrong and always being changed, but never for the better. When the flat became Ivor's all that was remedied. He had excellent taste.

Had Ivor scored his first success in peace-time, he might have made much more rapid progress, but he was in uniform—at least his body was but never his mind—and as money was coming in it did not seem to matter very much. Only ambition urged him, but he found it delightful to dream of what he felt was sure to come. He got one solitary song into the famous *Bing Boys* at the Alhambra, but it did not make much impact. Still, such a ringing success as "Keep the Home Fires Burning" could not be ignored. Hence his commission to write the score for *Theodore and Co.*, a commission which meant far more to him than the one he held in the R.N.A.S. Still, the laziness slowed him down. He worked fitfully on the score at Chingford. Admittedly the conditions were bad. He altered, he wrote, he re-wrote. The management became pressing. Then energy arrived and for a burst he worked day and night—and it was done! And even then, at the very last moment, disaster threatened and doom hovered. He left the score in a taxi on his way to the Gaiety and it vanished completely. He had to re-write the lot and against time. Maybe it was all the better for that, as happens sometimes. Nobody ever knew what became of the original manuscript. It has probably been destroyed long ago but if it does ever turn up from some corner of a garret lumber room, it will be worth something to-day for there is very, very little Novello manuscript music in existence.

The firm which gave Ivor his first real chance, and who commissioned his first complete score, was Grossmith and Laurillard. That Grossmith was George, son of the great Savoyard and entertainer at the piano, himself a pillar of musical comedy and of the Gaiety. He was one of the great George Edwardes's men; he was the supreme light comedian of musical comedy of his day and he was to the Gaiety on the male side what Gertie Millar was on the female side. Apart from George Edwardes, its inventor, nobody knew more about musical comedy than George Grossmith (then with " Junior " tacked on to his name to differentiate him from his father). He was an extraordinary man. He had all the gifts which go to the makings of real Theatre. He was the son of a great performer, and nephew of Weedon Grossmith, another actor and author of a classic in *The Diary of a Nobody*, who was also an artist of considerable ability. He was tall, thin and elegant. He was by no means a handsome man, but he had great charm and was the idol of the ladies for at least two generations. He could represent either brainless young men with perfect manners, oozing kindliness, courtesy, good intentions and complete vacuity, or terrific Casanova-like roués, which made him the envy of the men. He was supreme in both. He could not really sing but he could put over a song in the most perfect manner. Furthermore, the general public regarded him as a wonderful dancer, and so he certainly appeared to be, as stage dancing was then understood. It was before the days of the violent acrobatics imported from America, and when the term " hoofing " was unknown—yet he was a " hoofer " all right. He had great speed, he was long in the leg and he had the most active and energetic knees and elbows. His attack was superb and he could fascinate an audience. He led male fashions. He was, indeed, the Beau

Brummel of his day. He had all the air of an aristocrat—as understood upon the stage—but there was nothing aristocratic in his breeding, not that he was any the worse for that.

His father, who created the comedy roles in Gilbert and Sullivan operas, who was the first Ko-Ko, Lord Chancellor, Major General and so many more, had started life as a reporter in the Law Courts, with a vague idea of becoming a lawyer himself. But he had entertainment in his blood, for his father was a popular lecturer and so he gave up reporting and the law to become an entertainer at provincial Literary and Mechanics Institutes. He was very successful, giving recitals at private parties. He was noticed by Sullivan—and he never looked back.

Naturally his son went on the stage. George Grossmith Junior could write as well. He was responsible for many of the libretti of successful Gaiety shows; he was an unerring talent spotter—he found stars for George Edwardes who passed even that all-seeing eye, one of his many discoveries being the late and much lamented W. H. Berry, whom he found at Broadstairs. He had an equally unerring eye for feminine allure; his taste in girls was surpassed only by his chief's. It was George Grossmith who brought Gaby Deslys to London—and to the Gaiety. He knew all there was to be known about musical comedy. When George Edwardes died and the Gaiety suffered a decline George Grossmith teamed up with another man of the Theatre, as different from himself as chalk is from cheese. Of such combination are good partnerships made.

This was Edward Laurillard, a strange little man of Dutch extraction who had done lots of work in a managerial capacity, who had staged plays and managed them, and who had many ups and down but who was never defeated.

Laurillard was a small man, but very dapper. His face never betrayed the slightest emotion of any kind. It was quite pale, with no trace of colour and his hair was a pale sandy colour, polished with pomade. He would often negotiate deals for other people. Nothing deterred him. He might be literally thrown downstairs—it had happened—but he would get up and straightway resume the attack. Usually, he triumphed in the end. He always took up new things and he was one of the pioneers of the cinema industry. He had a cool, astute brain and was quite impervious to insults or threats. How he managed to succeed as he did was a marvel, for his speech was incoherent and often quite incomprehensible. He had his own way of pronouncing words and frequently did not know what they meant when he said them. He not only handled shows but he handled artistes and would pester managers to go and see them. His opening was always the same. He would remark, quite clearly and coherently, " Well, there you are, you see." What that meant nobody knew but it was the invariable opening gambit. He would then say quite a lot, but only a few words would emerge which were comprehended. Place names defeated him but he had a shot: he would speak of Glasborough, when he meant Glasgow—it was near enough for him, and Greenwood was easily distinguishable as Wood Green. But 90 per cent. of his remarks conveyed little or nothing—except when it came to figures. In the end his business opposite would find out that Edward Laurillard knew what he was saying even if his competitor or bargain-maker did not and that Edward Laurillard held the big end of the stick and the bargain. And at no moment of the negotiations had he shown the slightest emotion upon his face. The nearest one can get to his expression would be to compare it with one of those calves' heads, which in more bounteous and prosperous days would be seen in butchers' shops, with a lemon in its mouth. His hair was brushed to the back of his head and down the back of his cranium it formed a little ridge, but not a hair was out of place.

He never quite knew people's names, or at least he knew them but got them muddled. If he had several appointments, the first caller would be, so far as he was concerned, quite anonymous and never addressed by name. But the second person to be interviewed would be called by the name of the first caller. It was all most confusing, except to Laurillard. He was a little vain and once he feared he was putting on too much flesh—he was never slim at the best of times. That good fellow and inveterate joker, Tom Reynolds, uncle to Binnie Hale and a producer of merit, adored " Laurey " as he was called, but adored still more pulling his leg. Tom used to sup at the Savoy Grill, then the great theatrical rendezvous; so did Laurillard. Laurillard would stroll from table to table, sitting down with people whom he knew—and he knew everyone there—and perhaps eat a course with each before his next move. That these courses were charged on the bill of the holder of the table troubled him not a whit—quite the reverse in fact. One evening he came and sat at Tom Reynolds's table, which had two other occupants as well—myself and another theatrical friend. Tom led the talk round to avoirdupois and showed for an instant a medicine bottle filled with a reddish pink liquid, which he hastily thrust back into his pocket. That was enough for " Laurey "; in his own patois he wanted to know what it was. Except to hint darkly that it was a slimming mixture, Tom would not divulge. We who were in the joke backed him up. Laurey persisted and as he did so his speech got clearer and clearer too. Tom told him it was a secret which his doctor had prepared and as it was rather dangerous, except under certain conditions, he was not at liberty to say anything about it. Laurillard had now made up his mind. Tom said he had taken a stone off himself with it—he never had a pound of superfluous flesh in his life—and Laurillard was now grim and determined. Day after day he dogged Tom Reynolds. Day after day he questioned us. At long last, Tom said he would, as a very great favour, get him a bottle, but it was expensive and under no conditions must Laurey ever tell anyone. Laurillard swore on his oath. He was told the cost was £5, a lot of money then, but he paid up like a bird. We prepared the concoction for him: plain water, a little sugar, cochineal and a dash of cheap claret. Tom delivered the bottle at a secret rendezvous and Laurillard went off in glee. A few days later he was back for more. It was wonderful, he was understood to say; he had lost several pounds already. He had indeed. He had lost five, but not the sort he meant. He bought another bottle and it seemed to give him youth and buoyancy, and he became speechless with delight. Then we relented. We told him it was really slow acting stuff and he would not find the real results until some months had passed. He had taken enough for the cure, we said. And we bought him a supper, with champagne galore, which cost over £10—and considered the deal closed. He went to America shortly afterwards, but he was always grateful to us and would sometimes recall how much good our medicine had done him. Which shows there must be something in faith healing anyway.

He and Grossmith, the long and short of it, the eloquent and the taciturn, joined hands. Grossmith was as brilliant an after-dinner speaker as ever I heard, and his speeches were quite extempore. He had real wit, excellent delivery in his curious clipped voice with the suggestion of a lisp but remarkable diction; he was a delight to hear and an example to follow. Laurillard could never have made a speech to save his life. But each had what the other had not. They started their joint venture with *Potash and Perlmutter* of glorious memory, bringing success to the then unlucky Queen's Theatre—now bombed —in Shaftesbury Avenue. The bulk of their finance came from that amazing man George Dance, who died a knight and whose motto was " Do It Yesterday."

When the war of 1914-18 was at its height, Grossmith and Laurillard went into musical plays and *To-night's the Night* was the result. Produced first in New York—the whole company went over from England through submarine-infested waters—it was a success there, although some of the American critics found it a bit speedy. That first production is memorable to me because with Dance, who had much at stake in the venture and who was chairman of the Gaiety Theatre Company, I waited for a cable from New York to let us know the result. It was Boxing Day. Dance, never a patient man, got very restive. I explained that we could not get the cable yet on account of the difference in time between New York and London. This was something quite new to Dance and in which he flatly refused to believe. He told me I was mad or drunk—or both. How could time be different? Time was time, or so he had always been led to believe. The more I tried to explain, the worse things got. I was not too sure of the reason myself beyond that the curve of the earth and its rotation had something to do with it and I was within an ace of being dismissed with ignominy when I called up Arthur Collins, of Drury Lane, to support me. He assured Dance over the 'phone that I was right and Dance accepted his word very grudgingly. But he gave me clearly to understand that the whole thing was my fault and that he held me personally responsible for it. But at length the cable came and it was the best of news.

To-night's the Night came to the Gaiety and restored both fortune and prestige to that enchanting playhouse. It also provided our Theatre with a great comedian in the person of Leslie Henson, who had previously been in one of Dance's smaller touring companies and had been sacked out of hand for asking for a ten-shilling rise. He was getting £4 a week at the

In his photo album were these snaps of location scenes in the making of *Bonnie Prince Charlie* and *Scarlet Pimpernel*, the latter taken in Venice

Easily recognizable in this page of snaps from Ivor's private album are the Duke of Gloucester, Duke of Windsor (then Prince of Wales), and Mr. Lloyd George. Prominent in the comic scene is Ivor himself

time. Dance was never very pleased at his triumph in *To-night's the Night* and I had nearly been sacked for championing him.

When at long last a successor was needed for *To-night's the Night*, Grossmith and Laurillard decided upon *Theodore and Co.* and Ivor got the job of composing the score. How he did it has been told.

It had a most brilliant cast, including Davy Burnaby, Leslie Henson, Henri Leone, Robert Nainby, Frank Hector, Ralph Roberts, Joe Grande, Jameson Thomas (who became a famous British film star), Gladys Homfrey, Madge Saunders (who married Leslie Henson), Julia James, Peggy Kurton, a very lovely girl, and George Grossmith. And playing a tiny part was a girl named Joyce Barbour, now a star in her own right, and another, Mercia Swinburne. First performed on September 19th, 1916, it ran for 503 performances. It was Ivor's first theatre success, but there was just one tiny fly in the ointment. Jerome Kern had contributed some numbers, amongst them the big song hit of the show " Three Hundred and Sixty-Five Days." But that was as nothing. There was young Ivor Novello, scoring his first theatre success in that wonderful Gaiety Theatre, right opposite the flat in which he lived. In that theatre he had sat in the gallery and in the pit, watching those people with whom he now stood on equality in the world of the Theatre, watching Gertie Millar, a great friend to be and always one of his adored. Now he stood on the stage, behind the Gaiety footlights—the frontiers of Romance—taking a call himself. It was a thrill equal to that Sunday at the Alhambra when he had first tasted the champagne of public acclaim, perhaps even greater because that had been a concert while this was a show—and a show in a theatre, the Gaiety Theatre at that. He stood there a little awkwardly, with a shy smile, gratitude in his eyes and indeed in his bearing, and a mind in complete turmoil. He was at last past the Stage Door.

Now things happened. Now there was a demand for his songs. Despite the war and his war-work, he had to compose. But he was still in the R.N.A.S. He was still in the Service. For the matter of that, so was George Grossmith Junior. He had some job never quite explained, said to be very " hush-hush "—and so far as details went, it was very much so—but it entailed the wearing of naval officer's uniform, which became him very well and which he wore gallantly—although some of the jealous " knockers " said he wore spurs with it—and later it was whispered that it had something to do with tanks. But whatever they were doing in the Service both he and Ivor Novello were doing splendid work in the Theatre—and the Theatre was valuable to public morale.

To Ivor, the war was an unreal dream. There were air-raids, there were Zeppelins, Taubes and Gothas; there was one daring daylight raid on a Saturday morning when nothing was available to stop the raiders; there was desperate fighting overseas and casualty lists which made reason tremble. It was a very different war from the next one. But to Ivor, because he was now absorbed by the Theatre, it was unreal. What mattered to him, as to all theatre people, was what was going on in Shaftesbury Avenue, around Leicester Square and in the Strand. Who was making a success, who was suffering a flop? Who was going to do what? That was the real news. Life was hectic. Although it was nothing like the total war of 1939–45, it was, nevertheless, on the front doorstep and at night, when the wind set that way, those on the outskirts of London could hear the rumble of the guns in France. In the stalls sat men so young as to be mere lads, their faces flushed and excited, with one little star on their shoulder straps—one-pippers, second-lieutenants entitled to be called only " Mister," but proud of their uniform, proud of the fact that they were soldiers. They might be in training, but many of them, every night were on that precious embarkation leave—and probably, that very night, after the show, they went from one of the London termini, Charing Cross, Victoria or Waterloo, in a darkened train, away into the night from which they might never return. Some would be on leave from the vileness of the trenches, snatching at every moment of life, pushing the horror of war, too often mirrored in their eyes, resolutely behind them, whilst they revelled and gave themselves up to the joy of the sight of pretty girls, gay comedians, the colour and swing of smart frocks and dancing, and the music of Ivor Novello and others, with, perhaps, a little hectic short-lived love affair, before the end which was so certain for many of them.

London was gay on those war nights between 1914 and 1918, despite its semi-blackout, despite the tightening of the purses, the shortage of food, the new and entirely unexpected experience of rationing and the experience of surrendering coupons for meals in a land which had been so carefree, so full of plenty, and so easy and lovely to live in. But it was gaiety of the face and outward show, not of the heart. The main idea was to give the " boys " a good time, and, on the part of the " boys," to hide from those at home what it was really like over there and give a good time in return. Middle-aged people, who had never before entered a theatre and for whom playhouses had been places of sin, went to shows because the " boys " took them, and found they were not so bad as they had imagined. Indeed, they got the habit in most cases.

And to that state of things young David Ivor Davies was making his contribution. He was in uniform, but he was not going overseas. He was not dodging it, for he would have gone with as good heart as the others had he been sent, although he would have loathed it as he loathed his Chingford training. He was marked for home and he was helping to do just what he had written about—to turn those dark clouds inside out. He was succeeding too. He was now in real demand. He did a good deal of music for *See-Saw*, a revue by André Charlot at the Comedy; he wrote some music for *Arlette*, a production at the Shaftesbury Theatre. *Arlette* was a musical comedy and its star was Joseph Coyne. *See-Saw* was in 1916 and it ran for 158 performances; *Arlette* was in 1917.

During the run of *Arlette* unknown to either of us then, I got into opposition to Ivor. Grossmith and Laurillard had gone from the Gaiety which had been taken over by Alfred Butt. They carried on elsewhere. Butt had produced a musical comedy called *The Beauty Spot*, which was not at all a big success. Something had to be done. A little man from South Africa, who had already made history by introducing Sir Harry Lauder in revue to London audiences at the Shaftesbury, had gone to America and come back with a trio of musical shows. They were *The Lilac Domino*, *Shanghai* and *Going Up*. He could not get a theatre as managers were queueing up for them. His name was J. L. Sacks. It happened that I knew him.

In those days I ran the Globe Theatre—and others—for Sir Alfred Butt, booked all his provincial tours, and did a variety of other things for him as well. I suggested to Sir Alfred that if he would let J. L. Sacks into the Empire with *The Lilac Domino*—it meant a change of policy at that famous house—

Sacks would do *Going Up* with him at the Gaiety. Butt did not believe in *The Lilac Domino*, but he did believe in *Going Up*. I got the deal through, and getting it through was all I ever got out of it except personal satisfaction in two big successes.

To make quite sure about *Going Up*, it was necessary to get Joseph Coyne. Now Joe, a man of wonderful talent and charm, was an awkward customer to do business with. He was extremely erratic. He was, perhaps, just a trifle mad at times. For instance, he would have long conversations in the street with people invisible to other eyes—but these were just phases. Here he was, in a success and in which he had won a personal triumph, and it was necessary to persuade him out of it. I got that job, too. Night after night I would go in and see Joe in his dressing-room, chatting, making him laugh, laughing with him and always getting a little further along the path of agreeing to leave *Arlette* and come to us at the Gaiety. It might not have been fair, but all's fair in love, war and—the Theatre. I did not know Ivor then, nor he me. I knew all about him, but he had never heard of my existence: I was just a manager of a theatre and mainly behind the scenes. I had a war job to do as well, by the way, and a tricky, not too pleasant or safe one at that. *Arlette* was not Ivor's own show but he was its composer. It meant much to him—from prestige and income. And I, who came to know him so well, and to work so closely with him, was at that moment trying to do him indirect harm, because I had my duty to do. I got Joe in the end, but I need not have troubled because *Arlette* finished just at the time he would have had to leave and go to the Gaiety. But Ivor also wrote the music for another Charlot show, *Tabs*, at the Vaudeville, in which Beatrice Lillie starred, and made a tremendous success. That began another friendship for Ivor which lasted his life. And it was *Tabs* and his numbers therein which did him an immense amount of good with management and public.

Indeed, war, which ruins so many, lifted Ivor Novello to success.

CHAPTER SEVEN

THE BOYS COME HOME

BY the time that *Theodore and Co.* was produced and Ivor was through that stage door, there had been over two years of war. The dark clouds were still there, the silver lining very hard to detect, and the boys were still leaving home, many never to return. But life went on and, of course, the Theatre went on. That is always a world in itself, making reality out of its own illusions.

What was happening in the world of the Theatre when Ivor really entered it? In telling the story of a man's or woman's career, the background against which they move is all-important. It shows what they had to face, what competitors they were up against, and it also shows the quality of the public's mind. Ivor came in half-way. The old stability had gone, though it was not realized at the time. People were already used to paper money: a golden sovereign was already something strange and nostalgic. Unheard by the masses the doom of the old order had sounded. All those stately homes, all those old families rooted in them for generations, all had received notice to quit. There was already talk of the " New Rich " and the " New Poor." The former were the large numbers who were making money out of munitions and other necessities of war, for whom the bloodshed was being turned into gold. The latter were those who had fixed incomes, or capital in land and possessions, and upon whom taxation was pressing and for whom the future was dark. But the theatrefolk took little notice of that. Things in their domain were prosperous.

There had been a time, soon after the war broke out, when almost anything succeeded. That was gone but a show had to be pretty bad to fail outright because so many people wanted to go out, to " go to a show "—and they went to almost all of them. There were failures, of course, but, by and large, it was the straight play which lacked support, whilst anything musical flourished. There were exceptions, but not many. Revue drew big crowds: it was gay, it was carefree. Nobody wanted to think. But, also, it was delightful to be sentimental. *Peg O' My Heart* ran for years and years, charming but just a novelette with a good central character, written by an Englishman whose American wife created " Peg." *Daddy Long Legs*, the simplest and sweetest of stories, also ran for a tremendous time. Yet all forms of sentiment did not pay. The audiences lapped up the Irishry of *Peg* in which the English were largely unsympathetic and caricatures, but they would not have *Kitty Mackay*, despite a fine cast. Ireland was Ireland, although in revolt. Scotland, loyal to the death, did not get a look in. It took a Barrie or a " Bunty " to make Scotland a stage success. Laughter was in demand and shows which made them laugh were successes, too.

To get a proper background to Ivor Novello's entrance into the Theatre it is worth while to examine what occupied the London stages in 1916. Irene Vanbrugh and her husband, Dion Boucicault, were at the New Theatre, presenting straight plays, amongst them *Her Husband's Wife* and *Caroline* by Somerset Maugham. Arthur Bourchier and Sir John Martin Harvey were, until up to the summer, in alternate management at His Majesty's, with Martin Harvey reviving big Shakespearean productions, including *Hamlet* and *Henry V*. The Oxford Music Hall had gone over to revue. H. B. Irving was playing in *The Barton Mystery* at the Savoy, a play by Walter Hackett. Sir George Alexander was at St. James's with a revival of *Bella Donna*, including Mrs. Patrick Campbell, and a play called *The Basker*. Drury Lane staged *The Best of Luck*. At the Comedy, the Palladium, the Empire, the Palace and Hippodrome, revue was the attraction; at the Empire there was *Follow the Girls*, produced by Tom Reynolds, with Ethel Levey, Robert Hale, Joseph Coyne, Tom Walls, Blanche Tomlin and Fay Compton. Sarah Bernhardt thrilled audiences at the Coliseum in *Les Cathedrales* and there was opera, sponsored by Beecham senior, at the Aldwych. The Haymarket was not being too lucky; it had *Fishpingle* by H. A. Vachell, with Henry Ainley, Allan Aynesworth and Marion Terry as stars—Haymarket quality of casting as usual. A very amusing comedy called *The Boomerang*, produced by Charles Hawtrey, failed at the Queen's. There was farce at the Garrick in *The Girl from Ciro's* with H. V. Esmond, Lyston Lyle, Madge Lessing and Lottie Venne, and *Hobson's Choice* by the north-country author, Harold Brighouse, at the

Apollo. And after *The Boomerang* that wonderful couple Robert Yorke and Augustus Leonard came to the Queen's in *Potash and Perlmutter in Society* and success came with them. Gladys Cooper was at the Playhouse in *The Misleading Lady*, Gerald du Maurier and Hilda Trevelyan in *A Kiss for Cinderella* by J. M. Barrie at Wyndham's. The Globe staged a fine backstage play called *The Show Shop*, with A. E. Matthews at his wonderful best, Edmund Gwenn and Marie Lohr. It ran a short time and *Peg O' My Heart* came back again. *Daddy Long Legs* was drawing crowds to the Duke of York's with Aubrey Smith and Renee Kelly, and Dennis Eadie was playing *Disraeli* at the Royalty.

But it was the musical stage which glowed with success. Revue and musical comedy packed the theatres. Violet Loraine and George Robey were putting a new song into the national repertoire in *The Bing Boys*, the title of which was "If You Were the Only Girl in the World." Men in khaki sang that song in the trenches and women at home sang it too; it was every man's and every woman's song for the absent and loved ones. Mothers at home sang it to their babies with their minds on the man who was overseas. My own daughter—then a tiny baby—was lulled to sleep by it nightly. It had nothing at all to do with war, so it was a British war song. The Palace had revived *Bric-à-Brac*, with Madge White in Gertie Millar's part, and then produced *Vanity Fair*, one of the best of that wonderful series of Palace revues, under the management of Alfred Butt, which began with *The Passing Show* and ended with *Hullo America!* Even Old Drury turned to revue after the annual drama, de Courville staging *Razzle Dazzle* there, afterwards transferring to the Empire. And the same genius had *Flying Colours* at the London Hippodrome, in which were Little Tich, Bertram Wallis, Dorothy Waring, Gabrielle Ray and John Humphries. *See-Saw*, a Charlot revue, was at the Comedy, with music by Willy Redstone, Philip Braham and Ivor Novello, and Phyllis Monkman, Ruby Miller, Billy Danvers and Jack Hulbert in the cast. The unknown man who came from South Africa, J. L. Sacks, startled the world of the Theatre by presenting Sir Harry Lauder at the Shaftesbury Theatre in a revue called *Three Cheers*. He was to startle London often. C. B. Cochran, not Sir Charles then, had a couple of revues in two small adjoining theatres: *Pell Mell* at the Ambassadors', with

Alice Delysia and Leon Morton, and *Houp La* at the St. Martin's, the cast including Nat D. Ayer, Binnie Hale (then almost a child), George Graves and the one and only Gertie Millar. How he managed to make it pay was his secret—but perhaps he did not!

Of musical plays during that year there were plenty. The Shaftesbury had *The Light Blues*, with a young man named Jack Hulbert (later to go into *See-Saw*), Shaun Glenville, Cicely Debenham and also a very young girl called Cicely Courtneidge. In 1951 Jack Hulbert was to produce and Cicely to star in Ivor Novello's last play *Gay's the Word*, written specially for her. In the same cast was another young actor, destined to play a large part in Ivor's life and to rise to the heights on a parallel course, whose name was unknown then but is famous to-day—Noël Coward. The music was by Howard Talbot and Herman Finck. Mark Ambient and Jack Hulbert wrote the libretto. That fine comedian, W. H. Berry, who passed on recently, and who was always a fervent admirer of Ivor Novello, was the star of the Adelphi Theatre where he reigned for ten years. In 1916 Berry was at the top of his form, playing in a huge success called *High Jinks*, with music by Paul Rubens, Howard Talbot and Jerome Kern, and the book by Frederick Lonsdale. In the cast, too, were Tom Walls, Leon M. Lion, W. H. Rawlins, Maisie Gay and Nellie Taylor. Succeeding *The Light Blues* at the Shaftesbury came *My Lady Frayle* (music by Howard Talbot and Herman Finck) with Anne Croft and Cicely Debenham. Daly's had, first, *The Happy Day*, in which Jose Collins made a tremendous hit. The book was by Seymour Hicks, the music by Sydney Jones and Paul Rubens. Besides Jose Collins the company included G. P. Huntley, Arthur Wontner, Thorpe Bates and Winifred Barnes. But Daly's was to make history later in the year when *The Maid of the Mountains* was produced. Frederick Lonsdale was the writer, Fraser Simpson and Jas W. Tate the composers, and Jose Collins the great star, with Arthur Wontner, Lauri de Frece, Mark Lester, Thorpe Bates and Mabel Sealby. Robert Evett was in command, making a bold endeavour to maintain the Edwardes's tradition and carry on the Edwardes's quality. *The Maid of the Mountains* was a desperate throw, for finances were at a low ebb, but, as had happened in that theatre before (when Georges Edwardes produced *The Merry Widow*),

Fortune was favourable and success was in full flood. A record run resulted.

But signs and portents of the American invasion were visible, notably in *Mr. Manhattan* at the Prince of Wales's, in which London applauded Raymond Hitchcock. What was happening underneath Ivor's flat at the Strand? A great actor-manager had come there and Matheson Lang had revived *Mr. Wu*. And out at the Elephant and Castle Theatre, now no more, was a play by Sheila Walsh called . . . *Keep the Home Fires Burning*. One presumes Ivor knew about that?

Meanwhile the most romantic story the stage has told for years, where incredible and fantastic things happen so frequently, was coming to fruition at the stately and beautiful His Majesty's Theatre. The creator of that theatre, one of the greatest men our Theatre ever had, Sir Herbert Tree, was in Hollywood, filming *Macbeth*. He hated it but he stuck it out. He impressed the Americans far more than they impressed him. He created many sensations during his stay there but none so great as that which Constance Collier relates in her delightful *Harlequinade*. All the mighty ones of Hollywood sat agog and spellbound watching the first private run through of *Macbeth*. When it was over they turned to Sir Herbert Tree, who had been silent throughout, for his verdict before any of them spoke. They waited on his utterance with reverence and awe. He spoke no word. He was fast asleep. That was the real Tree.

Whilst he was in Hollywood, he received a cable from his manager, Henry Dana, informing him that £3,000 of his money had been invested in a play about to be produced at His Majesty's. He made no demur; he trusted Dana. Little did he know what that money was to amount to! For the play was a kind of Arabian Nights pantomime called *Chu Chin Chow*. Oscar Asche, who had won his spurs under Tree, had written it because it was raining in Manchester and he could not play golf. He wrote the first act there in a week and the second act in a similar period at Glasgow. Asche, of Scandinavian origin and born in Australia, had come to this country determined to be an actor. He slept every night for the first six months of his stay in England on a seat on the Thames Embankment. But he stuck it, and he became an actor. He went with the famous Benson company, he joined Sir Herbert

Tree at His Majesty's. He married that lovely woman and accomplished actress Lily Brayton. They did so well that they went into management. They were in management and playing Shakespeare when he wrote *Chu Chin Chow*. Asche was big in every way, in physique, in mind, in thought, in achievement—and in extravagance. Shortly after he had written *Chu Chin Chow* he had a sharp reminder from his bank concerning an overdraft. He asked his wife for help, who said she would buy for £500 half his author's fees—then very problematical—from *Chu Chin Chow*. She got them. He came to London, he approached a very clever musician who was also an actor, whom he hardly knew, named Frederic Norton, to write the music. Norton agreed. Asche promised him the other half of his author's royalties. He then offered the play to George Dance, then the most powerful and richest man in the Theatre. Dance said it might succeed as a provincial pantomime if George Graves played Ali Baba. Asche then offered it to Robert Evett who kept it some time and sent it back. Asche always believed Evett never even read it. But you could not beat Asche. By now he had got Percy Anderson, a splendid artist, to design the dresses and the settings. He went to his old friend Henry Dana. Dana liked it and got a few friends together to hear it read and to listen to the music with a view to forming a syndicate. Everyone was impressed. Asche estimated that £6,000 was needed to get it produced. Dana put in £3,000 of Tree's money and Lily Brayton put up the remaining £3,000. Now she had half the show and half Asche's royalties. Norton had the other half of them.

Asche, though he was to play the lead at £100 a week, had nothing at all left in the show he had created. But he was to produce it too. He asked for a producer's fee and was pooh-poohed. Asche, a tenacious man, argued. Dana agreed at last but had what he thought was a joke. He promised Asche a pretty high percentage after a certain sum had been taken and if the receipts rose beyond a certain figure. Both figures seemed to him fantastic, no such money had ever been taken at His Majesty's in its history. A little agreement was signed. Dana put it in the safe and forgot it.

On August 31st, 1916, *Chu Chin Chow* was produced. The rest is history. Certain critics jeered, one left after the first act. The public took it to its heart. It ran and it ran and it ran. It put up the record for 2,238 continuous performances at the same theatre. It is running still.

After an incredibly short space of time Asche reminded Dana of the little contract. The figures had been reached. Dana was appalled but had to pay. That contract brought Asche £200,000. Everyone made a fortune out of the play. Asche soon spent his and was penniless again. But *Chu Chin Chow* was an institution. No trip home on leave from France was complete without a visit to His Majesty's; people came time and again. Oscar Asche, Lily Brayton, Sydney Fairbrother, Frank Cochrane, J. V. Bryant and Courtice Pounds were the stars. And when at long last the incredible happened and it was to come off—an old lady asked for an interview with Oscar Asche, which he gave her. She told him that her son had brought her to the first night and that every time he came home from the trenches they visited the show. Then he had been killed but on the anniversary of his leaves she, his mother, had always booked two stalls. She sat in one and in the other was her dead son's cap. " We shall be there on the last night, Mr. Asche," she said. And so it came about. *Chu Chin Chow* was the highlight of highlights of that remarkable year 1916 when Ivor Novello first really entered the Stage Door.

Much space has gone on this record of plays and players but it is necessary to show what the stage was like and what it was doing when one of its most brilliant sons first joined it. It shows the calibre and type of the people with whom he was, as composer, in competition: such men as Fraser Simpson, Howard Talbot, Paul Rubens, Lionel Monckton, Frederick Norton, Jerome Kern, Sidney Jones, James W. Tate, Herman Darewski, Willy Redstone, P. Braham and Herman Finck. And amongst that galaxy of talent, after a sighter in *The Bing Boys*, he scored a bull's-eye with *Theodore and Co.* It was certainly a most promising début.

Among the many names I have mentioned are some who have made their last exit, but there are others who are now the big names on the bills. Their lives were to intertwine with Ivor's in that small but complicated maze which is the Theatre. Fay Compton, Frank Cochrane, Marie Lohr, Gladys Cooper, Gertie Millar, Cicely Courtneidge—many, many more, already prominent, used to be lifelong friends and associates. And already working to his music were Jack Hulbert, Ruby Miller and Phyllis Monkman. Noël Coward, who was to be his life-long friendly rival, was just emerging from the boy-actor stage. They did not know one another then. Ivor was six years older than Noël Coward.

Although Ivor did not realize it, did not even think about it, the Theatre which he loved then and all his life, was in the melting-pot. Changes were coming thick and fast. The stage holds up a mirror to Nature and Nature was changing too. The old order was on its way out. The actor-manager was in decline; the new men coming into the Theatre, men of commerce, get-rich-quick adventurers in many cases, were taking a gamble in what seemed a Tom Tiddler's Ground of wealth. Theatre rents were soaring. Theatres which could have been got for a modest £20 a week already asked and received three figures and, in many cases, it was not a One which led the row.

The actor-manager could not afford to compete. Tree never returned to his own theatre. *Chu Chin Chow* kept him out and he died of an accident in 1917. Sir George Alexander did not outlast the war, he died in 1918. Sir Charles Wyndham was already in retirement. Lewis Waller, that magnificent actor and manager, had died in 1915, at the early age of fifty-five. There remained still Gerald du Maurier, with Frank Curzon behind him. Charles Hawtrey, hardly managing now on his own account, was still a great producer and actor. Matheson Lang, Martin Harvey, Julia Neilson and Fred Terry spent most of their time in the Provinces to the great betterment of the provincial Theatre; Dennis Eadie was then in a partnership with J. E. Vedrenne at the Royalty Theatre in Dean Street; and Sir John Hare was practically in retirement. Cyril Maude had given up his lease of the Playhouse in 1915 and was in America. He returned later to London, not as an actor-manager, but as actor only. In 1917 Gladys Cooper was to become actress-manageress in association with Frank Curzon. Arthur Bourchier had left the Garrick but came back later as actor-manager to the Strand. Seymour Hicks made occasional actor-managerial descents on London, but also played in the provinces and on the music halls. Dion Boucicault, with Irene Vanbrugh, his wife, as star, was in management at the New.

The big managerial names were Sir Alfred Butt, Frank Curzon, André Charlot, Arthur Collins, Violet Melnotte, who took over her own theatre, the Duke of York's, on the death of

Charles Frohman (drowned in the *Lusitania* disaster in 1916), Robert Evett at Daly's, the Gattis, Frederick Harrison, Lady Wyndham (Mary Moore), who controlled Wyndham's, the New and the Criterion, with her son Bronson Albery, now very justly Sir Bronson, and Sir Charles Wyndham's son, Howard Wyndham, as her lieutenants, Sir Oswald Stoll and, behind the scenes, George Dance. But the new generation was entering. Leading the van of the new managements was the firm of Laurillard and Grossmith, who had given the chance to Ivor, and the strange little man from South Africa, J. L. Sacks. There was also the amazing and mercurial Albert de Courville, as well as another young man who came from America and who made a most promising début with *Daddy Long Legs*—Gilbert Miller. That was the balance of theatrical power.

Ivor was enjoying life now. The only drawback was the war job. But he did it mechanically for it hardly called for more effort than that. He revelled in success; he was a rising power, he was making friends, he was in the magical inner circle already and, of course, he charmed everyone he met and generally had a good time. There were changes in the Novello household. Mam was, of course, working hard and brimful of ideas. It was as well that Ivor was earning money, for at that time Mam was deprived of the man whose trained and careful eye watched her very tangled financial affairs. Fred Allen had joined up.

This stalwart and trusted friend of the Novello family has already made his entrance. Now he should have his proper place, for he was to serve Ivor so long and so well.

In 1908, when Madame Novello Davies took over her studio in Chatham House, Fred Allen was engaged in the great concert firm of Daniel Mayer in quite a humble capacity. Mam persuaded Rudolph Mayer, the charming son of the firm, to be her secretary. She hoped that by so doing she would gain additional pupils and that was, very probably, the case. In that year of 1908 Allen decided to take a wife—he was twenty-three years old then—and to help him along Rudolph Mayer handed over to him the Novello Davies job. It was a kindly gesture, but Rudolph Mayer had more important things to attend to. It helped young Fred Allen a lot and he helped Mam too. He worked for her and for the firm of Daniel Mayer, from 1908 until 1916, when he joined the Forces under the Derby Scheme.

By now Fred Allen had a wife and two young children. He was not bursting for military glory and Victoria Crosses, any more than any other man of his age and station at that time. He was prepared to " do his bit," but he hoped for the best. He had luck. He had friends. He was naturally in close touch with Ivor, and Ivor was great friends with Edward Marsh, who was not knighted then. Marsh kindly pulled a string or two—for Fred Allen, like everyone else, did not hanker after the infantry (the P.B.I. as it was called) if anything else was available. To his immense relief he was drafted into the Inland Water Transport Corps, and sent to Sandwich. He had only his army pay but he looked upon it as a fairly cushy job, despite the fact that he slept in a draughty marquee under some trees which held a rookery and would lie awake most of the night thinking he might have been better off in the Navy! He got a lot of very hard work as a navvy, building the huts in connection with the wartime port of Richborough. But his knowledge of shorthand got him along, and he was put to work in the architects' office. His best memories of those Sandwich days were the wonderful sunsets, and the suppers of bacon and eggs and apple tarts at Snellings, the bakers. There were still plenty of bacon and eggs in 1916 although the war was almost two years old and it was within reach of a private soldier's pay, which was pretty negligible then.

Allen could no longer look after Mam's affairs, but he kept in touch with her. And, from Sandwich, he wrote to Ivor suggesting that as Mam had helped him in his career as composer, he ought to put affairs between them on a business footing and they would both know, in those dangerous times, how they stood. But Ivor did not agree. Lazy he might be, artistic he might be and, already, he was practically Ivor Novello—but David Ivor Davies was wide awake and staring. He wrote back a firm refusal. He loved Mam, he said, and he would always see that she wanted for nothing—but he was not going to throw his money into " a bottomless pit." That was what he said, and he knew what he was talking about. On many occasions in after years, when Allen was back from the war and in charge of Ivor's affairs, he would remind Ivor and point out that by figures Ivor would have been better off had he taken the advice then given. But Ivor still knew better—and he was right. " Not on your life, Fred," he would answer, " you know I should have—as I have done—paid out far more than any 10 per cent. of my earnings."

Fred Allen was transferred from Sandwich to London when the office in which he worked, under the command of the now eminent architect E. Vincent Harris, came to Headquarters at the Hotel Cecil, which was a lot better than marquees or even billets at Sandwich. The good luck lasted a short time only. Cambrai and other desperate battles in France meant huge casualties and the need for more and more men. The " comb " got to work and all fit men were drafted into the Infantry, Fred Allen among them. He took it philosophically. He had a month's intensive training at Sheerness (and intensive training in 1914–18 was something, believe me), and then went to France. There he spent the rest of the war. He came through. And in the bitter winter of 1918–19, following the Armistice, he was informed that his old commander, E. Vincent Harris, wanted him to work on his new department, the Disposal Board. Allen was sent back at once and in February he started his new job. That was to last four years, years during which he saw little of Mam and little of Ivor. Ivor now had a Miss Chantry as a secretary—part-time. But it was Fred Allen who was called upon to battle with the intricate and increasingly difficult income-tax problems which were beginning to be Old Men of the Sea on the shoulders of most of the community. . . .

For Ivor they were years of progress and success. If 1916 had started him, 1917 and 1918 brought further advancement.

Other people destined to share his life were also entering it. He went to a first night at the Strand Theatre with Eddie Marsh. It was in January, 1917. The play was called *Under Cover* and in it was Margaret Bannerman. In the audience was another young man who was, like Ivor, serving in the Royal Naval Air Service and who was also an actor. He was introduced to Ivor by Eddie Marsh. That young R.N.A.S. man was Robert Andrews and that night a friendship began which lasted until death. Ivor had met Marsh in a theatre; he met Robert Andrews in a theatre: and it was always Theatre with Ivor for it was in his destiny.

In 1917, Ivor still had *Theodore and Co*. running and bringing in good royalties. He also had *See-Saw* to his credit, which ran for 158 performances at the Comedy from December 14th,

1916, roughly five months. In September, 1917, came *Arlette* at the Shaftesbury. The book was by Jose G. Levy (it was translated from the French, a job at which Levy, a dark, clever man who wore a monocle, excelled) and adapted by Austen Hurgon (a revue king in his own right and a splendid producer) and George Arthurs (a very clever, quiet, unassuming and pleasant little man with a north-country accent which he never lost), with music by Jane Vieu, Guy le Feuvre and Ivor Novello. Ivor did not write the entire score. The cast included Joseph Coyne, Joan Hay, Adrah Fair (who married Edward Laurillard), Mary Robson, Winifred Barnes, Stanley Lupino, Leonard Mackay (a fine upstanding actor whose son was later to play Ivor's part in the film version of *Glamorous Night* and also on tour), A. G. Poulton (a straight actor and a great character, known to everyone as " Aggie " on account of his initials and with a slight affliction to one eye, which shed constant tears), Wyn Weaver, Murray Moore, Strafford Moss, the old Savoyard, Johnny Fields, Lucien Mussiere and a very good French actor named Yvan Servais, whom Gaby Deslys had imported to appear with her in *Suzette*. The latter, her last show in this country, was presented at the Globe Theatre, which I managed at the time. As a result I became great friends with that remarkable woman. *Arlette* was a success and Stanley Lupino had a smash hit number called " I'm On the Staff." He, too, had been in *Suzette*.

During 1917 the war rolled on and life became more and more unreal. The submarine menace was at its height and few outside the High Command of this country knew how near defeat we were, not on land but on that domain which, by popular consent, we were supposed to rule. It was indeed a world war now, for America was in it and the Yanks declared their belief in victory in George M. Cohan's song " Over There." The streets of London and the audiences of the theatres were all besprinkled with an array of uniforms. The Americans were the latest note and their white gaiters made them conspicuous. There were also plenty of French soldiers to be seen and lots of small, swarthy Portuguese, who made quite a romantic show in their grey uniforms and comic opera cloaks. There were Italians, lean, brown-faced New Zealanders and the hard-bitten, smasher-hatted Australians, the " Diggers "—grand fighting men but a real headache to all theatre managers, for they were

A group of pictures of Ivor in uniform (and one in "civvies" about the same period) during his service with the R.N.A.S. On the picture below, he is seen in the centre next to Leslie Cahn-Rein (tall figure)

These snaps from Ivor's private album highlight his career as an airman. 1 On roof of Aldwych 1916 ; 2 With Edward German, 1916 ; 3 With Willie Canpers ; 4 " Self in cockpit " 5 " My Crash "

quite unruly and their idea of discipline did not match with ours. There were crowds of Canadians, too, whose attire was more like that of the British; and of the British in khaki there was no end. This mass of drab colour was enlivened by an array of " tabs," belonging to staff officers of various ranks. Everyone became familiar with the gradings and departments. It was amazing what a number of people seemed to be " On the Staff "—as Stanley Lupino sang in his song in *Arlette*. For tabs were everywhere. There were the red tabs of the General Staff, the high-ups, and those khaki-uniformed officers, with their beautifully polished boots and Sam Browne's. Their red tabs and their gilt decorated caps were at once the smartest and most soldierly looking of all the men of war. There were blue tabs for other branches of the executive: those on munitions and that sort of work; and green tabs for the men who worked on recruiting and Intelligence. The streets were positively lit up by these flecks of colour.

It was not surprising, therefore, that André Charlot, a King of Revue, should seize upon the word for one of his productions. *Tabs*, a revue in two acts and twenty-two scenes by Harry Gratton, additional scenes by Ronald Jeans, who also wrote the lyrics, and music by Ivor Novello, with additional numbers by Pat Thayer and Guy le Feuvre, was produced at the Vaudeville on May 15th, 1918. The star was Beatrice Lillie and others in the cast were Alfred Austin, Hal Bert, Guy le Feuvre, Ethel Baird, Tiny Gratton, Joan Emney and Vera Lennox. It was a big success and ran for 268 performances, the music which Ivor wrote for it contributing in no small part to that success, and to his own advancement. He was doing very well now and could endure those boring days at the Air Ministry softened by the frequent leaves he was able to wangle, for he was now a celebrity. He had some songs, too, in *The Southern Maid* at Daly's with which it was hoped to repeat the success of *The Maid of the Mountains*. But those hopes were dashed . . . it is seldom you can do it twice in the Theatre, although Ivor managed it later and the Aldwych farces proved that, if you had a team, it was possible to keep up continuity. Friendships were still being made and cemented. Ivor and Noël Coward had met; Mr. Coward recounts their meeting in his *Present Indicative* so there is no need to repeat it here. Beatrice Lillie, who had made a big success in *Tabs*, too, was also now a great friend of

Ivor's. José Collins, who was the great leading lady of musical shows and whose vibrant personality and remarkable voice put her in a class by herself, was another friend who was not only very much liked but also very useful.

The last year of the war was dragging along, but dragging only in the minds of a war-weary people. It was a year with plenty of shocks. There was the spectacular break-through around Easter, when the Germans made a tremendous advance and when the age-limit for the Army shot up to fifty years overnight, to the consternation and horror of a large class of men who had never ceased to pester younger male members of the community with tales of how they wished they had been young enough to fight and what they would have done if they had the opportunity. When that chance was provided them, there was no rush at all—just a lot of moans about responsibilities and inquiries as to what the country was coming to, and—when would the war be over?

The same year a childhood friend of Ivor's got into touch with him again, a man called Lloyd Williams. Ivor had a letter from Williams, who was serving as a soldier, telling him what a tremendous amount of good " Keep the Home Fires " had been as an aid to morale in the Middle East, where he was at the time. Lloyd Williams had studied under Mam and was a composer himself of no small merit and a first-class musician. Ivor remembered him hazily and wrote back. Later the two men met, liked each other and Lloyd Williams, known to everyone in the Theatre as " Lloydy " became Ivor's personal assistant and secretary, a post he held until his death, or almost until his death, for he became paralysed and lived at " Redroofs " until his death in August, 1948. Had Lloydy had more energy himself, or the slightest amount of personal push and ambition, he would have made his mark as a writer of light music. But he did not want to. He was supremely happy working for Ivor. His job was no easy one but he performed it magnificently. Quiet, unassuming, always in the background he possessed the keenest powers of observation. He knew whom to welcome, whom to exclude and whom to get rid of with the greatest tact and charm. He was the perfect Ambassador, the perfect Lord Chamberlain at the Court of Ivor Novello. He was here, there and everywhere, a tremendous worker, who never seemed to have anything to do and who never appeared to be in a hurry.

Yet he was always on the spot and was never late with anything. He was a very, very important part of the Novello machine. His judgment of voices at auditions was impeccable, his knowledge of music without question. If there were people in the audience whom Ivor wanted to see, suddenly Lloydy would at the right moment appear beside them and conduct them round to the dressing-room, making them feel very distinguished indeed. He could be in the room and never be noticed, but nothing which passed escaped him. He never appeared flurried; he never seemed to be ruffled or lose his temper; his voice was always low, calm and soothing. He was of the utmost service and value to Novello in his days of greatness and in his days of rapid growth. He could deal with Mam, too, without appearing to do so. He did almost everything for Ivor, save for that yeoman and sterling service in the financial and accounts line which was for so many years the job of Fred Allen. Of all his staff, of all the people working around him, these two men were the pivots and the rocks.

Lloydy had a sense of humour all his own and a power of making a remark which summed up a character in a phrase. He liked jokes, he loved laughter. He had a slow smile which was as quiet as himself, but as all-embracing. During Ivor's sojourn at Drury Lane, Lloydy would pervade that vast building. He was there talking to you—and then—he was gone. We christened him the Ghost of Drury Lane, a real opposition to our actual and much-prized spectre. He adored " going on " in a show. In *Careless Rapture* he would get into costume and go on with the chorus in " The Manchuko " number—and get away with it. Word would go round: " Lloydy's on to-night " and those not actively occupied in the action would go to the wings and watch. They always hoped Lloydy would go wrong and put things out, but he never did.

It was " Keep the Home Fires " which brought the two men together, yet another of the remarkable things that song accomplished. One of Lloydy's most arduous jobs was dealing with Ivor's voluminous fan mail. He did it splendidly, even to signing autographs which nobody could ever distinguish from the real ones.

That year of grace 1918 went on, and the German advance was checked. On August Bank Holiday Lloyd-George issued his memorable Message to the Nation, which was read on that evening in every place of entertainment of every kind throughout the entire kingdom—from theatres down to whist drives. It was delivered to the most important person at each of these in a sealed envelope with strict instructions that it was not to be opened until the time appointed for reading it. That actual time varied according to the time of commencement of the show. Leading actors, and actresses, stars of music hall and revue, musicians, managers, members of committees, film stars and cinema proprietors, all observed the rules. In front of their assembled public they broke the seals on that important looking envelope and read it to the expectant people—and the message was " Hold Fast." It made a great impression, although many had expected (for no reason at all) a message of Victory, imminent and immediate. As, indeed, it was, but prepared with the great caution which typified that amazing if flamboyant little Welshman. Lloyd-George knew when to counsel caution as well as when to wave the flags. He knew the value of a build-up. I had the honour and privilege of helping in the organization of that message and know all about it. And soon afterwards came the great and last advance: the Allies swept forward and entered Germany. It would have been nice to chronicle that when they marched in triumph over the frontier, the advance guard was singing " Keep the Home Fires Burning." But they were not. The first band to lead them—for they went over with flags flying and bands playing—blared out " The Robbers' March " from *Chu Chin Chow*. But Ivor had been to the fore, on an occasion almost as important. When the British forces entered Palestine—and that was the true beginning of the downfall of Germany—the troops had sung as they marched, and they had sung " Keep the Home Fires." Amongst those who sang loudest had been Lloyd Williams. . . .

Just when the Lloyd-George message was being given to the public, Ivor got an assignment of his own. German propaganda was still strong and nowhere stronger than in Sweden, neutral then as in the Second World War, but decidedly pro-Ally. But the Swedes wanted something with which to combat the constant infiltration of German ideas, which were being put over very skilfully by means of song and entertainment. The Germans were fighting their battles in the cabarets and night clubs which prospered in Stockholm, and important and far-sighted Swedes wanted this nullified. So they asked London to " show the flag," not with a demonstration of armed force, which, of course, was impossible, but by counter-efforts in the same field as the Germans. Only those who have served in Intelligence will realize fully the importance of this class of work. London listened and understood, for although our Intelligence has always been a joke amongst us, it has always been the finest in the world. Encouraging the idea that it was futile was by no means the least clever piece of Intelligence work either. So they decided to send over British entertainers. There was Ivor Novello in uniform, a popular composer, a handsome young man of tremendous charm—and he was in Service. So Ivor became a species of ambassador and went to Stockholm with a small but picked band of entertainers. He went in late September and he succeeded completely. He was still there when the Armistice was declared on November 11th, 1918, that unforgettable day when London went mad—all the Empire went mad—and when " Keep the Home Fires Burning " was sung (amongst other songs) everywhere and by everybody. He and his company heard the news in a Stockholm hotel. They celebrated in their own way, but their hearts were in London, with the cheering crowds, with those who had come through the great Ordeal, with those who, for the first time in four years and three months, no longer looked into the eyes of Death either directly or through the eyes of their loved ones. The war was over; Victory had come. Let joy be unconfined. Back again to the great days of old, to the gay, secure and wealthy days of Yesterday, with England as itself again. But that was not to be . . . although few recognized it yet.

For Ivor a phase had closed. The war had made him famous and the ball was at his feet. Now he could get out of uniform and enter fully into the Theatre: to compose, to write, and, as he told himself, above all, to act. His song had come true, the home fires had been kept burning, and now, at last, the Boys would come home. . . .

CHAPTER EIGHT

PEACE, FILMS, AND GREASEPAINT

IVOR was free of uniform in 1919. Before him stretched his future, and around him was a pretty good guarantee that things were going to be all right. Youth, health, marvellous good looks, imagination, friends, and talent as yet unguessed at and a good income from work already done!

It is of interest to look at old contracts and mark his progress thereby. On May 4th, 1914, he signed a contract with Ascherberg, Hopwood and Crew Ltd., whereby the latter agreed to pay him the sum of twenty-five pounds per annum, as retainer, payable in monthly instalments on the first day of each month during the continuance of the agreement and to spend not less than £100 on advertising a song called " Till the Boys Come Home "—the original name of " Keep the Home Fires Burning." The agreement was to remain in force so long as Ivor delivered to the company the complete manuscript of every musical composition he did, as soon as possible after completion and did not sell or otherwise dispose of any of his compositions or copyrights to any other firm, or until the company should have decided not to publish anything he had written, in which case he could offer it elsewhere. In respect of all material published, he was to receive £10 down, a royalty of 3*d.* on every copy of the pianoforte score sold in Great Britain and Ireland and half that for sales elsewhere, every seven copies to count as six and 250 copies to be free of royalty.

In the event of reproduction in newspaper or periodicals, Ivor was to be paid one-third of the amount received by the company. All copies of the music arranged for bands and orchestras were to be free of royalty. A composition entitled " The Moon is on the Water " was to be excluded because it had already been sold and each year Ivor had the right to sell eight, but not more, of his works to other firms, provided Ascherbergs had first refused them, but not more than four of them were to be sold to another publishing firm, whose name was stated.

All comic operas, musical plays or revues were to be submitted to the company fourteen days before their production in the West End and the company to have the right to acquire them on terms equal to those obtainable elsewhere, Ivor undertaking to submit to them any offers he received, for them to consider and beat if they so desired. They had a fortnight in which to make up their minds. The contract was to remain in force for five years.

This agreement was signed for and on behalf of Messrs. Ascherberg, Hopwood and Crew Ltd. by two directors, H. S. J. Booth and Wm. Abbott. Mr. Booth, whose name was Harold Sims Joseph Booth, was a very astute man of business. He had the appearance of a Frenchman and might have been taken, in manners and dress, for a Parisian boulevardier. His complexion was florid, his clothes immaculate—he affected morning coats and bow ties—he was dark and his hair was curly. His manners were what most English people, quite wrongly, expect from the French, and he had a persuasive and insinuating method of doing business. He was in all sorts of theatrical sidelines. He ran the Electrophone, by means of which, long before radio, plays were relayed to listeners over an attachment to the telephone. He ran the company which provided opera glasses in cases fastened to the seats of the Theatres. The cases sprang open when 6*d.* was inserted and a knob pushed and supplied a pair of very attractive looking opera glasses which, if they did not magnify greatly, at least encouraged the vision. He had offices in Gerrard Street and he knew everyone. He also had a habit of eating little violet cachous, which sometimes fell out of his mouth in moments of tension in business deals. George Dance, the theatre magnate, who also ran the refreshment departments of many theatres, could not tolerate Mr. Booth, but that was probably because of Booth's agreements in connection with the supply of opera glasses, which Dance could not get for himself. I had many dealings with H. S. J. Booth and found him as charming in business as in his manners, and also a man of his word. William Abbott, the other director, was for many years a pillar of the music publishing profession —or trade—of the utmost probity and honour, possessing a wonderful memory, an altogether delightful man to know.

Compared with Ivor's later earnings and royalties that £25-a-year retainer looks pretty meagre now. But it was perfectly fair at the time, inasmuch as Ivor was only just becoming known and even "Keep the Home Fires Burning" might have been a solitary achievement. Such things are frequent in the world of music and Theatre. It was probably a much fairer and more generous contract than he would have got elsewhere. Indeed, Ascherberg's have always had a high reputation for their dealings, a reputation that continues to-day with Walter Eastman in charge.

In the year 1918, actually on the first of May, that agreement was revised and instead of the annual retainer of £25, Ivor received one of £200. Thus his value had increased, in the views of his publishers, eight times over, in three years. That £200 he always gave to his father as pocket money to implement the very small pension which Mr. Davies senior drew as a retired rate collector. Ivor was not only a good son to his mother but to his father as well. They were lucky parents indeed.

Ascherberg's published the music for *Theodore and Co.* which, by the way, was called *Durant and Durant* before production. They got the rights for Great Britain and Ireland, its colonies and dependencies, including Canada and all other countries for which the rights had not already been disposed of (*Theodore and Co.* was from the French) and on written, printed, photographed or lithographed copies only sold elsewhere than in the United States, Canada and the continent of Europe. Ivor was to receive 8*d.* a copy on every vocal score, 4*d.* a copy on every piano score, 2*d.* a copy on any song selection or dance music arrangement, no royalty on copies of lyrics when combined with music—other, of course, than vocal scores—but ½*d.* per copy for copies of lyrics sold apart from music. In respect of sales by the publishers in United States, Canada, the Colonies and Europe, half the above rates to be paid, 250 copies being free and seven to count as six. All monies due for mechanical rights were to be divided in accordance with the rules regulating such things. If, after three years, from date of publication, sales should drop below 300 copies and the publishers decided to dispose of their existing stock, then Ivor was to have 10 per cent. of such sale, provided that this payment did not involve a loss on the publishers. He was also to get equal shares with them in any newspaper or periodical publication. The publishers were to make payments on the last day of January and July in each year. There were lots of other small points, but that is the basis of the agreement which Ivor signed and was, with every reason, very glad to sign. And it is pleasant to record that the utmost friendship always existed between the parties.

But here was 1919, he was free, he had plenty of money, or what was plenty of money in those days, some thousands in the bank, and an income as steady as that of any man who derived it from the sale of music. He was never at any time extravagant —his mother had the extravagance of the little family—but he had spent quite a bit from time to time. Among other expenditure he had the lease of a little house in the country. It is generally believed that until he bought his famous " Redroofs " he was simply a town bird and resided only at No. 11 Aldwych. That is not the case. During the war he leased a house at Downley, Bucks, not far from High Wycombe, for his father and mother to live in when they chose, and where he himself could go down for quiet week-ends to think things out or relax. He did not make as much use of it as did his parents (no doubt Mam recruited singing pupils from the surrounding districts) but Ivor kept that house on until 1921. His father always preferred the country.

But what he now desired was a change and a holiday. Memories of his previous visit to New York were vivid and that city beckoned to him. There he would find a complete change from the war-weariness of London and its somewhat brittle and hectic reactions to the coming of Peace, or, at any rate, cessation from hostilities. He wanted to be free from work for a bit, to relax himself and drink in the tonic of a complete change. So New York it was. He went with his mother, who already had an apartment there, which she had established during a trip whilst the war was on. You could not stop Mam from getting about, the war was not her business and must not be allowed to keep her back, submarines or not. With them went Bobbie Andrews and Fay Evelyn, a friend and vocalist. The holiday was a complete success although Ivor spent far more money than he had intended. He saw everything there was to see in the Theatre, he made hosts of new friends and he met Mary Ellis amongst others. Little did either of them think of the triumph which was to be theirs at Drury Lane years later.

Ivor let his lazy streak have full rein; he did no work at all.

But for all that, the trip did him an immense amount of good. His first visit to Canada and New York had made the profoundest impression on him, a lasting one, for it broadened his outlook and opened his eyes to things outside his own narrow sphere and his own country. It had laid a foundation which was to blossom later. This second trip sharpened those impressions and gave him a mental measuring stick. During his first visit he was young and unknown. Now he was already quite a name and a much more self-assured and socially brilliant person, with war experience and success on which to plant his feet. But whatever else it did for him, it achieved one thing: it revived that desire to act, which was always latent in his mind but which now became very active indeed. Seeing plays, watching first-class acting, meeting and mixing with famous players—these experiences made him desire to be an actor himself. He came home filled with that intention. And Fate met him half way.

Ivor was always a lucky man. All that vast achievement was, it is true, his own work, but he never had to contend with the set-backs, the heartbreaks, the grim despair and the biting poverty and hopelessness which so often fall to the lot of people in his profession. He always had comfort, a good home, and more than enough money. There is no hard-luck streak in his story, no cloud of tragedy, except once—and that he conquered where a lesser man might have succumbed. Always the luck of the game was his, always Fortune smiled on him. And this return voyage was no exception. Out of the wastes of mid-Atlantic a radio message reached the ship. It was from the firm of Daniel Mayer, so much bound up with the Novello fortunes. It was from Angus Macleod of that firm (they acted for Ivor as they did for his mother) asking him if he would consent to play in a film. Here was a thrill! Here was excitement! Only those of the stage stock can savour it to the full. In commerce, the chance of a good business deal is something which is never very unexpected, but usually the result of careful preparation. Even an unexpected offer of a big business contract has not the personal touch of a theatrical engagement which has not been sought and not even dreamed of. Here was Ivor determined to act and here was an offer from out of a clear sky, unsolicited, unasked for and from a branch of the profession which had hardly, if ever, been considered.

The offer sent the party into a state of complete turmoil. One can imagine the chatter, the talk, the gaspings and the excitement. Ivor, always a potential actor, had never yet played a part on the professional stage, let alone the studio. His one attempt to do so was when he tried to get into the chorus of Daly's—and a desire to be near his adored Lily Elsie may have been something to do with that—and that attempt had been foiled by his mother's suppression of the reply. Now, here, to a man known only as a composer, whose public appearances had been limited to accompaniments at the piano (and no appearance can be more self-effacing than that) and a very few " first-night " calls, was an offer to appear on the screen. It was, of course, the silent screen then. It was an offer, but not quite a definite offer, but it was good enough. Was it to be accepted? Was he to cable an affirmative reply? One can imagine Mam, Bobbie Andrews, Fay Evelyn and Ivor in conference. Mam was probably bursting with pride and complete assurance as to the certainty that her son would be a big star, though she would also be torn with anxiety that it might interfere with his music—and in her view nothing must be allowed to do that. Visions also of much wealth accruing would pass across her mind.

Robert Andrews, the actor, was all for it. All through their lifelong friendship, Robert Andrews—Bobbie to everyone—was Ivor's adviser and always a good adviser too. He is an actor and a good actor and he understands the stage. So he was aware of all the troubles and the difficulties which beset anyone—even the greatest—engaged in that most difficult and dangerous profession. He knew how personal it all was and how a false move would bring wreck and ruin. Devoted and loyal to Ivor always, he never allowed his deep friendship to obscure his vision. He was always able to see around Ivor, to see what it all meant. He knew Ivor through and through and his advice was always sound. Bobbie has a very good brain and a shrewd judgment of theatrical people and theatrical affairs. Sometimes when Ivor got obstinate—and he had a considerable vein of obstinacy—Bobbie would have a talk about things, see the points, assess them for and against, and get Ivor to see reason. Ivor never had any cause to regret taking his advice. And on this occasion Bobbie was for it: most decidedly, the answer should be " Yes." As the years went on and Ivor grew in greatness, Bobbie was still the best friend and his words carried the greatest weight. He was never blind to faults, nor to moods. Success never blunted his outlook. When he gave his judgment it was always sound, for Bobbie Andrews has a good mind and his advice was always entirely unselfish. So, amidst crackling excitement, the answer was " Yes."

It so happened that Ivor was selected not for his talent but for his type. His acting abilities were entirely unknown. The director of the film wanted a type. He called on the firm of Daniel Mayer to see what they had got. The man he wanted must look like a Sicilian. The firm of Mayer showed him what clients they had available and photographs of those not within immediate reach. The director, Louis Mercanton, a Frenchman, stopped looking when he saw a picture of Ivor Novello. Here was the type indeed. Here was everything he could ask for. Here was something beyond mere good looks—here was romantic handsomeness which was about all the silent screen needed. Here also was a young man who looked as if he might be Sicilian—or what the great public would regard as Sicilian. He brushed aside the qualifying statement that Ivor Novello had never acted. Mercanton reckoned he could teach him that if he had any brain at all.

Ivor landed and went over to Paris to see Mercanton. The film was a screen version of Robert Hichens's famous novel *The Call of the Blood.* He and Mercanton met and talked. It did not take the French director long to make up his mind that he had made a discovery. Ivor was signed up to co-star with Phyllis Neilson-Terry, the lovely daughter of that lovely and gracious lady Julia Neilson, an actress born of a great actress with a great actor, Fred Terry, as father. There began another of Ivor's friendships. He had great affection for Phyllis and great love and reverence for her famous mother. He treated Julia Neilson like a queen and, indeed, it is fitting that she should be so treated. I am proud that I have the privilege of being a friend of hers and that she calls me " Popie." Julia Neilson is a constant reminder of the grandeur of our stage as it was in her youth. Past eighty, she is still beautiful, gracious and graceful. Recently she sat in front at a lecture of mine and I said " What use is it for me, in poor words of my own, to try and tell you of the grandeur of our Theatre in my own youth? You can see for yourselves—for it is with us in person. There, showing you more eloquently than I could ever command is the Theatre as we knew it then—in the person of that wonderful woman and actress, Julia Neilson." There was a tremendous and sincere applause. My words were true. And Ivor felt just the same about her. Bless her, she is one of the truly Great Ones to whom he always paid tribute as, in my own humble way, I do as well.

Ivor made that film in Sicily and visited Rome and Venice too. The film was a big success and so was he. He became a film personality at once. But he was really working now, he was alive and busy. Ambition was awake. He wrote some music for *Who's Hooper?* at the Adelphi. *Who's Hooper?*, with W. H. Berry in the cast, was a big success. A fine, robust comedian, Berry was a man of foresight, for after hearing the music, he said " H'm, we'll hear more of this young man, Ivor Novello." We did, indeed. The book was by Fred Thomson, founded on Pinero's farce *In Chancery*. The play was produced by J. A. E. Malone, who had been for so long George Edwardes's right-hand man, and presented by Musical Plays Limited, Sir Alfred Butt and William Boosey. The lyrics were by Clifford Grey and the music by Howard Talbot and Ivor Novello. So the young man now stood beside the greatly popular and long-established composers. It was produced on September 13th, 1919, and ran for 349 performances. That was a very nice run then. And during that run Ivor had his first Royal Presentation—to King George V, who complimented him both on his music in the play and on " Keep the Home Fires Burning. " King George admired Ivor's work and came to his shows.

These were busy days for Ivor. He was wanted for films and he was wanted by the Theatre as composer. In films, he played in *Miarka* and *Carnival*. In the Theatre he composed the entire score for *The Golden Moth*, also at the Adelphi. That was in 1921. It was his first entire score. It ran for 281 performances. The cast was such as was usually gathered at the Adelphi in those days, first-class.

The presenter was an extraordinary gentleman from Bradford, who had made a fortune out of the war. His name was William Gaunt. He was reputed to be a wonderful man of business, but that is open to question. He had made tons of money because he dealt in stuff which was a necessity. He put much of that money into mills where weaving was carried on and when the slump came, he slumped with it. He put lots of money, too, into his theatrical enterprises. He descended on London, took over the leases of theatres in a wholesale manner and proceeded to show the poor " theatricals " what was what. Or so he thought. He, like other deluded folk, was under the impression that the Theatre is a business and can be run as such. The answer is that it is not and it cannot be. He, like James White, the ex-bricklayer from Lancashire, found to his cost that the theatrical profession is a gamble in gambles, not even a plain straightforward gamble on its own. White came from Lancashire, Gaunt from Yorkshire. White committed suicide, Gaunt lost his money, went back to Yorkshire and had the guts to start all over again and good luck to him. He was a large, kindly, nice man, a bit of real Yorkshire, and with all the true obstinate tenacity of the " Tyke." He professed a complete and deep-seated contempt for all Cockneys. Yet the real Cockney was the man who really ran him and did the work—the part of the work which succeeded at any rate—a man called Horace Fry, a Devon man who had become a complete Londoner.

Fry was the typical sergeant-major, who had sold programmes, done all the jobs on the managerial side of the Theatre and then began to run theatre bars and run them very well. He also ran William Gaunt, although William Gaunt never knew it. And Fry, being of the Theatre, was untouched when the Gaunt retirement took place. He carried on for years, right up to his death. Gaunt would sit in state and give advice. He would try and prevent would-be producers from taking his theatres and thereby run up the price. He would walk half a mile to get to a cheaper bus stage when going to the City and then waste thousands of pounds over something which a child could have told him would fail, provided that child was a theatrical infant. When guided, he gave excellent shows, though through no action of his own. To look at he did not seem worth a penny. He was never able, it appeared, to purchase hats which would fit him; they were always much too small and perched on his head like large pimples—they were very hard-looking bowlers. But he had a big heart and everyone liked him. However, he was the man—or by his means—at any rate, whereby Ivor got his first complete musical comedy score.

W. H. Berry was the chief comedian in *The Golden Moth*. He retired eventually to his charming house, Poplar Cottage, perched on the cliffs at Beltinge, near Herne Bay in Kent, with wide views across the North Sea. He grew his fuchsias, which he loved, he tended his garden, he gloated over his collection of Toby jugs and pictures from Dickens, and he played with his toy Theatre. The dust of the real theatre he shook right off his shoes. He had made his money and got out. Yet he hated to think he was forgotten. He never did the slightest thing to keep himself before the public, in these days of very short memories, and could never understand why he was not " news." I used to go and see him. He would run up a flag on his flagstaff to mark the event. He would greet me almost with tears in his eyes and crack lots of gags—rather old-fashioned gags it must be admitted, but he knew how to crack them better than most comics to-day. He adored my books and wrote me a constant stream of letters, always saying "Don't reply to this." But if I did not answer by return, I would get another saying that he knew how busy I was but he feared his note must have miscarried. It was safest to answer at once. As a rule I answer letters the day I receive them—that and my extreme punctuality are the two most untheatrical things about me.

Bill Berry, who adored to sign his letters " Bilberry," a typical Berry joke (and usually he put " Ahem " in brackets after his jokes in his letters) had the very highest admiration for Ivor and also claimed he was one of the first to take notice of him—he ignored the little matter of " Keep the Home Fires " and such like affairs. He wrote a book about himself and most of the copies got burnt in the blitz, to his abiding sorrow. He wrote another which I did my best to get published but it was too late in the day. For that, Ivor had written a foreword which he greatly prized. He died shortly after Ivor, at the age of eighty-one, and his age was the only thing which had changed about him. His ideas were still the same, his comedy of the same vintage. He was impervious to change and for years he had not left his little retreat. He became the complete creature of habit. He had his " shut eye," as he called it, at the same time each day and would not vary it for anything. I did a broadcast and paid him a great tribute. I wrote to him about it, suggesting that he listened, but he could not hear it. It was on the air during his doze! That was typical of dear old Bill, a magnificent comedian of the old school, God bless it, who was never in the least bit blue and who was always funny. He had " props," it is true, but he was funny with them; many comics have props and are not funny at all. He could dance with wonderful agility and neatness; he worked with every particle of his body, especially his face, and nobody could sing a topical song as he could. Dear old Bill, we were all very fond of him and I am particularly proud of the fact that my book *Carriages at Eleven* was his great favourite. He read it over and over again, rationing himself to so many pages a day so that he should not finish it too quickly. It is the greatest tribute I ever had.

With W. H. Berry in *The Golden Moth* were Robert Michaelis, as fine a juvenile lead as the musical comedy stage ever had, Thorpe Bates the actor-vocalist (and if Tommy Bates was a better vocalist than actor, he was still a better actor than most vocalists), Bobbie Comber, Nancie Lovat, Cicely Debenham, Sylvia Leslie and other clever people. The book was by Fred Thomson and P. G. Wodehouse and the music by Ivor Novello. Ivor gave Thorpe Bates a magnificent number called " Dear Eyes that Shine " and Bates sang it as it deserved to be sung. And for W. H. Berry he supplied a song called " Dartmoor Days," which seemed like a simple ballad but was very funny indeed and which Bill Berry made a little masterpiece of comedy.

In the same year Ivor had written much of the music for a revue called *A to Z*, with Helen Trix, of the Trix Sisters, as his collaborator. The same talented young lady wrote part of the book with Ronald Jeans and Dion Titheradge, and also played in the show with her sister. It was produced at the Prince of Wales's Theatre on October 21st, 1921, and it ran until October 7th, 1922—433 performances. It was a Charlot show packed full of clever young people; it would have been an all-star cast to-day. There were the Trix Sisters, Jack Buchanan, Gertrude Lawrence, George Hestor, Herbert Mundin, Herbert Ross, Elizabeth Pollock, Marcel de Haes and many others. Some of them became Ivor's close friends. And Jack Buchanan, risen to the very front rank of stardom, took over Ivor's last part when Ivor died. . . .

A to Z brought much kudos and coinage to Ivor, too. He was now a film star and a star composer. But there remained another world to conquer. Despite statements that he did not wish to be an actor, there is absolutely every proof that he did desire just that. How could he avoid it? Here were the films clamoring for him. But they could not give him what he wanted. Ivor was always audience-minded. He was of the audience himself and, without them, it was not a show at all.

True, they went to see his films but that did not put him into contact with them. Ivor was a most completely human person. He liked humanity around him, hating to be alone. It was not enough for him to see his shadow on the film and he was sure he could do better when in touch with humanity. He always wanted an audience—he adored them. He never really felt scared of them for he was too much of them himself. He might fear their verdict but they never presented themselves to him, as they do to so many players, as a mass of hostile personalities who have to be conquered and won over. Ivor felt them as friends to begin with—which was no small measure of his success. His success on the films only made the desire to act in the Theatre the stronger. And the Theatre was to him the complete epitome of life; it could give him all he wanted.

So naturally, and by all the laws of his Destiny, he went on the stage. He took the plunge in 1921. Many of his friends warned him not to do so. They besought him to be satisfied with his success, which would be continuous in the other media and not to risk failure and, perhaps, ridicule, as an actor. There was every chance of failure, they told him. The things which made him so good on the screen—the silent screen—would not have the same effect on the real stage. He was totally without acting experience, they emphasized. And without that, how could he hope to succeed? That was true enough. He realized it fully. But without experience, how could he ever become an actor? To that there was no answer, except that he had better leave it alone and be content. He was not prepared to do that. David Ivor Davies, that trenchant, tenacious young man, spoke to Ivor Novello and told him to take the risk and go ahead. He had had no experience of film acting, yet he had succeeded. This would be more difficult, but, nothing venture, nothing win . . . a start must be made. Why delay? Take the step now. Drop it if you are no good. You will soon know—you have enough sense for that. Follow your instinct. Thus David Ivor Davies to Ivor Novello, who listened, cogitated and agreed. The die was cast. He would be an actor—at least, he would try. It was that splendid actress Madge Titheradge who finally persuaded him and even made the opening for him.

A firm called Regency Productions was to stage a play at the Ambassadors' Theatre. The directors were H. M. Harwood (British) and J. L. Campbell (American). Their offices were at

Regency House, Warwick Street, W.1, but their registered office was the Ambassadors' Theatre. They were to stage a play called *Deburau*, written by Sacha Guitry, the English version of which was by that great man of the Theatre, Harley Granville-Barker. They secured a brilliant cast and it is worthy of being given in full; as it was Ivor's first appearance as an actor.

It is as well to see in what company he made it:

Deburau

Jean Gaspard Deburau	Robert Loraine
Marie Duplessis	Madge Titheradge
Monsieur Bertrand	Michael Sherbrooke
Robillard	John Howell
Laurent	Leslie Banks
Laplace	J. Henry Twyford
Justine	Gladys Gaynor
Mme. Rebard	Colette O'Neil
Clara	Jeanne Casalis
Clermont	Edward Mervyn
Amedee	Bruce Winston
The Money-taker	Cherry Carver
The Prompter	Harley Merica
Mme. Rabouin	Beverly Sitgreaves
Charles Deburau	Bobbie Andrews
A Young Man	Ivor Novello
A Doctor	Thomas Weguelin
A Lady	Cathryn D'Elaine
A Journalist	Stafford Hilliard
Marie Duplessis' Maid	Cherry Carver

The date of Ivor Novello's début as actor was November 3rd, 1921. The date of the play's withdrawal was November 26th, 1921. The run was twenty-eight performances. Neither the play nor the début set the Thames on fire. Despite the fine cast —many of the small-part players rose to be stars—despite the art of that tremendous actor-airman and fearless fighter, Robert Loraine and the tremendous ability of Madge Titheradge, *Deburau* was a failure. It will be observed that Bobbie Andrews was in the company, so he, the bosom friend, was able to help and encourage on that difficult occasion. He had the better part of the two. That entrusted to Ivor was small but not too bad for a mere beginner. It did not present much in the way of opportunity. But it was a beginning. He received the salary of fifteen pounds a week. The part he was to play was not even named in the contract. He was just engaged to " rehearse and play in the Comedy entitled *Deburau* at a West End London Theatre on such occasions and for such period as the Managers may elect to continue the performance of the said play in the West End of London." He was required to attend punctually " all practices or rehearsals which the Managers shall require him to attend and to have a competent and sufficient knowledge of the part assigned to him as aforesaid prior to the commencement of the run of the piece." He was to receive a salary of fifteen pounds per week of eight performances with an additional five pounds when the box-office receipts exceeded £1,000 per week (it sounds as though David Ivor Davies got that clause in, but there was little hope of it), any performances in addition to eight or less than eight being calculated as an eighth extra or less, as the case may be. All the other conditions were those in usual custom before the days of the Equity contract and any disputes arising were to go to arbitration. No disputes arose. No excitement was caused. Ivor gave a competent performance without making any mark; the play failed and that was that. But now—Ivor Novello was an actor. . . .

His determination to be one was marked by this engagement. Here he was, a well-known personality of the Theatre and films, content to play a small part for a small salary. He did it to try himself out, to get experience, to " have a reference " as it were. There are not many people in the position which Ivor then held who would have done as he did. Their heads would have been much more swelled; they would have wanted much more in the way of part and salary. And they would have been as wrong as he was right.

In those days, of course, the films were not so popular as now and had not the same vast following. Actors and actresses played for the films in their spare time and for extra money. Nowadays they specialize in films for the big money and come to the Theatre in their spare time and almost as if they were doing a bit of slumming. The dear old Theatre, one cannot desert it—let's go and do some plays—there is nothing doing in the studios! Then we hear about art and the love of the Drama. But they only stay until the big film chance calls again. In 1921 it was different. The Theatre was the Aristocrat of the Entertainment World, the screen the very young cadet of the house. There was little interlocking between the two. Yet the big stars of the silent screen were rarely real stage folk, although some of them had made their mark, and they were the people who lasted on the screen when the talkies upset all the calculations. A film star's following was negligible compared with to-day.

Ivor never really liked film-acting. He adored watching pictures; he understood their art and technique but, to him, they were as nothing compared to the Live Theatre. That was his place and he knew it even if his friends and advisers did not. Ivor was always far too human for the cinema. Those names appearing with him are noteworthy. Some, of course, like Loraine and Madge Titheradge were stars then, but several were to become stars and most popular players. There is Leslie Banks, now one of our foremost actors, who had learned his business the hard way, in George Dance's companies, amongst others. I remember him doing all sorts of jobs and playing all sorts of parts in the tours of Drury Lane shows. There was Thomas Weguelin, Stafford Hilliard, Bruce Winston, John Howell, all destined to do very well. And there was Jeanne Casalis—then without the de—now a star of stage and radio, the popular " Mrs. Feather." . . .

Ivor was quite contented. He had looked handsome (he could not help that), he had worn his clothes well, and he had spoken his lines clearly, audibly and with due sense of their meaning. So although there was no stir in the Theatrical World, he considered he was a success, for he had not failed. And he was determined to go on acting. That he would also go on composing went without saying.

Having been in a show, the rest was much easier. He had played in the West End and his age was twenty-eight. That was rather late to make a theatrical début. He should have been at it ten years earlier. But then four and a bit of those years had been filled by the war—and his music. But there he was, handicapped by lack of experience when compared with his other friends and competitors—compared with him Noël Coward was a veteran actor—but still with the tremendous asset of that magnificent profile, that immeasurable charm and that sturdy determination. His mother had surmounted every obstacle; so would he. It was her greatest gift to him.

He went on. The salary did not worry him. He was getting £100 and even £200 a week on the pictures; he had received £15 a week on the stage. But then, the stage was real and the films were not. And Ivor wanted to be in the Theatre.

In 1922 he got another stage job. *The Yellow Jacket* was revived at the Kingsway. This delightful Chinese fantasy had first been produced at the Duke of York's Theatre on March 27th, 1913, when it had run for 154 performances. It was written by George C. Hazelton and Benrimo. It was revived at the Kingsway on March 7th, 1922. Messrs. Benrimo, Blackden and Morley presented it and Benrimo himself produced, as he had done originally.

Benrimo was an amazing personality, a handsome distinguished-looking man with greying hair and an aquiline cast of countenance. He claimed that his ancestors had been Moorish princes—hence his name. It may well have been so. When he walked down a street in the West End, in perfectly-cut morning coat and trousers, light waistcoat, shining tall hat and patent boots, with a black satin stock as neckwear, everyone turned round to look twice at the spectacle. He took the pavement as if it were the stage, looking neither to the right nor the left but ahead into the future. He was well aware of the sensation he caused. He was also a wonderful producer. There were no airs and graces then, but he adopted methods of his own. Dressed in old clothes, flannel trousers, a Norfolk jacket and soft collars, he would lie at full length in front of the footlights, his head supported on one hand, and so direct the rehearsals. It seems as lazy as possible, but his eye missed nothing and he could impart his knowledge without fuss or ado. And when it came to a question of scenery, costumes and décor, he was all seeing and all knowing. His *Yellow Jacket*, performed in what he said was " the Chinese Manner "—and one was willing to take his word for it, so perfect did it seem—was a thing of beauty and charm. One of his productions, *The Willow Tree*, had one of the loveliest stage settings with which it has been my luck to be connected. It was a Japanese garden complete down to the last blossom, the final floweret. There were little bridges going over streams which were of glass but which appeared to flow so skilful was he with his lighting. And all over the garden were flowers. It gave me infinite delight to examine and name them, for I love gardens, gardening and birds as well. They looked exactly like their real counterparts, not like stage flowers at all. I was busy at this as soon as the scene was set. Benrimo came on stage and watched me. I called out the names of the blossoms as I came to them. Benrimo's eyes widened. " Here, Jones," he called to the stage manager, " come and look at this guy Popie; he knows the names of all the goddam flowers." And he viewed me with some awe. He knew what flowers ought to be there but not their names. . . .

This firm gave Ivor a contract, dated March 6th, 1922, which was brief and to the point. This is what it said: " It is understood between Mr. Ivor Novello and Messrs. Benrimo, Blackden and Morley that he is engaged for the run of *The Yellow Jacket* at a salary of Thirty-Five Pounds (£35) per week and that Messrs. Benrimo, Blackden and Morley have an option upon his next appearance in a stage play at the same salary." The Morley was Malcolm Morley, well known in the Theatre world, and he signed the agreement. What a different contract would be needed to-day! But there were no troubles or disputes. Ivor enjoyed that part, though once again no part was stipulated in the contract. He played the juvenile lead, " Wu Hoo Git." And he played it well, although he did not think so. It was during rehearsals of that play when I looked in at the Kingsway to see Benrimo, for we were considerable friends, that I first met Ivor. Benrimo introduced us. We did not say much, but he smiled and when I said I had loved the play at the Duke of York's, Ivor said that he hoped I would see it this time—and have mercy on him as he could never be as good as the one I had seen—and then he had to resume rehearsal. I thought he was just as good, when I saw the play at last. Ivor loved that play and that part. He was very happy all the time. He loved the Chinese costume and he looked the handsomest young Western Celestial one could see between here and China. He was acting again in something he liked. He was getting £20 a week more—and that was advancement—and the revival got a good press and it ran for seventy performances. This was much more satisfactory all round than *Deburau*.

CHAPTER NINE

PILGRIM'S PROGRESS

IVOR was now well embarked upon his stage progress, a pilgrim determined to reach his promised land. He was already determined to be an actor-manager, to write his own plays and act in them, and somewhere in his mind was the possibility—or probability—of an opera, with himself conducting at Covent Garden. And, although he never spoke of it then and very seldom afterwards, he wanted to be a great classical actor. Many of those ambitions he achieved, others might have been his had he lived a little longer, but one or two were beyond him.

He was a Chinese lad on the stage in *The Yellow Jacket* and he became a Spanish lad for his next venture, in a play called *Spanish Lovers*. The firm of Benrimo, Blackden and Morley exercised that option of theirs on Ivor's services at £35 a week, and he played the part of Javier. He had to look handsome, which presented no difficulties at all. He had also a good deal of acting to do, for this was not such an easy part as the two previous ones, and he managed very well indeed. In fact, he got a far better press than the play. It was in three acts by J. Feliu y Codina, adapted from the French of Carlos de Battle and Antonin Levergne by Christopher St. John. The music was by H. M. Jacquet, founded on the popular airs of the Province of Murcia. It all sounds a bit complicated. In the cast, besides Ivor, were Jevon Brandon-Thomas, Hugh Williams, John Tresahar, Seton Blackden, Malcolm Morley and Doris Lloyd—a very excellent actress indeed. Ivor really did make a personal success. He made an impression on playgoers. Requests for autographs began. He was already used to them as composer and film actor, but these were a tribute from playgoers. Also, there were people waiting at the stage door!

Those little knots of people at the stage door of the Kingsway in Parker Street did not have many evenings in which to wait, for the play ran only for twenty-eight performances, from June 21st to July 15th. But it was a very encouraging stage of the pilgrimage. It was a beginning of something which grew and grew and remained all his life. He had played three parts only: " The Young Man," who was afterwards called " Armand Duval " in *Deburau*, " Wu Hoo Git " in *The Yellow Jacket* and now " Javier " in *Spanish Lovers*. None of the plays had been successes and one of the productions was at the tiny Ambassadors' Theatre, the other two at the Kingsway, not one of the more popular playhouses, albeit a very charming one. Yet, with three parts (two new plays and one revival) and none of them to big audiences, this amazing young man had won a following already. It was not his acting; it was that penetrating charm and that classical beauty of feature. It was, indeed, Ivor Novello, then—as always. His popularity as a composer did not add much. Composers do not bulk very largely amongst what are now called " fans," unless they are American, and, even then, they cannot compete with the average actor or actress and not at all with a film star. Even Richard Rodgers, Irving Berlin or Cole Porter do not find their fans embarrassing. But with Ivor it had started already. It went on; it grew and grew. Long before he reached the height of his fame at Drury Lane he had the biggest stage-door following of any British actor—and of any American, either. And his following was of the Theatre, not gathered of the screen.

Only Lewis Waller aroused such wild and fervent admiration. All the great ones had their fans, but only Waller was in the class of Novello. And even he, for whom the first " fan club " was formed, never got such wild demonstrations as did Ivor—for the times were different and the fans much less demonstrative and hysterical before World War I than they were between the wars or during and after the Second World War. The public was quieter, better behaved. Sir John Martin Harvey, Sir Seymour Hicks, Matheson Lang of the older school, had excited followings, so had George Grossmith Junior. Owen Nares, in his heyday of matinée idolatry, was often hard put to it to dodge the eager young ladies who thronged the stage door. He would slip out at the scene dock, at side entrances or the front of the house. He never cared for fan adoration at all. Sir Gerald du Maurier had a host of fans and was very standoffish with them, which only increased their adulation. The utmost they got was a quick glare and a rather crooked smile as he hurried by, the whole thing rather sidelong. As for the big giants of the actor-managerial régime, they were worshipped from afar with respect and something of awe.

But with Ivor it was quite different. He adored the adoration. Indeed when asked if it did not worry him, he smiled broadly and said " What would worry me is if they were not there." Now and again when things got a bit too boisterous, he would try and do a little dodging, but by and large he enjoyed it vastly. He was for years the only actor so mobbed and certainly so greatly mobbed. It was open, flagrant, worship. It was not done by single spies but by battalions. It occurred in London and in the provinces alike, and perhaps to a greater degree in the provinces, because there was nothing stiff, starchy or " Well off, like " about Ivor or his personality.

At one provincial city, his fervent admirers nearly crushed him to death as he got into his car, and then, in their delight at his presence, proceeded to pull the door right off the car. On one occasion at Leeds he was almost torn to pieces and the belt of his overcoat remained in the hands of several young ladies as a treasured prize. They probably fought for its possession in the end. At Drury Lane, on first nights, the crowds of fans were so great that Russell Street was impassable. He would go out through Vinegar Yard at the finish or he would never have got home. It was the same everywhere. Many of the most regular he knew by name and would speak with them. He knew all about them and seemed to take the deepest interest, to their almost swooning delight. It was the same always. A few got an interview with him and never forgot it, enshrining it as a lifelong treasured memory. He gave autographs freely and joked as he did so. There was one thing about all these fans: they did not only hang about the stage door. They paid to go into the Theatre and see him and his plays. That does not always happen.

At times, something about a face or a personality would catch his attention and he would stop and speak to that favoured one; it was always one who was not pushing, shouting, calling out " Ivor "—they all called him Ivor—and trying to attract his attention. And the girl so selected would be the object of deep envy from all the rest, not to say hatred. However short the distance from the stage door to his car, it was a struggle. It could not be called a Royal Progress, as once it was described. They do not mob royalty so—there is an aloofness about that high eminence. There was nothing aloof about Ivor: it was his complete friendliness, unforced and genuine, which caused these crowds, as much as his art. It was as much his personality as his shows, which made him, for years, the No. 1 Box Office Attraction of the British Theatre, lengths ahead of his nearest competitor.

To Ivor it was part of his job, which meant part of his life, and he basked in it. His fans were of all kinds, and of all classes, but the majority were Middle Class. They loved to give him things and he delighted to receive them. It was not the value: it was the spirit, the offering. On him who had so much, gifts were showered. On his birthday and at Christmas there was a veritable deluge, a Niagara Falls of presents. On landmarks in his shows, like the 100th, 250th, or 300th performance, or on anniversaries of a year's run, the floodgates opened again. Everyone vied to give something unique. On first nights, it was perfectly incredible: fruit of all kinds, from luscious hot-house grapes, to humble oranges, from packets of tea to chocolates, from books to pictures, jewellery, samples of expert needlework and embroidery, huge baskets of exotic flowers and small humble bunches purchased in the street. You could not move in the dressing-room or in the passage outside. He saw and examined them all. He thanked everybody. Let him go away for a holiday, and the same thing happened. And on his return, it was repeated. When he came back from an operation, there were not only flowers but food and delicacies: sugar, honey, eggs, packets of chocolate and sometimes, *pâté de foie gras*, caviare and the like. On such occasions he could have set up a store. It gave him the keenest delight and he was always grateful. It was as if a very gracious and beloved Prince was receiving tribute from his loyal and devoted subjects; indeed it was so.

For Ivor had a way of awaking lasting loyalty in those who knew and admired him. He never strove for it; it came to him in perfectly genuine and sincere fashion. And it always lasted. Certain gifts he treasured more than others, some which caught his fancy and were apt; those he kept in his dressing-room. There was a sampler, worked in colour on a fawny-brown background, canvas colour, which had the names of all of his plays and the theatres in which they were performed, with the dates, embroidered on it. That always hung in the dressing-room. When he played *Henry V* I gave him one of those delightful tinselled Victorian prints of, I think, Creswick in the part. That got hung on the line, too—and so did my last gift, that programme of *Pygmalion and Galatea* all embellished by seed pearls in its mahogany frame. That he really liked. I have it back again now; it was a family heirloom anyway and has added value because he owned it for a while. I gave it to him on the first night of *King's Rhapsody*. It was on the wall before he went on the stage. . . . All sorts of things flowed in. I have seen soap and perfume, boxes of cigars and cigarettes. Ivor only smoked Turkish and many of us thought them horrible, but he could appreciate a good cigar. And there would often be a quantity of champagne.

Ivor never lacked for much, even in times of shortage. His most faithful entourage saw to that. Lloyd Williams and Olive Gilbert looked after him wonderfully. But I remember a sad scene when the childish streak which was in Ivor (he never really quite grew up, and was all the better for that) showed uppermost. It was in his dressing-room, after a matinée of *Perchance to Dream* at the London Hippodrome. I had gone to see him and he was having tea surrounded by the Court. The table, a low one so that he could recline beside it like a Roman Emperor, reminded one of that corny line in old books, it " groaned beneath the weight of good things." It was during the Second World War when there was a period of great shortage and when most of us got little of anything, especially those things we liked. There was bread and butter (not margarine, but butter), rolls of all kinds, piles of little cakes and complete cakes too, all sorts of scones, toast, sandwiches, fresh fruit, honey, jams and a very big dish indeed of strawberries. It made my mouth water. But there seemed something wrong; there was a distrait air over the whole gathering. There was almost silence instead of the usual chatter and laughter. Nobody seemed to be eating with any gusto and Ivor was just toying with some food. I came in with Lloydy and the greetings did not seem to have the usual warmth. I sat down and said nothing. But Lloydy, quick as usual, sensed something wrong. " Well, Ivor," he said, " everything all right? " Silence. Ivor gazed downwards like a child disappointed in a treat and the rest stared into space. Lloydy looked on with a sense of foreboding. " What's the matter? " he asked. One of the courtiers spoke up, in a hushed voice.

" No eggs," he said. It might have been an announcement of a royal assassination. Lloydy was thunderstruck. " No eggs? " he gasped. " No, no eggs—poor Ivor has not had an egg." One felt that tears were near. To say that Lloydy was shaken would be seriously to understate the case. He blanched, he even trembled. " No eggs," he gasped again. " But why? I sent them over—they must be here. . . ." But again came the voice of Doom: " No eggs." Lloydy, for once at a loss, fled to make inquiries. I felt that something must be done. I began to speak to Ivor about what I wanted to know. The spell was broken. The tea went on. I never heard what became of the eggs or who had taken them. Lloydy would not have failed. But it was as near tragedy as ever I saw in a dressing-room. Personally, neither I nor my family had seen an egg for many months. We had forgotten what they looked like. Nor did I have any of that tea. I was not asked. In all my long association with Ivor I had only one meal at his expense, of which more in its place. Sometimes Wright, his dresser-valet, would give me a cup of tea—and I was grateful.

But nobody grudged Ivor what he got. We would all have been only too ready to accept it had it come our way. I ought to add that there was, of course, no black-market business about it; it was simply the magic of his name. Stern, hard-hearted tradesmen and shop-keepers, who bullied their humble beseeching customers, dived below the counter when they heard that Mr. Novello was short of something. His power was amazing, his name opened all doors and unloosed all hoards. And he deserved it. It was, after all, a small return for the pleasure he gave to so many. . . .

Although Ivor seldom dodged his fans, except when the crush was too great or he wanted to get away quickly, he preferred not to be recognized when he was out on his own affairs. He was a very keen filmgoer and would always wear very large and dark glasses to avoid recognition in the cinemas when the lights went up, or when entering or leaving. I have seen him go down a busy street unrecognized when so disguised, until someone, keener-eyed than the rest, spotted that characteristic, loping walk and stared after him or pointed him out. But sometimes he got right away with it. Not often however; but, then, it was not very often he walked any considerable distance. If it was winter-time and he was thus engaged, he had his hat pulled down, his collar up and the black glasses did the rest. In summer it was less easy to escape recognition.

But the ordinary fans, those who paid him what he considered the compliment of coming to the Theatre to patronize his plays and waited to see him go in or out—those he did not attempt to avoid and with them he was very friendly.

He really loved it all and he liked flattery, provided it was not just sycophantic and fulsome praise. He liked to hear that he had given pleasure; he liked to hear people praise his work and his acting, to tell him he was the mainstay of the Theatre, that his music was adorable, that his acting was delightful, that he was ideal. Of course he liked it. Who would not? Who does not? Does anybody dislike being praised? I doubt it. Some deride it but they are not sincere. It is only human, and Ivor was intensely human. So he revelled in his fans and their adulation. Yet it was through this that his greatest distress, his one tragedy, came upon him. . . .

I think the very best and most significant of all the many stories which could be told of his fans and his manner with them, is the one which was almost the last of them, in importance anyway. It shows his attitude clearly and concisely. It shows, too, what manner of man he was.

It was the evening on which *King's Rhapsody* opened at the Palace Theatre. Ivor had been asleep, as was his custom every afternoon (like Hamlet's father). He woke—and found himself alone in the flat at No. 11 Aldwych. That was most unusual, but so it happened. He did not like being alone. He slipped on his things, he got into that shaky, sullen, dilatory little lift which never seemed quite safe and went down to the street. The Rolls was waiting, with Morgan his chauffeur, at the wheel. And by the front door as he came out, stood one of his faithful fans, a woman who night after night would watch him go to the theatre at that time and whom he knew by sight. As a rule she said nothing but just watched. On this occasion, as it was a first night, she said " Good luck, Mr. Ivor " with real sincerity in her voice. Ivor was touched—and he felt a bit lonely. A trial lay before him and he valued those words of cheer. He stopped and spoke to her. He asked her if she would like to jump into the car and drive to the Palace Theatre with him. Overcome with joy and surprise the young lady, gasping her thanks, needed no second invitation. He got in after her, with that gentle smile of his, and together they drove—the humble doorway fan and the King of the Theatre—to what was to be his greatest triumph.

That is quite typical of Ivor Novello. He always had the knack of doing the right thing at the right moment and finding exactly the right thing to say. It is a royal gift and he was Royalty of the Theatre.

To return, however, to Ivor's pilgrimage. In the earlier 'twenties he was very concerned with the films. Mr. Peter Noble, who wrote a biography during Ivor's lifetime, devotes a great deal of space to the screen part of the story. Mr. Noble is very much interested in films and knows far more about them than I do, who am purely of the Theatre. I do not propose to give Ivor's film career in very much detail, for I am concerned with the Man himself and his work in the Theatre, where his greatness lay.

For a time, of course, quite a considerable time, Ivor worked in both mediums, but it is by far the more important to put the spotlight on his work in the Theatre. All his life he liked watching films, but he was never very interested in making them. He used them as a means to get money to spend in the Theatre, as ammunition for his campaign therein, to further his ends and his ambitions. He told me that himself. And he certainly succeeded. He was busy in films in 1920 and for some years after that, even busier than he was in the Theatre, but it was just a means to an end. Once he was really established in the Theatre, he left the screen and never regretted it. Sometimes he wondered why Hollywood did not screen his big Drury Lane musicals. That was David Ivor Davies, with an eye to big money. The reason, of course, was that they were far too British for American taste and that the Romance he wove into them, most acceptable to British audiences, was to the American mind, what they called " hokum." *Glamorous Night* was filmed in England. Being a screen version of a play which had made history, it was altered almost beyond recognition. Ivor himself did not play in it, his part being portrayed by Barry Mackay. I am not a judge of films but I was not struck by it. Perhaps I was too close to the stage production. And, of course, much later came the film version of *The Dancing Years*, in all the wonder of technicolor. That will be dealt with in its place.

Ivor made *Miarka, The Daughter of the Bear* in 1920, under Mercanton's direction, and Rejane was in the cast. It was his second picture. That was made in France, and his third picture *Carnival* was made in England, a film version of the stage play in which, on the screen, Matheson Lang and Hilda Bayley played their original stage parts. To avoid confusion in the minds of filmgoers, this picture was made again later, as a talkie but this time without Ivor. The silent version was, I believe, a success, for Lang was a great name and, apparently, Ivor did pretty well too. Then he made a version of Balfe's famous old opera, *The Bohemian Girl.* Here he was amongst friends, for Constance Collier, Jean Webster Brough and Gladys Cooper were in the cast. Ivor had a great admiration always for Gladys Cooper, and his friendship with her was an enduring one. He had met her first at a big ball at Covent Garden and it was Constance Collier who had introduced them. Ivor, at that ball, probably enjoyed himself far more than he had done at the very first fancy dress ball which he ever attended. That was at the Albert Hall. He went as Orlando. He did not know a soul, he did not dance with anyone and never spoke to anyone during the whole evening. In those days, he was nobody and knew nobody. All that was changed. . . .

C. Aubrey Smith, that ultra-Englishman of stage and screen, that fine, handsome, tall actor who was also an England cricketer and who always gave the impression of wearing flannels and a blazer however he was dressed, was also in the cast of *The Bohemian Girl.* He remained perfectly English in Hollywood and was knighted. Ellen Terry herself also made an appearance in this film. She was, in fact, playing in another film at the same time, both of them at Elstree. To Ivor the mere fact of being near Ellen Terry was—as he would have put it—" Heaven." He watched her with wonder and adoration. And with reverence, too. Constance Collier remembers standing with Gladys Cooper and Ivor watching Ellen Terry play a little scene, one of great tenderness and tears. So wonderful was the grand old lady, such majesty of art did she display, such complete sincerity, that the three young watchers found the tears streaming down their faces as they stood spell-bound and speechless. The "shot" was over and Ellen Terry, all smiles (and a second before she had been all tears) came towards them. She spoke of them. " Can you tell me, my dears?" she asked " Which picture I am playing in now? " . . . That was the real Ellen Terry.

It was during the making of this picture that the friendship between Constance Collier and Ivor ripened very greatly. She was in grief at the time because of her husband's recent death, and Ivor's never failing care and kindness to her was something she never forgot. His understanding of women was one of his greatest gifts. It was uncanny.

The Bohemian Girl, probably the most enduring of British operas, was composed by Balfe. The libretto was written by Alfred Bunn, who was manager and patentee of the Theatre Royal, Drury Lane. Balfe had played in the orchestra there as a young man before he became famous. He and Bunn collaborated in *The Bohemian Girl* when it was first produced at the Theatre Royal, Drury Lane, in 1843. It was, after a rather sticky start, a vast success and it gave the egregious Bunn that " blaze of glory " he had always hankered after. It also gave Balfe immortality, for whilst his other operas are almost forgotten *The Bohemian Girl* lives on. It was of the Theatre Royal, Drury Lane, so it endured. Ninety-three years after the production of *The Bohemian Girl*, Ivor Novello stood on the stage of Drury Lane and was acclaimed as composer, as Balfe had been on those same boards. With *Glamorous Night* he had done what Balfe had done: given the Lane a success when it was badly needed. His achievement was even greater than Balfe's for he had needed no Bunn; he had written the libretto as well as the music and he had played the leading part in the show. He had done it all except the lyrics, which were the work of Christopher Hassall. But there he stood, where Balfe had stood and soared to triumph. Balfe had spent the evening conducting in the orchestra pit when *The Bohemian Girl* was produced. Ivor sat there later—for one scene—during *The Dancing Years*.

I took Alan (Jock) Dent, the kindly and erudite critic of the *News Chronicle* and a good friend of mine because he loves the Theatre, round Drury Lane once and, gazing at Balfe's statue which stands in the Rotunda, he said " Ah, Balfe—the Novello of his day." And Jock Dent spoke truer than he knew. The two were similar in many ways. Both were steeped in music from their birth. Neither of them were English: Balfe was Irish and Novello Welsh. Both had charm and both had lazy streaks interspersed with tremendous energy which made them, when they chose, men who worked like lightning. Balfe upheld the prestige of English Opera almost alone at a time when it sagged; Novello, single-handed, held the breach against the invasion of

our camera studies which mark the evolution of Ivor. The top right picture was ken at the time he wrote "Keep the Home Fires Burning." The picture below was one of the last he had taken.

Anthony Eden, Ivor and Bea Lillie chat together in the Garden Lounge of the "Queen Elizabeth"

The picnic party here includes Lily Elsie and Viola Tree

The portrait on the left was inscribed "to Ivor Novello: most sincerely, D. W. Griffith." It was sent at the time Ivor made his first picture for Griffith

American musicals. In essence, their music is similar: it is melody and romantic melody. Let nobody scoff at Balfe for his music was of its time and very good of its time. So was Novello's. Balfe will be remembered by *The Bohemian Girl*, while Ivor's *Glamorous Night* was of the same genre, far more operetta than musical comedy. In the Rotunda at Drury Lane, as I have said, stands a marble statue to Balfe. It was erected by Balfe's friends during his lifetime, at a cost of nearly £500. And by the time these words are in print, there will stand at Drury Lane a bust of Ivor Novello, the work of his friend Clemence Dane, to keep his memory always before the audiences and to stand as a permanent record of his services to that great theatre. Space forbids a closer study of Balfe and Novello but the resemblance was close. Of the two, Novello was considerably the greater.

Drury Lane has had, in its almost three centuries of existence, four outstanding musical figures amongst the hundreds of great players and dramatists. They are Dr. Arne, who was its musical director, that astounding man Charles Dibdin, who wrote over one thousand songs and did so much for the morale of this country during its desperate struggle with France, Balfe and Ivor Novello. They all worked at The Lane and created music there. It is a quartette of which any country might be proud and it is a bright jewel in Drury Lane's story.

But again back to the pictures. Ivor had made quite a mark on the screen. In 1922 he was in touch with D. W. Griffith, one of the greatest men the motion picture industry ever knew. It was Hannen Swaffer, then at the height of his critical fame, at once the best loved and best hated man in London, who brought them together. For you either adore Swaffer or detest him. It depends on whether you really know him or not. If you know him, then you understand and adore. But at that time he wielded a lash which hurt the actors, though it did them good too, for it kept them on their toes. Ivor had no cause to like him, but Swaffer liked Ivor and he put him in touch with Griffith. They met and Griffith told him that if an opportunity occurred he would send for him. He told Ivor he would have to work hard and Ivor said he did not mind that—and meant it, too. For Griffith was a giant. He did everything in an immense way. His silent films were not only breathtaking dramas, they were overpowering spectacles. *The Birth of a Nation*, *Orphans of the Storm*, *Intolerance*, *Way Down East* were all landmarks of film history. It was a tremendous chance for a young man. But as nothing materialized for a time, Ivor did a picture called *The Man Without Desire*. While he was making it, however, came the summons from Griffith. He was to go to Hollywood and play with Mae Marsh and Carol Dempster in a picture to be called *The White Rose*. It was to be made in 1923.

He completed *The Man Without Desire*, in which, incidentally, Lloyd Williams had a small part, and went to America. He met the usual blaze of publicity, but it was his good looks that won him the space. They hardly regarded him as an actor then—and maybe they were right. But he coped with the tough American newshounds and his charm beat them completely. As it was natural to him, it was a weapon no one could parry. Of course he was compared to Valentino and Ramon Novarro and the rest of them, but that did not worry Ivor. He was " news " all the time, for Griffith understood all about that, and, by a stroke of luck, two of his pictures were successes in New York, one of them being *The Bohemian Girl*. He then made *The White Rose* and he learnt a lot. The picture was a success and there was now a serious danger that the films would swallow Ivor. He also had a contract to work for Griffith again. And he was writing now, as well. To make money, he had done a film scenario which he called *The Rat*, though it did not materialize at that time. Meanwhile the contract with Griffith remained unfulfilled as Griffith laid off pictures for a while.

But the stage had got Ivor, not the films. He had made quite a lot of money and David Ivor Davies saw to it that some was saved. But before leaving the question of the engagement with Griffith, it is as well to record a cable which Ivor received from that great director when *The White Rose* was shown at the Scala, London. Here it is verbatim; the date is November 25th, 1923.

LCO IVOR NOVELLO SCALA THEATRE LONDON

" My best wishes to all and little picture comma the White Rose is notable perhaps in a small way in that the best talent of America and the best talent of England unite in a common cause period I only wish this small example might help point the way the best talent in England and the best talent in America can in a big way unite in great things statesmanship comma finance and philanthropy in accomplishment that tend for the best for everybody in the whole world D. W. Griffith."

Was Mr. Griffith expecting that cable to be publicized? One wonders. Anyway he gets it now.

Ivor came home from Hollywood on the crest of the wave of success. So far life had been full of roses and without a single setback. Starting without experience, his film career had been prosperous. His stage career, though without any outstandingly successful play, was very promising and he had received good notices for each of the three parts he had played (good enough mentions for the first two and extremely good ones for *Spanish Lovers*). He seemed to be what is known in the world of the Theatre as a "natural." Garrick was one, so was Kean, and so was Ivor.

He got another stage job in 1923, this time with his greatly adored Gladys Cooper, who was at the Playhouse, London, with Frank Curzon, a very astute and discerning manager-sportsman who eventually won the Derby. They were to do a play called *Enter Kiki* and Ivor was engaged for the leading role. It was not his cup of tea, but he took it. It was a character part at a time when his good looks were his greatest asset and his lack of experience his greatest liability. It takes experience to play "character": good looks and charm will get most people through a straight role such as he had played up to now, but not through a character part. Later, he became a very good character actor, but not in *Enter Kiki.* It was produced at the Playhouse in August 2nd, 1923—not a very auspicious date in those days. He got a remarkably good salary for such an inexperienced actor, but his films and his contract with Griffith were also standing him in good stead.

Here is the agreement. It is dated July 17th, 1923, from Curzon's offices at 37 Bury Street, St. James's, S.W.1:

"Dear Ivor,

Just a line to confirm your engagement to play the part of 'Victor Leroux' in the play entitled *Kiki* with Miss Gladys Cooper at the Playhouse, opening on or about August 2nd at a salary of Sixty Pounds (£60) per week of eight performances, subject to termination by a fortnight's notice from either side to the other, such notice however not to be given prior to the commencement of the run of the play.

If you will just send me a line in confirmation this is all the contract we need.

Yours ever,
(signed) T. B. Vaughan."

That was how the big ones did business in the Theatre before the days of Equity.

Ivor replied from 11 Aldwych, on July 23rd, 1923. The letter is actually dated, a rare thing with him:

" Dear Tom,

Thanks for your letter of the 17th inst, re my engagement at the Playhouse, which I now confirm.

With kindest regards,
Yours ever,
(Signed) Ivor Novello."

T. B. Vaughan, who signed the letter to Ivor was Frank Curzon's general manager, and he was a real power behind the throne. He was a north-countryman who never lost his accent, with a wonderfully level head, a keen sense of business and values, and a man who made fewer mistakes than any of his time in the Theatre. He was not a handsome man, fairly tall, dark, with a hard-bitten face and features and a complexion which looked as if it had been exposed to the weather. But although he never finessed and always spoke his mind, he was universally popular and his word was taken as gospel. It was kept as gospel, too. Nobody ever got the better of Tommy Vaughan and he never tried to " do anybody down," unless they were trying that process on him, when they invariably found the tables turned.

Although Vaughan calls the play *Kiki*, as doubtless it would be called in the Playhouse by those connected with it, the full title was *Enter Kiki* and it was adapted from the French of André Picard by Sydney Blow and C. Douglas Hoare (men of the Theatre who understood that job). It was in three acts. The locale was Paris. But the fact that the background was theatrical was against it. It was very well done—that was Curzon's way—and had a cast which included, besides Ivor Novello and Gladys Cooper, such people as Paul Arthur, Henry Wenman, Jack Raine, Drelincourt Odlum, Madeline Seymour, Daisy Elliston, and Eileen Earle. It ran for 155 performances. But Ivor got a very bad " press " indeed. He played Victor Leroux, a French theatrical manager. It did not suit him and he could not handle it. The critics were right. I saw him and he was bad. Although the play had quite a decent run, Ivor was very depressed. It was the first time he had fallen foul of the critics, or, rather, they of him. But not for long. He was back in the film world again playing *Bonnie Prince Charlie*, in, of course, the role of the Young Pretender, with Gladys Cooper as his Flora Macdonald. He got £350 a week. Master Ivor was not doing badly, with £60 on the stage and £350 on the screen.

It was his personal failure in *Enter Kiki* which first put the idea of being his own manager into his head. He wanted the Theatre even then far more than the films, despite his invariable success on the screen and the infinitely larger salary. And Constance Collier gave him excellent advice. She told him to find a play and go on tour with it. That way he would learn. For screen success was his. He had *The White Rose*, then showing in London, *Bonnie Prince Charlie* and *The Man Without Desire* all going at once. He kept receiving film offers, but he hankered after the Theatre, in which he had scored his only failure.

How was his music going? He had songs in *Our Nell* at the Gaiety, in which José Collins starred. One lyric, " The Land of Might Have Been " was Ivor's, with words by Eddie Marsh. Ivor had also written the score of a revue for André Charlot, called *Puppets*, which was done at the Vaudeville on January 2nd, 1924, running for 255 performances. It was a very good revue and Ivor did very good music. The book and the lyrics were by Dion Titheradge, and in the cast were Binnie Hale, Stanley Lupino, Arthur Chesney, Connie Emerald and Paul England. Ivor's notices for his music were as good as those for his acting in *Enter Kiki* were bad.

It was probably the touch of the whip he received in *Enter Kiki* which spurred him on. He was never one to bow to failure; not that he had had much opportunity of testing it; but he was tenacious, he was determined, and he was ambitious. He knew now where he was going—he was going right into the Theatre and right to the top. That was the goal of his pilgrimage, that was his Promised Land. He was now thirty-one years old, almost too old to be really starting an acting career. He knew already that experience on the screen was not very helpful in the real Theatre, but he was determined that it was in the latter that he would succeed.

Constance Collier, his friend and counsellor, had given him the right advice. She was—she is—Theatre through and through. She knew all about it. A great actress, a most understanding woman with a first-class brain, she had done it all, from chorus to Shakespearean tragedy and she had done it in company with the great ones. And as well as that, she knew Ivor through and through. She had appraised him skilfully. She knew that, gay, light-hearted and carefree as he always seemed, he could always take responsibility. She knew, indeed, that he was much better on his own than under any management or control, because he was a creator and not just a purveyor. That was why she advised him to get a play, manage it and play in it himself on tour. He would then have responsibility and that would be good for him and give him the pleasure of knowing it was his own.

She knew, too, how he adored the Theatre. Sometimes when they had gone to a show, or been backstage to see somebody they knew, he would say to her " Constance, let's just go and stand on the stage." And, together, they would do so. Ivor would stand still and gaze into the dark auditorium. Smiles would light his face, joy would be in his eyes and they would gaze ahead into the gloom of the empty spaces. To him it was not empty. It was alive with the ghosts of what had been and the spirit of what was to come. Ivor was steeped in it and he felt the spirit of the Theatre all around him. He was never completely happy out of it. Even then, when he had just a foot inside the door, it was everything to him and he was as sensitive to the lure of that extraordinary place as anyone who had spent a lifetime therein or who, by ancestry, was a complete product of the playhouse.

Those people who are real " Theatre " will understand. They know exactly what it is like: the joy of simply going into a theatre, of breathing the air therein, of sitting in an empty house, of crossing an empty stage. That is their kingdom. Here their feet are on their native heath. They have entered their Reality. The world outside is mere illusion, but this is real, this is what matters. Those real " theatre " folk move about a playhouse silently. Their feet make no noise, they never slam doors, they never raise their voices, for to them the play is always on, the playhouse always alive. You can never fail to detect the amateur, the part-time theatre person. They stumble, they make noises, they are ill at ease. But the real one, with greasepaint in the blood, is at home, in all that home means, and perfectly happy. Ivor was one of those real theatre people.

He thought over what Constance Collier had said. She was away in Switzerland, fighting for her life against a serious complaint which is all too common but which is now easy to control. Even that short time ago, it was difficult. But Constance, and the doctors, won. Then it seemed a miracle.

She came back to England, weak, a bit frail, but well, and fast becoming her old and vital self again. Ivor met her and was brimful of his news. He wanted to write a play, he was going to write a play, and they must do it together....

CHAPTER TEN

HOW NOW—A RAT?

IVOR was going to write a play. Though he had four stage parts behind him and a handful of screen successes, he had no special knowledge of the technique of playwriting. But his mind was made up. He felt the time had come and he must take advantage of it. All his life he believed in his instinct. He always let it guide him and it played him false only once. If he had a hunch, he let it have its fling. This was a characteristic he inherited from his mother.

It was his friend Constance Collier who finally settled his mind. She had just recovered from a very serious illness and was to come home to this country. She would want something to occupy her mind and what more perfect than that she should be his collaborator?

He had his idea, his plot, his story. Some time before he had invested some money—a good deal for him in those days—in a film company. The company had not had much success and Ivor had written a scenario for a film which he had hoped would put the company on its feet. But the film had never been made. Nevertheless, Ivor still believed that something could be made of the idea. He would turn that little story into a play.

It was a story of the Paris underworld, and he would play the part of an Apache called " the Rat." He was sure the part would fit him; he had that " foreign " look and he could make the character romantic, though why the Apache of Paris should ever have been romantic, and why Romance should ever surround criminals, brutes and crooks on the stage and in literature is one of those things, as Lord Dundreary used to say, " no fellah can understand." But Ivor knew full well they were regarded as romantic and he had reason to believe that his public, now quite considerable owing to his film success, would think it was just the stuff for him to give them.

It is probable that Ivor's film fans did follow him into the Theatre, for he was always unique. But in ninety-nine cases out of a hundred, the ordinary cinemagoer rarely visits a theatre.

Never was this better demonstrated than when Pauline Frederick, at the height of her screen success, played in *Madame X* on the stage of the Lyceum Theatre. Hordes of excited, extraordinary young things of both sexes packed into the pit, gallery, and the cheaper parts of the theatre. Most of them had never been in a playhouse before. They could not make it out and they gazed in wide-eyed surprise at the ladies and gentlemen, the first nighters, in the best seats. Who could they be, these distinguished people? And my friend Leslie Bloom, the President of the Gallery First Nighters, gave his imagination and sardonic sense of humour full rein by pointing out quite ordinary nobodies to these film fans as world celebrities, even though they did not resemble them in the least. The film fans hung on his words and believed it all. There were remarkable scenes, the wild young folk kicked up an enormous row and overran the stalls. But they did not appear to come again in anything like the same numbers. The revival was no great success.

Constance Collier came back to this country—and to Life. She had been right up to the gates of Death; indeed, the dark door had opened and it seemed to her that she had looked inside. And the miracle occurred. A medical discovery saved her. She was the first person in Europe and almost the first in the world to be treated with insulin. It saved the life of this beautiful woman and magnificent actress, to the joy of her countless friends and admirers. She came back fit and able to carry on.

To her Ivor confided his idea of writing a play and of becoming actor-manager. She not only applauded, she encouraged. They discussed the affair from all angles and Constance thoroughly approved the main idea of the plot and story that he had written for the film. So they decided to write the play together. She had plenty of experience, she knew all about acting and stage technique, though she had never written a play before. The fact that neither of them had any experience of playwriting seemed to them the best reason for collaboration. Ivor was pretty full up at the time: he was playing at the Playhouse in *Enter Kiki* and making the film of *Bonnie Prince Charlie*, playing opposite Gladys Cooper in both. But the creative urge was upon him.

Much has been written about the manner in which *The Rat* was evolved. There is little need to retrace all that ground. Ivor and Constance sat up to all hours, drinking innumerable cups of tea, quarrelling, fighting and insulting each other. But they made real progress. They understood each other and each other's ideas despite the fact that they constantly disagreed. Almost as soon as they began one of them got influenza and gave it to the other. But *The Rat*, repeatedly altered and rewritten, grew and took shape. Their battles over it formed the ideal way of collaboration, for the sparks lit their imagination and they both strove to beat each other in the supply of situation and dialogue. And it seemed to them that they did their utmost to make all the characters as bad as they possibly could. No trace of virtue or decent feeling was allowed. If they had drunk vitriol instead of tea, the parts they were creating could not have been more acid and biting. Ivor was very keen on this "Rat" character. Some years before he had seen the immense success and the tremendous artistry of the famous Apache Dance created at the Empire by Fred Farren and Beatrice Collyer, which had taken London by storm. He had seen innumerable adagio dancers do other versions of it and always with success. So they went to it with a will, striking showers of sparks from each other and igniting the tinder of the play. And, at last, they finished it.

Then came the matter of finance. The play had to go into rehearsal and it had to be produced. A date was booked at the Theatre Royal, Brighton. Ivor was hard up. He had money to come to him from films, but his ready cash was meagre. His savings were in a film company, Novello-Atlas Renters, which was non-productive. He had spent money freely for it seemed so easy to acquire, but here was the need for capital. Ivor found himself in the position of Mr. Micawber on another celebrated occasion. When her distinguished husband contemplated entering the Medway coal trade, Mrs. Micawber's opinion was that "it may require talent but it certainly requires capital. Talent, Mr. Micawber has, capital Mr. Micawber has not." It was the same with Ivor Novello. Mr. and Mrs. Micawber had inspected the Medway before delivering this weighty judgment. Ivor and Constance Collier had written the play. Now it was a question of capital. But they went to work and they managed to rake up just enough. They had just sufficient to cover production expenses and to pay the company and outgoings for a couple of weeks.

The show opened on January 14th, 1924, at the Theatre

Royal, Brighton. Up to that date £372 1*s*. 4*d*. had been expended. Second-hand scenery cost £40, and another £22 to convert. Repainting and odd jobs on the set cost a further £4 1*s*. 3*d*. The bills for costumes amounted to £43 3*s*. 10*d*., for furniture, cartage, etc. £16 1*s*. 7*d*., and properties £14 4*s*. 9*d*. Advertising, printing and other similar expenses stood at £136 17*s*. 6*d*. This figure included the salaries of the stage manager and assistant stage manager. The rehearsal expenses—the company got no rehearsal money in those days—ran to £66 12*s*. 4*d*., which included the full-dress rehearsal at Brighton. Other sundry expenses completed the £372 1*s*. 4*d*., which Ivor paid in four instalments as follows: a cheque for £100 on December 21st, 1923, further cheques for £150 on January 7th and £50 on January 13th, and the rest—as the note on the production account states—" by cheque and cash " on January 10th, 1924—£72 1*s*. 4*d*.

When his play was completed, it had first been read to friends. Some had approved, some had tried to be kind, others had shaken their heads. But Edward Marsh had been quite confident. Ivor and Constance did not put up their own names as authors; they put up the composite name of " David L'Estrange," David being Ivor and the L'Estrange Constance Collier. (L'Estrange was Constance Collier's married name; she had married the handsome, debonair actor Julian L'Estrange, a man full of gaiety and charm, whose tragic death had clouded her life and brought about her own almost fatal illness.) But all the " profession " knew who had written the play. It was pretty clear to the public as well.

Rehearsals were hard and troublesome. Constance Collier herself produced—or directed the play—with constant interruptions by Ivor. They had Isabel Jeans in the lead, with Dorothy Batley, James Lindsay, Jean Webster Brough, Nancy Pawley, Victor Boggetti and a competent cast as well. Everything looked all right, if the play was good enough.

Many of the cast became Ivor's lifelong friends, notably Jean Webster Brough and Victor Boggetti. The latter has special cause to remember *The Rat*. He was not exactly engaged but began by rehearsing on approval. He did not think he was giving satisfaction, and though he had not been told anything definite, he was quite sure he was going to be sacked. He left a rehearsal at lunch time and determined not to go back. After lunch he decided to go home. He was on his way to the bus when a friend met him and told him they were looking for somebody of his type for a part in *The Rat*. It was now certain that he was sacked. He reached the bus stop, but had to wait. While he was waiting, he thought it over and decided to go back. "If I'm sacked, I'm sacked, that's all there is to it," he thought. So he went back. He went on rehearsing. He was in the cast and he played the part. And from that time on he was always with Ivor Novello shows, right down to *King's Rhapsody*. Had he not obeyed his instinct, how different it might have been.

Tall, handsome and the possessor of an excellent speaking voice, Boggetti, who came from a stage family, had learned his job the hard way. He was with me in the George Dance days, out as assistant stage manager to *The Whip* and *The Hope*, doing tremendous jobs, playing odds and ends and whatever came along for the smallest of salaries, but with complete dependability and efficiency—all of which, except the odd jobs and the small salaries, remains to-day. Victor Boggetti thanks his stars over *The Rat*. His last job for Ivor was to act as usher at the Memorial Service at St. Martin-in-the-Fields and nobody had a better right or did it with better grace or fuller heart. He remembers many strange happenings during the run of *The Rat*, especially in London. He recalls how Ivor came upon one of the stagehands who was not only quarrelling with his wife but giving her a thrashing. Ivor acted at once. He threw himself upon that wife-beater and to the man's immense surprise gave him not only a pretty thorough mauling but threw him out of the theatre. He remembers, too, how one of the artistes came down to the theatre in a dream of alcohol. Quite drunk, but very quiet and extremely dignified, the said player was ready to go on when the stage manager found out the true state of things and informed Ivor. Ivor held an inspection, ordered the alcoholic case to be taken to the dressing-room to sleep it off, whilst the understudy played. Nothing more was said. The artiste slept off the potations and went on at the next performance as if nothing had happened. No trouble was made, no rebukes administered. All that happened was that the artiste found the salary cheque was made out minus one performance. Although Ivor was most abstemious himself and did not like drunkards about him, nothing more was said and the little affair was forgotten. Ivor was like that.

A similar thing happened at Drury Lane during one of his shows there. One of the chorus girls got much above herself. She came down to the theatre with a grievance. It seemed to her that she was a star who had been overlooked. It was obviously necessary to draw Ivor Novello's attention to the omission. She got into the theatre all right, went across to Ivor's dressing-room, walked straight in—and found him alone. At once she began her recital of fancied wrongs and woes. Ivor, understanding at once what was the matter, listened with patience. He knew that if William Abingdon, that wonderful stage director and martinet for discipline, saw the girl, her stage career would be ended. He also knew the girl was not in the habit of getting " tight." He made her sit down and rest, and then assured her of his help. Of course, she fell asleep. He hid her until it was time for the evening performance, when she went on and played. She had to account for her absence during the afternoon, but she managed to do that. He never said a word about it. He hated to get people into trouble. Above all, he had great understanding and patience.

He needed both during the rehearsals of *The Rat*. He himself had troubles enough then. Nobody had much faith in the play, and it did not seem to come to life. In the first place he himself was not a sufficiently experienced actor to take hold, and without Constance Collier's firm grip disaster might have happened. Scenes were cut and rewritten, temperaments were the order of the day. Most of the cast were certain they were in for a flop. The cast was, in the main, made up of very experienced people. James Lindsay, who played Detective Inspector Caillard was an excellent actor and a most charming fellow—an Old Rugbeian. He had built up a big reputation on tour as a "villain" in the great Drury Lane dramas, especially in *The Whip* in which, as Captain Sartorys, he toured for years under the management of George Dance. He was one of the very few actors who ever got concessions from that Dictator of Theatreland. For example, he insisted—and had it in his contract—that he should travel in a railway carriage by himself and that he should have Player's cigarettes supplied to him to smoke on the stage and not the Abdullas which were supplied by the management to the company. Dance was a pioneer of the line " Cigarettes by Abdulla " on programmes and daybills. It was generally believed that he himself was " Abdulla " but this was not the case; he was not even a shareholder. The firm got the advertisement and he got the cigarettes for nothing, which exactly suited his book. Rich as Croesus, he watched the pence. Let a big company spend more than 15*s*. a week on what is known as "Wardrobe Account" and the Heavens fell! "That wardrobe mistress washes everything but herself," he would storm. "Sack her and get somebody else. I'll be ruined." So the free supply of Abdullas was just right for him. Not that he smoked them himself; he did not. His own cigarettes came from Sullivan Powell, who became famous—or perhaps more famous—through the play *Raffles*. That expert amateur cracksman was an inveterate smoker. Producing his case, he would say, "Have a Sullivan?"

The Abdulla cigarettes used to come to Dance's head office at 48 Leicester Square, in boxes and by the thousand. It was one of my jobs to distribute them to the companies. There would always be some special boxes of their best brand. I am afraid the companies never got them. Jimmy Lindsay did not like Turkish or Egyptian cigarettes, preferring Virginian, hence his insistence on Player's. He meant no slur on Abdullas; it was just his personal taste. On the other hand, Dance's general manager, T. C. Wray, and I had no such objection. We did, in those days, smoke Turkish and Egyptian, as did most men, and we collared those boxes of the best brands. No harm was done, nobody was robbed. We argued that as we were at Head Office and in the West End, it was up to us to keep up the prestige of our revered boss. So we must have—and offer our friends—the best cigarettes. And we did. Ivor himself always smoked Turkish cigarettes. But most of us lost the taste for them during the First World War. We took to "gaspers," and we became chain smokers. That has endured with me.

Rehearsals struggled on for *The Rat*. Constance Collier was playing in *Our Betters*—one of her most outstanding creations—travelling backwards and forwards each day to appear at the Globe. Had this not been the case, she would probably have played Odile in *The Rat*. The outlook grew gloomier and gloomier. Both Ivor and Constance now began to think that dire failure was ahead. As a result they became very self-conscious with one another, each hating to think that they had involved the other in disaster. One day a very eminent dramatist dropped in to rehearsals. He said little then, but he took Constance Collier aside and begged her to stop the play opening. "You are very fond of Ivor," he said. "Well, so am I. You have influence over him, maybe. For heaven's sake stop him appearing in this. It will be disaster for him and for you both. But don't whatever you do, tell him I said so." This plunged Constance Collier into even deeper gloom. At the same time she noticed that Ivor was particularly distrait, too, and seemed to be avoiding her. Later, it came out that the dramatist mutual friend had said exactly the same thing to Ivor about Constance as he had said to her, and under the same seal of secrecy.

Worse was to follow. Lawson Lambert, who for years was the very popular and able manager of the Theatre Royal, Brighton, and was a man of great experience, said quite openly that he wished he could find another attraction to take the place of *The Rat* even at that late hour. And he delivered an even greater blow when he insisted that "profanity" played "far too great a part in the script." "This bad language," he protested, "this constant repetition of 'My God'—it won't do! It will upset all my patrons. It must come out, I insist." It was useless to plead that they had a licence from the Lord Chamberlain. Lawson Lambert, who looked exactly like an admiral and who could on occasions behave as one and did so now, was adamant. The co-authors had to strike out as much "profanity" and as many "My God's" as possible. When they got down to the task it seemed to them that the dialogue consisted of little else and they were at their wits' end what to write in its place. . . .

The dress rehearsal dragged on and on, all day and all night, all through a miserable winter Sunday right into the hopeless small hours of a worse Monday morning. The cast were exhausted, Ivor nearly dead and Constance Collier no better. She was under the additional strain of having to go to town on the last possible train every afternoon and returning to Brighton on the "midnight" to start all over again. That Monday she stayed until the very last moment, travelling to town in a daze and playing her part in *Our Betters* with her mouth and technique, her mind on the battleground at Brighton.

The Rat had been well ballyhooed. Attention was drawn to Ivor and his good looks, to his film success, to his spirit of adventure into the realms of management. The young ladies of Brighton were besought to look out, for Ivor Novello, in person, was coming to them. They looked out all right and they looked into the theatre on that fateful night. The Theatre Royal was packed from ceiling to floor. The tired, dispirited company experienced every ordinary first-night emotion, and only those who have ever undergone it can imagine what that is like. The Spanish Inquisition could not have been worse, there is no nerve strain to equal it. I know one great actress who is always violently sick shortly before curtain rise. And added to this they expected the worst. There is nothing quite so bad in the Theatre as that. But just to help there is the terrific spirit of optimism that always encourages theatre folk: " perhaps it may be all right—such things have happened." Indeed they have. Usually, it is a pretty safe bet to say that when the company are enchanted by a play the audience will dislike it and that when a show has " made the band laugh," there will not be a smile from the audience. . . . There was the usual excited chatter in front, the bustle of arrivals, the drinks at the bar, the continuous rustle of paper around the sweets and chocolates, the steady munching. And then, the house lights dimmed, the orchestra played its little piece, the footlights went up, the curtain followed them—and *The Rat* had begun.

Ivor Novello, whose feelings were now numbed as if he had been kept in a refrigerator, sat in the prompt corner, to listen and to hope. He sensed a feeling of tension. It seemed to him the play was holding: even the inexperienced can tell this in the Theatre. His cue came, he went on—that smile flashed out—and the audience roared a welcome at him. It was like a tonic, like a glass of champagne. He became Pierre Boucheron—*The Rat*—the creation of his own and Constance Collier's brain. This was his show, he was responsible. That feeling of responsibility which he always loved, took charge. . . .

Back in London, the curtain had fallen on *Our Betters* and Constance Collier was speeding to Brighton on the midnight train, her thoughts flying ahead. What had happened? Was it disaster? Was it—no it could not be. . . . And yet. . . . Oh, if the train would only fly, if the miles would only vanish more quickly! This suspense was unendurable . . . anything was better than this. And then, Brighton, the dark cavern of the station on a cold January night. She ran down the platform. Yes, there was the car and there was the faithful Morgan, Ivor's chauffeur until death. She hardly dared frame her question. Morgan spoke. " I'm afraid—" said he, and Constance's heart

Ivor as a girl in amateur theatricals

Above : Ivor and one of his favourite leading ladies, Olive Gilbert, in *Perchance to Dream* at the London Hippodrome

Ivor and Diana Wynyard in a war-front performance of *Love from a Stranger* at Bayeux 1944

Above : A big crowd outside the stage door at the Queen's Theatre, London, clamours for autographs

Centre : Ivor in his dressing room

Below : With Lady Kelly and the Marchioness of Headfort at the Literary Lunch to celebrate the author's book on the "Gaiety"

stood still, " . . . I'm afraid," continued Morgan, " that we have a success." She tells that story in her *Harlequinade*. Peter Noble tells it in his Novello biography. Quite shamelessly, I tell it again here. It is worth it. It is real Theatre.

And success it was! The first act had gone splendidly. Gladys Cooper, in a box, had sent Ivor round an encouraging note. The second act went even better. Confidence had returned, attack came with it, the company now had shaken off fear and fatigue and were giving all they had. So, of course, was Ivor. And when the last curtain fell, there was tumult. That curtain rose again and again; it is said there were thirty-nine curtain calls. Ivor had triumphed, his play was a real success. He was an actor-manager and he made his first curtain speech—nobody could make those little speeches with the same modest charm as Ivor—and everything in the garden was lovely. He hugged the company all round, he shook hands as if wrists were to be dislocated. He fought his way through the mass of excited girls at the stage door, as excited or more so than any of them, and it was then the unknown " fan " paid her compliments to his power of expectoration. He hugged Constance Collier as if to kill her and there were tears of happiness all round.

The next morning there was an ecstatic local Press and a constant crowd at the box office. Every seat for the week was sold by mid-day. Ivor and his manager got busy and the original tour, planned for eight or nine weeks, was extended to fourteen. Every provincial manager wanted *The Rat* and Ivor Novello. Beyond that, in the minds of Ivor and Constance Collier, gleamed the golden haze of the West End. . . .

Ivor, Robert Andrews and Constance Collier would walk along the Brighton front, talking, thinking, planning. They would lean over the rails opposite the Old Ship or The Albion and gaze out to sea, wondering if they could peer into the future. They would stand hushed and, like three Paul Dombeys, try to discover what the wild waves of Brighton were saying to them. And to all of them the message seemed the same: " Go on—go on. . . ."

But friends who had not the same opportunity of listening to these waves, because they were in the West End, thought differently. Practically everyone advised Ivor and Constance not to try their luck too far, not to expect the hard-bitten sophisticated West End audiences to endorse the verdict the provincial audiences, easier to please (so they said) and not so critical as those of London, were bestowing on *The Rat* and its leading man. They produced all the good old arguments. But about the provincial verdict there was no dispute. Excited audiences shouted their pleasure and put Ivor almost in peril of his life. At Leeds a fervent admirer got hold of his hair and pulled out quite a large lump, and with the very best of heart and affectionate feelings. . . .

Money was now coming in from *The Rat*, and Ivor was determined to bring the play to town. He felt now he was not only an actor but an actor-manager as well. Although he was praised for his performance in *The Rat*, both by public and Press, it was still a very immature effort. He had little technique. Jean Webster Brough bears witness to this. In the play he had to struggle with her. Experienced people can appear locked in a desperate death grip, with muscles apparently tense and veins standing out, whereas they are undergoing no exertion at all. But Ivor went for it and would grip Jean Webster Brough, throw her over chairs and often hurt her. There was one scene on a sofa in which he had to appear to strangle her. Every night she suffered pain and torment and dreaded it happening, every night she was bruised and sore. Finally, young as she was, she took him in hand, teaching him the trick of how to conduct stage struggles. And it did not take him long to learn. I asked Constance Collier, quite recently, what she thought of his performance and she smiled. " Well, you know," she said, " he had such power over audiences, especially the women in them, that when he really made mistakes which were clear even to them, they would just smile and say ' Poor dear, he's only young—he doesn't know. He'll soon learn '—and forgive him his gauchness and inexperience entirely and probably love him all the more." And then she made a remark which was dead right and absolutely expressed my own opinion. " Nobody ever threw his heart at the feet of every audience as Ivor did," she said, " and they always picked it up."

And that tells the whole volume of Ivor's power as an actor and his uncanny control of audiences. But he always learned quickly and he never forgot. He seldom, if ever, made the same mistake twice, so long as it was pointed out to him. He would listen, try the advice and adopt it when he had mastered it. And he never lost that feeling of being part of the audience himself.

I really believe that the more sensitive of them felt that he was sitting out there, next to them, in very fact. He could put that over the footlights. It is a dictum that an actor should appear unaware of his audience. Ivor may have appeared unaware but he never was and the audience always knew he was aware of them. He was able to keep his body on the other side of the proscenium arch and send his mind out there with his many friends in front.

Now, indeed, might Ivor have been forgiven if he had shown a sign of conceit, or swelled head. To be a foremost composer, a film star, and an accepted and successful actor-manager all off his own bat with no help or undue influence, with no powerful hand to open doors and fill in pitfalls, and to have achieved all this at the age of thirty-one, was something which might go to the head of anybody. Indeed, Jean Webster Brough tackled him about it. She asked him if he did not feel a bit stuck up and conceited over his exploits. He looked at her with something of surprise. "Conceit, ducky?" he said. "No, indeed. Why? You see, it's always been like this, hasn't it?" He just accepted it, he thought nothing of it. It did not occur to him that there was anything to wonder at, or that what he had done was in any way remarkable. It was, in a sense, his method of life.

And, of course, the part he played in *The Rat* was really a character part. He was always best in such roles, far better than in straight romantic characters.

But in that year of success, 1924, he was determined to add the scalp of the West End to his belt of trophies. He had actually had a taste of management before. He had done a short tour with *Spanish Lovers* under his own banner and had been very successful personally and made a little money. But this—this was different. He had written this play himself, with Constance Collier. It is difficult to say who wrote the most: Ivor had the idea of the character and from Constance came the situations and technique; it was, indeed, a genuine fifty-fifty venture. He believed that the verdict of the provincials would be endorsed by the public of the metropolis. Perhaps he knew even then where his strength lay, not in the seats of the mighty but in the palms of the gods. So he took the plunge. He took the Prince of Wales's Theatre and he opened with *The Rat* on June 9th, 1924. There was a large and fashionable first-night audience, all the regulars and all the now very considerable army of fans. The critics were there, in force, as in duty bound. By now it was perfectly well known who David L'Estrange stood for and it only added to the interest.

No mistake was made about the presentation. It was not overboosted, there was no pretence that this was a play of culture with a message to humanity; there was no suggestion that this was Art or a new form of Drama. It was just presented as an honest-to-goodness romantic melodrama, a thriller of the Apache section of Parisian life—and to the average Londoner, Paris is a romantic place where the most impossible things can happen and be real. (In reality, London is even more romantic and exciting, but one never sees what is in one's own home or on one's own doorstep. If a thing is Parisian, it becomes at once attractive to the average Briton and, consequently, to the average playgoer it has an appeal which is half-way to success.)

The plot was of the simplest and most conventional. It was almost the Cinderella story turned round the other way—the tale of a man of the Parisian underworld, dazzled by the charms of aristocratic beauty of refinement and allure, who forsakes his own stratum of society and his humble associates to mix with the strange world above him, finds it is all wrong for him, and returns to his old haunts and his old loves. There was a dash of François Villon, of so many romantic heroes about it all. It is a theme which always appeals. But there was woven into the story some very strong situations, some good, telling, straightforward dialogue and quite a lot of surprise and thrills. That London audience, on that June night, accepted it for what it was and gave it full marks. London heartily endorsed the verdict of the provinces. Crowds thronged the stage door and equally dense crowds surged at the box office. The experienced heads of the "Libraries"—the ticket-selling agencies—came into the game and bought, and Ivor was a West End theatre manager in his own right. He got a very good Press indeed, both as actor and as part author. His friends were confounded but delighted. Eddie Marsh beamed on all and said he had always known . . . and said it with perfect truth.

Ivor was not quite entirely his own actor-manager. In this venture he was associated with Julian Frank, who looked after the business side and "presented" the play. But virtually and morally he was on his own and loving it. Constance Collier's advice had been right, that was indeed the way for him to succeed. *The Rat* was a success. There was no doubt about that. And Ivor was in the front rank. He was the most talked-of man in the British Theatre at that moment. For personalities were lacking. The old giants had gone, shrouded in the smoke of the guns of the Great War, and the public was agog for new names and faces to take their place. The reign of the actor-managers, so good for the Theatre, seemed likely to return. This extremely handsome and clever young man looked like being the very person to do it, to bring the personal touch and the skill of craftsmanship, which the actor-managers had possessed, back into the now purely commercialized Theatre, which was also feeling considerable American infiltration. True, a great number of the knowledgeable people of the playhouse just regarded Ivor as a very good-looking, charming young man with a knack of making himself popular, and did not take him seriously. They were right, at the time, but there were a few who looked deeper and saw more. They, too, were right.

Meanwhile Ivor basked in success and in the floodlight of publicity. You could not escape him in the illustrated newspapers. His name and his face were both ubiquitous. But it did not turn his head. He was looking forward, he was planning fresh ventures and David Ivor Davies was keeping the ship of Ivor Novello on an even keel. At the moment the great thing was Acting. It was as Actor that he saw himself. That was the immediate goal.

The Rat ran through the summer. It was transferred from the Prince of Wales's to the Garrick on September 15th. In all, it ran for 283 performances, an excellent figure for those days, especially as conditions were anything but good generally. There was one snag. Ivor had contracted to fulfil some suburban and provincial dates and now did not want to take the show off in town as he would be compelled to do if he played them. Some saw reason and cancelled in the friendliest manner. Two, however, stood upon their rights and the financial forfeit was considerable. Ivor was still a poor man and, besides his royalties, had only his earnings. He had still not accumulated capital. There was a suggestion that, to help him, everyone should forgo a salary for a matinée. He did not like this but his company almost forced it on him. He agreed reluctantly, with the proviso that if it were done, it must be absolutely unanimous. He would not accept anything which was partial or not in complete agreement. The ringleaders who had put up the offer retired to consult their colleagues, quite sure of complete agreement. They did not get it. One member of the company flatly refused. Ivor had to be told. He was told—in writing—by Jean Webster Brough. And here is his reply:

> " Jean Dear,
>
> I can't thank you enough for so generously and sweetly wanting to help me out of my very grave difficulty and I was delighted to accept but I find there is one voice of protest which may conceivably be expressing other people's views. Therefore the whole thing becomes impossible. Nevertheless I shall always be proud to remember that you tried to help me over my first big stile.
>
> Love,
>
> Ivor."

But Jean got her way. Ivor accepted in the end and the one protestant received salary in full, while the others gloried in the help they gave. Nor did Ivor ever forget it—either way.

The Rat was the beginning of the Ivor Novello Stock Company, that little band of actors and actresses for whom he wrote parts and whom he loved to have around him right up to the end, whenever opportunity served. And he often made those opportunities. In *The Rat* were two of the staunchest Old Novellians in Jean Webster Brough and Victor Boggetti. And Isabel Jeans, who played the lead, was another fine actress with whom he played whenever he could. The cast of *The Rat* at the Prince of Wales's was as follows:

America	Dorothy St. John
Mere Collins	Hannah Jones
Rose	Jean Webster Brough
Mou-Mou	Kathleen Grace
Detective-Inspector Caillard	James Lindsay
Herman Stetz	W. Cronin Wilson
Odile	Dorothy Batley
Pierre Boucheron (Known as ' The Rat ')	Ivor Novello
Zelie de Chaummet	Isabel Jeans
Madeline Sornay	Nancy Pawley
Paul	Maurice Braddell
Alphonse	Victor Boggetti
Therese	Kathleen Grace
A Gendarme	F. V. Owen

Ivor got over the stile and *The Rat* ran on. He was now of the Theatre and in the Theatre and adoring every moment of it: the excitement, the personal touch, the applause of the audience, all the intimate life which goes to make the theatre in which one is playing not so much the centre of the universe but the entire universe itself. The Theatre is a mad place which believes only in illusion and considers reality unreal and, because it is not the Theatre, unworthy of the slightest attention.

What matters above all is what is being said in the dressing-rooms, the little contretemps which happen at performances, whether one was in good form or a " bit off " the previous night, what so-and-so said about such-a-one, and the curious excitement engendered by the real nothingness of it all—nothingness to outsiders but of supreme importance to those on the inside. The Theatre is the world and the home—life begins when the stage door is entered—and dreams start when the curtain falls. It is always a tragedy when a run ends, for it never seems possible that it should. There never seems a time when that particular dressing-room, that special stage door, that identical stage will not be the nerve-centre of existence. But the run ends: good-byes are said—often as if for ever—and then comes a new job in another theatre and life starts all over again. The first rehearsals, despite the fact that you may know every solitary member of the cast and management, engender much the same sort of feeling as one's first day at a school; there is always the odd loneliness of the new boy. But that is all part of that devastating charm which the Theatre lays upon its mad inhabitants and it is something which the film studio can never supply. It is Theatre. And Ivor was savouring it to the full. For him *The Rat* had been his new beginning. Maybe he thought of that Shakespearean line spoken by Hamlet:

How Now? A Rat? Dead for a ducat. Dead!

But this Rat was very much alive and certainly not behind the arras, but well in front of the curtain. . . .

CHAPTER ELEVEN

ALMOST AT THE TOP

THE stage had got Ivor now and he knew it was his true element. After the successful run of *The Rat*, he went into a revival of *Old Heidelberg*, also at the Garrick Theatre. In that romantic play of a gentler Germany when princelings were many and Dictators none at all, he played the part of Karl Heinrich.

He was greatly daring in this because the role had been created at the St. James's Theatre by Sir George Alexander himself at the height of his fame and career. There were very many playgoers still active in their theatregoing who had seen Alexander in that part, easily one of his best. *Old Heidelberg* had been produced at the St. James's in 1903, twenty-two years before. Owen Nares had played a very tiny part in it and afterwards played Karl Heinrich on tour. Those who saw Alexander, and I had that privilege, will remember a beautifully balanced performance of great charm and magnificent technique, all through the changing character—from the gauche young man nursed in the hot-house seclusion, convention and ceremony of a small German court and unaccustomed to the societies of youths of his own age, to the happy young student in love with the innkeeper's daughter and also in love with love, and then to the man who has to relinquish freedom to take up his regal position, and who returns, a man and a king, to seek his dead youth and memories only to find them sad and bitter. Oscar Wilde may have said that Alexander did not act but merely behaved, but he behaved as few people on the stage can behave to-day. Later the play was turned into *The Student Prince*, a musical play which is still very popular.

Ivor was not his own manager in this venture. It was staged by Julian Frank and money was lost. It was not a success. Ivor had all the part required, except the experience to play it. He looked extraordinarily handsome, especially in the dark uniform with the cross at the neck—and he never forgot that uniform, for he wore one just like it in his last great triumph, *King's*

Rhapsody—and it is no disrespect to say that he loved himself in it. So did his innumerable fans. He looked far more handsome in it than any ordinary man had any right to look. Yet, awkward and amateurish as was his Karl Heinrich, he increased his fans, who delighted to gaze at him and forgive the mistakes as usual. He had shoals of letters from admirers. One wrote: "I feel I must write and tell you, and I can do so being quite an old lady and having been a keen theatregoer for many years, what great pleasure your fine acting in *Old Heidelberg* last Tuesday evening, gave my husband (name given) and myself. There was such soul in your acting of the Prince that it did not seem acting but real. The only thing we missed was the Kitty of Eva Moore in the old days at the St. James's Theatre. We were very sorry to see so bad a house and only hope that more people will go to see such a beautiful play with so fine a character study in it. Yours truly——" That was a genuine letter from someone quite unknown and Ivor always kept it. It is before me as I write. The lady was wrong in the name of Eva Moore's part; it was "Kathie" not "Kitty," but that matters little.

Meanwhile, the houses did not improve and the play came off. But far-seeing eyes were on him, those of Frank Curzon and his astute manager, T. B. Vaughan. It will be remembered he had already worked under this management with Gladys Cooper at the Playhouse in *Enter Kiki.* Now came an offer to go into a revival of Pinero's play *Iris* at the Adelphi, under Frank Curzon's banner. *Old Heidelberg* had been produced in February, 1924. Ivor received the offer to play in *Iris* on April 7th of that year and the following day came a letter from T. B. Vaughan.

"Dear Ivor,

Confirming our conversation of last night, the following is the arrangement we have between us. You will open on Monday night April 13th. In lieu of a fixed salary you agree to accept a certain proportion of the surplus receipts over expenditure, but for the purposes of such charges it is understood that neither Gladys nor Ainley receive any fixed salary; nor is there any charge to be made in respect of rent or the weekly charge for production. After the payment of all other expenses incurred in the running of the play at the Adelphi Theatre, the surplus is to be divided up in fortieths and, on the basis already agreed upon, your share is to be at the rate of three-fortieths of such surplus.

" We shall continue the run of the play anyway until Saturday, May 2nd, and between then and now we shall discuss our future policy, which naturally would depend on the amount of success the play may meet in the meantime.

" You will of course be starred equally with Gladys and Henry Ainley in the newspapers, and we will get new printing out as quickly as possible, but owing to the Easter Holidays there must inevitably be a delay about this.

" Would you kindly send me a little line in formal confirmation. All the Best.

Yours ever
T. B. Vaughan."

That letter shows the way business was transacted as between management and stars in the inter-war Theatre. Ivor joined the play after production, replacing another actor who had left. It had been produced on March 25th, 1925, and despite the fact that Gladys Cooper and Henry Ainley were in it, it wobbled badly. Curzon and Vaughan thought that young Ivor, now on the way to the top in public favour, might do the trick and save the show. They offered a gamble, Ivor accepted. That gamble came off. The revival ran for 152 performances, longer indeed than its original run of 115 performances at the Garrick in 1901. Ivor Novello, as Laurence Trenwith, sent the receipts rocketing up by hundreds of pounds. It is not on record how much Ivor's three-fortieths came to, but he probably did fairly well. His advance in prestige was considerable. And he was happy playing opposite his adored Gladys Cooper, though it must be admitted that poor Harry Ainley was not an easy person to get on with.

But mere acting was still not enough for this young man who was becoming so completely " Theatre." He and Constance Collier wrote another play, called *Down Hill*. This was another fifty-fifty collaboration, as had been *The Rat*. They tried it out at the Palace, Manchester, in December, 1925. It did not, however, come into town, as did *The Rat*, with provincial success thickly upon it. For Ivor had to play in *The Firebrand* under the management of Gilbert Miller at Wyndham's Theatre. He played Benvenuto Cellini in this play which opened in February, 1926. Once again, he looked amazing, for the romantic Italian *cinquecento* costume suited him perfectly. He had seldom if ever looked more handsome. And he was playing opposite his dear Constance Collier. But in the Theatre, looks are not all. *The Firebrand* did not live up to its name and there was certainly no blaze of success. However, Ivor was not depressed. He had his own and Constance's play *Down Hill*, and he had a letter from the clever and powerful Frank Curzon under date December 29th, 1925, which read as follows:

> " Dear Ivor Novello,
>
> Confirming our conversation of last night I agree to engage you for the term of five years, with an option for another two years, on the following terms:—The agreement is to commence six weeks after you have fulfilled your present contracts with Gilbert Miller and Julian Frank. I undertake to pay you £200 per week and 25 per cent. of the profits. You are to give me your entire services with the exception of any salary you may earn as a film actor. If you write a play, or I write a play which is done under our joint management, we naturally take the ordinary author's fees. The profits are to be adjusted year by year. In all advertisements and announcements it shall be ' Under the joint management of Frank Curzon and Ivor Novello '."

That was a nice contract to get hold of when the stage experience only amounted to four years and the number of parts played was only seven. Frank Curzon had a great flair for joint managements. He it was who steered Gerald du Maurier at Wyndham's during that long managerial season there; he had Gladys Cooper in joint management at the Playhouse; and he had been associated in many other such arrangements, with Marie Tempest, Charles Hawtrey and real top stars like that. Curzon was a man who made very few mistakes in the Theatre and his activity was enormous, although he was a lazy man at heart, who really preferred the country to the Theatre. When hunting, shooting or fishing, he was in heaven. And also when racing. His greatest moment came when his horse Call Boy won the Derby. He was ill then and did not live long afterwards. But he had tasted life to the full. For some reason or another that contract between him and Ivor never became operative. Had it done so, the course of Ivor's life might have been different. But Curzon judged him, not from present achievement, though with *The Rat* and *Iris* to his credit it was quite considerable, but by the potentialities he saw in the future.

But the Novello life was clicking into shape and so were the people who were to play important parts in it. Miss Chantry, who had been looking after Ivor's correspondence, was leaving to take up another post, so Ivor now offered Fred Allen a job with him. It will be recalled that he had approached him once before in his very youthful days when attempting to give music lessons, and had offered Fred Allen a percentage. He now wrote in 1925 and offered Fred, who was at the time in the Civil Service, a salary if he would give him an hour a day on his way home from work. It was not a large salary by any means but it helped. Ivor hoped Allen would give it a trial. Fred Allen did give it a trial and from then on he controlled Ivor's finances up to and after his death. And that was twenty-six years ago.

Down Hill came into Town in June, 1926, at the Queen's Theatre, under the management of Julian Frank, Ivor playing Roddy Berwick. The author's name was announced, as in the case of *The Rat* as David L'Estrange, but everyone knew—public as well as friends—that it was by Ivor Novello and Constance Collier. It had a long cast which included Glen Byam Shaw, Master Walter Gore, D. A. Clarke-Smith, Jessie Bateman, Evelyn Roberts, Phyllis Monkman—to become a lifelong friend of Ivor's—Reginald Gardiner, Marjorie Mars and Frances Doble. Some were stars then, some just rising, some have reached the front rank since. It was a good cast, with youth predominating. That was usually Ivor's way. Produced at the Queen's Theatre, Shaftesbury Avenue, on June 16th, 1926, it transferred to the Prince's Theatre on July 26th. It ran until September 4th, ninety-three performances in all. It was definitely not another *Rat*.

Ivor had now eight parts to his credit and two plays of which he was part author. He was an established film star and also an established composer, although his music had now become subservient to his acting.

What was happening in the world of the Theatre, in which he had risen in four years, from a small-part-and-salaried artiste of £15 a week, to the possession of a contract to be partner with Frank Curzon, at a salary of £200 per week and share of the profits? That was not at all bad going; indeed, it was stupendous. Much of it had been accomplished in 1925. What was happening all around him?

The world had settled down into a new phase so far as the Theatre was concerned. The stability of the old actor-manager régime had gone. It was a shifting place now, with changing values. The old system of theatres with policies had almost gone too, but where a policy existed, success came with it. Theatres now played musical plays and followed them with drama; there was no rule or order, it just followed the life around it. Something had gone from the theatrical profession, something which had contributed so much to its true value. The barriers were breaking down; even the professionals were no longer a race apart, but were becoming just ordinary, every-day folk like their audiences. Life outside was brittle, nobody seemed to have much time, nobody seemed to care much about anything. It was now quite usual for plays to be billed to start at eight-thirty, to actually ring up about ten minutes late, to have two long intervals and to be over well before eleven. No actor-manager, none of the old school, would have tolerated that. If tradespeople had done it, they would have been prosecuted for giving short measure. It was happening because the Theatre had now really become commercial and not professionally commercial. There were some honourable exceptions but they were exceptions and not the rule. There were still some men who loved and believed in the Theatre. There was that brilliant period at the St. Martin's Theatre under Alec L. Rea when with Basil Dean (who was also producer) he presented a number of good plays with fine casts and acting. That was the highest spot in the inter-war Theatre. There was Frank Curzon, of the old school, there was C. B. Cochran and there was Gerald du Maurier.

Acting was changing too, and it was doing so because of Du Maurier. His own particular style had become the standard. His repressed, quiet manner, his lack of flamboyancy, his quick movements—they became the ideal for all young actors. But to achieve what he did Du Maurier acted all the time. The lesser lights almost gave up acting and thought they were playing in his way. Understatement and half tones were the rule, and to be vital and arresting on the stage was to be "Ham." That word had arrived. There stood a few rocks who were founded on the grand manner: Seymour Hicks, Matheson Lang, Sir John Martin Harvey, Lilian Braithwaite, Godfrey Tearle, Aubrey Smith, Madge Titheradge, Marie Tempest, Arthur Bourchier, Irene and Violet Vanbrugh, Julia Neilson and Fred Terry, though they were rarely seen in Town. But, by and large, the art of the Theatre had become as shallow, brittle and insincere as the life it mirrored. It was perhaps doing its duty, but it overdid it. It forgot that although the stage must mirror life, it must also magnify it. The microphone was already becoming a power. The day of the talkie was on the threshold. The Theatre was soon to suffer its severest competition, to fight desperately for its life. The provincial Theatre was to go into eclipse from which it is only just emerging.

But there were new names and one of those newer names was an actress of such power that at times one thought Siddons had returned. Sybil Thorndike had shown what Tragedy should be, and shown it at a music hall which played Greek tragedy in the afternoons: the Holborn Empire. She had already reached the great heights with *St. Joan*, a bare twelve months before. That was a first night nobody who saw it would ever forget: Shaw and Sybil Thorndike on the very apex of greatness.

It is as well to have a look at what was going on in 1925.

One young man of the Theatre stood out beyond the rest—Noël Coward. These were the days of success for him, when he was reaching maturity, working with a speed that amazed, showing a wit which dazzled and a versatility which was scarcely credible if it had not been seen. He seemed indeed a Titan, an Admirable Crichton of the Theatre. He and Ivor were in after-years to run parallel, but at this moment in 1925 and 1926, Noël Coward was streets ahead in achievement. He had gone on the stage young and had a tremendous technical start on Ivor. He made his début as a child in 1911, ten years before Ivor played his first part. And ten years was a priceless advantage in the learning and mastering of an art. He was away for two years out of that time, but he could afford that. He joined up in 1917 and was back in 1918, he was playing in his own play in 1920. He had been on tour, he had been to New York, he had burst into revue and first-class revue at that, both as actor, singer, author and composer in *London Calling* in 1923. In 1924 his play *The Vortex* showed everyone that here was a force to be reckoned with. And in 1926 he had gone right to the top with his performance of Lewis Dodd in *The Constant Nymph*. By then Ivor was well on the map, having covered almost as much ground as Noël Coward in a much shorter space of time, and having musical plays, films and many compositions to his credit. From that year onwards, the two may have been said to have marched together. They were friends, there was no need for rivalry, and they were so utterly different. Except for their devotion to the Theatre and their great gifts—indeed, their genius for the stage—they were as unlike in thought, manner and execution as chalk is from cheese. Noël was as sharp, clear-cut and incisive as a piece of steel. He bit, he pilloried, he knew, understood and was part of the age in which he lived. He could, and did, show it as it was. And he could do much more than that. He was the master of brevity, of meaning much and saying little, of making a few words do the work of many. His rise was rapid and studded with success. He went straight to his point.

With Ivor it was quite different. He was an incurable Romantic and remained so to his death.

Peter Noble, his first biographer, in his book *Ivor Novello* does me the honour to quote something I wrote: " The truth about Ivor Novello is that he is an incurable Romantic. And it is as well that he is incurable, for Romantics are valuable people and there are not nearly enough to go round." Mr. Noble's comment on that is: " As to his being an incurable Romantic, Macqueen-Pope is probably right, though with regard to his personal romantic life Novello is noticeably reticent. In past years the newspapers have linked his name with various of his leading ladies . . . like Benita Hume, Gladys Cooper and others. . . ."

Bless Mr. Noble's heart, but that is not what is meant by being a Romantic! The great gift of being a Romantic has nothing whatever to do with love affairs, personal or otherwise: quite the reverse. The great lovers of the world were not Romantics at all and could not have been. For being in love, having what are now called " affaires," is the antithesis of being a Romantic. That sort of thing withdraws one from life and makes for self-centred thinking. It reduces the Universe to the scope of just one other person, either temporarily or for all time. Casanova, Tristram, Romeo, Pelleas and Melisande, Paolo and Francesca, none of these were Romantics in the true meaning of the word. Their stories may have Romance but they are not Romantics. Sir Galahad, on the other hand, was a Romantic and Sir Launcelot may have been. King Arthur was undoubtedly one and so was Don Quixote, the greatest of them all. A Romantic creates a world which he considers to be better than that in which he moves. He wants everyone to have the benefit of his creation. He wants to show them that life can be magnificent and full of colour, even though it may not be happy to the outward eye. He wants, as Omar said, to grasp this sorry scheme of things entire, shatter it to bits and then rebuild it nearer heart's desire. He creates a world in which he is the prime mover, the master of Fate and he asks everyone to come and share his world with him, a world utterly unlike that outside the walls of his imagination, his play, his book or his music, wherein all shall find life as they would like it to be, as he believes it should be. The Romantic rises above the limitations imposed by everyday occurrences and makes beauty of idea, music, thought and sight. He believes in ideals, he hugs his own to his bosom. He is undeterred by failure and does not worry about success. He sets out to establish a standard and to live up to it, but to share it with others. He is always creative and always goes forward, even if his methods do not change when he has achieved his end. He always believes more in the past—as the foundation, than he does in the present—and he lets the future take care of itself. He is in the life around him but not of it. All the great Romantics were like that: Shakespeare, Betterton, Kean, Siddons, Tree, Martin Harvey, Fred Terry, Lewis Waller and countless writers, musicians, and painters too. But not Garrick, Kemble, Sheridan, Macready, Lang, Alexander or Pinero. Wilson Barrett, yes, but not Wyndham or Du Maurier. George Edwardes and Charles Frohman were Romantics to the last degree. So was old John Hollingshead who founded the Gaiety. Ivor Novello was the last—or at least the last within sight.

Being a Romantic has nothing to do with physical love or sex, it has nothing to do with being a great lover of ladies or a happily married man. It is a condition of mind like being a Bohemian, although not many Bohemians are really Romantics. The Music Hall had its Romantics and Albert Chevalier was perhaps the greatest of them. He created a type of coster who became established as reality. But the Chevalier type was the result of Romanticism—Gus Elen provided the real thing. In my humble way I am a Romantic too and I have been happily married to the same wife for just on forty years. . . . But Ivor was a great Romantic. Noël Coward, despite his magnificent *Bittersweet* and other romantic operettas, is not himself a Romantic. *Cavalcade* was reality. He is a genius—so was Ivor.

If one must make a grading, Noël Coward would be Richard Brinsley Sheridan and Ivor, Cervantes.

When Ivor was moving steadily to the front, Coward was already there. Indeed, he was the biggest thing in the Theatre with infinite appeal to the smart sophistication of the time, which he understood and which he always gave the appearance of belonging to himself, though my private belief is that he laughed at it behind its back. The sharp, staccato style, the quick gleam, the stiletto point of his plays was his own, and his sense of humour, if somewhat sardonic at times, was and is immense. Satire was in his hands a rapier blade. Coward, in short, represents modernity, while Ivor represented a firm belief in the past. There was nothing at all old-fashioned about him, except the fact that he was a Romantic. These two men understood each other and were friends, never rivals. There was room for both, for both moved in different spheres. And apart from their astounding talents, they were so entirely different in manner and outlook. Both immensely popular, the reason for it was different in either case. Their courses ran parallel in that circumscribed life of the Theatre and of the two Coward had the harder knocks, the more disappointments. But he is a fighter and always comes back for more only to win in the end. He never feared a hostile audience and he has faced them more than once or twice. No audience would have boo-ed Ivor, they just could not do it; they were too busy succumbing to that wonderful charm and picking up that heart.

In 1925 and 1926 Noël Coward stood on a pinnacle; he still does so, but then it was all new. He was regarded as the miracle of his age. He was, and is, so essentially West End—Ivor was far more universal in appeal. And yet, if Mr. Coward will allow me, a firm admirer of his talent, to say so, his best work was his film *Brief Encounter* in which he threw away the glamour, the richness and the mink and got right into the hearts of simple middle-class folk against a background not of Mayfair or romance, but ordinary teashops, railway stations and waiting-rooms. I am no film fan but I loved that film. And I am sure that Mr. Coward will one day soon show us the depths which he really has within him and of which we have been allowed only some flashes as yet. In *Brief Encounter* he showed he understood the stratum from which both he and Ivor sprang—and there is no finer stock in the world—as well as Ivor did himself.

There was at this time another great dominating figure in the Theatre, not an actor, although he had been one, but a manager, an impresario—a showman. That was C. B. Cochran, who before his end achieved knighthood. This is no place for even a brief résumé of Sir Charles's most amazing career. He has his own books and a biography written by my friend Charles Graves in that author's own comprehensive and revealing style, with all the facts presented clearly and concisely. Cochran—" Cocky " or " C.B." to all who knew him and many who did not—was pre-eminently a showman. He had done it all, been in every branch of showmanship, from fights to farces, from ballet to ballyhoo, from circuses to concerts at the Albert Hall, from spectacle to sideshows—a complete entity in himself of what is now called " Show Business." Wrestling or revue, opera bouffe, roller skating; it was all one. He handled it. Spectacular in everything he did, his failures were as vivid and resounding as his successes and almost as numerous. He was a pioneer and they have the hard way to travel. He could never stop, he could never let well alone. The creative urge in him, which in another might have expressed itself in authorship, music or painting, showed itself in the constant presentation to the public of what he thought it was best for them to have, what he believed they would like. He backed his judgment against theirs, to use the flair which he possessed in full measure in giving that many-headed hydra, the Public, the entertainment for which it ravened. Often he was right, sometimes he was wrong and very often he was just a few jumps ahead of himself, what he failed in turning into success for others at a later date. But he never failed in giving them quality, taste, and the best he could get.

Of his gifts, his genius for publicity was the greatest. He was the best publicity man of his lifetime and there is nobody to touch him now that he has gone. He impressed himself upon the public as none of his many rivals could do. His name on the bills often meant more than the array of stars printed thereon, too. In that he was unique in his time. He had many of the qualities of the great George Edwardes though he did not understand women so well. His " Young Ladies," lovely and glamorous as they were, never reached the supreme height and allure of the Gaiety Girls whom Edwardes glorified. Cochran boosted the " Young Ladies." The Gaiety Girls did it themselves by being just themselves. But the name of Cochran stood for so much. People would say " Oh, let's go to the Cochran show." That mattered more than the title. His first nights were amazing. They were packed with celebrities—a gossip-writer's and candid cameraman's paradise. P. L. Mannock, the well-known critic, once said with the greatest truth that on Cochran's first nights there were always two shows in the same theatre—one in front of and one behind the curtain. It really was so. He was his own opposition. And sometimes it turned out that the show in front of the curtain was the better and more attractive of the two.

Not only did he understand publicity but he understood Fleet Street, which is a difficult and complex place. He had many battles with the Press and he sometimes " barred " the critics from the shows, amongst them Hannen Swaffer when " Swaff " was at the height of his power. But he always made friends again and he never lost the affection, the esteem and regard of Fleet Street, who were with him to the end. You might adore C.B. and you might just as heavily dislike him, but you always held him in respect. Of all that he did, of all the vast enterprises, the great glittering shows, the multiplicity of productions, his best effort was the presentation of C. B. Cochran himself. He was his own best production. And it never failed, either, no matter what happened to the show; Charles Blake Cochran never lost prestige, or confidence. He was undaunted, he held on to the very last, his ante-penultimate musical show being his greatest success. It is pleasant to record that he leaves behind him a great memory in the history of the Theatre, in which he will always be a tremendous figure—a giant amongst mediocrity—and a legend which will not fade.

Coward and Cochran had many associations, while Ivor had none with Cochran at all in the way of business. But he had the greatest regard for his genius all the same. Noël Coward and Ivor were associated on the stage once: it was a complete and outstanding failure and will come into the saga before long. A link between Cochran and Ivor might have been productive but more likely not. For Ivor preferred being on his own, taking all the risks and responsibility. There was only one manager with whom he was happy and that was the man with whom he was linked in the last and most successful phase of his life, Tom Arnold.

And what sort of shows were holding the stages of the Theatre whilst Ivor was climbing its greasy pole with such sure grip? It was an odd crop in 1925. A remarkable man named Philip Ridgeway, a curious mixture of artiste and visionary and businessman, with a gift for publicity too, was making some extraordinary experiments and doing some extraordinary things. He is still an amazing man. He burst like a rocket on the world of the Theatre, forsaking acting for management. He rediscovered Chekov. He drew crowds of the smartest people to a little theatre in what is for West End theatre purposes the remote and outlying district of Barnes. He had that genius Komisarjevsky as his producer. Ridgeway took immense risks and got away with murder. He might annoy you but you always liked him. He is a friend of mine; he has annoyed me, but never lost my affection. In the year 1925 he brought off what was perhaps his most spectacular scoop. He got Thomas Hardy to agree to a stage version of *Tess of the D'Urbevilles* and not only to agree to it, but to see it. Hardy would not leave his beloved home at Max Gate, Dorchester. So as Mahomet would not go to the Mountain, Ridgeway went to Mahomet Hardy. He was after publicity—and he got it. He took down the entire company to Hardy's house and they performed the play in the great author's drawing-room. Hardy had told Ridgeway that no pressmen would be allowed. Ridgeway agreed. The Press were not admitted officially, but they were there—they were the "supers" in the show. Hardy approved the show and was delighted with Gwen Ffrangçon-Davies as Tess. Ridgeway got a tremendous scoop. He had oceans of ideas, some wonderful, some frankly ridiculous. He only just missed being a great magnate of the Theatre. He was in his prime in 1925. And during the Second World War this strange man showed that what he could do in the Theatre, he could also do in commerce—and he did it too. At the time of writing he wants to come back to the Theatre and I hope he achieves that ambition. The Theatre lacks excitement in these days, and Philip Ridgeway not only makes excitement but is the embodiment of it himself.

In 1925 A. E. Matthews was giving a lesson in the art of acting in a very good play which was before its time called *Beggars on Horseback*. Julian Wylie, king of pantomime and prince of revue had a revue at the Hippodrome, called *Better Days*. Later musical comedy took possession and *Mercenary Mary* was a success, with music by William B. Friedlander and Conn Conrad, with Sonnie Hale, June, A. W. Baskcomb,

Paddy Dupres, Lew Hearn and Peggy O'Neil in the cast. Evelyn Laye, Leslie Faber and Arthur Margetson were in *Betty in Mayfair* at the Adelphi, and W. H. Berry in *The Bamboula* (a bad flop) at His Majesty's. Berry had previously been in another short run, *The Blue Kitten* at the Gaiety but it was not that ripe comedian's fault, just the luck of the business. The Empire had a musical show called *Boodle* starring Jack Buchanan, whilst Cicely Courtneidge and Jack Hulbert were at the Apollo and afterwards the Shaftesbury in *By the Way*. *Charlot's Revue* was at the Prince of Wales's, with Beatrice Lillie, Gertrude Lawrence, Herbert Munden, Betty Stockfield and Peter Haddon playing in it. Daly's staged *Cleopatra*, music by Oscar Strauss, with Evelyn Laye, Alec Fraser and Jay Laurier. Evelyn Laye had also played in *Betty in Mayfair* at the Adelphi. *Clo-Clo* at the Shaftesbury had music by Lehar and Max Darewski, the former also being represented by *Frasquita* at the Prince's, with a cast including José Collins, Spencer Trevor, Ethel Baird, Thorpe Bates, Edmund Gwenn. Paul Robeson aroused interest in *The Emperor Jones* at the Ambassadors'. Gertrude Elliott and Jean Forbes-Robertson, mother and daughter, with Godfrey Tearle and Leslie Faber, were playing in *Dancing Mothers* at the Queen's. That famous partnership between Tom Walls and Ralph Lynn was in full swing at the Aldwych with Ben Travers's *The Cuckoo in the Nest*, and the very successful *Ghost Train* by Arnold Ridley had opened at the St. Martin's. Noël Coward had two straight plays in the year, *Fallen Angels* at the Globe, with Edna Best, Tallulah Bankhead and Austin Trevor, and *Hay Fever* at the Ambassadors'—transferring to the Criterion—with a fine cast including Marie Tempest, Graham Browne, Robert Andrews, Hilda Moore and Minnie Rayner. Both were successes. John Barrymore was giving a magnificent performance of *Hamlet* at the Haymarket, with Constance Collier as the Queen and Fay Compton as the ideal Ophelia, and Courtney Thorpe as the Ghost. A play by Michael Arlen was produced at the Adelphi, *The Green Hat*, the cast of which included Tallulah Bankhead, Beatrix Lehmann, Frederick Leister, Eric Maturin and Norman McKinnel. Madge Titheradge and Owen Nares were in *Grounds for Divorce* at the St. James's, and also at that theatre in the same year was Frederick Lonsdale's *The Last of Mrs. Cheyney* with Gerald du Maurier, Dawson Milward, Ronald Squire, Mabel Sealby,

Dame May Whitty, Ellis Jeffreys and Gladys Cooper. Henry Ainley appeared in *The Moon and Sixpence*, an adaptation of Somerset Maugham's story at the New Theatre. Sean O'Casey's play *Juno and the Paycock* attracted attention at the Royalty. There was a musical play of Jean Gilbert's at the Gaiety, *Katja the Dancer*, with Bobbie Comber, Ivy Tresmand, Gene Gerrard and Lilian Davies. Nigel Playfair—to achieve knighthood—was established at the Lyric, Hammersmith, where he was presenting *Lionel and Clarissa*. The Lyceum had a monster show called *The London Revue*, starring Pearl White, a queen of thrilling serials on the silent films, and also in the show were George Carney, Billy Danvers, Ivan Samson, that fine singer Jose Fearon and the really excellent comedian from Australia who died too soon and who made a big hit, John Kirby.

Cochran's revue at the London Pavilion was *On With the Show*, with music by Noël Coward and Philip Braham and Delysia in the cast. In the same year Cochran also had *Still Dancing* there, with Delysia, Massine, Hermione Baddeley and Douglas Byng. Another very successful revue was Archie de Bear's *The Punch Bowl* which played at the Duke of York's, His Majesty's and the Vaudeville in turn. *Rain*, dramatized from Somerset Maugham's story, " Miss Thompson " was at the Garrick with Olga Lindo, Marda Vanne and Malcolm Keen in the leading parts. Shakespeare at the Haymarket also found himself in less usual surroundings: at the Empire, where Sybil Thorndike staged a brave and excellent production of *Henry VIII* with herself as Queen Katherine, Lyall Swete as Wolsey, Norman V. Norman as Henry VIII, Lewis Casson, Arthur Wontner and O. B. Clarence. On the programme against the part of " First Serving Man " was the name Laurence Olivier. There was a thriller by J. Jefferson Farjeon produced at the New: *No. 17* in which Nicholas Hannen, Nora Swinburne and Leon M. Lion appeared. Lyn Harding, Haidee Wright, Madeline Seymour and George Curzon were in *Ordeal* at the Strand. A play by John Galsworthy, *The Show*, ran for only one month at the St. Martin's, but Frederick Lonsdale's *Spring Cleaning* with Cecily Byrne, Edna Best, Ronald Squire, Ian Hunter and Cathleen Nesbitt was a success at the same theatre. Revue held sway at the London Palladium where Albert de Courville produced *Sky High*, in which were George Robey, Marie Blanche, Nellie Wallace, Nattova and Myrio (wonderful dancers), and

Lorna and Toots Pounds. Leslie Henson with Heather Thatcher was at the Winter Garden Theatre in George Gershwin's *Tell Me More*—musical comedy, of course.

The two enormous successes of the year were *No, No, Nanette* and *Rose Marie*. *No, No, Nanette* at the Palace Theatre, starred Binnie Hale, George Grossmith, Joseph Coyne, Gracie Leigh, Irene Browne, Seymour Beard and Joan Barry. The music was by Vincent Youmans and, as everyone knows, the show made history. *Rose Marie* at Drury Lane, the first of Sir Alfred Butt's big American importations, had a glittering cast including Edith Day, Derek Oldham, Clarice Hardwicke and Billy Merson, the little comedian from the music halls who did what few comedians had ever succeeded in doing, making a tremendous success in the theatre which has killed so many comics. His *Hard Boiled Herman* was a *tour de force*, but it was also his downfall. It went to his head, he forsook his old methods, discarded the red wig and eccentric make-up which had been his foundation, went what he called " West End " and lost all his money in actor-management. But until *Oklahoma*, *Rose Marie* was Drury Lane's longest run.

That was the Theatre, those were the people, those were the types of play, composers and authors Ivor now stood in line with, after his very short journey into Theatreland, he who already had a contract for actor-management in the West End in his pocket.

And just now the stage and acting were both on top. He had done very little composing at the period, and his mother was not too pleased about that. But then Mam was a very busy person, dashing all over the place, like a piece of human quicksilver, impetuous, reckless, seeing everything in a mist of musical achievement, quite sure that nothing else mattered in the world but Music—and chiefly the importance and complete necessity of learning to sing. Her husband must have often wondered at his family. This easy-going, inherently lazy man, with a love for sport, must have been very bewildered at times. There must have been flashes of Celtic temperament surging through the comfortable indolence for Mr. Davies was first and foremost a Welshman and all that it means. But life went on at 11 Aldwych and elsewhere. That flat, now famous, was always being redecorated and was becoming more and more one of the important places in the world of the Theatre, the rendezvous of artistes of all kinds and a mecca for celebrities. Later—and probably then—when someone in the Theatre mentioned "The Flat" it was always 11 Aldwych they meant.

It was possibly those gatherings at the flat which gave Ivor the idea of founding a club. That club was the Fifty-Fifty Club in Wardour Street and Constance Collier was with him in the founding. His inherent good nature made him think of the less successful of his brother and sister players, the rank and file who had not had his good fortune, whose salaries were small and very intermittent, and who had little to brighten their lives in those 1920s when prices were rising and things were not too good in the "Profession." The Fifty-Fifty was founded so that such folk should have somewhere to go after the show, somewhere to have something to eat and drink at a price which they could afford and meet other people like themselves—and partake in what was really a free-for-all party, with entertainment provided by the members of the club—and there was plenty of talent. Every night Ivor was there, receiving, making friends, welcoming and playing the piano. Another of the founders was Henry Kendall. There was a nice orchestra and it was very cheery indeed. Talent overflowed, a good many things which audiences afterwards paid money to see and applaud—things like Douglas Byng's wonderful Pantomime Burlesque—first saw the light of day in the Fifty-Fifty. It became famous. And it paid the penalty. The smart people began to ask for a table as a favour; and it was difficult to refuse. By degrees the place was swamped by the folk for whom it was not intended and the needy, smaller fry, for whom it had been invented, were frozen out. It had been truly Bohemian in inception in the best sense of Bohemia: complete equality such as only the theatrical profession understands in that queer freemasonry which used to exist in the Theatre but is not so prevalent to-day. When Society began to enter the doors, Bohemia left, if not by the window, at least by every other exit. And so the Fifty-Fifty, which Ivor had loved and to which his friends had come so loyally, night after night to assist him, just degenerated into a very ordinary night club—and the Fifty Fifty of Ivor Novello died out. But it was great while it lasted and gave Ivor much joy.

Half-way through the 'twenties he was enjoying life to the full. But then, he always did that. The world to him was always a new toy to a child. And although David Ivor Davies grew with the years, Ivor Novello kept the child in his heart always.

CHAPTER TWELVE

FILM SUCCESSES: BUT BACK TO THE THEATRE

THE tide of Ivor's personal success swept on. He was the most popular man now in the theatrical profession and he remained so till the end of his life. At this time his professional life was shared between films and stage: there was not much music. He had made a film version of *The Rat*—with Mae Marsh and Isabel Jeans—a Balcon picture with Graham Cutts as director. Its film success equalled its stage success. But there was never the same appeal for Ivor in the studio as there was in the Theatre. He knew quite well that the Theatre was his kingdom and he used the films as a means to further that end. The money he made was to be the foundation for his ambition to be the complete actor-manager, with his own capital in his own shows. That was right in the forefront of his mind and the primary objective throughout his film career.

On December 30th, 1926, he entered into a contract with Gainsborough Pictures Limited to act in a series of three films to be made between January 1st, 1927, and September 1st, 1927. He was to receive £100 a day when actually in the studio or on location for work, and those days were not to exceed four in each week when he was fulfilling a stage engagement. But when not so engaged he was to work, if required, six days a week, Sundays excluded, and then he received £500 for the week instead of the £100 a day. He had the right to disapprove of the stories.

There were many conditions in the contract. In one he bound himself at all times to comport himself with both dignity and decency in private and professional life and not to commit or permit any act or thing which would bring him into notoriety or contempt or disgrace. If that happened, the Company could terminate the agreement. Another laid it down that he was to be the sole star artiste unless the Company decided to employ the services of a foreign star also, in which case Ivor would be co-star, though in the billing his name was to come first. And there was also a clause which guaranteed that his total salary from each of the three films should be not less than £2,000.

There was another contract between him and Gainsborough Pictures on April 22nd, 1927, to apply to films produced between January 1st, 1928, and December 31st, 1928. Again there were to be three films, although by mutual consent the number might be increased to four. This time Ivor was to receive 10 per cent. of all moneys the company received from the exploitations of such films and on account he was to receive £3,000 by weekly instalments of £600 each. Every such sum thus paid was of course to be deducted from the amount due in final settlement. He was to work twenty days on each film and these days were to be spread over five weeks. If he had to work more than the twenty days, then he was to receive £150 per day for each day in excess of the twenty. He bound himself not to work for any other cinematographic firm or even to be interested therein. Again, he was to be sole star, except under the conditions of the previous contract and his name was to appear before the title of the film. In the event of co-starring, his name was to come first in this country, Ireland and the Channel Isles, but elsewhere if necessary, that of the foreign star might precede his at the Company's discretion. He was to receive a minimum of £3,000 in respect of each film.

There was a separate contract entered into between Ivor and Constance L'Estrange (Constance Collier) and Gainsborough Pictures Limited on January 3rd, 1927, in respect of the cinema rights of their play *Down Hill.* Gainsborough Pictures got the sole film rights in this for £1,500, £500 down on the signing of the agreement and the balance on an agreed date. Gainsborough's had the right to adapt the story for film purposes subject to the author's permission, such permission not to be unreasonably withheld. If Gainsborough's failed to make and exhibit the film within two years from the date of the agreement, then the authors could claim it back, subject to repayment of the money they had received. The authors' names were, by the way, to be displayed immediately following the title and printed in type easily readable by the public.

There was yet another Gainsborough contract for Ivor which covered the period January 1st to December 31st, 1929. Again the films were to be three—or four by mutual consent. Ivor was to receive 10 per cent. of the takings and on account of that figure £150 for each day he was "called" and, if on location outside this country, £150 per day for each day on which he worked; and there was a minimum of £450 per week in that respect. He was also to have first-class travelling and hotel expenses. There was also a guarantee that the amount he should receive should not be less than £12,000 in respect of three pictures or £16,000 in respect of four. Otherwise the clauses and conditions were much the same as the rest.

What makes this latter contract of importance is the fact that whilst the other three were between Ivor Novello of 11 Aldwych, W.C.2. and Gainsborough Pictures Limited, this one, in respect of the year 1929, entered into on November 10th, 1927, was between Gainsborough Pictures Limited and Ivor Novello Productions Limited, of 72 Avenue Chambers, Southampton Row, W.C., and Ivor Novello of 11 Aldwych. Ivor had already started dividing his interests and activities up into a series of Limited Companies, which was his habit for the rest of his life—and a very wise precaution too.

In my view, as one who has had the making and handling of many such contracts, congratulations are due to Gainsborough Pictures on the fairness and the clarity of theirs. It is not always so, in the film world. But then, Ivor always had a very clear mind in such matters, because of the guidance of David Ivor Davies. He was not primarily interested in contracts but he knew that they had to be made. He was never complex in these matters and neither were Gainsborough, which was probably why they—through Michael Balcon (now very deservedly a knight)—and Ivor got on so well and so successfully together.

It is my view, also—although I may be wrong—that the film career of Ivor is not of vital importance in his life story. It was short and it was extremely profitable. As stated, it was to him a means towards an end and he achieved that end. I do not think it necessary, therefore, to give much space to descriptions of those pictures and their making. They were silent films and now a thing of the past. They will not keep their place before the public—for obvious reasons—as will his plays and his music. A list of the films should suffice. There was, as mentioned, *The Rat*, *The Triumph of The Rat*, *The Lodger*, directed by Alfred Hitchcock, *Down Hill*, *The Vortex* (Noël Coward's great success in screen form, with Ivor playing Nicky), and then the screen version of *The Constant Nymph*. Adrian Brunel had joined

Balcon and was working on these pictures. In the case of *The Constant Nymph* Basil Dean joined the outfit and supervised the whole thing. He had been responsible for the historic stage production and had indeed collaborated with Margaret Kennedy in the making of the play from her novel.

But the talkies had arrived and further pictures in which Ivor played—*The Gallant Hussar*, *The Return of The Rat* and *South Sea Bubble*—suffered therefrom.

However, Ivor had made money—a lot of money. He was desperately anxious to get back to the Theatre, wanting to write his own plays, act in them and present them himself. That was not going to be easy because of his film contracts, but Michael Balcon met him generously. Ivor always spoke of Balcon in the very highest and most affectionate terms, and a friendship between the two endured. Ivor grew a moustache for *South Sea Bubble* and I remember him arriving with Mam for a first night at the Duke of York's Theatre. I remember the gasp which came from the throng of curious people who crowd the pavement outside playhouses, where first nights are being held to gaze at the celebrities and nonentities who frequent them. Here was Ivor—and they all called him " Ivor "—in a moustache! There was quite a riot and he and Mam were pushed about a good deal as they came in. He was quite used to it and gave them all that smile of his, and Mam seemed to enjoy it too. Once inside, there was another rush at him, this time from first-nighter friends " Ivor, darling, what have you done to yourself ? " —" My dear, a moustache—Ivor in a moustache—just fancy "— —" Oh, I think it's sweet." Those who know first nights will be able to hear and to visualize it. Those who are not first-nighters should not have much difficulty either. The cameramen present —there were several—had a great time, and lots of people who knew Ivor and just as many who did not crowded round to get into the picture too. Ivor explained the reason for the hirsute upper-lip adornment and vanished into the stalls, followed by a crowd of admiring, exclaiming friends. He was never one of those who hung about in the vestibule. The general concensus of opinion was that the moustache was splendid—some, I think, said it was twee. Personally, I did not agree.

But Ivor was coming back into the Theatre. He had, during his film career, some stage parts as well. He had not yet been so lucky on stage as on the screen. True *The Rat* was most successful, but *Down Hill* was only moderately so. *Old Heidelberg* and *The Firebrand* had failed but he personally had saved *Iris*. He now had far more confidence and far more technique. He was pretty sure of himself and he never lacked belief in his powers, although on the whole he was extremely aware of his own limitations. But he was now a star and he had ideas surging in that handsome head, born of the vivid Celtic imagination fanned by his own Romantic viewpoint. But he was not going into Romance in costume. He was going to be of To-day and one can be a Romantic as easily that way as any other.

From the stage point of view, he had been at the Duke of York's Theatre in an ill-fated production of *Liliom* in 1926. This was a play by the distinguished Hungarian dramatist Ferenc Molnar, who has never been lucky in this country. This particular adaptation was by Osmond Shillingford and Anthony Ellis. A previous version of the same play, called *The Daisy*, had been seen before at the Kingsway Theatre in 1920. It had been done also in New York, at the Garrick, in 1921, but that was a different version by another man. It has been stated that the Duke of York's venture was solely Ivor's affair. It was not. It was presented by the remarkable Philip Ridgeway, always attracted by something which was out-of-the-way. But Ivor was also attracted to the play and the part, and he offered to go in with Ridgeway fifty-fifty and did. He also wanted to be " produced " by Komisarjevsky, who was acting in that capacity for Ridgeway. It had quite a remarkable cast, which included Stella Freeman, Douglas Burbidge, Violet Farebrother, Beryl Harrison, William Kendall, Ben Webster, Douglas Jefferies, Marjorie Mars and Fay Compton. Against the part of Ficsur—a minor role—in the programme, is the name Charles Laughton. That was a very early part of the great actor's. He had taken the Gold Medal at the Royal Academy of Dramatic Art and Ridgeway, who is a great talent spotter, gave him his first job at the Barnes Theatre in 1926, in *The Government Inspector*. Laughton played at Barnes in *The Cherry Orchard* and *The Three Sisters* and he came to the Duke of York's in the same year, 1926. It was really his first West End part in a new play although he had been at the Gaiety during the very brief transfer of *The Government Inspector* to that most unsuitable environment.

There is a good story about that show. Two ladies who saw it at a matinée were horrified. They assailed the box office, they demanded to see Philip Ridgeway. They told him they had been coming to the Gaiety for years and had seen all the great George Edwardes's shows. Never had they seen anything so disgraceful as *The Government Inspector*. Mr. Ridgeway tried the soft answer. Perhaps, he said, they had bad seats? Would they do him the honour of accepting two good stalls for an evening performance and thereby give it another trial? They were more furious than before. " What! " they cried, " See that dreadful thing again? Not if you gave us £2,000 each." They went out in high dudgeon. Yet the cast was excellent and included Claude Rains, who was, like Laughton, getting £3 a week and a percentage, though it is doubtful if that brought him in anything extra.

But when Ivor saw the salary list for *Liliom* he said he thought Laughton ought to have a little more; he was such a good actor. Ridgeway pointed out that he was giving the young man, straight from R.A.D.A., his first chance and that salaries should be based not only on apparent talent but on experience as well. Fay Compton upheld him in that, he reports (and they were right), so Ivor agreed in the end.

The play opened at the Duke of York's on December 23rd, 1926. It had a very bad first night. A novel effect which had been arranged for the Heaven Scene went all wrong. The idea of the supernatural, the idea of the ante-room to Heaven did not grip the audience. They did not understand it. Such things are always difficult. Despite some brilliant acting, especially by Fay Compton and an extremely good performance by Ivor in the title role, it was a failure. Business became very bad indeed. Naturally, the management " papered " the house, that is to say, gave away complimentary seats and asked their friends to come to the box office, where free seats would be available.

Madam Melnotte was all against this. Despite her familiarity with " flops " she always got very cross when involved in one. She did so on this occasion. She was on " sharing terms." One night, when only a few pounds in cash had been taken and there was quite a crowd of guests in the vestibule, she suddenly gave orders that the box office was to be closed. It was nearly half an hour before the curtain was timed to go up. The box office man and her own manager—I was not manager then—pleaded with her. Ridgeway tried his considerable powers of persuasion It was pointed out that very important people had been invited:

how would they get their seats, what was to be done about them? " I don't care," stormed Madam. " I won't have all this crowd of awful people with no heels on their boots trampling over my carpets. Close that box office, I say." And closed it was. Infuriated people, arriving afterwards, protested, argued, hammered on the window, but unavailingly. Madam stood there like a thunder cloud, with lightning starting from her eyes. She had been very unpleasant—she had got her own way. It was enough. *Liliom* had a very short run indeed. Everyone lost money, including Madam, the custodian of the carpets. *Liliom* has since been a success but not under that name. Those two genii of the Theatre, Oscar Hammerstein II and Richard Rodgers, turned it into a musical play, humanized it and brought their craftsmanship to bear. The result was *Carousel* which ran for over a year at Theatre Royal, Drury Lane.

Truly, the Theatre was not treating Ivor very well. But he did not despair. He was going to win. He revived *The Rat* at the Prince of Wales's, in February, 1927, and it ran for a short time. And then, in the November of 1927, he went into Noël Coward's play *Sirocco* at Daly's Theatre. That was destined to make history. *Sirocco*'s whole career, as became its name, was full of storm. Noël's friends were always talking about it and many of them believed it a masterpiece. The result is not likely to be forgotten.

I was mixed up in the *Sirocco* affair myself, and believe me, a hotter wind never blew from the desert than that particular play produced during its brief but violent career. I had joined Melnotte—Madam as she was always called—as manager of her theatre, the Duke of York's. I was regarded as a complete fool for so doing. Before I went there, managers had come and gone with monotonous regularity, almost as quickly as did the plays. For Violet Melnotte was a law unto herself, with no syndicate in support. She had her own method of choosing plays. If it had about eight characters—no more—and one set of scenery, she would chance it. The merit of the play had nothing to do with it at all. The expense of production was her test. She had plenty of good tenants and she fought with all of them. She was the great Obstructionist of the Theatre. At one time, just before I took over, she had had twelve plays in the Duke of York's in as many months. They would come in, open on sharing terms, at once fall below the amount of money required for continuance of the run, according to contract, and so at the end of the first fortnight's run she would give the presenter notice. He had to run two weeks longer and out he got on a Saturday night and she brought in just such another on the following Monday morning.

Some of her managers lasted a short while, some did not last one week. I think the record in-and-out of a manager was two nights. So things were in a pretty bad way. I knew her son very well, Frank Wyatt. Her husband was Frank Wyatt, Snr., a charming and clever man, who had created the part of the Duke of Plaza-Toro in *The Gondoliers.* But he could not control her. Frank Wyatt the son was on the staff of the Duke of York's and completely under his redoubtable mother's thumb. It was not his fault. He was easygoing and very handsome. The two famous Misses Gunning were Wyatt ancestresses; Madam adopted them as her own although they had nothing at all to do with her. Frank was not very fond of work. In the words of the poem, he found his greatest comfort in an inn—to put it nicely. Had he been allowed to stand on his own feet it might have been a different story. He made efforts, becoming actor at one time and not a bad one; but Madam always overcame him. She was a tremendously strong character, certainly far too powerful for him. And if she loved anything in this world, she loved Frank. So he figured on the programme as "Representative," though of whom or of what was never discovered. He received a weekly salary for this—not a large sum—and he usually had it brought to him on Friday mornings in the Long Bar of the Queen's Hotel, Leicester Square, where he partook of his morning draft. I had known him for years and from time to time I had met his mother.

One day Frank came to see me with a concrete proposal from her. The theatre wanted pulling together—it did indeed . . . would I take on the job? I made all sorts of difficulties. I had interviews and showed no keenness at all. In fact I was not too keen, but then I was not afraid. I once served Sir George Dance for many years, with him all day, too. After that nothing has really scared me, not even two world wars and a very intimate acquaintance with them. And further back in this book I said that I am a Romantic. I showed it then. I took the job. I have always been one of the stupid people who go in for lost causes, who espouse the weaker side, even when I do not believe in it.

At right: Juvenile lead in *Symphony in Two Flats*

Above: Ivor in a pensive part in *Symphony in Two Flats*

An interesting group: Edna Best, Robert Andrews, Zena Dare and Fay Compton with Ivor in his dressing-room at the Globe Theatre

At right: Ivor, disguised as "Prince Meilung" in *Careless Rapture.* He appeared in the programme as David Davies, his real name

Below: Ivor and Dorothy Dickson in the same show

Also from *Careless Rapture* is the picture on the right of Dorothy Dickson and Walter Crisham

Had I lived in the reign of Charles I, I should certainly have been a Cavalier, although all my instincts and sentiment would have been with Parliament. Here was a job in which practically everyone had failed. That was the job for me. I was in charge of the publicity at the London Palladium at the time. I threw it up and went to the Duke of York's. I had an idea I could do something for that odd theatre: for one thing, I remembered the great Charles Frohman and my joy and pride in him when he was there. I believed I knew the secret. It seemed to me that it was not a job of managing a theatre at all, but of managing Madam. I was dead right. I found that I could and did manage her. I have always had a way with difficult ladies, especially with elderly ones. After a while when she had tried all her tricks to break me as she had broken the others and had found them rebound on to herself, she even came to trust me, which is perhaps the greatest compliment I have ever been paid, for she trusted nobody else. She was even, at times, a little afraid of me. Eventually she sold the Duke of York's—Hannen Swaffer said she sold it because she could not sack me—and I remained on. Our association lasted until her death. If ever she was in trouble, she sent for me. I was one of the very few people to whom she ever gave a present. I have it yet as a curiosity: it is a gold and pearl stud for an evening shirt. In those days we wore three studs, but she gave me only one. That was typical.

But this is not my story. I have to intrude because all this has a bearing on *Sirocco*. Before my advent, just before, Madam had arranged with Basil Dean to present some plays at the Duke of York's and the implication was that they were to be by Noël Coward. I took over at the end of a pretty bad play and had to see it off the premises. I hardly remember the title now—it was something to do with divorce—but in the cast was a valued friend of mine, Charles Brown, a pillar of the old Gaiety, a man of infinite charm and talent who lived in the States, but who would come over here for a holiday and, if possible, play a part. This was one of them. Charles Brown is still in America and he flourishes exceedingly. I am glad to say we keep our link and correspond with great regularity. America has not touched Charles Brown. He is still England—and Edwardian England—at its best, as becomes an Old Carthusian and an Old Gaiety boy.

We began to prepare for the first of the Noël Coward sequence.

I was not only managing the Theatre but in charge of publicity, too. I always doubled those roles. I knew Dean well, and his stage manager, Wilson Blake, was an old friend who had served and suffered with me under George Dance. So we got on well. His manager was Guy Charles, also well known to me. The cast was excellent. It included Pauline Newton, Marda Vanne, George Relph, Nina Boucicault, Henrietta Watson, Helen Spencer, Madge Titheradge, Arthur Margetson, Tom Woods and George Curzon. A perfect cast. The title of the play was *Home Chat*. I read it and did not believe in it. To be quite honest, I doubt if anybody did. I may be doing him an injustice, but I rather doubt if Mr. Coward really believed very much in it either. At the dress rehearsal Mr. Dean expressed his verdict on the play in language more forcible than polite. But Coward's star was in the ascendant and the cast was magnificent.

We opened with our fingers crossed, on the night of October 25th, 1927. It was no good. It was superbly played and perfectly produced but it was just no good. It was booed. There was quite an uproar. Coward faced the music, as he always does. But they booed on. A leading dramatic critic of the day got embroiled with a section of the booers—who were not confined to the gallery—and they openly expressed their intention of lynching him. I pushed him into the Royal Room, out of sight, and placated the angry crowd. Still vowing vengeance the booers left. I had also the representatives of the ticket agencies—the " Libraries " or the " Trade " as they are called in the Theatre—in that Royal Room, according to custom. We were to try and do a bit of business over the show and it was my job to endeavour to get them to buy up blocks of seats. And believe it or not, with the boos still ringing in their ears, I got them to give me what is popularly known as a "guarantee" (though why so called is their secret) to the extent of £400 worth of seats per week for four weeks. They had always been good friends of mine but we were both gambling on the same thing; we were not altruistic. We were gambling on the name of Madge Titheradge—and we were right. The Trade sold their last ticket and got out of their liability on the last night of the run, which was on Saturday, November 24th—the thirty-eighth performance.

And that dramatic critic saw all the mysteries of the art of " doing a deal "—the only one to do so. He admitted it had completely mystified him and made his senses reel. One day somewhere else I will take pleasure in describing that remarkable rite, which like most things in the Theatre has changed today almost completely.

Now *Home Chat* was, by previous arrangement, to be succeeded by *Sirocco*. I had read *Sirocco* and in my view—and I can only speak personally—it was no better than *Home Chat*. Indeed, I thought it worse. But Madam Melnotte did not agree, for the reason that Ivor Novello was to be in the cast. That was a pretty good reason but still I did not agree. All through the rehearsals Madam had pursued her usual policy of infuriating her partner-tenants. The show was being done on sharing terms (that is, a percentage of takings to the producers—the larger share—and the balance to the theatre proprietor). Basil Dean, never the most patient of men, and in this instance nobody could blame him, was chafing at the management. It took me all my time to keep the peace. I was now chiefly concerned in seeing if that contract—which was a very loose one—could be broken and so enable us to get out of sharing in *Sirocco*. I decided not to intervene when clashes came, to let Melnotte do her worst and so further upset Basil Dean. I knew that he had had enough and was negotiating elsewhere and I knew that he could take the show to Daly's—no longer the Daly's of old—which wanted an attraction. But I also knew that to try and impose my idea on Melnotte would be to make her decide that at all costs *Sirocco* must be held. So, on the morning after the first night of *Home Chat* I went up to her office on the gallery level and began praising her perspicacity. I told her how right she had been when, the previous week she had said that we must get out of this arrangement and not do *Sirocco*. She had said nothing of the kind, but I knew her. I made her think it was all her own idea. She knew by this time that it was a very doubtful proposition. I played my cards with great care. My little gamble came off. Then I told her what I knew about Daly's. There is a kind of bush telegraph in the world of the Theatre—nothing is secret. Policies may be hatched behind closed doors, deals may be done with nobody but the two dealers within sight or apparently hearing, but within a few hours it is public property. And I had that link with Daly's too. I got Madam to agree to smash that agreement and to do it gladly.

Consequently, a little later when Dean came round prepared for a storm to break his news and his contract, he found a charming lady, all smiles, who could not have been better pleased, who told him a few home truths and who made her own disclosure to him—that she had arranged for a musical play to come in forthwith—an arrangement I had made that very morning, and which turned out quite a success.

Sirocco had rehearsed on the stage at the Duke of York's for a day or two and I had watched it. I had also chatted with Ivor Novello and with Frances Doble, who is a family connection of mine. But they vanished to Daly's.

It was produced at Daly's Theatre on November 24th, 1927. That first night has been written about often. In the cast of the ill-fated show were Ada King, Margaret Watson, Helen Ferrers, Blyth Daly, Frances Doble, Ivor Novello (whose character was called " Sirio Marson "), Aubrey Mather, David Hawthorne, Tony de Lungo, Margery Gabain, Doris Garrick, Arturo Gomez, George Coulouris, Mario Mariani and Elizabeth Vaughan.

There is little to add to the thousands of words already written about the play. It was one of those inexplicable nights in the Theatre when everything seems to be wrong. There was an air of unrest from the time the audience entered. There was never a moment when they were still. There was a rising crescendo of disapproval which, at curtain fall, led to one of the most amazing demonstrations of disfavour which has greeted any play in recent times. *One Night in Rome* at the Garrick and a night at the Shaftesbury before the Second World War came near it, but there were reasons on those occasions. At the Shaftesbury stink and smoke bombs were flung because the leading actor was said to be a Nazi. But there was no reason of that kind, or of any kind, at Daly's on *Sirocco* night. Yet these things can and do happen in that mad, unpredictable place which is the Theatre. The verdict became perfectly apparent quite early on and it was clear what was to come, during the second act when the outbreak became all too audible. One could only feel sorry for the cast and also for the author. *Sirocco* was not as bad as the awful ordeal it provoked. It was not by any means good, but worse plays have been treated more gently. A foreigner suddenly entering Daly's might have been pardoned for thinking a bloody revolution had broken out, that heads, crowns and empires were about to fall. Not even the riots of the eighteenth century at Drury Lane, Covent Garden and the Haymarket were more appalling, except that they often caused bloodshed. For the matter of that, so did *Sirocco*. I saw the play from the back of the upper circle. At the end, after the unfortunate spectacle of poor Frances Doble, who, by some extraordinary bad judgment back stage, came on to make a speech of thanks when the tears were pouring down her face as she stammered out that it was the happiest night of her life—there was real pandemonium. And there were plenty of free fights going on all round me, from people who were out for trouble and those who resented it. One man just by me, engaged in fisticuffs, got a lovely punch on the nose, which bled profusely. Once again, Noël Coward had the courage to face his massed and violent critics. It seemed as if he was in peril of his life. But he did it. It was one of the worst first nights I have ever seen. The most unperturbed person in the whole house was Ivor. He had, by reason of the play, to speak a very unfortunate exit line at the end of the show. It was the final straw. But how he stood there, listening to the grim, threatening din, which had a real note of menace, calm and unruffled and with even a smile. Bless you, they were not booing him! And he probably knew it. In fact, I am sure he did. Nevertheless, it was one of his worst evenings in the Theatre for all that and one he never had to face again.

But I went back and reported to Madam. She was overjoyed. She said she would mark the occasion. She considered she had had a lucky escape. Indeed she had, for *Sirocco* would have done more harm to her prized but threadbare carpets than ever did *Liliom*. She said she would send Basil Dean and Noël Coward a telegram thanking them for taking the play away from her and sign it " Yours delightedly, Violet Melnotte." She did indeed send such a telegram but either through carelessness or a last moment of repentance, she signed it " Yours delightfully, Violet Melnotte." Which was not the same thing at all.

Sirocco was withdrawn on December 17th. It ran for twenty-eight performances—ten less than *Home Chat*. Noël Coward was having a real bad luck patch, such as most people experience if they work in the Theatre for any length of time. He survived and surmounted it. He did a revue for C. B. Cochran which was an immense success. *Sirocco* was forgiven if not forgotten. That was what the Theatre was doing for Coward and Novello in the year 1927.

But both Coward and Novello remained true to it. Ivor had made up his mind, and he was more certain now than ever, that his future lay under his own banner.

Already much had happened in his life. He had conceived an ambition and he was in course of carrying it out. That ambition was to have a fortune of £100,000 invested in Consols. He had begun the accumulation in 1926 with the purchase of 7,000, which at 55 7/8th cost him £3,924 13*s.* 6*d.* That was in the January. By March of the same year he had invested in a further 3,000 and in the April another 1,000. His outlay on the whole 11,000 amounted to £6,119 7*s.* That was where the film money was going. He added nothing until 1932 when he bought 6,000 more. As the years went by he bought and bought these gilt-edged if depressed securities. He reached that sum of his ambitions in 1945, when a final purchase of 4,000 on July 23rd sent the figure up to a holding of 100,000. The Consols were rising in value from the time when he had first started to buy. In 1926 he had bought at 55 7/8th, then at 54¾. In 1932 they stood at 70 5/8th and they varied from then on in the seventies. In 1935 they were up to 84¾, but went down again in the late 1930s to as low as 70 11/16th, rising again to 82 1/8th in 1941. When in 1942 he bought 2,000 they were at 83 1/16th. His last purchase was at 83 7/16th in July, 1945, when he bought 4,000. Their cash value was £76,161 8*s.* 2*d.* Their face value the desired sum of £100,000. On August 29th, 1945, he sold the lot at 88¾, realizing £88,750.

That was David Ivor Davies. But it must be remembered that Fred Allen was there to advise as well, through nearly all that time.

There are some interesting income figures, too, for the period. During the year 1927–28 he had earned £11,618 and paid £1,351 in tax. During 1928–29 he earned £15,460 and paid £1,880 in income tax. Those figures represent success—and the cost of living was considerably less then—and the income tax can be seen from the quotation.

As the story proceeds, income figures will be given, for they are the visible index of his amazing progress, though his continually growing popularity and power of attraction cannot be assessed at all. There are remarkable fluctuations at times, but always with a reason. It was *The Rat* which enabled him to buy his first Consols. Once he was tempted to sell out, as will be shown hereafter, but wise Fred Allen prevented him from so doing. That was in 1931. Out of the profit on the sale of the Consols Ivor bought his Jamaican home and, out of other capital, annuities to the extent of £37,500. He said he did not want to have to go on the King George Pension Fund in his old age (instead of that he left it thousands) nor to be tempted into wild theatrical gambles. He never was. That annuity explained why he did not leave the large amount of money so many people expected. He had made over a quarter of a million all right. But £37,500 died with him. That was a nice profit to the companies, for he only held those annuities for a few years.

Though it was David Ivor Davies of Cardiff who had persuaded Ivor Novello to be so cautious and avoid the great extravagance with which Ivor was so often—and so entirely wrongly—credited, or debited (as you please to regard it), David Ivor Davies had now no legal standing at all. In the eyes of the law he was dead. On January 13th, 1927, he changed his name by Deed Poll from David Ivor Davies to Ivor Novello. So Ivor Novello, whom David Ivor Davies had created with such skill, now took the field entirely, and David Ivor Davies became a mere memory and a shadow in the background, with no right to sign the name and no right to anything. Nevertheless he remained the power behind the throne and he came to the rescue on many occasions. He was always there when wanted, legal or not. In the year 1926 Ivor had become a Life Member of the Shakespeare Memorial Theatre. The number of his card was 452. He was always very proud of it. Later we shall meet him in his Shakespearean wanderings and learn something about his views on the Bard, which will probably be quite illuminating.

There was another ambition biting him, too. He wanted to become a classical actor, a famous classical actor. That ambition he was never allowed to realize. That was impossible. But he never quite believed he could not do it. The temptation was always there to have a try. And he had one brave shot at it anyway. Nor did he fall very short of the mark. But his personality and great gifts were not of the classical kind—and were none the worse for that. There are many classical actors: there was only one Ivor Novello.

But another precious possession came to Ivor about this time and he bought it with his own earnings. All that he had, he acquired himself by his own labour. That was his country home, " Redroofs, " which he loved so much. He bought that on November 11th, 1927. He was playing a " live " scene out of *Down Hill* at the Plaza in connection with the film of that play at the time and he 'phoned to Fred Allen to come over and to bring the cheque book to his dressing-room there. When Fred Allen arrived, Ivor told him he had decided to buy the country house which was the property of his friend John Gordon. He bought it for £4,000, together with two cottages. The name of the house was then " Munro Lodge." It has been suggested that Ivor considered calling the house " The Constant Nymph " because of his recent success in that film, but nobody among his closest friends seems to remember this idea. If he had that idea, it remained in his own mind. There was a discussion over the name during the first week-end he spent there—Bobbie Andrews, Frank Leveson and Fred Allen were among those present. On that occasion either Bobbie Andrews or Ivor suggested " Redroofs " and the only dissentient was the practical Fred Allen who said that to him it sounded like something out of a novelette. But the rest of the party acclaimed the choice. " Redroofs " it was and " Redroofs " it remained until his death. He loved the place dearly. Much of his best work, masses of his best music, was done and composed there. He slept there the last night of his life. He came from there to the Palace Theatre and returned to his flat—to die.

During his lifetime " Redroofs " was the most famous theatrical country home in the land—in the world. For it was of world-wide renown. Artistes of all kinds from all parts of the world went there, stayed there, and signed its visitors' book, which was a Roll of Fame in itself. Every summer he entertained his company there, taking them all down, giving them a charming and informal garden party, with lots of strawberries and all sorts of food and delicacies—an invitation which was looked forward to eagerly and discussed for months afterwards. It was one of his ways of keeping boredom from his players during the long runs. He was always giving them something to discuss and anticipate.

Ivor was the host and he was probably the most informal and scantily attired host any garden party ever had. The swimming pool was always in demand and he loved the swimming pool. His costume on those occasions consisted only of trunks or very brief shorts. The rest was just Ivor Novello. He did not seek publicity on these occasions although, besides his "girls and boys," many great celebrities would be there. All were welcome, from the chorister to the star and all rubbed shoulders—titled folk, actors and actresses, managers, musicians, artists, sculptors, ministers of religious denominations, authors, poets—all alike and all treated alike in the true democracy of the Theatre. Nor was there any set entertainment. Everyone was free to do exactly as he or she liked in the lovely surroundings of that high-walled, extensive garden and grounds. They could just sit around, they could play tennis on the courts, croquet on the lawn, gossip, smoke, eat, drink and make merry, bathe . . . whatever their fancy dictated. Usually irrepressible Olive Gilbert would do a little clowning in the swimming pool, in Victorian bathing attire. But it was all informal, as informal as Ivor himself, who was King there as he was King of the Theatre—but a democratic king without pomp or circumstance—and who was elected to his high position for life with never a dissentient vote.

Everyone was as happy at " Redroofs " as he was. Those who had children brought them, too—and Ivor was introduced and was delighted, though perhaps he was not at his best with babies. . . . The informality also expressed itself in the attire of the guests. The dresses ranged from silken gowns to print frocks, from Bond Street to bathing dresses of the scantiest proportions. But everyone was happy. Littlewick Green, the village of which " Redroofs " is part, entered into the spirit of the occasion. It never crowded round the gates to see the sights but respected Ivor's privacy. Usually there was a cricket match on the green. But at tea time, there would be an ever-growing crowd of juvenile inhabitants hanging around near the entrance. The reason was an excellent one: for they got all the cakes and good things which the guests did not consume—and the catering was on a lavish scale. Those small Littlewickians had a gala feed.

Adjoining " Redroofs " are four cottages which Ivor also owned, charming little residences. Two he bought with " Redroofs," the other two he purchased on December 19th, 1928, for £500. In some of them friends of his lived, at rentals so ridiculous as to be hardly worth the mentioning. In others lived his pensioners, rent free—and Ivor had more pensioners than even his close friends knew. He never mentioned it—he let his deeds speak for themselves. It was his reward for good and loyal service—and he always got that.

CHAPTER THIRTEEN

STORM, STRESS—AND AMERICA!

THAT Daly's disaster scarcely checked Ivor's stage career. Despite his run of ill luck, he wanted the stage far more than the screen. But the screen was providing money. Moreover, the screen could never bring personal disasters, for, if a film turned out badly, there was no actual contact with the audience and the failure was never so near to one. By the time he had made those pictures with Gainsborough, however, he had had almost enough. His bank balance was swelling, he had bought "Redroofs" and a couple of cottages, he had gone ahead with his climb to the £100,000 Consols. And again came the call of the stage.

Before leaving the first period of his real stage career and accompanying him to the next phase, in which he became his own author and manager, there are one or two things of interest.

He filmed *The South Sea Bubble* in 1928 and *Gallant Hussar* in the same year. His flat salary for the former was £100 a day and for *Gallant Hussar* he received £450 a week for seven weeks and £150 a day for five extra days' filming, which brought him in a total of £3,900. Flat rate for *The Return of the Rat*, which he made in 1929, was £150 per day, the other details were in accordance with the Gainsborough contract. In September, 1928, he had a two weeks' engagement at the London Palladium in a sketch called *The Gate Crasher*, for which he got £1,150. It was not all profit; he had to pay his company—Phyllis Monkman and Gordon Gay. But he did pretty well. So he was not deserting the stage. Indeed, he was thinking about it more and more.

He loved acting. And a sidelight on his own feelings—one which shows his utter lack of conceit—is shown in letters he exchanged with Jean Webster Brough, a lifelong friend, who when away on tour not only corresponded with him regularly but, knowing his sketchy methods of writing, used to send him little questionnaires for him to answer. And answer them he did. Here is one she sent after the production of *The Firebrand* when she was with Owen Nares in South Africa. And besides answering the questions, he also wrote a letter, which is quite typical:

"Jean darling,

Adored your lovely letter. *The Firebrand* is *not* a big success it falls between too many stools, but thank the Lord I've made a big success and look most 'plezzunt.' It will run about another six weeks which, 11 weeks, is not bad for a costume play. I may not do my first play with Curzon until August. I hope you're having a marvellous success, darling—it was really marvellous of you to have cabled. Bless you darling,

Ivor.

"I answer the questions all fragrant with witchery. . . ."

That was a typical Ivor letter of the time—all enthusiasm, and darlings in the good old theatrical way. Though why a "duckie" or two did not slip in is curious. And here are the questions, or some of them, for there are one or two which it is not politic to include, especially the answers. But enough is given to show what this little game they played was like:

Q. Was *The Firebrand* a big success?
A. Biggish.

Q. Were the notices good?
A. Fifty per cent. excellent, 50 per cent. lousy.

Q. Did Ivor make a terrific hit?
A. The biggest yet.

Q. Constance?
A. Enormous.

Q. How many calls?
A. Dozens.

Q. Do you think it will have a long run? (very important).
A. No.

Q. Did Ivor make a speech?
A. Yes.

Q. Did you have a party afterwards?
A. Yes.

Q. What did Eddie think of the play?
A. Not the play but the acting.

Q. How did Ivor get through the fencing?
A. Marvellously in spite of dagger in the foot causing postponement of four days.

Q. Was his cold all right for the première?
A. Yes.

Q. Did he get a big reception?
A. They had to stand still for three minutes!

Q. Have the Libraries done a big deal?
A. No fear.

Q. When is Ivor going to do his next film?
A. Starting to-day, March 8th.

Q. Have you been to any new films?
A. Not many.

Q. What did Lloydy think of . . . (a film, name suppressed).
A. Loathed it.

Those answers are typical of Ivor's frankness over what went on. He never pretended. If he had a flop, he said so. If he was in one, he said so. Only, of course, to his friends; he did not blazon it forth to the public. He was quite open about everything and did not mind who knew how much money his show was taking. During his last play, *King's Rhapsody* at the Palace, he wrote each night's takings, in details, in greasepaint on his dressing-table mirror. Anyone going into his room (and everyone did, his dressing-room being always like a platform at Euston with throngs coming and going) could see the state of the business. It was open to a snooping journalist—if he succeeded in getting by me—to tell the world what business was like at the Palace. Ivor did not care, but Tom Arnold was never very happy about it, and quite rightly so. Shops, hotels, and commercial concerns do not publish their daily returns, nor do newspapers, although they are very curious about what theatres are doing. A newspaper may from time to time give details as to its circulation figures but never what that means in terms of income or what its revenue is from advertising. But they always clamour to know how much money comes into a theatre box office. I have often told such earnest inquirers that I would tell them if they would in turn tell me how much Woolworth's took on the same day—or how much their own advertising was worth at the time. But to Ivor it was a source of pride—and he did not care who knew. In 1928 he had no such figures to write on his mirror. He was just determined on breaking in as actor-manager-author. He did not like his experiences in the Theatre under other people's command. His own biggest success, *The Rat*, had been his own venture in his own play—with Constance Collier—and that is how he meant to go on. He knew the risk, he knew the gamble, he was aware that by devoting himself entirely to film-making he would have a safe income and no worries for many years, but he wanted to be in the Theatre.

He made up his mind. He wrote a play with no collaboration. He called it *Taken by Storm*. He had the money—just about enough—and he would add the troubles of actor-managership to those he had already. For his life was not all clear and limpid. He had his domestic difficulties, which came from his beloved Mam, to whom he was devoted but whose faults he always saw.

Mam was always taking plunges: doing thoughtless things, getting herself into difficulties, often through the expansiveness of her heart and her incurable optimism. She was constantly getting into quite serious jams about money, and then Ivor would be besought to get her out. Between them stood the faithful, conscientious Fred Allen, devoted to both. A crisis blew up in November, 1928, when Ivor had just embarked on his critical venture.

It had better come in its place, after the story of his own plunge, but it reveals the background against which he had to struggle, not only in his bid for public success, but in his private life, about which the public have known nothing until now.

Ivor wrote his play with certain people in mind. That had been his custom from the very first. What he wanted just then, more than anything else in the world, was to play opposite to Lily Elsie. He had always adored her since she had enchanted him (as a member of the audience) in *The Merry Widow*. To him she was glamour personified and he was quite right about that.

He had first met her when he was still in the Royal Naval Air

Service. The meeting had been arranged through the good offices of Mrs. Asquith, whose distinguished husband was then Prime Minister, and it took place at No. 10 Downing Street. Ivor wanted to get Lily Elsie to come out of retirement and was going to try to tempt her to play in an operetta he had written. He could hardly contain himself when she was shown into the room and Mrs. Asquith introduced them. He must try his best to get this exquisite woman to play in his show. It was called *The Argentine Widow*. But Fates willed otherwise. A military band was blaring just outside the windows and kept on all the time. Ivor got tongue-tied in trying to compete with the martial strains, which killed his music. Lily Elsie saw the funny side and laughed, and Ivor abandoned the whole idea.

But that meeting blossomed into a friendship, and here was a real chance. Here was a play and a part which would suit Lily Elsie, here was Ivor, no longer a sub-lieutenant in the R.N.A.S., but a popular star of stage and screen, and a known box-office draw, just about to embark upon management. With high hopes, he put the proposition to her. Or rather he paved the way and then Barry O'Brien, a well-known manager and entrepreneur, put up the business side. Ivor waited anxiously. The answer was " Yes." So he wrote to her on July 3rd, 1928:

" Elsie dear,

I have just seen Barry O'Brien and this is to confirm your conversation with him that you will play the leading part in my play *Taken by Storm* in London, beginning round about October 15th at a weekly salary of £150 (one hundred and fifty pounds) for the first three months and then, if business justifies the play continuing, at an increase of £50 a week or a substitution of 10 per cent. (ten per cent.) of the gross receipts—this alternative to be discussed later and left to you to decide.

Yours,

Ivor Novello."

(Incidentally, Lily Elsie is " Elsie " to her friends).

And Lily Elsie replied on July 15th, 1928—with two letters—she was in Biarritz. . . .

" Ivor Dear,

I received your letter of July 3rd engaging me to play lead in your play *Taken by Storm* at a weekly salary of £150 (one hundred and fifty pounds) and a further increase of fifty pounds a week or

10 per cent. of the gross should the play run over three months. Rehearsals to begin as near as possible September 15th—the play produced round about October 15th. I think this covers everything but of course it is very important to get the best and most suitable theatre possible. Do remember, Ivor dear, it is an intimate play and must have a lovely intimate theatre. How thrilling now I'm going to sign my contract with you.

Lily Elsie."

And on the same day she also wrote:

" Ivor my dear, here is my contract. At least it started by being my contract and then I started to talk to you in it. So like me! Just imagine this, you really engaging me as your leading lady (at least I hope I'm a lady). It is strange, Ivor darling, isn't it? I do hope with all my heart you are going to have a grand success with it and that I shall help with you and all the others to make it so.

" It is such marvellous weather here, blazing sun and ever so hot. I've been feeling so rotten I don't ever wish to eat and not sleeping well. However, it is all the result of a long, long time of worry and ghastly strain. I'm having sun baths, etc., etc., so I shall be well braced up in another three weeks. I expect I shall be here till August 2nd. Send me the play and part and when I feel more like myself I'll go through it quietly. Have you been able to get the Haymarket? Oh, I do hope so. Do get a lovely intimate theatre darling, please. Lily Elsie."

The charm of those letters, the goodness of heart and the perfect naturalness show why Lily Elsie holds her public to-day and why, when she is seen in public, hearts stand still and eyes get moist. She is still the same lovely person, still filled with the same glamour—for she really possesses that much talked of but seldom experienced quality—and still has the same serene, calm beauty of a summer morning, still the same straight gaze from the clear, compelling eyes. She was heart and soul for Ivor and his play. She was Ivor's staunch friend in what was to follow.

She was there at the end. As the great church of St. Martin-in-the-Fields hushed for the beginning of the Memorial Service for Ivor, a solitary figure of a woman stood at the foot of the aisle. It was Lily Elsie. I knew her. She had just managed to get through the vast throng outside. She was limping, for she had suffered an accident shortly before, but she was there. I would have escorted her to the seat in the front, but I dared not stray from my door, which in company with William Abingdon

Ivor as Lord George Hell in *Happy Hypocrite*. This role was a masterpiece of make-up

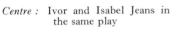

Centre : Ivor and Isabel Jeans in the same play

At left : Ivor and Vivien Leigh, also in the same play

Above : Ivor with Thea Holme in *Flies in the Sun*

At right : Film role in *Bonnie Prince Charlie*

Below : With Lily Elsie in *The Truth Game*

and my son-in-law William Sutton, both—like myself—Old Novellians, had been held against great odds. So I saw to it that an usher escorted Lily Elsie to her place of honour. I knew what she had come through. The holding of that door was not only a matter of great tact, but sometimes of physical effort. Just before Lily Elsie arrived we had been dealing with a rather violent person who insisted on her right to enter, because—she said—she was Mrs. Ivor Novello. She could not have found three harder cases on which to try that than we three. Erect as a wand, slowly because of the limp, Lily Elsie went to her place to pay her last tribute to the man she had held dear and who had held her dear, the man to whom she had been loyal when he most needed it—a friend had come to say good-bye to a friend. And if the shade of Ivor was present on that wonderful occasion —his face must have worn that slow, happy smile of his and affection must have shone from his eyes . . . truly the Captains had gathered to pay a last homage to the King. . . .

Ivor did not get the Haymarket for *Taken by Storm*. He got the Globe. Always a believer in quality and always believing in writing parts for people whose ability he knew and had tested—Sheridan had the same idea—he had his cast in mind when he wrote the play. He wrote the part of Rosine Browne for Lily Elsie, the part of the Lady Joan Culver for Viola Tree and he wrote the part of Evelyn Brandon for his dear Constance Collier. As he wrote, he could hear that characteristic voice of hers saying the lines. He secured the services of all those three ladies. And his heart was full—there would be Viola and Constance with him on this adventure—and, oh marvellous, there would be the adored Lily Elsie, playing opposite to him! Incidentally he wrote the part of Max Clement for himself.

One of Ivor's outstanding faults as a dramatist was that he never gave himself a good enough part. He always wrote so much better parts for his leading ladies. To them he gave exactly the right thing to do, and he knew to an inch, always, where their brightest talents lay. He so often starved himself and all too often just made himself a link. He seldom gave himself anything to do except lightness—and he was such a good character actor. He adored to get laughs and there was always in him a tendency to clown when possible. So he never gave himself a stupendous leading part in any of his shows. The nearest he came to it was in his last and best—*King's Rhapsody*. He very rarely gave himself the sympathy, as he should have done. Maybe he knew he would get it, all the same. . . . But Ivor Novello was a true son of the great actor-managerial tradition and did not hog the centre of the stage and the limelight all the time, any more than they did, no matter what people who never knew or saw them may think and even say.

Ivor took the Globe Theatre from Sir Alfred Butt and paid over a cheque for £900 on account of rent. That cheque is before me as I write. It is in his life quite an historic document, and it is intriguing to see that it is endorsed by R. E. Gray who, in later years became and is now, the secretary of Theatre Royal, Drury Lane, and who was closely connected with Ivor during his triumphs there. That cheque for this play was the first link between them.

The story of the battles and heartbreaks which preceded the production of this venture have been told so often. Mr. Peter Noble tells the story in his book vividly, as Ivor told it to him. Ivor himself told it when he wrote his own story for the *Sunday Chronicle* shortly before he died. It is quite a usual sort of theatrical story, taken by and large. But it has to be set down in some form and I will be as brief as possible, for it occasions heart burnings, quarrels and, for some time, angry feeling and open breaches between old friends. They all got patched up and forgotten, for Ivor never bore ill will and nobody could be cross with him for long either. Let the sequence of events be stated and let the details go.

Ivor was lucky to get the Globe, a charming and intimate theatre so desired by Lily Elsie. I managed the Globe for many happy years, but that was long before Ivor went there with his play. He had altered the title now. It was no longer *Taken by Storm* but *The Truth Game*.

Viola Tree got her friend Sir Gerald du Maurier to undertake the production. The cast was thrilled, and Ivor overjoyed. " Gerald " was the best producer of his day—and " production" was becoming more and more important in the eyes of the profession and the public. Whether that is really to the good need not be argued here. A play produced by Gerald du Maurier got off to a flying start. The first rehearsal came, but no Du Maurier. They made a start without him. It was not a good start. Trouble showed itself in the ranks. Constance Collier apparently did not like the part which Ivor had written for her.

The rest revelled in theirs, but there was something wrong somewhere. Days came and went, the play shuffled forwards or even backwards. Still no signs of Sir Gerald du Maurier. Ivor had by this time committed himself to £450 a week for rent and all the countless and often quite unexpected expenses which crop up at rehearsals and as production proceeds. Still no Sir Gerald. And, one day, no Constance Collier.

Ivor was rung up by Noël Coward and told that Constance Collier did not want to play. He said his heart stood still—and well it might. He had written that part especially for her. But he spoke to her. He told her not to worry. He decided to get Ellis Jeffreys. He could not understand what had happened. Actually, Constance Collier, in her deep affection for him, was sacrificing herself. She did not believe in the play. She thought he was heading for disaster. She wanted to save him from that and she believed that if she withdrew, he might cancel the whole thing and proceed no further. So Ivor Novello might have done—he was an emotional creature then. But David Ivor Davies was still there, although nowadays with no legal standing whatever. He stepped in and took the decision to go ahead. So Ivor rushed round to see Ellis Jeffreys, a superb actress who had at that time not been seen in town for far too long. He told her the story, he read her the play. She was enthusiastic. She came back with him to rehearsal and went right ahead. Ivor breathed again.

But a fortnight of the precious rehearsal time had gone by and still there was no sign of Sir Gerald. The interval between then and the time of production shortened to ten days. But no Sir Gerald. Things were desperate. And they got worse. For now Ellis Jeffreys rang Ivor up and said she could not go on. He reeled under this. He wanted to know why. She told him she did not understand either her part or the play. He reasoned with her and told her she had been splendid at rehearsal. She replied that she would come down to the theatre and explain. Ivor went to the Globe in a turmoil. He could not think clearly—his brain was awhirl. And when he got there—there was the long missing Sir Gerald du Maurier. For one moment hope shone. But Sir Gerald promptly blew it out. He told Ivor that he had not even read the play. And that he could not produce it. That was enough to stagger anyone. Ivor, dumbfounded, demanded to know how Sir Gerald could decry a play which he had not even read. He pleaded that it had such a good curtain to the second act. Sir Gerald replied, grimly " My dear boy, you won't even get to the end of the second act." And then Lily Elsie intervened. She told the great Sir Gerald she did not believe a word he said; but she did believe in the play and she was going on with it. Telling Ivor, with a lovely smile, to let her know when rehearsals began again, she made her exit. No wonder Ivor held her in adoration. Ivor was now quite determined. All right, let the mighty Sir Gerald turn down the play, let Ellis Jeffreys go, let them all go, so long as he had Viola Tree and Lily Elsie. Opposition always drove him on.

Now, he decided, he would get Lilian Braithwaite. By the time he reached her she knew all about it. That bush telegraph in Theatreland had been working overtime. One of Lilian's great assets was her complete self-control and calmness. She was quite unperturbed at his tale of woe. Two great actresses might have turned down the part he now offered her—she did not care. " What are they doing to you, you poor darling ? " she asked. And then Ivor broke down. All the Welsh fire, all the strung up Celtic temperament, dissolved in tears. And no wonder. Lilian understood. She petted him, she gave him wine, she gave him encouragement; she gave him courage and, above all, she said she would play the part. The elasticity of the Theatre was at work in Ivor—like most stage folk, he bounced from the depths to the heights. He took another decision and rushed the play to W. Graham Browne to produce it. " Wally," as most people called him, came down at once to rehearsal. He watched the first scene. " What are you worrying about, Ivor?" he asked. " This is charming." He took on the job, and they worked against time.

The play opened almost in a frenzy on October 5th, 1928. Lily Elsie got a reception a queen might have envied and there were plenty of cheers for Ivor, too. The final curtain fell and they waited, but for a second or so only. The real, deep applause and the cheers told them—told Ivor—they had been right and the objectors completely wrong. *The Truth Game* ran for 162 performances, a good run in those days of 1928. It had a most successful English tour and Ivor played it in New York for six months, too. Besides that, it was filmed—twice, as it happened—and it is in great demand for repertory companies to-day. In actual hard figures, the run at the Globe showed a loss. The production cost £2,902 5*s.* 1*d.* and Ivor had a partner who backed it with him. But they got their money back many times over in the long run from tours and film rights and Ivor, personally, did well, for he got a salary as actor and author's fees too.

Those were curious days, those late 'twenties, which are so close in time but seem so far away. Living then was ridiculously cheap as compared with the costs of the post-Second War period, yet the people who had lived and paid bills before 1914 were then grumbling at the terrible rise in prices. But you got a theatre supper at the Monaco for 4*s.* and at the Florence, in Rupert Street (it became the Merchant Navy club during the Second War) you could lunch for 3*s.* 6*d.*, dine for 4*s.* 6*d.*, and have a supper and dance from 9.30 p.m. until 12.30 for 5*s.* Romano's in the Strand was still open and had dancing from 9 until 1 a.m. (with an extension until 2 a.m. every Wednesday). And Morris cars, new, cost £142 10*s.* Theatre prices at the Globe were £4 4*s.* to £2 2*s.* for boxes, stalls 10*s.* 6*d.*, dress circle 10*s.* 6*d.* and 7*s.* 6*d.*, upper circle 5*s.*, pit 3*s.* and gallery 1*s.* 8*d.* There was entertainment tax on top of that.

Ivor was now of the Theatre and although there were still films to make, and a visit to Hollywood in the near future, the Theatre was his domain. Films were just an extra. He had quite made up his mind.

His next play was *A Symphony in Two Flats*. This, of course, he wrote and played in himself. This time he gave himself a heavier role, one with a tragic note, a composer who was going blind. He kept almost the same cast, except Lily Elsie who had needed a rest after the long tour of *The Truth Game*. Benita Hume played the lead. *A Symphony in Two Flats* played at the New Theatre in St. Martin's Lane. Produced on October 14th, 1929, it ran for 153 performances. His mascot, Minnie Rayner, was in the cast and she was with him afterwards until her death. Whether she really did bring him luck is a moot point, but it is a stone cold certainty that an introduction of hers to him was the cause of the one great outstanding tragedy in his life. But he loved the cheerful stout personality—she was a good actress too—and always wrote a part for her from then on. She was with him right up to *The Dancing Years*. *A Symphony in Two Flats* was filmed, too.

Ivor was now an outstanding figure in the British Theatre and a tremendous box-office draw. He was an actor-manager when actor-managers were few—and he was carrying on the tradition of quality.

But he had his worries, as already mentioned—and one of those worries was Mam. A crisis blew up during the run of *The Truth Game* when, despite the outward semblance of success, he had worries in the Theatre. Mam had decided to go to Hollywood where she was going to make a sensation and a fortune. Or so she declared! She was going to take a pupil with her—whether that pupil was to be a joint sensation is not at the moment clear. The pupil had made payments over the trip. Mam was broke. She wanted help from Ivor. She appealed through Fred Allen and to Fred Allen, who bore the brunt of these things. She had taken new premises in town and she had, as usual, got into debt. The only resource was Ivor. But Ivor was worried and money was tight with him. He was making her a generous allowance anyway, but he certainly did not see his way to finance this trip to Hollywood, nor did he believe in it. He knew his Mam. So it was Fred's job to tell Mam that Ivor had increased her allowance to £20 per week, of which £7 was to be set aside to pay rent and rates, leaving her £13 per week, which she would receive every Friday. Fred mentioned to her that he had told Ivor he had already made her certain payments and Ivor said they were to be disregarded and written off, so the £13 a week was hers. He pointed out that he had now to find £125 per week for Ivor's outgoings and there was the production of the show *The Truth Game* to be paid for, so. . . .

That brought a genuine wail. Mam was heartbroken. She had no money sense at all, only a terrific belief in herself and her "flair." Now she moaned that nobody wanted her, all that was left to her was a life of seclusion, which would mean her end! (that was true enough). She knew that her wonderful darling was straining every nerve to make good and get out of debt himself and that, she declared, distressed her beyond words. If she had one glimpse of hope of making money in this country, she said, she could stand it, "but here I am with so much to give, in myself I have never been better, and beautiful singers, all ready, I am working hard for nothing—*no money—nobody wants me or my choirs if they have to pay for it*!"

She said she had gone too far in her arrangements for Hollywood to draw back and that her only object in going there was to be able to send money to Ivor to put away for her and to stop him having to send money to her. She said she really felt she would go anywhere in the world to bring that about. Then she admitted it might be as well if she did not go to Hollywood at once, as it would give her a chance of finding out what the prospects were. She admitted it would have been a mistake to carry out this intention of rushing there without knowing something definite and admitted that Ivor had told her so. But it was her anxiety to help which drove her on. She should have listened to Ivor, she said, and been patient as he told her (she should have done so often, indeed). And then she says in her letter: " I am sure you will understand my feelings when the enclosed is a specimen of what I have to face every day. I am only sending it for you to see, not to ask you to help me pay it, please return it. I feel better now I have poured out my troubles to you! " What that bill was is lost to history but whenever Mam was asked to pay anything she always seemed amazed. She ends up her letter by calling down blessings on Fred Allen and his family and sending her love. Then, womanlike, comes the postscript—like a trumpet call. " I tell you not to worry about me—I shall be all right when I get to Hollywood!!! N.B. I paid a ten pound account out of the thirteen you sent me yesterday "....

Fred Allen's reply was a masterpiece of diplomacy. He consoled her on the non-demand for the choirs and blamed it on the jazz age. He returned the document she had sent him and sent her one which he had to pay for Ivor, so that she could see for herself. And ended up by sending her, too, some very sound further advice from Ivor. There, for the moment, the matter rested.

I have told this story in some detail so that the picture of Ivor and his domestic life may be clear to all. There has always been the belief that his mother was his guiding star and helpmate. Now the true position can be judged. That was only one instance out of many. Some others will crop up when necessary to the story of his life.

In his lifetime Ivor never said a word about this, and would not have allowed it to be mentioned. But the real truth does not detract from him, quite the reverse. He was a model son, he adored his mother, he really adored her despite all her failings. He understood her, he regarded her as a child who had never grown up; indeed, there was much of the child in him, too. He was grateful to her for what she had done in his youthful days, although it was actually by encouragement and enthusiasm that she inspired him more than she actually helped. Nobody helped him at all—he did it off his own bat. But Mam was near enough to being a genius to have all the eccentricities of one. Ivor Novello actually had genius, but he also had a useful brake in David Ivor Davies, who kept the ship to the wind and contributed an excellent business sense to go with the artistry.

Ivor never wasted money—he hated that. And he soon saw that if money were continually given to Mam it was tantamount to waste. There was now no real demand for her choirs and although she was a wonderful teacher of singing she should have been able to do that without getting into debt. But all too often she scented genius amongst her pupils and did not care if she didn't get paid. Ivor had that talent spotting complex in him too. He often made startling discoveries of stars, but it was not very often that they shone out of his reflected light. But Mam would dash and plunge where Ivor never did. But all his life he denied her nothing at all within reason.

After the run of *A Symphony in Two Flats* Ivor got an offer to go to New York from the Shubert Brothers. He jumped at the chance as he wanted to play on Broadway. He took his play from the New Theatre over to the States, via Montreal, where they had a try-out and a successful one too. When they opened on Broadway, Viola Tree was not with them; she could not go because of ties in London. Ivor regretted this for Viola Tree was another of his mascots. He had quite a few—I was one myself for years. Or so he told me—and truly they were successful years for both of us. Ivor had the theatre superstitions—as all true theatre folk have. His belief in mascots was complete though usually his mascots were people.

I believe in people in the Theatre who believe in mascots. Mine are not people but things. I have a threadbare old tie, which I always wear if I have something very difficult to do. The first time I wore it I achieved what had seemed an impossibility. It is a disgraceful sight now—over twenty years old—but it never fails me. I have a tiny wooden black cat which has brought me luck and which my daughter carried with her to every examination. She never failed in one; indeed she took honours always. I have a waistcoat pocket full of mascots which never leave me. Amongst them is a very small bronze figure which was given me by one of the barmaids in the Palladium Palm Court when I worked there. I had told her of the persistent bad luck which was pursuing me—and it was really very grim. She gave me that mascot. My luck turned the next day. I would not lose it for worlds. And I also have a big lump of shellcase which caught me a nice clout on my tin hat whilst on duty during a raid in the Second World War. It was red hot when I picked it up and I dropped it to let it cool. But it has brought me luck. I have many more, all of which are tried and precious, but the little bronze figure is the most potent—that and my tie. Tom Walls had a great and abiding faith in the number thirteen. There were thirteen letters in the name of *April the Fifth* with which he won the Derby, thirteen letters in his own name (Tom Kerby Walls) and the thirteen plays which he did at the Aldwych, all successes. Walter Hackett, the playwright, would fly from any building when he heard the strains of the Barcarolle from "Tales of Hoffman." "The Count of Luxembourg" does the same to me . . . one could go on for ever, especially with lucky and unlucky tunes. Julian Wylie never did a pantomime—and his pantomimes never failed—unless he included some music by his late partner and friend James W. Tate. Ivor always had a few bars of "Keep the Home Fires" in all his scores, tucked away, but there all the same. To be really Theatre you must have superstitions—it is part of the divine madness of the place.

A Symphony in Two Flats moved into New York. It opened at the Shubert Theatre in September, 1930. So did a heat wave. Thunder roared as the first-nighters almost swam to the Theatre through torrential downpours of rain. All through the first act half-drowned playgoers straggled in and those that were there could hardly hear for the thunder. It was a dreadful opening. They got a much better press than they might have expected, and they tried to outrun the heat wave. The weather is very hard to beat in the Theatres. Fog or snow empties them, so does the first spell of real cold and the first spell of fine spring sunshine. So does the first hot day. Only a heavy shower just before a matinée can help. And not always that. It has to be a terrific success to beat the weather. And *A Symphony in Two Flats* was not that. They battled on for seven weeks—that was the extent of the run. But when they came off, the heat wave was still running merrily.

Ivor was distressed. He liked New York, he wanted to conquer it. He liked everything about it and he liked the playgoers. He believed he could win if the weather would allow him. Fortunately for him the Shuberts thought so too. There had been a kind of option to do another play. Ivor asked them about it. They were willing, like good theatre gamblers. So he decided to do *The Truth Game*. He cabled to Viola to come out at once. He was not going to miss a trump card like that. And Viola, who was most understanding and who was very fond of him, made it possible, despite difficulties, and went across. But now he wanted someone to play Mrs. Brandon, the part which Constance Collier and Ellis Jeffreys had not played but which Lilian Braithwaite had. Lilian was not available. Who was he to get? His luck held. He got Billie Burke. This gave him great joy for he was a fervent admirer of this delightful, lovely and very clever red-haired woman, so full of charm and grace. He had always admired her and had been enchanted when he met her. Now here she was, to act with him. In this production, the wheel of Time was going round and old troubles were being healed and forgotten. Constance Collier and Ivor had buried that old misunderstanding. It was Constance Collier, in New York, who helped in the production of *The Truth Game* as Billie Burke tells in her book *With a Feather on my Nose*—into which she has poured her own enchantment—and, with gratitude, I quote from it:

" Of my plays during these three seasons, *The Marquise* was by Noël Coward, which means that it was smart, but *The Truth Game* was the most important to me. It came at a time when I felt more than ever that I needed to get back to the Theatre. It was made possible for me by those two brilliant, excellent old friends, Constance Collier and Ivor Novello and it marked the first time that I played a character part. . . . I had enjoyed knowing Ivor for years and I had seen a lot of Constance during her brave fight to produce *Peter Ibbetson*. . . . Constance helped Ivor to stage *The Truth Game* and did it beautifully."

The Truth Game opened at the Ethel Barrymore Theatre in December, 1930. Its first night was as brilliant as that of *A Symphony in Two Flats* had been eccentric and unlucky. The play was a big success; so was Viola Tree; so indeed was Billie Burke; and so was Ivor. The whole thing was acclaimed. Ivor was a figure in New York as he was in London.

Metro-Goldwyn-Mayer bought the film rights. Everything in the garden was lovely. Ivor was walking on air and the air of New York is invigorating, especially for the successful. The play despised and rejected by Sir Gerald du Maurier was now a success on two Continents. Du Maurier had long ago admitted his mistake, and true to type Ivor had borne no malice nor felt any bitterness over what might have been a crushing blow. And when, in 1950, Billie Burke wrote her book, Ivor wrote a foreword for the English edition. In it he laid the success of the American production of *The Truth Game* at her dainty feet. He gave me a copy of the book inscribed " To Dear Popie, with Love From Ivor." And all that he said in it about this wonderful woman is true.

My own memory of her goes back to the time when, from a humble seat in the gallery at the old Prince of Wales's Theatre, she made me a slave to her auburn loveliness when singing " My Little Canoe " in *The School Girl.* She was little more than a child herself then. I was even more humble than I am to-day. But I never forgot that vision and that charm. Incidentally my own dear wife is very like Billie Burke and I hasten to say that there was what was then known as " an understanding " between us even then. It is one of my regrets that although I have met and known most of the famous ones of the Theatre, it has never been my luck to meet Billie Burke. But I go on hoping.

The success of *The Truth Game* did more than wipe out the disappointment over *A Symphony in Two Flats.* This victory of a play that had cost him so much trouble and strife was a quiet triumph for him. New York loved him and he loved New York. For the moment it was the complete centre of his life. Ivor was like that. When he succeeded somewhere, when he was happy in a place, that was the only place in the world, that was where he wanted to be and wanted to stay. The bigness of America captivated his fancy. The big ideas, the big scope, and—incidentally—the chance of the very big money. When in later years—not so far away—he was to reach his real greatness at Drury Lane Theatre, he said that he never wanted to leave it. It must be his home for ever, there was no other place, no other theatre in the world. But the war cut his stay, in his greatest success. He grieved. But he became very happy at the Adelphi when the play moved there. And he thoroughly enjoyed the London Hippodrome during *Perchance to Dream.* And, on the first anniversary of *King's Rhapsody* at the Palace, he told me how happy he was there, how in many ways it was his ideal theatre and how he thought he would like to go on playing there for the rest of his life.

In 1930 England and London had receded. Here was success in America. Here was a new continent to conquer. Here was a chance for a young man with big ideas . . . America was the place for him.

Metro-Goldwyn-Mayer not only bought the film rights of *The Truth Game*, they offered him a job in Hollywood as script writer and as actor. Ivor was dazzled. Here was the chance, here he would have all the vast resources of that miracle city behind him. From Hollywood he could show the World and conquer it. Of course he accepted it. Who, in his position, would not? He had been there before and thought he knew the ropes. At the end of the run of the play he took a brief holiday—and then went to Hollywood to work—so he thought. He went there to conquer—so he thought—as so many brilliant Englishman had thought before him. He arrived there in 1931 eager and straining at the leash. He would now work wonders. He was to learn.

CHAPTER FOURTEEN

HOLLYWOOD HEARTACHE

BEFORE Ivor's adventures in Hollywood come up for chronicle—and they are not very exciting anyway—another musical success must be mentioned. In 1929 he had become composer again, and had written most of the music for a revue staged by Jack Hulbert and Cicely Courtneidge, called *The House that Jack Built*. It was produced at the Adelphi on November 8th, 1929, and it ran for 270 performances. This combination of Ivor, Cicely Courtneidge—the finest burlesque artiste of our stage—and Jack Hulbert was important, not so much at that time, but in view of what was to come later. Ivor was full of admiration for Cicely Courtneidge's genius, and he made her a promise that one day, when she needed it, he would write a play for her and compose the music as well. That promise was kept, in the year 1950, twenty-one years later, and it resulted in *Gay's the Word*, the last work Ivor ever wrote and the last of his shows to be produced. It was one of his greatest successes. But we will come to it later in the story.

In 1929 the Hulberts—for they are man and wife—were the King and Queen of Revue. They were an ideal stage partnership, real foils to each other, the crisp, sparkling speed of the lady being contrasted with the very English, leisurely, nonchalant method of the man. Jack Hulbert was also the leading revue producer, his shows bearing a hall-mark for efficiency, rapidity of movement, exciting dance routines and even his own individual colour scheme of lighting.

The House that Jack Built succeeded *Clowns in Clover*, another Hulbert-Courtneidge success which had run, also at the Adelphi, for 508 performances. This had been notable for magnificent performances by the two of them and for the fact that the one and only Elsie Janis came over from America and appeared in it—with no success at all. It was one of the only things which Mother Janis arranged for Elsie without my knowledge and consent for I looked after their business here in Europe. It made me furious when I heard, for I thought it extremely bad policy that Elsie, at that stage of her career, should go into a show which contained the brilliance of Cicely Courtneidge who could do all that Elsie could do—except those superb imitations—and who had the advantage of immediate popularity and youth. But Elsie went into the show. She brought no new material. She gave her imitations and they consisted of people whom we did not know in London, however famous they were in the States. She did her dancing, which was almost of the old fashioned " skirt dancing " variety, a thing of lovely movement and grace but even then a bit old-fashioned, especially against the background of the speed supplied by Jack Hulbert's routines.

Mother Janis was ill and could not attend rehearsals, or it might have been different, but I doubt it. She sat in a box on the first night when she ought to have been in bed. It was almost her last visit to a theatre, for very soon afterwards she took to her bed at the Carlton Hotel, where she and Elsie always had the same suite. But so long as she could struggle to the theatre where Elsie was playing, there she would go. In the ordinary way she would have been in the wings whilst Elsie was on the stage. But that night she had to remain in the box. With her were Hallie, the coloured maid (who used a lot of rouge with astonishing results), and Frank, the chauffeur, who was always treated as one of the family. At the end of the show, my wife and I went up to see Mother and we took Hannen Swaffer up, too. That afternoon I had taken him to tea with the Janis's and we had had muffins spread with jam. Another visitor to the box was Ivor, with whom we chatted. It was a sad occasion, for we all knew what had happened, although Mother bravely pretended she did not. Elsie did not remain long in the show. She and Mother went to Paris and that was the last I saw of either of them, although I still hear from Elsie—whom I admire and adore—and I heard from Mother regularly up to the time of her death. And every year came a Christmas card, from " Elsie and Mother." Those joint cards only stopped recently, though Elsie's still come and the other day when I sent her a photo of myself to show her what I now look like (God help her!) she wrote back and said I had improved. . . .

But Ivor visited Elsie on his last visit to Hollywood—a holiday this time, the one on which poor Lloyd Williams was stricken down. They were delighted to meet again and, according to

Elsie, Ivor saw Mother too. I have not the slightest wish to hurt anyone's feelings, especially people of whom I am very fond, so I refrain from telling the story as Ivor told it to me—wide-eyed and amazed even then, a long time afterwards—but it was certainly an extraordinary story. Shakespeare, who knew everything there was to know, said that there were more things in heaven and earth than were dreamed of in Horatio's philosophy, and Shakespeare was right. On all these matters, I have a most open mind.

Ivor did some very good numbers for *The House that Jack Built*, including one for Cicely Courtneidge, in which she depicted a Fairy Queen.

Anyway, *The House that Jack Built* brought Ivor £2,262 in royalties, a nice little sum. He had a knack of coming out on the right side. *A Symphony in Two Flats* actually showed a loss on the London run of £169 12*s*. 6*d*., but against that he drew £2,212 10*s*. as salary and £1,544 4*s*. 9*d*. in author's fees, making a profit of £3,587 2*s*. 3*d*. That business acumen of David Ivor Davie's always turned up trumps.

In the year 1928 Ivor had tried to bring about that desire he had for classical acting. He entered into an agreement with Bertie A. Meyer, a well-known theatrical manager who had built the St. Martin's Theatre in West Street, London, near the Charing Cross Road and the famous Ivy Restaurant, and Barry O'Brien, another prominent manager. The three of them put up a capital of £1,333 6*s*. 8*d*. each, for the purpose of staging *Romeo and Juliet* with Ivor as Romeo and Fay Compton as Juliet. Fay Compton was to receive a fixed weekly salary and Ivor was to have 10 per cent. of the gross weekly receipts. The profits were to be divided: 40 per cent. to Ivor and 30 per cent. to each of the others, and Meyer and O'Brien were also to have weekly fee.

The project was subject to Fay Compton being available to play the part on or about October 15th, the date fixed for the tour to commence for the production was to tour before coming to town. If she was not available, then the whole matter was to be reconsidered. And it had to be reconsidered because Fay had a contract to go to America. On July 6th, 1928, Ivor wrote to Bertie Meyer saying, how sickening it all was but hoping that they might do a tour in the future " when we get a nice, strong play suitable for the provinces with a possibility for London sometime later." That did not materialize either. The pity of it was that London—and the provinces—were thereby prevented from seeing Fay Compton as Juliet. In my humble estimation, Fay Compton would have been the greatest Juliet of our time as one could judge from her performance of the part over the air. There was the beauty of face and voice and there was the experience and the ability to play this difficult, elusive role. She would have been our greatest Juliet as she was our greatest Ophelia, in which role she gave performances of amazing loveliness and tragedy.

About the Romeo of Ivor one is not, by any means, so sure. He would have looked every inch of it; no more handsome or romantic Romeo could ever have taken the stage. But, frankly, he had not the depth nor the variety of voice and expression to play that headstrong, love-mad young man. In company with some two thousand others, I saw him do the Balcony Scene at a matinée at Drury Lane, with Jean Forbes-Robertson as his Juliet. There was an offer to him to play it in a production, but wiser friends gave him counsel, which prevailed. He wanted to play Petruchio, too. He did, in the end, play Henry V—the wisest choice of the three and the safest. But, on tour, his Romeo would have played to capacity.

All these things had gone on during the very active period before he went to Hollywood, years which produced *The Truth Game* and *A Symphony in Two Flats* as well.

Ivor got to Hollywood just when the new " talkies " were getting right into their stride. He had been met at the station by Joan Crawford, and she and Douglas Fairbanks junior introduced him round. He was always grateful to them for making his first entrance there so easy and for breaking down the complete strangeness, for there was a strong streak of shyness still in Ivor.

He had gone to Hollywood to write scripts and to play in pictures. The first script was to be his own play *The Truth Game*. He was allotted an office and he was given what I believe is called a " treatment " of the play as seen through the eyes of a Hollywood scriptwriter. To Ivor's astonished gaze, it seemed that the play had received very rough treatment indeed. He said so, too, and his frankness was rewarded. They discovered he had no illusions. He did not consider his script was sacrosanct and that not a line should be altered in any circumstances.

Indeed, they found him receptive, easy and, above all, charming. But he did not know much about Hollywood, its ideas, its extraordinary mentality, its *idée fixe* that what appears on the screen must, except for the title, be entirely different from what has made a big success on the stage. Ivor knew as well as anyone that a mere photographic version of a stage play did not make a good film, but he had, as yet, no idea that the last thing cinema folk desire is to retain anything faintly suggestive of the thing which they have considered it worth their while to buy at a high price. He put in nine months of solid work on that screen version and, at the end, nothing of *The Truth Game* remained at all, not even the names of the characters, and certainly not the title, which became *But the Flesh is Weak*. Those nine months were a revelation to him. He was not even allowed to play the part which he had created. It was played by Robert Montgomery. He also worked on the script of a picture called *Lovers Courageous*.

And, of all things, he worked on the dialogue of a film, which was probably the first of that everlasting series, the hero of which was no less a person than Tarzan. They ought to have gone completely mad and asked Ivor to play Tarzan as well. He would probably have had a shot—and who knows . . . ?

He did not enjoy Hollywood from the working point of view, but he loved the sunshine and the bathing, spending most of his leisure in the sea. He made many friends and he started a kind of interchange of hospitality. Those who had been hospitable to him in Hollywood found that when they came to London, 11 Aldwych and also " Redroofs " could be their homes. Whilst he was still in Hollywood, Lilyan Tashman and Edmund Lowe came to London. They arrived at the flat with Ivor's instructions that they were to stay there. Fred Allen cabled to Ivor as to the extent of the hospitality. Ivor replied " Lowe pays for nothing except food and drinks." There was more in that cable too. Mam was on the warpath again. She had acquired another studio, this time in Paddington. She sent a vague cable to Hollywood about it: she wanted Ivor's grand piano or—at any rate—one of them. The studio was in Porchester Terrace but Mam just said Paddington. The calm, cool judgment of Fred Allen was invoked. Ivor had been writing him to sell Consols, too. Fred Allen was against that. He placed the facts about Mam before Ivor and his advice that Consols should be retained. He cabled this advice and also about Mam and he wanted to know about Lowe. So Ivor sent the cable, an extract from which has been quoted. It said:

> "Lowe pays for nothing except food and drink. Mam can have piano is studio actually in Paddington Station it ought to be what's wrong with Euston Kings Cross and St Pancras keep Consols."

That shows Ivor very typically. Mam had the piano and the studio and the Consols were kept, and no more was said of their being sold until the 100,000 mark was reached.

Other guests who used the flat as residences at various times when Ivor was away were Lilian Davies, Constance Carpenter, Beatrice Lillie, Gwen Ffrangçon Davies, Marda Vanne, Edmund Goulding, Barry Sinclair, and Cyril Ritchard and Madge Elliott. They, the last named, stayed there whilst Ivor was in South Africa. And when they left and he returned, they bequeathed to him the housekeeper Ellen Ashman, who gave him such splendid service up to the very end and for which he was very grateful. He always said that he had "the best of the bargain" through this.

Among those who occupied "Redroofs" during Ivor's absences, were Edna Best and Herbert Marshall and Mr. and Mrs. Owen Nares. Ivor knew how to be host; the terms were always the same: nothing to pay except for food and drink.

However, Hollywood was wasting Ivor's time. He was getting nowhere and that creative urge of his, that constant desire to be on his own and take responsibility was being starved. But he was making many friends—he was, indeed, the friend of all the stars. One made a tremendous impression on him, an impression which remained clear and vivid all his life. One day Lilyan Tashman drove up to his bungalow in a car with Paul Lukas, Kay Francis and another. This other wore trousers, a sweater all stripes, a kind of reefer coat, dark blue glasses and a beret pulled over her hair. It was Greta Garbo. It was their first meeting. Celebrity though he was himself even then, Ivor was always thrilled at meeting other celebrities for the first time, and he admired Garbo of all the artistes he had seen on the screen. Here she was actually in his house, and talking to him. He thought it wonderful. Apparently he broke down her traditional reserve and shyness and desire to be alone—for they talked on and on—and were still talking when the rest of the party went away. Garbo was alone—with Ivor. Ivor had learnt a little Swedish while in Stockholm during the First World War. He tried it on Garbo, who was delighted. It is probable that Ivor did nine-tenths of the talking, but Garbo stayed. That was the point. At last she had to go, and she stood up to say farewell. She smiled at him and said, " Auf wiedersehen." " Really auf wiedersehen?" replied Ivor, who was completely under her spell. " Really auf wiedersehen," she smiled—and was gone.

It was fifteen years before they met again, but there was a friendship between them which endured. They were to meet again in London, and whenever she came here, it was to Ivor that she went for her welcome and he who took her about, disguised in the glasses which she firmly believed rendered her unrecognizable. Ivor had the greatest admiration for her as a woman, a beauty and an artiste. But it was not now in Ivor to be idle. If he was not given enough to do for the film people, he employed himself and he wrote some plays. He did not believe in waste—of time or anything else.

Then came really bad news—the first touch of tragedy in his life. His father died. This was a very, very sore blow to Ivor, who loved him dearly. He died at No. 43 Aldwych, where Mam had taken a flat—one of the causes of the correspondence between her and Fred Allen, over the deductions from her £20-a-week allowance which had already been quoted. It was a flat similar to Ivor's but over the Aldwych instead of the Strand Theatre. Mr. Davies had been suffering from his heart for some some time but the end was unexpected. The doctor wrote the details out to Ivor in Hollywood on October 16th, 1931.

" Dear Mr. Novello,

The sudden death of your father must have come as a shock to you. It was rather unexpected. On Monday last he began to show real progress, in so far that the dropsy was receding and the heart was showing a more definite and regular action. His best day was from the Wednesday morning to the next morning, the morning before he died. On the Thursday morning he was rational and was enjoying a joke at the expense of the nurses and also myself. Altogether conditions seemed favourable. What happened at the end was a little clot in the coronary artery, the vessel supplying the heart itself and its action on the organ is swift and with absolutely no suffering. I have attended many such cases but I have never seen any patient whose illness was so free from any unpleasant and disturbing sequelae. Instead of the dropsy increasing and lung trouble setting in, the former was considerably relieved and the latter was never present. I am so sorry you are so far away but you can take much comfort from the fact that all through this last illness there was the minimum amount of suffering. Your mother was in seeing your father before 6 a.m. and as a matter of fact he spoke to her just before the end. She was then holding his hand. Your mother has been wonderful and most courageous right through. I have just returned from seeing her and she is bearing her great sorrow most bravely. Her one thought is for you.

Let me add my sympathy. I know how deep your sorrow is at not seeing the passing of your devoted father. Believe me, etc."

Ivor's end was from the same cause as his father's and he died only a stone's throw away at 11 Aldwych.

Mr. Davies had been ill for some time. So many men who have been athletic, as he had, die that way, though that was not the case with Ivor. Mr. Davies had been a good cricketer in his youth. Later in life he took up bowls and became first class; indeed, he became a Welsh International. He had the privilege of playing bowls with no less a person than the mighty W. G. Grace, when that Grand Old Man of cricket took up the game late in his life.

Ivor's own sporting activities included an occasional attempt at golf. His clubs were always kept in perfect order by his butler, John Crawford, to whom, after Ivor's death, they were given by the executors. It was not a particularly hard job to keep them clean but it was a labour of love and pride with John, who came from the north, from Berwick-on-Tweed, and who venerated the game. Ivor's golf was mostly confined to putting greens, but if he felt like it and could find a member of his company who could put up with his efforts he would sometimes try a round. He also played tennis a little, egged on and instructed by Peter Graves, an excellent player indeed, of Wimbledon standard; but he was not much good at it. Swimming was Ivor's sport—if the day and the weather were both warm. Ivor was not very fond of the open air. Nor the fresh air—there is not much of it in a Theatre. But he worshipped the sun.

Those slow heart cases with dropsy engendered by the weakened action, and the consequent battle for life with choking lungs, can be most distressing—I speak from close and painful experience—but Ivor's father was spared that. He was cremated and his ashes strewn in the Garden of Remembrance at Golder's Green. Later, Mam was to join her husband there—and later still. . . .

Ivor decided to come home. Hollywood and its ways were no good to him. He was feeling the frustration which so many others have felt. There was, for example, the case of Hugh Walpole. After resisting the lure for many years, he went, hoping to do good work. He was given a splendid office and magnificent terms. He sat in that office waiting to be given work to do, week after week. Nobody ever came near him except the cashier who brought him his large cheque each week. That was not what Walpole wanted. He began to agitate, he demanded to see the head of it all. The head could never be seen; he was either in conference, on the set, or on location. But Hugh Walpole was a determined character. He won. He broke through and he got right into the office at a time when the Great One was neither on the set, in conference, or on location, but was having a rest and a big cigar as well.

To him Walpole the famous—world-famous—novelist, poured out his wrongs. The Great Man of the Motion Picture Industry blinked and could not understand what was the matter. Was the office not good enough? It was not that, protested Walpole. Was it not furnished as he wished? Walpole brushed that aside too. Did he not get his cheque regularly? That gave Walpole eloquence. In clear calm English he told the Great Man that he was a writer and that writers just had to write. He was wasting his time and that was sinful. He wanted to write. He must write. If they did not want him to write in Hollywood then, for God's sake, release him and let him go home so that he could work as he desired. As regards his cheques, that had nothing to do with it; he had received them as per contract and had no complaints in that direction. But he wanted to work and would not take money for nothing.

The Great Man had a glimmering of an idea at this. "Don't worry yourself, take it easy," he said. "We aren't philanthropists here. We know what we are doing. Don't fret about not working, that doesn't matter. It's not so much your work. It's your NAME we want Mr—er—Wrapsle." Hugh Walpole took the next train away from Hollywood, contract or no contract and came home.

Dame May Whitty had a similar tussle on the vexed Hollywood question of nomenclature. When she became Dame of the British Empire, the publicity men of Hollywood and those responsible for the film credits and casts got into a fine mess over this—to them—incomprehensible title. Dame May sought the Chief. " Listen," she said, " About my name. My name is May Whitty. That's all I want. I don't want to be called Dame May Whitty, or Dame Whitty or May Whitty Dame, all of which have appeared. I just want to be called May Whitty. It's very simple. I'll spell it: M-A-Y W-H-I-T-T-Y . . . May Whitty. That's all I want. Do you understand?" The Chief had listened with all ears. " Sure, sure," he said. " I understand. You won't have no more trouble over that. I'll give orders myself, Mrs. Whittle ". . . .

Ivor had no troubles like that. But he was wasting his time and he knew it. He had hoped not only to write films but play in them. He played in one only, opposite Ruth Chatterton, who persuaded him into it. It was called *Once a Lady*. It can be left at that.

He went to Irving Thalberg, the chief of production for M.G.M. who was a friend of his, as was Norma Shearer, his wife. Thalberg listened and he understood. But he asked Ivor not to be rash, to stay another three months. If nothing happened during that time to make him change his mind, well, they would release him. It was during that time that he played in *Once a Lady*. That completed it. He went again to Thalberg and he was released.

He said good-bye to everyone, for he had now many, many friends. They had all come to his home to parties, he had been to all of theirs. He had met and liked Edgar Wallace, that amazing man with an even more amazing career, the master of impossible but compelling thrillers, the record holder of output of words, journalist, editor, newspaper proprietor, war correspondent, dramatist, theatre manager, ex-private soldier and ex-newspaper boy. Wallace died in Hollywood when Ivor was there. Ivor was shocked and mourned with the rest.

He caught the train for New York and he took along his dog Jim. Jim was put in the guard's van and Ivor went to see him. Then he discovered that he had a compatriot and fellow dramatist as his fellow traveller. Edgar Wallace's body was on the same train. . . . Ivor came home and travelling with a corpse did not bring him bad luck.

What a difference between those two men, Novello and Edgar Wallace! Both men whose output of work was enormous; but Ivor's was done by hand and Wallace's by mass production. It was craftsmanship versus machine. Despite his preoccupation with the Theatre and films, Wallace remained always the slave of the printing presses; his soul was in Fleet Street where very rightly his memorial stands, marking the spot where once he sold papers. News meant a lot to him; news meant nothing to Ivor unless it was news of the Theatre. Wallace's work was a succession of glorified paragraphs, expanded at most into serial stories—a quick, breathless business, extremely ingenious, with a master hand at suspense but a complete disregard of probability or carefully linked continuity. Wallace was a master of thrills—thrills of violence. Ivor knew all about thrills too, but his were the thrills of Romance. In the Theatre, the plays of Wallace were subordinate to his own personality, whereas those of Ivor's had his personality welded into them with skill. Both men made vast sums of money, but in business Wallace was careless and was possessed of an overpowering, flamboyant generosity, whether from his heart, or from his sense of publicity. Ivor kept his money, invested it with skill and was never over generous. He gave to a few with an open hand, but not to the many. Wallace promptly doubled the salaries of players who had pleased him and gave gold cigar boxes to his stars to mark milestones in the run; on similar occasions Ivor more often than not was the recipient of presents instead of the giver. He was not mean or tight-fisted, but Wallace's kind of generosity just did not occur to him. And instead of paying his actors and actresses inflated salaries to mark success and thus overloading the play, Ivor got his to run and kept re-engaging those who had pleased him—by far the better way.

Wallace had bitterness and intolerance; he nursed grievances and he was jealous of success in others. Also, he could be—and was—extremely rude and insulting to those whom he did not like. Ivor did not know the meaning of any of these things. He was never jealous of a soul. At no time was there ever any bitterness, though after his imprisonment he had good cause for it. He had, of course, a very happy youth. That of Edgar Wallace had been hard which accounts for much. The conditions of one's childhood can colour the whole of one's life. The names of both men were—still are—household words, but they were the diametric opposites of each other. When Wallace died he was heavily in debt and his affairs were in the most dreadful mess imaginable. When Ivor died his affairs were in perfect order and he did not owe one penny. Even the current income tax, amounting to over £40,000 was there, provided for. Three men—all authors—were the outstanding figures in theatres and films during the 1920s and early 'thirties: Edgar Wallace, Noël Coward and Ivor Novello. It would be hard to find three more different personalities.

Despite his usual immersion in his immediate surroundings, Hollywood had cast no charm over Ivor Novello. He was glad to be back in London, his home. He had found success here; he had his flat here. And there were also his friends, ready and eager to welcome him: Eddie Marsh, Bobbie Andrews, Noël Coward, Viola Tree—all the host of Novellians. No doubt there was a crowd at the station to meet him: there always was.

To meet Ivor returning from a journey was quite an experience. There was always an air of expectancy and subdued excitement around, similar to that which pervades a town's notables awaiting the arrival of Royalty. Nobody kept still, everyone was fidgeting. As the time drew near, the excitement grew intense. Then the train steamed in, the carriage doors opened, and there would be a shout of " There he is—there's Ivor "—and a rush. It was a two-sided rush. For the home-coming of Ivor was never an affair of dignity and high hats. He would leap from the train and dash towards his friends. It was just like a schoolboy coming home from school after a long term to eagerly anticipated holidays. His face was alight, his smile radiant, his eyes agleam. Everyone was embraced—man or woman—everyone was hugged and the women were kissed. There was a hubbub of exclamation—the teeming crowds forgotten—for here was the only important thing on the platform—Ivor. " Ivor," " Ivor," " Ivor " was heard on all sides, the excitement was overpowering. Ivor's voice was as loud as the rest: " Duckie " and " how marvellous " would resound. One would have imagined that he had not seen these people for years, or that either he or they had escaped from the valley of the shadow of death. Cameras clicked or flashed according to the time of day, a reporter or two would get a hurried word and a smile which made him feel that Ivor was as glad to see him as anyone else in that crowd—and so he was—and then the little maelstrom would surge towards the car, that Rolls with the red " I.N." on the door. Then off it would go towards 11 Aldwych, with the rest in full cry after it. And when Ivor came into a well-loved place, he would stop still for a second or so, his face alight with a smile, gaze around him and draw some deep breaths, whilst he spread his arms in wide embrace of his surroundings. He was Home. The King was back—all was right with the world.

However that may all seem in the reading, the amazing thing was that everyone was quite sincere. They really felt the pleasure and joy, and so did Ivor. He was not putting on an act, nor were his friends. He had that power over everyone because he himself really felt it. He never lost his enthusiasm, he never surrendered to boredom; he found something fresh always and he made quite simple things into an adventure. Like his mother, he never really grew up. He was also utterly without self-consciousness.

When Ivor came back from Hollywood he became immersed once more in the Theatre. Films, so far as he was concerned, were at a discount and he was not giving much time to music, although all through his life he composed when the fit was on him, and the list of his works, many quite unknown to the general public, is amazing.

He had written two plays in Hollywood, on which he now did some further work. They were *Party* and *I Lived With You.* It is probable that Ivor liked the latter the best of all his straight plays and he always loved playing in it. This light comedy was something more than superficial amusement. It told the story of a penniless, refugee White Russian, of most exalted rank, meeting a nice, rather lower-middle-class English girl in the maze at Hampton Court. He is starving, she gives him some of her sandwiches—made with " Gentleman's Relish." (That was a joke which, for Ivor, never lost its savour. The mere idea of " Gentleman's Relish " convulsed him.) The Russian was penniless but he had a piece of jewellery with magnificent diamonds. He was taken into the family of decent, ordinary suburban folk, proceeding, with the utmost innocence, thoroughly to upset them. They became snobs, they flaunted him to their neighbours at tea parties—at which the Russian got them tipsy—and the moral fibre of the family cracked under this completely exotic and disturbing influence. But it ended happily, for he went as he had come and just as mysteriously. And when he and his dangerous philosophy had gone—all was well.

Ivor just adored playing the Russian. It gave every chance. And moreover it gave him an opportunity, in certain scenes, to clown to his heart's content and that was what he liked. There was a scene in the suburban villa between him and the little maid-of-all work, whom he did not like and who was scared to death of him. To see him chase her, hissing like a snake, whilst she fled in panic, was something to remember and always got yells of laughter. He adored that scene.

The last time I saw him play it was in 1940, when after Drury Lane had been taken over by Ensa and before *The Dancing Years* was revived he took *I Lived With You* on tour. He had a good company which included, amongst others, Olive Gilbert, Minnie Rayner, Lloyd Pearson and Maidie Andrews, who gave a truly excellent performance. Olive Gilbert, who likes a bit of comedy too, was memorable in the tipsy scene which she handled like an artist, managing to get her hat to suggest genteel tipsyness too. I remember that night well. I had taken my wife with me. I was an Air Raid Warden and, being conscientious, went fully equipped. We had not got uniforms then, but I had my tin hat, all my other " props " and was ready for anything. Managing for Ivor then was Leonard de Renzie, an old friend who had been stage manager at Drury Lane. The blitz on London had not started but the suburbs were getting raids nightly. In the second act the sirens wailed and just as the moan was dying away Minnie Rayner had an entrance and a line to the effect that she thought she had heard a funny noise. That got a nice laugh. A pretty brisk raid proceeded, the show went on and the " All Clear " had not gone when the final curtain fell. As was the custom then, the audience were asked to stop in the theatre, if they so wished. And Ivor made a little speech saying that he and the company would do their best to entertain them. Ninety per cent. of the people stayed on—they would get a treat. I put on my tin hat, went outside to have a look round and then went backstage to see Ivor, who was delighted at the sight of me in my armoured headgear. He then went to the piano and the audience had a wonderful concert. My wife and I left about eleven in the car—we had a long way to go—and the concert was still in full swing. We drove home and it seemed that we were accompanied by a hostile plane which kept abreast of us. It was quite an exciting ride. The " All Clear " did not go until about midnight. Ivor revelled in the concert.

I Lived With You was first produced at the Prince of Wales's Theatre on March 23rd, 1932. It got an excellent Press and so did Ivor personally. He was given a hearty welcome home. The show ran for 120 performances. He looked upon the Prince of Wales's as his lucky theatre for it had seen his first big success in *The Rat*. It transferred from the Prince of Wales's to the Shaftesbury. The production cost Ivor £1,400 6*s*. 4*d*. and the run at the Prince of Wales's and the Shaftesbury showed a loss of £3,926 19*s*. 8*d*., but the tour more than paid for this, and the film rights were sold. Ivor came out well on the right side. He got £2,000 out of the film rights alone.

He was getting bigger ideas now. He decided to get *Party*, the other play written in Hollywood, produced whilst *I Lived With You* was still running. And produced it was, at the Strand Theatre, right underneath the flat. He was not so certain about *Party* as he had been of his other shows. To begin with, he had to some extent flouted a good old crusted theatre superstition. *Party* was a theatrical play. It was about theatrical life and theatrical people. The general idea in the profession is that such plays do not succeed. There is a modicum of truth in this, but there are also many exceptions. It all depends on the play. If it is too much " back stage " it is unlikely to succeed, for theatrical shop and technicalities however delightful to the members of the greasepaint calling, mean very little to the paying public. Indeed, they feel rather out of it and consequently resentful. It seems to them that the players are having a nice little joke all to themselves in which the audience has no part. As a simple background, or for a scene or two, it may get by; but for a whole story and evening's entertainment, most managements would doubt very much.

Yet many films have been backstage stories. Moreover, it would seem that the public now knows a lot of theatrical slang and shop, for quite recently a play called *On Monday Next*, which was about rehearsals in a local repertory company, ran on and on, with Ivor's friend Harry Kendall as lead. *A Pantomime Rehearsal* and *Trelawney of the Wells* were other outstanding exceptions which proved the rule, though they were not given up entirely to Theatre. The first was a farce, the other a magnificently human high comedy, with contrast as its keynote.

However, Ivor, who had enjoyed writing *Party*, and who had as usual written some magnificent roles for actresses therein, was a bit dubious and considered a production at the semi-private Arts Theatre. It went into rehearsal under the polished direction of Athole Stewart and there were few better producers of this sort of play than that first-class actor. Ivor got his beloved Lilian Braithwaite to play the lead. Both she and Ivor—and everyone else—knew that the character she was playing was in reality drawn on Mrs. Patrick Campbell. And when, eventually, she saw it, Mrs. Pat the tempestuous, knew it too, and, unlike Queen Victoria on another occasion, she was amused. There was a first-class cast, including Benita Hume, Sebastian Shaw, Joan Swinstead, Victor Boggetti and others. Once in rehearsal Ivor began to like *Party* as a play and as a potential success; the pleasure he had in writing it was now eclipsed by the pleasure he now derived from seeing it come to reality. He thought it worth while risking a full West End production. It so happened that Leslie Henson and Firth Shepherd, then in partnership at the Strand, wanted an attraction. They came down to rehearsal. They watched—and they took it.

So it opened at the Strand Theatre on May 23rd, 1932. It was a big first-night success and it received a very good Press indeed. Ivor himself had no risk in this production for he was on a good royalty. He played Lord Bay Clender, the male lead and got a good salary. He joined the company on August 1st and played it until the 29th when the play transferred to the Gaiety Theatre. By joining the cast he had kept up the tradition of always playing in his own plays.

Ivor Novello, like many other playwrights, had some favourite jokes and situations which he used over and over again. In *Party* there was a situation in which two women turned up at a gathering, both wearing identical dresses. Even mere men will understand what that means to feminine feelings. Ivor, who understood women as few men have ever done, understood that situation and its repercussions to the full. It delighted the audience. He used it again in *Full House*, a later play. A gag line he enjoyed was in the form of a comment, " Does that still go on? " He never tired of that, and as spoken either by Lilian Braithwaite or Zena Dare, it never failed to delight him and his audience. " Living together? " queried Zena Dare in *Careless Rapture*—" Does that still go on? " Shrieks of delight. " Embroidery? " murmured the same actress in *King's Rhapsody*—" Does that still go on? " Howls of laughter. Well, it is funny, especially as spoken by Zena Dare who knows better than most people the great stage secret of inflection, point and timing. It is far better than W. S. Gilbert's oft-repeated joke, " I saw him kissing her right under my nose, " with the retort " Under her nose, you mean." Other playwrights had such favourite jokes as well.

Party was a success. Ivor left it on August 29th to go on tour with *I Lived With You.* That was a success too. The film rights of *Party* were sold to M.G.M. for £8,000. Ivor was delighted that it was to be a vehicle for Joan Crawford, who had been so kind to him and whom he liked so much. But Hollywood was never very lucky to Ivor; the film was never made. But still, £8,000 for their rights was not so bad.

Ivor enjoyed the tour of *I Lived With You*, but the spirit of unrest that governs the Theatre had got right into his bones now. His natural laziness was conquered by it. Had he merely been a composer, the laziness might have won; but the Theatre was too strong. Whilst on tour he wrote another play, which was *Fresh Fields*. Success at home was running with a flood tide, whatever Hollywood might have done to try and check it.

CHAPTER FIFTEEN

THE GREAT YEARS BEGIN

IVOR NOVELLO was now in the last twenty years of his life. The year 1931 which began the last of the two decades, was almost wasted in Hollywood. The year 1932 brought full recompense with his two successes *I Lived With You* and *Party*. And now in 1933 he stood on the threshold of his biggest play success to date. That was *Fresh Fields*.

These were the years of true achievement, when he had gained the experience he had missed when young, when he was really maturing and when he was going up the hill of Fame with a sure and rapid step. He never knew what it was to pass over the summit and commence the descent, a process so common and so tragic to so many. He never felt his powers wane, his imagination falter, his creative ability fail or even hesitate. He never had to use the whip or the spur, his abilities always went at full gallop. It could never have been said of him that he was "slipping." Indeed it is certain that he never reached the zenith of what he could have attained, for when he died his work both as dramatist and actor was still improving, as was his music, too. The note of maturity and the polish of experience were there. There was not a trace of fatigue or effort.

In 1932 and 1933, Ivor was living and enjoying every moment of his life. He was full of restless energy. He worked hard, he kept late hours, but he took care of himself. He took his afternoon rest to make up for the late nights, never missing it except when strenuous rehearsals interfered. Right up to his end this held good, and between a matinée and an evening show the notice that he was resting and not to be disturbed would hang on the handle of his dressing-room door. He did this not only for his own sake but because he thought it unfair to go before an audience and give a tired and indifferent performance. That was one of the secrets of his success.

In all the years I knew and worked with him, I never saw him give a bad performance. It was one of the things which made him Number One Box Office. That cannot be said of all the great stars, of either sex, but it was another thing which he shared with the older actor-managers, and especially with Tree and Lewis Waller. Waller never showed signs of fatigue even if he felt it; he was always on his toes, he never lost that swinging stride; it was as if his muscles and sinews were of steel springs. And, like Ivor, Waller never lost his temper. Whenever things went wrong, no matter how great the provocation, he never showed anger. The only way to tell was to watch his neck. When he was furious but still outwardly calm, his neck would go very red. He was a living example of that peculiarity which the Boers deemed general amongst us and which made them call us "rooineks." Ivor never went red in the neck, however, He would be serious, a little sad and extremely polite, but there would be a sarcasm which only dawned on its recipient later.

In 1932 he toured *I Lived With You.* He was making money fast. Losses, if any, on the London runs, were turned into handsome profits in the provinces. He was very wise indeed to undertake those tours. It was another proof of that acute business acumen which this amazingly artistic person possessed. It was, of course, David Ivor Davies showing Ivor Novello the way to make money. He never surrendered to the stranglehold of the West End, wherein he showed his wisdom. He was already a big box-office attraction and in 1932 he was acknowledged Number One Box Office in the provinces.

We know how the fans mobbed him, tearing his hair and clothes, damaging his car, and sometimes putting him into a position of peril. But he did not mind; he just adored it. He was all the time steadily building up and solidifying his popularity. He never fled from his admirers as did Lewis Waller. He never dodged them as did Owen Nares. Nor did he force himself upon them: he did not have to; they did not meet him half-way, they came the whole distance. All Ivor had to do was to stand still, and the fans were attracted like steel filings to a powerful magnet. There was something in his personality which made him welcome in any country, in any town, wherever he went and in any stratum of society. Even in the dark days of his imprisonment, he was the most popular man there. Popularity like his does not come to those who seek it; it is a natural possession and that is how it worked with Ivor. Everyone, whether they knew him or not (except a tiny minority of jealous curmudgeons) looked upon him as a friend, just as everybody called him Ivor.

He never deserted the provincial Theatre, even when he was absolute King of the West End and ruled Drury Lane. He would go out with his latest success and playhouses were besieged. Indeed, it was hardly a tour then; it was what Christopher Hassall described with such truth and beauty when he spoke his address at Ivor's Memorial Service as " a royal progress." Christopher Hassall spoke of him as a Prince but, in his own province, that of the Musical Stage, he was undoubtedly a King. It was not just the West End that loved Ivor Novello, it was the whole country; Scotland as well as England and, of course, his own Wales. He never went to Eire nor to Northern Ireland when at the peak of his career. But the Irish, whether of north or south, came to see and applaud him when they came to Town.

He was doing very well financially in the early 'thirties. His earnings in 1927-8 were £11,618; in 1928-9, £15,460; in 1929-30, £12,995 and in 1930-1, £12,440. The big jump in 1928-9 was accounted for by film earnings.

Whilst he was touring with *I Lived With You* he wrote *Fresh Fields*. He nearly always wrote plays or composed music whilst on tour; there were fewer social distractions and golf made no calls upon his time. He wrote it quickly, how quickly he will state for himself later. He had an ambition in this play, which was not realized. He wrote a part for Lilian Braithwaite and another part of equal magnitude and importance which he designed for Marie Tempest. That was the ambition. He wrote this play, as he wrote them all, very quickly, because he always knew where he was going and could always see the end quite clearly.

The great Henry Arthur Jones, one of this country's great dramatists, laid it down that the definition of a good play was the same as Euclid's definition of a straight line—the shortest distance between its two extreme points. Whatever the merits of Ivor's plays from the purely artistic standpoint, they certainly subscribed to that. He would have been the last person to claim greatness for them or literary distinction. What he wanted to do was to effect a workmanlike job for the Theatre and give amusement to the public. He very seldom failed in that and, when he did, it was either because he ventured on to ground which he did not understand, or allowed his love of backstage life to swamp his sense of public values. What he did, and always

Top : A gay gathering at Ivor's house in Jamaica

Centre : With Fred Allen in the garden of "Redroofs"

Below : Robert Andrews, Ivor, Lord Beaverbrook and Beatrice Lillie at Ivor's Jamaica home on his last holiday

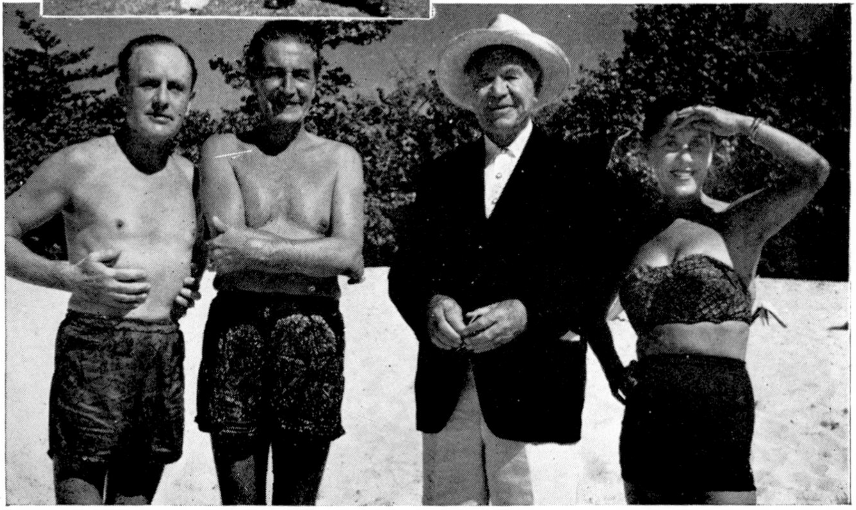

Ivor and Fay Compton in scenes from *Proscenium*. He played two roles in this comedy

did, was not so much to create original characters, as to create characters which certain stars could play superbly well, characters designed for them, their peculiarities, their mannerisms, their very tone of voice. He fitted the parts to the players like a skilled costumier. He had written a part for Minnie Rayner, who was now his mascot and whose comic abilities he loved and could exploit to the full. And now he offered the play to Marie Tempest with a part which he had written expressly for her. He encountered difficulties. It would have been strange indeed if he had not done so. That great actress was always one of the major " headaches " of the Theatre, just as difficult but in a very different way as was Mrs. Patrick Campbell. Ivor knew her and adored her—it is so easy to use that word when writing about him for he always used it himself. Not only did he want her in his play for his own sake, but he wanted to give her a part in which she could make a major success. He believed he had written the part, too.

Marie Tempest did not always have successes, despite her fame and her art. Indeed, she appeared in many failures. Her art, though perfection of its kind, was limited and very personal. She had not the power to lift a second-rate play into a popular success, although when she was on the stage the audience would be entranced. In all her long career, she never played a great role, she never triumped in one of the classic successes. She played " Marie Tempest " parts, and, naturally, nobody could play them like her. She was, despite this limitation, a very magnificent actress within her sphere. Towards the end of her life, she was a perfection of technique. She knew the business of the stage backwards. Every movement, every inflection, every pause was exactly as it should be. Nobody, since Mrs. Kendal, could cry on the stage as she could; nobody could pour out tea or drink it like Marie Tempest. These sound small matters, but that is how great acting is built up. She was terribly incensed on one occasion at the Haymarket because they would not let her play Queen Gertrude in *Hamlet*. I think it is a pity she was not allowed to do it. She probably understood the acute feminity of that character, for Gertrude was pre-eminently a woman driven by sex. Marie Tempest in the role might have been a revelation to everyone. But she did not play it. She appeared in so many plays which were quite unworthy of her because they contained a " Marie Tempest " part.

Marie Tempest's last and best part was in *Dear Octopus* by that dramatist who really understands life and people and who can make them perfectly natural and life-like and still give them the necessary magnification which the Theatre demands, and who has the knack of keeping it out of sight—Dodie Smith. This clever little woman is really one of the major dramatists of our time and posterity will grant her her rightful place. Whilst appearing to write what are theatrically known as " nudgers "—which means that all the characters are so real that members of the audience nudge each other in recognition of husbands, wives, relatives and friends—she always had a true underlying theme. Her plays were always about something. There was always a motive. The past tense is used—more is the pity—because she has not written a play for a long time. May that omission soon be rectified for the contemporary stage can do with the works of Dodie Smith. In the future, people who want to know how the middle classes of this country—the true backbone of the nation—lived, thought, spoke and behaved will find a truly accurate and perfect picture of them in the plays of Dodie Smith—more so than in the works of any other contemporary dramatist.

In *Dear Octopus* Miss Smith gave Marie Tempest a magnificent character and Marie Tempest played it magnificently. It was the best thing she ever did. But the storms and stress of rehearsals had to be seen to be believed. I know. I saw them as I was part of the outfit. I was on the side of Dodie Smith, for whom I have not only admiration as a dramatist but affection as a friend. In the Theatre Marie Tempest was a tyrant who ruled by fear and who oppressed the younger members of the company, especially if they were girls. I do not abate my admiration for her as an actress one jot by saying that. I only want to show what Ivor was coming up against. I doubt if even he could have ruled her, despite his charm and the affection she had for him. At rehearsal, or during the run, she was a real terror. I will admit that she was the one person in the Theatre of whom I was afraid. And I learned my business in the hard school. She was so unpredictable; you never knew what was coming next. Yet I managed to get on very well with her, but I never shed my armour or dropped my guard for one split second. This is not the place for the story of Marie Tempest, which I shall tell elsewhere. She could be, she often was, quite ruthless. Ivor would have had a trying time. But whatever her faults, she was in her time Queen of the British Theatre and, as such, must be honoured.

Ivor sent his play to W. Graham Browne, who was Marie Tempest's last husband, a dear, nice fellow who understood her but had his work cut out. He was an actor of charm and a fine and sensitive producer. It will be remembered that he had stepped in and produced *The Truth Game*, doing Ivor a very great service and doing it supremely well. It must be remembered that Marie Tempest had praised that play, too. Here was Ivor paying his debt and writing a perfectly gorgeous part for Marie Tempest. But now the trouble started.

Marie Tempest made all sorts of conditions, some impossible, some very onerous and she went in for long and vexatious delays. What she did not like, of course, was the presence of Lilian Braithwaite in the cast, for Lilian could have held her own with Marie Tempest and probably have emerged victorious. Nor did she like the idea of Minnie Rayner. There were talks, letters, arguments, delays. She wanted the Haymarket Theatre—she wanted all sorts of things. Now, with a play one has to get the right theatre and in 1932 it was not so easy to just walk into a theatre and say " We're here." Theatres have commitments, they are costly to keep shut—ruinously costly. Owners of theatres have to look ahead and indulge in a long-term policy. Ivor knew all this, of course, and so did Marie Tempest. But she liked to be awkward. Ivor saw the chance of his play missing the right moment for production and the right theatre, too. He was abroad in Paris. His manager, at that time M. E. Benjamin, had interviews which were fruitless. Reports went to Ivor in Paris. Time was getting very short. So Ivor wrote himself to W. Graham Browne. Here is the letter, which places the full facts on record in Ivor's own words:

Hotel Majestic,
Paris.
23rd November, 1932.

" My dear Willie,

Forgive typing but I am in bed with a slight cold. I have just had a long twenty-five minutes' talk with Benjamin who has tried to give me the full position, and it seems to me that there are too many difficulties in the way of our original plan working out the way I had hoped and I should like to enumerate them if I may.

"The opening at Brighton, which I negotiated at Mary's original suggestion, is out of the question without a guarantee—the worst week in the year facing a loss of possible £300—a very high price to pay for what will be hardly more than a series of dress rehearsals—this I have turned down.

"The other alternative was Blackpool where they would give a guarantee and it was a week further off, which was all to the good; we could have had the theatre for as long as we liked during the previous week for rehearsals, and if we liked, opened on the 24th, the Saturday evening.—This idea Mary did not like, so I turned it down.

"The Haymarket. Certainly a grand theatre with a definite date but, with a proposed play going in first with Madge Titheradge, as remote as Buckingham Palace!—because, as we all know, the very plays we have no confidence in run for years and the others we believe in, three weeks, also

"I had discussed and obtained very favourable terms with Bronson Albery—and I could not tell him calmly we had fixed somewhere else—and let's face it, the Criterion has, at the moment, a much more successful record than the Haymarket, though naturally we could not play to nearly the money, but at Christmas time theatres are impossible to get, and if the Haymarket happened to click, or indeed ran six weeks, which it might easily do, we should be properly in the soup.

"The question of cast. Now, Willie, you know I am the last person to blow my own trumpet or shout about being the author of the play, but the fact remains that all my plays have been successes and have made a great deal of money (you helped me enormously with one for which I was very grateful) and I venture to think that this has been mainly because I have taken the trouble to write good parts for people whom I *know* could play them, and this I have done in *Fresh Fields*. And I have written the part *for* Minnie Rayner just as much as I wrote the others for Mary and Lilian. Because I *see* her in it, and she has proved in two plays of mine how invaluable she is both to the satisfaction of the public and to the author, I do not swerve from the idea for one moment. Mary and you do not see her in juxtaposition to Mary but I do. You see, Willie, I am not in the Theatre—who is?—for purely altruistic motives; I like to back my fancy with my own money, my own plays and my own idea of casting—and this I was going to do in this play. I love and very much fancied Mary and Lilian together with Minnie in comic contrast, and I believe the idea would have been completely successful, but as I am silly enough to be putting up money for any theatrical venture just now, I am silly enough also to want my own way about it.

"If I was some down-trodden young author trying to get a play done, I should have no alternative but to turn the whole thing over to be done as other people wished, but I am not at this moment (this may come later) unknown or down-trodden, which brings me to the question of re-writing. I quite admit I wrote the play quickly, three and a half weeks, but I have always written quickly, I can't write any other way. *Symphony*, three weeks—*I Lived With You*, three weeks—*Party*, two and a half weeks. Noël wrote *Hay Fever* in ten days and *Easy Virtue* in two weeks, so that what you find wrong in the play is not from hurry but probably from my intention. When I read the play to Lilian she had only one suggestion: a slight tightening up as to how Minnie and Una came into contact with Lady Strawholme, with which I quite agreed, so that I am afraid that I couldn't manage anything drastic in the way of re-writing.

"Now, Willie, *please* don't think for one moment that I am belittling in any way Mary's great position on the stage, or my adoration for her as an artiste, bless her, or as an enchanting woman, bless her again, nor that I should not be more than honoured to have her playing in a play of mine. I am only trying to tell you that I've got an instinct about this play, done in the way I see it. If you and Mary don't agree then do please say so, and we can call the whole thing off with no bones broken, only with me left with a great regret at losing an exquisite artiste. You can call me obstinate, extremely swollen-headed and spoiled, but that won't prevent my continuing to be

Your very loving
Ivor Novello."

That letter is typical Ivor; it shows his whole character and his method of work. It is a very illuminating document. There, clearly expressed, is his business sense, his acumen, his belief in his method of work, his demonstration of how he worked and his determination to be master of his own fate, to shoulder all the responsibility, come what may. It is as firm as a rock, yet entirely free from offence and not even the most sensitive artiste could really have felt hurt. But it brought the affair to a head. The deal was called off, so far as Marie Tempest was concerned. Events proved that Ivor was right and that she was entirely wrong. If he lost his chance of having the Queen of our stage in one of his plays, she lost her chance of a very big—perhaps her biggest—success. The letter also shows what Miss Tempest—or Dame Marie Tempest, as she became—had in mind in the way of desires and objections. No words of mine are needed to underline it.

No reply came to that letter. Ivor got on to Fred Allen, his trusted lieutenant, and told him to go at once and see Marie Tempest and Graham Browne at their home in Avenue Road and make it clear that he wanted a very quick decision. Their decision was give to Fred Allen, as stated above.

The play was then sent to Irene Vanbrugh. That gracious lady wasted no time, raised no awkward objections, but dealt with the matter at once. Fred Allen had telephoned the Tempest refusal to Ivor and acted at once on Ivor's instructions to take the play to Miss Vanbrugh. Miss Vanbrugh's reply, which is so typical of herself, came without delay and here it is.

Dudley House,
Westmoreland Street, W.1.
29th November, 1932.

" Dear Mr. Allen,

I have read the play and think it quite delightful. As I told you last night, I had to give another decision this morning to a management with whom I had been negotiating, and they settled in my favour the points that were under discussion, so that now is fixed and this means that I shall not be able to appear in Mr. Novello's play.

"I will write to him personally, as you tell me he is coming back from Paris at the end of the week, thanking him for thinking of me and telling him how very sorry I am and I do hope the opportunity will come to be in one of his plays another time.

"As to the play itself, I feel sure it is a ' winner '. It quite delighted me—also a delightful part.

Yours very truly,
Irene Vanbrugh."

There is a typical letter from one of the very great ladies of the British stage, with as much right to be considered Queen thereof as Marie Tempest. Both Irene Vanbrugh and Marie Tempest became Dames of the British Empire. Neither of them appeared in *Fresh Fields* nor in any other Novello play. Lilian Braithwaite, who did, also became a D.B.E. as well. Dame Irene uses the word " delightful " in her letter, and no other word is so apt as a description of herself. The word " lady," like the word " gentleman," is sadly misused but there is really no other word which adequately describes Dame Irene. She was an English gentlewoman of the very best kind, with a charm and kindliness which was innate and a dignity which was all her own. It never obtruded, though it was there just the same. There is no space here, nor is this the place, to try to do justice to her acting. Those playgoers who had the inestimable privilege of seeing her saw acting at its best. Those who were doubly privileged to see her play Nina in Pinero's *His House in Order* saw one of the finest performances ever given by a British actress—be the others who they may.

But here was Ivor in search of a joint leading lady. He had turned down Marie Tempest's difficulties and demands. The " worst week " to which he refers is the week prior to Christmas. He had remained loyal to his Minnie Rayner (it will be noticed that Dame Irene raised no objections) but he still had to find someone who could play that part. There remained the actress to whom he had turned in his stress over *The Truth Game*—Ellis Jeffreys. The part was offered to her and this time she made no demur. She accepted it. So the play went into rehearsal, with Athole Stewart as the producer. *Fresh Fields* opened at the Criterion Theatre on January 5th, 1933. It ran 464 performances, Ivor's biggest success up to that time. And it is in constant demand to-day for both amateur societies and repertory companies. Lilian Braithwaite, Ellis Jeffreys and Minnie Rayner all scored very big successes. The Criterion was packed to capacity for months and months. Ivor had been right all along over this play, despite the short time it had taken him to write, at which Marie Tempest cavilled. He had a knack of being right about such things. Whether the combination of Lilian Braithwaite and Marie Tempest or Lilian Braithwaite and Irene Vanbrugh would have been better than that of Lilian Braithwaite and Ellis Jeffreys, does not matter now. Miss Jeffreys was a splendid actress without equal in her own line. The best might have been Lilian Braithwaite and Irene Vanbrugh. The parts were those of two sisters and there was a certain similarity between these two ladies—perhaps because they were both daughters of the Church—not so much in their art as in their manner and demeanour. Again that word " lady " is necessary.

Ivor did not play in *Fresh Fields* which was unusual for him. He watched the first-night performance from a box, with Mam by his side and she shared his triumph. That was in 1933. He never saw another first night of one of his own shows from

" the front " until he sat in a box to witness another triumph in *Gay's the Word* on Friday, February 16th, 1951, eighteen years afterwards. That was at the Saville Theatre. It was his " first night "; he died seventeen days later. . . .

Fresh Fields was by way of being his best play. It was an " inspiration " about which he always had a " hunch," and, like most of his " hunches," it was right. The production did him much good, for critics almost began to take him seriously. Up to then he had been regarded as a very handsome young man who could act a bit and write tuneful music, and who had a flair for writing amusing plays which were not to be taken too seriously. But *Fresh Fields* had quality. A few of the discerning men of the Theatre, whose years of experience taught them to look below the surface, began to expect a lot more from Ivor Novello. It revealed an improvement in craftsmanship and a sign of real maturity. He was really to be reckoned with as a dramatist. And in 1933 the Theatre was not in these ways in a very flourishing state, although there were some good names. The giants of old, the Pineros, the Henry Arthur Joneses, the Grundys, the Hubert Henry Davises, the R. C. Cartons seemed lacking. But there was Rudolf Besier, J. B. Priestley, Emlyn Williams, Walter Hackett, Ben Travers, Ashley Dukes, James Bridie and, of course, Dodie Smith, to mention a few, with Terence Rattigan just round the corner. And Somerset Maugham was still writing for the Theatre, so was a giant called George Bernard Shaw. There was as well, Noël Coward, whose *Cavalcade* two years before at Drury Lane and whose *Bittersweet* had made history, to say nothing of many other successes. Noël Coward and Ivor Novello were now the two most significant figures in the British Theatre: two young men who were both actor-dramatist composers. And, what is so very important in the Theatre, both were " news."

Being " news " is dangerous. It can upset balance, poise, and level-headedness quicker than anything else. But it did not do that to either of these two. There they stood in the world of the Theatre which reflected to some degree the world around them, in as much as it was far from stable, far from feeling solid ground beneath its feet and, generally speaking, far from prosperous either. But both Coward and Novello were firmly rooted. Money was still plentiful when compared with the years to come after the Second World War, although prices had never gone back to the old pre-1914 level. It was a dancing world, which did not pay much heed to serious things and, for many, many unfortunate people, a world in which there was little or no work. People still clung to the belief that there would be no more war, and that gay parties, speed, travel by air, and luxury cruises were all that mattered.

The real clash between the old order of Capital and the new order of Labour was in full swing. There had been much talk of a Gold Standard, which few people understood but all talked about, and which this country had abandoned. A royal visit by that wise king, George V, with his family, to Noël Coward's *Cavalcade* at Drury Lane Theatre had done much to allay a financial panic. Money was shaky all the world over and in Germany a new force was rising, where a man called Hitler was making his harsh, grating, and most unpleasant voice widely heard. They were not good years, those middle and late 'thirties, although they were the years when Ivor Novello reached his greatness. But he was not worrying much about the world outside. Like all true " professionals " he was only concerned with that very circumscribed world of the Theatre, the rest being illusion whilst the illusion of the Theatre was real. But before he had this big success in the Theatre, he wanted to reach another ambition: the urge to become a classical actor was upon him again. He had, as yet, never brought that production of *Romeo and Juliet* to fruition.

He went off now on another Shakespearean track. Why should he not play Petruchio? Why should he not stage *The Taming of the Shrew*? That was comedy—indeed, farce—and would not demand the tragic intensity of *Romeo*. Surely it was within his scope—and it was Shakespeare! Here was the true actor-manager spirit coming out in Ivor. His heroes, Tree, Waller, Ainley, Forbes-Robertson, Alexander, Matheson Lang had all played Shakespeare, and as he desired to carry on the tradition, he felt he should do so too.

He thought about it and he liked it. So he wrote to Tyrone Guthrie, asking him to come and discuss it with him. He got no reply. He wired to Tyrone Guthrie and an answer came, written on Westminster Theatre notepaper (where he had recently produced *The Anatomist*) with the address scratched out and his own substituted. It read:

23 Old Buildings,
Lincoln's Inn, London,
September 19th, '32.

" Dear Mr. Novello,

I have been away in Ireland and—may they be devoured by pigs—the post office people have been very erratic about forwarding things, with the result that your letter and wire were both awaiting me when we got back last night. *Yes:* I am very intrigued by the notion of producing *The Taming of the Shrew* for you. I don't remember the play very well, but the idea of yourself and Miss Jeans in Shakespeare's comedy at Xmastime is grand. I'd love to have a go at it. Meantime I'll read the play again and perhaps when you come back to London you will let me know and we could discuss it all further. I hope that my delay in replying hasn't caused you to look for another producer.

Yours sincerely,
Tyrone Guthrie."

It had not. Ivor knew what he wanted and he was wise to want Tyrone Guthrie. Ivor was away on tour with *I Lived With You* when he wrote to Guthrie and *Fresh Fields* was as yet unproduced. He was busy, too, with another idea for a play, but the Shakespearean urge was there just the same. He wrote back to Guthrie, who replied:

23 Old Buildings,
Lincoln's Inn, W.C.2.
September 29th, '32.

" Dear Mr. Novello,

Thanks for your letter. Yes, delighted to meet you on Oct. 10th at 11 Aldwych. I'll have read the play by then and we can have a lot of talk. Yes, I'm looking forward to this *very* much. And I'm glad you're not going to be the least like the sort of Petruchio that anyone ever thought about. That's as it should be. And there must be no purple velvet, and no Mary Queen of Scots caps and no gentlemen in ' Tammies ' with ostrich feathers and above all—*no fur*—anywhere. I think Messel's a grand idea but surely he's doing *The Winter's Tale* then for Cochran and is also very expensive—but then again, perhaps not. Anyway, Oct. 10th at 11 Aldwych at 12 o'clock.

Yours sincerely,
Tyrone Guthrie."

It was Isabel Jeans who was to be Katherine the Shrew to Ivor's Petruchio. It seems a pity that this projected production never came off. The reason for that is not known now. Probably Isabel Jeans got involved in another play and there are signs that Ivor wanted Gladys Cooper to play it. Anyway, although he and Tyrone Guthrie had several talks about it over breakfast, it was never done.

I have my own idea about it, though. It is in my mind that, secretly, Ivor wanted the velvet, the Mary Queen of Scots caps, the Tammies with ostrich feathers and the fur—they all had their appeal for him. . . .

Anyway, if he did not play Petruchio he had his reward in *Fresh Fields*. That was real success. And he wanted it because just before its production he had suffered one of his few setbacks, one of his very few " flops." He had written a play called *Flies in the Sun*. It was not a bit like his usual work. But he appeared in it with Gladys Cooper. She was then at the Playhouse as actress-manageress and it was under her management that it was produced. It was not a very lucky theatre for Ivor Novello. He had not shone when, as a young actor, he had appeared there with Gladys Cooper in *Enter Kiki*. But the two of them had made a very big success in *Iris* at the Adelphi when, as chronicled, Ivor's box office value saved the show. Anyway, to quote his favourite word, he " adored " Gladys Cooper (how right he was) and felt great joy at being with her again. Indeed, at one time a gossiping public had linked their names with a view to marriage.

Flies in the Sun brought no sunshine to anyone. This play about a lot of most unpleasant people in the South of France was no good. Ivor was writing about something he did not understand, even if he thought he did. He could not be unpleasant himself, even if he tried, and the characters never rang true. They were mere filmy shadows without semblance of humanity. Not even the tremendous popularity of Miss Cooper and Ivor could save it . . . it was bad. And, more dangerous than that, it was not what the public expected from Ivor.

Much is heard of the iniquity of the theatre managements who insist on " typing " players. It is really the public who types them far more than the managements. That has been proved over and over again. Charles Hawtrey shaved off his moustache—almost his trademark—to play in a delightful costume comedy at the Vaudeville Theatre called *Mr. George* and entrancing Billie Burke played opposite to him. The public would have none of it. This was not the Hawtrey they adored, the Hawtrey of the easy charm and familiar moustache, lying his way with ingenuity out of all sorts of difficulties. They did not want him in powdered wig and sentiment, although it was one of his best performances. So off came the play and back went the moustache as soon as he could grow it.

Owen Nares, at the height of his fame as matinée idol, went into management at the Queen's Theatre, Shaftesbury Avenue, in 1919. He started with a not too good play called *The House of Peril* based on a novel by Mrs. Belloc Lowndes entitled *The Chink in the Armour*. It got a rapturous reception and the Libraries did a deal right away. He followed it with a piece of American sentiment, all about a poor composer living in the garret and falling in love with the sweetly charming little rich girl. It was entitled *The Cinderella Man*. Nine months run to big business! Then he did the best play he presented there, *Mr. Tod's Experiment* by Walter Hackett. It was one of the very early flashback plays and Hackett had used the idea really ingeniously. It had a splendid cast including Holman Clark, Fred Kerr, Marie Polini (Mrs. Owen Nares), Tom Nesbitt, Meggi Albanesi, Marion Lorne and many other distinguished people. It was a lovely production and got " rave " notices. But Owen played a young man with no backbone, unsympathetic and, in the first act—he wore a beard! There was a shudder all through the house when he first appeared. We had that beard off with every expedition, but the damage was done. Although he gave an excellent performance, it was not the type of thing they wanted to see Owen Nares appear in. And certainly not in a beard. I was as much to blame as anyone. I was general manager of the undertaking and was all for the play. Despite the splendid acting and cast, despite notices which said " the best comedy for twenty-five years " it ran about sixty performances and would have run less but for Walter Hackett and I conspiring together and Hackett putting in cheques to purchase seats to bring the takings just over the danger line. Despite all that, despite floods of publicity and despite that most dangerous of all remarks in the Theatre " I don't know what's the matter. Look how well it *goes*," the show came off and lost money. Indeed, it closed Nares's season of management.

So it was with Ivor in *Flies in the Sun*. It was not even a good title, this picture of " rotters " on the Riviera. It flopped. And it probably did Ivor good. One learns more from failures than from the successes. Indeed, almost all one can ever learn in the Theatre is " what not to do "—and then it is easy to be wrong.

The success of *Fresh Fields*, following hard upon it, put Ivor right back where he belonged. Although he did not play in it, it was an Ivor Novello show. And that was what the public always wanted—right up to the end.

CHAPTER SIXTEEN

STAGE, FILMS AND DOMESTIC STORMS

FRESH Fields cost Ivor Novello £1,073 9*s.* 8*d.* to produce a sum which seems fantastically small to-day, but which was then, in 1933, quite large though not extravagant. Ivor did it well, as he always did, but he never wasted money, because he knew what he wanted. The complete cast at the Criterion was Gwen Floyd, Martin Sands, Lilian Braithwaite, Ellis Jeffreys, Robert Andrews, Minnie Rayner, Eileen Peel, Fred Groves and Martita Hunt. It was produced by Athole Stewart.

Ivor had been quite right about the Criterion Theatre. That playhouse, although small, stands in the very centre of the world, in Piccadilly Circus, and is a wonderful theatre for what are theatrically known as " Doors." That means money taken over the box-office counter for the actual performance between the time the doors open and the start of the show, as against seats booked in advance. In this respect the Criterion is remarkable. I know from personal experience. I have done plays there which, when the doors opened, had only £5 on the booking sheet but which at the final return showed over £100. Ivor had known what he was doing when he decided not to risk waiting for the Haymarket. That beautiful theatre was having rather a run of bad luck at the time: it comes to them all in turn. The play Ivor mentioned in which Madge Titheradge was to appear, and which stood in his way, was *Business with America*, which was not a success. But *Fresh Fields* was a success, most emphatically.

And its success led to a nice little row with Mam. It is as well to get the relations between Ivor and his mother into full and precise focus and to set them on record.

Business at the Criterion was of the " capacity " nature. That means that every seat in the house was sold. That mattered little to Mam. This was her son's play and, therefore, hers as well. So one Saturday night—the night on which it is absolutely tabu to ask for complimentary seats in any theatre, even if business is not good—M. E. Benjamin, who was business manager at the Criterion for Ivor, was faced with a rough scrap of paper, torn from a letter-heading, on which was scrawled "Please give Mrs. Hayes two or three seats and oblige, Clara Novello Davies." There was hardly a seat at that moment and the few remaining were being queued for. Mr. Benjamin had been faced with these demands before and on one occasion had, very rightly, turned down the bearer of a similar demand. This led to his being reported to Ivor and a whole lot of trouble. He did not want a recurrence of this, so he passed in Mrs. Hayes, for three stalls. But he spoke to Fred Allen, who at once saw the justice of the manager's complaint.

Fred Allen wrote a tactful but firm letter to Ivor, pointing out the difficult position in which Benjamin was placed and also underlining the fact that it was not only the loss of revenue from the seats which mattered, but the bad effect of giving away seats for plays which were in popular demand. He drew attention to the fact that women were apt to talk and that the idea of free admission got round and did harm to everyone. He suggested that if this was tactfully explained to Mam—and Ivor was the only person who could do it—she might be made to see reason in this matter. He had just emerged from a pretty tough battle with her himself over financial matters and did not want to enter the lists again. He had won the fight but had been quite unable to convince Mam that Ivor had reached his eminence by his own efforts. She was, on her part, firmly convinced it was entirely owing to her. Ivor took action—there was a pretty good row—but no more "chits" came to the Criterion box office.

As stated earlier, Mam had absolutely no money sense. She lived in a world of her own, roseate of hue and always saw a glowing future before any project which leapt into her brain, however fantastic it might be. She would win, she was quite sure. She seldom did. She got herself into the most frightful tangles, the most complicated of difficulties. This did not happen only in this country but in America. She decided to teach singing over there. She took premises far beyond her means on the slenderest of foundations; in fact, with no foundation at all. That had been going on for years. She was in great distress in New York as early as 1916 which brought a cable from her to Fred Allen which read:

Thankful for news very worried over money last hundred went for advance rent colossal possibilities impossible continue without money to start cable one hundred and fifty pounds immediately to 519 Westend Ave for advertising and living can then go ahead otherwise must return at once don't worry Ivor writing full details

Davies

That is only one of many such incidents. There was another crisis in 1924 when Ivor had to cable here pretty strongly and which drew this reply:

Your long expensive letter just arrived biggest shock of my life finding I am your last consideration read again my letter that you have now answered the only proof of love is sacrifice and don't forget you will reap as you sow will you send Theresa immediately to me by next boat God guide you all love

Mamsie

There was a much greater crisis in 1925. She was really in a bad fix and her attorneys cabled and said so on her behalf. Ivor, had, of course, helped her out on all previous occasions, and this was in addition to the allowance he gave her, but this time he took strong action. He cabled his attorneys who, of course, were Mam's as well and said that she was to be helped but that she must come home, give up this succession of panics and submit to being told what she was to do. A cable to him went over wires which probably sizzled with her rage:

Your cable to your attorneys concerning me monstrous and amusing no one has or ever will rule me and certainly not my only child goodbye

Mam

Fred Allen was always trying to get her to see reason and sometimes succeeded; but it was for the moment only. Soon she would be off on a new track again. A letter to him from Ivor reveals how much Ivor himself was doing for her with absolutely no result. It also shows Ivor's own thoughts and character, and how he lived up to them. It is a sad letter from a worried young man doing his best. Here it is:

Two romantic attitudes in *Perchance to Dream*

Ivor and Vanessa Lee immediately after her success on the first night of *King's Rhapsody*

Ivor tries Shakespeare: an impressive-looking Henry the Fifth

With Roma Beaumont in *The Dancing Years*

Ivor, with Madge Titheradge, in his first stage role, *Deburau*

A poetic pose in *The Firebrand*

A Quartet of Roles

"' My dear Fred,

I'm really most unhappy about Mother's letter! Does she really think I haven't done enough? I'm afraid she does. No one is more sensible of the enormous work she did with 'Till the Boys' and all my other compositions than myself, and without wishing to throw bouquets at myself, I think I have shown it. I have, as you know, since last October given her about £800 (£500—£100 to go away—£90 to Ascherbergs and £50 I cabled to her and £60 odd with which I intend paying the rent). That is more than one-third of what I have made: and how much further is she towards getting clear of her debts?—hardly any at all. It is frightfully disheartening to feel that all I have done has been practically *no* use and to think that I am actually expected to *go on* throwing money into what seems a bottomless pit is really more than I can face, and nothing will induce me to make a business arrangement, as I feel that I ought to be allowed to use my judgment as to when and what to give. I personally am never going to drift into the hopeless muddle of never having any money that Mother has, through her marvellous but utterly foolish goodness of heart. I've got my whole life and career before me, and I simply *won't* cripple myself at the beginning by ladling out money continuously which seems to bring back no return at all, and it is not fair that she should think I've an inexhaustible supply. I feel most strongly about it, and have thought of nothing else since I had yours and her letter, and I feel sure that you, in your heart of hearts, agree with me. I am very proud that she has succeeded in making a position in New York because I feel that in a large measure I have helped, and now that she has made it, I shall only be guided by my own judgment what and when I shall give.

Yours ever,
Ivor."

That was a letter from a very sensible young man who was still striving to get his footing firmly on the ladder. He was already making her and his father an allowance, but she was always clamouring for more. He was dead right about Mam's goodness of heart. She had very great love for and tremendous pride in Ivor, but she never looked where she was going and was probably the greatest wishful thinker of her time.

Fred Allen would patch things up. Nonetheless he would come under her lash very often, although he was very fond of her and tried valiantly, often with success, to keep her on the right and economical road. She knew it, too, and after a big battle would send him charming letters of thanks for what he had done. But the battles went on and on. In 1937 there was a very severe one, when Mam behaved in a manner which was beyond reason. This drew from Ivor the following latter:

25th October, 1937.

" Darling,

I didn't want to answer your letter until I had read and re-read it and fully considered what I feel about the whole situation, and even now I am pretty bewildered about the whole thing as I did think I had done everything in my power to make your life as comfortable and even luxurious as it is possible for anyone's life to be.

" For this tremendous financial outlay that Paris has cost me I have myself partly to blame as I clearly remember mentioning to you how exciting it would be if you were able after thirty-seven years still to take a Choir to the Paris Exhibition, but I must confess now that I did not think that you would go so wholeheartedly and a little rashly into a scheme that although it has given you—and rightly—very great personal gratification has resulted in your affairs being in a state of chaos. You speak of your paying pupils being at a standstill—surely some sort of compromise could have been effected and you could have continued teaching those pupils who were still paying and still trained the Choir to the extent you have. After all, pupils are only human beings and having paid for their lessons expect to have them.

" However, you think that the outlay of, I should say, roughly £1,000 on one spectacular but very unremunerative visit to Paris is worth while, and although I do not agree with you, I must bow to your decision. What concerns me far more is the personal side. You have always adored " Redroofs " just as much as I do; I have adored your being there, and so have *all my friends* and you have been greatly missed through those weeks in which you have chosen to absent yourself. You have let grow in yourself a feeling that there has been and is antagonism and as you put it yourself ' toleration ' in the minds of the staff and my friends, when the very reverse is the truth, and all this because of one word of criticism from me, and even that word of criticism only sprang from the fact that you never asked me whether it was convenient to have your pupil stay there, and when she was you never told me. The first I heard of it was when I rang Milly up to tell her I was coming down with friends during my strenuous weeks of rehearsals and to my surprise she asked ' How many friends? ' and ' What rooms? ', to which I replied, very naturally, ' When I come down to my own house I want all the rooms when and wherever I choose and on asking for an explanation of her question was told that you had someone staying in the house apparently permanently of whose existence in the house I had never even heard and on this small incident you take yourself off from the place you profess to love and you are not only and naturally welcome, but much beloved.

"Now, my reason for writing to you at all about this is that my foremost idea in my mind about you is that you should, without giving up your work of which you are justly proud, only live in absolute comfort and luxury and these ideas of mine of comfort and luxury do not coincide at all with a basement in Park Lane where you have no proper quarters for yourself and in which there is not even inside sanitation. I quite admit that you took it with the idea that you would be living at "Redroofs" and merely teaching in that particular place, and this is what you should be doing.

"Believe me, darling, the sooner that you dismiss the idea that you are not wanted at "Redroofs" the better. Your lovely room is there, waiting for you. It has, of course, remained unused since you decided no longer to occupy it, and what is most important of all, you can there continue your treatments with Mrs. Murray which are so vitally important to your health—and that is my chief consideration—so darling, please let me know when you would like Morgan or James to take you and all your belongings back to where you belong.

"Also, don't forget that if Fred is to make any headway with your debts he will have to use as much of your allowance each week as possible; if you sincerely wish to be economical, to live at "Redroofs" and to come up to London for two days in the week to teach, going back and sleeping at "Redroofs" for the night in between those two days is the only way to start doing so, to say nothing of the fact of the benefit to your health after these exhausting and strenuous weeks, which is my main anxiety.

"Now, darling, don't let us have any more letters, recriminations and reproaches about all this. I am battling with one of the most strenuous tasks of my life and I can't stand it.

All love,
Ivor."

Even that row got itself smoothed out, Ivor's purse-strings being loosened to do so. But it always went on, more or less.

There was another occasion at "Redroofs" when a crisis blew up and Mam was deeply in debt. Ivor put his foot down. Mam took to her bed and announced her intention of just passing out. She would eat or drink nothing; this was the end. Life had nothing more for her: let the end come. And she actually kept this up for three days. Then Ivor went into the room and said, " Mam, everything's all right. I've paid all you owe and there's no more trouble." She was out of bed like a flash, embracing him and jumping about with pleasure.

Yet, with it all, with full knowledge of her little foibles, her absolute disregard of money and her rather pathetic but quite sincere belief in her own judgment—for she was always quoting it and supplying instances where she had been absolutely right whereas she had been absolutely wrong—Ivor just worshipped her. His moments of—not anger—but hopelessness, soon passed. He loved her and he wanted her to have everything. He understood her, and knew she was a child. And like a child he humoured her if he sometimes chided her. Nothing was too good for her. And the homage he paid her was not only in the face of the world but in private life.

I was behind the scenes in that little trip to Paris with the Welsh Choir. Ivor asked me to arrange a Press reception for Mam and we did so. A room was hired at the Waldorf Hotel and scores of Press men and women were invited. They all came, for it was a good story. Refreshments were served all the time. Mam was late but made up for it by extreme volubility, volatility—and exuberant excitement. She chattered away, she told snatches of her life story, she exhibited a crown which had been presented to her as a trophy when she had been to Paris before. She was going to wear it on this occasion. She took off her hat and put it on. It kept falling off because she jumped about so and it bounced all over the floor, greatly to the detriment of the jewels within it, and Ivor kept picking it up and giving it back to her. He treated her throughout with the utmost consideration, like a child at her party. There was considerable publicity—and she actually flew to Paris—being much photographed at the air port. This visit, according to her, was going to make history and put her choirs and choral singing generally on top of the world. All that really came of it was the disbursement of £1,000 by Ivor. But, as he stated in his letter, it gave her joy and he did not grudge it. All the same, he had been led to understand that Mam had been invited. Nothing of the kind. She invited herself. Hence the £1,000.

She wore amazing dresses: flamboyant was perhaps the word. She always cut a figure, with her silver hair, her rather high-coloured face and her general air of being on the bubble-over. She had a penchant for white dresses at first nights—Ivor's first nights—and she would sit in the box which he bought for her, well forward for all to see and framed in the flowers with which he had decorated the box. There was a kind of glitter about her and she rarely sat still; she was far too excited. She was, indeed, quite a disturbing feature of the audience. At the first night of *Crest of the Wave*, she came back rather late after the interval and slammed a door loudly in a very quiet and tense scene, which did not help the scene at all. She meant no harm, she did not know what she was doing. She was in Heaven, for her Ivor was there, acting in his own show and, she was sure, heading for triumph. Her smiles were as bright as a whole row of arc-lamps, but to most people she was a rather frightening old lady. And at the end, when Ivor came forward to acknowledge the plaudits of the cheering house, the first bow was always for her—towards her in her box—and everyone knew, and saw and understood. That was her moment of supreme triumph. It was no " act " this homage of his. It had nothing to do with publicity or gestures to the world. To his mind, it was her due; she was his mother, the woman who had encouraged and fostered and taught him in his childhood days, the person in the world that he loved most and to whom he bowed his head first. At such moments, for Mam, there was nobody else in the theatre.

At other times, too, she considered herself the centre of interest. When Fred Allen's daughter got married, Ivor and Mam came to the wedding. He looked very elegant in his morning coat as he led her to her seat. Mam was all smiles and bestowing bows right and left like royalty. At the reception afterwards, Mam took the limelight. She was sure she was the one they had all come to see and was quite delighted with everything. The King and Queen Mother are here—that was her attitude. And believe me, she was not far wrong. For Fred Allen's wife had learnt singing from her and was proud to have her, and Ivor, there.

It cannot be stressed too much that Ivor's affection for his mother was real and deep. What he said in his letters about wanting her to have every luxury and comfort was sincere and heartfelt. His only worry was that she seemed to think he was not doing enough. He was not right there. She never realized what he was doing at all; to her, money spent on her schemes, or the clearing up of them, was a long-term investment, bound to pay a hundredfold. Her eyes were always fixed upon that elusive El Dorado. And all the while El Dorado was there, in the person of her son. It was Mam's extravagance which led to the installation of a telephone call box at "Redroofs," for she would ring up New York, Hollywood, Barcelona, or where you will, on the spur of the moment and as the fancy took her and indulge in the longest conversations.

And now let Mam and her excitements rest until she makes her exit. It is time for the remnants of Ivor's film career to be got out of the way to leave room for his complete triumph in the Theatre. This is not in chronological order but that matters little; the films were subsidiary; they gave him money to spend in the Theatre and that was his chief reason for doing them.

He had started his film career in the days of the Silence. His first talking picture was *A Symphony in Two Flats*, screen version of his own play. He made a talkie *Once a Lady* in Hollywood in 1931. He had plenty of offers when he got home. So he made *The Lodge* at Twickenham, which he had made as a silent film years before. He made *Sleeping Car* for Gaumont British, and also *I Lived With You* at Twickenham. He was pretty busy at this time for he was also writing plays and appearing in them too. And he soon found it was too much. Something had to go. Naturally he jettisoned the films, decided to make no more, unless by some chance things failed in the Theatre. He had now taken his final decision: it was Theatre, not films. But he did make one more picture and that was the screen version of Dodie Smith's *Autumn Crocus*. He adored the play, and he enjoyed making the film. If anyone wants the full details of Ivor's film activities, let them read Mr. Peter Noble's *Ivor Novello* where it is all clearly and very well set out. Mr. Noble knows far more about films than I do. It would puzzle him to know less. For I am completely of the Theatre.

And, really, so was Ivor. Despite the big money, he preferred the gamble which he took with his plays, he loved the upward surge of the curtain, the hushed, dim auditorium from which came ripples of laughter and crackles of applause. He loved the warm personal feel of it all because that was like himself. He liked the dressing-room, the company coming in and out, the friends coming round in the interval and after the show with their praise. And he liked to feel they were there, in front, when he was playing. He loved that last look in the glass, the last few words and backward flung smile as he went towards the stage, the few moments in the wings, then the deep breath, his entrance and the roar of welcome. The films could not give him that. It was not conceit; it was the sheer joy of his job and the knowledge he could do it. Pride maybe, but that is not conceit. He loved to hear his own words being spoken, his own music being played.

The whole play came to his dressing-room at every performance over a loudspeaker. It was hardly ever turned off. It served two purposes, nay, three purposes. It enabled him to judge how the others were performing, to know when his entrance grew near . . . and to give him the supreme thrill of listening to his own work. An artist may stand before his own picture and admire; an architect gaze at his masterpiece with perhaps reverence and pride; an author get real satisfaction from seeing his words in print, his books in a row on a shelf (but I wonder how many authors read their books after they are published? I never do)—all this is the pride and joy of achievement, just as a composer feels when a great orchestra brings his music to life, as a poet feels when a lovely voice declaims his works and as a dramatist feels when expert players speak his words.

Ivor felt all that to the full. He loved his own work, because it was his. Keneth Kent, one of Ivor's friends from boyhood, relates how when the records of the music of *King's Rhapsody* came to " Redroofs " he was there and listened to them with Ivor. Ivor stood whilst they were being played, wearing the battledress of dark blue which he affected latterly for ease, convenience and speed of dressing, and listened with gleaming eyes and face alight, until tears came down his cheeks. This was his offspring talking to him. He had the same feeling as a father hearing his son's first words. There was no affectation. Ivor loved his job.

That battledress was very popular with Ivor. He got used to it when he went overseas for Ensa soon after D-Day to play on the Normandy beaches. I have known him arrive at the Palace in it, very often, during the run of *King's Rhapsody*, especially on Monday evenings when he came up from " Redroofs." He would come out of the car and right into the dressing-room, wearing it. Then he would take it off and underneath were his pyjamas. That was his favourite attire. He never liked dressing up formally. He did not care about clothes, although he liked silk shirts and had an enormous number of them. He was much happier in loose shorts and flannel slacks than anything else. Yet he looked elegant and well-dressed in whatever he wore. On the stage, it was very much the same. He would wear easy clothes. He also liked Tzigane costume, and was never happier than when wearing it, as in *Glamorous Night*, and a near approach to it *King's Rhapsody*. But perhaps his favourite costume of all was that dark uniform in the same play, which repeated that worn in *Old Heidelberg*. In that, perhaps, he looked his best.

He liked dressing-gowns, too, but the one he used in the theatre was sanctified by long and faithful service.

The flop of *Flies in the Sun* did not deter Ivor from writing plays. He took his few flops as easily as he took his many successes. He knew he had made a mistake. He went ahead again. In 1933 he wrote *Proscenium*. Here he might have been on dangerous ground, for he wrote about life in the Theatre and it was even a more dangerous bet in 1933 than it would be now. But Ivor used his theatre sense. He superimposed a perfectly credible and intriguing love story over the backstage atmosphere. His people were of the Theatre, but his story was of their emotions towards each other. He did in this play what he adored to do: he played two parts—and that always gratified his acting sense. He played a middle-aged man in the Prologue and the same man's son in the main play. It was a good story, if not extraordinary in its originality but Ivor did what he always did—got in new twists, a warm humanity and a deep accurate understanding of women.

Briefly, a middle-aged Lieutenant-Colonel (that rank was not so common in 1918, when the prologue of *Proscenium* took place, as it became in the Second World War) named Sir Geoffrey Bethel is going back to France. He has long been in love with a successful actress, Norma Matthews. He is a married man with a son at school in his teens. He and his wife are not in love; they are apart. On the night of his return to France he invites Norma to Ciro's and he proposes that at last they should live together and let his wife divorce him—and then marry. But Norma, although she loves him, refuses. She thinks of his career, her own, and she thinks of his son. It is not to be. So the soldier goes back to France, and it is the end for him. But the son grows up. He takes his mother's name and is known as Gray Raynor. He becomes a great admirer of Norma who, whilst he was at school and at his father's request, had sent him her photograph. She is now an actress-manageress. Gray not only admires her, he falls in love with her. She is still a lovely woman—Fay Compton played the part—and she resists him. She tells him his father loved her. That does not deter the boy. His enthusiasm, his devotion and his handsome face make her surrender. They marry. Gray takes to the stage. But he finds that he is simply " Miss Matthews's husband" and, in theatrical parlance, the man who carries the music. That does not suit him. His love for Norma does not alter but his stage ambition grows. He wants to play Romeo. There is a young actress who attracts him and whom he wants for his Juliet. The perfect Juliet would be Norma, his wife, despite her age. But Gray does not see it; nobody sees it but Norma. In the end she sacrifices herself to make Gray happy in his stage aspirations. Thereby she can hold him, thereby she can keep his love.

It was a good play and beautifully played. Ivor got a chance as Romeo, the part for which he always hankered, although here it was only in the form of a " Masque." It enabled him to look the part without betraying the vocal limitations and lack of real depth which would always have debarred him from being a successful Romeo in reality.

Proscenium was produced at the Globe Theatre, June 14th, 1933, and presented by Moss Empires and Howard and Wyndham Tours Ltd., the firm from which sprang H. M. Tennent Ltd. It ran for 227 performances. Ivor had two successes in town at the same time: *Proscenium* and *Fresh Fields*. It was produced by Athole Stewart. The cast included besides Ivor himself, Andrea Melandrinos, Fay Compton, who, of course, gave such a beautiful performance, Lena Maitland, Pat Woodings, Hargrave Pawson, Joan Barry, Henry Crocker, Zena Dare, Margot Sieveking, Margaret Watson, Madge Snell, Dorothy Boyd, Harold Cheshire and Keneth Kent.

This was the first time Zena Dare had been in an Ivor Novello play. She played Lady Raynor, Ivor's mother. It was Lloyd Williams who suggested her and Ivor apologized for asking her to play his mother. But Zena, who is one of the sweetest women in or out of the Theatre, did not mind a bit. She was a bit doubtful if she could really play the part, doubtful if she could compass a character which was really in the Lilian Braithwaite range. But Ivor was sure she could—and she did. She played it superbly.

As the Lieutenant-Colonel in the prologue of *Proscenium* Ivor looked exactly like his own father. As one compares the photographs to-day, the resemblance is most marked. And in *Proscenium* Ivor made his declaration about his views on the Theatre. It was his creed, like that declaimed by Dubedat in Shaw's *The Doctor's Dilemma.* He did not speak the words himself, he put them into the mouth of the character of Mr. Hyman, a theatrical magnate, which was very well played indeed by that good actor Keneth Kent. This was the declaration and it is worth reading and remembering:

> " Now, my dear, I want this plan—it's very near my heart—I've been searching hard for someone who will help me realize a long cherished ambition. I believe in the Theatre—I believe in beauty in the Theatre—I believe that in the Theatre lies a road back to sanity—but the road will only be found through endeavour—the highest standard—nothing but the best. I want to give the people the chance to dream again—and I want to show them that there is an art beyond the reach of mechanical devices and black and white shadows chasing each other round a white sheet.

That was really Ivor's own declaration and one which he lived up to from then on, one which indeed had always been his belief. In it he threw over the films, and swore complete loyalty to the Theatre and to that standard of high quality which had been the standard of the older actor-managers and which he upheld nobly and grandly to the very end.

Quite a lot happened during the run of *Proscenium.* Ivor did the hat trick, for he had another play produced whilst it and *Fresh Fields* were still running. This was *Sunshine Sisters.* It was produced at the Queen's Theatre (the first London theatre to be bombed during the Second World War) next door to the Globe, the home of *Proscenium* on November 8th, 1933. The three companies, those of *Fresh Fields*, *Proscenium* and *Sunshine Sisters*, all had their names engraved on a large mirror which was presented to Ivor and which he fully appreciated. But two of the cast of *Proscenium* carried it a bit further. Ivor was chaffed a good deal about his invasion and occupation of three London theatres at once and, on the evening of the presentation, when he dashed off to make a very quick change, he found, just off-stage, Harold Cheshire and Dorothy Boyd who played Vaughan and Helen respectively, standing with palm boughs to make an arch for the conquering hero to pass under and a carpet laid for him to walk on (the carpet was an old one which Mr. Cheshire has supplied), whilst the rest of the cast threw paper rose petals over him. Ivor halted in his career, took in the idea, bowed right and left in stately fashion, as he passed between the ranks, taking off his coat and vest as he went, and then dashed into his dressing-room—to dash out again at once almost and shout " thank you "—but minus his trousers!

An incident in the rehearsals of *Proscenium* shows a typical Ivor act. It is Harold Cheshire's story and let him tell it in his own words: " One of my two scenes in *Proscenium* in which I played Vaughan, the dresser, was with Miss Zena Dare, and after the dress-rehearsal Ivor said he would re-write it, as Vaughan had most of the lines leaving Miss Dare to stand and listen (and, of course, look lovely!) This new version of the scene reversed the situation—except for the loveliness—and Miss Dare objected, generously, on my behalf. Whereupon Ivor handed us the script and said we could settle it between us. As he reached the wings he turned and came back, saying he wanted us distinctly to understand that this did not mean he would share his royalties with us or bill us as " co-authors." That was typical Ivor Novello—and typical Zena Dare as well. . . . "

Ivor did not have three plays running together for very long. *Sunshine Sisters* was not a success. It was again a story of theatrical people, Ivor making the fatal mistake in the Theatre of trying to get away with it twice. In *Proscenium* he had succeeded because it was a real flesh-and-blood story of emotion and life; if the background was theatrical the emotions were not. But *Sunshine Sisters* was just a piece of light-hearted nonsense about a theatrical mother and her daughters, who were professionals and went to live in an aristocratic home. It was all far-fetched and it never rang true. Ivor could get away with a lot, but not this play. Despite its cast, which included Dorothy Dickson, Phyllis Monkman, Irene Browne, Joan Clarkson,

Maidie Andrews, Jack Hawkins, Veronica Brady, Sebastian Shaw and Joan Swinstead, it never got the sunlight of success. But many of that cast were already Ivor's firm friends and others were to become so and form a niche for themselves in his companies. Dorothy Dickson was to be his leading lady at Drury Lane itself, Joan Swinstead was to play there for him, too, and so was Maidie Andrews, already an Old Novellian. Veronica Brady was also to be in his shows and Phyllis Monkman was an old and valued friend, the friendship lasting up to death. But *Sunshine Sisters* was a Novello failure.

Ivor Novello was financing his shows himself, but he had as partner Richard Rose, a young American who was greatly interested in the Theatre. Richard Rose—Dickie to most people who knew him—was (and for that matter is still) a charming man, slight, dark and given to wearing very dark glasses. He always appeared extremely cool and unperturbed, no matter what was going on around him and had a tremendous admiration for Ivor. He took life easily and paid scant attention to what was happening unless it concerned the play in which his interest lay, or what Ivor was up to. He would cross a busy London street entirely oblivious to the roaring traffic, quite rapt in his own thoughts and it was the wonder of all his friends that he ever reached the other side in safety. He always did and never had the slightest idea of his many escapes. He was financially interested with Ivor, but Ivor always took the biggest risk.

I met Dickie Rose whilst writing this book, in Ivor's flat. He had got thinner—but so had I. I knew him at once, but he scarcely recognized me. But then, suddenly, he knew me and was just as delighted at the meeting as I was. He was then living in Rome and drew a wonderful picture of life there. He made one's mouth water. He seemed to be looking for something or someone in the flat. It was, of course, Ivor he sought. For that flat, once so busy and populous (Ivor could make himself seem like a crowd by his own personality and vitality) now seems, despite the people in it, to be empty and like a place just inhabited by a caretaker while it awaits the next tenant. Such places seem emptier than those entirely uninhabited. For No. 11 Aldwych meant Ivor Novello: and he was no longer there. It did not matter how many people were about—and there were six of us there at the time—I knew that to Dickie Rose it was quite empty, and so it was to me.

For *Proscenium* Ivor put up £1,000 of the capital required—or he and his associates did—and Moss Empires and Howard and Wyndham Tours Ltd. put up £625. The profit-sharing was in proportion. The salaries of the artistes amounted to £318 per week and Ivor's salary was £150. He drew a 5 per cent. royalty. Nobody can say he was exorbitant in his demands. A glance at the balance sheets, haphazard, reveals that for the week-ending July 22nd, 1933, at the Globe—not a good week for business as a rule—the gross takings were £1,410 5*s*. 5*d*. The total expenses were £1,248 10*s*. 9*d*. and the profit was £161 14*s*. 8*d*. Such a production could not be run at those figures to-day; it would show a loss. Everybody did quite well out of *Proscenium* and they deserved to.

When it came off at the Globe, it went on a tour which showed a handsome profit. After that Ivor went with Lloyd Williams, Bobbie Andrews and Richard Rose for a holiday. They went cruising in the Mediterranean to Cairo and to Jerusalem.

And whilst he was away, another play was taking shape in Ivor's busy head. This was to be *Murder in Mayfair* which he eventually presented in conjunction with Moss Empires and Howard and Wyndham Tours Ltd. The moving spirit in Howard and Wyndham Ltd. was A. Stewart Cruikshank, a very charming and pleasant man and a most astute and keen man of business. Tall, strong, fresh-complexioned, with a ready smile, he did not look at all like a theatrical magnate.

He had, indeed, become one by chance. He was originally a builder and contractor. Amongst his undertakings and contracts he built the King's Theatre, Edinburgh. At that time he had no thought of becoming a theatre manager but the fates intervened and he was destined to control the theatre which he had built; not only that, but many others. By 1933 he was managing director of the King's Theatre, Edinburgh, director of Robert Arthur Theatres Co., Ltd., and of the firm of Daniel Mayer Co., Ltd. (the firm which had looked after Mam, found Ivor his first film job and for whom Fred Allen had worked), managing director of Howard and Wyndham Ltd., his company controlling the King's and Lyceum Theatre, Edinburgh, the King's and Theatre Royal, Glasgow, the Opera House, Manchester, and Theatre Royal, Newcastle-upon-Tyne. No provincial theatres were ever better run or controlled.

Mr. Cruikshank really exercised personal supervision. He had personal contact with all details. He had a London office but his head office was at Edinburgh, his native town where he was born in 1877. His son Stewart, who inherits his father's charm and ability, looked after London interests. When the new Board of Directors, with Prince Littler as chairman, took charge of Theatre Royal, Drury Lane, Mr. Cruikshank and his son were also members of the Board. Mr. Cruikshank knew all about making a bargain but he also knew how to keep it, too. His word was his bond—you did not want it in writing. What he said he would do, that he did, to the last penny. But he expected the same quality in others. He was extremely popular in the whole profession. He met his death jumping out of a taxi to see a fire and was run over and fatally injured. He was sincerely mourned, for many people in the profession could testify to his kindness and when in need, assistance. Kindness they always had. Even a humble person like myself was made to feel a friend of his; and that is a great thing. His son carries on his tradition and is just such another.

Such people as this were good associates for Ivor, whose instincts and whose actions were the same. *Proscenium* and *Fresh Fields* did Ivor much good. *Flies in the Sun* and *Sunshine Sisters* although failures did no harm at all. Indeed, they did good, for he learnt from both of them. The utmost one can learn in the wild, insane game of the Theatre is what not to do —and not always that.

The play which he was busy on during and after that Mediterranean holiday in the sunshine was to advance him still further. Managing the business of Moss Empires and Howard and Wyndham Tours Ltd., was H. M. Tennent—with whom was associated Hugh Beaumont, the now all-powerful Binkie. Harry Tennent had been to Oxford and was, I believe, an Old Etonian. He was a tall, slightly-built man, with a scholarly air, given to reflective gazing and the smoking of leisurely pipes. He looked far more like a schoolmaster or a don than a theatre manager. There was a rather birdlike air about him; not perky but rather in the nature of an elderly eagle taking a well-earned rest or a secretary bird on holiday. He had not started his career in the Theatre; he had been with the firm of John Broadwood and Sons, pianoforte manufacturers. He knew a lot about music and was a composer of no small merit with some charming songs and pieces to his credit. In the First World War he did some excellent executive service. Then he joined Moss Empires, as booking manager for their provincial theatres. The theatre business was not very flourishing at the time and his activities in that line drew a jibe from Sir Seymour Hicks, with whom he had a misunderstanding, a very easy thing to do when dealing with Seymour. That volatile actor-knight described him as " The Tennent of Empty Houses."

Harry Tennent was regarded as a strong man. This was because he was a fairly silent one and so often silence is mistaken for strength. One of the famous " Tite Barnacles " in *Little Dorritt* enjoyed a similar reputation because he was " buttoned up." Dickens missed nothing. Tennent was anything but a strong man. Almost anyone could talk him over. He had to be bolstered up with care and tact and what to say instilled into his mind. Then he would often not do it but something different. Tennent became, however, the titular head of a production firm which bore his name (H. M. Tennent Ltd.), the driving force of which was and is Hugh (Binkie) Beaumont. Tennent was the figure-head and everyone trusted him. In that they were right, for he was an honest man and quite straight in his dealings. He was supposed to be able to say " No." So he could, but he seldom said it at the right time, or to the right people. I had a long and happy association with him, both at Drury Lane and with H. M. Tennent Ltd. I knew him well and understood him. We had at least one taste in common—the *Times* crossword puzzle. Despite his university career and his classical education I was rather better at it than he, and he would come to me with the knotty problems.

When Drury Lane Theatre was in a very bad position, H. M. Tennent was made General Manager, to get it on its feet again. To his credit, he did so, in a manner shortly to be told. He was at the same time still managing Moss Empires and Howard and Wyndham Tours Ltd., and as such in touch with Ivor Novello. Ivor believed in him too. He did indeed inspire confidence. He was retiring and disliked publicity. At the first nights of his shows he sat in a seat at the back of the dress circle. Most theatre managers have amazing dress suits for such occasions—Tennent did not—it never looked new and he usually had a bit of difficulty with his tie which seldom if ever kept straight. But he was immensely popular with the artistes, who had blind belief in him. He took over Drury Lane when there was not an attraction in sight. He was looking after—or his firm was—Ivor Novello's *Murder in Mayfair* at the time. It was an association of ideas. For Harry M. Tennent was the man who gave Ivor Novello the chance which secured his lasting fame and put him on the top of the world. Tennent gave the opportunity; but it was Ivor who took it.

CHAPTER SEVENTEEN

ON WINGS OF SONG

IT was now the end of the summer of 1934. The world was not a happy one. Germany was again on her feet; Hitlerism was growing and growing, but nobody seemed to care. There had been a succession of crises of various kinds. Russia was still regarded as a sinister régime run by the Bolsheviks, and to most people Bolshevism was some kind of a local complaint. Italy was, so Mussolini said, resurgent and powerful. The Duce was going to found a new Roman Empire. He was always putting Europe into fits of nerves. But to the majority of the inhabitants of this country, he was a big joke. They could not take the " Wops " seriously. Hitler, too, was regarded as a rising comedian. And by now the League of Nations was a thing of the past. Few foresaw what the next four years were to bring forth. Few realized the closeness of the Second World War. There was a general idea that " something ought to be done about it," though who or what was another matter. What seemed of great importance was that the Duke of Kent married Princess Marina of Greece and Denmark, and Fred Perry, of England, won the Men's Singles Championships at Wimbledon. The summer was one of extreme drought and many reservoirs dried up completely. Two hundred and sixty miners lost their lives in a disaster at Gresford Colliery, at Wrexham, North Wales; the Mersey Tunnel was opened by King George V; Campbell Black and Scott flew to Australia in just under three days; Belisha Beacons, traffic lights and the establishment of a thirty-mile limit in built-up areas were instituted.

In the world of the Theatre, the folk of course thought only of the Theatre. A big success, entitled *The Dominant Sex*, written by Michael Egan, saw the light at the Embassy, Hampstead, which was to come to the West End and have a very long run. J. B. Priestley had *Eden End* at the Duchess; *Family Affairs* was at the Ambassadors'; the London Coliseum presented a very bad if elaborate show in *The Golden Toy*, although it managed to run for a bit; *The Greeks Had a Word for It* was at the Duke of York's; John Gielgud played *Hamlet* at the New Theatre; Walter Hackett wrote and presented *Hyde Park Corner* at the Apollo; a very successful musical play, starring Frances Day, Arthur Riscoe, John Mills and Louise Brown, with music by Vivian Ellis, entitled *Jill Darling* was produced at the Palace; a play called *Libel* was a success at the Playhouse; *Living Dangerously* was being played at the Strand, underneath Ivor's flat; and afterwards *Lucky Break*. There was a play called *The Maitlands* at Wyndham's, and one called *Mary Read* at His Majesty's; Noël Coward's *Conversation Piece* was also there; *Men in White*, a play about doctors, had a run at the Lyric. *Merrie England* had a successful revival at the Prince's. The London Hippodrome staged musical productions entitled *Mr. Whittington* and *Yes Madam*. The Haymarket had *The Moon on the Yellow River*. But after *Mary Read* at His Majesty's came *Music in the Air* and the art and voice of Mary Ellis was fully realized in London. She made an immense success a fact which is important to this chronicle. Earlier the Lyric had had that delightful play *Reunion in Vienna*. *The Shining Hour* was produced at the St. James's; *Sporting Love* was the attraction at the Gaiety.

That autumn, the Palace staged *Streamline*, a Cochran show, with music by Vivian Ellis, and the book by A. P. Herbert. At Wyndham's, in the October of 1934, Diana Wynyard made a triumph in Joyce Carey's *Sweet Aloes*. Marie Tempest had played in *Theatre Royal* at the Lyric. Dodie Smith's contribution, and she was now a major dramatist, was *Touch Wood* at the Haymarket. Seymour Hicks presented *Vintage Wine* at Daly's Theatre, in which I was heavily involved. All those plays had respectable runs—exceeding one hundred performances—and are listed in John Parker's invaluable *Who's Who in the Theatre*.

For new plays, as will be observed, it was not a very vintage year. But there is one more play to add, by one of the important people in the theatrical world, and that was *Murder in Mayfair*, by Ivor Novello. It was produced at the Globe Theatre on September 3rd, 1934, and it ran for 163 performances.

Ivor kept his company around him. He had Fay Compton, Zena Dare, Robert Andrews, and dead against the type of part she played, Edna Best, who made a very big success indeed. Ivor gave himself a French character who played the piano. He was a good character actor—much better character actor than a " straight " one—and a very good pianist, so he made a considerable success. Robert Andrews was the young man who did the murder showing the public that he was a very much better actor than they knew. He is, indeed, a very good actor.

Murder in Mayfair was, like *Proscenium*, presented jointly by Ivor Novello and Moss Empires and Howard and Wyndham's Tours Ltd. That brought H. M. Tennent and Ivor nearer together once more.

Tennent had by now been appointed General Manager of Theatre Royal, Drury Lane. That great playhouse was right in the dumps. It was really suffering from what Dick Swiveller called " an accumulation of staggerers." For a considerable time nothing had gone right. *The Land of Smiles*, in which Richard Tauber had sung his way into the hearts of Londoners, had brought a snatch of sunshine, but Tauber was then very unreliable and his constant absences from the cast spoilt real and lasting success. Then the Lane had staged one of its biggest and most resounding flops in a musical play called *The Three Sisters*. On paper this looked like a success. On the stage it was an out-and-out failure. There was an excellent cast, but it was not a " Lane " show. Money was tight. Things were desperate. Tennent was called in. Very wisely he played for safety. He booked Julian Wylie to do a pantomime, a safe card at Drury Lane, which is the real home of pantomime.

But that could not be done until Christmas, and meanwhile the Lane was closed. Julian Wylie went to see *The Three Sisters*. I sat with him. A man who had his whole soul in the Theatre, and who was one of the greatest stage technicians of all time, he could not endure to see so much feebleness on that hallowed stage. Julian did not drink. So he turned, for solace, to ice cream, his favourite form of nourishment. To the astonishment of all seated around, he ate a dozen during the interval. They did not cheer him up; quite the reverse. They—and the show—plunged him into deep depression. Julian was a strange man when one of the audience. For him, there was only the person with him, and what was taking place on the stage. He would keep up a running commentary, annoy everyone, fidget with irritation or rage and be all the time, blissfully unconscious that anyone was near. I had quite a job to keep him quiet during *The Three Sisters* and did not succeed too well. The only way was to give him toffee drops to eat. He loved them, he never refused and whilst he was sucking or chewing them, he could not say much. Usually I took a tin along to rehearsals and often to shows. I had not any with me that afternoon—and I was sorry!

Poor Julian! His despair at the failure of *The Three Sisters* —which had nothing to do with him—was counterbalanced by the fact that he was to do the pantomime at the Lane at Christmas. That filled him with pride and joy, because he revered that majestic playhouse and all it stood for. He had done one there before, with immense success. He could hardly wait to triumph again. But he never saw that pantomime. He died whilst it was in rehearsal. He went from a rehearsal on the stage at Drury Lane to his flat, and in the small hours of the morning he passed away. That famous stage door was his exit from the world of the Theatre. He would have liked that. And, as it so happened, Ivor Novello had a hand in that pantomime as well. He wrote a song called "Echo" for Phyllis Neilson-Terry, who played Principal Boy. It was the first time any work of his had been heard from that stage, except at charity matinées, which don't really count. It was not a big success, for it was not really a pantomime song. But it was his introduction.

Pantomimes are only seasonable entertainments and Tennent had the very formidable task of keeping Drury Lane open. That vast place means equally vast expense. Closed or open, it eats up the money. When a show is running the gap can be closed; when it is empty the pit is bottomless. Tennent made up his mind that he would repeat the old tradition of a pantomime every Christmas at the Lane, but he had the interim to think of. There was nothing in sight: America, so long the supply ground, seemed to have run dry. All sorts of people put up all sorts of ideas. But the Lane is a strange place. It almost seems sentient at times, kindly to those it likes, brutal to those to whom it is allergic. In 1934 thoughts ran only on the old tradition at the Lane. For so many years it had purveyed spectacle. It was expected to do so. Indeed, there was a formula which for many years had spelt success. It was not a difficult formula but it needed a mind of size and flexibility to compass it. Small things ruled in 1934. The last real success the Lane had had was *Cavalcade* which fulfilled all the spectacular demands of the old régime, even if the treatment was modern Noël Coward.

Where was such a thing to be discovered? Where was a man who could conceive a Drury Lane show to be found. Julian Wylie might have filled the breach, and had he not died, Drury Lane history might have been different. But Tennent did not like Julian Wylie much. They were opposites, in every sense. Tennent, like most people, regarded Julian and his work as "provincial." Julian, on his side, professed not to understand what they meant when they talked about being "West End." He knew his job; he had many successes quite apart from pantomime, and in the West End too. But he never went in for the smooth glitter and polish which gilded the shows of men like Cochran. He was a plain, down-right, honest-to-goodness sort of man and he believed in that sort of show. He liked highlights, not half tones and subtleties. The word "sophistication" drove him mad. He ridiculed it. He said he had looked it up in the dictionary and it meant upside-down, topsy-turvy. All right then, he *was* sophisticated, for he was King of Pantomime (he was, too, and I had the honour of crowning him) and so, as pantomime was entirely topsy-turvy, he must be sophisticated. He never said what dictionary he used. Julian was trying very hard to get Drury Lane. He laid plans for a show with J. B. Priestley and he laid plans with Dodie Smith, too. He had Gracie Fields at the back of his mind. He would have done a wonderful show, but it is doubtful if Tennent would have agreed. Julian was a very awkward man, bless him, until you understood him. And, anyway, he died.

So Tennent was looking elsewhere. He was looking for a success—the most vital thing in the Theatre. There was Noël Coward—who had done the trick with *Cavalcade*. But Noël was busy with *Conversation Piece* at His Majesty's, playing in it himself. He had other fixed plans and commitments. *Conversation Piece* was not a very big success. Perhaps Mr. Coward did not fancy the job of tackling Drury Lane at that time; anyway, he did not do so. But there remained that other Success of the Theatre, who was on top of the world, Ivor Novello.

Now the tradition at Drury Lane, though still that of spectacle, was also, since the production of *Rose Marie*, musical as well. What was wanted was a big spectacular musical play on the big lines demanded by the Lane. Ivor was a composer. True, he had not done anything musical for a long time, not since he had written some numbers for Jack Hulbert and Cicely Courtneidge in *Clowns in Clover* in 1927. That was seven years ago. But what of it? Ivor was a composer, a popular composer. He had devoted himself to straight plays, writing and acting in them, and had let the music go, except when he composed to please himself. But the great talent was there: with the right touch and the moment of inspiration, it would flare up.... He was, moreover, immensely popular and a great box-office attraction. Could he do a show for Drury Lane? Harry Tennent mused and wondered. He was very fond of Ivor and admired him. Ivor liked him very much, too. They both loved music; they both composed. They met constantly. They talked about the Theatre: professionals always talk shop—no matter what their profession, but none quite so persistently as members of "THE" Profession. They talked about Drury Lane. Ivor's friends had talked about Drury Lane, too. They had even suggested that Ivor should have a shot. Very likely he had given it thought. He would not, however, consider writing a big musical play, or any musical play for that matter, in which he himself should appear (for that was what his friends advised), because he could no longer sing. The youthful nightingale had become a bird of paradise maybe, a bird whose plumage glittered but whose voice was mute. At that time, Ivor considered this a complete bar.

One day, in 1934, Ivor and Tennent were lunching together. Tennent was more depressed than usual. Under those conditions his neck seemed to grow longer and his chin to rise in the air. Ivor had some animal pictures at the flat and one of them, a lama, he always swore was a portrait of Tennent. The man who was at that moment guiding the destinies of Drury Lane did not know what to do or where to look. He had not chosen the last flop, *The Three Sisters*, but it seemed to him that if a play with a book by Oscar Hammerstein and music by Jerome Kern failed so miserably, then the times were out of joint in the kingdom of the Theatre. He gazed speculatively at Ivor.... Now this was one of those moments fraught with Fate.

The setting was the Ivy Restaurant—the table just facing

the door, with the broad pillar at the back. The coffee stage was reached. Neither of these two men was ever quite clear how it all came about. It is still a moot point as to whether Ivor planted the idea or whether Tennent really meant to ask Ivor to take the plunge at the Lane. I asked Harry Tennent once; he just smiled, nodded, looked a bit wise and said " Oh, well. . . . " I asked Ivor. He said he had gone to the lunch with absolutely no thought in his mind of what was to happen but that, all of a sudden, when Tennent was bewailing the failure of supply from America, he had a kind of warm feeling and a quiver of excitement. . . . Anyway, according to him, he decided to give Tennent a little advice. He said, his own words, " What do you expect if you persist in going to America for plays? Now, if you'd asked me . . . " and Tennent, sitting up said quickly " And why should I ask you? " . . . Ivor took the plunge. He had not really meant to say what followed. But it was impulse, fate, kismet, inspiration, what you will; he was somehow controlled by stronger forces than himself and and he said " Well, I've got plans for Drury Lane." Tennent gasped. " You have? " he said, " Why didn't you tell me before? " Ivor replied, simply " You never asked me, did you? " Tennent became aquiline with excitement. " Do you mean to tell me that you have a play which would suit? " Ivor was more excited than Tennent now. He heard opportunity knocking, he felt that here indeed was that tide in the affairs of one man; his mind was working both ways, one urging him forward, the other—probably David Ivor Davies—reminding him that he had nothing at all and not to be a fool. But this time Ivor Novello won. . . . Outwardly quite calm, but inwardly surging with excitement he replied " Well, I've got an idea." And, really, he had nothing of the kind. For once Tennent was a man of action—fate was taking a hand with him too; it was the spirits of the old Druriolanians taking charge of these two men. Fixing Ivor with his eyes focused through the horn-rimmed glasses, his mouth working a bit with nervous tension, he said " Let me hear it, then."

There was the challenge, direct and open. In that popular restaurant, with people of the Theatre all about, many gazing at these two men—wondering what they were up to, but little guessing the truth—there, at that moment, one of the worst crises in the centuries-old history of Drury Lane was hovering on the brink of settlement. There Disaster was being defeated by Triumph, there Ivor was to take the step which brought him his real greatness, his eternal niche of fame in the Theatre, and for Tennent, full justification for his job at the Lane and a piece of tremendous kudos. Yet, a few moments before, neither had any idea of it. That is how things happen—in the Theatre, anyway.

For Ivor it was a titanic moment. His mind was actually a blank sheet, but across it ideas were rushing to and fro, the creative talent working like a dynamo. His quicksilver brain was becoming crystal clear and functioning like a machine-gun, spitting out little fragments of notions which were fusing into a whole. He said to me once that it was like what he had heard happened to people when they were drowning, only, instead of his life passing in rapid review, across his mental vision went flashes of plays he had seen at the Lane and elsewhere, fragments of ideas he had had and discarded, bits and pieces of thoughts he had stored away. He was playing for time and every second was precious. He had said something, he had been challenged; he must pick up the gauntlet which Fate in the person of H. M. Tennent had thrown at his feet. He ground the cigarette he was smoking into the ashtray. It was one of those Turkish things which he always smoked, abominations to most ordinary men.

He asked the usual, rather banal question, just to gain a second or so. " Are you really interested? " he said rather naïvely, knowing quite well Tennent was gasping for more. And Tennent had no suspicion that Ivor had no idea. He thought Ivor was just being the " author " and a bit " up stage." My own idea is that he did not believe Ivor really had the stature to do a show for Drury Lane. He probably regarded him, as did most people at that time, as a very clever young man and a very handsome one, a grand fellow who was quite a useful actor and who wrote amusing plays which made a bit of money. I have never believed that Tennent thought of Ivor seriously as a man who could write a Drury Lane show, but I give him every credit that I believe he meant to sound him out, for he was not going to leave a stone unturned. After all, Ivor was in the front rank—but—the Lane was the Lane—the most difficult problem of all—unless you knew it. . . .

Ivor knew that too. His brain was working like lightning,

now choosing and discarding, measuring, appraising, and hoping, desperately hoping. . . . Still, he stalled, for his mind suddenly froze hard: it was a block of ice, nothing was happening. " Well, you know, it is difficult to tell it in cold blood," he said. " It might not sound at all right, just told here—things look so different in writing but—but give me just a second to get my thoughts in order. . . . " And then the icepack broke, the sun of inspiration melted it and ideas rushed forward like the rivers in Canada at the touch of spring. . . .

Out of that brain of Ivor's poured a story, which he told with urgency. It seemed to him that the words formed without his thinking or even knowing how they came; the ideas leapt into shape like the pieces in a kaleidoscope when the handle is turned; he seemed like a machine, a gramophone retailing a record which someone—he knew not who—had placed on the drum . . . and he told something which in due course became *Glamorous Night*. He told it well. Ivor could always do that. His Welsh fervour seized him, he was himself carried away, and he carried the open mouthed, wide-eyed Harry Tennent with him . . . and then—he stopped. The record was over. He looked at Tennent, he got behind a shield of casualness. He lit a cigarette. " Well," he said, calm outside, exhausted with anxiety within " will it do? " Tennent drew a breath. " It sounds just like it," he said. He became the business manager facing the author, both on their guard, friendship not in this at all. " Of course, I cannot say ' yes ' myself. I must put it before the Board. When can I have it on paper? "

Having plunged so deeply, Ivor went deeper still. " Oh, to-morrow," he said. And David Ivor Davies gave a despairing cry whilst Ivor Novello smiled in triumph. Tennent rose to go. " Splendid," he said. " I have a Board Meeting before lunch. Send it over to me at the Lane. I will put it before them." Ivor thrust the word " Impossible " behind his back. He was on the flood tide. He began to make conditions. " Listen," he said. " I want everything my own way. I went no interference. I want a simply huge orchestra, I want a star cast, I want everything the Lane—and money—can do in staging and mounting. . . . " Would that gain time? Not a bit!

" Let me get your synopsis by the Board," said Tennent, " and you can do what you like—and how you like." They shook hands. The die was cast. Ivor had opened the door, could he climb the stairs on the other side? Tennent went off—no doubt happy and relieved. But the job was up to Ivor.

The moment the tension was over, the flash of inspiration spent, he got very frightened. What had he let himself in for? He went back to the flat not seeing anything at all. He walked in a daze. His subconscious mind, which belonged to David Ivor Davies, nagged at him. He had never done anything like this: this was entirely different to his comedies, which suddenly seemed very small and tiny indeed. He had not written a note of music for ages, he had not composed a score for years, and, anyway when he had, it had never been on this scale. He felt like a writer of pretty drawing-room ballads suddenly told that he must rival *Tristan and Isolde* or die, like a man who wrote the words on Christmas cards being sentenced to outdo The Sonnets or be hanged, drawn and quartered. He reached his flat and flung himself down and gasped. Atmosphere started to work. There was a Theatre downstairs. This was a Theatre flat. There was his piano. He had done things before. He must try—he must try! Why on earth had he said " To-morrow "? . . . . And then David Ivor Davies took charge. " Look here, young Ivor Novello," said he, " You've got us into a pretty mess. I'll help you out of it. Get on with the job you've landed. It's your doing—entirely—but you can do it, if I give you the guts to tackle it. And I will."

Ivor had less than twenty-four hours and not a word was written. All he knew was what he had recited to Tennent as it came into his head. But David Ivor Davies stiffened him and gave him confidence. He set his teeth. It should be done. Ivor was forty-one years old when he faced his biggest task to win the glittering prize. He sat down at his desk and he began to write—in pencil. Fate was still with him. Inspiration glowed. He wrote and he wrote. It flowed like a millstream, sparkling, foaming and shining too. He did it in two hours. It differed a good deal from what he had recited to Tennent at lunch, but the theme was the same, the basic idea was there; above all, it was a better story. And even above that, it was Drury Lane.

There it was, done and completed, so far as present needs went. But it wanted a title. A real man of the Theatre, a genuine author and dramatist, Ivor knew the value, the immense value, of a good title. He knew it should be short and he knew it should be arresting, intriguing. He knew that there was one thing which never failed with the public, and that was " Romance." He knew it must suggest that, and also that it must suggest music. He leaned back and closed his eyes. He visualized the front of that beloved theatre at night time, with its big electric sign ablaze: he wanted to see the words he so desired flame upon them. His mind worked like a well-oiled engine: What was it to which the public of 1934 responded so well, what was the " word of power " so much in use? " Glamour "—ah—and when was Glamour most glamorous, most pregnant with Romance? Why, at night. He saw the words in lights outside Drury Lane. He wrote down the title above his synopsis " Glamorous Night." He always swore that it was the title which sold it to the Drury Lane Directors.

That synopsis of *Glamorous Night* went over to Harry Tennent by hand. He took it to the Board and explained it. It is doubtful if they went into details at that time. But the title appealed right away. Ivor knew it would. And Ivor was in his flat and as it was lunch time, he was probably up and about. He was waiting with anxiety not unmixed with fear. The telephone rang. He answered it himself. It was Tennent. Everything was all right. Ivor could go ahead. He had *carte blanche* (to take that decision the Board must have felt immense relief at something tangible which had a real chance) and the show was to open in May. Tennent expected the pantomime to run until April. . . .

So there it was. Ivor had grasped his chance and he was to write a show for Drury Lane, compose it and play in it himself. At the moment however, it was to be kept a secret. That meant that everyone in the West End knew before night.

It was November. We were in the full flush of pantomime publicity. Julian Wylie adored publicity and I loved doing it for him. I was getting columns and columns of space, pictorial and otherwise, for this pantomime which was *Cinderella*. Julian was the ideal man to publicize. He would do exactly as he was told and he understood that publicity has to be " timed." He knew all about timing on the stage and so it was easy to make him understand about publicity. He revelled in it. He swelled with pride as he saw his name and his pantomime constantly before the public. He had the supreme gift of being able to make himself "news" when faced with a press man. He always had something to say and said it clearly. He always answered a question and answered it well. He could always evade giving away a secret before the right time, by supplying some other bit of information—also new, which he and I made so interesting that the news-hound forgot his first quarry and gladly seized on the red herring. Julian never spoke out of his turn, he never, in publicity matters, did a thing without consulting me, but he never sent a reporter away without a story. Ivor was the same—up to the last few months of his life.

Our close association in the business of publicity began with *Glamorous Night* and ended only with his death. Seventeen years of personal contact and understanding. You see, if you are to get the best publicity, you must treat your publicity man as you treat your doctor or solicitor. He is the expert (he really is, although everyone thinks they can do better) and he must decide. Technically you instruct your solicitor—so you do your publicity man. You tell him your story, but he does all the rest. You follow his prescriptions as you do those given you by your doctor. Then you get real publicity, publicity which helps. There is another kind and that is what you get if you do not leave it to the man who knows. If you flout your solicitor, you lose your case. If you go against your doctor's orders, you get very ill indeed. It is the same with publicity. I am proud to say that I taught Ivor that and he was a willing pupil. Only at the very end did he . . . but that comes later.

Tennent instructed me on the matter of *Glamorous Night*. I saw Ivor. I told him my views. He listened and understood. We would just give it a break, to stop leakage and then we would leave it until the right time. Publicity spilt too soon is wasted. He understood and was charming. I gave it a break—it got headlines—and then pumped in the pantomime again. And Ivor got to work. He had seven months to write, compose, cast and rehearse the play. He was starting from scratch. The time was short enough but he was a quick worker and could take quick decisions.

Now, one of Ivor's strong points—because he understood the Theatre—was his ability to write parts for people, rather than to write parts and find the people afterwards. His leading lady, around which the whole plot and essence of the play revolved, was the most important thing. He was not worrying at all about himself or his own part; at that time and for some period afterwards, he never did. He concentrated on the women. He understood women; there was a streak in him which responded to their emotions and their character which made him see them very clearly indeed. His leading lady must be chosen. And the choice presented no difficulty to him at all. He must have a woman who was beautiful, who could sing like a prima donna and act like a Bernhardt, and one to whom he could fit the character he had created. That sounds difficult. But he knew one. She was not British born, although she had become British by marriage. He had met her in America, he had seen her act, heard her sing there. But he had fallen right under her spell when he saw her in a play presented by C. B. Cochran at His Majesty's called *Music in the Air*. She was a big star in America and had been the original " Rose Marie." Over there, she had done it all, from musical shows to Shakespeare. Over here she had played in straight shows; *Knave and Queen* at the Ambassadors' in 1930 and in *Strange Interlude* at the Lyric, with great success, in the same year. She had gone back to America but had returned here in 1932, playing at the Haymarket in *Queer Cattle* and at the same theatre, in 1933, in *Double Harness*. Neither of those two plays succeeded. Then came *Music in the Air* and she captured London. So Ivor knew who was to be his leading lady.

She had just been playing in *Josephine*. It had not been any good and she had gone away to the country. He rang her up. Now he had to be careful. He must tell her it was a musical play and she would immediately want to hear the music before deciding. He had not written a note. However, he had chanced so much, he would chance some more. His star was shining. Mary Ellis answered the 'phone. Ivor told her who he was and came straight to the point. Would she like to appear in a play of his at Theatre Royal, Drury Lane? There was no hesitation. She would love it, she said, but only if he played in it too. Ivor assured her there was no doubt as to that: nothing would keep him out of it. But he had to mention the music. He took another chance—he had taken so many that he did not care. " I've written you some wonderful music," he told Mary Ellis. He had not written a single note. She thrilled back over the 'phone, asking when she could hear it. Ivor rushed headlong—he invited her to tea the following day, to tell her the story and play her the music! She would be there, she said. Ivor put down the telephone. Then he thought—Oh well, perhaps it was best this way. Now he just *had* to do it—no chance of delay—no putting off!

In his brain, in the creative cells a reservoir of unwritten music, of what would have been the output of eight years, was dammed up. He sat at the piano. He played, he scribbled on his music paper, he played and scribbled, he played and scribbled, and then he sat back. It was six on the morning. He had worked all night. But there were six of the big numbers done. Achievement was approaching hot foot.

And in the afternoon Mary Ellis arrived. Ivor was very excited, so was she. It was a great undertaking. Tea was served, but that did not matter. Ivor told his story. Mary listened, then he played her the music. Both of them were in heaven. Ivor asked her if she was satisfied: would she play in the show? Then he got his first shock. Mary Ellis said she would love to, but when did rehearsals start? He wondered what was wrong and replied, "In the middle of March." Mary looked thoughtful. "What's the matter?" asked Ivor. Mary Ellis told him she had a film contract. She was sailing back right away, but she thought it would be all right; the film would be done and she would be back, at the latest, a week after rehearsals had started. Ivor gave a sigh of relief. "That's all right," he said. "My darling, I'll send you the script and the music over, and when you come back you will know the play." Everything was settled. Mary sailed a day or two later, and from the ship she sent Ivor a cable: "I'm sailing away with waltz music in my heart."

Ivor got down to details. There was much to do. He had to get the script into proper shape and complete the score. He was bubbling with ideas—he wrote and composed, wrote and composed, wrote and composed. Nightly masses of material accumulated. When the script was finally done, it was bound like a book and photostat copies were taken. In due course I received mine and read it. I fell for it right away but knew there would have to be a lot of cutting. What I had read would play for well over four hours. . . .

There was a producer to choose, a dance arranger to settle, the scenery and décor to get in hand. Ivor's choice for décor fell upon Oliver Messel, which brought a modern touch without destroying the fundamental Drury Lane tradition or the romance. Tennent was already getting shocks, for this was going to cost a lot of money. He had promised Ivor a free hand but this did not extend, he had to point out, to real ermine for the " borders " in the Palace scene! It would have meant miles of fur and the Royal Mint, let alone the Bank of England, behind it.

Then there was the all-important question of a producer. Ivor, however, had made his choice. He wanted Leontine Sagan. He got her. This was revolutionary. Never before had a woman produced a show at Drury Lane. There was much head-shaking. Ivor did not care. He believed in Sagan. She was, therefore, engaged. Ivor sent for her and asked her to do it. Leontine Sagan asked him was it was all about. He explained. She accepted. She had produced, in this country, *Children in Uniform*, a most distinguished, sensitive piece of work, but that was at the Duchess, a small theatre. She had produced *Richard III* for the Oxford University Dramatic Society. That was something to see, and Ivor had seen it. She had, of course, handled all sorts of shows on the Continent and she had worked for Reinhardt, who was her Master. She herself was Viennese. There were grave doubts amongst the staff at the Lane, which was very conservative, and very naturally so.

William Abingdon, the stage director—even the Lane never had a better—made no comment. That was his habit. He had to cope, he had to provide all the works. That was enough for him. Trained under Sir Herbert Tree in the great days of His Majesty's, there was nothing he could not do. He was prepared to tackle a woman producer, and a foreigner at that. He had a splendid staff and Freddie Munns, the Master Carpenter, was by way of being a genius in the matter of stage " effect." Bill Abingdon saw no difficulties. When Ivor told him there was a scene where a great liner first exploded and then sank in flames, he just nodded and said " All right." This was Drury Lane, it could be done. Leonard de Renzie was the stage manager: it was he who would have to battle with the producer at close quarters. But the staff at Drury Lane in the days of Novello was one of sheer magnificence in the matter of being expert.

Alick Johnstone was busy as soon as possible on the scenery, which was of course painted on the immense frames at Drury Lane, which is a place complete in itself. The properties were made in the property room, under the eagle eye of E. Boxall, and from that room you could have anything from a battleship to a lobster salad, which would look even better than the real article. Did you want armour, statuary, period furniture? Right, you had only to say the word! Ivor could not have been better served. And Boxall had been property master for Ivor in *The Rat*. And up in the wardrobe was Miss Field, daughter of a famous wardrobe mistress and famous herself. It was all set. The show would not suffer on the technical side.

The dances were to be arranged by Ralph Reader, who was on top of the world in that line of business. He was the creator of the famous *Gang Show*. He had learnt his business the hard way, and knew all about it. He might issue his instructions in sharp, staccato terms, interposed with such phrases as " chick-etty snitch "—whatever that might mean; he might address the dancers as " slaves " (he made them willing ones), but he knew what he wanted and how to get it. He might appear quite oblivious to his surroundings and to be gazing into the week after next, but out of his brain came exactly the right things and he could make the people do them in exactly the right way. He brought with him as assistant a youth with ginger hair, a cheerful smile and an unruffled calmness of demeanour. His name was William Anthony Sutton. Little did either of them dream then that fourteen years after they had worked on that production of *Glamorous Night* they themselves would, as producing managers, take it on tour and make further history with it. Yet so it was to be. Indeed, the production of *Glamorous Night* accounted for a lot.

Leontine Sagan is a remarkable woman and one of the most charming I know. She is, in her own way, a genius. Her mastery of crowd movement is a thing at which to wonder. She has her own way of producing. She can charm the players and she can drive them. She can praise them and she can condemn. Neither of these things are done by halves. " Why do you do it like that? " she would demand of an actor, " you are such a stupid man—you do such stupid things. I have shown you time and again—still you are stupid." They would do it again: the actor would get it right, and she would praise. Star or super, both felt the lash, both were called " stupid." She is quite fearless ;

The famous Rose Ballet from Ivor Novello's *Careless Rapture*

Ivor in the Hampstead Heath scene from *Careless Rapture*

Ivor in *Old Heidelberg*

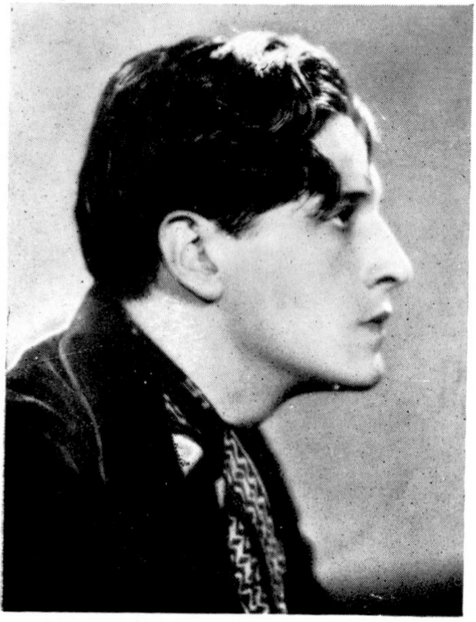

A picture of Ivor as " The Rat "

Ivor in *The White Rose*

she sees what she wants and she goes towards the achievement of it without counting the cost. Nothing must stand in the way. She is handsome and distinguished with eyes which shine with artistry, a voice which can speak music or rasp like a saw. She could have moods which varied from the calm of a summer evening to an equinoctial gale. The staff soon learned to look for a storm signal which she flew. If the petticoat showed beneath the skirt, then look out! The two things always seemed to synchronize.

I am sure that Leo Sagan, whom I count as a very dear and valued friend, will not mind if I disclose that, during the periods when she drove all before her in a fury of production, the staff christened her " Madame Hitler." But they liked her none the less. Sometimes nothing would satisfy her. She wanted a record for a crowd effect. Dozens were tried over but none would do. She found fault, she condemned. So we tried a little trick. We said there was one more she had not heard. This might do. And we put on the first one we had played over hours ago. Bill Sutton had the job of putting them on the panotrope. This particular record was one I knew well. It had, indeed, been made specially for me, for a play called *Take a Chance* at the Whitehall. That had a racecourse scene and this record was actually made at the Alexandra Park racecourse during a meeting. If you listened closely, you could hear the thud of the horses' hooves. So good was it that it had been the first one played, but Leo had condemned it. Now we trotted it out again, as a special discovery, and at once she said it was the very thing. How stupid we were, why had we not tried it before? We said nothing. We were only too glad to get it by.

Leontine Sagan and Oliver Messel went across to the Balkans to get ideas for the costumes to be worn by the inhabitants of Krasnia, the Ruritanian kingdom in which much of the action passed. They came back not only with ideas but with stacks of actual costumes. No expense was being spared. Meanwhile, the pantomime was running and Ivor was playing in *Murder in Mayfair*.

There was still a cog wanted in the wheel. Someone had to write the lyrics. Now this is a most important job. Writers of lyrics do not get nearly enough tribute for their work. True, in these days, the words they write are seldom heard with any clarity, diction being distant from stage technique, but those words really matter very much. Ivor was quite capable of writing lyrics himself but he thought there could be better than this. He had taken a lot of chances so he took another.

In his company was a young man playing a small part and understudying. His name was Christopher Hassall. He had been at the Old Vic, he had toured Australia, he had played in Shakespeare. John Gielgud had sent him to Ivor. The idea was for him to understudy Ivor in a projected production of *Romeo and Juliet*. He had called at the Globe to see if Ivor had anything for him, had been told to go to the dressing-room and had lost his way in the corridors. He was trying to find his bearings and was humming, rather loudly, a melody by Fauré. Suddenly he heard a voice call out " Who's that." It was Ivor's voice, the tune having attracted him. He saw Hassall and at once gave him a job. And now young Christopher was playing in *Murder in Mayfair*. He had very humbly presented Ivor with a slim little volume of poems which he had written—everyone always gave Ivor everything. He did not expect Ivor to read it. But Ivor did.

One evening, when Hassall came to the stage door, a bit late, he was told that Mr. Novello wanted to see him at once. He got a shock. This summons to the dressing-room of the great man was quite unexpected and quite frightening. What had he done? Was it the sack? He went along, his heart in his mouth. He knocked on the door and went in. Ivor looked at him and said " We've just got time for a cup of coffee. Come over to the Prompt Corner." The Prompt Corner was a café a few yards from the theatre. Hassall was more than ever perturbed. Why was he being taken out of the theatre? Why did they have coffee at all and why not in the dressing-room anyway? He was sure he was in trouble. They sat down. Ivor opened up by asking Hassall if he had ever written any lyrics for musical plays. Hassall said he had not. He also admitted that he had only seen a musical play once in his entire life, and that was *Bow Bells*. That did not daunt Ivor. He was taking chances. He told Hassall he was going to do a musical for Drury Lane. He produced a rather dirty, crumpled piece of paper, with the top line of a tune scrawled on it. " Here you are," said Ivor. " See what you can do with this. It's in the key of C. It's called " Glamorous Night," and he just outlined the situation. " You have plenty of time before you go on," continued Ivor, " just see what you can do with it—and bring it to me at the end of the show." They went back to the Theatre, Hassall in more of a whirl than before, Ivor pleased because he was following a hunch, trusting his instinct. " See if you can get the words ' Glamorous Night ' into it," was his parting instruction.

Hassall went off to his dressing-room. He was not taking it too seriously. He did not realize that his own moment was upon him, the turning-point in his career. He went up to his room, he made up for his part, he kept the tune in his brain and he began to fit words to it. But by the time the show was over he had set the lyric to the music. He took it down to Ivor. Ivor read it and he gave Hassall one of those smiles of his which meant so much when you understood them. He was satisfied. More than satisfied. He had been right. This was the man to write the lyrics to his songs—and here before him was the song which everyone now knows . . . " Glamorous Night."

CHAPTER EIGHTEEN

KING IVOR OF OLD DRURY

GLAMOROUS NIGHT took shape. The casting was complete. Mary Ellis was leading lady, Militza Hajos; Lyn Harding, that grand veteran actor, was Lydyef, the villain; and Barry Jones, an actor of real quality, was King Stepan. Now a film star, Barry Jones was not then nearly so well known as he deserved, despite his big success with his partner Maurice Colbourne in their own production of *The Queen's Husband.* There were also Elisabeth Welch, Victor Boggetti, Trefor Jones (in the tenor role), a handsome young actor named Peter Graves, whose chief occupation in the play was to have his face smacked by Mary Ellis (and often it was a really good hearty smack), Olive Gilbert, appearing for the first time with Ivor in a musical play, Clifford Heatherley, who played "Lord Broadcasting," Minnie Rayner, an army of smaller parts and, of couse, Ivor himself.

Mam came to the auditions and flooded them with her pupils. Sitting in the stalls, she acclaimed each one, saying in her husky voice "Ivor, darling, you must engage them all." Lloyd Williams's tact came in very useful at these junctures.

The final chorus and dancers, when selected, had many of the regular Drury Lane people amongst them. The *Glamorous Night* chorus, which became, with very minor alterations, the chorus of all the Novello musicals at Drury Lane, was certainly the finest I have ever heard or seen in musicals shows—and I have a long experience. The same can be said of the dancers, both male and female. There are still—or there were still, when *King's Rhapsody* was running at the Palace—many of those "Girls" and "Boys" in the chorus of that show. Some of them spent their lives from 1935 in Novello shows, wanting no change, asking no better. Charles W. Prentice was musical director for *Glamorous Night* and all the other Novello-Lane shows.

Glamorous Night was news. A carefully prepared campaign

of publicity was worked out and gradually built up. It received all sorts of unexpected but welcome help. It very soon became apparent that the show would not be produced in March. Mary Ellis was not available; that film was still hanging about. There was much anxiety, but it was all grist to the publicity mill. Ivor had a script sent to her and had all the music which concerned her recorded and sent over, so that she could study when in Hollywood. Nothing was left to chance. The vast production grew and grew; so did the expense. So did the excitement and the interest. But Mary Ellis was still required in Hollywood, and it began to look as if another leading lady might have to be found. The Lane could not wait for ever; it could not afford it.

Meanwhile the songs were ready and Christopher Hassall found that his Fate had overtaken him. He was to do all the lyrics. He kept getting them, top line on rough paper, from Ivor, and had to work at full speed. He would get the music one day and have to deliver the lyric the next morning. Somehow he did it, or nearly always. He was not married then, and had not much money. He lived by himself, and sketchily, like most young men. His food was taken when and how he could get it, and he would drink Guinness to keep up his strength, smoking innumerable cigarettes and drinking countless cups of tea. He had a habit of cutting himself whilst shaving. He scribbled the lyrics on odd bits of paper, and these suffered in the confusion and muddle, which led to Ivor demanding " When are you going to bring me a lyric not covered with Guinness, tea and blood?

" Fold Your Wings " was nearly his Waterloo. He struggled with it; Ivor made suggestions; Lloyd Williams made suggestions. At last it was Ivor who thought of the line " Fold Your Wings." It was the second most popular song in the show.

Hassall worked wherever he could, at " Redroofs," during week-ends with Ivor at Brighton, at the flat. At " Redroofs " they had the unsolicited assistance of Mam. Hassall did not find that helped much. But Ivor explained matters and put it straight. After a long discussion one night, when Mam had been laying down the law, Ivor said to Hassall, " Don't ever listen to what Mam says. Follow your own instinct. That's what I've always done."

" Shine through My Dreams" was an accidental inspiration.

Before Trefor Jones was cast as the tenor, Ivor heard many other tenors, some sent to him by H. M. Tennent. One of these, a foreigner with a fine voice who was well known in his own country, came to the flat. Ivor played to him a tune which he was suggesting for the show. The tenor listened and shook his head. " No, no," he said. " That is not the sort of song you should write for me to sing—you should write a song like in *Tosca*." Like a flash, in Ivor's head, came the melody of " Shine through My Dreams." He composed it, but that tenor never sang it. Ivor had not a title for that tune, nor had Hassall. But at Brighton, where they spent the week-end, Ivor suddenly said " I've just thought of a scrumptious title—do write it down—' Shine through My Dreams '." And there it was, all complete. The lyric flowed easily . . . Christopher Hassall was quick; he had to be. At one time he was turning out eight lyrics a week. . . .

The show was in rehearsal, but still no Mary Ellis. Cables flashed backwards and forwards; there was growing anxiety and fear. It was obvious that *Glamorous Night* could not be produced as soon as had been hoped. But rehearsals went on. The stage hands at the Lane were singing " The Militza Guard " song, that fine marching number, old-fashioned in type but a tower of strength, sung by the male chorus in long line across the stage in the striking uniforms of the Krasnian Guard. That was the stage hands' favourite.

It was also the favourite number of Lord Lurgan, the Chairman of the Board of Directors, who attended many rehearsals. It was usually my job to sit by him, keep him engaged and head off too many questions. Lord Lurgan was a tall, distinguished nobleman of the old school. He had been a soldier in his youth and spoke of the Foot, never a regiment's name. That song was redolent of comic opera, and that is what he had liked as a young subaltern. He was a most decorative chairman. A director of many companies, he did not really know much about theatre business. Nor was there any reason why he should. But he did know how to conduct a meeting and that was his job.

Ivor had been clever to put in the " Militza's Guard " number. The Mounties' Chorus in *Rose Marie* had started a fashion at Drury Lane and he followed it. Indeed, *Glamorous Night*, despite its romantic story, was conceived on the formula which had always succeeded in Drury Lane drama. It was indeed, a romantic Drury Lane drama, with music added. Those dramas had always been topical, and so was *Glamorous Night*. Ivor's leading lady was thinly disguised from a certain red-haired beauty who had made romance and excitement in a Balkan state. Ivor also featured something which was in the news, but not yet achieved—and that was television. Nobody knew anything about it then, outside the inventors, but it was much discussed. So Ivor put it in. His hero, " Anthony Allen " whom he played himself, had invented television, but the B.B.C. would have none of it. This led to Allen's disappearance (plus £500 left lying about by " Lord Broadcasting " as a bait for his invention) to the troubled and stormy land of Krasnia and excitement after excitement. The burning and sinking ship was inspired by the tragedy of the " Morro Castle " still fresh in the public's mind.

Ivor had studied the Drury Lane formula, and added his own touch as well. His hero was unromantic, a contrast to the romance all around. His love scenes were mainly light comedy, or quarrels. He eschewed sentimentality, but he did not forget drama. Nor did he forget spectacle. There was the attempted assassination outside an Opera House, with his leading lady in a carriage drawn by two horses—real horses; there was a mob stoning the Royal Favourite's villa, with crashing glass galore and the singing of revolutionary and patriotic songs; there was another attempted assassination, this time by knife-throwing, on the deck of a luxury liner when a cabaret was in progress, with an amazing skating dance having a surprise *dénouement;* there was a scene in Broadcasting House only slightly more fantastic than the real place; there was the ship being blown up; there was a wonderful scene in the mountains culminating in a Gipsy wedding (Ivor and Mary in Tzigane attire, and Ivor loving it); a Palace scene which occupied the full depth of the Drury Lane stage (seldom used in its vast entirety); a rescue in a dungeon with the villain shot just as he was about to kill his King, who was making trouble about abdicating; and a Royal Wedding as seen by television. It was all astonishing and it was all Drury Lane.

Ivor never used a low comedian. Instead he played comedy himself and also used his beloved mascot, Minnie Rayner, who was the maid to Militza and got a lot of laughs. And just for full spectacular measure, Ivor threw in a scene behind the scenes at the Krasnian Opera House, and a scene on the stage as well, where an opera was being played and the King sat in his Royal Box. It was Drury Lane right enough.

But what of Mary Ellis? At last came a cable announcing that she was sailing. Hearts beat high and things went with a swing. I went down, with pressmen and cameramen, to Waterloo to meet her. The station was crowded and the platform at which the boat train was to arrive was packed. We found Mary Ellis and, as we found her, the crowd swirled and broke like waves of the sea. Through its broken ranks burst Ivor. He rushed to Mary Ellis, flinging his arms around her and shouting with delight. They embraced and kissed over and over again. "Darling," "Lovely," "Glorious" filled the air. Cameras flashed, the crowd cheered. Ivor and Mary were whisked away. My cameramen fled back to Fleet Street, well satisfied. I took H. M. Tennent back to the Lane in my car. (I ran a big Daimler then. I can't afford it now. But I had a vast amount of work then, and taxation was not what it is to-day. Also, I had not started writing books. . . .) We went as fast as we could for I had the more dignified characters of Fleet Street coming to meet Miss Ellis in the foyer, men whose importance did not fit in with waiting about upon a platform. Tennent was quite cheerful during that drive. But I thought he looked rather curiously at the car. He had not seen it before. His firm used it often enough afterwards, in all conscience.

Back at the Lane, I escorted Mary to meet the Press. She was perfectly delightful to them and charmed them all. She created a sensation of the first water. She refused a cocktail and asked for a cup of tea. She got it and she drank it and she enjoyed it. Here was a staggerer for the Fleet Street boys. The film men had come as well as the theatre men because Miss Ellis was a planet of both spheres. Here was a film star, a great leading lady, refusing a cocktail. That was a "story," too, and a good one.

Mary started rehearsals right away. She had learnt both music and script from what Ivor had sent her. It was only a matter of fitting in with positions and of getting the costumes done. Things worked at fever heat.

And then came another Sensation. Equity, the actors' trade union, was growing in strength. They had decided that they were now powerful enough to declare for a " closed shop," that nobody except their own members could be employed in any theatre. Quite reasonably, from their point of view, they wanted to make this an affair which got much publicity. Here was Theatre Royal, Drury Lane, in the news every day. Here was an eagerly awaited production, expectation of which was on tiptoes. Here was the ideal sounding-board for them. They told the management of Drury Lane that there must be a closed shop. The management replied, with courtesy and common sense that, in principle, they had no objection. But before Equity could dictate terms, Equity must be in a position to prove that she could get and enforce a " closed shop " in the " Profession." Equity went to it. They worked on the cast at Drury Lane. They almost succeeded, but not quite. One member of the cast—an important member—stood out resolutely against them. Equity tried every means. Drury Lane was urbane. Equity was not powerful enough to call a strike, and it had apparently not the power, as yet, to make people join who did not want to. Her officials tried every way. The Drury Lane management never ceased its courtesy nor its stand that a " closed shop " was agreeable if it were 100 per cent. closed.

I was besieged with queries. Who was the actor—or actress—who was standing out? I would not say a word. A man who considered himself the arch-cross-questioner of Fleet Street put me through a cross-examination which would have done justice to Marshall Hall, F. E. Smith, Carson, Birkett and Sir Patrick Hastings rolled into one, or so he thought. He never got one word out of me. In the end, Equity had to withdraw its closed shop demand, and there were no hard feelings and no strike. But a whole lot of publicity. Nobody knew the name of the stalwart who stood out with such rocklike resolution. There is no harm in disclosing it now. It was dear Lyn Harding. Nothing shook him: the fear of a strike and the damage to the show, the fear for his own future, nothing. He did not believe in trade unions. He was an actor, he said, not a labourer nor a miner. No trade unions for him. And, bless him, he won.

Excitement and thrill followed excitement and thrill. The day came when the full Drury Lane orchestra played the music. Ivor sat entranced. Here was an ambition come true. And the music moved us all as it swelled and soared in melody through that great auditorium. Some of us were carried away. Then came the costume parade. The eye was dazzled by colour and beauty, both by the dresses and the scenery, though one member of the Drury Lane staff denounced the pillars of the Palace scene, which were a little modern and fantastic. But the scene was gorgeous and satisfying, all the same. The sinking of the ship was rehearsed with great care: it actually did sink by means of Drury Lane's famous " lifts." The explosions were timed and considered from the safety point of view. It was Bill Sutton's job to be the person experimented upon. He was put in a little cabin whilst bombs exploded all around him and red fire and smoke filled the air. If he did not get hurt, it was all right. He survived safely. He took things like that in his stride.

The dress rehearsals came. First without audience and with the company and staff being fed on coffee and sandwiches in the foyer at the expense of the management—for these rehearsals lasted all day and far into the night.

It was Bill Sutton's job to " call them." It was the habit at the Lane jokingly to refer to the chorus and small parts as " Scum." Indeed, they did it themselves. So Bill Sutton called " Scum in the foyer, sandwiches and coffee please." They all went up. But the mother of a new girl came down and wanted to thrash young Sutton for insulting her daughter. " Scum " indeed!

Through the whole of this vast complex piece of work Ivor moved as if on springs. He was at the summit of delight; he was in heaven. Here was his work taking shape on that revered stage of beloved Drury Lane. Here was his music being played by a magnificent orchestra. Here were great singers singing his songs and fine actors speaking his lines. His name was in every paper, his name was headlined. His name was on the lips of all Theatreland. Inside the Lane he was at home; he was almost a King already. Everyone, from stage hands upwards, was calling him Ivor. He spoke to them all, he knew them all; they were all his friends. He was installed in Garrick's dressing-room, from whence issued the prince of valet-dressers, Bill Wright, with endless cups of tea, with cigarettes all ready, with everything Ivor could want, foreseen before he asked. Mam was always bobbing about, though those who could avoided her. Lloydy pervaded the scene, always there, always busy, always watching points. And for three days before the opening night, the queue began to form for the pit and gallery. Yet there had been no overboosting: there had simply been a succession of news stories and such details as it was good to tell in advance. Nobody had said officially, least of all the publicity man, that this was a great show or was bound to be a big success. That is Bad Publicity. Overboosting kills more often than it helps.

Apart from talk of success, the " knockers " were quite busy. There are a lot of " knockers " in and around the theatre. They are of both sexes and their business is to belittle a show. They don't damn it outright; they whisper; they say so much and no more, leaving the rest to the imagination, as they know that most people always think the worst. They are the folk who, on a first night, go round to the dressing-rooms and say " My dear, its perfectly marvellous. I think its a certain success, but. . . ."

These good folk did not know their Ivor. They only judged him by what he had done; they did not know that of which he was capable. They gave him grudging full marks for his success, adding " But, my dear, this is the Lane, you know. Ivor's a darling, he's so charming, he's so clever—BUT—the Lane, you know—a death trap, if ever there was one . . ." and a shrug of the shoulders completed it.

Ivor displayed no sign of nerves, whatever he felt. He never said he was sure of success, but he communicated quiet confidence to all around him. He worked like a beaver and was gentle and kind to all. He gave Leontine Sagan a free hand; they had conferences at which his experience was at her disposal and she, like a wise and clever woman, would listen to what he said. He felt friendliness and good wishes all round him.

He had not given himself a very good part, but he had given a sign of genius. And more sign than one. He had abandoned any pretence at the romantic hero so usual at the Lane. He was playing a modern, middle-class young man with an offhand, rather impertinent manner. He made his first appearance in lounge suit, raincoat and umbrella. One of the signs of his genius was the way he fitted himself with that part, not spectacular but with just the right dialogue for him, lines from which he knew he could get every ounce, lines which were right up his street.

He did not attempt a big spectacular opening scene, such as was customary at Drury Lane. Instead, the curtain rose on a suburban street, with little houses all in a row, all just like each other and the life going on in that street just as it does, all mimed to music. And he had contrived a logical ending, with the right finale to it, although apparently unhappy. But on top of that he played his trump—his Ace of trumps—he had his "Vision." He had given himself only one major entrance—in the Palace Scene, when, in a plain blue lounge suit, he walked the whole depth of the stage between crowds in brilliant uniforms and Court dresses. That was a sop to him as an actor. He gave his leading lady an exit which he himself had adored when he sat in the pit: there she was, torn between duty and love, and choosing, as she must, the path of duty. Turning her back on her audience and on love, in her gorgeous gown with its sweeping train, she mounted, slowly but steadily, a long staircase treading the path of duty, leaving love behind. . . . It never fails—it did not fail in *Glamorous Night*, especially as Mary Ellis played it.

We saw her, through television, married to her charming king and acclaimed by the populace, whilst her loved one—played by Ivor—watched his loss through the medium of his own invention . . . and then . . . and then the lamps dimmed down, the stage was almost dark, and a gleam of blue light crept in like rising moonshine. Shadowy figures filled the stage, waltzing, waltzing, changing partners, and waltzing on until the stage was crowded with a whirling mass of dancers. The light grew stronger, but always blue—and blue is the colour of Hope. Hope was always Ivor's theme. And, through that throng, came the two lovers whose paths had parted. Here, in the land of Hope, of Memory, they met again; they took each other in their arms and they waltzed through eternity. That was the trick of Ivor's genius. He used it several times and it never failed. . . .

The first night of *Glamorous Night* arrived: May 2nd, 1935. Crowds besieged the theatre. Through the stage door came an endless procession of telegraph boys bringing those sheaves of telegrams to all concerned, or nearly all concerned (few people ever send the publicity man a telegram) with good wishes for success—telegrams which, according to theatrical superstition, should not be opened until after the show. That night even I had two telegrams, one from my wife and daughter, and one from Ivor himself.

And in a stream as endless as the telegrams came the flowers, great bouquets, baskets in cellophane, clusters, sheaves and humble bunches. It might have been a flower show. " Woody," the then stage door-keeper, and Cavell, his assistant (but now in full charge) could not cope. Nothing like it had been seen before even at the Lane. Crowds of fans waited for the company and for autographs—and for Ivor. His name was heard on all sides— " Ivor," " Ivor," " Ivor." In the front of the house, into that spacious and noble vestibule, the first-nighters of stalls, dress circle and boxes filtered. Here again, it was " Ivor," " Ivor," " Ivor." Cameras flashed at the celebrities. Those amazing people who go to first nights, and who make such a to-do over getting their seats, were following their usual procedure. They were not occupying the seats for which they had clamoured. That was their last idea. They stood and stared at each other, at the other celebrities, for in their own minds everyone attending a first night, themselves included, is a celebrity. But that night there were celebrities indeed. The footmen in their Royal liveries could scarcely push between the ranks of the starers, who, of course, all congregated in doorways or on staircases, causing as much inconvenience as possible. The critics dribbled in, some going straight to their seats, with a professional and detached air, others greeting friends, and some, of course, had lost their tickets and wanted duplicates. Amazing that so many of them do this. Theatre-going is their job but they give more trouble over their tickets than the ordinary playgoer. Gossip writers besieged me, gazing and questioning. The bar bells shrilled, but nobody heeded. There were shouts of " Take your seats, please. Curtain going up " and at long last the crowd thinned, late-comers—some of them critics, too—making a last minute rush.

Inside, the noble auditorium was packed and excitement seethed. You could cut it with a knife. Old Drury stood on the verge, a failure would be terrible. Ivor stood on the verge too. Could he do it? This young man—he was forty-one—was taking a vast risk. Many did not believe. In the Royal Box was Jack Joel, who really owned the Lane, despite the shareholders, for he had so often come to the rescue with money when things were bad. There he was, a little man with his head hanging downwards and sideways. He was never likely to press for his money in Drury Lane, for whatever faults he may have had, he loved the grand old theatre and we all liked him. Opposite, in the Prince's Box, sat Mam, Madame Novello Davies, all smiles and beams and brilliance, embowered in flowers placed there by her son, that son who to-night took such a chance, had such a tremendous responsibility.

For never before in its two hundred and seventy-two years of history had one man written and composed an entire evening's show for it—and played the lead himself. There was an air of tenseness, of vast anticipation and excitement. . . .

And what of Ivor? He had come in very quietly, his hat pulled down, his coat collar up, to dodge the fans. He loved them but he did not want a fuss just then; afterwards, perhaps, if he earned it. He had gone round and wished everyone luck. William Abingdon had visited him in his dressing-room to say a few words of cheer and to assure him that everything would be done. Leonard de Renzie was in the prompt corner: he had to run the stage from now on. Everyone was at their post. Bill Sutton called the " quarter." And Ivor made up. There was over £25,000 of Drury Lane's money at stake. For him the risk was higher: there was his reputation in the balance. For a failure at the Lane is apt to resound very widely. He was outwardly calm, and rather quiet. He says his hands trembled with emotion. I had slipped in to see him and had been thanked and got one of those smiles. Anyway, there was nothing he could do about it now. For good or ill, the curtain must go up. . . .

And up it went. I stood in my usual place, just inside the right-hand entrance of the Grand Circle. I saw that curtain ascend. And what followed was history. . . .

When that curtain fell again, there was such a scene as the old walls around us had hardly witnessed. That night is a piece of treasured memory. One recalls the massed excitement of it, the welcome Ivor received, the applause for them all and the roar for Mary Ellis. But transcending all that was the amazing roar which followed her singing. Mary Ellis, that night, touched the heights. She is not a tall or a big woman, but she dominates. She is force and energy personified. If I had to describe her, I would say the tirelessness and energy of a Shetland pony and the grace and fire of a pure-bred Arab, joined to personal beauty, immense talent and knowledge as to how to use it, and a voice which came from heaven. She was a revelation. She tore the house into roars of enthusiasm. Seldom has such a performance been seen or heard as hers in *Glamorous Night*. There was not a slip nor a false note.

Everyone of that vast cast, down to the most unimportant member of the chorus, down to the humblest stage hand had done their best and done it superbly well. And now they received tribute. Emotions ran riot. This was an Event; this was notable. It was not just a first night; it was a milestone. Not only was Drury Lane back where it should be but a new force had entered the Theatre—Ivor Novello. They cheered and they cheered, the curtain went up and down. The company stood in serried rows, smiling, bowing their thanks. Ivor led them forward to take their bows, to receive their acclaim. He led Mary Ellis forward last and she swept a curtsey to the house —and to him. He raised her and kissed her. People went mad with delight.

Again his name was everywhere. " Ivor," " Ivor," they shouted—not only the gallery and the pit but the stalls and the boxes. And then he came forward. He did it in that usual way of his, that modest, quiet, almost humble manner. There was no stride forward with look of triumph, like a conquering hero. There was that slightly awkward, almost sideways, almost slouching step, as he stepped down to the footlights to received his reward. He was like a schoolboy coming forward to take a prize. He stood there with his quiet, friendly smile, and he bowed to the house and to Mam, and then he spoke his gratitude. It was a modest speech, such as he was to make so often thereafter. It was a heartfelt speech of thanks and gratitude. He had thrown his heart at their feet and they had picked it up. The applause was deafening. " The King " crashed out, as excited throngs poured out from the theatre, and once again " Ivor," " Ivor " was on the air. Russell Street was just a solid pack, and it was impossible to get anywhere near the stage door. And in the eyes of the folk of Drury Lane Theatre there were tears of pride and thankfulness. Once again, the man had come at the fateful hour. Colley Cibber, Garrick, Edmund Kean, all had done it. And now, so had Ivor Novello.

Ivor eventually went home the side way, after an almost endless stream had gathered on the stage to congratulate him. With him went some of the company and friends, back to the flat to live it all over again, and to wait for the morning paper. I did not go to the flat. I went home. I knew what was going to be in the morning papers. . . .

And of all his successes to come, of all his many triumphs, nothing was ever to equal that night for Ivor Novello. That night of May 2nd, 1935, was his night of triumph: the first flush of real, enduring and immense success. Such things come once only. He had tasted success before, he was to taste it many times again, but that was the vintage of vintages. Such joy comes once only in a lifetime. . . .

He was still Ivor Novello. He had been that in the morning. But now he was in the eyes of the world a very different Ivor Novello. He was one of the great People of the Theatre. Yet, to himself, to them and to everyone, he was still the same Ivor, not proud, not the least bit puffed up, only a little tired, very pleased and very, very grateful. . . .

The Press notices were "raves." The Libraries—ticket agencies—plunged heavily, and away went *Glamorous Night* for a prosperous run, to the joy of all connected with Drury Lane. Yet, strange as it may seem, it did not jump to capacity at once. For some reason, the cheaper parts were slow. The stalls, dress circle and the boxes sold out, but the upper circle, pit and gallery hung fire. But, after a week or so, these came in and business was magnificent. The Lane was itself again. *Glamorous Night* and Ivor were the talk of the town, the talk of the country.

Actually, the business with *Glamorous Night* fluctuated considerably. It ran into a very hot summer, for one thing, which, although it did little to thin the stalls, did affect seriously the cheaper parts. The production had been very costly and the running expenses were high. Drury Lane was not making a fortune, for all the success; indeed, it was finding it difficult to recoup its production costs. All this will appear later. But it did not take anything away from the fact that *Glamorous Night* was a triumph for Ivor as actor-author-composer and that it had restored the lost prestige to Drury Lane.

It was indeed a great, glittering show. Ivor had conceived it on the right lines. His music was the best he had ever done,

The Dancing Years was one of Ivor's favourite plays. He was at his romantic best in this gay and colourful musical

A scene from *The Dancing Years* at Drury Lane

This picture, taken in the show, was Ivor's favourite portrait of himself

This scene and two studies of Ivor are from the lovely and ever-popular *King's Rhapsody*

miles away ahead of his previous works. And much of the success, apart from the basic creation of Novello, was due to Mary Ellis. She played superbly; she dominated, she gave everything, and she sang like an angel. She swept the audience off their feet. Ivor's songs had full justice done to them. If it was Ivor's triumph, it was no less a triumph for Mary Ellis. She brought the audience to their feet. Those of us who had heard it at rehearsal, over and over again, were yet thrilled to our hearts. Christopher Hassall, whose lyrics she was singing and who therefore knew it all backwards, found himself standing up and cheering. There is only one word which can sum up Mary's performance of Militza and that is—Perfection. She was a revelation of Beauty in every form. She was a revelation to the playgoers. Here, at last, was a real leading lady, who could do it all. Ivor had been right in his choice.

Mary Ellis and Christopher Hassall made a special celebration of *Glamorous Night*. It was a presentation to Ivor. She bought a bronze plaque, and Christopher Hassall wrote some words which were engraved thereon. It was to go on the sundial in Ivor's garden at his beloved " Redroofs " but it proved too large, so it went on the door of his special workroom-studio in the garden. That enduring bronze is there still and may it remain there for centuries, to mark a night of triumph in the Theatre, a night when a man reached the peak of his achievement, presented to him by two people who helped him and who reached peaks of their own too. Here are the words which Christopher Hassall wrote:

"We read the silent language of the sun
We fill the hours and seasons as they run
How Spring returns and Summer swells the vines
How ripe July to Winter's rains declines
How all things alter with the alt'ring year
Save wit and music, laughter and good cheer
Indeed, most happy owner of this ground
Where harmonies resort and friends abound
The Sword of Time can put the world to flight
But not the splendours of your *Glam'rous Night*."

Alas, that it was not true in actuality . . . and yet it was, in the long run. Something was to put those splendours to flight and to blot out the sun of success in the very noontide of its glory, as will be seen. . . .

Glamorous Night was technically as near perfection as such a thing can be in the Theatre. There had been, there were, no hitches. Everything worked like clockwork.

Lyn Harding gave a memorable performance as the villainous Lydyef; he is an actor of the right generation trained to his profession, experienced to the hilt, and knowing exactly what to do and how to do it. And he was no stranger to Drury Lane. He had been a " villain " there before, and once, in one of the melodramas, nearly lost his life (his horse did) by being overwhelmed by an avalanche. That was in *The Marriages of Mayfair* in 1908. He was a casualty in *Glamorous Night* too. A minor one, but a painful one all the same. In the scene of the Castle dungeon, where he stood over the King, demanding abdication or death, at the very climax of the drama came a shot, and Lydyef staggered back—killed. The King was saved. The shot was fired by the hero in the person of Ivor Novello. At one performance, the shot rang out and there came a most realistic cry from Harding, as he reeled and fell to the ground. The scene went on, the curtain fell and it was then discovered that Lyn had really been shot. Ivor had shot him. He lay there all the time the scene was being played, shot in reality, although the audience knew nothing of it. The property man responsible for the rifle always put in an extra amount of powder in the cartridge to obtain a louder report. Owing to the continual refilling of the cartridge the brass edges became jagged and a piece had become detached and acted as a bullet. It had pierced the leather belt which Lyn wore and all his clothing and entered the small of his back. Ivor was appalled and Lyn was furious. " Take that young man's gun away," he thundered. " He does not know how to handle a rifle." Ivor was frightened at the best of times when it came to guns and he always shut his eyes when firing. He did not aim at Lyn but just pointed the gun in the general direction in which he stood. He was now most contrite. He sent for a doctor for Lyn and, on arrival, the doctor ordered an X-ray photograph to see where the piece of metal was lodged. It was discovered that a triangular piece of brass was much too near the kidneys to allow for an operation to remove it. It was decided to leave it where it was—and there it is to-day. Lyn Harding will carry that souvenir of his friend

Ivor Novello to the grave—and he treasures it, too. But it might have been very serious. After that, Ivor always fired in the air—and hated it!

To Barry Jones must go praise as well. This actor could, and can, play royalty in a manner so lifelike as to create the belief that he must be a king indeed. Despite the charm and courteous kindliness, there is always that air of remoteness which surrounds kings, that is when Barry plays a king, of course. In the ordinary way he is a perfectly charming man with a tremendous sense of humour, given to belittling himself and to telling stories of which he is the butt. Trained in the Benson school, he and his friend Maurice Colbourne, also a good actor and a sensitive producer, joined forces after the First World War (in which they both served with distinction) and, eventually, after many adventures, took the plays of Shaw backwards and forwards across Canada, which was almost without a theatre, making quite a bit of money in so doing. Greatly daring, they entered the West End as actor-managers, quite unknown to the public. They took the Ambassadors' and staged a play by Robert E. Sherwood, called *The Queen's Husband*. Grace Lane was their leading lady and played the Queen. Barry Jones played the King, a quiet, delightful man dominated by his wife who finally takes action and wins the day. They opened with no flourish of trumpets but the next morning's Press brought them fame. Since then they have done much splendid work for the Theatre. Barry Jones is now a film star of the front rank and Maurice Colbourne writes very good books, and plays, also, when he feels inclined. One hopes to see them together again in the Theatre, for the Theatre can do with them. It was Maurice Colbourne who revived the famous O.U.D.S. after the First World War.

Those days at the Lane, beginning with *Glamorous Night* and continuing the whole time that Ivor was there, were amongst the happiest we of Old Drury ever knew. Ivor had the knack of spreading happiness, and success. We were one big family, without any family quarrels.

But that joy which *Glamorous Night* brought was not to endure. Ivor, living in a golden dream, and planning the future, had a rude awakening. He heard a rumour—it was more than a rumour, it was fact—that despite the success of his play, it must come off because a pantomime had been booked for

Christmas. He was furious. He could not believe it. He went to H. M. Tennent and he learnt the truth. That pantomime had indeed been arranged, and the arrangements had been in progress, though not settled, before *Glamorous Night* was produced. Tennent had played for safety—and who shall say he was wrong? Pantomime at Drury Lane was a certainty. But pantomimes have to be arranged well in advance. They are huge, costly undertakings and the proper stars, mostly music hall and variety performers who are well booked up, have to be secured early in the year. It had all been done; it was a *fait accompli.*

Ivor was nearly stunned. Anger battled in his mind with incredulity. He heard the news first from Bill Sutton, who was callboy and general assistant-assistant to the assistant stage manager. It is always the callboy who knows the secrets of the theatre first. If I want information it is the callboy I ask; and the callboys of to-day are the theatre magnates of to-morrow (it worked that way with Bill Sutton, too). One night he expressed his sorrow to Ivor that the show had to come off, and that was how Ivor found out. Nobody had told him: they probably did not dare. But there it was. Ivor nearly went mad. His castle was falling about his feet, his dreams turning to nightmares. He demanded that the pantomime be cancelled, but that was impossible. So he offered to guarantee profits that might be made over the pantomime to the extent of £8,000 with his own money. He had no financial interest in *Glamorous Night* for he was on a salary and royalty. But that offer was not enough; even the sum of £10,000 would not meet the case. Ivor knew the risks he might run; he knew how snow or fog could wreck the greatest success. He might be involved in heavy financial loss; he could do no more. But it rankled; it hurt him badly. He appealed to Jack Joel, for he heard that Drury Lane had disposed, or was disposing, of the touring rights. This is what he wrote:

" Dear Jack,

Thank you for your message. The only thing I wanted to know was how much Tom Arnold had offered for the production, as thinking it over you said that if I bought the production at the end of the Drury Lane run I could do what I liked with it. You also said that if the show was doing well in October and November you would try to arrange to transfer it to another theatre and then, if still doing well, bring it back to the Lane after the pantomime when you will need a fill in very badly. But how can these things happen if the production is sold to a Touring Manager? So in fairness to me, whose only object is to keep a great show running—don't you think I should be told what Arnold's offer consists of, so that I might at least have the option of saving the thing I cared about most in the world from going down the drain? I do see quite clearly that the pantomime is settled and possibly quite sensibly too, but must that mean that *Glamorous Night* is killed for London, all that love and enthusiasm we all have for it just pushed aside? You, as a human being, can't do this, and as Managing Director of Drury Lane must see that *financially* it's the same; then surely I—who have created the play—have more right to be considered than a Touring Manager. So all I'm asking you, Jack, is how much are you getting for the Production. Please tell me this: it isn't very much to ask.

Yours,

Ivor."

But nothing came of that. Tom Arnold did not get *Glamorous Night*. Prince Littler secured it; he also did the pantomime which drove *Glamorous Night* from the stage. He is now Chairman, Managing Director of Drury Lane Theatre. It was not his fault. It had nothing to do with him. It was really nobody's fault. It is one of the gambles one is forced to take in the Theatre, especially with a place like Drury Lane. Tennent had played for safety. So *Glamorous Night* ended whilst playing to capacity on its 243rd performance, equal to twice that run in an ordinary theatre, having regard to the capacity of Drury Lane.

But Ivor had one piece of satisfaction. King George V and Queen Mary came to see the play, and came unexpectedly and at short notice. King George was a great theatregoer, and Queen Mary, bless her, remains one to-day. It so happened that *Glamorous Night* was the last play King George V ever saw. He told Ivor his views about it when Ivor took Mam to the Garden Party at Buckingham Palace that summer. Ivor and she stood in the ranks as Their Majesties passed down them. The King made towards Ivor, who heard Lord Cromer say to him " This is the young man whose play you saw the other night, Sir—Mr. Ivor Novello." Lord Cromer and his wife were great friends of Ivor's. The King stopped before Ivor. " So you wrote the story and the music and acted the principal part yourself. Don't you find it very tiring in the hot weather? " Pride and joy almost choked Ivor. But he made the right reply (trust him for that): " Not when you are in front, sir," he answered. The King was amused. Then he said, " We enjoyed ourselves very much—with one reservation . . . " (Ivor was terrified) . . . " we could have wished a different ending. We found it a little sad, the Queen and I." The King turned to Mam " Don't you agree, Madam? " he asked. " Oh, yes," said Mam, with emphasis; she probably did not but tact saved her for once. " You made the Queen cry," said King George. Ivor murmured apologies. " Make it a happy ending next time." And the King and Queen moved on to greet other guests, leaving a very proud Ivor behind him. It was typical of King George V. He said what he thought but he said it kindly.

Just after that conversation the blow fell and Ivor learned that *Glamorous Night* was to die. He remembered the King's advice, however. His next play did have a happy ending. But there was to be storm and stress before that. Ivor was now a sad man; he looked like a wistful child, deprived of a long promised treat. But he determined to do another show at the Lane. This one must perish and it left its mark. And as to the new one? Well, Shakespeare, who said everything, said the thing about this, too: " Thus bad begins—but worse remains behind. . . . " For battle, grim and desperate, was to be joined before Ivor trod the boards of the Lane again.

CHAPTER NINETEEN

A FAMOUS VICTORY

TO get the true perspective and to be perfectly fair to both sides in the battle of *Glamorous Night*, some correspondence between Jack Joel, the Chairman of Directors and Ivor is worthy of consideration. Ivor wanted to do another show for the Lane. He had proved himself. He thought he was entitled to security of tenure. So, on June 14th, 1935, he wrote to Jack Joel:

" My dear Jack,

I do want you to know how sincerely delighted I am at the success of *Glamorous Night* and to tell you what a joy the whole thing is to me and how very pleased I am to have been able to give you something for Drury Lane which seems to be fulfilling the traditions of that grand theatre. *But*, and there is a big but, I do wish you were getting your Production back a bit quicker; in fact, so strongly do I feel about the matter that I want to do something to help. Naturally I want the play to have a long run—partly because I want it for my own personal satisfaction but—and this I mean sincerely—because I think Drury Lane *needs* a long run which will lead to more long runs and which will establish the theatre again as the leading theatre of the world. If this play (which is the only one doing business at this difficult time) were to have a run of only about seven months it could easily be classed with *Wild Violets*, *Ball at Savoy* and *The Three Sisters* and the public who are now being won back to Drury Lane would never have the same excitement about the next big production if this one did not have an outstanding run. Now I know that in order to have a run expenses must be a possible figure, therefore I am prepared, naturally upon certain conditions which I will outline to you, to reduce my percentage to five per cent. in each capacity even while the show is making a profit so that you will get your production back so many weeks sooner, and this arrangement is to continue *until* the production is paid back, and after that the percentage is to return to what it is now. The receipts are bound to suffer a bit during the summer but I feel quite confident that the early autumn will find us as big if not bigger than now, then will come the pre-Christmas drop followed by its automatic enormous Christmas business (this is essentially a Holiday attraction on account of its excitement and spectacular qualities) so that with any luck, the production being paid off, the Christmas season should show a nice profit with no fresh money expended.

"Therefore my proposition stands this way, that I will make these big reductions if you will guarantee that *Glamorous Night* runs until the end of February, at which time I understand that Mary Ellis will have to go to Hollywood to fulfil her Hollywood contract. Then, in accordance with an idea I've long cherished, a spring production of *Romeo and Juliet* with Edna Best and myself. I have a strong instinct that this would not only be extremely distinguished but a big popular success, and that with a simple, economical but beautiful production we should do a big three months with running expenses down to a minimum—a small orchestra, no author's fees and a cast of not more than fifty. I do honestly feel, that this is a wise and popular idea. You know that I am no highbrow but have always gone out for what the public wants, and in the course of fifteen productions, I have only had two failures. During all this time I shall be preparing the big autumn production for Mary Ellis and myself, about which you have already spoken. As you will see, this is a letter addressed to you, but if you like to show it to Lord Lurgan, Mr. Tennent and the members of the Board, please do so, as I could not explain to them more clearly than I have to you. I shall be awfully glad if you can make a decision as soon as possible, as although I love being at Drury Lane and feel I can be of use to you there, I must, if you have other and better plans, make my arrangements for returning to management on my own and this as you know takes some months' planning.

With kindest regards,
Yours ever,
Ivor."

Now it will be agreed that this was a very good letter. Not only was there a very generous offer but the main idea was good. It shows Ivor's keen business sense. He was "selling himself" to Drury Lane but not in a cheap way. He was convinced he could do the job better than anyone else, but he was underlining all the facts to drive it home to Jack Joel. What Ivor wanted was a long run for *Glamorous Night* and security of tenure for himself at the Lane. And he was trying after that ambition to play Romeo in a wonderful setting. I am sorry he regarded Shakespeare as highbrow. There was never anything less so in the Theatre (that may have been a sop to Mr. Joel). Also, to be fair to *Wild Violets* it should be stated that it ran at Drury Lane for 291 performances, a very respectable run indeed, actually longer than the truncated run of *Glamorous Night* (243), whilst *Careless Rapture* ran for 296 performances and *Crest of the Wave* for 204. *The Dancing Years* had its Drury Lane run stopped by World War the Second. I wish Ivor had not included *Wild Violets* in his list. *Ball at the Savoy* ran only 148 performances and *The Three Sisters* was negligible.

However, it was clear as to what Ivor meant. He meant a really long run. The letter drew a reply from Jack Joel, fairly promptly and here it is:

24th June, 1935.

" My dear Ivor,

I received your letter of the 14th instant to which I would have replied before but, as you know, last week was Ascot Week and, secondly, I wanted to get in touch with the other members of the Board and get their views.

" In the first place, old man, I want to thank you for your kind offer to meet the Company in the matter of expenses, and your suggestions that you should reduce your percentage to 5 per cent. in each capacity, until such time as Drury Lane get back their production expenses, is gratefully accepted by them, it, of course, being understood that the percentage is to revert to that of the original agreement as soon as the production expenses are recovered.

" I am afraid, however, that I cannot get them to agree, and neither can I agree myself, to your contingency that we should guarantee the run of *Glamorous Nights* until the end of February. I know how keen you are to run the show as long as it is humanely possible and so are we, but it is not reasonable to expect anyone in these times to guarantee to run any show for any period. Such a lot of things, my dear Ivor, can happen which would interfere with such an arrangement; the future must take care of itself. Obviously though, if it is found to be a paying proposition in the autumn, we should have to reconsider the position at that time, and I do not think it unreasonable to suggest that we should not take off a great production, such as this, in the height of its success, but time again can only tell us that. I think you will have to cut this out.

" Then there is the matter of your suggestion of *Romeo and Juliet* and that again I am afraid the Board will not stand for one moment. The ‘ Lane ’ has always been essentially a home of drama, musical comedy and pantomime, and I fear Shakespeare would not go there. At any rate, that is the view of my fellow Directors.

“ By all means, get busy with the new play which we should like to have the first refusal of. If we found that we were justified in running *Glamorous Night* through into March or, alternatively, if we decide to take it off in say, November, and put on a pantomime, we should still want a new show in March. Nothing would give me greater pleasure than to see you continue your wonderful success at the ‘ Lane .’

All good wishes,
Yours sincerely,
Jack.”

That is the answer. Mr. Joel does some curious things. He calls the show, in one place *Glamorous Nights*—that might have been the typist, for many of the public always called it that. He uses the word “ humanely.” Did he mean “ humanly ” or was it a little sardonic joke? But he knew very little of Drury Lane history if he thought Shakespeare would never draw there! There had been such people as David Garrick, Edmund Kean, Mrs. Siddons and Macready. He was looking no further back than Gus Harris; or perhaps he remembered poor Chatterton's wail that “ Shakespeare spelt ruin and Byron bankruptcy.” However, there was the position. He stated it clearly and concisely.

Ivor got in his reply quickly—the same day in fact.

11 Aldwych, W.C.2.
24th June, 1935.

“ Dear Jack,

Thank you for your letter, the contents of which surprise me very much. The suggestion came from me that, on certain conditions, I would reduce my percentage when, as you know, there is no need for me to do so, and I had thought this gesture would have been responded to in a similar manner by the Board of Drury Lane. Therefore, as my offer was conditional, and the Board can give me no kind assurance that this play will run through an inevitably prosperous Christmas season, I have no option but to withdraw the offer and hope that the autumn business will justify the show running the length that it is certainly justified in doing. I have, however, an alternative suggestion to make, viz. I am prepared to reduce my percentage to a flat 5 per cent. under each category until the production is paid back but on the condition that should the play finish before Christmas, any payments due to me on the old basis that I have voluntarily given up shall be made good to me at the conclusion of the run. (This of course, I repeat should occur only if the play finishes before Christmas.) If you will work this out you will see that it is a fair suggestion as otherwise I should be amply justified in saying, 'Alright, I will stick to my contract and chance the length of the run,' but I think you know me well enough to know that I am much more grasping about kudos, both for Drury Lane and for my own reputation, than I am about money.

"With regard to *Romeo and Juliet* I completely accept the Board's decision that this does not conform to the Drury Lane policy, though I hope in future to prove that this proposition is a big financial one in any theatre. Now with regard to your suggestion that I should 'get busy with the new play which you should have the first refusal of,' this naturally I could not consent to do. I feel quite convinced, Jack, that you personally would never intentionally hurt anyone's feelings, but you have evidently been overruled into treating me as a beginner. Therefore, I consider the suggestion that I should work on a show for Drury Lane 'on appro' most surprising, as having proved that—in addition to not being entirely unknown as a dramatist—I know the measure of Drury Lane, I ask you if you can give me any reason why I should put in a lot of work on a show which being designed for Drury Lane would be quite useless anywhere else? If you cannot after *Glamorous Night*, which, as you will see on the programme, was 'devised, written and composed by Ivor Novello,' trust to my judgment and talents to provide something that stands more than an equal chance of success with anything else, then I don't care to discuss the matter further. Nothing would please me better than to continue at Drury Lane, but I have had twelve years of extremely successful activities elsewhere, and doubtless can continue to do so. I, too, sincerely wish for the continued success of *Glamorous Night*, and hope that when a successor is needed, it will prove to be to everyone's satisfaction. Please don't think I am being in any way unreasonable; I am the first to admit that I wrote *Glamorous Night* 'on appro' as I had never written for Drury Lane before, but having—so to speak—proved myself in this most exciting theatre, I cannot consent to be treated as an experiment. For the reasons stated in my letter of the 14th instant, I shall be glad if you will let me know your decision as soon as possible, so that I may make my plans accordingly.

With kindest regards,
Yours ever,
Ivor Novello."

Jack Joel had written a personal letter to Ivor the same day as the official one—that to which Ivor replied as above—to lessen the blow. He said: " We had a meeting of the Board this morning and I have sent you practically an official letter embodying their views, which honestly I consider reasonable and, I think, old man, if I were you, I should accept them without any comment. You can rest assured that *Glamorous Nights* will *not* be taken off if it is paying sufficiently well to keep it on. I am going away to my house at St. Albans to-day where I am in residence but I shall be up in town to-morrow if you want me. Take care of yourself old man, hoping you are keeping fit, Yours always, Jack."

That was written in Mr. Joel's own handwriting and was his unofficial comment and advice on the letter previously quoted. He got Ivor's answer by return and on the following day, June 25th, he wrote, also in his own hand:

" My dear Ivor,

I am in receipt of your letter, the contents of which I will discuss with the Board at the earliest possible opportunity. I don't quite understand the purport myself and think you and I ought to have a chat over it, so that I shall be in a better position when meeting the Directors. I am going to the country to-night but shall be back in town on Thursday. Give me a blow through in the morning and then perhaps we can fix up a meeting for the afternoon.

All the best, old man,
Yours,
Jack."

They had their meeting, this millionaire and this brilliant man of the Theatre—and both of them loved the Lane, even if they did not see eye to eye. And on July 1st, 1935, Jack Joel wrote again to Ivor, and again in his own hand:

" My dear Ivor,

I do so hope you were not upset by our interview the other day. Nothing, my dear friend, would delight me more than that you should stay at the Lane for ever, but one must not allow a really wonderful production to carry one away without thinking about the financial side. I am sure we shall never get anything like our production money back. Last week's receipts, I see, are down again, and I am afraid that this week we shall not be far away from the £3,200 mark. I do wish you would listen to me, my friend, and agree to let this show run as long as it will give us a chance of getting the production money back, you writing a big musical play for the autumn—if possible with Mary Ellis in it. I can think of no one else at present. If we have to take *Glamorous Nights* off, as I told you, we should put on a pantomime, or if *Glamorous Nights* runs over the pantomime season, fill the gap in the spring with some show or other until your autumn production is ready. I am sure it will be a very great mistake to continue show after show by the same author—the public would tire of it.

" Sleep on what I have written and I am certain eventually you will come to the conclusion that I am right. In any case do not allow it to strain our friendship."

Ivor's reply came very quickly. He had slept on it:

July 3rd, 1935.

" My dear Jack,

Thanks for your letter with which I agree entirely, particularly as I want to be on the top of my form for the big musical show that I will write for you for the autumn of 1936. I quite agree that there is no one to touch Mary Ellis, and I will concentrate on writing for her—and I believe Harry Tennent is fixing up a lunch date with her to arrange things. The autumn is so *much* the best time for a big Lane production as it has so much more chance of carrying right through until the following autumn and then the Theatre gets into its stride again. Of course we were down last week but you must admit that our business is phenomenal considering the heat and the fact that people *will not* go indoors (except to see *Glamorous Night*) and you *just wait until the Autumn!!*

All the best,

Ivor.

" PS. I'd like to get some sort of arrangement set about the next ' big one ' as I must plan my year next year in case ' Glamorous ' doesn't go through Xmas—so will you talk to Harry about it?

Ivor."

That was the state of things, peaceful and harmonious. Jack Joel was not right in thinking it inadvisable for the same hand to turn out the plays—continuity is the safest card in the Theatre—at the Lane or elsewhere. The Aldwych farces, with Ben Travers as the resident author for most of the thirteen of them, and a stock company is proof, and there are very many other instances.

The business fluctuated at the Lane, but despite heat-waves

it was quite remarkable for what had been done there for some time past, and there is little doubt at all that Ivor was right in his conjecture that when the autumn came, things would be splendid. But the Board would not take the risk and the definite negotiations about the pantomime began. Then Ivor got to know that they had decided on pantomime and he wrote to Joel making his offer of a guarantee. That was in August and Jack Joel sent him this letter on August 14th:

> " My dear Ivor,
>
> I did not intend to see you but I thought it better to put on paper the result of my going into the matter of the pantomime. I am given to understand that negotiations have been commenced but so far as I can gather, nothing has been definitely settled. I had a talk with Mr. Johnson about your offer re continuing the run of *Glamorous Night* and your suggested guarantee; he has a perfectly open mind on the matter and is quite agreeable to anything that will benefit the Theatre. *Now* would you be prepared to guarantee us against loss for the period from say the last week in November until Christmas Eve (the date the pantomime would be produced), practically four weeks, and also guarantee us a profit of £8,000 over a period of eight to ten weeks, which I understand, is the usual run of the pantomime? Think it over and if you can see your way to do this send me a letter officially and I will call a special Board meeting for Monday next and I feel sure that I will be able to carry it. There is a hell of a lot of opposition but *I want to* get it through.
>
> " I am writing this letter to you, strictly confidentially between us two. I would have come over to see you on the matter but I thought it better to put it on paper and let you digest it. I shall be at Childwick all day to-morrow if you wish to ring me up or if you desire to see me, I shall be in town on Friday and can see you at any time, as if you agree a special Meeting *must* be held on Monday.
>
> All the best, my dear Ivor,
> Yours,
> Jack.
>
> " Think this well over my friend, I should like you to do it for many reasons, it's up to you.
>
> Love,
> Jack."

The last few lines are marked Confidential and are in Jack Joel's own hand. The rest is typed.

There is no doubt that the reason for the Monday Board meeting was that the pantomime was on the verge of being signed up. There was no guarantee forthcoming from Ivor. And, as fate willed, the moment the arrangements were made for the pantomime, the business for *Glamorous Night* shot up and up and at the end of the run it was actually playing to capacity. That was what made it hard for Ivor to bear. His actual terms were 7½ per cent. on the first £3,500 and 10 per cent. on all over: he got that as actor and the same amount as author-composer, so on average weeks he was drawing 15 per cent. and on good weeks 20 per cent. of the gross. He deserved it. Ivor made money out of *Glamorous Night* but there was not much for Drury Lane, for the production costs were well over £25,000 and running expenses very high. But it was success and it was prestige. It was a million times better than it had been for years. And, of course, on top of the house receipts the Lane got the bars, cloakrooms, programmes, etc.

It was during *Glamorous Night* that Ivor got Romeo out of his system. There was a big special Shakespeare Matinée. The present Queen and the Princess Elizabeth attended; it was the first time the Princess had been to a theatre. The Queen was then Duchess of York. As an item therein Ivor played the Balcony Scene, with Jean Forbes-Robertson as Juliet. He looked the best Romeo ever, but there had been very many who played it better. He knew it, too. There was not much talk of it afterwards and it died. It was just as well. It was beyond him, as it is beyond so many.

Nor had he, whilst he was so busy at Drury Lane, divorced himself from his dramatic and managerial activities outside that theatre. He knew better than to become submerged in Old Drury. He meant to keep in touch with the straight Theatre. In the August of 1935, on the evening of the 21st, he presented his play *Full House* at the Haymarket. There he was, occupying two of London's Theatres Royal, for although the lovely Haymarket's Royal Charter really only held good during the lifetime of that genius Samuel Foote, it stills keep its title and still remains every inch a Theatre Royal. Nowhere is tradition and grandeur better maintained. This play of Ivor's was a light-hearted comedy with his beloved Lilian Braithwaite in the lead in a part written for her, and a cast which included Isabel Jeans, Heather Thatcher—valued friends of his associates in plays—Robert Andrews, Frank Cochrane (who had sung the famous " Cobbler's Song " in *Chu Chin Chow* but was as good an actor as singer), Maidie Andrews and Hubert Harben. There was a delicious scene in which Lilian Braithwaite was given a lesson in Bridge and defeated all attempts to instruct her. Also, a scene in which Ivor worked one of his favourite jokes: two women turning up at a function wearing identical dresses, and one in which Isabel Jeans spanked Heather Thatcher in full view of the audience. It ran for 185 performances.

As usual, all Ivor's friends had to go and see it. The cast of *Glamorous Night* visited *Full House* as Ivor's guests and the cast of *Full House* visited Drury Lane in similar capacity.

Ivor had not forgotten the idea that he was to write a new show for the Lane. He would not write on approval, but he never got a definite contract in writing from the Board. It should be mentioned here that the Board then was entirely different from that which controls Drury Lane at the time of writing. In Ivor's time, practically all the Board, with the exception of H. M. Tennent, who was not a Director but simply General Manager, and of one other who was much involved with theatrical affairs but not actually in management, were all men of commerce and not theatre men at all. It is entirely different to-day. But Ivor went ahead; he had the implied promise of Jack Joel, who owned the Lane financially. Jack Joel had asked for Mary Ellis as leading lady, and Ivor had agreed enthusiastically. But it could not be arranged for Miss Ellis's Hollywood commitments stood in the way. So Ivor devised the show with another actress as leading lady, somebody in whom he believed and whom he knew he could suit. And when this play was ready for the Board to hear, he went to a Board meeting to read it to them and play over the music. Christopher Hassall had written the lyrics. He was taken along by Ivor to stand by, make himself generally useful and distributed typed copies of the lyrics to members of the Board so that they could read them as Ivor played them.

Christopher Hassall remembers that day very well. He said he did his part and it was like a verger giving out hymn books. But he (and Ivor) were both conscious of a curious " atmosphere " which seemed anything but friendly. There was a feeling as if the corpse was in the next room and that nobody present had been remembered in the will. Well as Ivor read, well as he played, good and charming as were the lyrics of Hassall, nothing registered. The gloom seemed to increase rather than disperse. Hassall felt frightened. This sort of thing was new to him. Ivor began to regret that he had ever consented to read the play and indignation swelled within him. He should never have put himself in such a position. But he stuck grimly to his task, reading and playing *Careless Rapture* to the, then, bitter end. At last it was over. There was silence. Then he was told that, of course, they could not decide just right at that moment—he would understand that—but they would let him know. He went out of the room his head in a whirl with anger and wounded pride. . . .

The last night of *Glamorous Night* arrived—that awful audition had been just a week or two before—and that last night was even more brilliant than the first night. There was a packed house, cheers like Niagara Falls in volume, and, of course, speeches. It was a sad night. We who worked at the Lane all loved Ivor, and we all loved *Glamorous Night*. We were hoping to keep him at the Lane, that he would return after the pantomime, for we, unlike Mr. Joel, knew that continuity was the best thing for the Theatre and that here was the man who could do the trick in that sometimes difficult Theatre. We knew, too, that the Lane liked Ivor. No decision as to his next show had been taken. But four of us, who were mainly responsible for making the Lane's wheels go round, banded ourselves together into a pro-Ivor gang and made up our minds that we would bring him back. Those four were William Abingdon, the stage director, R. E. Gray, the secretary, S. F. Webb, the manager and myself, the humble publicity man.

Almost immediately after the withdrawal of *Glamorous Night* the blow fell on Ivor. Tennent had to tell him that the Board had turned down *Careless Rapture*. Tennent was bitterly disappointed. He wanted Ivor at the Lane; so did the public; so did everyone but the Board. They had their reasons and they were to be proved wrong.

Ivor took the blow. David Ivor Davies again steadied Ivor Novello. He put his last hope behind him and went straight on. If the Lane did not want him, all right. *Careless Rapture* was for the moment folded away, but he meant to do it somewhere all the same. He would show everyone that he could act in a manner they knew not. He had proved what he could do musically and he had proved he could write and compose a show for the most famous theatre in the world. Now he would show the public a new Ivor Novello and if the Drury Lane directors happened to be watching, so much the better. He would show everyone another side to his talents. He hovered between the choice of two plays, neither of which he had written. They were *Charles the King* by Maurice Colbourne, in which Ivor would have played Charles I and *The Happy Hypocrite*, a stage version by Clemence Dane of Max Beerbohm's most delightful story, concerning the Regency Rake who was conquered by sweet love and innocence and who was transformed by that love from the ugliest man in London to the most handsome. Ivor took His Majesty's Theatre for this production for he would only have the best. I asked him why he wanted to play " Lord George Hell "—the leading role, why he was going to appear with the face crimsoned by excess and hard and ugly of feature instead of the Ivor Novello of the beloved profile. Ivor looked at me and laughed. " You've said it, Popie," he replied, " there will come a day when the profile will not be so maddeningly perfect, when I shall no longer be young—and I don't want to give up acting. So I am going to prepare the public for it by degrees. See, duckie? " I saw, and humbly approved. There spoke the real man of the Theatre.

Maurice Colbourne produced the play and had just the right touch. Ivor saw to it that it had a beautiful setting, mounting and décor in general. He gave it a magnificent cast. Marius Goring gave a grand performance as Cupid; Carl Harbord was Mercury; and an outstanding performance as the old Mask Maker was given by Stafford Hilliard. In the cast, too, were Viola Tree, Isabel Jeans and, playing the innocent little heroine whose purity reforms and transforms the wickedest man in London, a young actress with one success to her name: Vivien Leigh, whose stage name had been given her by Ivor—a very good theatrical godfather. The masks were made by Angus McBean, who also took photographs of that production and enabled me, by his wonderful work, to make a little bit of publicity history. With his pictures of *The Happy Hypocrite* I achieved the front page of all the five " glossy " weekly papers which then showed an interest in the Theatre in the same week.

Ivor had a wonderful make-up. He transformed himself. His red, bloated face would have borne comparison with that of the famous Duke of Cumberland—" Butcher " Cumberland, the blood-thirsty but clever soldier Duke who defeated the Young Pretender at Culloden Moor and whose empurpled visage, when seen in the street, used to frighten children into fits. Ivor altered the very shape of his nose by putting little glass balls up his nostrils and making the nasal appendage swell and distort. In the end, of course, he was the handsome Ivor. The whole thing was a production of really great beauty, and distinction. It held its place with all the productions of the great Sir Herbert Tree. It was a thing worthy of the best traditions, in every way, of the grand theatre in which it was performed.

It opened on the worst night in the year, at Easter, 1936, on the day before Good Friday. It was acclaimed by public and Press alike. Ivor's new strength of acting made a big impact. His success at Drury Lane had placed him high in public and critical regard. He was now taken seriously. After the curtain fell on the first night I fought my way into his dressing-room through the teeming mass of friends showering congratulations and thanked him for giving us all one of the finest nights in the Theatre we had had for years. He seemed a bit mystified. But the notices proved what I had said. Alas, that thing of delicate beauty, that piece of gossamer idealism, was not for the general taste. It was caviare. But it was a memory to treasure as long as one lived. This was the way to do things, this would elevate the Theatre—and at that time it needed it—but it was obviously not to be a popular success with *hoi polloi*. Many of the ordinary Ivor fans, too, did not like to see their hero made ugly even for a moment. But the discerning knew that he had arrived, and as an actor-manager stood in line with the great ones of yesterday, keeping their tradition bright.

The rehearsals were long and often stormy, but the result was superb—from every point of view except finance. I suffered a defeat too. We got Max Beerbohm, for whom I have a tremendous admiration, down to a rehearsal and we got him to agree to see the Press. He is of a most retiring disposition. But he agreed, on this occasion. Ivor charmed him into it. All the important men from Fleet Street gathered in that dignified bar in the Dress Circle of His Majesty's, wondering if Max

Beerbohm would really come. He came all right. He talked to them for a long while, telling wonderful stories with that command of which he is a master, flashing with wit and amazing reminiscence. It was going to be wonderful publicity. Then he rose to go. He reached the door, and turned. With a nice little smile he said " Of course gentlemen, nothing I have said is for publication. You understand that, don't you? " And he vanished . . . it was a heartbreak for us all. But we respected his wish . . . although we were sorely tempted.

Clemence Dane had done a fine job with this little masterpiece of imagery, this fairylike fable with the bloom of a butterfly's wing. It could not have been done better. Richard Addinsell's music was right in the atmosphere. Ivor did not write a word or note. Alas, that *The Happy Hypocrite* should have had only a short run and lost money. But that money was a good investment. The kudos was tremendous. It impressed the people of the Theatre. Ivor Novello was a force with which to reckon. He was a man who did things in the Grand Manner. And that was just what he wanted. He was playing about in his mind with varying projects, with Shakespeare again, but this time *Henry V* and he asked me for ideas. I suggested that it might be worth while thinking about a stage version of Maurice Hewlett's romance *The Forest Lovers*, a favourite book of mine which I always wanted to attempt to stage, with himself as Prosper and Vivien Leigh as Isoult. But we never got round to that and, indeed, I do not think it is feasible. Ivor was now seeking to satisfy that hunger to be a classical actor and his personal success in *The Happy Hypocrite* urged him on.

At the end of the run, he went off on a holiday with several plans, including *Charles the King*. But the Fates were taking a hand, too. He had pushed Drury Lane right to the back of his mind. Meanwhile, what was happening there? Drury Lane had got itself into a jam. It staged a pantomime for which Prince Littler was responsible and a very good one it was, too, the subject being *Jack and the Beanstalk*. Binnie Hale was Principal Boy, Shaun Glenville the Dame, Marjorie Brown was Principal Girl, Douglas Wakefield, Billy Nelson, Charles Heslop all provided excellent comedy, Gavin Gordon was a suitably villainous Giant's Henchman and the Giant was of such vast proportions that only a bit of him could be seen at a time. A real Drury Lane pantomime. It was followed by a musical play entitled *Rise and Shine*. The best that can be done is to draw a veil over that. It did not rise and it did not shine. It was beautifully mounted and produced, it had a fine cast, but it was not a Drury Lane show. At the Hippodrome it might have been a big success but not at the Lane. A fatal mistake was that all the pre-arranged spectacular and mechanical effects, which included an avalanche and a parachute descent, were cut out. That did not help at all. Horses for courses may or may not be a sound Turf maxim, but plays for theatres is a great truth with no doubt about it at all. *Rise and Shine* only scored forty-four performances.

Here was a situation! The Lane was going " dark " again. That is where the four members of the staff who had banded themselves together in a pro-Ivor Novello Fellowship came in. They worked hard and, at the last moment, Ivor was persuaded not to sign for another theatre—and he was within an ace of so doing—but to come back to Drury Lane which wanted him so badly. Peace was patched up with the Board. But this time they had to deal with David Ivor Davies far more than Ivor Novello. That tough Welshman was going to have no nonsense. The artiste of sensitivity who was Ivor Novello might be over-persuaded but not clear, cool, hard-headed David Ivor Davies. No more would he put himself into a subservient capacity. No more would he allow others to dictate to him. That old and ever-present desire to take responsibility was blazing up. All right, he would come back to the Lane. He would stage the previously scorned *Careless Rapture*, but on his own conditions. He would be in charge; he would have the full say-so. And to that end, he would be mainly responsible for financing the show. He was going to have no more tragedies like the withdrawal of *Glamorous Night*. Things should be run his way.

And so, when the agreement was made over *Careless Rapture*, Ivor, through his private company, shouldered 75 per cent. of the production and running cost and Drury Lane the other quarter. Profits, of course, if any, in proportion. Drury Lane limited its liability even then: they would be responsible for only 25 per cent. of the production up to a total of £20,000. If that were exceeded, Ivor was to bear the whole of the surplus. That did not daunt Ivor. Where his own money was concerned he was not extravagant. His rough notes to Fred Allen concerning the heads of the contract made it all very clear. He wanted his full rate for services as actor and composer, on a sliding scale. Here are the notes:

(1) No flat rate—I'm risking enough, God knows.
(2) I will deliver MS.
(3) Harry to sign contracts if he will please.
(4) In association with T.R.D.L. please. I don't want this above the Title but at the foot of the bill as in *Hypocrite* [this meant the billing as to presentation; he would be in association with Theatre Royal, Drury Lane Ltd]. " Presented by I.N. and T.R.D.L." is as bad as to have " I.N. Presents I.N. in . . . by I.N." except in the programme matter where it shall be as you suggest

" In Association with T.R.D.L.
Ivor Novello
Presents
Careless Rapture "

(5) Preliminaries

" In Active Preparation
Careless Rapture
Devised Written and Composed by
Ivor Novello."

(6) Quite satisfied with letter press but would prefer design if we can get it done cheaply.
(7) 12 per unit maintenance I prefer.
(8) Let Abingdon O.K. everything, and I will tell everyone to refer to him.
(9) You and Gray arrange anything you like about the finance and running but I agree we should have D.L.'s £5,000 intact and you and he sign jointly.
(10) Note W.A.'s difficulty about the roundabout—but knowing him, he'll get one, even if it's shabby it can be redecorated.
(11) Let there be no change in the policy of the way things are run. They are all much more experienced than I am and must decide themselves about first-night seats. Prices I suggest as in *Glamorous Night*, both first-night and after and *not* the reductions as in *Rise and Shine*, because if the play's a success the upper circle will sell out as it did in *Glamorous* without reduction. We will use every economy with regard to rehearsals and over *my dead body* will the orchestra be kept when unnecessary.

Well, there are all the answers!!

Love,

Ivor.

There were all the answers indeed. That is the way to do it. The reference to the orchestra is most illuminating; that is where the big money goes. After the free rehearsal times which the musicians give by arrangement, the costs of a big orchestra are terrific. So often they are kept hanging about whilst other things are being dealt with and production costs soar and soar quite needlessly. Not for Ivor, despite the fact he was the composer. Over his dead body, he said.

Ivor got his own way. *Careless Rapture*, which had been despised and rejected, was to go to the Lane, and cast exact by as Ivor had wanted it. He won. It was a famous victory. Also an insight into theatre secrets and methods!

CHAPTER TWENTY

THE HAT TRICK

WHEN it became known that Ivor was to do yet another show at Drury Lane, there was a fresh outbreak of "knocking." "H'm, is he?" said the knowing ones; "Well, we'll see. He had luck once, but you can't do it twice. It's a pity, for his own sake." But the public did not agree. Directly the headlines—and we got headlines—appeared announcing the production of *Careless Rapture*, the applications for seats started to pour in.

The show went into rehearsal. Dorothy Dickson was the leading lady, Ivor having written the part for her. The "knockers" were busy over this too: could Dorothy play the Lane? A clever girl, a very pretty girl, oh yes, but the Lane was the Lane. Ivor had no doubts at all. Ivor was right. The title, moreover, was a good one: Ivor had a genius for such things. This time it came from Browning, *Perchance to Dream* from Shakespeare, but the others were his own.

He came back to Drury Lane in triumph to start rehearsals and he got a welcome from the staff as if he were the victorious general entering a liberated country, or a king who had been exiled but who had won back his own. The staff was the same as that which had worked *Glamorous Night* almost to a man, for the Lane made few changes; you go there, it gets hold of you, and you stay. The chorus and dancers were mostly the same. Many of them had been in *Rise and Shine* and were overjoyed that Ivor had returned. In every theatre in which he worked, it was like this. He was treated like royalty, and indeed, he was royalty of the Theatre. But it was very friendly royalty, too, with a close personal touch. He won loyalty and affection not by being lavish and generous with tips and drinks, but just because they liked him and amongst themselves called him Ivor. To the heads of departments he was not Mr. Novello, but the Guv'nor, and so they addressed him. They liked him for himself and his invariable kindliness and good temper, and also—and really more importantly—because he knew what he wanted, did not waste time, and was a real Professional. Nowadays that is not always the case. There are stars who are not " pro's " however brilliant they may be . . . but Ivor most definitely was.

He was now at the Lane in a quadruple capacity: actor, author, manager and composer. I took a composite picture of him in all phases, on the one plate. Edgar Wrather, of the Stage Photo Company, actually took the picture under my direction: he was sitting at the piano marking a music sheet, he was standing with a script in his hand saying lines, he was busy with a pen writing, and he was signing a cheque—that was the managerial capacity. It was one of my cheques he used; he never carried a cheque book himself and only signed one on the very rarest occasions: Fred Allen did all that. I wish I had been able to sign that cheque of mine for a fraction of what his name would have meant thereon. That picture went well.

Leontine Sagan was again the producer. She was well known to the staff by now and she, too, was liked and respected. Although there were frequent storms, they never lasted long and her smile afterwards was sunshine after rain, and no hard feelings. Joan Davis did the dances. And again Ivor had Zena Dare with him, which delighted him, and his mascot Minnie Rayner. Zena played one of those roles in which she excels and he gave her one of his favourite jokes: " Does *that* still go on? "

Walter (Wally) Crisham joined the cast, and made a success too. Olive Gilbert had much more to do than she had in *Glamorous Night*, Peter Graves had a part and Ivan Samson played the villain. In the cast, too, was Mr. David Davies. And that perfect player of such parts, George Elton, as a Chinese priest. He lifted the whole show in the one scene; he looked like a piece of old ivory and gave an exquisite performance.

Poor George Elton has passed on. He was a lovable man with a wonderful character who endured much and said nothing of his troubles. You hear of people being Christians—quite apart from being Gentiles. Well, George Elton was one. I only saw him at all put out once in all the years I knew him and that was during *Careless Rapture* at the Lane. He was standing at the entrance to the Green Room, just inside, all made up—and he was a master of make-up—ready to go on. But he did not notice the fire bucket hanging on the wall. He backed against it and he tipped the water all over himself in a cascade. He was really annoyed that time, and said so quite forcibly.

Now, Ivor had for years refused to write himself a musical play because he could no longer sing. Then he found out, in *Glamorous Night*, that it did not matter. So, being himself, he decided that it would be a greater improvement if he could sing as well as act and he would have a try. He took lessons from a very eminent master of singing and voice production. Those lessons were given in Ivor's dressing-room, during the breaks between shows on matinée days and sometimes before the show. Very strange were the noises which issued from that room. Just across the yard from that dressing-room is a large block of modern dwellings, Siddons Buildings. In Siddons Buildings are many children whose bump of reverence is not noticeably developed. Its large yard was a noisy place when the kiddies came back from school, and across the shrill clamour of the children's voices would cut the shouts of maternal parents: "Ed-ie tea time—come on in now—or must I fetch yer?" Not perhaps the best background for singing lessons for a star. But the lessons intrigued the kiddies greatly. Whether or no they knew who it was who was learning mattered little. They adored it. The moment Ivor started his scales and exercised, there was a hush, a pattering of feet and a gathering by the wall. For a short while, an entranced silence—and then the children gave their most emphatic and enthusiastic imitation. It was as if hundreds of cats were at battle. They just adored it.

In the end Ivor decided not to sing. We who loved him rejoiced, quietly, but rejoiced nevertheless. Nevertheless, he had a scene where Dorothy Dickson, Olive Gilbert, and he did a burlesque opera act, as it were: and thus was his ambition salved. And if he could not sing, he decided there was nothing to stop him dancing. And dance he did, to the astonishment of all beholders, public and private, friends in front and friends behind. There was a great Chinese ballet, which embodied in its action the legends of the temple in which it took place, as recited by George Elton as the Priest. Dorothy Dickson, delightful dancer, was the "Princess" of the legend, a Princess Priestess at that. Ivor was the young lover-Prince who came to woo her. Together they danced in real ballet style. Ivor had trunks, some arm and neck ornaments and sort of ballet boots reaching above the ankle. In his hand he carried a dead bird—we decided it was a partridge—for he had been hunting. And Ivor Novello and Dorothy Dickson did a solo ballet on the boards of Drury Lane. Considering that Ivor had never had a lesson in ballet dancing in his life, he did not do so badly at all. The musician in him kept perfect time; and the actor in him got him through. But after a while he decided he had had enough and a real member of the ballet should do it. Anyway, he had danced ballet at the Lane and he could add that to his achievements. It made a good story for me, too. He was attracted, I believe, by the costume, or lack of it. He adored wearing a minimum of clothes, and he wore very little in the ballet. He was almost plump then, too.

The big spectacular scenes in *Careless Rapture* were many. They included the interior of a smart shop in Bond Street, a wonderful Chinese Garden, a most marvellous temple interior with an enormous Chinese God (that was where Ivor danced), and scenes in a dressing-room. There was also a scene on an actual stage of the Lane itself (a play within a play, as it were, such as Ivor delighted in), in which Dorothy Dickson danced and sang " Wait For Me " with the use of the " lifts " for effects. Other scenes were in the mountains, where bandits held Ivor and Dorothy Dickson to ransom, and in caves where desperate deeds, worthy of any Drury Lane melodrama, were done.

The finale was just like a Drury Lane pantomime—so right for the Lane. It was all white, and it dazzled with its splendour. It might have been the magnificent culmination of a super *Aladdin*. Th huge chorus, all arrayed in white, filled the stage and there was a tremendous bridge with Chinese turrets from which Olive Gilbert—all in white, too—sang . . . and there stood Dorothy Dickson, looking very beautiful and all in white as a bride waiting for her groom. Music filled everything. The voices and the orchestra soared and swelled, the fine organ tones of Olive Gilbert dominating as soloist; it was a pantomime producer's dream of a finale. Then, from the o.p. side, in sharp and dramatic contrast, came Ivor. Ivor, escaped from the bandits, tattered, torn, weary, stumbling and his ragged dirty clothes, stained by travel, and prison caves, but going, like a homing bird, to his bride. What an entrance he gave himself there, although through most of the show the others had had all the jam! In the centre he collapsed and fell. Zena Dare, all in white, stepped forward: the Fairy Godmother (there isn't one in Aladdin, but it does not matter), lifted him up and helped him towards Dorothy, who now extended her arms. And hero Ivor staggered and stumbled into them as the music and voices reached a great crescendo, and the curtain fell on as beautiful and well contrived—if as highly improbable—a finale as ever the Lane had witnessed.

But that was as nothing to the really big scenes. There was the best representation of Hampstead Heath ever seen on any stage. That roundabout Ivor mentioned in his instructions to Fred Allen was there. Of course Bill Abingdon had got it and of course it shone resplendent. It was a real one and it behaved as such. Everyone had rides on it during the show. There was all the fun and noise of the Fair. There were the 'Arry's and the 'Arriet's; they were almost extinct in real life, but they were still lingering at 'Appy 'Ampstead on a Bank 'Oliday, and Ivor had them at the Lane. They did the traditional coster dance and Ivor wrote some delightful Hampstead music for them to sing. One number was a good as any real gem from the old-time Halls. " Winnie Get off the Colonel's Knee " was the title and first line, and it gave every opportunity for the final " er " which should end each phrase in true Cockney. " Hampstead Heath " never failed to bring the audience to its feet cheering; it was one of the best stage scenes ever done anywhere. Once before the Lane had staged it in *The Great Ruby* (it had a balloon ascent as well then) but even that paled before the Heath of *Careless Rapture*.

How Ivor loved that scene and his ride with Dorothy on the roundabout! How we all loved it. What fun we all had! Olive Gilbert (always a comic at heart) and Maidie Andrews (who was also in the show) used to go on disguised and create havoc. I went on myself night after night. I used to take distinguished people on with me who said how dearly they would love to walk the boards of the Lane. How they fared depended on how much we liked them and whether they showed a proper deference to the honour done them. If they were off-hand, I had a little scene all ready rehearsed which brought about their downfall and confusion. Two of the chorus boys played policemen. If they saw me bring on some people and if I had my black hat pulled down over my eyes, it meant I was a detective and they would watch me closely. Then, suddenly, I would beckon them forward, denounce the surprised walkers-on, who would be seized by the police and hustled off in the most undignified manner, to their own bewilderment and to the joy of friends whom they had brought to see their triumph at the Lane and who would be in the stalls. We stood for no nonsense there. That scene was always looked upon, when done, as being part of the show as far as the audience was concerned and they thought it marvellously realistic. They little knew!

On Baddeley Cake Night—Twelfth Night, January 6th—I had plenty of cameramen in the house all waiting to take pictures of the time-honoured ceremony after the show. I took one of them on the stage and when Ivor and Dorothy entered stepped up and said I was from the Daily whatever-it-was and could we have a picture. Ivor adored it. He and Dorothy, well used to such things, posed and the cameraman took his flash—one of the strangest pictures he had ever taken. His colleagues in front, who had been let in to see it, cheered until the roof rang. It was grand fun. Alas, in the excitement afterwards, the negative got broken. . . .

The big effect of the play was, however, the Earthquake. Storm and heat had been gathering during the previous scene, gusts of wind blew fitfully and an atmosphere of sultry heat foreboding peril was created. Then one saw the crowded street in a Chinese city at the Feast of the Moon. Multitudes jostled each other, all sorts of types filled the eye, tourists from Europe gaped around. A procession of priests carrying a palanquin came through an arch; the crowd bowed in worship. And a rumble of thunder shook the tense air. The procession halted, the Priests chanted, the High Priest muttered incantations, and that thunder was there again, louder, more menacing. The moment came for a piece of ritual. The High Priest approached the palanquin and, as he did so, there came a roar, a rush, the heavens opened, thunder crashed and lightning flickered blindingly—the Earthquake was on. Panic stricken crowds dashed to and fro; seemingly solid buildings shook, telegraph poles fell in splinters and then the buildings crashed in clouds of dust and the great centre arch itself broke into total ruins. The curtain fell to shouts of applause. It was a terrific effect. There had been Lane earthquakes before. That in *The Hope* took three scenes to show. But we did as much in one scene in *Careless Rapture* as had been done in the three of *The Hope*.

To tell the plot of *Careless Rapture* is not possible in cold blood. Ivor took it at top speed and the public had no chance to think of the many complete improbabilities. Kidnapping by Chinese bandits had been much in the news so he had it in *Careless Rapture*. And there was a moment at the end of the Temple, when he and Dorothy Dickson, after one of those insolent, offhand little comedy love scenes which he wrote and played so well, fell asleep on the Temple steps and two crouched, menacing figures, silent, fearful and resolute as Death itself, crept towards them—when he achieved a high spot of drama. He gave himself the satisfaction of playing two parts. The action started in London and went to China. Ivor, though penniless, got to China too, after his beloved. How he got there was a mystery—there was some talk of cattle boats—but who could have believed in Ivor as a deckhand on such a vessel? Anyway, there he was and for the purposes of the plot he disguised himself as a Chinese Prince. This was not given away even on the programme. Thereon, the character was assigned to Mr. David Davies, and so David Ivor Davies played a part that evening and played it so well that most of the audience were quite deceived. Ivor loved that. So did David.

Careless Rapture was by no means the best of Ivor's shows, nor was the music in the *Glamorous Night* class; the latter was some of Ivor's very best and it will live on. *Careless Rapture*, musically and dramatically, is not destined for immortality. It had its moments in both genres, but not very high spots. The little Rose Ballet was a thing of dainty beauty but, of course, ephemeral. There was a duet for tenor and soprano, which Ivor thought would be a hit number and was not; " Why Is It Ever Good-bye? " sung by Olive Gilbert; " Music in May " for Dorothy Dickson; the Chinese ballet music and Olive Gilbert's songs therein (repeated at the end); Dorothy Dickson and Walter Crisham's dancing (the big ensemble " The Manchuko " never quite came off, apart from their dance therein, although Lloyd Williams loved to go on in it and held his own too). Those were the high spots, apart from Zena Dare's acting and the wonderful décor and scenic effects. But it did not matter. Ivor had given them a Drury Lane show, full and brimming over. The whole was successful, never mind the parts. And thunderous applause greeted the end as once again he led them forward to take their bows and then made his own graceful, modest speech, with triumph surging in his heart, a special bow for Mam and perhaps a sharp look at the Royal Box where sat Jack Joel, as much as to say " You see . . .? " Again a magnificent Press. Again a Novello triumph at the Lane.

That first night had been hectic. It was a very brilliant gathering indeed. Marlene Dietrich attended it. Crowds fought over her at the entrance and we battled to rescue her and by a trick we did. For a few moments, I held that lovely creature in my arms as I got her through the surging mass of fans. . . . But once inside, it was Ivor's night again.

The next day it was a tired but happy voice which came over the 'phone to me from him, purring over the notices. " Ivor," I said, " what about the Trade? They are coming down this morning to do a deal. You have a say in this. Let's be sure Harry Tennent doesn't give them too much!" " Popie," replied Ivor, " you know so much about deals. I don't. Go in to the meeting as my representative. Be tough. I'll back you up, duckie." Well, I could not do that. I was on the staff at the Lane and Tennent was general manager. He went in and he, the man who could not say no, gave the Trade far too easy terms!!!

The whole of *Careless Rapture* from the first rehearsal to the last night was a time of great happiness for everyone concerned. The only person who did not enjoy the rehearsals, or some of them, was young Bill Sutton. In his position of junior official of the stage department, he was again the lay figure to be experimented upon. It was his duty during the rehearsals of the earthquake to lie on the stage and find out where the debris fell, so that spaces could be marked where the actual performers could stand or lie in safety. He soon found out the right spots by personal experience. But it was a fairly painful experience whilst it lasted. He took it in his stride however. And in that same show his future wife danced too. She was learning her job the right way, in the chorus. Her name was Moya Macqueen-Pope, carrying on a family tradition.

Careless Rapture lived up to its name for Drury Lane. It ran ten months, from September 11th, 1936, to June 5th, 1937. During its run King George VI was crowned. This event was celebrated at Drury with a special interlude which included a song composed by Ivor with the lyric by Godfrey Winn. It was called " We're One Big Family." It was to be sung on Coronation Night. The company lined up on the stage, the audience were given leaflets printed with the words, and it was put over very well. But there was no noticeable enthusiasm. Getting an audience to sing is not an easy matter. It takes a skilled pantomime or music hall artiste to do it. It did not come off that night, so far as communal singing went, but it got plenty of applause. It was during *Careless Rapture* that Ivor had the idea of playing " Aladdin." We stopped that. . . !

Ivor took a holiday after *Careless Rapture*. He was working on the next show, too, the terms for which were 50 per cent. Ivor, 50 per cent. Drury Lane up to a £20,000 production. He had done it twice at the Lane and now he had to risk a third attempt. This time his title was *Crest of the Wave*. Again Dorothy Dickson was his leading lady. In the cast also were Marie Lohr, Peter Graves, Olive Gilbert, Walter Crisham, Ena Burrell, Maidie Andrews, Clifford Heatherley, Finlay Currie and, naturally, Minnie Rayner. Again Leontine Sagan produced. Again the lyrics, as for both the preceding shows, were by Christopher Hassall, now becoming famous as became the son of John Hassall, the best perhaps of the artists of his day. But Christopher worked in verse, while his father drew marvellous illustrations and excelled as a poster artist; seldom if ever has there been a better and never one of such distinction. There is the same quality in Christopher Hassall, too. Again the staff and chorus and dancers were all Old Novellians, and again Charles Prentice was musical director. And again the knockers knocked. " Third time pays for all," they said. For Ivor was now about to attempt the Hat Trick. If he succeeded, it would be the first time it had been achieved by one man devising, writing, composing and acting in the whole show. Garrick and Sheridan had written many successes for the Lane, although really only two of the latter's were outstanding. But they wrote no music and Sheridan did not act. Cecil Raleigh and Henry Hamilton had written many of the dramas, but they did not act or compose either. Here was Ivor Novello doing the lot, and attempting a third time to put his fate to the test.

He called it *Crest of the Wave*, prophetic of his state if he

The full extent of the vast Drury Lane stage was used for this set in *Glamorous Night*

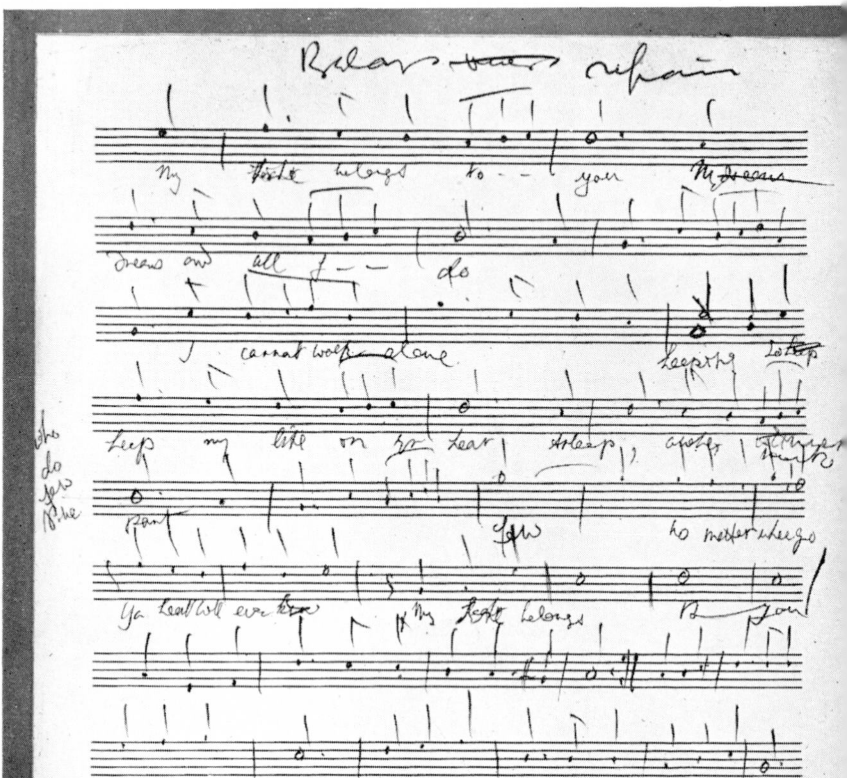

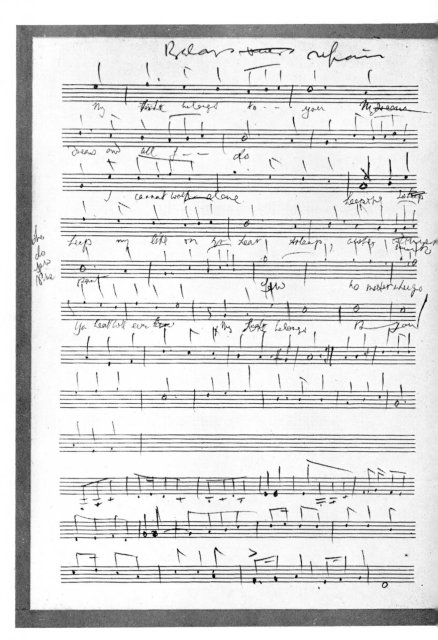

Ivor's original manuscript of " My Heart Belongs to You "

succeeded. He filled it with spectacle. It was full of surprise and effect. But, musically, it was his weakest. There was only one notable tune in it: that was very notable and is likely to remain in our musical annals always. But it came too early in the show. Ivor had spread himself on the plot and effects. The story was most complicated once again, concerning an impoverished duke and a rather—shall we say—common little girl of the films. It went from an ancient and decayed stately home of England—Gantry Castle—to the fantastic glories of Hollywood. It ended where it began, back in the Castle, again with its hero—the Duke—now rich, thanks to the films, and the little rather Cockney girl, who insisted she was " reserved," as his bride. There was one lovely piece of music: a delightful nocturne to which Dorothy Dickson and Walter Crisham danced—to my mind, one of Ivor's best efforts. There was an equally stirring and rousing mazurka which the one and only Sokolova " set." The first half ended with Ivor prostrate and presumed dead, after a revolver fired by a jealous woman. But, of course, the hero cannot die in the middle of the show, so he was back again after the interval. There was some splendid comedy and not a little clowning. Ivor loved to clown. There were some of those clever, modern, touch-and-go love scenes of which he was master, and which he and Dorothy Dickson played so well. And Ivor rejoiced because he gave himself two parts, the hero—and the villain! He loved playing that villain—a Hollywood film star in decline, a murderous man with a taste for train wrecking, in which he indulged during the show. That was heaven to Ivor! Scenically he spared nothing. There were scenes in the Castle, scenes on a liner, a Spanish fiesta which was a blaze of dance and colour, scenes in film studios, in Hollywood gardens with swimming pools, and a song, " Oh Clementine," for Peter Graves who acquitted himself very well and showed that he would be the star he has become.

But the two high-spots were a really beautiful and imaginative scene in which the great aisle of a ruined Gothic cathedral took shape before the astonished eyes of the audience and then the ghosts of the past trooped through in silent array—one of the best scenes I ever saw at the Lane and I have seen so many during the last half century. Clifford Heatherley, a charming fellow and good actor, played the ghost of Henry VIII. But within a few days of the opening of *Crest of the Wave*, poor Clifford died suddenly. That night the part was cut out. But most of the company in that scene, portraying ghosts themselves, saw Clifford play it that evening, just the same. Drury Lane, which has a ghost of its own, was in the way of having another. But the next night another man played Henry and Clifford was seen no more. He was faithful to the last, even in death. He was not going to stop the show or miss an entrance. I give this for what it is worth. Believe it or not, there were many witnesses. . . .

The big spectacular smash scene was a train crash. One saw "The Chief," the great Transcontinental Express, travelling at speed. At the lighted windows sat passengers. The big, full-sized train dashed through the night—and then came disaster. An ear splitting explosion and that express was a jumbled heap of flaming smoking ruins . . . real Drury Lane! Nobody was hurt by the smash itself, but Bill Sutton had to try it out at rehearsal. He escaped scot free. But one night, as the train was apparently dashing along, one of the steel wires which worked the revolving scenery and the trees and bushes which hurtled by—they moved but the train did not—snapped and came back into the wings like a whiplash. It might have killed one of the staff, for it struck him in the face like a thunderbolt. He escaped with his life, but had a damaged eye. . . .

Another sensation in *Crest of the Wave* was the transformation of a liner into a great battleship complete with 15-inch guns in the winking of an eye with the company singing and dancing, as sailors, a number called "Nautical," very well set by Ralph Reader. It had nothing whatever to do with the plot, but it was a fine piece of stagecraft and showmanship. But then, the whole of *Crest of the Wave* was very loosely knit.

Like all Ivor's shows, it was far too long. At the first dress rehearsal it went on and on. There was a scene outside Grauman's Chinese Theatre, so famous in filmland. Here Ivor was going to help himself to a slice. He had decided he was an excellent mimic. He wrote this scene which showed famous film stars going into the theatre to witness a film première. He had Angus McBean make masks exactly like the great ones of Hollywood and he was going to stand hidden and out of sight and imitate their voices as they spoke to each other on entering. It was a bad scene anyway—not scenically but technically—and the worst of it was that Ivor was not at all a good mimic. They mostly sounded just like Ivor Novello. Certain people he could imitate well, but not these. It was decided that the scene must come out. But Ivor adored it. Who was to persuade him? Many tried and failed. I got the job. I sat in his flat. We had supper there—a little ham, some cold water (I don't drink alcohol anyway) and a rather tired lettuce. We talked and we argued. I persuaded, he resisted. At four o'clock in the morning he gave in. I had won. I drove home more dead than alive, but it was worth it. Ivor admitted that afterwards.

Crest of the Wave opened on September 1st, 1937. It ran until February 26th, 1938. The vast theatre was packed with celebrities. The curtain rose and disclosed the exterior of the old castle. Across its front stretched a line of armoured knights, and they sang a male voice song " Rose of England," one of Ivor's best and most lasting numbers. But, musically, it never reached anywhere near that again. And the end, instead of the big eyefulls to which the audience had become accustomed in Ivor's shows, was a very quiet domestic scene, in which the domestic staff of Gantry Castle welcomed back their Duke and his new bride, against an interior scene backed by an enormous Christmas tree. Carols were sung. It was quiet and it was altogether charming, but it was not quite Drury Lane—nor Novello. Yet there was a fine reception and when Ivor stepped forward at last and asked if he had done it again, the answer was " Yes." But if truth must be told there was a slight dissent in a small portion of the " gods." One or two of the stage-door fans expressed disappointment. But the Press was good, a big Library deal was done, and " Crest," as we all called it, went on with big success. Ivor had done the Hat Trick.

When it finished, Ivor went with it on tour. Tom Arnold toured it and it went forth practically as at Drury Lane. Tom Arnold naturally wanted big publicity. He and I decided to fire the first shots in two of the biggest and most important cities, Glasgow and Manchester. Ordinarily it was my job but I could not be in two places at once and we wanted neither of the places to feel slighted by a previous announcement in the other. So we decided to make a simultaneous release in both. Now, to which was I to go? I look upon both those cities as spiritual homes. I have been there so many times, the Press boys and girls are my old and beloved friends. It was a hard choice. But I decided upon Glasgow, for Tom Arnold was not so well known there then as in Manchester. It was best for him to go where he was most at home. I went up to Glasgow on the night train. I had a press conference at the Glasgow Alhambra at 11 a.m. I told my story to my friends of the Glasgow Press. I distributed my pictures. I paid a personal call on one or two of the big men of the papers, who had not been able to come to the conference because of the cares of their office, and I caught the 1.20 p.m.—the Coronation Scot—back to town, having lunched on board. I was home before 10 p.m. That is how we worked in those days. Glasgow did me—and Ivor—proud. So did Manchester, but when Tom Arnold and I measured it up, I had won. Well, no credit in that. It was my job. Publicity means quick movement; that was my usual way of working Glasgow. If it was Manchester, I went up on the breakfast train and in pre-war days came back the same evening on the old 5.45, having dinner on board. It meant hustle and organization. But one has to think of the local conditions and editions, too.

Of course, when the show one was publicizing opened, one spent some time in the town for rehearsals and first night. But for the preliminary campaign, I found those few hours in both cities most effective. It was entirely due to the friendship and co-operation of the pals on the Press which made it possible. And I would like here to pay tribute to the Manchester-Glasgow Press, to the help and consideration I have always received at the Central Hotel Glasgow and the Midland Manchester, to my friend Fred Ferne at the Glasgow Alhambra and Harry Ashton at the Kings, to Bill Taylor and Douglas Bush at the Palace Manchester. They are companions of many a hard-fought field. And Ferne and I worked together as far back as 1911.

There is something else to chronicle as to Ivor's ceaseless activities. The old laziness was gone—conquered, although deep in him it was still there. He kept it under, however. And whilst *Crest of the Wave* was running, his creative urge was on him again and he wrote a straight play, *Comedienne*. This also fulfilled an ambition of his. He always adored Mrs. Patrick

Campbell, as actress, woman and " character." There had been some of her in *Party*. He collected stories about her, and he could give a very good impersonation of her—better than those he wanted to do of the Hollywood stars. He put all that knowledge of the incomparable and unpredictable Mrs. Pat into the leading character in *Comedienne*, and Lilian Braithwaite played it at the Haymarket, where it was produced on June 16th, 1938, by which time *Crest of the Wave* had finished its Drury Lane run. It has been stated in print that all the Ivor musicals at Drury Lane, including *Crest of the Wave* ran for a year. They did not—any of them.

To run a year at Drury Lane, with its big capacity, is a considerable event and before the Second World War a year's run was quite an event anyway, at an ordinary theatre. But these musicals of Ivor's restored success to the Lane, restored prestige, showed that there was a man in the Theatre who understood his job from A to Z and who could do what had only been regarded as possible by the Americans. For, since the First World War, the latter had gradually advanced in the science of musical plays and were turning them out better than their inventors, the English.

All the Ivor plays had an aura of success about them, even if they did not make much money for Drury Lane. They brought the people back and in an exciting manner, for whatever Ivor may have lacked in the theatrical art he never lacked that important quality of being able to excite. He had an immense following which was very loyal to him, as he was to them. He filled Drury Lane with happiness as nobody had ever done before—or since. There were no grumbles, no fights, no quarrellings whilst he was there. Even if his plays did not perform to " standing room only " every night—as has also been chronicled—they did so often enough to be satisfactory to all concerned. And the greatest thing was the knowledge that a man existed who knew and could supply the needs of that mighty if difficult theatre, a man whom Old Drury liked, who was a true son of its tradition. He won his greatness and lasting fame at Drury Lane and by it will be remembered.

Ivor got another little chance at this period of indulging his fancy as classical actor. He played " Charles Surface " at a matinée for the King George Pension Fund, a charity in which he took the greatest interest and of which he was a director.

His Charles Surface was a lot better than his Romeo. That was at the Winter Garden Theatre.

To return to *Comedienne*. Lilian Braithwaite made a big success. The cast included Barry Jones, Kathleen Harrison, Alan Webb, Fabia Drake, Ralph Michael, Edgar Norfolk, Mervyn Johns and Cecily Byrne. It was produced by Murray Macdonald. To mark its success—and hers—Ivor gave Lilian Braithwaite a brooch. She expressed the greatest pride and pleasure and she wore it. At the Ivy she showed it to her friends. " Look," she would coo, in that drawling characteristic voice of hers, " this is the brooch dear Ivor gave me " . . . and then, after a momentary pause, " you *can* see it, can't you? " Typically Lilian. . . .

Ivor himself got a presentation during *Crest of the Wave*. To mark his hat trick at Drury Lane the whole company and staff, under the organization of Dorothy Dickson, collected money and gave him a silver cigarette case, with a map of the West End of London engraved on the back, and the theatres marked thereon, those at which his plays had been produced being marked with a jewel. It turned out to be costly and some of us —myself for one—had to foot the bill! It was presented to him on the stage at curtain fall. He was very touched. He told us all that he had many such things and often he lost them; but that this one he would always keep and carry near his heart.

There is another little story in *Crest of the Wave* to show how Ivor always kept his company on their toes and how he encouraged young players. Instead of having all the understudy parts allotted by choice of stage directorship, he had competitions. Those who fancied themselves competed at an audition for the chance to understudy the part they coveted. Ivor sat in the stalls as judge. There were some excellent results. In one case he could not make up his mind between two girls; one of them was my own daughter. In the end, he gave it to them both: they shared it and had they ever had the chance (they never did) would have played alternate nights. This procedure of testing understudies might be more widely tried. It is good for morale and initiative. And it is an example of Ivor's encouragement of the youth of his beloved profession.

The tour of *Crest of the Wave* brought Tom Arnold and Ivor into touch and into business together for the first time. From then on every play of Ivor's but one was presented by Tom

Arnold. He is the only manager with whom Ivor worked with real pleasure and complete understanding. They were complete opposites, in ideas, in mind, in manner and probably in thought. That is why they got on so well together. Tom Arnold understood this genius to whom he was yoked with such excellent results. He knew how to handle him. If at times Ivor's ideas scared him, he would meet the case and make a job of it. And he could use his persuasive powers to good effect, too—and Arnold knows all about that. He is a commercial manager and despite all the glamour and the glory and the romance and adulation of the fans, Ivor was a commercial manager as well. If he was more lavish in his ideas of spending sums on production than Tom Arnold, that was because he was of the older school and also because he was an actor and knew what that really beautiful background meant to an actor. But he was never over-extravagant when dealing with his own productions. David Ivor Davies with the keen business brain kept the more idealistic Ivor Novello in check.

Tom Arnold and Ivor were friends in and out of the Theatre. Ivor was godfather to Tom Arnold's son; not for reasons of business policy but because he wanted to be. And he left that godson the rights of his biggest success, *The Dancing Years*, when he died. He did not leave that—in reality—to the godson alone. It was a gesture of affection and friendship to Tom himself. Arnold is a most successful man and is therefore presumably rich (if he is not it is his own fault, and one cannot conceive that he is not rich for he understands how to make money) so Ivor could not leave him a few thousand pounds. But he could show his feelings towards Tom in his bequest to the son—and he did so.

Tom Arnold had first become really aware of Ivor Novello many years before they ever met. He had a show on tour and he was in Leeds. It so happened that Ivor was on tour too, with one of the straight plays and was playing at the Grand, Leeds, whereas Tom Arnold was at the Theatre Royal. Arnold went to see Ivor's matinée. He marvelled at the crowds, he knew that Ivor was No. 1 Box Office in the provinces. He watched Ivor carefully. He thought to himself (he recalls it with pride): " I wish I had him under my banner. I wish I was presenting Ivor Novello." That was many years ago. That wish came true. Starting with the tour of *Crest of the Wave* in

1938 Tom Arnold " presented " Ivor Novello until the latter's death in 1951.

It was over that tour of *Crest of the Wave* that Ivor came into contact with Roma Beaumont, who was to reach stardom in *The Dancing Years*. It was Tom Arnold who brought them together. He had noticed Roma Beaumont himself. He thought she was good. He asked Ivor to go down to the Saville Theatre, where she was rehearsing and have a look at her. Ivor did so. He was not impressed. He had a chat with her in the stalls. He did not enthuse. He told Tom Arnold so, but Arnold did not change his mind. Roma Beaumont played the part on tour, and Ivor saw then what she could do. It was enough for him. He wrote a part for her and she was a star overnight.

Poor enthusiastic Ivor. He was always finding stars. I was constantly taking along cameramen to photograph him rehearsing young ladies and clasping them in his arms in admiration of their artistic powers. All too often they did not turn out to be stars at all. The success they achieved was entirely due to him, and to the material he gave them, for he knew exactly how to fit them out. It was often just reflected glory. It was like a girl looking ravishing in a dress by Hartnell, Schiaparelli or Dior, but not being nearly so good in a dress off the peg from her own dress shop. That did not always apply, of course, and certainly not in the case of Roma Beaumont or Vanessa Lee. But there were others. . . .

Ivor made up his mind to do that tour almost at the last minute. But go he did and much was to come of it.

His touring was not like that of an ordinary actor-manager. It has been best described by Christopher Hassall, who in his beautiful Address at the Memorial Service used these words: " Ruling his Kingdom of the Theatre, he would go a progress through our great industrial cities, but all the time the voice of the inner man that spoke through his melody was the voice of a place far away where there are wild woods and hills and ancient traditions of song." That is very beautifully true. His tours were Progresses. His visits to cities were Occasions: they excited the entire place. The theatres were packed; the stage doors thronged; people crowded for a glimpse of him. He brought them something they all desired, consciously or not. That inner man spoke to them, and, although the voice of that inner man came from that place of woods and hills and music—

which is Wales—it also came from the Land of Romance, both Wales and that intangible idealistic kingdom which lies in the soul and heart of most people, even if they are not aware of it until a man with Ivor's gifts awakens them.

Whilst Ivor was on tour he began to write his next show for Drury Lane. It was all arranged that he should do another. The show he was preparing was his most outstanding production, *The Dancing Years.* He wrote most of it and composed much of the music whilst on that tour. He created the part of Greta especially for Roma Beaumont. And he had got Mary Ellis for his leading lady, so he was feeling very good indeed.

Meanwhile things were happening at Drury Lane. Walter Payne, head of the Society of West End managers, a theatrical magnate and son of the famous Adney Payne of music hall fame, a charming, handsome and very knowledgeable man, had joined the Board as Chairman. Harry Tennent was on the way out, although he did not know it. He thought Payne had come in to help him. The Lane staged, with O'Brien, Linnit and Dunfee, a stage version with music of one of the Edgar Wallace stories *Sanders of the River*. It was entitled *The Sun Never Sets.* Basil Dean produced it. It did not live up to its title . . . the sun set fast on that big show. There was a season, brief but brilliant, of Russian Ballet to fill in. Then Ivor came back. He made another sensation. It was announced that he and Tom Arnold were to present Shakespeare's *Henry V* with Ivor as the victor of Agincourt. Thus was his urge for classic acting to be assuaged. He was to play one of the great parts at the greatest theatre.

There was a bit of backstage bargaining over that production. Even Tom Arnold needed some persuasion to venture on it. He made a good bargain, however ; he got the job of presenting a pantomime at Christmas. I had a considerable hand in those arrangements myself.

If there had been wonder and doubt before as to what Ivor could or could not do at Drury Lane, there was more now. He had proved himself as a master of the spectacular musical, but what would he be like as the Warrior King? Much speculation was aroused. Another surprise was that Dorothy Dickson was to play in Shakespeare at the Lane too! Ivor cast her "Princess Katherine of France." Once again Ivor was right! Dorothy was excellent, beautiful and charming. The love scenes between the two were a high-spot of the production.

Tom Arnold deserves praise and remembrance for this venture. The production, by Sir Lewis Casson, was excellent and imaginative. One remembers the endless chain of victorious English soldiers entering Harfleur to the tune of a march composed by Ivor (who here collaborated with Shakespeare). One remembers, too, an impressive Southampton scene with the ships and banners and what was the best stage representation of the actual battle of Agincourt I have ever seen—and I know this play and its various productions backwards. It was an affair of clash of arms, gleaming armour, the flutter and surge of banners backwards and forwards, and the turmoil and noise of battle seen in glimpses through splendid lighting. . . . Again, one remembers Gwen Ffrangçon-Davies as " Chorus," a gay speedy Chorus dressed like a Page.

The whole thing got a surprisingly good Press. So did Ivor. One paper condemned but the rest praised. All things considered, Ivor managed very well indeed. It was all new to him and his voice had not the requisite range, nor his powers the depths demanded. He looked magnificent. He spoke his lines well, especially the Prayer and " Upon the King." It is no use pretending he was within miles of Lewis Waller, the best exponent of this role the stage will ever know. He was not. The " hand props " worried him a lot for he hated carrying things. But it was a most creditable performance. The lighter scenes were excellent and the " Honour " speech well spoken, even if the famous speech at Harfleur lacked the true, trumpet-like urgency which greater vocal powers and experience could have provided. But it must be accounted an Ivor success. It did not make money. It struck the Munich crisis and the bottom fell out of the world of the Theatre.

I used to sit in Ivor's room discussing the chances of war and peace. I did not believe war would hit us then but I regarded it as a certainty later on. Maybe there would be a year or two of breathing space. Ivor hated war and the thought of it. I remember getting a laugh from Bobbie Andrews's simulated terror: " If there is a war they will find out how old I am," he said. . . . But although war was averted, Munich killed *Henry V*. Nevertheless, it had served its turn. Ivor had achieved a desire. He had spoken of *Henry V* whilst doing *The Happy Hypocrite*, in which he showed everyone his real powers of acting. That was a character part even though he ended up as himself; he had to play " character " to do so. " Lord George Hell " was essentially " character." Henry V is straight and Ivor was always a much better character than straight actor. *Henry V* closed down. Tom Arnold did his pantomime, which was a grand one and a big success.

Ivor lost money over *Henry V*, as did Arnold. It worried neither. It worried Ivor not at all. What did depress him was that his hopes of doing a series of Shakespearean shows had vanished again. He never got that desire. He bowed to the verdict of the outside world. The failure was not his but caused by world conditions. He himself wrote the notice of withdrawal which was posted on the theatre notice board. He wrote therein the farewell to his Shakespearean hopes.

CHAPTER TWENTY-ONE

THE DANCING YEARS—AND WHAT THEY LED TO

BEFORE Ivor enters upon his last appearance at Drury Lane, which was also to be his greatest, there should be a little assessment. That of finance is important. His earnings varied but were always considerable, as the following table shows:

Year	*Earnings* (£)	*Tax* (£)
1927–28	11,618	1,351
1928–29	15,460	1,880
1929–30	12,995	1,568
1930–31	12,440	1,962
1931–32	14,711	1,155
1932–33	17,007	2,527
1933–34	23,335	4,107
1934–35	15,943	2,948
1935–36	23,758	3,413
1936–37	7,573	1,870
1937–38	14,926	1,041
1938–39	8,002	582

In these figures can be read the success of his shows, as well as the amount of risk he took when financing them at Drury Lane, which depleted both capital and income considerably. The drop in 1936–37 is accounted for by *The Happy Hypocrite* and the fact that he did little until the opening of *Careless Rapture*, most of the expense of which he bore himself. The drop in 1938–39 is accounted for by the fact that he did little until *The Dancing Years* was produced; moreover, he received only a moderate amount from *Henry V*, and, of course, *The Dancing Years* was cut off in its prime by the war. It should also be remembered that in the later periods he had finished with film-making.

It is also as well to take a glance at his methods of work and thereby see how these came into being. Most of the work he did himself. The only other person who contributed in a creative way to these triumphs was Christopher Hassall, who wrote the lyrics. Hassall knew Ivor and his ways of creation better than most people. When once started, Ivor worked very fast and it took Hassall all his time to keep up with him. Practically always the tune came first. Hassall would get the music from Ivor—just the top line—and be told to provide a lyric, and quickly. Sometimes he would suggest the titles, but often they were Ivor's and they provided the opening line, as it were.

Hassall was in a real fix once. They were working on *Crest of the Wave*. One evening he was given a piece of music and asked to bring the lyric to 11 Aldwych without fail the first thing next morning. Hassall went home and was involved almost at once in a pretty serious domestic crisis. He could not write a line. But he kept his appointment—with a blank piece of paper. When he arrived, Lloydy told him to his immense relief that Ivor had only just woken up. That gave Hassall breathing space, for there would be coffee and telephone calls. All he had as guidance was a title. He sat himself down, took a grip of himself and concentrated as he had never done before. The Muse was kind. When Ivor called him in, he had the completed lyric. It was " Rose of England." Ivor had told him that he wanted something as English as Elgar, whose music he worshipped. Lehar, he said, had given Tauber the right stuff, and that had been some inspiration to him for " Shine Through My Dreams." But now he wanted something really English. He got it: " Rose of England " is as English as bacon and eggs.

Ivor was very fond of Chris Hassall and often pulled his leg. When company was at "Redroofs", they used to play a game called " Analogies " and everyone had to find analogies for everyone else. Viola Tree said of herself that she was a horse's bedstead at the bottom of the sea, and she likened Ivor to a gardener's boy in the sun. Ivor's description of Chris Hassall was that he was a cross between Romeo and Rowton House.

He enjoyed working with Hassall, for such work was creative. He said to him once, when Hassall was at the war and could not work for him, " What fun it all was. You could bring in a lyric and give it to me, and I would say ' No, it stinks.' Then you would clutch your head, alter a word and I would read it again and say ' It's heavenly.'... That's the way to work." It really was very much like that. Hassall wrote his lyrics under all sorts of conditions. He would be sent for when Ivor was on tour, go up North and write madly to keep pace with Ivor.

Ivor gave him the title for " Some Day My Heart Will Awake," the big hit number in *King's Rhapsody*, and also for " I Can Give You the Starlight " in *The Dancing Years*. Sometimes the idea sprang to the mind at once, for Hassall always found Ivor's music lyrical. Such things as " My Dearest Dear " were instantaneous as soon as the tune was played. They were ideal collaborators. Hassall would sit and listen to Ivor at work on the piano. He would be working on a tune. He would play it over, he would improvise upon it and then, out would come the melody he wanted. It would be played on to the recording-machine and he would listen. Maybe he would improvise again but usually it was what he wanted. He worked quickly and with inspiration.

Ivor would tell Christopher Hassall his thoughts and he confided to him his difficulties about Shakespeare. He said he often came upon long tracts in the plays which he failed to understand, even individual words in them. He said he understood fully the rhetorical and emotional value of these words but their precise meaning eluded him. And then he would give an imitation of a celebrated actress playing Shakespeare, making up the words as he went along, and make everyone die with laughter.

On his piano at " Redroofs " (it was a piano of fumed oak) there always stood a large signed photograph of Lily Elsie. Also on the piano was a glass vase, a really ancient Roman vase, in perfect preservation and glowing with the rainbow's colours when it caught the light. It had belonged to James Elroy Flecker, that great poet who wrote *Hassan*, who had given it to Eddie Marsh, who in turn gave it to Ivor. And at " Redroofs " he kept a book which he called " The Lectern," which contained all sorts of odds and ends and scraps, including a poem which he himself had written when very young and of which each verse ended with the words " For we were the happiest."

To Chris Hassall, Ivor seemed two people in one, as, indeed, he really was. But his view of them differed from mine. He says that to him, especially when in London or in one of his favourite restaurants, the Ivy or the Caprice, Ivor always gave him the impression of being a distinguished visitor from the Balkans. That impression was deepened for him by the main room at " Redroofs ", which, although beautiful and artistic, always seemed to be the refuge of an exiled heir to a Balkan kingdom who had made this home in England. This was chiefly on account of a huge expanse of bright scarlet satin curtains and an immense eighteenth-century mirror framed in blue glass. The effect was essentially Baroque and it always prevented Hassall, he says, from feeling completely at home there. Yet the key of the workroom in the garden was kept in an enormous and brightly coloured china duck which stood in the hall and was called " Birdie." That workroom was added after the success of *Glamorous Night*. It was in a sequestered spot of the garden, with latticed windows and an old oak beam across the roof. There was a piano there and a recording-machine and on that Ivor and Chris Hassall worked on *Careless Rapture*, *Crest of the Wave* and *The Dancing Years*. And just outside was a small recess, probably intended as a place in which to grow vegetable marrows. But Ivor used it for lying naked in the sun. He loved to do that: he loved the sun and he loved sunbathing. Hassall tried it but found it made his head swim.

Hassall also said that he had an impression that Ivor was always made up ready to go on the stage at any minute. I had that impression too. It was his darkness, for there was no actual make-up, and the sense of the Theatre which always radiated from him. There was a gipsy look and that Balkan *motif* was strengthened by his love of and his penchant for writing gipsy music; he loved it and used it whenever possible. His love of the sun, too, was gipsy. Hassall always regretted that when Ivor described him as a cross between Romeo and Rowton House that he had not replied by likening Ivor to Apollo and a gipsy fortune teller. Ivor at " Redroofs " was a completely happy person. Sometimes in London and at work he would have phases of an almost royal aloofness, though always very courteous and polite, but at " Redroofs " there was always a great gentleness of manner.

Near the workroom in the very English and very peaceful garden at " Redroofs " was a little rose garden. Here Ivor had placed the sundial given to him by Mary Ellis. The bronze plaque on which was inscribed Hassall's verse was to be fixed to the sundial, but it was too large. It went instead on the workroom wall and it is there to-day.

During the first three shows for Drury Lane Hassall not only wrote the lyrics, but also worked at the recording-machine on which Ivor recorded his music as he composed it. The machine was in a little lobby with a glass door and Hassall would watch

Ivor as he played, noting the expressions and gestures of despair or satisfaction. When the record was made, Hassall would carefully brush the thread clear of the cutting needle, wipe the disc with acid and run into the room, putting the record on the gramophone for Ivor to hear! Ivor would light one of his Turkish cigarettes and probably say " I think this is going to be IT." If, however, he did not like it, he would take it off in the middle and say " That was foul! Let's have some coffee." And sometimes he would show that extreme consciousness he possessed as to the actual passing minute. Ivor hardly ever lost himself or became unaware of his surroundings, however hard he was concentrating. For he would say " Isn't this heaven? Can there be anything more enjoyable than what we are doing? How perfectly frightful to be anyone else. I can't wait to play this to Mary! " That would be after he had got things to his satisfaction. It showed how he enjoyed his work compared with those composers who find their creations things of storm and stress. To Ivor it was pure joy. That is why his music sounds as it does; that is why, although no claim is made to classicality, it has the pure freshness of a gushing spring, of a morning breeze, or the beauty of an old and sunbaked wall. Whilst composing he wore a shabby dressing-gown with sleeves so long that one wondered how he could play the piano in them. But he managed somehow.

Hassall recalls how their session would nearly always end with Ivor suddenly walking off—sometimes in the middle of a sentence—to shave, or to have his afternoon sleep, that sleep which enabled him to keep awake most of the night. . . .

These are some of Hassall's own impressions, and I want to place on record my gratitude to him for them and for much more in this book to come later which comes from his own contacts with Ivor.

Ivor worked on *The Dancing Years* on tour, at " Redroofs " and at the flat. He had found a new star in Roma Beaumont and he wanted to fit her perfectly. She had not a powerful singing voice, although she is a good actress and can dance like an angel or a piece of sunbathed gossamer. Ivor, however, had to fit her with a song. It will be remembered that in the play this child of Vienna came to England and became a star of musical comedy. Her return to Austria years afterwards caused the dramatic moment of the play, when misunderstanding broke

The tasteful dining-room, the cosy study and the elegant main bedroom at "Redroofs," Ivor's lovely country home near Maidenhead

Top picture shows Ivor's bedroom in his Aldwych flat: the one below his massive and beautiful bed at "Redroofs." Bottom picture is a view from the study in the Aldwych

the romance between Rudi (Ivor) and Maria Ziegler (Mary Ellis). He asked her what she could do and got her to sing an English musical comedy song in what he referred to as her " Shepherd's pipe." The song she sang and the dance she danced to it was called " Primrose." It was a perfect example of a tune by Lionel Monkton or Paul Rubens of the 1910 vintage. It was a most popular number, but all too short.

Ivor's idea was to do a pastiche of a period musical comedy. He asked Hassall for the lyric. Hassall had to admit he knew nothing at all about the Edwardian shows, or what their lyrics were like. So Ivor sat down at the piano and played all his favourite tunes from these shows, which Hassall had never heard of. He sang the words too, as well as he could. And then there was no difficulty at all in Hassall's way, with the result that " Primrose " might have come straight from a Gaiety show. And *à propos* of that event, Hassall remembers that Ivor's favourite of his non-theatrical songs was his setting of " The Tan Faced Prairie Boy " by Walt Whitman, to which Bobbie Andrews had introduced him. It was probably never published but it was a prime favourite with him.

The Dancing Years went into rehearsal and there was happiness at the Lane again. Mary Ellis was back, to everyone's joy. Here is the leading lady of all the leading ladies of the musical stage; here is a woman who can do it all. Since the days of Evie Greene, there has been no one like Mary Ellis. She had triumphed in *Glamorous Night*. She did it again in *The Dancing Years*. Ivor had Minnie Rayner with him again, as always. He had a good part for Peter Graves (who, incidentally, had put up a good show as the Dauphin in *Henry V*, although he admitted to being scared out of his life) and all the old chorus and dancers were back. A newcomer to the company was Anthony Nichols, who played the Prince and played it very well indeed. Dunstan Hart sang the tenor role and is still at the time of writing in Ivor's shows, in *Gay's the Word*. For Roma Beaumont Ivor had written a delightful part: she was a very young girl, practically a child at first, with a blind hero worship for Ivor, who as Rudi Kleber was a struggling musician and composer. It was her childish freak of making him promise not to marry anyone until she had the first refusal which caused the main trouble in the play. Joseph Carl did the *décor*. Freddie Carpenter arranged the dances and once again Leontine Sagan produced.

In this play, which Tom Arnold presented and in which Ivor was financially interested (he and Arnold were eight-thirteenths of the show and the Lane five-thirteenths, an odd calculation but satisfactory to both parties) Ivor broke all the rules. Times were unsettled. Neither Arnold nor he, nor the Lane, wanted to embark on one of the old big spectacular shows, for those big effects cost much money. So Ivor put all the effects into the plot. There was not a single stage effect of a mechanical kind in it. But he got drama—and how he got drama! He started off the play with the introduction of the Nazis. This was almost the first time, certainly the first time in a musical play, that Nazis had been brought upon the stage. It was quite unlike anything he had done before. This time he had written a play which was " about " something, which had a much deeper note than any of his others. He had not merely a story: he had a theme. And that theme was that although Cruelty, as symbolized by the Nazis, could kill a man, it could not kill his achievement. However much they might suppress that achievement in the reach of their own power, it would triumph over them outside their realm and eventually be victorious.

Beauty must always beat ugliness—that was what he meant. In this case, the theme he chose was Music. He gave himself a good part for once; indeed, he gave himself almost two parts: himself when young, gay and in love and himself when old, weary and a prisoner of the Nazis facing instant death. And he played them both very well, the older man better than the, younger. He achieved another ambition, too, for he had a scene—he always liked the idea—of a stage within a stage, of an opera being performed in Vienna composed by Rudi Kleber whilst the composer conducted the orchestra. And when that scene arrived Charles Prentice laid down the baton and left the conductor's chair whilst Ivor Novello as Rudi Kleber went into the Drury Lane orchestra pit and conducted the Drury Lane orchestra. How he loved doing it. And how well he did it, too!

In *The Dancing Years* Ivor departed from the advice given him by King George V and returned to the unhappy ending of *Glamorous Night*. But, as in that show, he sent the audience away happy with a Vision, once again a vision in blue with the reunion of the lovers, in each other's arms, to dance away the years of eternity.

There was never any doubt about *The Dancing Years*. Ivor

had learnt the lesson of *Crest of the Wave* when he so nearly slipped. Here was a well-made, absorbing tale wedded to some of his very best music, music which will endure the passing years and always be heard. He showed the old carefree romantic Vienna. He showed the coming of the Nazis and, by means of a series of little masques, first Vienna in the old days, then Vienna under the Nazis and then Vienna ruined, starving and penniless but striving to keep her soul. Those masques were mimed and danced to really enchanting music, perfectly fitted to the mood. The rehearsals were a joy.

The first night came, and a most brilliant first night it was, both back stage and in the front of the house. Maybe the audience was not so glittering as that which had attended *Careless Rapture*, but the times were different. Anyway, everyone who was anyone was there to see Ivor bid for success for one of his own shows for the fourth time at Old Drury. I don't think anyone dreamed of failure, certainly none of us who knew the show. The scenery, although not ultra-spectacular, was beautiful. There was the garden on the hilltop overlooking Vienna and the Danube, which quite rightly was not painted blue at all, there was a lovely interior in Maria's house, a glittering operatic production, a rehearsal scene (in which Lloydy took part), a lovely château on a lakeside with mountains around it, the delightful masques—and the vision at the end.

The big scene was in the grounds of the Castle of Schoenbrunn, with a fête in progress in which was featured " The Leap Year Waltz," one of the most popular tunes and danced by Roma Beaumont. This was a vision of loveliness all through. Mary Ellis had never been in better form: her singing of " Waltz of My Heart " and especially of " I Can Give You the Starlight " (my own favourite of all Ivor's tunes, and Chris Hassall's too) were memories to cheer one's life and one's old age. Seldom does such beauty come from the Theatre.

When at last the curtain fell, it fell to a deep-throated cheer such as one seldom hears but always longs to, for it is the note of real triumph. Again and again the curtain rose, again and again the whole company bowed. Again Ivor led forth his principals one at a time, to take their bow. There was no need to wonder if Roma Beaumont had succeeded. The cheers and the ecstatic applause told that. And he led forth Mary Ellis who swept her curtsy like the Queen of the Theatre she is and received her just and clamant meed of appreciation. A new star had been born in the person of Roma Beaumont—and Ivor said so—but Mary Ellis was a fixed planet in her own sphere. And still the cheers, still the applause. And then Ivor came forward with that shy, sidelong smile, that look of grateful happiness, humble but content, with that slight shambling, boyish lurch forward, to say his speech of thanks. Waves of friendliness rolled from him back to that audience and back again from the audience to him. It was Triumph—total and complete. At last the curtain fell. He stood on the stage as usual, like royalty receiving, whilst crowds came up to congratulate. Some merely stood and stared, some shook hands, some he embraced. Breaking away from the people he was talking with he would plunge forward to greet a favourite with a shout of " Darling. How wonderful! And did you really enjoy it? " hugging them the while. Even I got hugged that night. Outside, the crowds jostled and milled, eager for a sight of the hero, the man who had " done it " four times at Drury Lane. Ivor managed to enshrine that moment, that crowning point of his career. He had the whole show recorded as it proceeded from start to finish, including the applause at the end and the speeches. Millions have relived that experience, for it has been frequently broadcast. It was a great Theatre moment and it is good to know that it endures.

In the morning, a grand Press, a big Library deal—happiness all round!—a box office at Drury Lane which could hardly cope with the queues dashing to book—success had come in full measure.

There was, however, one moment during the rehearsals which I am not likely to forget. It was the only time I ever saw Ivor lose his temper and get really cross in the Theatre. He spent quite a lot of time in that show playing the piano. As he was a composer in the story there was every reason why he should. And of course, to him, it was heaven. But Leontine Sagan dropped a brick, the only one I ever knew her drop. She did it with the best of intentions for she did not know Ivor as well as we did, even then. She suggested that he should cut out some of the piano playing. Smilingly, he differed. She insisted, saying that she thought the audience would get tired of it. Ivor stiffened. He went a bit pale. He got dangerously quiet. " Leo," he said, " I know *exactly* what my audience will stand from me.

I know they like to hear me play. And I shall go on playing." The tone of voice was steely and cold, and the whole company became taut. And Leo immediately realized what she had done. There was no more said about it. But it was the only time I ever saw him really angry.

When we had the "photo call" for that play (that is a special rehearsal at which all pictures the public sees outside the Theatre and in the papers, are taken) the Drury Lane Ghost took it upon himself to walk round his usual promenade at the back of the upper circle. Many saw him, many did not. It is like that with ghosts—you either can or you cannot. The only time I ever used to get annoyed with Ivor was at the photo call. It is a long and rather weary job and everyone, including the publicity man to whom it is of vital importance, likes to get it over. Ivor would come down all bright, although the call was early. He would have a picture or two and then he would seize the heaven-sent opportunity. Here was the stage, here was his company, so "Let's rehearse." And he would waste much precious time making little alterations in position. Thoroughly enjoying himself, he would become completely oblivious of the real reason why we were there. It always ended in my taking him by the arm, talking severely to him and leading him off the stage, whilst he apologized profusely. But he always did it again: it was no use.

The Dancing Years was a real solid success. It seemed that it would run for ever. But Hitler saw to that. Crisis followed crisis, the nations armed and the world was rushing headlong to war. Business fell away to nothing. It was a tragic affair. The takings dropped from many hundreds to a few pounds. Then to help the worries of the company, who did not know what to do, Ivor put a notice on the board:

1. 9. 39.

Needless to say I am making every effort to continue and I hope that as the news of world conditions improves that I may have good news for all of us who have worked so hard on this production.

Ivor Novello

He wrote and signed that himself. But nothing could be done, a stronger hand was at work. On Friday, September 1st, 1939, there was no doubt at all. The show must finish. It was the end. I went down to Drury Lane. Outside, the street lamps were coming down and the barrage balloons were going up. People were walking about in a dazed manner. It had come at last then? There was nothing of the wild, patriotic scenes which had marked the outbreak of the First World War. People glanced at the skies, which the barrage balloons were already flecking. Would there be a surprise attack before war was declared? Inside the Lane was a mere handful of people. The takings amounted to £49 16*s*. 8*d*. in that enormous auditorium. All that week it had been tumbling—as the war clouds thickened: the takings had been £126, £130, £128, £135, £164—and then—the end!

None of us will ever forget that evening. We watched the curtain go up. And it might have been the last time the curtain was ever going up at the Lane, for all of us expected the war to break out with a terrible and concentrated blitz on London. We got through the show. Ivor went down to the footlights and invited that sparse audience to come down into the stalls and sit near to him and the stage. They did it. But he and the rest gave a performance like a first night, though off-stage most people were in tears. I saw the curtain fall, and again, it might be the last time the curtain would ever come down. I had a mental vision of all the times I had seen it go up and down at my beloved Lane. . . . I went round and said good-bye to them all, and to Ivor. For all we knew, we might never meet again. The mist of war, blood red, blotted out our vision. And then, through the rapidly darkening streets, I drove home. . . . Even that night there were two or three fans standing faithfully at the stage door to see Ivor. . . . I went out that way. *The Dancing Years*, Ivor's greatest success so far, was over. We had played to as much as £685 one night—very big money then. I did not realize at that time that I should move into the Lane and work there with Ensa until I escaped and became, in the joking parlance of those war-time years, a fugitive from Ensa. All I knew was that the Lane had closed, and that Ivor's reign was at an end. An era closed that night, never to be renewed.

Ivor left the stage at Drury Lane that evening and never trod it again, save once, in public, at the matinée given by the Royal Academy of Dramatic Art in 1951, when he and his *King's Rhapsody* company gathered in the final masque. He led them on gaily and at the run. He also rehearsed there when he went with Ensa to France just after D-Day, but then the Novello

Dynasty had ended. He had loved it so much and had risen to greatness there.

As I drove home I recalled memories of him and his shows. I remembered that long, drawn out rehearsal of *Crest of the Wave* when one of the chorus boys, tired and hungry, suddenly spoke up " I wish I was a woodpecker," he said, " I'd get my supper off the scenery." Ivor at once gave them a break. I recalled another rehearsal when the whole company was exhausted and lying about in heaps. There was some delay—it was not Ivor's fault—and he walked on to the stage and began to play the piano. He played all sorts of tunes and amongst them he started some of the numbers from the Lane shows. That tired mass of humanity stirred and began to sing, softly. He played on. He broke into a number which had been cut out of *Careless Rapture*. That company remembered the number and sang it softly, too. Ivor said, " Ah, boys and girls, you remember it? Will you sing it with me?" And they did, at the top of their voices. He played on and on and they sang with him, resuming rehearsal refreshed and happy. That was the touch he always brought. There was also the time in *Crest of the Wave* when Ivor missed an entrance —a unique thing for him. He had altered some dialogue and had forgotten it. His cue came—he was not there. Finlay Currie, on the stage, gagged on. Still no Ivor. Peter Graves rushed on and off. Still no Ivor. Bill Sutton was hunting for him madly; so was Bill Budd, the assistant stage manager. Leonard de Renzie, the stage manager, was climbing up the curtain in a frenzy. Going along a narrow passage Bill Budd encountered two stage-hands carrying a table, but he dived over that table in the manner of Richard Hearne. And then Ivor was found. He had forgotten the cut, and was changing his costume, as had been the custom before the change was made, but doing it in a corner upstage and not in his dressing-room. He was bustled on—and he laughed himself silly. It was his own fault and he admitted it. It was the only time I ever knew him miss an entrance.

I remember those crowds of first-night telegrams pouring in on opening nights. Ivor alone had thousands, and I use the word advisedly. I remembered the flood of flowers, the girls and boys who had become a real family party, the pride and joy with which Ivor walked that stage and his love for his room, which had been Garrick's. I recalled all the times we had sat in the stalls at rehearsals, working on the shows. Now it would never happen again. It never did. That company broke up, though some of them stayed with Ivor right to the end. But that wonderful chorus and company of dancers never came to Drury Lane again. Indeed, an era was over. . . . For on Sunday, September 3rd, 1939, we were at war and over the radio came the announcement that all theatres and cinemas were to close down. . . .

To Ivor, to all the theatrical profession, this was a staggering blow. Never before had such a thing occurred. The last time there had been a general closing down of theatres, except for the short period of Royal Demise, was during the Great Plague, from June 5th, 1665 until the Special Order was rescinded on November 29th, 1666. This time it did not last so long. When the expected blitz did not materialize, provincial theatres and suburban theatres were allowed to open and eventually the London theatres and cinemas followed suit. But the King of Drury Lane had lost his realm, for that had been occupied by the Entertainment National Service Association, which Leslie Henson christened Ensa.

Ivor was almost heartbroken. Here was his major success cut off in its prime. He hated war, he hated cruelty. Here was the very thing he had inveighed against in *The Dancing Years* taking place. His music was being suppressed by the Nazis, so far as the Theatre was concerned. He was a very sad man. But he could not remain idle. He took *I Lived With You* on tour. He sent *Full House* on tour with Zena and Phyllis Dare in it. He played in *I Lived With You* himself.

A year after the outbreak of war, Ivor Novello and Tom Arnold decided to take *The Dancing Years* on tour. Out it went with all the glamour of Drury Lane success upon it, a big-scale production, to brighten the black-out. The tour opened at the Palace, Manchester and that Progress of Ivor lasted for eighteen months, all round the country. Business was immense. He and his play brought fresh hope and colour into lives dulled by the care of war and the depression of the black-out. They flocked in to see him, they cheered and they applauded. Business was magnificent.

William Newman, who was in charge of all stage affairs, will tell of the difficulties they encountered in those days of makeshift and improvisation. How the journeys were long and trying and often dangerous, too. How they played in air raids and under adverse conditions. How sometimes there was a very great shortage of stage hands which caused delay in setting and changing the scenes and how Ivor would speak to the audience, always getting their sympathy and often help change the scenery himself, and how, on one occasion, the local military authorities sent a squad of soldiers to lend a hand. Ivor was doing magnificent work. So, for the matter of that, was Bill Newman. Ivor wrote a song to mark the war. He had written " Keep the Home Fires Burning " in World War One; he must write a song for World War Two. He did so. It was called " We'll Remember." The words were by my old and valued friend, Collie Knox. But times had changed. The country was not yet ready for a war song, even by Ivor and on his theme of hope, remembrance and return. It did not succeed. He was, however, to write the great war song—later.

And Ivor wrote another play. He took it on tour first, before the tour of *The Dancing Years.* He had with him some of the stalwarts and Dorothy Dickson was his leading lady. He had, as a curtain raiser, some of his songs, which Olive Gilbert sang. The name of the play was *Second Helping.* It was comic but very, very light. It came to London, to the Lyric Theatre in April, 1940. The tour had gone out in October, 1939. He altered the title, for London, to *Ladies in to Action.* It was not a good play and it was not a success. It was well played, he gave a good production as always and a good performance (one always remembers an excellent piece of work by Maidie Andrews), but it did no business—and it struck Dunkirk. Ivor took it off. And it was after that failure that he did his tour of *I Lived With You.*

In the March of 1942, Tom Arnold and Ivor Novello decided to risk London again and bring back *The Dancing Years.* Ivor told his company and they re-echoed his enthusiasm. They had been through great hardships in travelling round the country, sleeping and living where they could, battling with the unaccustomed black-out in unfamiliar towns. But they stuck it out, largely because of the example of Ivor himself. He would always find a means of cheering them up, of reviving dropping spirits, of making bearable incredibly slow, long, uncomfortable train journeys. Those who had the misfortune to travel during that period of the war—and any other—know what it was like even on the best trains, to say nothing of those taking "professionals" on Sundays. The news that they were coming to town was greeted with joy.

Then began a short break in my association with Ivor from a business point of view, but not in our friendship. When the theatres all closed down, I had done the only thing in which it seemed that I could be useful. I was well over military age. I was an Air Raid Warden. I joined Ensa at the very beginning, and was one of its original members, for it seemed a grand thing to do. I became what they were pleased to call its Public Relations Officer. In the early days I loved, it too. There was not a lot to do in the Public Relations line: there was little space in the newspapers. I was mainly engaged in repelling quite unjust attacks on Ensa. It was something new and therefore suspect. That is the way in this country. When theatres began to reopen, I resumed my publicity work on shows, doing the Ensa work too. But the unpopularity of Ensa grew, especially in the profession which was supposed to support it. One by one my clients left me, the excuse always being that I had too much to do for Ensa, which was very far from being the case.

So when *The Dancing Years* was brought back into London in March, 1942, I had nothing to do with it. For the first time for years, Ivor was in town and I was not with him. I had helped launch this show and I loved it. I had no part in that experiment with war-time London, an experiment which was crowned with immense success. It opened at the Adelphi and repeated its Drury Lane triumph. The cast was different in some cases. Mary Ellis was not there. She had taken up war work; she was in the wilds, helping in hospitals, doing wonderful work, quite unheralded and unsung. She did not appear before a London audience for some time. I was associated with C. B. Cochran in a big one-night show at the Albert Hall, called *Seventy Years of Song* which C.B. created and staged. I wrote the second half of the show, from the end of the First World War down to the then present time. The fact that I am a recognized authority on the old time songs was sufficient reason—in the Theatre—for not being allowed to handle them. But of course that second half had to mention Ivor and his work. And I saw to that. I got into touch with Mary. I asked her to sing "Glamorous Night." She agreed at once. The show took place at the Albert Hall on Wednesday, June 16th, 1942, in aid of Toc H. It was an outstanding success, despite a dreadful rehearsal. Indeed, we never got a rehearsal of the second half at all. Geraldo, conducting, performed wonders. But the outstanding memory was Mary Ellis, looking very tiny in that vast place and all by herself, singing "Glamorous Night," whilst that enormous, massed audience roared their approval. She was quite wonderful. The most nostalgic event on that programme was when dear Violet Loraine and George Robey sang once more "If You Were the Only Girl in the World." The people cried as they cheered. . . .

Mary's original part in *The Dancing Years* was played by Muriel Barron, who had "stood by" for her at Drury Lane and who played it on tour. She is a first-class artiste and a principal boy of the front rank. She made a big success. She is also an Old Novellian. Roma Beaumont, Olive Gilbert and many of the others were in the show, so were the girls and boys. There was no doubt about *The Dancing Years.* It was the big hit of London, the big hit of the war. The Adelphi was packed. It did bigger business than it had done at Drury Lane, despite the difference in capacity. It became to London in the Second World War what *Chu Chin Chow* and *The Bing Boys* had been in the first war. Ivor was king again, if not of Old Drury, at least of the Adelphi and perhaps of the London stage. He was Box Office No. 1, be the other whom he might. There were crowds in front and crowds at the stage door. His dressing-room was packed, as it always had been: as packed as Euston Station.

The brass plate bearing his name was on its door. Lloyd Williams was officiating, pervading the Adelphi as he had pervaded the Lane or any other theatre in which Ivor appeared, taking round people Ivor wanted to see, getting tea served to them in the intervals, attending to the vast fan mail, doing wonderful work in the quietest and most unassuming manner. Fred Allen was in charge of the accounts. All that was different was that none of the Old Drury staff were around. Bill Newman and Winnie Newman were there in executive capacity.

It soon became apparent that this experiment, this measure which had been looked upon as temporary, was to become almost permanent. Ivor was in his seventh heaven of delight. He loved that show. He loved everything about it: his gay, carefree performance of the young and penniless composer in his Tyrolean clothes and lederhosen; his tired, weary but still unconquered elderly man still fighting the Nazis who represented that Evil which seeks to destroy Beauty. *The Dancing Years* was a household word. To Ivor it was Paradise. But there was trouble to come in that paradise, though he did not realize it at the time. That Eden which was the Adelphi was to see the very blackest days of Ivor's life, when calamity befell him, a calamity which was grimly tragic and so absurdly foolish that the absurdity just heightened the cruelty and horror of it all. Nobody realized it as yet. Meanwhile I was to rejoin Ivor. I left Ensa having had more than enough. I joined Tom Arnold. Ivor and I were together again. Much was to happen but neither he nor I, nor anyone else, dreamed in those happy if bomby days at the Adelphi how all Ivor's world was to smash in confusion and chaos, from which might have arisen the greatest tragedy of all. . . .

CHAPTER TWENTY-TWO

RETROSPECT—BEFORE THE STORM BREAKS

SO far, for fifty years, it had been sunshine all the way for Ivor Novello. Small setbacks, little troubles, no great loss of friends or money and a steady upward rise to the top of his Profession. His name was a household word, he was the greatest male box-office attraction of the day. He had, indeed, achieved more continuously concrete success than any of his contemporaries. He was universally popular. He had a fan mail which was staggering in its size and continuity. He was rich both in wealth and affection. He was—Ivor. The First World War had brought him his first fame. The Second World War was to bring about what might have been, to a lesser man, complete and utter downfall, but in his case, although he tasted the dregs of bitterness and mental horror, he was to shine even brighter when, almost in his own phrase, the dark clouds were turned inside out—and rolled away for ever.

It is as well to look back and to assess and remember. Ivor was at that time one of the few completely happy men in the world. Only his father's and mother's loss had clouded his horizon. How he felt about his father he showed in a letter to his old friend Jean Webster Brough:

> " Darling Jean,
>
> I so loved your letter, darling, about my darling Dad—oh God, how I shall miss him. It is so lovely to know he was spared any suffering and just slipped away with a smile. He would have hated *feeling* old—I'm sure he never would have *looked* old—would he ? "

He was in Hollywood when he wrote that. The multiplicity of " darlings " will be observed. Typically Ivor.

He had his staff around him, who were staunchly loyal. The little financial worries occasioned by Mam kept cropping up but he always dealt with them. There was a cablegram from

New York in 1924, where Mam had been chasing that fabulous fortune always just beyond her grasp, which read:

> " AM YOUR MOTHERS LAWYER SHE IS IN DIRE FINANCIAL DIFFICULTIES CREDITORS PRESSING HER COURT PROCEEDINGS INSTITUTED LANDLORD EVICTING HER FROM FLAT YOU MUST CABLE HER FIVE HUNDRED POUNDS IMMEDIATELY TO AVOID EMBARRASSING PUBLICITIES FOR FURTHER DETAILS CABLE ME FANHOLTLAW (signed) HOLTZMANN "

That was on June 12th, 1924. On June 22nd came another:

> " MOTHER WILL SAIL WHENEVER YOU HAVE PROVIDED YOUR PERSONAL ASSURANCE HER DEBTS WILL BE PAID CABLE SUCH FINAL AUTHORITY AS YOU DESIRE. FRANKOHL "

It is obvious what had happened. Ivor had again shouldered the load and eventually, promptly too, paid up. But he made Mam come home. It was much cheaper, and safer, to have her under observation. Poor Mam, she was always oblivious of the trouble she caused. She never dreamed it was her own fault; she never realized that the world had gone past her. She never ceased to chase the phantoms her vivid and enthusiastic imagination constantly conjured up.

But Ivor did not mind much what Mam did. He just adored her. He would be cross and a little hurt at the seeming fruitlessness of his efforts to check her, and then remember that she had never grown up. Well, neither did he, completely. He was always a Peter Pan. He had her enthusiasms, but not her carelessness—far, far from it. For one thing, Ivor was never a spendthrift, and was never extravagant. He would give generously to friends, and look for no thanks. But he did not give indiscriminately. He would frequently fail to do the obvious thing. When the Staff Bar under the stage at Drury Lane was redecorated and reopened, he was asked to perform the ceremony—I think it was during the run of *Crest of the Wave*. He went down with pleasure, he admired and enthused and declared it open most charmingly and graciously. But he did not " push the boat out." It just did not occur to him. I did that, in his name, immediately afterwards. It cost me quite a bit, but I never said anything about it.

Yet there was the other side. He tipped generously—call boys attest to that—and when he thought people might be in difficulties, he never hesitated. They did not have to ask. He demonstrated that most Christian-like characteristic that he who gives quickly gives doubly. When that friend of all the theatrical profession, Mario, for so long a presiding genius at the Ivy Restaurant, left there, Ivor sent for him. He asked what Mario was going to do. Mario, rather at his wits' end at that very time, said he wanted to start a restaurant of his own. It is as well to ask Mario what Ivor did then. Mario now controls the Caprice and shows that the art of the restaurateur is no lost one, seeing to it that not only the best of everything is served but also that from the moment a client enters until he leaves, he is the object of care and service. To hear Mario on the subject of Ivor is an inspiration. . . .

There are letters attesting to the kind actions he did, how he saw to it that friends in need got the best medical attention and ready help, even to expensive trips abroad to climates in which they had that chance of recovery which seemed doubtful here. The cost was not counted then. I should like to give chapter and verse, but many of the names are well-known. . . . But there is an instance of immediate kindliness. *Careless Rapture* ran over Christmas and Ivor, to his great delight, was one of the chief celebrants at the ancient ceremony of the cutting of the Baddeley Cake—that unique Drury Lane ceremony bequeathed by old Robert Baddeley the pastry-cook actor. His leading lady was Dorothy Dickson. When Dorothy got home to her flat that night, burglars had favoured her with a visit, probably just when the cake was being cut and had stolen a valuable jewelled wrist-watch. Ivor knew that watch. A short time afterwards he took Dorothy out to lunch. On her plate was a little package and in that package was what amounted to a replica of that watch which had been stolen. He did things like that. But he seldom saw what was right under his nose: he missed the little things all too often. However, what did it matter? Everyone was pleased to be with him. He could say " Thank you "—which is rare in Theatreland. For instance, on Sunday, February 27th, 1938, he wrote to Ronald E. Gray, the Secretary of Drury Lane Theatre (or of Theatre Royal, Drury Lane Limited, the company which owns it) and said:

" Dear Mr. Gray,

This is just to tell you how very deeply I appreciate the wonderful way you have worked with me and for me at Drury

Lane. It is so rare to find that the business end is also the friendly end ! And now what ?

Yours sincerely,
Ivor."

That letter was written just after the end of the run of *Crest of the Wave*. " And now what? " refers to what Ivor was going to do there next, when and how. He went on tour with *Crest*, and *The Sun Never Sets* went into Drury Lane, and set very quickly. Ivor came back that autumn with *Henry V*. But he wrote that letter of thanks which is a most unusual thing for a man in Mr. Gray's position to receive. It rather shook him. He was not used to it. But he has always kept and treasured it since. The point was that there was no need for Ivor to write it—but he did.

Mr. A. Gilbert Clark, who had been with Ivor as costume designer in *Fresh Fields* and knew him well, was understudying Peter Graves in *Crest of the Wave*. He was one of those who subscribed to that silver cigarette case with which Ivor was presented. He remembers the speech Ivor made. He finished by saying " We are going on tour. Unfortunately I cannot take you all with us but I hope the time may come when we shall all be together again. Children—I have had many presents in my time—I assure you I don't know where half of them are but I promise that this will be always here." And he did really value that case.

Some of his plays gave Ivor more happiness than others. *The Happy Hypocrite* was a case in point. He lost quite a lot but the prestige was enormous. It did him more good, as actor, than anything he had done before. Praise poured in and he kept all those letters. Particularly did he treasure a note from dear old Cyril Maude, in his own characteristic and extremely difficult handwriting which said:

" Dear Novello,

Well done ! And I expect you'll be filling another dozen or so theatres soon.

Yours sincerely,
Cyril Maude."

How well I knew that handwriting.

Clemence Dane (to him Winifred) who wrote the stage version of that charm of Max Beerbohm's, wrote to him in pencil just before the curtain went up (on the day of the production, that is) and said:

" How idle it is to wish you luck. You know already so perfectly well how I feel about your strong and beautiful playing of L. G. (' Lord George Hell ') and how I feel about the whole adventure as regards your share in it. It has been one of the happiest times I've ever had in the Theatre. I do feel that whatever publicity or financially comes of to-night that you and I have both had something personal out of it and out of our association that we shall greatly value. I know I have. And you have so constantly and generously shown me that you have, too. So I say only, Thank you, bless you, love and good luck. . . . I see a parcel on the piano in your hand. But I am opening my excitements last thing. . . .

Affectionately,
Winifred."

All too often relations between author and actor-manager are severely strained by the time the curtain rises. But not when Ivor was the actor-manager. Ivor sent a typical telegram to Max Beerbohm to announce the beginning of the rehearsals. . . .

"We start our dear Hypocrite on Monday at the Kingsway Theatre : please bring us luck by coming some time during the day. Ivor."

That was how he did things, with the graceful personal touch of homage. Barry Jones wrote him a letter and Ivor appreciated that fine actor's judgment. Barry Jones knows all about his business and is not given to shallow enthusiasms. If he does not approve, he says little or nothing. But if he does, then. . . .

" Dear Ivor,

I am not going to send you a telegram—too like a mere gesture. But I must send a note of complete blither about my hopes for the show. We all know what we all thought of its original charm, frailty *and* its chances. Saturday's complete delight in the 2 performances I saw, has made me feel very differently about the whole thing.

It is an amazing string of pearls which you and Dick are offering the public (and I won't say ' swine ' yet!!) The whole show is an amazing blend of things, the plot appearing stronger than I thought possible, the music enchanting and nothing intrudes on anything else. The delightful scenery, colours, period, production, acting—none of you can offer more—and it is up to the public now.

I repeat my impertinence of Saturday night (I know you'll know how sincerely I mean it) that in this, you have jumped and landed with both feet, on a far higher plane than ever—and

> glorious feat—in a new medium. . . . Keep it up old man, it is all perfect and you all are, but above all it is the NEW NOVELLO who'll kick the bastards in the pants—Hooray, hooray and already thousands of thanks for the joy I've had out of it. And I'll give you hell if you don't keep it up.
>
> Barry."

And by the side is a footprint of a dog, done with an inky paw—the signature of " Judy," Barry's beloved beagle. There was no need save sincerity for Barry Jones to applaud. He meant it and he says what he meant. Actually, Ivor had been considering staging Maurice Colbourne's *Charles the King*—and Jones and Colbourne were and are partners—so Barry might not have been so enthusiastic at all for the substitution of *The Happy Hypocrite*. But they never weighed with him. When he saw good work, he applauded. He is always like that and his recent film successes have not altered him an iota. He is like Ivor in that success never goes to his head. He will appear in the witness box of this book in a later chapter, too. The " Dick " to whom he refers is Richard Addinsell, whose music was on the high level of the whole beautiful thing. Alas, that the public did not rally to that string of pearls. It was too soon. To-day there is more sensitivity: poetry has come home. Ivor might have had financial as well as an artistic success.

Maurice Colbourne, Barry Jones's partner, had produced *The Happy Hypocrite* with the perfect touch. I linger on this production to stress how right Barry Jones was; it was the beginning of the more mature Ivor Novello. It was the first time the public had seen Ivor Novello, the charactor actor.

It is worth while to take another glance at *The Dancing Years*. That show was always very near his heart. He wrote it for two women, Mary Ellis and Roma Beaumont, who had toured with him in *Crest of the Wave*, playing the part created by Dorothy Dickson. He composed much of the music whilst playing a Christmas season in Edinburgh with *Crest of the Wave*. Mary Ellis went up to hear it. It was there she first heard " Waltz of My Heart, " one of her big numbers with which she electrified Drury Lane audiences. And on that last, sad night of *The Dancing Years* at the Lane, when Ivor sat at the piano to play the accompaniment for her—such was the situation in the play—instead of doing so he strayed into the song from *Glamorous Night*, his memories getting the better of him. Mary Ellis could not restrain her tears. There she stood, struggling for command of herself. Ivor realized what he had done and swung into the right melody. The chorus saw what had happened and joined in. Mary recovered herself and her voice soared out into that auditorium, singing that song for the last time in the show. . . . That September 1st,1939, was indeed one of bitter memories. But, nevertheless, *The Dancing Years* went on, as has been chronicled, and ran in all for ten years, in town and on tour. When he died, Ivor left the rights in it to his godson, Tom Arnold's boy—and it will go on and on. . . .

But during those years before his troubles came to him, Ivor had had one more sorrow. His beloved Mam had died in February, 1943. Something went out of his life when she passed. He never minded the troubles she caused him: she was Mam and that was that. He was very sad, for indeed she had seemed immortal and so very, very vital. Anything so lively as Clara Novello Davies has rarely been seen by the present generation. She had all that vitality and that urge which was typical of the Victorian Age, about which the young ladies and gentlemen who describe it to-day know nothing. They are obsessed with visions of over-furnished rooms, walls crowded with pictures, heavily curtained windows, lack of fresh air, heavy food, antimacassars and aspidistras. It never occurs to them that the age was one of tremendous urge, of new invention, of sweeping commerce and industrialism, and, consequently, immense energy. All that was in Mam. She looked like a Victorian, she dressed like one. She had the Victorian figure; she was plump and not ashamed of it. She had that enthusiasm which marked the Victorians and Edwardians. The Victorians took the flag and commerce into the unexplored places of the world. And that urge of Mam's which always got her into trouble sprang from the same basic idea. Ivor mourned her deeply. She had her funeral service at Golders Green. Her ashes went into the Garden of Remembrance there to join her husband's. And now the ashes of the man who was their son has joined them too. That united family are united again.

Ivor paid her a last tribute when he wrote and played in a broadcast programme about her not long before he died. It was a very charming programme indeed and typical of him. He gave all the credits to her and there was no sign of the strife. He never mentioned that to anyone. He let the world believe that she had helped him always. He appeared in the programme playing himself and his father.

He would not have approved of much that I have said herein, but my concern is to show the truth and to give him the credit he never dreamed of taking. But Madame Clara Novello Davies was a remarkable woman of remarkable achievements, and her peculiarities do not detract from her deeds. That vital spark of hers she passed on to her beloved son. But he was also beholden to his father for a great deal, including a great amount of that shrewdness which led him to success. His mourning for his mother afterwards had one bright spot: she died before his dark hour came upon him. That was almost the only grain of comfort he derived: that his mother had been spared the suffering. What would have happened to Mam passes belief. He was grateful she was dead. One of the truest things which can be said of Ivor Novello was that he was the ideal son.

In 1943, at Christmas time, in partnership with Tom Arnold, he presented a stage version of *Alice in Wonderland* at the Scala Theatre. The beloved book was dramatized by Clemence Dane, who did a really wonderful job. No liberties were taken, and not one grain of the charm, the wonder, or the supremely human inhumanity was lost. The music of Richard Addinsell was just the music one had always dreamed should go with those verses of Lewis Carroll's. The décor by Gladys Calthrop was level with the book and the music. The characters were those of the Tenniel illustrations in right perspective and hue. The White Knight was superb, the Lion and the Unicorn magnificent, the Gryphon and the Mock Turtle just as one had always known they would be, if they came alive. It was by far the best of all the many stage versions of that classic. Roma Beaumont was the Alice, again right out of the book. Zena Dare was the Red Queen, and there could not have been a better. Sybil Thorndike was the White Queen, with all that lady's vagueness and untidyness. And to see Dame Sybil fly—on wires—as if to the manner born and as if she had been flying in ballets all her life was breathtaking! Anything of the stage is natural to dear Dame Sybil. Crowds flocked to the Scala Theatre to see *Alice* despite bombs and flying-bombs. The first show (it was played twice daily) was at 10.30 a.m. It was always packed out. It was repeated the next Christmas at the Palace for matinées. This time Peggy Cummings was Alice and Margaret Rutherford the

White Queen. And Margaret Rutherford flew too—and enjoyed it. Artistically, *Alice* was as good as *The Happy Hypocrite*, but then the same team had worked on the book and music. To me, who knows both " Alices " by heart, the whole thing was a complete joy. It effaced all the previous versions I had ever seen, except a vision of Ellaline Terriss as Alice and the genius Seymour Hicks's Mad Hatter—that was the zenith of midsummer madness.

And as 1943 merged into 1944, Ivor was still playing in *The Dancing Years*. When he took time off his part was well and truly played by that actor in his own right who always undertook the job, Barry Sinclair. But he was not writing, he was not composing—at least, not seriously. That did not seem right to me. So I will disclose a little bit of backstage diplomacy. Mary Ellis had not been seen in London since the outbreak of the war. I thought this was all wrong. She was sent a play and she liked it. She consulted with me. I knew the play—I had seen it before. It had its points but I did not think it was right. Not but what it could be got right. A distinguished composer, a man of the Theatre, was also interested. He came to see me. The proposition was that I should see if Ivor could be got to do something about it, financially and artistically. I knew that Ivor would not back any shows save those which were his own work, but there was the possibility that he might do some work on the show. And I admit I had another thought at the back of my mind. I reckoned that if Ivor could be made to understand that there was a chance of Mary Ellis doing a big musical play for somebody else, he might be inspired on his own account.

I brought the two men together. Ivor was charm itself. He read the book. He assured the composer that he knew the music would be all right, as he had the highest opinion of that clever man's work (and he had; too; he was, rightly, quite sincere). He explained that he did not enter into theatrical speculations except for his own plays. He also explained that he did not believe it was in anybody's interests for him to work on the book. So they parted with expressions of mutual esteem. But I had watched Ivor. I had taken a chance on this. I did not want to do any harm to my friend, but I did want Ivor to write another musical for Mary, for both their sakes. Nothing came of that introduction, although I made it in good faith and I believe that for some time that man, for whom I have a regard, thought I had put Ivor against the play. I did nothing of the kind, but I do admit I hoped that Ivor would wake up and write for Mary. I banked on it—and I was right. Very shortly after that interview came *Arc de Triomphe*. Ivor wrote that for Mary Ellis, and also to satisfy an urge to try out his operatic music. It was, as stated, one of his ambitions to write an opera and to conduct it himself at Covent Garden. Ivor usually led up to things; he seldom took his fences blindly. There is little doubt that at the back of his mind was an intention eventually to write an opera about Joan of Arc. Here was a chance to try it out. He took the chance.

Arc de Triomphe was a story of an opera singer who fell in love with a young man who played in cabaret and musical comedy. She was a country girl who was discovered by a great teacher of singing. The locale was Paris. She turned out to be a nightingale. She lived in an attic in sight of the Arc de Triomphe. The young man lived in an adjoining attic. There was a charming love scene on the Parisian roofs: Mary Ellis played the girl and Peter Graves the young man. But Ambition interrupted Love. And Ambition had a strong representative in the manager of the Opera, well played indeed by Raymond Lovell. The girl chose the way to Fame. The First War broke out; the young hero departed for the war and was killed. The heroine went on, and eventually gave up singing. But she came back to save the day when the girl who was to sing St. Joan in a new opera lost her voice—or she thought she had. Actually the girl, her close relative, did it to make the prima donna sing again. And the last scene was an excerpt from that Opera of "St. Joan." It was one of Ivor's musical highspots, as well as one of Mary Ellis's triumphs both in acting and singing. She reached superb heights. Peter Graves came into his own in that show and had a delightful number called "Paris Reminds Me of You," which he sang and danced in the real spirit of the period of 1914. The dance routine was set by Cyril Ritchard. Harcourt Williams, that actor of all the graces, played the Music Master. Maidie Andrews and other faithful Novellians were in the cast. Leontine Sagan produced, and Tom Arnold presented. It opened at the Phoenix Theatre on November 9th, 1943, for 222 performances.

Despite the lovely settings, the real Novello music and the perfect playing and singing it cannot be set down as a Novello success. On the face of it, it had all the makings. It had the Novello qualities and it had its share of spectacle. One scene, a fancy dress ball on a barge in the Seine in Paris when war was declared, finished with the male populace of Paris marching to war, accompanied by their female relations and the "Marseillaise," whilst the silent and tragic figure of Mary Ellis stood, her hopes and dreams dashed around her. How William Newman got that big scene on the Phoenix stage is his own secret but great credit is due to him. But there were several reasons why *Arc de Triomphe* was not a Novello triumph. Firstly, for once he made a mistake in his construction. He killed off his hero midway through the play and with him went the love interest, the Romance. The future career of the ageing prima donna and her scheming impressario did not hold the audience, beautifully performed though it was. They wanted the Romance of Novello, that story of hope which he had always given them. But there was no vision at the end, no shadowy reunion of the star-crossed lovers. A vast success for the prima donna, true, but that was not Romance; it was not genuine Novello. Another serious defect—the most serious of all—was that Ivor himself was not in it. That was the real reason why *Arc de Triomphe* did not fill the Phoenix for months and months in a time of boom in the Theatre. They always wanted Ivor in an Ivor play. But he was at the Adelphi in *The Dancing Years*.

He tried to help the show. He put in a scene to carry a special number for which he wrote both the words and music. He gave the number to Mary Ellis. It was not Mary's song, it helped but little. But Ivor loved that little song and he kept it by him. It was his habit to do this. Discarded songs were always cropping up, even those from that first immature musical operetta of his, written in his youth. He used that song again in *King's Rhapsody* and he gave it to Phyllis Dare to sing. That song was "The Mayor of Perpignan," a failure in *Arc de Triomphe* but a smash hit in *King's Rhapsody*. Just as there are horses for courses, theatres for plays, so there are certain shows for certain songs. Nobody remembered that song when it was enthusiastically encored in *King's Rhapsody*—nobody amongst the critics or the public, that is. Those of us who were around Ivor knew. Yet Ivor did make an appearance in *Arc de Triomphe*. One afternoon he sneaked into the Phoenix and walked on in the café scene, to the delight of everyone on the stage but to the complete mystification of those in front. There is another factor which harmed *Arc de Triomphe*, the mention of which is approaching rapidly. . . .

Yet memories of that show endure amongst the Novellians. It was during its preparation that in his dressing-room at the Adelphi Theatre Ivor afforded me with another opportunity of witnessing—with delight—his method of working. The scenic designer brought in a model for a scene. With great pride he laid it before Ivor. Ivor gazed at it and clasped his hands. " It's marvellous," he said. " It's real genius. It's just as one visualized the scene when writing it. Really, it's wonderful. One would not have thought it possible." He sat and gazed raptly at the model, whilst the designer beamed, glowed and shuffled his feet with gratification. Ivor gazed on, his whole face alight with pleasure. Then he turned one of his charm smiles on the designer. " Of course," he said, " I may be wrong, I usually am—but don't you think—it's only a suggestion—perfection could be made more perfect if that door—instead of being there—was there? (he indicated an entirely different position in the scene and hurried on). You see, when I wrote it I knew So-and-so used it as an entrance and had to come down to this table—here—and if the door was where it is and not over there—it might be just a little difficult, don't you think?" . . . The designer could not agree more. Bit by bit, with gentle charm and courtesy and by the merest and most apologetic suggestions, Ivor proceeded to demolish the entire set-up of the scene and indicate the way he wanted it. Everything was agreed to with acclamation, and finally the designer departed the happiest of men, quite convinced he had done the job of his life and was now going to do even better. Which he was. He was a first-class man and models are always altered anyway. That was how Ivor got his wishes carried out. How much nicer and more abiding than the ordinary way. . . . Often, of course, he had altered his mind about the scene whilst the model was being made; he had done so in this case and no fault lay with the designer. But he was made supremely happy in his second effort, and it made Ivor happy to see him happy too.

There was a moment at rehearsal which lives in my mind. Mary Ellis was playing a scene, in which she was saying what amounted to good-bye to her career. She stood at a piano, she struck some chords, and then her hand ran down the scale and came away from the keyboard with a gesture, half despair and half farewell. It was done beautifully. At the next rehearsal she did not do it. I went on the stage and asked why. She looked at me with a smile. " Did you notice that?" she asked. " Nobody else did." " Keep it in, Mary," I replied, " it was a little gem." She kept it in. I don't suppose the audience noticed it, but it was one of those tiny touches which make perfection. . . .

Everything conspired to bring bad luck to *Arc de Triomphe*, which was in many ways a beautiful piece of work with the reservations mentioned above. It struck the flying-bombs, too, which did no good at all to the Theatre. During its run Ivor and Tom Arnold organized Sunday afternoon entertainments for the troops in defiance to the redoubtable champion of the Lord's Day Observance Act, which forbade such things. He had inflicted a severe defeat on me a short time previously when I was a spearhead in the attack to get the Theatre the same freedom as granted to the films—the right to open on Sundays. That right might never have been exercised, but justice at least demanded the right. That effort was beaten in Parliament by a mere handful of votes; I think the majority in the " No " Lobby was eight.

But the shows went on at the Phoenix and the place was packed with men and women in the Services who otherwise might not have spent their time so pleasantly, or so well. On the first occasion the bellringers of the nearby church chose that time for practice. The bells were very audible inside the theatre and did not help matters at all. Ivor was really cross. He was convinced it was done on purpose to annoy him. I could not persuade him to the contrary. He wanted me to go round and have it stopped. I did not do so. I do not suppose for one moment those bellringers even knew we had a show. But nothing would convince Ivor to the contrary. However, it only happened that once.

But although *Arc de Triomphe* was not a financial success, it was so artistically. And in that year (1943) Ivor was indeed on top of the world. He had in his way conquered the war. His plays were filling theatres, he was doing his job. He was well and truly at the apex of popularity. His earnings for the year 1941-2 were £16,249 and he had paid £7,204 in income tax. His earnings for the year 1942-3 were £24,937 and his taxation was £12,292. Indeed, that year was the one in which he earned the biggest money up to that date. The future seemed to shine brightly. *The Dancing Years* was to the Second World War what *Chu Chin Chow* had been to the First. It seemed to be as immortal, too. Ivor would take holidays whilst Barry Sinclair played—nothing altered the business—which was " capacity."

Ivor's fan mail was fantastic, and the crowds at the stage door resembled a football match. It was an incense to him.

But out of that blue sky, out of the crowd of fans, was to come disaster—sudden, shattering and with almost blinding unexpectedness . . . and it was to come through fan worship, one of the things Ivor liked best. . . .

He had not been too well. Not long before he had had an attack of pneumonia. He threw it off after treatment but it left him weak. He kept going by spending his week-ends at " Redroofs," travelling to and fro in his Rolls. Ivor loved that Rolls. It was one of the famous cars in London. Everyone knew that black Rolls-Royce with the red " I.N." on the top of the door panel. It was part of Ivor's life, like the flat, Lloyd Williams, Bobbie Andrews and his friends—and " Redroofs." It was essential to him. Yet, that cherished possession was, in conjunction with fan worship, to be the means of an experience which might well have broken him and brought him, his career and all his work into utter and irreparable ruin. That thunderbolt fell on March 23rd, 1944. But it had been gathering force for some months beforehand, quite unknown to Ivor or to his friends.

Petrol was a vital need for the prosecution of the war. Nobody needs to be reminded of the fact that its use was severely curtailed. From time to time the restrictions would be enforced more rigorously than before. And it so happened that Ivor had been refused a petrol licence for the use of that car of his to take him to and from " Redroofs " at week-ends only. He did not want to go each night. He stayed at 11 Aldwych for the bombs never worried him. But he needed those week-ends of rest in his own home and in the fresh country air. He applied for a licence both in London and at his local office at Caversham. He had been running the car on gas, as did other people, but now the use of private cars was banned. He wanted just a little petrol to enable him to go to and from Littlewick Green, four miles beyond Maidenhead, once a week, so as to keep him fit for what he imagined, from the public demand, was quite important work from the point of view of morale. Had not the troops in the field been given entertainment to that end? Was not Ensa created to provide it? And did not that organization have petrol when it wanted it? But both Caversham and London turned down Ivor Novello's appeal flat, backed though it was by his indifferent health and the full knowledge of the work he was doing. Ivor lost his temper. He said the car was no good to him. He would give it away—to the Red Cross—to anyone!

So far as can be ascertained, the conversation took place in Ivor's dressing-room, admitted to be crowded at the time, on Christmas Eve, 1942. That is probably correct, for his application for the use of the car—then gas driven—had been turned down by the Ministry of War Transport on December 22nd, 1942. He was informed that the Ministry considered the railway facilities adequate for his needs, but that they might be prepared to consider the granting of a limited facility between Maidenhead and Littlewick Green, if Ivor could make out a strong enough case. But Ivor lost his temper.

Sitting in the room at that time was a fan who was in his good graces, and whom he knew as Grace Walton. In his statement later, he said he did not remember when he first met her but that she had been pointed out as repeatedly sitting in the same stall during the run of *Crest of the Wave* at Drury Lane in 1938. and that she used to wait at the stage door to say good night, in which, of course, she was by no means alone. Naturally, Ivor was delighted: the more who did so the better. Miss Walton got to know Minnie Rayner, Ivor's beloved mascot, and would come backstage to see her. Minnie Rayner introduced her to Ivor, and what better introduction was needed than this? It will be remembered that Ivor had risked losing Marie Tempest in one of his shows, had indeed lost her, rather than sacrifice Minnie Rayner. Miss Walton seemed to him intelligent and very interested in the Theatre.

When Ivor went on tour with *Crest of the Wave*, to his considerable astonishment, he saw her sitting in the front row of the stalls, not in one town, but in several towns they visited. They were in Edinburgh at Christmas time and there was a party. Minnie Rayner came naturally and Miss Walton came with her. She said she was now employed by a big commercial concern of which she was private secretary. That firm had branches all over the country and she went to those branches on business; hence her constant appearance at the show.

The Dancing Years was produced at Drury Lane. It was now 1939. Miss Walton was constantly in the stalls, as she had been during the production of *Henry V*, and was in frequent correspondence with Ivor, telling him of all her personal troubles.

During 1940, the early days of the war, Ivor was not much in the Theatre at all, so he saw or heard nothing of her. But when he took *The Dancing Years* on tour again, she began to see him again. There she was, sitting in the stalls, sometimes on successive nights. Such devotion to his play—and himself—would have stormed the barriers of a harder-hearted man. She begged to be allowed to come now and again and talk to him for a few minutes. He consented. She told him of her work for her firm and the big part they were playing in the war effort which necessitated her travelling so much.

By the time Ivor came to the Adelphi with *The Dancing Years* she was a pretty constant caller at the dressing-room. She never stopped long, for nobody was allowed to do that. She was never alone with Ivor: that was an almost impossible thing even on important business. But she was there when Ivor reported the turning down of his car application and his resentfulness over it. Nobody has an absolutely clear remembrance of what words were actually used on that occasion. According to Ivor, Miss Walton asked him if he really meant to give the car away because, if so, she was sure her firm could use it for war work and she would see if she could get it taken over.

Her own version was that she wanted to help him in his deep despondency at not being able to use the car and, finding no way of doing it, suggested that her firm should take it over.

The outcome was the same, except that Ivor denied despondency, but admitted great annoyance, pointing out that the matter was not all that urgent because, by means of a doctor's certificate which his health at that time would have secured without trouble, he could have hired a car to make the journeys.

She made a statement later to the effect that Ivor was constantly pressing her to get the car taken over, so that he could use it as an authorized passenger. That he totally denied. Certainly, to those who were intimates of Ivor, it seemed impossible that he could have entered into a "wangle," for he would not have known how, and he would have been scared out of his wits. But there it is: one word against another.

Eventually the news was brought by Miss Walton to Ivor that her firm would take over the car. Ivor gave instructions for the transfer to be made—insurance, everything. As several people had to be involved in this, it would have been a pretty dangerous wangle and little like the hole-and-corner conspiracy which was later represented in the Courts. He insisted, however, that his chauffeur Morgan, who had been with him then over twenty years, should drive the car and, when told the firm could not afford the salary, said he would pay it himself as he was not going to have a servant like Morgan suffer for war difficulties. The re-registration was carried out by Miss Walton, ostensibly on behalf of her firm and she also accepted the transfer of the insurance, which had been effected and handed over to her by Fred Allen. It all looked quite square and above board.

Now, according to Ivor, when Miss Walton told him that her firm had accepted the car she added: " Now, I have got a nice surprise for you. You know we have a branch at Reading (he did not but was not surprised for he met her all over the country apparently visiting branches) so that any time you like, you can get a lift down to Littlewick." This astounded Ivor: it sounded too good to be true. (It was and one wishes he had gone deeper into the matter then.) He asked if this would be possible on Saturday nights? She replied " Why not? The car can always go to Reading on Monday morning, if required." And now and again that did take place. It was garaged at " Redroofs " on the Sunday and Morgan stood by. Also, it would call on its way back from Reading on Mondays and give him a lift back to Town.

Now it is only fair to state that Miss Walton's statement differed in some details. She swore that Ivor pestered her to get the car transferred—after she had suggested it—and that his insistence made her take the course she took. When she carried the transfer through, by bluffing the Petrol Board into believing that the car was now the property of her firm and would only be used by them on urgent national work, Ivor agreed that the firm could use it on certain days when it was not giving him a lift. As against this, one can comment that this arrangement does not sound very much like Ivor, who could have hired a car and need never have troubled his head. He himself deposes that having transferred the car, as he thought to its new owners, he never gave the matter further thought, except to avail himself of lifts when needed—about two or three times a month during the period of " the transfer." Miss Walton said that Ivor asked her to accept a present for her hard work: " anything in the world she wanted." She said she refused and Ivor then gave her a pair of earrings " the treasured property of his late mother." Ivor's version was that she asked him as a favour for something of his mother's and that he had nothing left (he had distributed his mother's jewellery amongst her friends) except a pair of earrings which he never remembered seeing her wear and which he gave to Miss Walton. In the matter of gifts he thought the position was the other way round: her firm had obtained the use of a good Rolls and all he got was an occasional lift, when he could fit it in.

In his manner he dismissed the thing. He was like that. A thing was done, it was over. He was a pretty busy man too and did not worry about things which he regarded as settled. So the time went on—until October 8th, 1943, when he got a rude shock.

CHAPTER TWENTY-THREE

TRIAL AND ERROR

On October 8th, 1943, Ivor received a telephone call from the Managing Director of the firm whom he believed held his Rolls, asking him to come round: it was important. He went. To his horror, he learnt for the first time that the Managing Director and the firm had known nothing of the transaction at all, and had not been aware of it until just before they sent for him. He learnt also that the lady had been misleading him and that she never held the position she claimed. She had no power to do as she had done, and the firm had no knowledge at all of what had happened. She was a clerk in the firm who also did secretarial work at a place they had in the country. She was known to them as Dora Grace Constable, and it was in that name she was jointly summoned with Ivor. She gave to her employers and to the authorities as her reason for what she had done her complete infatuation for Ivor.

Here was a pretty kettle of fish. Here was this firm involved with a car which they had never used, which had been drawing petrol and with a licence from the Petrol Board obtained by illegal methods. Here was Ivor involved in using his own car under the impression that he had transferred it and was a mere passenger, while, in fact, the petrol had been obtained for no other purpose than to give him those lifts. He was filled with horror . . . and well he might have been! If only he had made inquiries, if only he had not trusted, as he did all too often. If only one of his immediate staff had taken the trouble to try to probe into this extremely coincidental matter! But it had not been done.

He and the Managing Director discussed what should be done. Ivor suggested, and it was agreed to immediately, that the Petrol Board should be informed of what had taken place. This was done by their respective solicitors. But Ivor told none of his friends who could have helped him. The Board began its own inquiries. They were rather prolonged—such Boards are not renowned for speed—even though they administer petrol.

The police began inquiries too, on their behalf. Statements were taken. Ivor worried a bit but not much. His conscience was clear. The woman had admitted that it was sheer, complete infatuation for him which had made her do what she had done, and he could not help that. He had given her no more encouragement than to many, many other fans, indeed, less than many. So after a time he began to let it go from his mind. Those who had bad thoughts of him were those who did not know him or that almost childishly simple mind of his. To those who knew him, Ivor's mind was not one which could bluff a Board always on the look-out for evasions, and do so successfully.

And then came an even ruder awakening.

On the morning of March 24th, 1944, a policeman in plain clothes called at No. 11 Aldwych. He asked, in the polite manner of his kind, for Mr. Ivor Novello, stating that he must see him privately and personally. Ivor was not up. In the ordinary way the visitor would have been asked to call again. But you don't do that to policemen. It would not be much good for they have a wonderful way of seeming immovable and of expressing their fixed determination to come in and see their man—all done without words or gestures and more by implication than expression. This caller got in. He had mentioned the fact that he was a police officer and he appeared very nice, very friendly but quite determined. So Ivor was told and the police officer was shown in. After going through the formality of asking Ivor if he was Ivor, the police officer handed him a document. and this is how it read . . .

No. 1 Court

In the
Metropolitan
Police District

Ivor Novello
11 Aldwych W.C.2.

Information has been laid this day by
The Director of Public Prosecutions
for that you, between the 22nd day of December 1942 and the 11th day of October 1943 within the district aforesaid, did unlawfully conspire with Dora Constable to commit offences against Paragraph 1 of the Motor Vehicles (Restriction of Use) Order 1942 Contrary to Regulations 70, 90 and 92 of the Defence (General) Regulations 1939

Three views which indicate the exquisite taste of Ivor's home in the Aldwych. He leased the flats over the theatre

Top : A corner of the Hall

Centre : Ivor's desk. The blotter has some characteristic "doodles"

Below : The elegant drawing-room and lovely grilled doors

The charm of "Redroofs"

YOU ARE THEREFORE hereby summoned to appear before the Court of Summary Jurisdiction sitting at the Bow Street Police Court on Thursday the 13th day of April 1944 at the hour of 10.30 in the forenoon to answer to the said Information

Dated the 23rd Day of March 1944
(signed) Harold McKenna
one of the Magistrates of the Police Courts of the Metropolis.

Sch. 1—2.
General Form
Indictable and Summary Cases

The receipt of this summons should be acknowledged to the Clerk of the Court forthwith on the tear-off slip on the back hereof. Please sign and return this slip. The correct postage, if the envelope is unsealed, is one penny.

That was a nice start for anyone's day. Anyone would have been shaken, most of all a man living as he did, in a world of his own, more artificial than even the Theatre to which he belonged, in which policemen, summonses and Courts of Summary Jurisdiction, let alone the Public Prosecutor, had no being at all. Ivor was soon in a panic, and when the full purport of his position struck him, when he got an explanation from the courteous police officer, he was in a worse panic still. A prosecution at Bow Street with him in the dock: it was horror! And another thing occurred to him: the awful publicity it was bound to receive. Thoughts coursed across his brain and what he saw ahead terrified him.

It was then he made a fatal mistake and acted like a fool. He suggested to the police officer that this might be kept quiet if made worth while.... The police officer stiffened, shook his head, and took his leave. But that officer gave evidence later in Bow Street as to the execution of the summons and had to mention what had taken place. It did Ivor no good. It was just a foolish, thoughtless, action of a man in a panic, but it did not sound so good in the grim surroundings of Bow Street Police Court.

There was upheaval in the flat. The scene can be imagined. Ivor went to his solicitor. That was very sensible. But he did another foolish thing. He kept very quiet about it. There was, of course, no need to blazon it from the housetops, but he should have told some of those who worked with and for him. He never told Tom Arnold. He never told me. Both of us were men of the world and used to meeting emergencies. True, this sort of thing had never occurred to either of us, but we did at least know how to cope with trouble.

The first I heard of it was by reading a paragraph in the *Daily Telegraph* which had got hold of the story. I rang Ivor at once. By that time he had cooled down. He was inclined to pooh-pooh it all, to play it down. He was perfectly convinced that he had nothing to fear. But he did ask me to keep it out of the newspapers. I told him I would do what I could but there was little hope of that. Had he got a lawyer used to dealing with such things? He said he was perfectly satisfied. Indeed, he seemed fairly happy about the outcome of it all. He had not the slightest fear at that time that there was the remotest possibility of his being found guilty. It never crossed his mind, except as a kind of nightmare hallucination. He knew he was innocent and was sure everyone would find it so.

I was a bit wiser in the ways of the world than Ivor Novello. I got out of him as many of the facts as I could, much stress being placed by him upon the point that he had at once told the Petrol Board. Would a guilty man do such a thing? But it dawned on me that what the authorities might want was a case which would get wide publicity and help to stop the obtaining of petrol by dubious means and in the Black Market, which was rife. There had been some cases and some heavy fines. But put Ivor Novello—No. 1 Box Office, the biggest name in the Theatre—in the dock meant nation-wide publicity; indeed, in times of peace it would have been world-wide. I told Ivor this and it shook him a little. The idea of this publicity was hateful, and very naturally. But he was quite convinced he could prove his innocence with a minimum of trouble: the whole thing was fantastic. I told him the Law was a funny thing—you never knew what might happen. Technical points which laymen overlooked, won or lost cases. The Public Prosecutor was a man who made few mistakes. Not for one moment did I think—any more than I do now—that Ivor had been doing the slightest bit of conspiring, that he was the least bit guilty. I thought he had been very foolish and that he was being foolish now. I told him so. But he did not listen, at that time. Later, when the seriousness of the charge of conspiracy came home to him, he was a bit shaken. When he realized fully that this was not just a charge of getting petrol which he should not have had but of conspiring to break the law made and provided in such cases, he was worried. But he shook it off. He thought that even, if by some technical catch, he was found guilty, it would be a matter of a fine. What he had done, he had done unwittingly. The idea of imprisonment never crossed his mind. His friends rallied. It got round. There were paragraphs. Those hurt him. The legal machinery got into action; there were statements and counter-statements, new statements and longer ones. Counsel was briefed.

Ivor played on and did not say much about it. But he began to look a bit hunted. He began to know fear. Not the fear of guilt, but the fear of that day, so rapidly approaching, when he, Ivor Novello, must stand in the dock at Bow Street—following after some felons, some street walkers, drunks and disorderlies, pickpockets—in that narrow space between iron rails, a gaoler at his elbow and beside the woman who had got him into this mess. It began to haunt him night and day. He could visualize it even if he had never been in the Court, and I do not suppose he had. I never asked him. He knew he would have to stand there like a common criminal and be gaped at. He knew he would be photographed going in and coming out. He knew there would be columns in the Press. " Ivor Novello in the Dock "—" Famous Actor Manager on a Charge of Conspiracy "—for all the world to read. He who had never harboured a hard thought against a soul must be treated like a hardened offender. It haunted him day and night. He looked ill; he was ill at the time for he had not shaken off the results of pneumonia. But he knew the day must come, and the moments between it and him fell away relentlessly. It was enough punishment for a man like him, a creature of illusion, of music and the make-believe of the Theatre, always aloof from squalor and the seamy side now to be plunged up to his neck in both. We did what we could to cheer him, but you could always see it in his eyes, behind the mechanical smile and in the long and sudden silences. It was a terrible thing to see. The man who gave pleasure to multitudes and found his pleasure therein was on the rack because of a woman's infatuation.

April 13th came in due course. I went to Bow Street and waited outside. His band of immediate friends began to arrive.

The photographers came. I knew them all, but it was no use my asking them to go away; they had their job to do, it was their duty. They were not a bit keen on it. They all knew Ivor and they all liked him. They had all taken his photograph and been thanked, on much happier occasions. Said one of them to me, " Sorry, Mac, but we've got to do it. You understand. The only thing which could save Ivor from big space to-day would be if the war suddenly finished, and even then, perhaps not. . . ." I understood. All press photographers call me Mac. About three generations of them have done so. I do not mind. I answer to anything. The usual form is " Popie "; there are a few who call me " Queenie," but that I don't like. I told them that they need not expect him to pose for them. They did not expect it and would not have asked it. There was a rush by them when Miss Constable arrived, but little comment. A little, but not much. I was asked a few questions about her but would not answer. Then Ivor arrived with a handful of friends. . . .

We went upstairs. Tom Arnold joined us. Ivor went to consult his legal defenders. We went into Court.

I had been there many times—as spectator, I hasten to add. At one time I had much to do with the Royal Opera House, Covent Garden, and sometimes in the afternoons I would go over to the Court and hear a case or two. One learns much that way. One learns to marvel at the patience, the knowledge and the rectitude of magistrates. I remember one being given a dreadful time by a woman demanding a maintenance order against her husband. She would not stop talking. She was sure her husband had means, she said, because she had seen him getting into a train at London Bridge Station. This did not impress the gentleman on the Bench but no reasoning could elicit more from her. To her, it seemed enough. He granted the order, at her importuning. He wanted to know her husband's address. " London Bridge Station," she replied. " But surely he does not live there " said the patient Beak. " Do you mean he works there?" " That's where I saw him getting into a train," replied the woman. " I keep telling you. If he can do that, he can pay me." It went on and on. He granted the order and tactful police officials got her out. I have often wondered what happened. . . .

But that morning there was a star attraction. The small public space on the floor of the Court, behind the dock, was packed. Tom Arnold and I managed to get a place of vantage. I did not see upstairs, but it was full.

The Magistrate was dealing with a man of no fixed abode who had been found in possession of some knives and forks belonging to a restaurant. The vagrant had much to say and said it earnestly. The Magistrate listened. He gave the man every chance of stating his case. He asked pertinent questions of witness and police witnesses too. He examined the man and listened to the rambling replies. He showed the greatest consideration and patience. To me it seemed a case of guilt, but he remanded the man for medical examination. . . .

Ivor was the next. His counsel and those in opposition were already in Court. His name, and that of Dora Constable, was called. The charge was made. Police evidence was given. Ivor and Miss Constable pleaded " Not Guilty." I looked at him as he stood upright in that small dock, as far away as possible from the woman with whom he was charged. He was pale under that dark, southern-looking skin of his but he seemed calm to the outward eye. But those of us who knew him knew, also, the signs, the little signs Ivor gave under trying circumstances. But he stood there firmly and answered his charge. The case opened. The police officer mentioned the suggestion of a gift and the Magistrate took a note. The case went on. The Court was full. This was a star performance indeed. Never before had a famous actor-manager, a man whose music was known to everyone, a man whose success was phenomenal, a man who had set armies marching and sent them into battle with his song on their lips, lightening their weariness and their staring at Death by his gift of melody, never before had such a man stood there. This hardly seemed real. It seemed like a scene in a play; but it was real enough; that Court with its Royal Arms, its faded light, its general air of the stuffy, acrid squalor of crime was real enough. So was the man on the Bench, so used to the underworld, so used to all sorts of tales, all sorts of wrong-doings. He had not looked at Ivor when he came in, he was writing, but he looked at him when he pleaded " Not Guilty." It was the impassive, incorruptible look of a man who deals in Justice and lets nothing sway him.

The case went on. Evidence was called. Various witnesses gave their stories; there was examination and cross-examination. The Magistrate would join in. Miss Constable elected not to give evidence. Ivor was called. He went into the box and took the oath. He gave his evidence. I have seen many cases. I have been witness in many myself. I have seldom, if ever, seen a worse witness than Ivor Novello proved himself that day. He was an actor by profession and he never gave a worse performance. He was not so bad, naturally, when answering his own K.C. But when cross-examination began, he was really terrible. He was in a panic. He kept turning to his own counsel as if for help. Every answer he gave was muddled. One felt cold and sweaty with fear. The reporters from the news agencies were scribbling and sending away their flimsies. One or two newspaper people in Court were impassive as usual. Ivor was doing himself no good. He was doing himself every possible harm. He was creating an impression that he was trying to shelter himself behind the woman. That was not his idea, but he was hemmed in. The questions gave him little chance. It began to look black for him. Evidence which would have made everything plain could not be elicited because it was held to be irrelevant to the case. All that could be done was done. It seemed to me that Ivor prosecuted himself. He looked like being "for it"—a very large fine indeed.

I had begged him to plead "Guilty"—guilty through inadvertance. To plead that he had broken the law, but unintentionally. But he had done it and now realized it. Therefore guilty without intent—and ask for the consideration of the Court. I had not mentioned this to his legal advisers. I had not been asked. Indeed, why should I be? But I had suggested it to him. He would have none of it. He must be cleared entirely. Well, it did not look like it now. I was sure mine would have been the better way as I am sure of it still. One could feel—see—the sympathy going from him as he floundered and made his case seem worse. At last his ordeal was over. It was stated on his behalf, all that he had done for the war effort—his entertainment of the troops, his unblemished reputation, his high standing. . . .

The Magistrate said he had no doubt at all about that. He proceeded to sum up, briefly, very briefly, and to give judgment. He dismissed Miss Constable with a fine of £50. He sentenced Ivor Novello to two months' imprisonment. . . . Ivor's counsel gave immediate notice of appeal which was granted. So was bail, in Ivor's own recognizances. It was over. . . .

I hardly dared look at Ivor. He was turned to a stone. His friends took him away. I devoted myself to the newspaper people, to do what I could.

As I had expected, the newspaper reports were bad. They made it look as if he had tried to shift all the onus on to the woman. They were read eagerly—evenings and mornings—all over the country. Letters began to pour in to Ivor—thousands of them, and the overwhelming majority protested their belief in his innocence. But there were those—he never saw them, care was taken on that score—which jeered, which called him names (all anonymous, of course) and which threatened reprisals in the way of breaking up his show.

To say Ivor was stunned is to understate. He seemed not to be alive, to be in a trance. His nearest and dearest did all they could. His legal advisers railed against the sentence: a miscarriage of justice, they protested. Ah, if only certain evidence had been permitted, if only certain facts had been elicited, how different it might have been. My own feeling in advising him to plead guilty was that, if technicality had come into it and been persisted in, he might have got one day's imprisonment (which meant the duration of the hearing) and have left the Court a free man. There would have been a black mark in official records, but nowhere else. But he would not see it. Now. . . .

His friends were wonderful, Sir Edward Marsh, Lloyd Williams, Fred Allen, Bobbie Andrews, Peter Graves, Olive Gilbert—all the Novellians—tried to bring sunshine to him. They were as staggered as he was. Tom Arnold, his manager and partner, had stood by in the Court and stood by loyally all the time. Sir Edward Marsh never ceased his efforts. Ivor had his firm unswerving friends who believed in him and would fight on. There was the Appeal. That would pay for all.

I won one thing and it was a great victory, too. I got him to come back right away and play in the show. " The guilty man hides, Ivor," I said, " the innocent man carries on." He did it. What it must have cost him to face an audience with his sentence hanging over him, to face the mass of humanity with a feeling in his heart that amongst them—how many nobody knew—were people who held him a convicted criminal who had resorted to conspiracy to have the luxury of his Rolls whilst they fought for trains and buses or walked through the blitzed streets. I know what it cost him. I know the agony of mind.

But it says much for him that he did it. It was, of course, David Ivor Davies, from gallant little Wales, who came again to the rescue of Ivor Novello. He played in *The Dancing Years* and his company hid their tears and played up grandly. And the applause came as warmly and loudly as ever. That cheered him.

But his agony had begun. He suffered much later; but he suffered most, I believe, during that dreadful period of waiting, waiting for his appeal. Suspense is the worst of all mental stress: it breaks more hearts than sorrows, causes more defeats than armed force. One has to be strong, or dull and unimaginative, to stand it. To Ivor with his vivid imagination, it was a time of pure hell. He had seen the prison door gape, he had seen dishonour, disgrace—unmerited but threatened—more than threatened—almost engulf him. Now he had another chance. This was mere respite. All around him assured him that things would be all right. But he was low and despondent. He seemed to lose hope. He seemed to lose faith in almost everything. At times he would rally and would appear gay, talk and laugh. But he never laughed with his eyes, or with his mind. That mind was always searching, questioning, wondering, doubting: the eyes were always trying to pierce the secrets of to-morrow. He slept badly—and at times one began to fear for his reason.

It was the grimness of punishment unmerited that hurt him, the stupidity of it all. His mind seemed dead and the creative urge seemed crushed. But behind him stood David Ivor Davies determined to see it through, determined not to be beaten, not to be crushed, keeping up a semblance of hope and courage against fearful odds. Ivor had imagined that by his work, by his shows and music, he was helping the national effort. He had given time and talent freely and largely. He had done all a man could do. And now, for something of which he deemed himself perfectly innocent, he was to be crushed. The iron heel of the Law was to stamp his Art out of existence. Why try? Why fight on? It was over—and then a gleam of hope would come. Surely, surely, somebody would see sense. Surely proper councils would prevail, surely Life could not be so cruel. He had paid so much into the Bank of Good Fellowship and Humanity and had drawn so little out—surely this moderate draft would not be dishonoured? He thought of other cases of similar prosecutions. He thought of all sorts of things which had not been said but for which there was yet time. They now knew the worst the other side could do. They were doubly armed for the new fight. He had his moments of hope, he who did so deeply believe in hope and always preached it in his songs and plays. . . .

Meanwhile much was being done. There were conferences with Counsel, there were conferences with friends. New witnesses were brought in, people of the highest repute and standing, in and out of his own profession, who would gladly go into the witness box, speak of his upright and honest character of their own sure knowledge, testify as to the impossibility of his having done this thing. Answers were prepared to points made by the prosecutors and new questions and points framed and made. There were amongst Ivor's friends not one who doubted him, not one who was not confident in his ultimate victory.

It had been stated in Court that if the facts of the case had been as Ivor protested he believed them to be at the time the offence was committed, then no breach of the law had taken place. He could have ridden in his car, he could have had his lifts with legality. But, alas, such had not been the case; the licence had been got by falsehood. What he had to prove was that he had no hand in that. He had, of course, no actual and visible sign of proof. He had his word, the word of his supporters that they believed as he believed: that should be enough. But the charge was Conspiracy. He had to make it clear that at no time had he ever been aware of irregularity. That was the difficulty. It was a case of word against word, unsupported otherwise. Still, there was plenty to fight with, plenty to hope for. There was the fact of the immediate report, on discovery, to the Petrol Board.

And the time of the appeal grew nearer and nearer.

April had turned into May—a favourite month of Ivor's—but not this May. As the time approached, Ivor's state of mind gave his friends considerable anxiety. It was not that there were any violent scenes, any ragings or railings against fate, but he seemed to lose grip. That terrible anticipation of an ordeal so repugnant, and, beyond that, the ever-present dread of what might happen. His eyes were opened wide now: it was possible for people to think him guilty. Consciousness of his innocence only made matters worse. He was in that serpentine grip of the Law, that tenacious octopus with so many tentacles, whose suckers hold so fast. That grip is made secure not only by the large salient facts but by the little trifles so hard to explain, so easy to escape notice, except from the hawk-like eyes of legal men. He knew now that no concern was paid to temperaments, to gifts, to conditions of life and habits, or even to intentions, let alone impulses. No allowances were made for lack of foresight, for a state of mind which was trusting and tender-hearted, which people took at their own valuation, which looked only for good and did not seek evil, which did not suspect ulterior motives.

Here was a man used to homage, used to adoration by fans, accepting it was something quite usual, grateful for it, but at the same time not at all surprised by it. It was not conceit which made Ivor take such infatuation, as that displayed by the woman in this case, in his stride. It was quite the usual thing. He lived in a world of his own of which he was the axis. If he wanted a thing, and expressed the desire for it, well, there it was. It may be remembered that earlier in this book I drew a pen picture of an occasion when there were no eggs for tea. It was all like that. He had wanted his car, which he loved. He had never completely grown up (he was like his mother there) and this car was his favourite toy, and it was taken away. Like a child he rebelled. The infatuated woman stepped in, and he accepted the thing as naturally as a king—in the days when kings ruled and did not merely reign—accepted tribute. It was not his habit to look below the surface. He wanted a thing: it was there; that was good enough for him. The pity is that, like a child, he would have got over his disappointment quite soon and been happy with something else. He was easily thrown into the depths as lifted to the heights. When he had to leave Drury Lane his spirits dropped to the nadir. Life could never be the same again. Yet, when he filled the Adelphi with success, he was just as happy there. And he told me, not long before he died, how he " adored " the Palace Theatre. " It's just my cup of tea," he said, " just the right size. One does not have the overwhelming expense of a large stage, one does not have to sacrifice intimacy to big effects. I hope I stop here always. I think I like it better than the Lane." Well, it was his last theatre. He will never play elsewhere.

But as the day drew on which was to decide his immediate fate—freedom against imprisonment—he got more and more into himself. It was quite apparent that serious harm had been done. This man might never create again, this man's well of inspiration might be so defiled and choked that it would never flow any more. A Tragedy was in the air. Already, voices were being raised against what was considered the harshness of the Police Court sentence. Already people were saying that it was unjust. Even if he had done as the Law believed, he had done no more than many others—very many others—some of whom had never been caught, and some who had been laid by the heels, had merely been fined. The public, by and large, paid no attention to the charge of conspiracy. To them Ivor Novello was a man who had wangled a little petrol to ride in his own car occasionally, backwards and forwards to his own house in the course of his employment. Most of them who had cars had wangled some petrol. They felt deep sympathy. And, it must be remembered, those amongst his friends best qualified for the job had been very busy, if unobtrusively busy, in working on public opinion through the most useful channels.

Directly after his sentence, business at *The Dancing Years* had fallen off. But it began to pick up. There was an evergrowing portion of the community who considered that justice had overdone it. They shared this view with his own legal advisers.

New points had been discussed at conferences, and Fred Allen, then an Official of Civil Service (Ministry of Agriculture and Fisheries), was to go into the box, by permission of his Ministry, and give his evidence about Ivor, and tell of vital matters concerning car insurance and payment of certain bills, which should dispose of the question of conspiracy and any sort of collusion. Sir Edward Marsh, Sir Lewis Casson, Dame Sybil Thorndike were to be called, and a whole army of stars of the Theatre were in readiness as volunteers, if required. Confidence in the vindication of Ivor grew and grew. But he responded little, although he hoped. He was still stunned. That he should be considered guilty took his reason away from him. Meanwhile everything which could be done was done.

The appeal was heard at the London Sessions, Newington Butts, on Tuesday, May 16th, 1944. By a strange coincidence that building stands almost on the site of an old Elizabethan theatre. The site is not absolutely established, but it was thereabouts. But the theatre, to which Londoners thronged in the days of Thomas Kyd, Christopher Marlowe and Shakespeare, never showed a play with the same dramatic value.

I went over early. I met the photographers and the pressmen. I talked to them. I did what I could. The friends of Ivor arrived. The Court was going to be packed, for the public arrived too. It was obviously going to be a case of " House Full " and many being turned away. There was no chance of a reserved seat but I knew I was all right for the Press Box. At the finish Tom Arnold took my place therein and I entered with Ivor's K.C., who very kindly found an official who got me a good seat. Not that I wanted to be there at all, but it was Duty.

The London Session House is a very much larger court than that at Bow Street. It is lighter, brighter and much more airy. It was packed from ceiling to floor. There was a large muster of magistrates on the Bench in support of the gentleman who was to hear the case. Counsel this time wore wigs and gowns, not worn in a police court. The Majesty of the Law was now fully apparent. The atmosphere was tense, even electrical. But it was shocking to be there: to see a man whom one knew and for whom one had affection, on the rack in such a cause. There have been many days in my life I would rather have not lived, and that was one of them. One felt so angrily desirous of helping, yet impotent to do so. . . .

The case was called. Ivor this time sat at the solicitors' table. He was under appeal, so not in the dock. This time he faced the Court alone. The Law had dealt with his so-called "fellow-conspirator." She had gone free, on payment of £50. He was fighting for his future, and those of us who knew him understood that he was fighting for his reason and his life as well. My prayer was that he might retrieve his previous failure in the witness box. He wore rather light, summery attire. He looked exactly what he was, a shining light of the Theatre Profession. I glanced at the Justices. There was a large sprinkling of women. Those who have been in courts where Justices of the Peace sit, will known what I mean. My spirits sank.

The case started. The opening statements were made. The evidence began. Ivor went into the box. His rehearsal had not done him much good. He was not quite so bad as before but he was not a good witness at all. He was right on the cue in answer to his own Counsel but he was not easy or confident under the quiet, deadly questioning of the opposition. Ivor was always better at asking questions than answering them. He never had the gift of quick expression in few words; he always elaborated. His brain was not calm. Had he been cross-questioned on his own profession nobody could have shaken him. But here he was frightened; he was a rat in a corner, surrounded by dogs, looking all ways for escape, never perceiving it. He never grasped what was behind certain questions and fell into traps. When re-examined by his own Counsel afterwards, he did something to retrieve himself, but it was too late.

The other witnesses were called. Dame Sybil gave her statement with shining enthusiasm and answered her questions like the wonderful woman she is and one felt she carried the crowd with her. Sir Lewis Casson was firm, unshakable and clear, a perfect piece of integrity. His fine voice was a pleasure to hear, and he got the one laugh of the day. He was asked if he agreed with the evidence given by his wife and replied " Certainly." " I suppose you always agree with your wife?" queried Counsel. Sir Lewis paused and smiled. " Well, no, not always, nor of necessity," he answered. It was a human touch in inhuman surroundings. Fred Allen gave his evidence with the clear-cut knowledge of fact peculiar to the business mind. He was suffering great pain and was asked if he would like to give his evidence seated but he elected to stand. He was at this time under doctor's orders and there had been some doubt as to whether he could stand not only the ordeal but the journey. His wife was with him. But Fred would have come to that Court, or anywhere else, on a stretcher to have defended Ivor.

The Court adjourned for lunch. There was a buzz of excitement, comment. Hopes, fears, what you will. Nobody was sure yet, but there seemed hope. I did not go with the Ivor contingent. I went off with members of the Press. We adjourned to a pub where we had quite wonderful sandwiches, considering it was war-time, and where we talked and talked. I laid seeds useful for whichever way the case went. I will freely admit it: I had not much hope. I did not like the look of that Bench. I knew that Ivor was innocent of what he was charged with, but I knew Life as well.

The Court reassembled. The Bench filed in and the public stood. Then there was the usual bowing and the shuffle of reseating . . . and the tense moments of waiting began. . . .

Ivor was now standing in the dock. He had to receive the judgment. . . .

Why prolong the agony we passed through then? The verdict

was quickly given. He was not acquitted, but his sentence was halved. He must go from that place to prison for one month. There was a gasp, a rustle. There was a flicker of handkerchiefs. There were tears. . . .

Ivor stood like a statue. A gaoler touched him on the shoulder and turned him round. He pointed to a door at the top of some stairs beside which stood another man in blue. Ivor gazed round that Court like a man looking his last on life. Reason, movement, seemed to have deserted him. But, under the gentle, almost kindly, urge of that gaoler, he left the dock. He climbed the stairs with his head bowed down—one's mind flew to Sidney Carton—he reached the top, and the other gaoler indicated the open door, which led to obliteration. Then Ivor stopped. He stood for a moment. Then he turned, and faced that crowded court. He flung wide his arms in a gesture—it seemed of renunciation, of appeal, of farewell, of despair—who knows? It was pure Theatre—but then, of course, it was Ivor. For one moment, for one second, it seemed he might speak. There was a slight movement from the gaoler by the door, a step forward from the one who followed, and Ivor's arms dropped. He turned his head sunk low, his hands clasped before him and he passed through the door, which closed behind him. . . .

His closest friends were allowed to go down to where he was waiting to be taken to gaol, to say good-bye to him. It was a terrible quarter of an hour. What is one to say? What is one to do? There is a ghastly feeling of being completely powerless, of being shackled in thought and speech. The few people around him were those who shared his life and his happiness—at the flat, at "Redroofs," in the Theatre. But what to say? What to do? He sat at a table, staring into nothing. There was no expression on that face, it was a ghastly drawn mask. All the boyish charm which was so much of him had vanished. This was a stricken, middle-aged man. He was fifty-one, and this had come upon him. His eyes were quite blank and staring into a void. He did not move. One by one we spoke to him—those who could do so. I put my arm round his shoulders. "Ivor," I said, "this is nothing. This is one of those pieces of misfortune which fall upon us all. Keep your head up and your chin up. It will pass, and you will be the better and the stronger. Stick it out, old man. I know it's easy to talk but I am speaking the truth. You will be better afterwards, and everyone believes in you! The world will be with you. Remember that. We shall be working for you and your welcome will surprise you. Good luck, and remember: it will be all right." I pressed his shoulder and there was a slight movement of response.

I hurried away. There was nothing more we could do there. Our work lay outside. I walked with Tom Arnold and Bill Newman to a bus stop, and then found a taxi. We did not say much. We did not want to discuss what we had just seen. My memories are that we talked about the extreme shortage of food, which was the main topic at the time. We did also wonder how this would affect business—we should not have been human otherwise—or theatrical—and we were all dyed-in-the-wool members of our profession. We came to the conclusion that it would kill *Arc de Triomphe*. It did. But *The Dancing Years* survived. It was one of the most painful scenes through which I have ever passed. I never want to take part in such another. The worst of all was that terrible feeling of impotence. One knew that what had happened was morally unjust—in every sense—even if the vice-like inhumanity of the Law was justified in its own view. It is not for me to impugn British Justice, which is the finest and most shining and withal the most merciful Justice in the world. But all of us felt that it had been human this time—and erred. We were not concerned with the strict letter of the Law which can apparently prove as many things as figures can in the hands of a skilful accountant.

We took up our lives again and worked on. It was all we could do. If we could not give Ivor freedom, we could at least pave the way for his return to it and bring him back in triumph.

Bad as that moment of parting was, there is never a thing so dark but that some gleam brightens it. Unconsciously maybe, but to be remembered afterwards with a smile. On this occasion a gaoler provided it. He was standing in charge of Ivor and keeping well away, showing feeling and tact. What he did—what he said—was the best thing he could think of. He knew all about Ivor, of course. It is quite possible he was a fan of his and went to his plays. He looked on in a kindly manner. He saw how upset everyone was. He selected Lady Juliet Duff, that charming woman who was one of Ivor's oldest, closest and dearest friends. It was to her he spoke as she left, showing her emotion . . . " I shouldn't worry too much, Mum, if I was you," he said, " it'll be a nice quiet 'oliday for 'im . . ."

CHAPTER TWENTY-FOUR

INTO THE DEPTHS

IVOR NOVELLO was driven in a black Humber police car from the Assize Court to Wormwood Scrubs Prison to serve his sentence. He had passed within sight of that prison many a time when travelling to and from Maidenhead by train. The car entered the massive wooden gates, slowly swung open for it by a warder, who had also unlocked the two immense iron gates which form a sort of courtyard between them—and a triple defence against escape. The car entered, the gates clanged to and Ivor was a prisoner. Those gates shut him off from the world he knew and loved and placed him face to face with another world, a world then beyond his comprehension, an incredible world, full of bitter anguish and suffering. Then he was driven away to the Reception Office, through which all new prisoners must pass.

What he had thought of on the way down nobody knows. What fragments of impressions went through his reeling brain must be his own secret. He probably never knew himself. The car stopped at the Reception Office, where he was told to get out. He found himself facing two men: the Deputy Governor and the prison Chaplain—the Padre—the Reverend Meredith Davies. Ivor did not know it but that Padre—a true Christian in the real sense of the word—and a good Samaritan who did not pass by on the other side—was to be his guardian angel and saviour in the time of his direst need. It was their first meeting and at that moment it meant nothing at all to Ivor. But, by all the luck in the world, that Padre was a brother Welshman.

He was asked the usual questions, registered, and his clothes were taken from him. He had then to put on the prison garb: a suit of ill-fitting grey cloth, a coarse white shirt with a lay-down collar, and loose, by no means well-fitting, shoes. On the shoulder is a red patch—the badge of a prisoner. One thing, they are no longer numbers, they retain their names. But imagine these clothes on Ivor, always so elegant, so debonair, so carelessly immaculate. He had to take the disinfected bath,

First draft, notes and alterations of a number called "I Can Give You the Starlight"

There is a tragic interest in this picture. It was the last ever taken of Ivor. The snapshot was taken by Lady Juliet Duff at " Redroofs " (seen above) less than 24 hours before Ivor died

and was then taken to his cell and given a mug of cocoa, which he did not drink. He was still stunned. Maybe realization in all its grim detail had not come yet.

Ivor's cell was No. 242, " B " Hall. He was put inside and the heavy iron door clanged to. He was alone, a prisoner in real earnest.

The halls—so called—in Wormwood Scrubs are long buildings of immense strength, with three tiers of platforms running along each side. An iron staircase climbs up from the floor. The platforms, or corridors, naturally face each other and are fenced in with iron bars and netting where they overlook the well of the hall. Door after door of the cells seem to stretch along in an immense vista. Ivor's cell was on the second tier.

But the walls in the Scrubs are not grey or drab. They are painted, the lower part is green, up to a white dado, and then above that they are yellow. The colours are crude and harsh and show the brick beneath, but at least there is colour.

The cells are the same. They are narrow and not very long. There is a pallet bed on the floor with a rough mattress and pillow, two sheets and coarse, heavy blankets like rugs. There are two small tables, one bearing washing utensils, and one for the eating of meals or carrying what small articles or possessions the prisoner may be allowed in his cell, a book from the library, for example. High up and out of reach, at the end farther from the door, is a small, semi-circular window, heavily glazed and barred which lets in the light. The artificial light is out of reach too, controlled from outside. Each prisoner has a large, heavy earthenware mug, holding a pint, an enamel bowl and plate, a tin knife, a fork and spoon and a tin can for vegetables, etc. That is the entire outfit. And the inmate of the cell can be and often is under complete supervision. In each door is a small circular hole, about the size of a five-shilling piece, glazed with thick glass and covered on the outside with a circular piece of metal fastened by a nail or staple, so that at any moment, the warder can push it aside and look in. He can see every inch of the cell through that hole. There is no privacy.

It was eight at night when Ivor entered the prison. He went straight to his cell after the usual routine and there he stayed until roused, as are all prisoners, at 6.30 the next morning.

What he did that night nobody knows either. Imagine this

man, used to every luxury, to silk pyjamas, the finest bedclothes and eiderdowns, to sleeping in a bed that Le Roi Soleil might have envied, surrounded by everything for which the heart could desire, able to satisfy every whim, whose mere wish was a command often anticipated by eager, loyal servants, imagine this man now plunged into the surroundings described, and all around him hundreds and hundreds of men branded as criminals by the law, amongst whom he was now counted. To most of them such a place as that in which they now found themselves meant nothing Many were old lags, many found the conditions better than those in which they lived outside. They are certainly clean and healthy, weather and windproof. But to Ivor. . . .

I am not trying to excuse or extenuate. I am not for one moment suggesting that there should be one prison for the rich and another for the poor. They must all be treated alike in the great democracy of crime. The wrongdoer must suffer, and suffer he does. But Ivor's greatest and only fault had been folly; a seeming guilt which was not real guilt at all, a carelessness induced by overtrustfulness on the part of one who never looked for wrong in anyone because he thought no wrong himself. But the Law had not believed him, and a harsh sentence had brought him to this place where his sufferings must be—and were—far, far deeper than those of the hardened habitual criminal serving a five years' sentence. He had a month, a month only, true, but a prison sentence does not depend upon its length for its punitive power but upon what it inflicts upon the person serving it. To Ivor that month was eternity.

At 6.30 he was roused and given his breakfast, but he did not eat it. He had to clean out his own cell and then go to the yard for exercise. The yard is a large one, partly paved, partly gravel, with buildings and walls all around it. At one end is a line of lavatories, wide open to view. Nowadays the prisoners do not walk round and round in circles, so many feet apart. They can walk how they like and they can talk. Not that Ivor wanted to do much talking. He was stared at, of course, as a newcomer, and without doubt many knew him. But they left him alone, they did not pester him. In the end they held him in respect.

He had no work assigned to him that morning, for he had to go before the Board again, for interrogation. And at 9.30 he was in the Reception Hall. His name was called and he shuffled

EXIT

forwards in his shapeless prison shoes, his head down in despair and sorrow. The same two men sat before him, the Deputy Governor and the Chaplain. He was asked his name and replied. The next question was "Occupation." Ivor answered "Actor-Manager." That was the Chaplain's chance, "Isn't that lucky now?" he said brightly, and Ivor heard the tones of Wales, "this is the very chap for us. He can give us some advice and help about that stage we are building . . ." Ostensibly he spoke to the Deputy Governor but in reality he spoke to Ivor. At the mention of the word "stage," he saw a little gleam of light come into Ivor's face and the eyes raise themselves and show just a flicker of life. It was as if a ray of sun had entered the room, something from outside. It seemed incredible to Ivor that there could be a stage in here. Something he thought he had lost for ever seemed to lean forward and touch him. It pulled him together. When asked if he would like to help, he replied quite eagerly that indeed he would. That little occurrence, so carefully timed, that little stroke of genius, of real Christianity on the part of the Padre, maybe turned the scale of the whole thing for Ivor. It was a straw for a drowning man to clutch, a particle saved from something which seemed to be utter ruin. It brought him round: it was the first time he showed any sign of awareness. And he did give advice about that stage, although he never trod it. He gave expert advice and that stage, a good and workable one, is now a treasured possession of the prisoners. It was built as he advised and it remains a monument to him. There is a projection box and a screen in that theatre, too. And the prisoners have their own orchestra which plays there. When, sometimes, a company does come from outside and gives them a show, the players little know how much good they are doing, or more and more would go and render such service.

The theatrical profession always gives its help nobly for deserving causes. It went all over the world to entertain soldiers; it goes to hospitals to cheer the men wounded on the field of battle. There is fine work for it here amongst the casualties on the battlefield of Life: men wounded by faults and by crime and for whom the only cure is an understanding of humanity. The more of that they can be got to understand, the more they can be made to feel that they are not outcasts and moral lepers, the better hope of their recovery. That is why prison treatment grows more humane every year. There are some, of course, beyond cure, just as there are those who are mortally wounded. But these touches of brightness, these glimpses of outside, of the life lived by those who have freedom, mean more than is realized by most people. And those who go to this prison will be playing on a stage which one of their own great ones once helped to make when he, too, was in the depths, and found therein a step to salvation.

He was put to work in the library. The Deputy Governor, wise in the judgment of men, knew it was useless to give him heavy labour. So to the library he went, to help there, to work on mending torn books, repairing broken backs and things like that. A mere glimpse of his hands showed labour to be out of the question, even if they had not known who he was.

In the library the Padre visited him and asked him how he was getting on. Ivor was despondent: he feared he could do little, he said, he was not used to it and had never used his hands that way. The Padre knew that what to an ordinary man was a light, easy task, was to Ivor a real labour. But he knew what to do. He smiled at Ivor. " Now look," he said, " here is a useful job that you can do. In here many are almost illiterate. Those who can read often don't understand what they are reading about. But they all like looking at pictures. We will put you on to making scrap books for them. I will see you get the illustrated papers, *Picture Post* and the like. Then you can cut out the pictures and paste them in books. They will like looking at them. And you will like doing a useful job like that, won't you now?" Again a Christian thought of great understanding. Prison padres, and this one in particular, are wonderful men, all too seldom recognized and all too seldom recompensed. Not that they look for either recognition or reward. They just do their job.

Ivor worked industriously on his scrap books. He did not want to think and the work enabled him for a time at least, to concentrate on it. It was not quite so monotonous as some jobs; it gave him a little scope, a little choice for display of selection and taste. It probably saved his reason. For there were times in that seemingly eternal month when that was feared for and it seemed to tremble in the balance.

For some time he hardly touched his food, so coarse, rough and ready and so far removed from that to which he had been accustomed. All he ate and drank were bread and tea and sometimes a little porridge. Ivor was never a big eater, but he liked good food, well served and cooked to perfection.

His day was made up as follows. Rise at 6.30, clean out the cell, then breakfast at seven. Then exercise and work at 8.30. Break for dinner (lunch time) and work again until 4.30. Then locked in his cell until 6.30 the next morning. That long, solitary time in the cell was the hardest thing for him to bear. The break for lunch was at noon. On Saturdays they were put in their cells at the latest at 4.30. They did not come out, except for chapel, until 6.30 on Monday morning. And that was what nearly broke Ivor for ever.

He got through his first week somehow, although he had terrible fits of depression. The Padre would visit him and do his best to cheer him. But one night there was a collapse. On being put in his cell, Ivor found they had left a mail bag for him to sew. He could not do it. He broke down; it seemed the last straw. The Padre was fetched. He told Ivor not to worry. That would be altered. He must do what he called " home work," and it would break the monotony, but it could be arranged that he could work on his scrap books. Obviously not only he but the mail bags would suffer if he tried them. That was all a mistake. By degrees he got Ivor calm. And he did it by mentioning choir practice. Would Ivor like to help at that? It was right up his street, wasn't it? And he could be very useful. Ivor rallied to that—here was a chance to touch music. He agreed eagerly.

He not only went to choir practice, but he was soon conducting the choir, training them, getting wonderful results. He made a suggestion. Why should not the choir face the congregation when they sang, instead of doing so with their backs to it, as heretofore? It would help them and it would help the audience. He got his way. And it was a vast improvement all round. He taught them anthems, too, and they sang them well. He went to chapel every Sunday morning and afternoon service and played the piano at the services. He sometimes recited Shakespeare to the inmates as well.

Those things did much to keep him sane. The chapel was his refuge. It is a large place, although called the chapel, being as spacious as a small cathedral and seating over 1,000 people. It has a lovely altar and chancel, with murals painted mainly by prisoners and well painted, too. The altar cloth was given by Her Majesty the Queen and is a beautiful and costly thing. It glows like a jewel. At the opposite end is a large gallery and the organ.

Directly after Ivor's release he sent some of his company down to the prison to give the inmates a show. Olive Gilbert recalls with emotional pride how she sang Handel in that church, and how the audience applauded.

But Ivor had one great crisis. It was on the second Saturday night. The Deputy Governor told the Padre he had better go over to Cell No. 242. He hurried there and Ivor had collapsed. He was lying on the floor, crying bitterly and moaning. He was practically at the end of his tether. The stunned period had gone, thought had returned, he had been weighing things up. He saw no future. He saw only complete oblivion ahead, the end of his plans, of his creative life. The Padre sat on the floor by him, comforting and reasoning. Ivor told him it was the end. There was nothing left for him. If he got out sane, he must leave the Theatre, leave the stage and go into retirement. He said he had £100,000, therefore he would not want; but that was not what mattered. It was the end of a career which he had made himself, of which he was so proud, of the ambitions he cherished. All was gone—gone. Ivor Novello was finished. . . .

Gently and with infinite tact the Padre talked to him, reasoned with him, encouraged, praised, began to break the chains of despair which bound him. Time passed, but still they sat on and by degrees the Padre got him calm and more reasonable. He told him he had done so well, he deserved a little reward (and he managed to get Ivor the *Sunday Times* for him to read on Sundays, the crossword helping a lot, too). He told him the Governor was very pleased with him: he had not gone sick, he had not applied to go into the Infirmary, he had done his work, he had helped them in many ways, and he had never given the slightest trouble or asked for a vestige of favour. He gave Ivor courage, and he gave him back hope. It was a scene fraught with real drama, that talk between those two men in that grim cell in those even grimmer surroundings—the one, a brilliant, perhaps the most brilliant, figure of the British stage, fighting for his reason, the other, a man used to despair and to the tragedies of life but always keeping a high heart and a God-sent ability to impart his courage to others. And by the time Sunday chapel came Ivor was almost himself. The storm had passed. The Padre got him some music paper for his cell, should he want to compose, the Governor permitting it for health reasons.

Ivor did not use that music paper to compose. But he wrote, and he wrote something in prose comparable to " The Ballad of Reading Gaol." He put his thoughts down on paper as they crossed his mind. It is rather a terrible document in the insight it gives to his suffering, but to understand what that sentence did to him, it is as well that all who would, should read it. Here it is:

" I forget when I wrote last, it must be some day sago. Anyhow, it's Sunday evening, the 28th May. I think with all its beauty I shall always hate the month of May. Until the last two days I've not been warm *once* since last Tuesday week when I came here; also my bed being on the floor makes it a target for all the draughts. I've not felt hot to-day. The week-end's much the worst —in 48 hours we're locked in for 38. Double summer time! I've always loved it best—not now, not here, because it's really 2.30 in the afternoon when the key turns. . . .

Why aren't Padres knighted or made saints with £2,000 a year free of income tax—I mean some Padres—well, anyhow—one Padre.

How long is it going to take me to forget this—I mean *my* actual feelings? I don't ever *want* to forget what other people are suffering: they talk gaily and bravely about 61 more week-ends! What can I do for them? Precious little, until the whole rotten pernicious system is turned inside out and completely reorganized under humane ideas instead of all this death dealing red tapery and sheer childishness. There must be something so vitally wrong in a system that the man who is sent here for two weeks for an oversight or breach of war regulations is treated exactly as the most habitual robbery with violence, sex outrage, sub-human creatures who unfortunately over-run our prisons. Things are being done. The courage and pertinacity of one man has steadily broken down some barriers and the rest will fall if he has his way and I fancy he will.

When I talk to people with long sentences—five years, eighteen months, mine seems a fleabite, but as I said before the relative quality doesn't impress me at all. I just hate, loathe and despise every second of it and I pray God to let me forget it all as soon as possible. Of course, I shan't be able to avoid talking about it at first and my friends will be curious, but I shall never be betrayed into rushing into print. In fact officially I shall say nothing.

One thing has disappointed me. I have always been surrounded by people—never alone—had an idea that if I was alone I should 'find myself'—discover some rare new philosophy, some staggering new revelation—find a new depth of soul—but no—not at all. I have learned nothing. I'm just the same—only very angry and resentful. Perhaps—and it is possible that when I get home, my having suffered a lot and having been so terribly lonely, *will* do something for me but I very much doubt it. However, we shall see!

Of course, one's appreciation of the little ordinary taken-for-granted things like warmth, open doors and windows, food when you like, sleep as long as you like, cigarettes, sugar (oh *dear* regretted sugar), hot water (not one drop for fourteen days), shaving cream, a chocolate perhaps—and millions of others that will for the time increase amazingly and I hope it stays there—we all take too much for granted. I'm told one has to go *very* slow with food at first. How my soul and my stomach revolted at first but I'm eating now—most days—funny—I've got fourteen more days and nights. Oh, Christ Jesus help me to get through this and come out *sane*—I think the root of insanity is sheer utter futile black boredom. . . ."

That was what he wrote in his cell and it illumines like a flame both the life he led and what he felt about it all.

He used to lie on the pallet on the floor and go over in his mind what was happening on the stage at the Adelphi Theatre in *The Dancing Years*. He would take it almost word for word, note for note, timing as the moments passed by. He tried to project his spirit there. And one night he had a vision. He told his lifelong friend Keneth Kent about it. Keneth Kent is a Spiritualist and believes, as do most of us, Spiritualists or not, in an after life. Ivor had no great belief in that; we used to argue about it. But after he came out he told Keneth that one night, as he lay on his bed, following that show with his mind, Mam suddenly appeared to him. She was wearing a yellow gown, an evening gown. She smiled and said, "Ivor, how do you like this dress? I want your opinion. Do you think it fits behind?" and she turned round. Ivor said he leapt up with a cry of "Mam" and stretched out his arms, but she seemed to fade and vanish through the floor. Keneth Kent told him that, of course, Mam would have come to him and that, knowing his interest in dress—and always in her dresses—would have done as she did to cheer his mind, rather than make reference to his surroundings and trouble. But Ivor made no comment. Nevertheless, he remembered. Personally, I am not a Spiritualist although I have many friends who are—Keneth Kent amongst them—and I respect their belief. I give the story exactly as it was told to me, by one who had received great comfort.

Whilst Ivor was in the Scrubs, we who were outside were anything but idle on his behalf. Sir Edward Marsh never ceased his efforts, everyone worked, and I did my bit. I was constantly doing my best to inform public opinion of the real facts, to dissipate the unfortunate impression that he had, at his trial, endeavoured to hide behind the woman in the case, which he most certainly did not. And I was succeeding. As the days went by, as calmer reflection took the place of first impressions, more and more people began to understand. Public opinion came his way. . . .

On June 1st, 1944, I wrote a letter to Fred Allen, from which I may be permitted to quote because it is part of this story now. I was concerned with public opinion. And I was just as concerned with Ivor's state of mind. I wanted to prepare him for the publicity which must accrue on his release. I wanted it explained to him and I wanted him to understand what, in my humble opinion, should be done about it all. I was also determined that he must come back to the stage, to *The Dancing Years*, with the least possible delay. And this is an extract. . . .

> " It has to be borne in mind that Ivor is ' news ' and his release from prison will be regarded as just as big a story as his sentence. There is no dodging it so it is just as well to take advantage of it. In a long, worrying and arduous experience of Fleet Street I have always found it best to have something to say. If you say nothing, they have a chance of saying a lot or construing your silence in the way they desire. It has always been my policy to say something and to say that something emphatically and in very marked terms so as to make an impression. We do not want any more stuff about the trial, the sentence or the prison. Ivor is an innocent man and he has paid a debt. . . . His innocence and the payment must be made clear to the public. This can be achieved if he returns to the stage *as soon as possible* after his release. Public sympathy had veered to him as soon as it was known that he was serving his sentence like anyone else and undergoing the ordinary hardships of a prisoner—doubly and trebly hard, of course, in his case.
>
> He has nothing to be ashamed of—he has done nothing wrong. At the very worst it was a technical offence and would carry no further stigma even if he were guilty. I told him after the sentence at Bow Street that he must face up to the public as an innocent

man would do—and he did. It got him good marks and had much to do with the fuller and better reporting of the Appeal case as compared with the Bow Street case, for now the idea had got about that he was in fact innocent. He can come back to an even greater height of public favour if he takes the plunge at once and shows the public that Ivor Novello, the actor or the playwright, who has given them so much pleasure is again doing his job, as the servant of the public, and does not mean to let his private life interfere with his professional duties. That, I think, will disarm any lurking hostility there may be, and that would be confined to a very small jealous minority, and would make people regard him as a man desirous of doing his job, come what may.

Next week I shall be inundated with inquiries and I am sure that it is desirable to say something. What I propose to say, in the absence of any line from Ivor, is that ' Mr. Novello will resume his part in *The Dancing Years* at the earliest possible moment. He has, during his detention in Wormwood Scrubs, fulfilled the ordinary duties and routine according to regulations, without any relaxation or privilege. He was at no time in the prison infirmary. It will be readily understood that he will require a few days for rest and recovery but his reappearance before the public in his capacity as actor, author and composer will be made at the earliest possible moment. He wishes to thank the innumerable friends who have written letters of sympathy and understanding and to tell the writers how much they have done to cheer him after his unpleasant experience. These letters he will read and hopes to answer at the earliest possible moment. They are waiting for him on his release but he has been told of them. An announcement will be made in due course as to the date of his reappearance in *The Dancing Years* at the Adelphi '."

That letter was sent to the Prison Governor, who was able to inform Ivor because it affected what was going to happen to him after his release. Ivor agreed that the policy suggested should be adopted. Certain paragraphs he considered were excellent and he agreed that the matter should be copied in its entirety. . . . He planned to play on the evening of Tuesday, June 20th. He agreed completely with my message to the public.

So that was done.

But there was something else to be done. I wanted to save Ivor from the barrage of publicity which would show him coming out of the prison gates, from the attempts to get him to speak and give interviews, from the garbled statements which might ensue. Anxious as I have always been to help my friends of the Press, I have never let that cloud my views as to the feelings of my clients. So we made plans whereby this could be avoided.

An idea occurred. Ivor was to go free on Monday, June 12th. Now the point was, when did Monday legally begin so far as prison regulations were concerned? We knew the time of ordinary release and that was what we wanted to avoid. It seemed possible, that, with proper representation, a little aid might be given to Ivor on his becoming a free man. He had not asked for a favour, he did not now—we did it for him. We made the tentative suggestion that as soon as midnight struck on the Sunday he might be considered a free man. If he could leave then, we would take him away and it would mean so much. It says a tremendous amount for the helpfulness of the good Padre and for the humanity of the Governor that this was granted. So, just before midnight, there was a car outside Wormwood Scrubs and very shortly afterwards Ivor was in it, amongst friends, and speeding to "Redroofs." Later I went to the prison gates. Photographers and pressmen were waiting. I told them not to waste their time, Ivor was out. They grinned. "No good, old boy," they said. "We understand what you want to do, but we are waiting." I told them they were a lot of idiots and that I was going to bed. I got into the car and I went home to bed. About 8.30 my 'phone began to ring. It was those who held the vigil outside the gates. They wanted to know where Ivor was—I laughed at them and reminded them I had told them.

Ivor went home, a free man. Some of his nearest friends greeted him. He went to bed, to a real bed in his silk pyjamas. He sank into the comfort. After a while he slept. And then he woke up, at the time prison had made usual. He stared around him and realized where he was. He looked at the door. He said to himself, "That door is not locked. I can open it and go out. No door is locked any more, I can go through any of them freely. I can open windows, I am free; I can go anywhere and do what I like!" He got up and he crept about the house. Then food occurred to him and the realization that he could have any food he liked. He wondered what was in the pantry! He went on tiptoe to see. And there he found—oh heaven!—some of his favourite food which he ate then and there with devouring relish. And what was that favourite food of Ivor Novello's, surrounded on all sides by fortune and luxury? Cold rice pudding. . . .

Ivor was all right. He was a bit gaunt and there was a new expression in those deep, dark eyes. But he rallied. He revelled, he luxuriated. He seemed himself again—almost. There did not seem bitterness in his heart, but I think that deep down there was always a feeling of bitterness there, and it is very understandable. But he never showed it at all. He took up life again where he had left it off. Whilst he had been in prison the weather had been atrocious, May or no May. In the prison screed of his, he mentions the change to warmth, and how he did not feel it even then. But now the sun shone for him, and the flowers bloomed in his garden at " Redroofs." Spring was there, melting into summer: the sweet of the year was welcoming him back. He knew very little about Nature, very little about flowers or birds, but he appreciated their beauty in the whole scheme of things and he loved to gaze on them. He looked his fill.

It was also the time of the flying bombs, the latest horror which Hitler was inflicting on this country. Hardly any need to recall those days when the sirens so frequently wailed, when the semi-human machines came over with their noise like a wild beast worrying its prey, then the sudden cessation and the grinding roar of the explosion. It became a part of one's life. Those things worried " Redroofs " very little. But they would not have worried Ivor had he been, as he was to be soon after, in the thick of them. And one of them actually played a big dramatic part in his life.

I made all the arrangements for his return, so far as the publicity side went. He spent his time resting and reading the tens of thousands of letters which had been sent to him, all expressing their complete belief in him. Some of them were remarkable, some very funny which made him laugh. Some were sad in their intensity. There was one from someone who had suffered as he had done and wrote of the feelings such things engendered. They came from people of high degree, from working people, from many thousands who had never so much as seen him but who loved his music. Many of these people had written to the Press maintaining their belief in his innocence and quite a few were printed. And many thousands came from men and women serving in the Forces. That gave him great joy. I have been through thousands of those letters (they were all kept) whilst collecting materials for this book. I wish there were pages of space to quote from many of them, to mention names. But it is best not to make any choice. They gave him such comfort and courage, all of them. But I was touched to find amongst them the letters which my wife and I sent him to greet him on his release, to put our feelings on paper. Those, too, had been kept.

But time drew on. I made my arrangements. I did not want Ivor too worried when he made his reappearance. The date was announced and there was a tremendous rush for seats. We did not " paper " the house at all, it was left to the general public. Just his nearest friends were there—and, of course, Tom Arnold, his partner and friend, and his immediate staff—such as could come. Bill Wright had his dressing-room just as he had left it—as if no hiatus had occurred.

I had not seen Ivor myself, since he had come out. I did not intrude on " Redroofs." But I spoke to him daily on the 'phone. I told him what I wanted him to do and he agreed. He said he placed himself entirely in my hands. I told him that on the evening of his reappearance I would meet him at the flat and that we would walk along Maiden Lane to the Adelphi stage door. I told him I wanted him to stand there for the photographers but that I would see that he was not worried about interviews. He was quite willing to do all I said.

I arranged things with Fleet Street. I explained the ordeal facing him and they played ball, as they always do when the approach is right and when they know the man with whom they are dealing. They appreciated fully what lay before Ivor, the ordeal he must face. They would be welcome " in front," I told them, and they came. I would get a message for them, I told them, and I did. The photographers were informed that at a certain time he would be at the stage door, arriving on foot with me and that he would give them a picture. They understood.

It was a lovely sunny evening. Curtains rose early in those days and it was double summer time as well, so really it was just very late afternoon. It was to me a time of great anxiety. I knew what it might mean. A false move, a bit of trouble, an untoward word, and that scared, scarred mind of Ivor's might take fright and a further disaster befall. That was why I was going with him. I had every hope of his reception for I had had my ear very close to the ground—but one or two malcontents . . . one or two badly disposed people—you never know for sure. . . .

He came with me, walking as he had always done, with that individual gait of his, part spring, part lope, part slouch—impossible to describe it. We met with deep pleasure and we grasped hands. I would not let him say much, I did the talking. He made no pretence at concealment. He did not wear his dark glasses. For all the world to see he was Ivor Novello, going back to work. We walked along talking. Here and there a head turned to stare. And twice passers-by called out " Good Luck." I could have hugged them. Ivor was taking the plunge and taking it well. We went along Maiden Lane and there the photographers met us. Some took pictures of him as he walked along this time with a smile. It was such a different occasion to the last time they had met him outside the Appeal Court, when he had not been pleased to see them at all. We got to the stage door. He stood there and he smiled at them. They took the pictures—quite a battery of cameras, of course, and the usual request for " just one more." He stood quietly smiling until I said " That's all boys, he must go in now—and work." They all called out " Thank you " to him and he thanked them back again. Then we went through the stage door. His passage to the dressing-room was like a Royal Progress. The company and the stage staff were there, many in tears, but tears of joy. I saw him into his room, and then I left him and went to the front of the house, where I met my wife.

People were crowding in. There was a buzz and hum which exceeded that of a big first night. Tom Arnold was there. I greeted the Press, I explained again about no interviews either before or after and repeated my promise of a message. They were all friends. As regards going backstage after the show, there was one exception. Ivor agreed to it. That was Philip Page, then of the *Daily Mail* and an old and valued friend of both of us. I told " Peter," as we called him, that I would take him round.

And then began such an evening of drama as surely nobody has ever witnessed before, and may—almost certainly will—never see again.

I wrote a description of that night which I gave to Ivor, and he thought so much of it—humble as it was—that he had it printed and he sent it to friends all the world over. I wrote it personally for him. But I did mention in it the most dramatic event of the whole thing although that had no direct bearing on him at all. He did not engineer it: none of us could have done so. It was just one of those coincidences, maybe heaven-sent, which not even the most gifted of publicity men doubly inspired with genius, could have brought about. It is recorded here. It sounds incredible but it is true. So many will remember it. It completed an evening never to be forgotten by those who lived it.

CHAPTER TWENTY-FIVE

UP TO THE HEIGHTS

THE story I wrote about that return to the stage and which pleased Ivor so much is reproduced herewith because it is a piece of plain reporting of the occasion. It was called " A Night of Real Theatre " :

" In forty years of service in the Theatre, one imagined that every emotion, every thrill, every excitement had been tasted and experienced. But the Theatre always surprises and has something up its sleeve. It had a surprise on the night of June 20th, 1944, when it provided such an evening of emotion that comes only once in a lifetime—in a lifetime? No, in centuries—perhaps only once in all time.

" The occasion was the return to the stage of one of the most eminent and popular of its servants, just released from serving a sentence for something which he did not do, although the Law held him guilty. We, his friends, knew that. But the vaster public, whose servant it was his pride to be, had not our means of knowing the truth, and had, maybe, formed their own opinions from hastily scanned newspaper reports even more hastily written.

" He was coming back, this man, to face them again, not knowing what his reception might be, not knowing what mass judgment they might pass upon him, but he was coming back to act in the play which he had written and composed, which had brought joy to countless thousands in conditions of total war. He had spent a lifetime in the service of the Theatre and its public. He had deserved well of them. In their last great war he had given them a song which heartened and sustained and which had become a classic. In this war he had given them the play they liked best. His music had been a most valuable contribution to the music of our country. His plays gave delight, he had given employment to thousands for years. He had set a standard and he lived up to it. Then, out of the blue, came something which might mean destruction.

" But he was coming back. He knew now that he had enemies

as well as friends, enemies not of his own making but created by those jealous of his self-won success—the envious Casca's who stood around every Caesar. Yet he would face them, for he was the servant of his public and until they cast him off it was his duty to serve.

" There was a setting for drama—a play within a play—a situation in real life beating and surpassing most of those contrived by a dramatist! And the theatre in which it was played was worthy of it. Nearly a century and a half old, it had made a tradition of its own. It has given a name to a brand of play—' The Adelphi Drama.' And here was a real life Adelphi drama taking place in it again. The long arm of coincidence showed itself. It was the 1897th performance of the play being presented. In the year 1897 the hero of those Adelphi dramas had been stabbed to death by an envious madman when entering that same theatre. Was Ivor Novello to meet the same fate, not by a butcher's knife but by butchery from evil wishers?

" That was what we felt as we took our seats. And as we did so the sirens outside called, to show us what the world and human minds were really like.

" The auditorium was packed. An air of suspense, so strong that it could be felt touching one, hung over the whole theatre. There was an excited hum until just before curtain time, and when the lights began to dim one noticed that there were very few late comers. Practically everyone was seated. That, in the theatre, means a great deal.

" The lights dimmed right down, the orchestra struck up, the curtain rose and the well-known opening of *The Dancing Years* showed itself: the dark stage just before the dawn, the voice of the watchman with his lantern, the swell of the orchestra. The house was very still, its attention riveted on the stage. A few rows behind a man choked back a cough, a woman blew her nose. A young playgoer, a girl, moved a little and whispered, ' Oh dear—oh dear.' Suspense was affecting them. That many friends were there, one knew, but there might be others. To-night a man was to survive or to be doomed. Which was it to be? A flying bomb passed over and exploded not far away. Nobody heeded it. The tiny figure of Roma Beaumont ran on, as the lights gradually increased. Now the moment was coming. For this star wrote himself no carefully prepared and long awaited entrances, he just came on the stage. The audience stiffened to attention, one could feel it and sense it everywhere. A middle-aged man and his wife, who felt this occasion very strongly, clasped each other's hands. And then . . . Ivor Novello made his entrance. Now. . . .

" It came. It came like a peal of thunder which starts apparently afar off and grows in intensity as its climax approaches. Those who knew the play applauded at once. Those who were seeing it for the first time and were perhaps taken by surprise at the early entrance now realized and began to join it. A hurricane of applause, a vast wave of enthusiasm, swept across the huge theatre. It came from all parts, it grew in volume, not merely hand clapping, but shouts and cheers—a warmth of friendly feeling, long pent up, but now finding a public outlet. It was the verdict of the public who knew the man.

" What Ivor's own sensations were must be his own secret. But the thunder of welcome seemed to take him by surprise. He stood facing the audience, stooping a little, looking his usual charming self, but very strangely young and a little helpless. His smile flashed, there was a trace of nervousness in it, and in his hanging arms. And who could wonder? For it was an ordeal in itself to stand up to such applause at any time—and at a moment so fraught with emotion, a harder task still, however gratifying. But the applause lasted for over two minutes—an unprecedented time—and he recovered quickly. His smile got its genuine beam, he bowed his usual boyish bow—and then he turned and started the scene . . . he was Ivor Novello again. . . .

" And, as if in complete sympathy, the ' All Clear ' sounded outside. . . .

" In the interval they talked. ' He looks much thinner.'—' He seemed a bit nervous'—' Well, wouldn't you?'—' I've seen the play more than a dozen times and he's better than ever '—' My dear, what a thrill '—' My hands are still sore with clapping '—' I called out " Welcome back " Ivor. I hope he heard me.' ' He's O.K. by me,' said an American soldier, ' *and* his play. Prison? So what?' A newspaper critic, who had seen many strange sights in the theatre spoke: ' The danger to-night was bigger than most people imagine,' he said. ' We might have lost a man the Theatre can ill afford to lose. There's been too much spite. Did you see that article in " The . . ." condemning a letter or a statement, whichever it was, by one of the cast? That man should be punished for condemning what was merely a grateful tribute to someone who is evidently a model employer.' All round, the theatre buzzed now. The suspense was over. It was ALL RIGHT, as it should be. But the depth of feeling was shown when the bar-bells rang, for everyone hurried back to their seats again. And usually, they are so reluctant.

" The last scene came. The penultimate scene was perhaps Ivor's greatest difficulty, for here he had lines to speak which seemed strangely apposite. But never had he played the scene better. He was the persecuted idealist fighting for his country and his people with the only means that he possessed; he gave the performance such as he had never given before. He showed a depth of feeling, a power and gift of character beyond any he had ever shown us. He spoke the difficult lines with fearless intensity. Nobody stirred. A nervous laugh (and it was so easy) might have broken the spell, but Ivor's sincerity and acting overrode it.

" Then came the vision scene which has contributed so much to this play's success. Through the blue mist is seen the figure of Roma Beaumont, and gradually as she dances, she is submerged and swallowed by other waltzing figures, as the stage fills and fills. The tempo quickens, the atmosphere clears. Roma goes up-stage and beckons, and into the midst of the throng come Muriel Barron and Ivor Novello, whirling in a gay, unheeding waltz. The lights go up. And now feelings were really let loose. As soon as Ivor appeared it began. It drowned the final bars of the orchestra as the rest of the principals trooped on. The applause grew and grew—cheers, bravos, hurrahs, resounded, handkerchiefs waved—until by its very volume it checked itself, as the leading members took their bow. Still it was generous enough, but it was holding back. Ivor, according to custom, pushed forward Roma Beaumont, who got her meed, then Olive Gilbert, then Muriel Barron, who got theirs. But the great moment was not yet. Standing in line, he faced the expectant crowd, smiling. The crescendo rose again. A section of the house struck up ' For He's a Jolly Good Fellow,' but it was lost in the roar of applause. So—at last—Ivor came down to the footlights and made what should be the model curtain speech for all time, gentle, unassuming, poignant, from the heart, gracious and tactful, supremely tactful. Then, because he was Ivor Novello, he gave praise where it was due: to

Barry Sinclair, who had held the fort . . . and at long last, the curtain fell.

"When the house lights went up, one could see traces of tears; women were openly crying and men blew their noses, too. One felt that what Ivor Novello had said was true, that from his experience he had indeed gained something and that we and his public would benefit thereby. 'Well, the best of luck to him—he deserves it,' said a man as he went through the door. Happiness had come back to *The Dancing Years*—and upstairs they were cheering still, even after 'The King'."

Those cheers were still going on when I got round to him, with Philip Page. He was standing on the stage, entranced. "Listen," he said, "they are still cheering." "That's for you, Ivor," I said, "the real verdict at last." He smiled just a little and looked a bit mystified. "But I haven't won the V.C.," he said, "I only did a little time. . . ."

He chatted to Philip Page, who wrote about it with his kindness and grace. He gave me the message to the rest. And I left him in a crowd of friends, welcoming him back to his kingdom.

The passage which ends with the reference to the cheering still going on after "The King" had been played, for such was the case, was what I wrote at the time and what pleased Ivor so much. I give it for what it is worth. Ivor was back and triumphant. But despite his despairing heartcry written in prison he did learn something and there was a deeper, stronger note in his plays and music. Of all the success which he achieved afterwards, nothing ever touched that night. It was his complete vindication. And that "All Clear" right on the cue! Astounding, but true!

The prison theme must vanish, after a few more words are said. Ivor on his release, sent a handsome cheque for the use of the men who had been his fellow-prisoners. He sent them a piano, too, and he sent one to Holloway Gaol as well, when he heard one was wanted there. And although he arranged for many visits to entertain the unfortunate people, he never went himself, which one can readily understand. Nobody ever spoke of it to him, and he mentioned it very rarely. And not at all as time passed on. It was to be a closed book. The only written reference to it which exists is an entry in the Visitors' Book at "Redroofs," a book which contains autographs of practically every celebrity of our time—and a great many who are plain nobodies, for he was no snob. That entry, under date June 12th-13th, 1944, says: "Ivor's Return to Civilization" in his own handwriting. Those also signing included Olive Gilbert, Ernan Forbes Dennis, Sir Edward Marsh and Peter Graves—and there were others.

Everyone who had written him a letter relative to that imprisonment got an acknowledgment from him. He said "My most grateful thanks for your thought of me during the past few weeks and for your faith in my honesty of purpose. If my painful experience has shown me any way in which I can in the future help to better prison conditions, it will not have been in vain. Ivor Novello."

And a word about that Padre who was his true friend. The Reverend Meredith Davies is now Vicar of Shoreditch. He has his links with the Theatre. His noble church carries a monument to the Burbage family, who were buried there, to the man who built close by the first Theatre ever erected in Europe, in the world—called rightly, The Theatre. One does not class as theatres the Grecian and Roman amphitheatres in the open air. The Theatre was the first playhouse and it arose in 1576, in Shoreditch. The Burbages worshipped at that church and there are the names of many of their company on the memorial. Richard Burbage, son of the founder of the theatre, was the man for whom Shakespeare wrote his plays, the original *Hamlet*, the first actor-manager. In and around the church, traces of their graves now lost, lie many of the old actors who founded our Theatre. The church records are full of them. I am proud of the fact that an ancestor of mine played there too, although he is buried in Southwark Cathedral, for he was one of those who helped the Burbages to dismantle The Theatre because of civic prosecution—transport the materials across the Thames to Southwark and rebuild the materials there as the famous Globe.

The Reverend Meredith Davies is proud of his church and of its theatrical connections. He will never forget another actor-manager whom he was to help so much. His days as prison chaplain are over, but he goes back constantly and helps. Just before these lines were written I went with him to Wormwood Scrubs and, at his request and with him as chairman, gave a lecture to the prisoners, to make them laugh, and I am proud to say I succeeded. They laughed, they stamped, they hit each other in joy and they yelled Encore. I hope to go again with Meredith Davies. He still brings brightness to their lives. And as I spoke to those men the spirit of Ivor seemed very near indeed.

That Padre now lives in a fine vicarage to which one is welcomed by his charming, smiling wife. There is a spacious room, with comfortable chairs, nice pictures, an old sampler, and a signed photograph of Ivor. All is bright and shines like the polished brass candlesticks on the shelf. There is a television set. There is an air of comfort, charm and friendliness. There is no great show of religion about: that is there in the person of the Vicar and his wife. Outside, there is a large square in which still remain old houses. Industrialism girts it all about—factories, workshops, roaring traffic—but that vicarage is peace, peace surrounds the church too. For the churchyard is now a shady garden, bright with flowers and with old, leafy trees, beneath which children play, tired housewives snatch a moment's welcome rest and old men dream away Time. It is what Christianity should be. And the Vicar is the epitome of it all. He was a close friend of Ivor's right up to the end. It is not too much to say that but for him there might have been no more plays, no more music, no more Ivor Novello.

That year, 1943/44, during which Ivor had his trouble, proved by the paradox of fate to be, financially, the highest point he had touched up to then. His income was £35,400; he paid £19,948 in income tax. And they sent him to prison.

The story now draws towards its close. There is no need to go into all the details of those last years of Ivor. He sent plays on tour, he helped younger and struggling managements. And whenever he could, he spent much time at "Redroofs," that beloved home which will become a haven for the ailing people of his profession.

"Redroofs" stands on the edge of Littlewick Green, about four miles from Maidenhead. It is shut off from the world by a mellow brick wall. You have to know where it is to find it, for it lies remote from the main road. A lane runs past it down hill, a typical country lane of England. It is not a big house; it is long, low and rambling. Ivor had built on to it and made many alterations and you can detect the new work from the old. But it is a kindly, welcoming place, just the right frame for him. He had not a large staff: housekeeper, chef, butler and gardener, with occasional help. He owned some of the cottages nearby—in some of which lived old retainers of his. All his staff always adored him. The inside of the house – his furnishings and the contents—is a thing of beauty. Some idea can be gained by the pictures in this book, but naturally they lack colour and Ivor liked colour. None of the rooms are large in the accepted sense, except the lounge. The entrance hall is quite small and low—Ivor had it heightened—and leads right on to the staircase. In the dining-room are pictures, some by famous artists like Epstein, some by famous players such as Bea Lillie, and amongst them a genuine Noël Coward. On the piano in the lounge stood, as it has always done, a signed picture of Lily Elsie. In the corner was his collection of jade articles which he loved, many of them given him by Olive Gilbert. There are many things and much furniture—far too much to describe.

The last time I went there was in this summer of 1951, when we expected the place would be sold and none of us would see it again. I took my wife with me. She was enchanted, especially with the curtains, the general fittings and the covering of the beds. Each room had its own colour scheme, each bedroom its own individuality. He chose everything himself. Those rooms have their names. There is the Married Quarters, a double room for married guests; Lloydy's room, locked up since Lloydy's death; Bobbie's room, and Constance's room, kept always for Constance Collier, whenever she liked to go. What delighted my wife was the quilted satin in the lime-green decorated married guests' room, the celophane covers over the bedheads to prevent staining and the enormous amount of cigarette boxes which were all over the place, all kinds of cigarette boxes which are made of all sorts of material. She fell in love with Olive's room, too, which is in a lovely shade of pastel blue.

Ivor's own bedroom is a beautiful place with its own private bathroom. There is a picture of the bed in this book. It is indeed a regal couch. The main scheme is grey and silver, with touches of blue and red—blue was Ivor's colour. The bed was covered with glazed chintz, sent to him by Joan Crawford. In the room hangs a wonderful clock and an equally wonderful mirror, the edge of which is blue glass. The curtains were apple green. There is a balcony to that room, from which he could gaze at his little kingdom—a flight of steps leads down to the garden and into a glass room where there is a piano and a suite of furniture given him by members of his company, furniture which is built to stand the open air. There is a piano, too, and he would sometimes work there. He could go down those stairs and away to the studio and be quite apart from his household for the staff sleep in an annexe. Everywhere there is light, beauty and freshness; it is indeed a home from which melody can spring. And although when we were there last, he had been dead for some months, that room was kept ready for him as if he might come home: the windows were open, everything was spotless and clean, there were fresh flowers all round. It was ready for the Master, who would return no more. In the house, were Mabel, the housekeeper, Tommy, the chef (her brother-in-law,) and John the butler. No need to ask them about Ivor; they bubbled over with talk, with story, with reminiscence and with deep affection. He was the best employer ever. Morgan, the chauffeur, had said the same every day of his life and said so at a Christmas party on tour when everyone had to make a speech. That was his contribution. Tommy would tell of Ivor's taste in food: how he liked cereals, fried chicken, lobster cooked in the American way; how for breakfast it was just toast and coffee; how Ivor did not like cold meats, but adored all fruits; of his favourite sweet dishes, crème caramel, rice soufflé, and, most of all, cold rice pudding. And also Ivor always craved fried chipped potatoes. When they were being cooked he would come out into the kitchen and help himself to them, straight out of the pan. And, of course, there were the endless cups of tea—"cuppers" as Ivor called them. Ivor drank little else; some champagne when he felt the need but his favourite wine was Château Yquem.

John, the butler, would recall his delight always on arrival, his invariable kindness to them all, the constant succession of celebrities always coming and going. He would tell of the games of Canasta which held Ivor in complete thrall: how he would get up early and play it before breakfast. And he recalled that last morning, when Ivor went to town and gave them all a cheery good-bye, that he had played Canasta that morning, too. They never expected that they had looked their last on him. All of them mourn him deeply. But Tommy the chef remembered something else. He was used to all the celebrities and took little notice. Still, once he got a big shock. He had a film star who was his heroine. He was in the kitchen making the soup. He heard people coming in; he knew it was Ivor and a guest. He looked up and saw the guest staring at him. " Oh, my God," he cried, and dropped the soup, for it was his film divinity—Garbo!

There was another inmate of " Redroofs, " too—" Nikki " the dog. He missed his master. One would call him a spaniel, a nice, lovable mongrel with spaniel predominating. A friendly chap, a new inhabitant, and called " Nikki " after Ivor's part in *King's Rhapsody*.

And outside, stretching in front of " Redroofs," is that English garden which he loved. There is no room behind the house, but in front and at the side is the garden, the grounds. Away to the left are the swimming pool, the tennis courts, the big flower-filled borders, the stretch of lilac bushes which inspired his great song, and the kitchen gardens. There are the tree-decked lawns, across which run pied wagtails, with their jerky, tail-flirting movement, their sudden darts and swoops at insects, and where flycatchers perform their aerobatics from the trees. Flowers, birds, space, sunshine and shade, and, above all, that peace which one finds in a garden in England. It was a fitting setting for him and for his work. No wonder he loved it.

There are a lot of clocks at " Redroofs " and an immense number of mirrors. Ivor was not vain, not given to standing and gazing at himself, but mirrors give light—and he liked light.

There was a curious vein of nonsense in him, a delightful, childish nonsense, for, as it has been said, he never really grew up. There was a strain which, had he encouraged it, might have brought him further fame and fortune had he ever felt the urge to write books. But he always said he could not. He would not know how to manage it: the conversations worried him. " I could not go on writing ' she said ', ' he replied' and things like that. Plays, yes, you have your characters nicely tucked into the margin—they just speak." But had he wanted to, he could have written beautiful nonsense. Christopher Hassall knows all about that and would listen with joy. Ivor invented a thing called a " Slubbock". This, according to Ivor, was a very springy suitcase made of soft plastic material, grey in colour but with no clips. You had to hold it in your arms, otherwise the

" murbins " which it contained would fall out and be lost. " Murbins " were a kind of bone knitting needle and apparently the chief use of a slubbock was to contain them and their mission in life was to be carried in the slubbock. Nobody ever knew the real reason for either, but it was felt that they had a sort of mystical significance. They passed into the speech of Ivor and " Redroofs." If Ivor was ever worried what to give for a Christmas present, he always decided on a slubbock and the gift eventually selected became one, *ipso facto*. He also invented all sorts of words which he used habitually. He wrote to Chris Hassall when he was working on *Perchance to Dream*. Hassall could not do the lyrics for this, for, at the time, he was serving in the Army. There has been one slight quotation from this before but it will bear repeating! There was, of course, no date . . .

" Dearest Chris,

I can't tell you how I adored your letter. I'm so sick of eighth-hand news of you. What an incredible time you've had, and a badly bombed wife and baby on top of it—it's too much. I hear Eve was wonderful—she would be. I don't know what to say about the lyrics, much as I long to contrive something—our time together was always so productive apart from being sheer bliss, wasn't it? You bringing a lyric to me and I saying ' No, it stinks '—then you clutching your head, altering *one* word and I saying ' It's heavenly.' That's the way to work. I'm doing a few—starting as dummies then improving on them a little, but they do fall so far short of you. . . . Shall we leave it like this. If I get absolutely stuck, I could write you a letter explaining the circumstances which you could show to your C.O. and he might give you a little more compassionate leave (fancy them still daring to keep that word in use while this staggeringly cruel nonsense is going on). Anyhow, let's hope. I've missed *you* more than I've missed anyone and my groops are practically becraped with lack of stoskins. All my swerb.

Bargrope."

There was more Carrollian nonsense. In another letter he wrote:

" I expect Eve is busy knitting a brand new flexible slubbock which can accommodate anything from a marmoset to four tins of Lyle's Golden Syrup—with which passing reference to the war I will close—ah, but what? All screrp.

Ivor."

When Sir Edward Marsh was given his well-deserved knighthood, a dinner was held for him which Chris Hassall organized. He wrote to friends for subscriptions, amongst them, of course, Ivor. And Ivor replied:

" Dear Mr. Hassall,

Of course I am only too delighted to subscribe, and enclose a cheque for £5 5*s*., thus setting aside the insulting suggestion that One Guinea is enough. I shall unfortunately be unable to attend the dinner as I am playing the leading part at Drury Lane in a play called *Turgid Rancour* (limericks by Christopher Hassall). As Sir Edward has been a close friend of mine for many years, in fact, for almost too long, I am sure neither he nor the Committee would object to a shower of leaflets advertising the above play being let down from the ceiling just at the moment when Sir Edward gets up to respond to any good wishes that may be handed out. I have chosen this moment as the most romantic of the evening. Regarding the work of art which it is proposed to offer Sir Edward, I suggest a bound volume of the vocal score of *Turgid Rancour* and if this appears too slim a volume add another six copies of the same score to puff it out a bit. What I really mean is ' Let us use every occasion to advertise.'

Yours most sincerely,
Ivor Novello,
President of the S.P.C.E.
(Society for the Prevention of Cruelty to Eddie)."

There was another joyous bit of nonsense occasioned by a clock. Chris Hassall had been admiring one of those sort of gold sunray clocks with rays bursting out on all sides. Chris said to Ivor, " How do you suppose those clocks are made?" Ivor replied, quite solemnly " They come from Brazil." " Oh, from what part?" queried Chris. " From the lakes," said Ivor, even more solemnly. Chris scented nonsense and asked " How do you mean " and Ivor told him, " Well," he said, " the men who find them tie balloons on their shoes and wade about round the edge of the lakes." Chris " bought it". " Why do they wear balloons?" " So as not to hurt the clocks." " Oh, I see," replied Chris, " like looking for cockles. Then what happens?" " Every so often they feel with their feet hard lumps of clay which they pick up and put in their baskets," Ivor assured him. " But," said Chris, " what are those lumps?" and received the reply, " Clocks." Hassall tried again. " But surely not like the one on the wall." " Ah," said Ivor, "they take the lumps of clay to a nearby wall and then throw them violently against it. Each lump spreads out, leaving a sort of nucleus in the middle. Along comes the sun, bakes the splashes into the glass rays while the lump in the middle becomes the clock." And after that the word " clock mud " got into the private language, the Novellian tongue. The clock was at "Redroofs" a very beautiful thing with glass rays to it.

Hassall gives many glimpses of Ivor at work and his methods. Despite Ivor's dictum about never taking Mam's advice, he kept one of her rules—" Always keep the vocal line simple. If there are two alternatives, the simpler one is always the better." Ivor often quoted that when Chris had expressed a preference for a composition played several ways by Ivor. He very rarely gave himself a solid session of composition. He would come dashing in from a game of tennis—he played it sometimes with vigour but pretty badly—would go to a table, take a chocolate, eat it, and then turn to the piano and try something out. " I say," he would exclaim, " What about this?" If Chris said it sounded so simple as to be almost a hymn, Ivor would say " Then it's bound to be good."

Whilst Ivor was touring with *Perchance to Dream* Hassall received an urgent message to go up to him at Glasgow. He had started on *King's Rhapsody*. The hotel was so full that there was no room for Chris, who finally slept on a camp bed in Ivor's room. Ivor never went to sleep until well into the small hours, when they were not small any more, and he had the light kept on. Poor Chris therefore could not get to sleep. So he read too, until his eyes ached and then fell into a kind of coma. He could still hear Ivor turning over the pages and coughing the little dry cough that affected him when he was really interested. . . . There was a piano in the bedroom and another in the sitting-room.

That hymn-like quality which always invaded Ivor's work expressed itself in the National Anthem he wrote for *Glamorous Night* and *King's Rhapsody*. He told Chris once that they ought to go into business writing national anthems for the new countries to be established after the war. So Hassall went to the piano and played a parody on a characteristic Ivor tune. Ivor roared with laughter and said, " You know what that is? The National Anthem of the Polish Corridor."

One flashback to the trial. During the war Hassall told Ivor a great secret. He had been asked to write the lyric for whatever melody won a competition for a song to be launched with our Forces on D-Day, dropped by planes over the Continent and translated into all sorts of languages. The composers had been approached privately and had been asked to submit their work anonymously. Ivor was a little surprised that he had not been asked. He said he thought that something like " Keep the Home Fires Burning " was the sort of thing wanted. He slipped into his slippers and dressing-gown—he had been in bed—and then and there played a melody. That melody won the competition. Hassall wrote the lyric and the title was " Clear the Road to Glory." Chappell's published it. It had one broadcast. There was a little heedlessness by Ivor. Thinking there was no need for further secrecy when the competition was won, he told a reporter who quoted the words and Ivor's and Chris's name on the front page of *The Daily Telegraph.* On top of that almost immediately came Ivor's sentence. So it died and was pulped. It was one of his greatest disappointments.

The last time Hassall spent any period with Ivor was just after his return from Jamaica from that last holiday. He went down to " Redroofs " and would have been better to have stayed in bed at the flat. But he was anxious to return to *King's Rhapsody*. Chris Hassall heard him his part. It was the last thing they did together. It had been a perfect combination of composer and lyric writer. These two men knew, understood, liked and respected each other—and each other's work.

One play of Ivor's escaped London's notice. He wrote it in 1940 and it was produced at the Windsor Repertory Theatre the year afterwards. Ivor took a great interest in that place, which is quite a nursery for promising actors and embryo stars. The play was called *Breakaway*. Peter Graves and Frances Rowe were in the cast. Ivor had a great opinion of this actress. He was right. She went to America, played with Maurice Evans in *Man and Superman* and became the rage of Broadway. When she came home Bernard Shaw was pleased to see her and gave her tea at Ayot. But all the work she could get was at the Bristol Old Vic. One day Frances Rowe will really be discovered by the West End. She is a real actress. Peter Graves is a star in his own right now—of stage and screen. He is the first to give the credit to Ivor.

But, despite his triumphant return at the Adelphi, Ivor was still very unsettled in his mind. He wanted to do something more. So he went to Ensa. He had previously done an enormous amount of troop entertainment, but off his own bat. He was not very fond of Ensa. When I was at Drury Lane with that organization, I asked him why, as he was so near, he never came in to see us all. " What," he said, " and be asked to fill up a silly little pink slip at the stage door before I was allowed in? I should spit."

But he went to Ensa this time. He went over to France, very soon after D-Day with *Love from a Stranger*, a most unusual part for him at the time—a murderer—with Diana Wynyard, Margaret Rutherford, Robert Andrews, Esma Cannon (who had scored a big success in the West End production of this play) and Joan Benham. He played through Normandy and Belgium for four months. It did him good for he was getting depressed again, and some of us feared that he would not have worried if a stray bullet or raiding bomb had brought his life to a close then. But he was very successful. They played almost as soon as they got ashore; there is a picture in this book of the performance. They played anywhere and everywhere in all sorts of places—barns, sheds, in bombed buildings—anywhere, as did all the Ensa shows. They ended up in Brussels in a blaze of glory. But he came home in the autumn to play again in *The Dancing Years* and to write and compose *Perchance to Dream*.

Like so many of his other works, he did most of this whilst on tour. It was destined for the London Hippodrome. Ivor consulted with me on certain historical aspects of this play, which began in the days of the Regency and travelled down through time, with each character repeating itself in different periods: Regency, Victorian and the present. It was for *Perchance to Dream* that he composed " We'll Gather Lilacs," and the song was first heard, before the play was actually produced, by means of a broadcast one Sunday evening, from the Criterion Theatre in a series of programmes which Tom Arnold presented and with which I had a good deal to do. It was sung by Olive Gilbert and Muriel Barron. There was no doubt at all what was going to happen to it.

Perchance to Dream went into rehearsal, with Ivor starting as a dashing Regency nobleman, who had an ancestral home called

" Huntersmoon " which he loved. He was impoverished and to get money he took to the road as a highwayman, always evading capture. He had living under his protection an actress from Drury Lane who loved him truly, played by Muriel Barron, and a friend of hers, also an actress, lived with them, too. This part gave Olive Gilbert a chance not only to use her lovely voice to great advantage but also to display her very considerable gifts of comedy and pathos. " Huntersmoon " is coveted by a relation of Ivor's whom he heartily dislikes and who means to bring him down. This was well played indeed by Robert Andrews. Sir Rodney (Ivor's character) stops a coach and takes a necklace, only to find that the people robbed are his rich aunt (Margaret Rutherford) and her ward and protégé (played by by Roma Beaumont). They meet at " Huntersmoon " and Sir Rodney falls deeply in love with the girl he has robbed. From then on complications ensued, with Ivor dying at the end of act one (he wore a red wig and it became him), being a composer in another period of existence, and being married to the reincarnation of his actress lover—and again meeting the girl with tragic results. This time she died. Gradually it came down to the present day, and at last ended happily for all. It was very long and very involved. Sir Edward Marsh worded out a genealogical table which was shown on a drop cloth. I doubt if it made it much clearer. But nobody minded. It was a big sweeping colourful show with plenty of action, plenty of romance, plenty of very good music, plenty of Ivor Novello, and what made much of the success, " We'll Gather Lilacs," which became to World War II what " Keep the Home Fires Burning " had been to World War I.

Produced at the London Hippodrome on April 21st, 1945, *Perchance to Dream* had the longest unbroken run of any of Ivor's shows, 1,020 performances. There was chaos at the dress rehearsal. It went on and on, with interminable delays; people fell asleep all over the place. But the axe was taken, whole chunks were cut out, including a scene in which Ivor appeared (as his mother had done in reality) before Queen Victoria. I regretted the loss of that scene. It was short and it was good. But, anyway, the thing was a triumph. Ivor had done it again. In the cast, besides those mentioned, were Margaret Rutherford (succeeded later by Zena Dare, who in turn was succeeded by Maidie Andrews when she went on holiday),

Dunstan Hart, Victor Boggetti and many other Old Novellians. Also in the cast was Gordon Duttson, who succeeded Lloyd Williams as Ivor's personal secretary and was with him up to his death. There was some charming stuff and décor in *Perchance to Dream* which was, of course, presented by Tom Arnold. It was produced by Jack Minster. When Muriel Barron left the cast the part was played by Sylvia Cecil, and also by Hilary Allen. *Perchance to Dream* was announced as a Victory production. It lived up to that, for it was running when the war ended and Germany and Japan surrendered unconditionally. During its run, a special performance was given in aid of the King George Pension Fund for Actors, and Ivor arranged a scene at the end, which introduced a lot of stars outside the show. Her Majesty Queen Mary honoured the performance by her presence and sent for Ivor, giving him an audience in the Royal Box. What that most gracious act meant to him can be guessed.

Both Ivor and his public loved *Perchance to Dream*, so everyone was happy. And the sales of " We'll Gather Lilacs " were fabulous. . . .

CHAPTER TWENTY-SIX

TOWARDS THE END

DURING the long run of *Perchance to Dream* Ivor found other outlets for his activity. He was not yet worrying about a play to succeed this smash hit. But he wrote a comedy called *We Proudly Present*, which Peter Daubeny presented at the Duke of York's. Ivor made his old, enthusiastic mistake of going too far backstage for the general public. It was the same trouble as in *Sunshine Sisters*, delightful for those who talked theatrical shop but not so interesting for the ordinary theatre-goers. It was well played by a company mostly composed of members of the Royal Ivor Academy: Peter Graves, Phyllis Monkman and an old and dear friend of Ivor's, Ena Burrill; also Anthony Forwood, Irene Handl, Mary Jerrold, Anna Turner, Edward Sinclair and Leo de Pokorney, a good actor indeed. It ran for six months and also had a tour. So it did pretty well. He also presented a revival of *Our Betters* by Somerset Maugham, at the Playhouse, with Dorothy Dickson and Cathleen Nesbitt in the leads.

He was always thinking of things to help the Theatre to improve the lot of actors and actresses. It was he who conceived the idea of " The Ellen Terry Award "—a silver statuette to be presented to the actor, actress and playwright, all of them to be British, who in the opinion of an appointed committee did the best work in each year. The first committee consisted of Robert Lantz, Sir Edward Marsh, Hester Chapman, Leslie Bloom of the Gallery First Nighters' Club and Alan Dent, critic of the *News Chronicle*. Ivor was sure that such a thing would get big publicity as did the Oscar for the films. He gave the first statuettes himself, at a cost of something in the region of £500. It is to be hoped this Award will go on in his memory too. He was very proud when, in 1949, the Duke of Edinburgh made the presentations.

Ivor said of the scheme: " Our earnest hope is that this scheme will prove to be one more stimulus to good work in the Theatre and that it may also further excite the interest of the public into

FF

going more regularly to the theatre and making their own awards."

The scheme never got the success it deserved. It did not seem to capture the imagination of the public like the Oscar, although that is in America and this of Ivor's was for home.

Arrangements were made by Tom Arnold and Ivor that at the end of the run of *Perchance to Dream* the whole show, with Ivor, of course, should go to South Africa. And there is a pendent story to that. Whilst *Perchance to Dream* was still running, there was a revival of *The Dancing Years* at the Casino Theatre, with Barry Sinclair playing Ivor's part, which he had played so often. Her Majesty Queen Mary payed it a visit. It was during that terrible winter. But soon after its production the leading lady got laryngitis. She could speak, but she could not sing. Her understudy, a girl called Ruby Moule, stood in the wings and sang for her, synchronizing the whole thing. The emergency action was a big success. But the laryngitis got worse and the understudy played. She was a most competent artiste; indeed of some us thought she was much more. She had done it all, young as she was. She had been employed in a telephone exchange. The B.B.C. wanted a girl for what they called "The New Voice" in the very successful radio programme, "Band Waggon". She applied—she got the job—she sang like a lark in spring. But it was not radio that was her ambition. It was the stage. She set about learning. She did everything. She was in Ensa, in repertory, in musical comedy; she played opposite Tauber in a tour of *Old Chelsea*; she was in concert party. There D. L. Murray, the famous novelist, saw her and mentioned her to me. She played Principal Boy in a Birmingham pantomime and did well. But somehow, she never got the break she needed. Then came this understudy job, and the chance of playing. She played and sang the part beautifully. Ivor was told how she had kept the curtain up at the time the leading lady lost her voice and how well she was doing now. He was playing at the Hippodrome, but the matinées did not clash. He went, and he saw. He told the girl he would engage her, but she must change her name, and he christened her Vanessa Lee. He had been stage godfather to Vivien Leigh, and it was Lee again, although spelt differently, that he bestowed on this new find. He did all sorts of things for her, had her groomed for stardom, and he took her with him to South Africa, as his leading lady in *Perchance to Dream*. The whole thing, visit and play, was a big success. So was Vanessa Lee. Back in England, the show went on tour, with Vanessa Lee in the lead with Ivor. He decided to write a part for her in his new show. He roughed it in but he wanted a holiday. He went to America and with him, of course, went Lloyd Williams. They went to New York in 1946 and saw all the shows. They got on the train for California.

One Sunday morning my telephone rang. It was Fred Allen. " Popie," he said, " I've just had a 'phone call from Ivor from California. Lloydy had a stroke on the train and he's dead." I was horrified. " Are you sure, Fred?" I asked. " Ivor has just 'phoned me," he said, "asking me to get in touch immediately with Lloydy's sister, Mrs. Secretan, to get her to cable authority for autopsy. I've got to do something about it, but I can't do much at this long range! But I thought you ought to know." Now, my job is publicity. Lloyd Williams was a celebrity on his own and by his nearness to Ivor; he was known to hundreds of famous people and to thousands not so famous. It was obviously a story. I gave it out and it was in the papers on Monday morning. Then we heard from Ivor again. Lloydy was not dead but he was stricken. There was little hope of life. Ivor was in a terrible state. Gladys Cooper helped him tremendously in this crisis. We gave a correction in the press, and we waited. Ivor brought Lloyd Williams home, still alive. He could do little, poor man. He lived down at "Redroofs." He improved slightly and he could go about in a wheeled chair. He was taken to shows when possible. All that could be done for him was done. He had been a good and faithful servant and friend. His days were spent in sitting and listening; he could move a hand sufficiently to smoke a cigarette. It was little more than mere existence and it saddened Ivor terribly. He died in 1948: his reported death was in 1946. But he never knew of those reports: he was never allowed to read his own obituaries. And they were nice ones, too.

But one thing more, which throws a light on Ivor must be chronicled before *Perchance to Dream* leaves the stage.

One Saturday afternoon, I had to see him before the matinée. It was pretty important. I got to the Hippodrome early and he had not arrived. Rather than go and sit in the dressing-room I waited outside. It was summertime and a fine day. As I stood there waiting, I fell to musing about all the people of the Theatre whom I had been to see in my time—a long, long list—and began to compare them with one another, and also the times in which we were living, as contrasted with the times I had known before. Members of the company passed into the theatre and I thought of those of the older days, of the girls and boys I had known and of the great ones, too. I thought of the Gaiety Girls of my youth, who had such grace, such poise and allure and who lit the Strand with their beauty as they floated along, of their hair done in its special style, of their hats to suit their personality and particular style of feature. Most of the girls going into that Hippodrome stage door were pretty enough but wore trousers and no hats or had handkerchiefs over their heads. The war, of course—they were all efficient and worked maybe far harder than the girls of old—but there was not that essential, that terrific, femininity. And I thought of the leading people, the stars and especially the actor-managers—for it was an actor-manager for whom I waited, the last of the truly creative actor-managers. I thought of those old timers' dignity, of their pride in their calling, of their approach to the Theatre and their profession, of their clothes, their smart suits, their tall hats and frock-coats, and their general air of aloofness from the ordinary life around them. It was not a pose, not assumed for showmanship; they really were like that—the Theatre was, then, a thing apart. It was their kingdom in which they ruled, cut off from ordinary life by the footlights. Their theatres were thrones, which they graced and at which their subjects worshipped with reverence. When caught sight of in the street they looked always what they were—celebrities—and were saluted as such. I thought of Tree, Alexander, Irving, Wyndham, Cyril Maude, Martin Harvey, Waller and the great actor-managers of my Yesterday, and up the street came a figure. He was wearing a shapeless brown hat on the back of his head, his coat he carried over his shoulder, slung from his finger through the tab, his white shirt was open down to the waist and he wore old grey flannel trousers. On his face were dark glasses and as he came towards me he was eating an ice-cream with evident relish. It was Ivor Novello, actor-manager of my To-day, approaching the theatre wherein he reigned. . . .

Yet, once inside, the aura of the actor-manager shone around him and he became the same as those who had gone before him.

Once past that stage door and something happened: he was at once Royalty of the Theatre. He was of the right line, the right descent, ruled in his own right, and he contributed as much, indeed more, of what was actually bringing the people into the theatre than any of the great ones of old. It did not matter what Ivor did, or how he dressed: nothing stopped him being Ivor because he never assumed anything, and nothing ever stopped him being pure Theatre either. He was one of the few who could eat ice-cream in the street and sacrifice nothing by so doing. Yet I always wish he had not done so . . . not that it matters to anyone but such a stickler as myself. His fans loved him for it, just as much as the older epoch's " fans " would have swooned with horror at the sight of George Alexander eating a hot baked potato *en route* for St. James's, Tree consuming winkles from a bag whilst proceeding down the Haymarket, or Cyril Maude with a toffee apple. Yet Ivor got away with it. A remarkable man. Other times, other manners. But he had a foot in both periods.

He had had an illness whilst on tour which had pulled him down. But he recovered. He took a holiday in his Jamaican home with a party of friends. He adored that. And he looked upon Jamaica as his refuge against the English winter. It was apparent to us all that since those hardships in Wormwood Scrubs he had not been so strong and that the winters tried him. The first little crack had come when he had pneumonia and that crack had not healed when prison came to widen it. He disliked the cold more intensely than ever.

He had escaped to Jamaica during that terrible winter we had when the snow never melted, when light and heat were always being cut off. And it was as well that he did, for although he came in for the tail end of it he was fortified by tropical warmth. Ivor loved warmth. He loved the blue skies and heat of Jamaica, he loved his house there, and he loved his friends to enjoy it with him. He loved swimming and splashing in the tropical seas. Jamaica gave him joy and a look came into his eyes when he spoke of it.

But he was now approaching his last phase and his last, triumphant success. In the meantime, Ralph Reader and William A. Sutton had taken *Glamorous Night* on tour. I had asked Ivor to let them have it and he did. I asked him for a message to use during the tour, for publicity. He wrote to me from Brighton, and this is what he wrote:

" Dear Popie,

Will this do? How I wish I could sit in on the production—I know so little about it all—who's designing it and who's doing the costumes and the cast? I know nothing. How I *love* your books.

Best Love, Ivor."

and the message was:

" *Glamorous Night* was the first of a series of my musical plays at Drury Lane followed by *Careless Rapture*, *Crest of the Wave* and *The Dancing Years* and is in many ways my favourite of them all, partly because it brought prosperity back to music on the big scale and partly because it brought prosperity back to Drury Lane after some considerable time; and I am more than happy that it is being restored to the stage at this present moment. In my opinion it contains all the colour and excitement we badly need in the Theatre in these unsettled times; it takes one 'out of oneself'—a pleasant and rare experience. I shall be more than anxious to have the opinion of the present-day public of this full-scale operetta-drama. Ivor Novello."

Well, the public approved very highly indeed, and it was a great success on tour. Ivor was not really worrying about those rehearsals, otherwise he would have been there; nothing would have stopped him. He knew we knew the show. Ralph Reader had produced the dances and Bill Sutton had been callboy at the Lane when *Glamorous Night* was first produced, and I had been " in " on every moment of it. He knew them, he knew me, so he left us alone to do it. But had he not done so, had he attended rehearsals, it would have cost much more than it did—and it cost enough anyway!

It will be noticed in his message how Ivor believed in " escapism " in the Theatre. It was the only " ism " for which he had any time. Then he wrote to me on October 11th, 1948:

" My dear Popie,

First of all, congratulations to you and yours over the success of *Glamorous Night*. I have had ecstatic accounts both from strangers and friends and am truly glad that this courageous venture should have turned out so well. One thing about Ralph, he has got the true tradition of doing things on the big scale, and I was awfully touched by a letter from Bill Sutton remembering that it was in

Glamorous Night that he started as call-boy—and was the pet of the entire Theatre.

Will you do something for me personally? I know there is no need to ask—but I think there could be some publicity, if only in *The Feathered World* about the fact that for the first time in history there are three ' one-man ' shows careering round the Provinces and breaking records everywhere. Incidentally, we have so far visited eight towns with *Perchance to Dream* and have broken the records for each theatre since it was built; so if you could do something with all this I should be ever so grateful. It might actually tie up with the advance publicity for *Glamorous Night*.

This is for your ears personally. My own new show—which is from a libretto point of view complete—will not be until the early autumn next year. This time I have gone very spectacular. How lovely it would be if the gods thought fit to send me back to the Lane!! But I suppose all this is too much to ask!

Ivor."

Bless him, what did he think I was made of? In reply I sent him a sheaf of cuttings all pointing out that *Perchance to Dream*, *The Dancing Years* and *Glamorous Night*—all Ivor Novello shows—were on the road together, so on and so forth. He was delighted! If I had not thought of that myself I should not have been worth my salt! True, I was not looking after his other two shows whilst on tour, but it was all the same. I did not get it into *The Feathered World*, though! And Ivor saw *Glamorous Night* for himself. It was his own opposition for the Christmas Season at the other theatre in Edinburgh whilst he was there with *Perchance to Dream*. And every night, when he made his curtain speech, he advised the public to go and see it. And they did. But the gods—in this case Tom Arnold—did not send him back to Drury Lane with that new show, which was *King's Rhapsody*. It went through to the Palace instead.

Ralph Reader Limited also toured *Careless Rapture*. I got both those shows for them from Ivor, and they brought him in handsome royalties I am glad to say . . . Ivor came to the opening night of the tour of *Careless Rapture* at Lewisham Hippodrome. He saw the show from a box. He had never seen it from the front before, of course, and it was an experience for him. But he was delighted and he made a speech from the box—after the spotlight had shone everywhere else than upon him—and expressed his satisfaction to the large audience which acclaimed him. He was to make one more speech from a box, a year or two later, and that was to be his last first-night speech.

That night he and I discussed the new play, *King's Rhapsody*. He told me the plot, and the next day sent me the script. He had been to South Africa a second time, with *The Dancing Years* and had thoroughly enjoyed it. He was ready for London again. Little did he know that he had done his last tour, had seen the great provincial cities, except for two, for the last time and that he was upon his last phase and on the verge of his best and most artistic play of them all. None of us had a suspicion. He was his old self—happy, busy, excited at the prospect and pretty confident, as usual, although he always kept his fingers crossed and took no chances.

King's Rhapsody began to take shape. Vanessa Lee was to be his leading lady with a magnificent provision for Zena Dare and Olive Gilbert. Ivor was very happy, too, because once again Christopher Hassall was to do the lyrics. It was to be presented by Tom Arnold, of course, and it had been decided that it came to the Palace Theatre, London, after a try-out at the Palace Theatre, Manchester. Except that Lloydy was gone, it was almost the old Drury Lane set-up managerially. Of the immediate staff Fred Allen, Bill Wright, Chris Hassall and I had fought side by side on all the battle-fields with Ivor.

It was the summer of 1949 and it was a very hot summer. Casting was complete and Ivor was overjoyed because Phyllis Dare was to play as well. She and Zena were to appear in the West End together for the first time. He was delighted with his cast, delighted with his book and his music. He had no fault to find with anything. He wanted the world to know—and they did. When Ivor was really happy, he shone! Murray Macdonald produced, doing his first musical play. The care of dialogue and situation he brought added much weight. Bill Newman was in charge of production for Tom Arnold, Winnie Newman was in charge of the company. Harry Acres was the conductor. All was set. Outside the summer blazed as, one day, I sat in the stalls' bar at the Palace and watched Ivor, Zena, Olive, Vanessa Lee and Bobbie Andrews rehearse the now famous Abdication scene. Even under those conditions it "got" me and I felt my eyes fill with tears. I told Ivor I had never seen him play better. He hugged me. It was quite true—I never fill up artistes with praise—and it went for all of them.

The time came near when we should go to Manchester to

open for three weeks' trial run. I went down for a few hours to see the Press. I was quite sure of this show. I met the "boys and girls" as usual in the office of Bill Taylor at the Palace, Manchester, where they had been invited by Douglas Bush, the publicity man of that theatre—both old friends of mine. They all came. Even dear old Harry Lomax, the veteran, came to see his old pal. I told them my story. "What's going to be the smash-hit song?" asked one. "'Some Day My Heart Will Awake'," I answered. "Seem to have heard something like that before" was remarked. "You haven't heard this song," I assured them, "just you wait." They remembered that and on the first night they told me I had told the truth. "But I always do," I assured them, and that got its laugh.

Just before we went Ivor decided he must have some friends in to the dress rehearsal. All the scenery had gone but that did not concern him. He loved friends in front. "Just a few," he said, and, of course, half the profession crowded in. They saw *King's Rhapsody* under the worst conditions, played practically in "tabs" and without all the costumes. But it did its work. It held them gripped.

And so, on Monday morning, August 23rd, we all set off for Manchester. It was one of the hottest days within living memory. All the principals were on the train. Ivor could have gone by car in the cool but he came on the train. There was the show to talk about! The train was packed. We sweltered as we went along, there was no coolness anywhere. In the compartment with my wife and me were two very charming people from South Africa, whose daughter had come over here to dance and who was in the show as a dancer. They were friends of Zena Dare, who is well known in South Africa, and she introduced us. The gentleman—for that is what he was, and of the old school—was more than unwell and feeling the heat badly. We helped as best we could and when the time came we got them places in the crowded restaurant car. His wife, handsome and smart, was very concerned about him. When we got to the Midland Hotel he went to bed and then he went to a nursing home. He had travelled many miles to see that first night—and his daughter's début. But he never saw it. He died on his way back to South Africa. . . .

Next day we were all down at the theatre. I had been to a newspaper office on my way and as soon as I walked into the dark stalls I heard Ivor's voice: " Where's Popie?" I was there, and we went on. It was the old gang at work again and Bill Wright produced an endless succession of " cuppers." It was really great joy, those days away with a big show like this, especially when Ivor was there too. His enthusiasm was always on the boil; he kept everything and everybody on tiptoes and he always knew exactly what he wanted. That night there was a dress rehearsal. We went to bed quite happy.

King's Rhapsody opened at the Palace, Manchester, on the night of Wednesday, August 25th, 1949. The house was packed from ceiling to floor and was in holiday mood. The overture was loudly applauded. The curtain rose. I was sitting with my wife at the end of a row in the stalls handy for the PASS door, that is the private door which leads backstage. The curtain rose on that bright scene in the Royal Palace at Norseland. Olive and the rest got their applause on entrance, and then the chorus and dancers entered to present their gifts to the Princess on her birthday and to dance for her entertainment. A man in rough clothes brushed past me down the aisle. I thought he was one of the staff, maybe an electrician, going backstage. But instead of turning through the door on the right, he sprang up the little flight of steps which leads actually on to the stage . . . all was not well. There was a scream from the back of the theatre. I started up and hurried forward—but one of the boys in the chorus, one of the old Druriolanians, had got the interloper, who had taken hold of one of the girls, and pushed him into the wings. There I arrived to see him being rather roughly handled. It turned out he was an epileptic and not accountable. He was taken off to hospital, but it was a nasty minute.

It did not affect the show. That went from triumph to triumph. Vanessa Lee got prolonged cheering for " Some Day My Heart Will Awake " and Olive Gilbert's voice held them tight. " Eh, but she can sing, tha knows," came from just behind us . . . and everyone was in the mood of success. Ivor's own reception was something to hear: there was goodwill and happiness everywhere. In the interval, on all sides one heard glowing comments on him. The Press made no secret of their verdict. And the final curtain fell to such enthusiasm as is seldom witnessed. There was not a seat in the house for the entire visit.

Back in the hotel there was a supper of celebration. My wife and I sat apart with a friend, D. L. Murray, come to see the triumph of the girl he had spotted. Our place is in the background and we know it. But Ivor left the big table and came over, sat and talked, asked questions, listened, sat for a long time. Those after-the-show suppers on try-outs can be joyous or tragic . . . it all depends. I have seen strange things happen at the Midland after a show, even fights! But this was one of the happy nights.

King's Rhapsody opened at the Palace Theatre, London, on September 15th, 1949. It was an immediate and complete triumph. One critic begged to differ, and his paper was flooded out with letters from an indignant public. Another was a bit snooty, but he was young and modern and he said some nicer things afterwards; anyway, he was entitled to his opinion. It made no difference. The public were pro-Ivor no matter what he did and this time he had done them proud. His story was a good one. For the second time he had entered the realms of Ruritania. Strange how the newspaper men always thought all of his plays were Ruritanian, but only two of them were, actually: *Glamorous Night* and *King's Rhapsody*, two of the best he ever did. There was much in common in some ways between those two shows. In *Glamorous Night* the King's mistress was the heroine who saved the country. In *King's Rhapsody* the Queen did that, after the mistress had previously saved the King from losing himself in exile. But of the stories, *King's Rhapsody* was by far the better. It could have been divorced from its music and still enthralled. It was a success all round, everybody scored. Zena had never been better. Phyllis was delightful as always and she sang the song which had failed in *Arc de Triomphe* with such knowledge and charm that she could have taken as many encores as she liked. Olive Gilbert, so reliable, so sure, so fine of voice, gave that air of reality it needed. As for Ivor, he had never played so well, he had never had such authority, such variety. His seduction scene with Vanessa Lee, who became a star overnight, was played with the surest and most delicate of touch; his abdication scene was perfection—nobody, not the biggest star of the straight stage, could have played it better. And the last scene, in the Cathedral, brought down the house. It was a scene worthy of Drury Lane. It appeared as if the Palace stage had acquired new depth and acreage. One seemed to be in that vast House of God, to feel the atmosphere and to smell the incense—to be aware of the high roof and the dim vista of the nave. It was a scene worthy of the great days of Tree, too.

The Boy King was crowned and the procession passed down the aisle. The Queen Mother, as she left the altar, dropped a white rose thereon. When the great ones had gone, out from the dusk of the pillars came the populace, to follow their new king, and then, a solitary figure—the king in exile, who had risked his life to see his wife for one moment, to see the crown he had discarded held above his little son's head. All in black, singularly like Hamlet, he went to the altar. He saw the rose, he picked it up and knelt on the altar steps, his rose between his hands, his head bending in prayer, as the curtain fell. It could not possibly fail and it did not. It was Ivor's moment of great triumph. The cheers went on and on. He went through the usual routine of handing forward his stars to take their applause, of bowing to them, of kissing them. And then he came down himself, looking so handsome but smiling with boyish glee, with that loose-legged walk, those swinging arms, and made his speech of thanks to the cheering multitude. It was a moment to remember, even if it had not been the last time that Ivor was to make a first-night speech in thanks for the last play in which he appeared, in the last character he ever played.

Queues surrounded the Palace daily. People quarrelled over the possibility of returned seats. It went on and on: *King's Rhapsody* was a smash hit. Its lovely scenery and décor, the Ball Room scene especially, were things of quality and of the true tradition of the actor-manager. Edward Delany had painted the scenes—he had done so many Ivor shows—but this too was his high spot. It was triumph for All Concerned.

It ran and ran. But there was bad luck somewhere. Illness attacked the principals in turn. We never seemed to get a long period with a full cast. We did not worry much because so long as Ivor was there, nothing else really mattered. He could truly say " The show—it is I." But he would not have done so. Princess Margaret came to see it and spoke words of praise. Queen Mary attended a special charity matinée and sent a most gracious letter which transported Ivor to the heights. He nearly got into trouble over his enthusiasm. He stuck that letter on the call board, so proud of it was he, for all to read. Of course someone saw it who told the Press. Such things are not done without permission, but Ivor was forgiven.

And then, in the summer of 1950, when the second birthday of the show approached, he fell ill. He had taken a holiday but it had not done him good. He entered a nursing home and underwent a very severe operation indeed. We did not publicize its nature nor its severity. But he was very ill. His part was well played by his understudy, John Palmer, who deserves credit. Ivor recovered, took a short rest, and came back. Immediately the business soared. But he still had to receive treatment, and drastic treatment, which was taking its toll. He was not himself. Outwardly the people who did not know him might not notice, but he was visibly thinner and gaunt. And to those around him, there was a certain look. . . .

He was changed but it was difficult to put one's finger on the change. He was possessed of a strange urgency, a desire to get things done. He did not rest, he worked, he bothered; he was anxious over things which he had not previously worried about at all. He appeared like a man with something to do against time, like Cecil Rhodes: " So Much to Do and so Little Time to Do It." He had been writing a show for Cicely Courtneidge. She had been ill which held things up, and then his illness delayed it again. But now he set about it and, with Alan Melville to do the lyrics, he wrote and composed *Gay's the Word.* And all the time he seemed hurried. He gave me the script to read, asked me to let him have it back as soon as possible with my comments, ringing up for the verdict the next morning. As it happened I had sat up to read it overnight.

He did things he would never have dreamed of doing. He seemed avid for publicity; he went out of his way to get it; he entered upon undertakings without asking any of us, as heretofore. This might not have been apparent to the casual eye but those of us who knew him, and liked him so well, saw it.

Gay's the Word opened in Manchester, too. We went down there as usual. Ivor, playing at the Palace, could not come to either the first night or the dress rehearsal. But he did the next best thing. He flew up on the morning of production, after as bad a dress rehearsal as it has ever been my misfortune to see, and he set about his own work, cutting, suggesting and altering. It was all there but it wanted his pulling together. In a few hours he did it, and then he flew back, to keep faith with his public at the Palace. And the curtain went up that night to another

Novello triumph. Never had Cicely Courtneidge been better, and that is saying a very great deal. Never had such vitality been seen, and her great song of that name " Vitality " brought the first half to an end. There were eight curtains but there could have been eighty. The chorus work was superb. Here was a show which under the expert guidance of Jack Hulbert could challenge any American production. And that in effect was what Novello had done! He had not written an ordinary Novello show: he had set out to write a part for his much admired Cicely Courtneidge, the finest burlesque artiste the stage has to-day. She can do it all and she does. He had set out to show that when it came to slick, up-to-date musicals, they could be done here as well and better than they could be in the States, and played by British artistes, too. His book, based on a story Jack Hulbert told him, Alan Melville's lyrics of wit and shine, the excellent company, Lizbeth Webb, Thorley Walters, Maidie Andrews and the rest of those talented people, made another Novello success, not only for himself but for home-made shows, too. This was the sort of thing George Edwardes did and Cicely Courtneidge challenged comparison with any of the great ones of those days. It was her triumph as well as Ivor's and—Britain's. It was a smash hit.

I telephoned the news to Ivor at the flat where he had come hot-foot from the Palace. He had been having messages during the evening and from me he heard the final scene. I can hear his purr of gratitude and satisfaction now. I could almost see his smile over the wire. . . .

But he could not go and see his own show. He was wanted at the Palace and *Gay's the Word* was to tour for quite a time before coming to town. Of course, Tom Arnold presented it—the last act of active partnership between him and Ivor. But Ivor could not wait. He took a night off, a most unusual thing for him, and he went down to Coventry. Everyone was sworn to secrecy. We did not want the London public to think he was playing truant, natural as it was. He went to Coventry; his understudy played. He sat in an obscure seat. He revelled in the show, but they knew him. The audience spotted him and he had to make a speech. There was a London critic in the house having a pre-view. He is a man I know and trust. I did not know myself, when arranging for him to go down, that Ivor would be there. For the matter of that, Ivor had not then selected the date. But I told that critic and he kept faith. No word appeared in London.

So the autumn drew into winter and Christmas approached. Ivor was not well, and not looking well. Apparently elated at the success of *Gay's the Word* he still had that curious look, and would go into long and unusual silences. He was going to play up to Boxing Night at the Palace and then go to Jamaica for a rest and holiday. He would be back for the opening of *Gay's the Word* in town, to which he looked forward eagerly. We were worried about him. I would sit chatting in his dressing-room at the Palace, and would watch him out of the corner of my eye, unknown to him. There was always that odd urgency, that seeming hurry. The old repose, the old boyishness had gone. He would arrive later than usual. He would come up more often from " Redroofs " in that battledress of his beneath which were his pyjamas. He seemed tired, too, and he had a bit of a cough at times. He admitted he wanted a rest. He seemed to be grasping at the fleeting minute; he seemed to want to do so much. He would sometimes say that he thought the time had come to give up acting. Then he would laugh at the way he had foreseen the march of time and gradually given himself middle-aged parts.

He did so in *King's Rhapsody*. This part was far removed from the light-hearted young composer of *The Dancing Years*, the debonair Regency buck of *Perchance to Dream*. He had got level with the years and had beaten them. His portrayal of a man in his forties, slightly embittered with life, cynical, hard and yet tender in love, which he played in *King's Rhapsody*—" Nikki of Murania "—had got him greater kudos and more appreciation than anything he had done before. His fans just ate it up. He had beaten the years' ravages on the profile—he joked about it in the play—and had made a new man of himself, a more mature Ivor which was so much finer than the younger one. In *Gay's the Word* he burlesqued his own work, he poked fun at his romantic plays and he even burlesqued " We'll Gather Lilacs," and " Keep the Home Fires Burning." People roared with laughter. It was as if he was burning his own youth, making a clean sweep. . . .

And then, having discussed retirement, he would begin to talk about the next play, to outline *Lily of the Valley*, a tale of Wales with himself as an ageing teacher of music and musician and Vanessa as a young singer, or to explore a play which had the South of France as its venue, which I believe was the outcrop of an idea he once had whilst at the Lane, which he called "The World" and in which he played first a father and then a son. He loved that dual role always. Anyway, he was shedding his youth. He was not dependent on the profile; he was meeting age and beating it and had never stood on a higher pinnacle. There was no question of the beauty of his music in *King's Rhapsody*, there was no question of his dialogue and story, and no question of his looks. His appearance in the Ballroom Scene, in his dark uniform, always drew an "Oh" of admiration. He liked himself in it and he knew they liked him too. On his breast he wore a star which Naomi Jacob had given him and which had belonged to Edmund Kean. He used to smile at me when I touched this with reverence, for Edmund Kean, despite his wildness and tragedy, is one of my great heroes and my great-great-grandfather played leads opposite to him. If that star had adorned Kean, as it undoubtedly had, it still shone on the breast of greatness, greatness of a different kind, but still greatness, and on a man who could pull the public into the Theatre with as much certitude and power as Kean ever did.

Just after the production of *King's Rhapsody* Ivor wrote me a letter, thanking me for what I had done—and, believe me, I had done a few things although I say it. That Christmas he sent me a present—the first—and last I ever had from him. It was a bottle of sherry and a bottle of whisky and I am a teetotaller. But he meant it well. That gift, apart from a gramophone record and a book to which he had written the prologue, were the only gifts I ever had from him. That never troubled me. I am one of those foolish people who get joy out of doing their job, even if reward is inadequate or wanting altogether. No wealth ever comes their way, but they grow rich in achievement. That they cannot lose, nor can a Government which specializes in taxation take that from them. They cannot take it with them when they die; neither can they take the money, so what does it matter? Satisfaction makes a light heart even if the pocket is in a similar condition. But it has no money troubles and nobody squabbles over the remains.

There was a party on the first anniversary, and the company and guests watched a film made of the show and themselves.

There was much guying and back chat, some champagne and sandwiches and a lot of good feeling. There had been the customary Garden Party during the summer at "Redroofs." Meanwhile, things went on just the same at the Palace but still Ivor did not seem quite as usual. He did not seem to go into those uncontrolled fits of hilarity which had so often overcome him when he really enjoyed a joke. He seemed a lot more thoughtful, and much quieter. He read a tremendous lot of novels, but he did not remember them, I am sure. He went to all the plays whose matinées did not clash with his own and to every film he wanted to see. He played Canasta; he gave the parties in his flat and at "Redroofs"; but those sudden absences from the party, those mysterious disappearances and reappearances after an interval, seemed to become more and more marked. But he still smiled at the fans who waited for him. He still got the thrill from the applause and his nightly curtain speech, and he still had the entire show relayed to his dressing-room, all the time.

He began to look forward to his Jamaican holiday. There was the little informal Christmas party at the theatre. There were the masses of presents for him and he sent gifts to his close friends. And after Boxing Day, he would be away, New York first, and then Jamaica, sunshine, friends and relations: Bobbie Andrews, Phyllis Monkman, Alan Melville, Olive Gilbert, Bill Wright his dresser valet, Bea Lillie—that and more was to be the party.

He played to a packed holiday audience on Boxing Night, which roared itself hoarse with approval. He made his speech. He was off the next day to the shows of New York, to his friends there, to the sunshine. Barry Sinclair would play for him—Ivor had been best man at his wedding to Nicolette Roeg—a romance started in *The Dancing Years*.

I went to say farewell. As I left I turned at the door and said, "Now take great care of yourself, Ivor. You are very precious, you know." He smiled, a real Ivor smile. "Thanks, duckie," he said, "I'll be back. God bless." And I left him.

CHAPTER TWENTY-SEVEN

LAST ACT

IVOR went to Jamaica with his friends to his home, "Wyndways," Montego Bay. We did not hear much from him. The news I usually got from overseas was sent by Bobbie Andrews, who was always witty and to the point. Ivor did not shine as a correspondent. Meantime business dropped at the Palace.

Although the weather in Jamaica was absolutely tropical and the heat and sun quite unusual, Ivor did not seem to respond. Olive Gilbert, who looked after him so faithfully and well, noted a lassitude, so unusual in him at any time. As a rule, he took the lead; he drove his parties from amusement to amusement; he would keep them on the go; everything he suggested was going to be " fun." He would make them paint, swim, bathe, drive, go wherever he wanted. It never dawned on him they might not want to do it. They never rebelled. There was enough of the child in Ivor to make it difficult to deny what to him was evidently pleasure. But on this last holiday he did little. He sat about and he did not seem inclined to bathe, though as a rule that, to him, as he said, was " heaven."

He went about wearing as little as possible. At such times he was the nearest thing to a nudist, but he was always quite unself-conscious; I think, indeed, he was the least self-conscious person I ever knew. But he was thin, tired and seemed very weary. Although he was tanned almost black, it was not the hue of health for beneath it was a pallor. Nor did he sparkle at the parties. A picture in this book shows that: he is sitting looking into space as if he could see the end too clearly, well in sight. On this trip he saw a good deal of his neighbours, Lord Beaverbrook and Beverley Baxter, M.P. (who loves the Theatre although he is a critic), and a friendship and understanding sprang up. Lord Beaverbrook was impressed by Ivor, whom he said he found " different." He was right in every sense.

I would occasionally ring Fred Allen to ask if there was news, but the news he had was a demand from Ivor for £500 to be sent to him, which rather irked Fred Allen's careful and economic mind. " But it's his money," he granted, " I suppose he can spend it as he likes."

Towards the end of the holiday I did get a letter. Bill Wright came back in advance, with Alan Melville. Bill Wright is the man with the dark moustache and the white coat at the other end of the table at the party shown in this book—it was always democracy in Jamaica. And Wright came straight to me with this letter from Ivor:

" My Dear Popie,

Bill Wright is bringing this to you—not that there's ever any need to ask you but just try and get everything you can in about my return on the 19th and the redressing of the show as we want business to go up with a bang. But really what with the flu epidemic and the world situation and the weather and the meat rationing I don't see why it should. Max B. is delighted with the enclosed so I'm sure the *Express* will publish it. Try to get Olive's name mentioned as she's such a favourite—then of course *Gay's the Word*—I shall be at the first night. It's been wonderful holiday but of course I'm dying to get back to the Theatre. I really am insatiable.

Best Love,

Ivor."

I got his name in—and Olive's—but not the photo. I did not like the photos of him for he looked so ill. But the best of them I have used in this book, as it does not matter now, anyway.

That letter shows Ivor's care of business. He was aching to see it go up. With all respect to Barry Sinclair, the meat rationing, the epidemic and even the world situation, all that was needed was Ivor's return.

And at length he came back. He was to come back, wait until the first night of *Gay's the Word* and then rejoin *King's Rhapsody* on the following Monday. He arrived home on the evening of Monday, February 12th. Olive Gilbert recalls he had not been well then. I went down that evening to Waterloo to meet him. It was a cold, bleak, horrible night, with a searching wind and flurries of sleet and snow! No sort of night for a return from Jamaica. I waited for the boat train to arrive. It steamed in and the usual horde streamed out. I was looking for Ivor but he saw me first and called to me. I went towards him in the dim light but I stopped in my tracks for a moment. He looked brown enough, but drawn, ill, lean and gaunt—and he was coughing badly. Then I went up to him. He smiled, but I did not like the look in his eyes. " Ivor, what's the matter " I asked when he had, as usual, hugged me. " I've got a chill, caught it on board the boat," he replied. " You get into the car and off to the flat, quickly," I said, " this is no place for you." He wanted to look after the girls, but I said we would do that, and took him towards the car. Bill Wright was there, and there were Bobbie, Olive and Phyl Monkman. I took Ivor towards the car. A photographer asked for a picture and Ivor stopped; a reporter spoke to him and Ivor briefly mentioned his intention of being at the first night of *Gay's the Word*, and of going back to *King's Rhapsody* on the following Monday—the show having been re-dressed for the occasion. In answer to questions: " Oh yes, a marvellous holiday, did a lot of painting—going to exhibit? Well, I don't think so—not yet . . . ." And then I got him in the car and sent him off. He did not resist. He was coughing most of the time. I went home and my wife asked how Ivor looked. I said nothing for a moment and she looked at me. " My dear," I said, " I believe I saw death in his face."

Ivor had the doctor and was sent to bed. I was really shaken. It is my misfortune to have seen a great deal of illness—in other people—and a great deal of death, too. I have an uncanny feeling about it: I have had it always—a premonition which has seldom failed me. I was really frightened about Ivor. I did not see him again until the first night of *Gay's the Word*, which took place on the Friday of that week, February 16th, 1951.

He did not go to the dress rehearsal on the evening before production and that to him was a terrible sacrifice. Every care was taken of him. He could not have had better medical attention, nor is there any more careful guardian in this world than Olive Gilbert, in whom he trusted completely. None of them wanted him to go to the first night of *Gay's the Word* at the Saville. He had a temperature of 102. But he had made up his mind and when Ivor did that nobody in the world could alter him. But he rang me in the afternoon. It was then he asked me to keep the Press away from him on the first night—and broke off with a cough. " Don't worry, Ivor," I said, " I'll look after it. You won't be worried. Go into the box through the side door and I'll take care that nobody comes near you. But you know you ought not to go, don't you? It's no good asking you not to?" "You just try," came back over the 'phone with the ghost of a laugh. Of course it was no good. And who would blame him? Here was his own work; here was the play he had promised Cicely Courtneidge as long ago as 1929 coming to its climax. He had not seen a first night of a play of his own since *Fresh Fields* at the Criterion in 1933. Of course he must go.

There he was, in his box watching every moment of the show, joining in the applause, as excited as anyone there; indeed, more excited. He was carried away, as they all were, by Cicely Courtneidge's wonderful performance and by "Vitality"—that grand song rendered so grandly. And at the end, when the curtain rose and fell, rose and fell, and Cicely made a speech, there were yells for him. In the interval, everyone had gone to the side of the theatre opposite his box and stared up, as they do at Royalty. They knew where he was—and they demanded a speech. He stood in the box, graceful and charming as ever in his dinner jacket and the dark red carnation in his button hole. He looked wildly exultant and smiled with all the old glamour. "But don't applaud me—don't look at me," he said, with a sweeping gesture of his left arm towards the stage where Cicely Courtneidge stood with the company. "Look at her—applaud her—give it all to her—she's worth it—she deserves it. . . ." It was an evening of real triumph for all and especially for him. He deserved it, for it was to be his last. He could not have wished a better. He was indeed right on the crest of the wave: two successes in London at the same time—and his popularity greater than it had ever been before. . . .

He should have gone home to bed, but instead he gave a party. He would do it and nobody could stop him. He read the notices as soon as they came out; they were all "raves." And then he was ill again. It was obvious that he could not, as expected, take up his part again in *King's Rhapsody* the following Monday, it was postponed for a week. He got rest and he always got attention. But really he did not improve although the cough lessened and the temperature went.

He was not too fit the following Monday (February 26th, 1951), but he came back. We had invited the Press to see the show again, and they were anxious to do so. Business had been so enormous during the greater portion of the run, except when he had been away, that they had not had an opportunity of getting seats. So they were there in force. I had to deliver a lecture that night. It had originally been fixed for the previous Monday but I had altered the date to leave myself clear for his reappearance. When that was put off I could not alter it again.

The theatre was packed when the night came. I went round to see Ivor. I had not seen him since the first night of *Gay's the Word*, although we had spoken on the 'phone. He looked better and was very excited. He was glad to be back. The dressing-room was piled high with gifts: flowers, chocolates, all the usual offerings. There were telegrams galore. The members of the cast poured in and out to welcome him. We had a little chat as he dressed. Then I told him I must get back to see the Press and explained that I could not wait until the end as I had my lecture to deliver. But if wanted, I could come across, for I had only to go to the Arts' Theatre Club. He understood all about that. Now, I had recently had my first set of new teeth other than those I grew myself. Ivor had taken the greatest possible interest in the whole undertaking. I had to explain all that had been done and then when the night came and I was able to display my new dental apparatus in all its glory, he was quite enchanted. He examined them carefully and said he would never have believed them not to be real . . . (he was right there!) I had been terrified at first and had made him laugh with my descriptions of terror but it so happened that the man I went to was a wizard and I never felt a pang. The result pleased Ivor; he had his own out and compared them and was like a child with a new toy. That night, February 26th, he referred to them again. As I went I turned at the door and said, " Well, you know I wish you all the best. Go on and win—and take care of yourself." And I gave him a smile. He flashed one back. " Popie," he said, " it's like old times to see you smile that way again. I love your new teeth. God bless you." I went out of the room: and that was the last thing I heard him say, face to face.

He got a royal welcome. The show had been redressed and looked even more sumptuous than before. As usual, every principal got a special reception as they made their entrance in the Ballroom scene, and this evening, too, there was an " ooo-h" of admiration for the lovely dresses. Ivor entered in that black uniform and got a reception all over again. He played as usual, perhaps a little better than usual. He was so glad to be back in the play and the part he loved. And as he left the stage in that scene, it was the last time I saw him alive. In the interval I talked to the Press and then my wife and I had to go to the lecture. Neither of us wanted to, but there is no chance of putting on an understudy for a lecture. . . .

The last curtain fell and it was like a first night. Ivor made his speech and thanked everyone. He said he felt like the prodigal son surrounded by the fatted calves. He was back and all was right with the show. During the week which followed I did not see him. We wanted him kept quiet; visitors were kept to a minimum and I had nothing pressing to see him about at all. If he wanted me, he knew he had only to ring.

He played all that week. He went and spent the week-end at "Redroofs." Lady Juliet Duff was there, Bobbie Andrews, Alan Melville and Tom Gill. Life went on as usual and there was a lot of Canasta. Ivor even played a game that Monday morning before he had breakfast. It was an obsession with him. Before Lady Juliet left she decided to take a photograph. Ivor, Alan Melville, Gill and Bobbie Andrews lined up. Lady Juliet looked in the view-finder. "Funny," she thought, "I cannot see Ivor." She looked up, he was there, smiling. She tried again; still he was not in view. "Ivor," she said, "you must come in a bit. It may be your grey clothes against the background or something but I cannot see you." He moved—and then she saw him—and took her picture. It was the last he ever had taken. It is in this book.

He got to the theatre at the usual time. It was usual for me to see him on a Monday evening, but that night something prevented me. He told Bill Wright that he had bad pains in his upper arms and bad pains in his chest, but that they had passed off. "I suppose it's rheumatism," he said. "Well, we all get it you know, as we get along," said Bill.

Ivor played the show through and made his curtain speech as usual. He went back to No. 11 Aldwych and had supper with Tom Arnold. But Ivor did not seem well. He opened a bottle of champagne, but had difficulty with it. Tom Arnold helped.

"Are you all right, Ivor?" he asked him. "I've got some pain," replied Ivor, "but I'll be all right." They had some supper. Still Ivor did not seem well and Tom Arnold persuaded him to go to bed. He did so. "Shall I get the doctor?" he asked. But Ivor said, "No." Olive and Bobbie would soon be in.

He was sitting on his bed and was obviously in pain. Tom

Arnold heard Olive and Bobbie arrive, and then he went. He had not gone far before he found he had taken the wrong hat. He went back. Ivor was still ill but Olive was with him and Bobbie. Tom Arnold left. That was well after midnight on the night of March 5th/6th, 1951.

The telephone beside my bed rang. I am quite accustomed to that. It happens so often to those who deal in news. I have also the gift of being wide awake at once; there is never a second of drowsiness where I am concerned. I picked up the receiver. I heard Tom Arnold's voice. "Is that you, Popie," he said and I told him, yes. "Are you awake? Can you stand a shock?" he asked. By this time I thought I knew. "I can stand anything but waiting," I said. "What is it?" "Ivor," said Tom Arnold. ... "Dead?" I asked. "Yes," he said, "just a short while ago."

Although I was semi-prepared, it was still a terrible blow. I switched on the light: it was just 3.15 a.m. "Tell me what happened," I said. He told me what he knew; how he had been rung up and called back and how the doctor had come. Bill Wright was there too. It was thrombosis. Tom Arnold told me his story plainly and well. I realized the terrible shock he had suffered and all it meant to him. "Leave the rest to me," I told him. "I'll see you at the flat at ten o'clock. You get to bed and get some rest." My wife was awake now and wanted to know what it was. We have a couple of grand-children we adore and she, of course, feared for them, I told her—as gently as I could....

I had to decide what to do. I rang the flat. I spoke to Bill Wright, a tower of strength at that moment with his grief under control, efficient and clear. He gave me details, telling me the doctor's name and 'phone number. And now I had to tell the world.

I looked at the clock. Still time for the late editions. But I said to myself. "No, I'm not going to let Ivor get just a couple of lines in the fudge. His story shall be done as he deserves. It shall be done well." I made a cup of tea for myself and my wife. She was terribly distressed. I have had to do this gruesome, heartbreaking job all too often. I checked up with the doctor, who was helpful in every way. I wrote out my story. I knew they would ask me for the usual "appreciation." It is my fate to be always writing appreciations and obituaries for the great ones of my profession as they pass on. I knew them all and am almost the last of their generation who can do them real justice. I waited until all the daily papers had "gone to bed," which means they had closed down and were through the press. Then I rang my friends the Press Association and I told them. Long years of association with this great firm makes them take anything I say as true and they do not confirm. This time I gave them the flat number and the doctor's number too, and asked them also to ring and pick up anything I might have missed. Then come back to me, I said, and I will give you an appreciation. Within three minutes they were back. It was then 4.15 a.m. And I read them this over the 'phone:

> "Ivor Novello died in harness as he would have wished. His whole life was wrapped up in the Theatre, which he loved. To him the world held little else. An actor-manager for nearly thirty years, he was the most outstanding stage figure of the time and the most deservedly and consistently successful. Author of many brilliant comedies, an actor of grace, ability and polish, it is as author-composer of brilliant musical plays that his name will live. He gave this country a succession of brilliant musical shows; he gave it songs and tunes which will be for ever in the memory. He enriched his time with melody and almost alone he upheld the prestige of English musical comedy. He was himself a man of golden quality and quality was what he stood for. He was 'Ivor' to everyone—he was everybody's friend. His name will be enshrined as one of the great ones of the Theatre. . . ."

I left it at that. I knew I should get the 7 o'clock news. I knew that the evening papers would give it columns on the front page. But I slept no more that night.

At seven o'clock I heard my news come over the air. And then the 'phone began to ring. Everyone wanted details. I told them all that I knew: how he had had a very bad attack of thrombosis at 2 a.m. and had died at 2.15. He was unconscious at the end. . .

Then the evening papers got on. My friend Frank Starr, of the *Evening News*, asked me to do him a column. I said I would. I went down to the office very early. I typed that column with one hand, answering the 'phone with the other. When they came, my secretaries rallied nobly. The 'phone never ceased. The column went down to the *News* and went on the front page. There was a siege at the office: everyone wanted stories, and pictures. But we coped.

I went over to the flat at ten a.m. It is quite handy to where my office was then. There was Fred Allen, Gordon Duttson and Bill Wright, to whom I had already 'phoned. The question which had to be decided was what was to happen at the Palace that night? I had to make an announcement. We asked Olive and Bobbie—we knew their answer. We 'phoned Tom Arnold, who was just starting for the flat himself. The decision was taken. The theatre was to be closed that evening. It was necessary for none of those people could have played. . . .

Before I went, I wanted to see Ivor. Bill Wright took me into his bedroom. He lay there on the lovely bed with the mirrored wall beside it—at rest—with the nobility of death upon him. There was just that slight smile which most dead people have without sign of age or suffering. He was a boy again. His age was fifty-eight. I gazed for a moment and I said my farewell. Then I went back to work.

The story of the last scene he played in this life belongs to Olive Gilbert. Ivor owed much to Olive who, for a long time, looked after him, controlled his staff and his flat, to say nothing of " Redroofs." She would see that he got the food he liked and all the dishes he fancied. It was Olive's mission in life to do this and not only did she love doing it but she did it nobly. She will forgive me if I say she was the ideal housekeeper and artiste combined, for her care of Ivor was artistry as much as her singing and acting. She knew all about him, all his moods, all his tastes. She worshipped the ground he walked on and he thought the world of her. There was nobody like " Ollie." He had one taste she rather deplored but with which she never interfered. He loved that curious looking sweetmeat called " Candy Floss." To her it resembled cotton-wool. She recalls how, during his last visit to Brighton, they went on the pier where he saw Candy Floss being sold. He—the idol of the Theatre—promptly joined the queue and waited patiently for his turn. He bought two pieces of it. Then he and she walked down the pier in triumph whilst he devoured it with every sign of relish. Crowds looked on. It did not matter to Ivor. He was doing something he liked, he was eating something he liked. Let all the world see. And because he had absolutely no self-consciousness, his wholehearted enjoyment was so perfectly apparent to all. And that is a pretty good highlight on Ivor.

Olive was present all through that last scene. She had not gone down to " Redroofs " with him that week-end. She had a cold and wanted to save her voice. But she had seen to it that all was as he liked and the staff there knew what to do so well. She rang up and all was happy. He arrived back at the Palace much earlier than usual on the Monday and came in to see her. He told her everything had been grand and that the food was wonderful. But she thought he looked ill. His colour was ashen. She asked him about himself. He said he had had a fright. A horrible pain had attacked him in the chest (which was his weakest spot). He thought it was indigestion. He had gone to bed and propped himself up and felt better. She told him he must keep some brandy by his bedside. He promised he would. But on the whole he seemed all right. He had a new uniform for the show—that uniform he so adored. When he got into it, for the last scene of the first act, he came to see Olive again. He said, with a laugh—he thought he looked fine—and that he was giving a good performance. At the end of the show she told him that she had ordered oysters for him and Tom Arnold for supper. She thought he seemed all right then but she was a little worried because she had noticed he had had just a sip of brandy during the show—a very, very rare thing for him indeed. But she remembered she had advised him to keep some by him and thought he was taking her advice. She and Bobbie Andrews went out to a supper party together. When they got back to No. 11 Aldwych, Olive went up to Ivor's flat—hers is the one below his—to see that everything was in order. She was told that the supper had been wonderful. Ellen (who looked after the flat) asked her to look at the kitchen and see the mess. Ivor had tried to open a bottle of champagne and could not do it. So he just gave it a whack with a hammer and it had exploded like a bomb—all over everything. Nobody cared, they all laughed. The next bottle proved more amenable. But he had only drunk about half a glass. Olive did not see Ivor then—he was still talking to Tom Arnold; knowing that Bobbie was in and that he seemed all right, she went down to her own flat. But before she went she suggested that perhaps it would be as well if Tom Arnold did not stay too late because Ivor was not well. There was no need to worry. Tom Arnold knew that himself.

She went downstairs and prepared for bed. It was about 1.15

a.m. and all was silent. She had heard the lift go down. Later she heard a bell ringing and thought somebody had got locked out. And then, when things were silent again, her telephone rang. Those stabs in the silence of the night are terrifying things, so wide awake she rushed to the 'phone. It was Bobbie Andrews. " Olive, come up quickly," he said, " Ivor's terribly ill. Come at once." She threw something on and rushed upstairs. Ivor was in bed. He looked terrible and felt cold and clammy. But he smiled a little when he saw that Olive had a brandy flask clasped in her hand. She propped him up as comfortably as she could and he seemed to rally. He said he had had some brandy. She gave him a clean handkerchief with some eau-de-cologne and it seemed to help. But there was no doubt he was very ill indeed. Olive told Bobbie to 'phone to the doctor at once, and he did so. She had some smelling salts but Ivor said they were too weak: he could not smell them. Bobbie Andrews brought in some more and Olive sniffed them first, finding them very strong. She held them in consequence some distance from Ivor's nose. But he took them from her, and putting them to his nostrils sniffed hard and said he could not smell them at all. His pain seemed to have passed. Although weak, he said he would get up and go to the bathroom. She tried to make him keep in bed but he went. Then the doctor arrived. He got Ivor back into bed again. He examined Ivor with the utmost care. He asked if there had been similar attacks and was told " No, only the previous night." Whilst the doctor was treating Ivor, Olive stood away, but in the door ready to help if needed. Ivor asked the doctor if he was going to be ill again (it will be remembered how bad his health had been for most of the previous year). He told the doctor then how some time before he had had a similar attack but had told nobody about it. He had thought it only a passing affair and did not want to cause alarm. Olive thought that the doctor was going to give Ivor an injection and for the second she turned her head away. The doctor had previously whispered to her that Ivor was very, very ill indeed. He continued to work on Ivor. Then she heard a gasp—a kind of long drawn out sigh. She came forward anxiously. The doctor looked up and she read the message on his face before he spoke. Ivor Novello had made his exit. He was dead.

There was no pain at the end. He was unconscious during the

last short phase. But he had gone. It was the end. He had said one significant thing before the last attack. He had said: " I'm afraid I've had it." Poor man. He had. And there is little doubt that he knew. Peter Graves came to help. Nothing more could be done. But they called everyone they could think of in the emergency. They called Tom Arnold, who called me.

There were no last, lingering words, no farewells. That sentence of death he passed on himself was almost the last thing he said, save faint replies to the doctor's queries. That doctor knew him and did all that could be done. But it was too late. And it is now known that had he lived he might have been bed-ridden for months, perhaps, for years. It was better that he should go as he did, for it would have been a living death for him. His end was as he would have wished it: with applause still ringing in his ears, a supper party with a dear friend and plenty of laughter, his nearest friends around him at the finish. He would have asked no more—save the wish, perhaps, that he might have died on the stage as the curtain fell.

A light had gone out of the Theatre and when such a light will shine again is unknown. It went out like a lamp at about 2.15 a.m. on the morning of March 6th, 1951.

CHAPTER TWENTY-EIGHT

DE MORTUIS . . .

EVERYONE knows the old cliché about speaking nothing but good of the dead. It is more honoured in the breach than in the observance. Shakespeare said that the evil that men did lived after them and the good was oft interred with their bones.

Let it be seen what not only the members of his profession but the general public thought of Ivor, and not only when dead but alive. He had an extraordinary postbag. And as soon as he was dead, letters poured in. People who wanted to express themselves did not know to whom to write; there was no widow, no family and nobody knew of relations. So his friends got letters. I got thousands. These good folk had to write to somebody and they chose those whom they knew were his friends. But first of all look at some he had received in his lifetime. It helps to assess character. Here is an extract from one he received in 1936, the writer being unknown to him:

> " May I add my thanks to the many others you must have received, for one of the most beautiful productions that I ever remember seeing and I have been a theatregoer for years. I have seen *The Happy Hypocrite* three times in as many weeks and feel that I could joyfully go on seeing it, if I were not leaving London. I cannot convey to you in words the intense delight that you have given to me, and others, in this play. Not only is it on a far higher level than the ordinary play, both in its lovely English and in its theme and the way in which it is developed, but the whole production is exquisite, acting, music, scenery and lighting all fitting perfectly into a whole, so unusual, original, artistic and beautiful that it will remain in the minds of those of us who saw and loved it as a very precious and lasting possession. We do truly ask you to accept our heartfelt thanks for a most beautiful gift and wish you all future good. . . ."

That might be dismissed as a fan letter except for the excellent composition, but it must be borne in mind that Ivor was the only actor-manager with the courage to do that play when he did.

There was a dear lady much attached to the Theatre, of whom we were all very fond. She was the most regular of the regular first nighters: one put her name down for two front row stalls without her needing to apply and that name was Mrs. Higson. She and her charming daughter were first-night land-marks. She had strong likes and dislikes and was not averse to airing them, but she liked Ivor. She used to write to him very characteristic letters. Here is one:

> " Well, my dear, I hope you are pleased with yourself—very good notices. I am coming soon—any time between the acts?—and I'm so glad it ends well. I know two cases of men who married women much older than themselves and it answered quite well. . . . Bless you, I am glad of your success. . . . I always admired you and knew you were clever in spite of your looks. Curious people, critics, why should they talk about your age? You'll never read this. Affectionately,
>
> Nell Higson. (The Old Lady of the Theatre).
>
> " PS. Do you open your letters? How many roofs has your house got? I am not fishing for invitations. I never can get away. . . ."

In another letter she besought him to save money:

> " Now for good advice, which you won't take—*do*, *do* put away something every week even in a box and invest it at 4 per cent. when you get £100 (Bless the woman, does she think me a fool?) Bless you, dear Lamb."

Mrs. Higson need not have worried: she did not know David Ivor Davies.

When Ivor gave Ralph Reader and Bill Sutton the rights of *Careless Rapture* to tour, Ralph wrote this letter:

> " Dear Ivor,
>
> It is kind and generous of you to help us with ' Careless '. I have always believed in Santa Claus but I didn't realize he came from Wales. I think you must know what is in my heart so when I say ' Thank You ' it really means much more. God Bless you always,
>
> Yours devotedly,
>
> Ralph."

If I were to attempt to give even extracts from the numbers of letters I have seen in working on the material for this book—

from the many from people with famous names, thanking him for favours, thanking him for help, thanking him for making it possible for them to get ease from pain and struggle back to health because he had paid for medical treatment or because he had sent them and theirs abroad to a better climate to recover strength, I should need another book. Ivor never said " No " to a call for help where pain or suffering was in question. Those two things he hated.

There was one letter which Ivor treasured very much and which he received from his friend Lord Cromer on New Year's Day 1951. Lord Cromer, whose service and devotion to the Theatre are well known and who was such a popular Lord Chamberlain wrote:

" My Dear Ivor,

My handwriting being no longer as easy to read as it should be I have taken to typing my own letters and this one is to tell you that I am reluctant to allow the New Year to begin without telling you how much I think the theatre-going and music-loving public owe to you for the genius of your compositions and productions over a long series of years. From the vast and enthusiastic audiences that incessantly crowd to your plays night after night, you have the measure of the deep appreciation felt for your work, and hard work it must be never to disappoint your public. It is then that, as the old man that I now am, I should like to pay you this inadequately worded tribute, as also of an old friend, to what you have already accomplished in a sphere you have made your own in the Theatre. Besides this, I want to wish you all good fortune, prosperity and above all, good health to allow of your continuing to enchant your listeners not only in 1951 but for long years to come.

Cromer."

I had decided not to print any of the letters which Ivor received as regards his imprisonment, but I think Constance Collier, his very dear friend, his mentor, theatrical guide, and collaborator in early success, should be allowed her say. Her letter to him came from New York. It is full of her sound good sense and philosophy and is written with a full understanding of him—she said:

" My Darling,

If it is true, I wish I were with you. We could have long talks as we used to. Anyhow, I know you will turn it into a great experience and write a wonderful play about it. It is all very silly, but I supposed they used you because they want to make a point, so you are a casualty of these stupid, cruel times. It is so unfair, as I suppose nobody in England has done as much as you to keep up public morale and help the theatre people to earn a living. Don't mind, darling—*everything* in life is an *experience* and you have the talent to make use of it. All my love, dear love,

Constance.... I am practising my typing on you...."

It was just the sort of letter he should have had. And as I sat with Constance Collier not long ago, she told me the truth of her non-appearance in *The Truth Game*. She did not believe in the play and thought it would fail. She did not want Ivor to do it. She wanted to use every means in her power to save him from what she thought was failure. She went to Noël Coward for help. He saw how terribly upset she was and prescribed tea at once. She knew he was right and longed for the tea, which Noël Coward made for her himself. She sat gasping out her story whilst that tea " drew." And then Noël Coward poured out a — cup of hot water. He had forgotten to put in the tea! Anyway, he helped her. He told Ivor she could not play the part; he read the play and did not believe in it either. So Ivor, without waiting to see Constance and have any further explanation, gave the part to Ellis Jeffreys, who did not play it either. Constance Collier had hoped that she would see Ivor then they could argue it out, possibly make some alterations, as Noël Coward had kindly suggested. But he took her at her word and went elsewhere. There was a rift, but it did not last. Always that room at " Redroofs " was " Constance's Room " —ready for her. And she so readily admits she was quite wrong about the play. So does Noël Coward.

She keeps his memory fresh and lasting in her heart. She has as a further memento that jewelled cigarette case with the map of the theatre given him at Drury Lane—which is fitting, for she helped him in the Theatre so much, as she has helped and does help, so many others. He and she wrote *The Rat* and *Down Hill*. She is still to-day that Grand Lady of the Theatre, still the perfect Cleopatra, the only actress I ever saw who not only looked it but played it as it should be played. Age cannot wither her, nor custom stale: she is Cleopatra and kindliness in one.

HH

But Ivor's hold on his public was best shown when the news of his death was known. Letters rolled in and I can deal only with a handful. We asked for no flowers, but the money to be sent to King George Pension Fund for Actors, and this came:

"Dear Sir,

Will you please except my small donation. I am an old-age pensioner. I marched to the tune of 'Keep the Home Fires Burning' in France many times and I am sure that tune helped us to win the war.

An old Buff,
R. Harriss."

That came to me, as did all those from which I now quote:

"As a great admirer of Ivor Novello and of everything he has done for the British Theatre, I feel I must send some personal expression of sympathy to all his many friends in the theatre world who must now be missing him so much, and I think that I can do no better than to send this message to you as one of his closest associates and one who is also known to me in a modest way. His genius as an actor, author and composer will surely make him immortal but to many thousands he will be remembered for all those little acts of kindness which came to him so naturally. I remember most vividly his great patience in answering every one of the letters I wrote to him as a small girl and that he was never in too much of a hurry to spare a few words and a smile to that same little girl who spent much of her time at Drury Lane stage door. His loss is a cruel blow to the British stage and he can never be replaced.

Yours sincerely,
Valerie L. Ripley."

I am sure Miss Ripley will not mind my using her letter.

"Dear Sir,

I was so sorry when I heard that Dear Gentleman passed away so sudden—he was very famous gentleman although when he wrote very famous song 'Keep the Home Fires Burning' until the Boys come home it went all over the world and my Brother who was in the Battle of Mons, they all sang that gentleman's song as they went into battle as he done 25 years in the army he has six medals—he saved the guns as the sergeant was shot who had charge of the guns poor man and my Brother he took charge of the guns—he saved the guns. . . . I am so sorry for the Dear Gentleman that has gone—God Bless him."

And both the writer and her brother who saved the guns signed that letter which would have made Ivor proud. Their name is Nodes.

Albert and Mabel Day, who had been valet-dresser and housekeeper respectively to Ivor, wrote to Fred Allen, who answered, and here is their reply:

" Dear Mr. Allen,

Many thanks for your nice letter, it was so nice hearing from you again. I have always wanted to come up to town and see Mr. Ivor and everyone but our days are so full and my word how they fly that we never get much time for visiting; we rent a rather nice house with my sister and husband; we have a large garden back and front with fruit trees and a lawn, also keep chickens and rabbits so you see we have our work cut out, not forgetting queuing, etc. I have been ill myself too, several times and just could not get round to coming up. I am so very sorry now as I should have loved to have seen Mr. Ivor again but there it is. He was always so very nice to us both and thoughtful he was to us whilst in U.S. He would always wait for us in a taxi and take us to and from the theatre and always put any pleasures he possibly could in our way. It was a wonderful experience for us both and we have always been grateful to him for it all and we always worked together so well and enjoyed every moment of it all."

That was a letter from someone who appreciated Ivor and shows his appreciation and kindness to good service. Marie Tempest had recommended Mabel Day, who wrote the letter, to Ivor, and he always felt grateful to her for that, too. Not one of Ivor's servants but say the same. And it is the servants who know true character.

There is also a letter from a lady who happens (heaven bless her) to be a fan of mine:

" Dear Mr. Macqueen-Pope,

I feel I must add a tribute to the many you must have received about Ivor Novello. During 1941 we were living at Brighton and in June Ivor Novello was playing in *The Dancing Years* at the Hippodrome. One morning a message was received at the Battery where my husband was stationed asking if one of the officers could take Mr. Novello and a friend to bathe at the private beach used by the men of the Battery. The C.O. said he'd never met an actor in his life and did not know what to say to him and asked my husband if he would go, as he had had some contact with ' pro's ' during his amateur theatrical days. In due course my husband went along to the Norfolk Hotel where Ivor Novello and Barry Sinclair were staying and they all spent the morning bathing and sun bathing. Before my husband drove them back to the hotel Mr. Novello asked my husband if he would like tickets for the show. We had already booked seats. He said ' That's a pity,' but would we come round afterwards and see him in his dressing-room? During the performance I thought, ' Oh dear, how bored he must be seeing strangers and listening to fatuous compliments when he is probably longing to go home.' However, the show ended and I being a rather shy person at meeting strangers, would have welcomed an excuse to go straight home without seeing him. We went round. Outside the dressing-room door, I took a deep breath and hoped I would not appear as dumb as I felt. We went in; immediately he made us feel as though we were two old friends he'd been waiting to see all the evening. I look upon the half hour we spent with him as one of the pleasantest in my memory and we both came away feeling what an exceptionally nice man he was. We never saw him again, of course, but we feel that, apart from his great talents, what a great loss he must be to his friends—as a friend. We both send our best wishes,

Yours very sincerely,
Nancy Wells."

And the following also touches me closely, but it is so sincere and from that large part of society which is the backbone of this country and the backbone of Ivor's following too. It came to me:

" Dear Sir,

I hope you will not find this letter an impertinence. I am a very ordinary ageing suburban housewife with an intense love of the Theatre and a great admiration of your writings. Recently I read in the *Barnet Press* that you live not so far away and also that you are a friend of Ivor Novello's whose career I have followed since I saw him in *The Rat*. I feel sure there must be soon a memorial service for him and as I have no connection with the stage I write to ask if you can possibly help me to obtain a ticket, either for myself alone or with my daughter. I am not very well fitted to cope with the crowds I am sure will be there. I realize there will be a great demand for tickets from stage associates and friends so if it is impossible for you to grant me this favour perhaps you will be kind enough to let me know when the time and church are fixed and if there will be any places for the general public. . . ."

And she sent me a passage from Shelley's " Adonais " copied out by herself, including those wonderful lines:

" He has outsoared the shadow of our night,
Envy and calumny and hate and pain,
And that unrest which men miscall delight,
Can touch him not and torture not again. . . .
He lives, he wakes, till Death is dead, not he."

And I remembered how Maurice Hewlett had loved that poem too, as I do.

Tom Arnold received this one, with which I dealt:

" Dear Mr. Arnold,

Ivor Novello's passing! What a shocking blow this is to the musical world! As an old Cardiffian of 84 years I well remember him born having then recently started singing lessons with Madame Clara Novello. What a genius Ivor was! And too sad to think he is no more. I did contribute to the Chorus when Madame had her Jubilee Concert and Ivor was present. That was a wonderful event! And now to think they are gone; it is difficult to realize its sadness. Will you please accept my deep sympathy always to be remembered and if I can be spared a card to his memory it will be very much treasured. I do possess Ivor's thanks when his mother passed on. With sincere sympathy. . . .

Mrs. Frances Foster."

There's Welsh for you in every sentence, but also sincerity. She got the card.

Miss Dollie Broadbridge wrote and suggested the formation of a Repertory Company of Ivor Novello's musical plays on the lines of Gilbert and Sullivan. It is a suggestion which might take shape some day and will be remembered.

One gentleman made another suggestion:

" I was wondering if you would consider it a magnanimous gesture to the memory of Ivor Novello and the fact that his last play is running at your splendid theatre to rename the Saville—

the Novello Theatre. If this is not possible, perhaps *when* the next theatre is built and opened in the West End, it may bear his illustrious name."

It is not such a bad idea. And a young lady wrote to me as follows:

"As a very close friend of Ivor Novello's I can imagine the great shock you have experienced at this tragedy. Please accept my very sincere sympathy in the overwhelming loss of such a wonderful friend. I have admired him for years, especially his great kindness and patience to us—his public. I remember some months ago while I was waiting at the stage door of the Palace seeing him in a hurry to get to his dressing-room (it was seven o'clock). As he passed I pushed a parcel of chocolates, etc., into his hand, never expecting him to stop. But he turned and in spite of his hurry said a few words to me as if he had all the time in the world. Truly we have lost a very dear friend of the Theatre. . . ."

A lady spoke to me in the vestibule of the Saville Theatre, asking how she could obtain a photo of Ivor Novello. I sent her one—she wrote:

"I feel I must express how deeply shocked and saddened I was to know of Mr. Novello's sudden passing. It was like losing a very near and personal friend. His work and art have given me so much pleasure that it is almost unbelievable that I shall never see that generous elegant figure again nor hear his gay, bantering and caressing voice which I found so enchanting over the years. I know of no one worthy of wearing his mantle in these days in which violence and sex in the worst possible taste are flaunted for all they are worth. And I fear his like may not pass this way again."

That lady, when she heard I was writing this book, wrote to me and asked if she might have the pleasure—if it would be any help—of assisting in the typing of it. For that I am grateful and I should like friends of Ivor's to know of her concrete offer of service to his memory.

John B. Meikle, of Larkhall, Scotland, wrote to me:

"He was a great national figure and in the realms of music was the undisputed Master. I was reading the story of his life in the

Sunday Chronicle and I realized how fine, how sensitive and how kindly a disposition he had. Naturally I have been impressed by the tribute of praise and the sense of bereavement expressed on all hands in the Public Press, and the emotional effect on the mourners at his funeral was a genuine augury of devotion to a hero of supreme lovableness and genius. Three weeks ago, at one of the lectures I helped to conduct in the Community Hall at Larkhall, during discussion time the audience was questioned as to what was most conducive to happiness in each member's life and one young lady surprised everyone by answering ' The music of Ivor Novello.' At last Tuesday's meeting the same pretty girl was in tears when she discussed with me Ivor's sad ending. Ah well, he has gone to gather the other world's lilacs."

From every class and denomination and calling they came, those letters. We tried to answer them all.

Mrs. Godbold, housekeeper at His Majesty's Theatre, that dear lady everyone knew as " Goddy," paid her tribute:

" I just cannot realize even now that he has passed on and can only say that out of the literally hundreds of ' pro's ' who passed through my hands at H.M.T. he was one of the very few who gave so little trouble and was always most gentle and courteous to us all."

And that from " Goddy " is a tribute worth having. He was gentle and he was courteous, two characteristics so rare to-day. The Church paid its tribute too. The Reverend Herbert T. Lewis, M.A., of the Marylebone Presbyterian Church, wrote:

" I feel I must write to someone on the passing of Ivor Novello. You in the Theatrical world have lost a great figure, and as *The Evening News* expressed it, ' there was no one quite like Ivor.' But we have all lost someone who has thrilled us with his lovely melodies and it's sad to think that we shall see him and hear him no more.

" One of my most vivid and happiest recollections of a Garden Party at Wadham College Gardens, Oxford. It was in the autumn of 1914 and the gardens were illuminated. A young man, comparatively unknown, came forward and sat down at the grand piano. He played ' Keep the Home Fires Burning ' which, he said, he had composed. The atmosphere was electric; many people were in tears; I shall never forget that experience. That song went round the world, as indeed so many of his melodies have done. I gather that you have lost a good friend and I was glad to read your tribute in the *News*. I am so glad that you and he saw *Gay's the Word* on the road to success in Manchester. ' Gay ' is not the word just now, and yet Ivor's tunes will help to keep us gay when the ' dark clouds ' are about. . . ."

Mrs. Reed, the postmistress of Beltinge, in Kent, wrote to me. I used to go and see W. H. Berry, the great comedian, who lived there and she knew me:

" Forgive me writing you but feel so much regret at the death of Ivor Novello that I just had to write to someone. How you must all feel the loss of such a wonderful genius. I just cannot forget it myself, and what you must all feel that have been in close contact with him for so long I cannot imagine. My daughter and I saw *Gay's the Word* and enjoyed it very much. Cicely Courtneidge is really wonderful. We listened to the radio when you all paid your tribute to Ivor and just felt we had had a great loss ourselves. I remember Zena and Phyllis Dare when they wore their hair in pigtails and have sold them many stamps but I don't suppose they would remember me. Do hope you won't mind my writing to you but I am glad I've done so. . . . "

When I was down there she asked me many questions about Ivor and she and her daughter listened eagerly to the replies. They did not know him, had never spoken to him, but they mourned just the same.

There is a letter of unusual interest and importance from Norman G. Phelps, who wrote to Tom Arnold, saying:

" Dear Sir,

It occurs to me that it might not be inappropriate to have a plaque erected to the memory of the late Mr. Ivor Novello in his flat in the Strand and that the attached words might, perhaps, be considered in that respect. It is just an idea of mine which I pass on for your consideration.

Yours faithfully,

(*signed*) NORMAN G. PHELPS.

PS. I am not certain of the dates of the years and therefore leave them vacant."

" Here From . . . . .To . . . .
Lived Ivor Novello
And Here, in those Years
Was Pleasant and Lovely
Music Born
That Comforted the People."

It is devoutly hoped that this idea will go further. But the plaque I think, should not be inside the flat but on the outside so that those throngs which pass up and down Aldwych may see for themselves where was born such lovely music which did indeed comfort so many of them. There are plaques on houses of people who did far less than Ivor. He is indeed entitled to such recognition. Representations are being made whilst this book is being written to the proper authorities, and it is hoped that such a plaque may, one day before very long, mark one more spot in London of interest to such a multitude of people.

It has been stated in these pages that Ivor had a habit of saying " Thank You." He always did this in a very personal manner. Notes of thanks would be photostated in facsimile of his own handwriting and the following are examples. They are firstly, the letter he sent after his release from imprisonment (the one quoted further back was to those who wrote to him after his sentence and pending the appeal):

> " Thank you for your most dear thought of me during the last few weeks. I have been quite overwhelmed by the love and loyalty of my friends and their precious qualities have made my bitter experience possible to be borne. My most loving thanks.
>
> IVOR."

And after he had done the broadcast concerning his beloved " Mam ":

> " Thanks for your very kind letter about ' Mam's ' broadcast. It was a great joy to do and I know she would have been proud and pleased. Again many thanks. Ivor Novello."

Lastly his final letter of thanks for those who sent him telegrams, gifts and messages on the occasion of the production of *Gay's the Word.*

> " Thank you most awfully for remembering the first night of *Gay's the Word.* It really was a wonderful evening and I'm extremely happy.
>
> Yours,
>
> IVOR."

Poor man, his happiness was to be shortlived.

A letter came for Fred Allen and his wife from Sybil Vane, the vocalist, who was the first to sing " Keep the Home Fires Burning " long ago at the old Alhambra. She wrote from her home in Los Angeles, California:

" My Dear Folks,

Thank you so much Fred for your sweet note, with Ivor's Memorial enclosed. Yes, I can well understand how you must feel, for as far back as I can remember you were in his life. How faithfully you served him, this I knew. I know you both understand what a part in each other's lives we played. You both must know what his passing has meant to me. When he visited here I felt we had never been apart, but knowing Ivor like we did, he could never live and suffer. I feel now something snapped inside me. Of course, I was not with him all these many years but he was just as dear to me—only you both know his last letter to me, saying how thrilled I would have been with the broadcast of Madam's life. He said I kept cropping up . . . Leon joins me in sending our our love to you both,

Always,
Sybil."

Miss Vane's real name was Elizabeth Jenkins, but Ivor, who always had a great flair for names, told her and her parents that she would never make a name in opera as " Lizzie " and he suggested that she should call herself Sybil Vane. That was his first effort at theatrical godfathership and it was as successful as the other two. Miss Vane not only became a concert singer in great request but made a big success as a " pocket prima donna," especially as Gretel in *Hansel and Gretel* at Covent Garden. She went to America during the First World War where she married a clever pianist named Leon Dunn, and their life remains happy to this day. She was of great assistance to Ivor when Lloydy was lying prostrate in Hollywood and it was impossible to send Ivor money from this country to pay for doctor and hospital charges. She and her husband paid them until matters could be straightened out.

There were thousands of letters from all ranks and grades. But those selected and used have a certain value. They show not only the affection of the public for this man, but they also throw a light on his character, which, coming from outside sources and being entirely unsolicited, has a greater value than any opinion expressed by anyone nearer to him or a close friend. There was no need for any of them to be written; they were written because the urge was there. They show so many things: the value of his song " Keep the Home Fires Burning " and what it meant to the actual fighting man, so well expressed by the gallant old " Buff " who sent 2*s.* 6*d.* for charity, a gift of great value from him, as well as by the gunner who took over in extremity and saved the guns. Presumably it was not at Mons he saved them, for " Keep the Home Fires " was not written then; but even if it was, that song heartened that stalwart gunner throughout the whole campaign, which he survived.

That story of the girl pushing the packet of chocolate into Ivor's hand is typical of the kindness he always showed and also of the overpowering desire on the part of so many people to give him something as an outward and visible sign of thanks. And the letter from Miss Ripley is just another instance of the patience he always showed to genuine people and of his courtesy, which never deserted him. His old housekeeper and valet-dresser prove how constant was his care for those who worked for him. He never forgot them. They were in a strange land and he saw to it that they had comfort and were looked after.

Mrs. Wells, who tells of his bathing at Brighton and of her visit with her husband to his dressing-room, does more than she knows. Ivor was not happy by the seaside if he could not get into the sea, provided the weather was warm. At that time, when he was playing at Brighton, the whole of the beach was closed, barb-wired and mined. But he saw this spot occupied by a battery and wondered. He asked, and he received.

And when that charming couple of shy people got into his room, Ivor's real self showed clearly. He had the wonderful gift of making anyone feel at home at once. He had the equally wonderful gift of giving the impression that of all the people in the world, they were those he most desired to see. He could make conversation, he had a wonderful knack of making others talk, and it was impossible for the most retiring of souls to be uneasy with him for more than a moment or so. Mrs. Wells shows this clearly.

In passing, one is delighted with the glimpse of the C.O. who was apparently a bit scared of actors. . . .

The girl in Scotland who found her greatest joy in his music—all these things are real and vouched for. They are not padding by a biographer anxious to show his subject in the best possible light. They are facts. They speak for themselves. They speak volumes, and they could be made into a volume by themselves.

His obituaries in the Press were excellent. They did him justice. Only one or two mentioned his imprisonment. Hannen Swaffer did so; but he spoke very kindly and well of Ivor and drew attention to the injustice of the whole thing. But there was one journalist who could find nothing to write about except the fact that he had been imprisoned. The fact that this man was what he was, the idol of the public, someone who brought happiness and joy to thousands and thousands, who had never a black mark which he deserved, who stood for quality and for the defence of the British musical stage against the ever-increasing flood of music from overseas, who was so kindly, so beloved—all that meant nothing! What appealed to him was the fact that Ivor had been in prison. He was tackled by a friend of Ivor's and he admitted he had never seen Ivor nor any of his plays, let alone ever met him. One was irresistibly reminded of that part of the great English work *The Pilgrim's Progress* (also written by a man who was put in prison undeservedly) in which was drawn such a vivid picture of the man with the muck rake. That unfortunate creature never looked up; he never saw the Angel standing by, offering him a gleaming crown. He could not lift his eyes from the muck which he raked amongst so eagerly, so busily. Indeed John Bunyan drew Life and Truth. The man with the muck rake still lives on and still rakes assiduously, never looking for good but only for garbage. That man, who writes anonymously, got his answer over and over again. He gets it again now. Fortunately, such men do no harm, save perhaps to themselves. What a miserable life it must be, unless they like it. Perhaps they do. Anyway, Ivor's memory is quite safe. He did more in this world than a "bit of time"—and much more that is worthy of remembrance.

CHAPTER TWENTY-NINE

PERSONAL TRIBUTE—AND ASSESSMENT

HAVING dealt with the letters, there remain the Personal Tributes. Again, only a selection can be used, for the friends were so many and all so anxious to bear witness. Sir Edward Marsh, for so many years Ivor's close friend, has already been mentioned. He it was who did so much for Ivor in many ways, who tried to form his taste in Art. Indeed, many of the pictures which grace the walls of "Redroofs" are Sir Edward's own property and he is leaving them there for the benefit of those who will now get health in that place—and that is just like "Eddie."

Lady Juliet Duff, another very old friend, first met him one snowy afternoon on Sir Edward's doorstep in Gray's Inn; they had both come to tea and that was their first meeting. The friendship was instantaneous. She remembers having dinner often with Ivor when he was in the R.N.A.S. at the Crystal Palace during the First World War. They used to sit on the terrace and look out over London, and he would dream dreams of one day conquering that City, dreams which came true and by his own efforts. Both those people knew Ivor backwards, forwards and inside out. They both testify to that clarity which was Ivor's, that transparency of mind and character, so easy to understand, so easy to see through, and they both adored him. Lady Juliet says that the Crystal Palace was a fitting place for a Phoenix to have sprung from (how right she is!), and that we shall never look upon his like again and that we who were his friends were fortunate. Her sorrow is that anyone that the world needed so badly should be taken away.

And now let Keneth Kent take the stage, which in real life he does so well and with such talent. He also is a very old friend of Ivor's. One of the oldest, for he knew him when they were both boys. Keneth was staying with his mother (he was sixteen) at the Cairn Hydro, Harrogate. He was about the only boy in the place, which was filled mostly with more elderly people undergoing the cure (Harrogate's gift to humanity) and was therefore rather the pet of them all. One day he and his mother saw a fly draw up to the Hydro and a lady get out with another boy. That boy was so good looking that Keneth thought he would probably dislike him very much. He found, on acquaintance, that he was wrong. A firm friendship sprang up between them which existed to Ivor's death. They were both mad about the Theatre. It has been related how they called on Sir Johnston Forbes-Robertson and how, on going back to London, they used to go in the pit and see all the shows, especially at Daly's and the Gaiety. They would wait at the stage door for Lily Elsie to come out and beg her autograph.

But at Harrogate, Ivor, whose voice had not then broken, instantly displaced Keneth as the pet of the ladies. He would sing at the concerts and transport them to joy and tears, which made Keneth a bit jealous at the time. Ivor had become the beloved of all. And after one concert the old ladies collected a sum of money and gave Ivor a pair of gold cuff links—one of his very early professional earnings, as it were.

But momentary pangs of jealousy notwithstanding, that friendship endured, for Keneth Kent is a big-hearted, sympathetic and understanding fellow whom one is proud to know and to be able to call friend.

It was he who told me the story about Ivor seeing Mam in Wormwood Scrubs. Ivor went ahead faster than Keneth in the profession when they were young, and sometimes Keneth sitting in the front row of the pit, would see Ivor in the stalls. He always attracted his attention—and jeered at him! Keneth heard that story of Mam in the garden at "Redroofs," which he remembers so well, because it was very often a difficult job to get Ivor out into the open air, if not for the purpose of sunbathing. Ivor was not an open-air man at all. Keneth remembers Ivor, in his siren suit, listening to the first recording of *King's Rhapsody* when they arrived at "Redroofs" and of the tears of pleasure and emotion which streamed down his face as he did so. He says that in Ivor there was a love of and a desire for children, which he showed plainly in *King's Rhapsody* in the scene in the box at the Opera when he speaks of his son—to be crowned—and says "He is only a little boy." Ivor certainly showed the deepest feeling in that scene, which was also tenderly and beautifully written. It may well be so. But Ivor knew my intense love of little children and my great delight in my grandson and granddaughter, to say nothing of my own daughter whom he knew well and who worked in his shows. He never mentioned such a thing to me, but then I never asked him and there was no need for him to do so. I would bow to Keneth's knowledge in that respect. He certainly always liked to hear the latest " gags " about my two little ruffians, bless them. He knew their father well, too—that same Bill Sutton already mentioned.

Keneth Kent recalls a fancy-dress ball at that Cairn Hydro. Ivor went as a girl. So nice did he look that a man chased him and stole a kiss, getting a good sound wallop over the face for his pains.

There was at " Redroofs " a figure held to be lucky but of no prepossessing appearance. It was often going to be banished but it held on. And then banishment fell upon it; shortly afterwards Ivor went to prison. And Keneth remembers too Ivor's pleasure when he saw his friend score a success on the stage. Kent made an outstanding success in the last play ever produced at Daly's Theatre, that theatre in which he and Ivor had so often sat in the pit. Now Kent was leading man and Ivor was in front. The times had changed, music had left Daly's and a strong drama was one of the last things ever played there. It was *St. Helena* and Kent played Napoleon and played it very finely indeed. Round to the dressing-room came a note scribbled on the back of an old envelope, all that Ivor had in his pocket. It said:

> "Buddha. It's marvellous and you are superb—far finer than I hoped. You're most moving and I'm proud of you and happy to be here.
>
> Love.
>
> Ivor."

Ivor had nicknamed him Buddha for he said there was a resemblance. Keneth Kent treasures that impulsive typical but sincere note. Kent was as fine a Napoleon as ever I saw, and I have seen many. His summing up of Ivor Novello whom he knew so well is that he was always unspoilt, and always grateful.

Hannen Swaffer, who introduced Ivor to D. W. Griffith, has his own version concerning that. He was sitting with Griffith in the Savoy when Ivor came in. He believes that he and Ivor were at that time quarrelling, no unusual state with " Swaff " at any time and more especially then. But it often happened that although someone might quarrel with Swaffer, he saw no reason to quarrel with them. He always liked Ivor anyway whatever he said—or did—about him and Swaff never bears malice. He says on this occasion Ivor chose a table in full view of Griffith and gave a beautiful performance of a young actor having supper. Everything was most perfectly done, with such grace and charm. Anyway it attracted Griffith's attention. He asked the journalist-critic who the young man was. He was told, and said he had never heard of him, but he added thought he was good and would like to see him. When Ivor had finished his meal the two men were still sitting at their table—Swaff seldom goes to bed at all. Ivor got up and made a very good exit. Swaff followed him out. He told Ivor that Griffith wanted to see him and told him how to get into touch. He says Ivor fell on his knees and said his prayers were answered. . . . Swaff is a man who speaks the truth. Who shall blame Ivor? He was young and he was ambitious. Here was the greatest man in movies in full view. What was the good of being an actor if you cannot act and make an impression? It says much for his powers that he did attract D. W. Griffith's eye, that he did get that interview, and that it led to a contract. That is not the only time Swaff has done things like that for people he likes, and he likes far more people than most imagine. I am proud of his long friendship. I have found much inspiration in his fearlessness and his outlook on life. But there have been times—there are now—when we differ very greatly. That makes no difference to either of us.

Barry Jones, who was a great friend of Ivor's and who played in two of his shows, whilst his partner Maurice Colbourne produced *The Happy Hypocrite*, met Mam in New York in the early 'twenties. He saw Ivor play in *Symphony in Two Flats* in New York but did not meet him. In September, 1931, he and Colbourne decided to attack London. They had played all over America and Canada, from Halifax to Vancouver, from Los Angeles to New York; but apart from the fact that Maurice Colbourne had taken over from Owen Nares in *Milestones*—years before—nobody knew them. When the news of this managerial venture broke in London there was a good deal of " knocking " in professional circles—how dare a company which had been messing about on the prairie dare enter the sacred West End? They opened their show, *The Queen's Husband* by Robert E. Sherwood with Grace Lane as their leading lady and both Jones and Colbourne in the cast, at the Ambassadors' Theatre on October 6th, 1931. Barry Jones had a long telegram of welcome and encouragement from one star only—Ivor Novello. And they did not know each other. That was typical of Ivor's love of the Theatre and his pleasure in courage. He was the first to encourage newcomers—and talent. *The Queen's Husband* and Barry Jones scored a triumph.

Barry Jones attests to Ivor's gift for making people easy and " at home " at a first meeting. He met him first some months after the telegram, and at the Ivy. He also attests to Ivor's gift for making people think they really mattered to him. And they did, if he liked them. Barry Jones holds that no composer has had Ivor's gift, in music, for making his melodies fit the moods of human beings. Nor has any of them ever spread more happiness; he says that if you saw anyone whistling or humming a Novello tune, you saw a happy face. He comments on Ivor's intention to play " Charles I " in Maurice Colbourne's play of that name and does not think that the public would have liked it. I agree there. Barry Jones played it eventually and played it beautifully, too. And Ivor brought a party of friends to see it. Barry Jones remarks that they were a wonderful audience and Ivor brought them all round to the dressing-room afterwards. They all praised and made their comments, but Ivor said practically nothing. Then they went off to Gwen Ffrangçon-Davies's dressing-room, Ivor being the last to go. Jones, left alone, had a feeling that someone was standing outside his door. He opened it, he was right. Ivor was standing there. He had not followed the others; he was stifling great emotion. And he wrote and apologized to Barry afterwards, apologized for paying him the greatest compliment an actor could receive. And those who saw Barry Jones as the ill-fated king will remember that tender human performance which nevertheless never lost that aloofness which surrounds royalty and was always wrapped about the man who sacrificed his head rather than allow his Divine Right to be questioned. His farewell to his children was one of the most affecting pieces of acting I have seen in a long theatrical life. Barry Jones played King Stefan in Ivor's *Glamorous Night* at Drury Lane. Ivor told him he must not get any laughs (Barry was then known as a comedian); it must be played dead straight. Ivor had the comedy part. Jones respected his frankness and played the part as a king should be played.

But let him speak for himself, this good actor and sincere man:

"Throughout the years a Novello opening night and a number of other visits became a 'must.' The last time I saw him was, I am glad to say, a very worthy occasion. Several hundreds of stars were crowding rather self-consciously towards the footlights at Drury Lane, pretending not to push and pretending not to be aware of Her Majesty when she came backstage after the performance. Nearly at the back, smiling happily, flanked by those two most gracious ladies of the Theatre, the Dares, stood the man who had had more success than anyone else had probably ever had in that theatre and over a longer period, the man who had perhaps saved the grand old playhouse's life when he swept into it with *Glamorous Night* and gave it the new life it enjoys now. There stood Ivor Novello, no speech to make, no claiming acquaintance with anyone but everyone, just happy to be in a Theatre. I was proud to be standing with Olive Gilbert and others in that little obscure group at the back when we all sang 'God Save the King.' On the stage at Theatre Royal, Drury Lane, is my last memory of one whose loss I think is the biggest loss the British stage has had or is likely to have. A man who always gave his attention, who chuckled quietly and had no swank, and the only person I have ever met in the profession who, however he appeared to enjoy the party he was at, or giving—appeared far more to be waiting politely until he could withdraw—to a dressing-room. He had to live somewhere and did so very comfortably. But I always felt that he relaxed most and was most content in the excitement of a dressing-room. When my mother, then about eighty-five, saw *Glamorous Night*, Ivor had heard of it and decorated the box with orchids as he did for Mam. Orchids could hardly have been wronger than for my mother, but the thought was there. I have always felt that Ivor was the leader of our Theatre. For sheer solid popularity, provincial, West End and Empire without any social ambitions or 'smart' publicity he held a position unrivalled. For that reason when sailing for the U.S.A. and Canada for the British Council in November, 1939, I drove myself down to "Redroofs" to say good-bye. Exactly why I cannot say. I had never been there before, or since, but on that occasion I felt I was saying 'Au Revoir' to the top of our profession who had been kind enough to ask me into *Glamorous Night* and later to offer me 'Comedienne' with Lilian Braithwaite at the Haymarket . . . in return I was able to do the same play under another name with Constance Collier in United States. . . ."

Barry Jones, by sending me that, has saved me writing much myself: I agree with all he says. He puts his finger right on the spot, especially as to the dressing-room part of Ivor's life. That was indeed where he was most himself and it was in his dressing-room that I saw most of him—and so got to know him clearly and well.

Philip Desborough, another good actor, wrote to me:

" While lately in the South of France for five weeks, friends and acquaintances died one per week. Yet one—and one only—do I find impossible to believe as no more with us—Dear Ivor. There was something about him that made it difficult to believe in death and that alone should stamp him as an unusual person. There was surely seldom a more universally beloved man in any specific profession. I knew him for most of my life and played with him in *The Happy Hypocrite*, surely one of the very best performances he ever gave and one of the loveliest productions. . . ."

Philip Desborough's sister is Teresa del Riego, the famous composer. She wrote to me:

" There is little I can say of my dear friend Ivor Novello which has not already been said by his many friends and admirers more eloquently than I could say or write. We had a sense of comradeship from the first although I was some years older than him. Both began writing music in our very early youth and music was responsible for our meeting when Ivor was about eighteen. We were both singing and playing our own songs on concert platform. I remember one of Ivor's visits to me in the early years of my marriage and how interested he was in a new invention in my possession called 'The Musicograph.' It claimed to be the sort of typing machine for which many composers had yearned but it never proved of use to either of us. A clever idea but quite impractical. I believe I was the only purchaser and it never came into the market since. Being an Italian production it vanished during the First World War. Ivor was very generous in his admiration and appreciation of other song-writers' work, and full of that warm praise which makes the heart glad—because it is sincere. He had a marvellous memory for all kinds of music, classical or otherwise.

" I so well remember during our last visit to "Redroofs" (his fascinating country house) how, after tea, he sat down at his lovely piano and played a few phrases from several composers, wandering from Wagner to Elgar motifs—to modern songwriters and finally playing the opening bars to my own ' Homing ' (a compliment to me). Upon which we persuaded that charming singer Olive Gilbert to sing the whole song through and most beautifully did she render it. An incident which I am sure amused Ivor occurred to a friend recently. She asked in a music shop for a song from one of Ivor's musical plays: the reply was, ' Sorry, we don't stock the Classics.' Ivor Novello's music may indeed become one of the classics in the way that Arthur Sullivan's and Edward German's light operas now are. Of a different category, no doubt, but in its own line, inimitable. There was always the stamp of individuality upon Ivor's music; not ' great ' perhaps but unique in its sheer luxuriance of melody and gracious harmonization. In the words of several of his friends I end my small tribute. There will never be another Ivor. . . . Teresa del Riego."

Mary Ellis, the greatest of his leading ladies in his musical plays, spoke a beautiful poem which she had written as a tribute to him during that broadcast in the week of his death, when many of us paid our public tribute to him over the air. And she recalls the hours at " Redroofs, " too, when they never dressed for dinner but he loved to see a new frock which made a picture. He had an artist's appreciation of a beautiful dress. The days, she said, went like poems, to soft music. And she was completely happy, nothing jarred; he was the perfect host. Mary understood Ivor and he understood her. He knew her gifts and he gave her songs—and parts—which she made into jewels.

On that occasion, too, Tom Arnold paid his tribute. He said:

" Between Ivor and myself there was more than a business partnership; there was very close personal friendship. In all my long and wide experience of the Theatre it has never been my good fortune to meet with anyone with whom it was easier or more delightful to work. He was a man of great humanity, of great understanding. He could always see the other man's point of view. In all the productions which we did together from 1934, there was never an argument. And in the Theatre that is saying a great deal Nobody could ever be despondent or cast down in his company. He had courage; he had conviction and the unusual quality of seeing his own mistakes, on the rare occasions when he made them, and of agreeing that they were mistakes. To me, he was the Theatre in person. He lived it, he breathed it, he loved it. To be in his company gave one a sense of well-being: it was a tonic and he lit the dark days of the present world with his belief in the fact that one must always do one's best. That he always did. I am proud that I was associated with him and proud that he was my friend. To me, as to everyone else, he was always Ivor. His music will always remain. . . ."

That was the tribute from a man of the Commercial Theatre who nevertheless always saw eye to eye with Ivor. Arnold says Ivor wrote the shows and he sold them: it was fifty-fifty in that. . . .

Fay Compton, who always held Ivor very near her heart, said very much in very little. He held her in as high affection and admiration as she held him. She and Barry Jones were on the air together on that broadcast and Fay said:

"I don't want to be sentimental about Ivor now because he'd have hated it. But in a peculiar way I find myself for the first time for nearly forty years without Ivor to go to with my troubles. Now and then, of course, I used to go to Ivor with my troubles—and found they were his troubles too."

And Fay Compton, that lovely woman and equally lovely actress said a great deal. That was perfectly true of Ivor. And he liked people to take their troubles to him, which is more amazing still. He adored Fay and she was leading lady in two of his plays; and both of them were very happy. In the broadcast Barry Jones mentioned to her that he had heard "We'll Gather Lilacs" being sung by German prisoners-of-war and that he had heard Ivor's music being whistled in San Francisco and Nantucket, and in Australia. And Fay remembered how she had heard a gondolier in Venice sing his own version of "We'll Gather Lilacs" too. Olwen Brookes, Peter Graves, John Palmer, Olive Gilbert, Barry Sinclair, Barbara McFadyean, Fabia Drake, Cicely Courtneidge, Roma Beaumont, Christopher Hassall, Phyllis Dare, Vanessa Lee and myself were others who paid tribute, and every word we said was from our hearts, sincere and true. The broadcast was produced by Douglas Moodie, Spike Hughes, and Audrey Cameron and was a piece of inspiration.

And now comes the hardest part of the writing of this book about Ivor. It is necessary for a man who writes a book about a personality to make some personal assessment. I maintain that this is not a biography; a biographer must have a much different approach than mine to this subject. What I have tried to do is to present the story of Ivor Novello from his youth to his untimely death, and to show what he did in that time and how he did it. It is, as my sub-title shows, a story of achievement, or at least I hope it will prove so. For Ivor did achieve so much, as much and maybe more than any of his fellows in his profession in that long and glorious story which is the history of our Theatre. He did not reach the greatest heights of immortal glory some attained, maybe, but for steady achievement in his own limitations he did as much. I shall be accused of repeating myself at times in this book. I want to say that I often do that on purpose because I know there is a habit amongst readers of "skipping." So whenever I have a fact which I want to drive home it is a habit of mine to mention it more than once. To those who have not skipped—if there are any such—I apologize. The others will not know.

The final biography of Ivor Novello will perhaps be written several years hence. It is not possible to get such a thing into focus when a man is so recently dead, when he still pervades the Theatre, when he still seems to be with us, and when we still expect—as I do often—to hear his voice calling on the 'phone, or to walk into what was his dressing-room and see him. It is only when a man's work has stood the test of time and that acid factor has shown what has endured that a true assessment or appraisement is possible. That time is not yet. But one can hazard a guess based upon one's knowledge of the Theatre, of human nature and of the man himself. So what I must do is a species of summing up of points and new angles still to be presented and let the reader have my own impression of Ivor, for what it is worth. I have called so many witnesses in this book to speak and so much that they have said coincides with my own views. Yet it is possible that I saw certain things others did not and that by the detachment from his private life, from his parties, from the constant visiting at the flat or to "Redroofs", may have a picture of the man which is not tinged with social polish.

The great thing about him, the big outstanding truth, which I have already said but say again, as that he had a dual personality composed of David Ivor Davies and Ivor Novello. It was David Ivor who was tough, who stood up to the world, who was shrewd in business and careful of money; it was he and not Ivor Novello who saved that £100,000 in Consols, who left that handsome fortune in the end. But it was largely Ivor Novello who earned it. The two were often inextricably mixed. Yet there were moments when David Ivor did more than peep out, but came into full view. He would do so when anything occurred which merited disapproval, or when decisions had to be made. It was David Ivor Davies who killed the germ of laziness which was there by overlaying it with achievement. And it was David Ivor Davies who came forward and served that grim term of imprisonment. Ivor Novello went to gaol but David Ivor Davies served the sentence. For in the identity whose name was annulled by deed poll, was the essence of that land of Wales which gave him birth, that sturdy independence, that retention of national characteristic and language and that hardiness of spirit drawn from the mountains. And I think, too, it was David Ivor Davies who really composed the music. Ivor Novello wrote the libretti, of that there is no doubt. And it was Ivor Novello and Ivor Novello only, that the public saw and loved. It was the driving force of David Ivor which sent Ivor Novello on that path through the Theatre which led him to the very top, a position he attained by his own unaided efforts, or by the efforts of the two of them put together. It was David Ivor who would go right to the point in one of those interminable discussions which arise in every production, and see clearly what must be done. And do it, come what may. I think it was Ivor Novello who was often so very obstinate, who would not listen to good counsel and who would, all too frequently, go off at a tangent and do just the thing which should not have been done.

You had to be a bit careful in giving Ivor advice. If you did not know the way, opposition was the surest way of making him do the very thing you were striving to prevent. He took quick decisions, he jumped his fences. The best way was—not to say flat out, " No, Ivor, don't do that," but to create a doubt in his mind, to make him uncertain. Then he would think and, if you have sown your seed properly in that mind, it would grow and he would be all right. Direct opposition was quite useless. Ivor Novello was a creature of impulses; they were good impulses, but often a good impulse leads to trouble. He found that out for himself in the one dark phase of his life. It was always difficult to get him to say "No." He would say it quickly enough to things of bad quality, indifferent value, to anything cheap, nasty or mean. But let sympathy be aroused, let there be a suggestion of undeserved bad luck, of pain and suffering and off he would go, no matter how clearly his friends and would-be advisers saw the folly of it. That was what got him into trouble. And having got himself into a mess by his own actions, it was very difficult to give him help. He would shut himself up within himself, he would not admit the error, he would tighten up and try his own way—and get further into the mire. That he also did in his trouble. He took no advice there until the awful revelation came to him.

But really his faults were very few. He would very often quite overlook the obvious thing to do in small matters and take no notice of what, had the affair been bigger, he would have seen quite clearly. He saw things his own way and seldom, if ever, through another person's eyes. Very largely he created his own world in which he lived. That was where he was so child-like, not childish be it understood, but child-like. He created a life around him which did not exist outside his own sphere but which he firmly believed as being the whole of existence. He did not peer below the surface; he did not ask what was the general opinion of anyone he met. He formed his own conclusions. If he liked them, it was enough. If he did not, that was enough also. That is why so often at certain times in his life he had hangers-on who were drawbacks. But in the end he would see. Something would be said or done which did not conform to his standard and then—that was the end. He had all the impulses of a child and all a child's gift of vivid imagination. He saw things as he wanted them to be far more often than as they actually were.

Yet—that was one of his great strengths. He was able to make that into the real illusion of the stage. He knew and he would maintain, as Tree had done before him, that the whole business of the stage was Illusion: that that was what it was for. He created his own visions into his musical plays and he let the people see, through his eyes, life as they would like it to be and not as it was. Not for him the greyness and sorrow of the world. That it was there, he knew, but he did not believe its right place was on the stage, in the Theatre. For the Theatre to him was Life where Life was lived as it should be. There he could be a god and create; there he would dash the sorry scheme of things to bits and remould it nearer heart's desire. And he could do that supremely well. . . .far better when aided by his music than when he wrote straight comedies. Let the cynics jeer, the sophisticated sniff. What did he care? He knew that myriads wanted to see the sort of life in which he believed, and in which they believed too, when he showed it to them. He knew that Romance is latent in almost every heart, only awaiting the touch which he could give to make it blossom into life. And he had the surest touch of that magic that was ever known. There have been many musical plays from many lands, but never such musical romances as those of Ivor Novello.

He kept a balance in them; he never used a low comedian. Whilst Minnie Rayner was alive, she had a comic part, but it was a naturally comic part. It was not put in just as comic relief. And the rest of the comedy Ivor supplied himself. He was careful about sentiment. He always sheered away from sentimentality, especially in love scenes. Those in his hands, became things of light comedy: flippant, amusing, joking, which he could play with just the right touch, for when depth was not required Ivor was a very good actor. And yet, with all their flippancy, which is perhaps not quite the right word, there was never any doubt as to the sincerity of the two people's feelings towards each other: most definitely they were in love. Scenes of this nature in *Glamorous Night*, in *Careless Rapture*, and in *Crest of the Wave* were little gems. And in *The Dancing Years*, which had much more sentiment than the others, it was not the brilliant young composer of the gay waltzes who endeared himself so much to the tempestuous " Marie Ziegler " as the gauche, rather awkward young man in the perfectly awful ready-made suit (with the tiny bit of handkerchief cut off from the tie) which really won her heart by awakening a desire to mother him. One was conscious of that always. But Ivor, in that play, as the ageing composer, fighting for freedom and for his music against the cruelty of the ruthless Nazi gave a splendid performance indeed. He was a very good character actor.

But his best performance was his last in *King's Rhapsody*. There he did not put a foot wrong and he gave himself almost the whole gamut of emotions. And he succeeded. For he was always sincere. Some people disliked the way in which he would twist a scene from sentiment, straight sentiment, to something they thought was far too off-hand. But what Ivor was doing was employing that rigid dramatic law of contrast. He knew just when to change a mood. . . . There was not much about the art of stage craft he did not know. And apart from that perpetual hankering after the great classic roles, which he could not have played—for he had not the variation or the depth of voice, art or character—he knew his limitations.

His music was essentially tuneful and melodious. He eschewed the modern idiom. Not that he disliked it, but it was not his. He believed in melody and he filled his life with it. His pet of all forms was gipsy music. How he adored a *czardas* in his shows, always doing his best to work one in. But the waltz was his especial joy, as also was the ballad. If his music had no great depth, it had swirl and movement, it had size, it could capture and it could enchant. It could touch the heart and it could stir. He was in his own music. It was happy music, even if it was in the minor key, which sounds a paradox. It never stopped down there for long for it would come bursting out with chords and cadences and great floods of melody which caught the heart and made it bound. He knew what the people of this land wanted in the way of music and he gave it to them. It was characteristic of him. Yet his best song, written in a plane as he flew the Atlantic to Jamaica, was called "Pray for Me." To my mind it was prophetic—and he knew it!

He was, I think, the most completely happy person I ever knew. Life had been good to him. He had made his life as he wanted it and he was able to live it that way without interruption. He could shut out the world of men and live the life of Ivor Novello. He created an atmosphere of beauty wherever he went, and he brought a smile with him and imprinted it on the faces of others. His enthusiasm was tremendous and almost impossible to resist. He adored giving help. He would often say to me " Such and such a play is not doing well—it is a shame, for it is a good play. Is there anything we can do to help them?" And he meant it. He had a genius for saying the right thing at the right moment to the right person, a quality which sprang from his complete and utter unselfconsciousness—the root, also, of that perfectly amazing charm which surrounded him like an aura. Many people can create something like charm and turn it on and off. Ivor's was part of himself, real and enduring.

I have sat with him in his dressing-room, in which as observant Barry Jones says, Ivor was most at home. I have seen him in all sorts of stages of dress and undress. I have seen him when the ravages of time were not obscured, though heaven knows Time treated him lightly, but when he was not in the ordinary way looking his best. I will not alarm his sincere fans by going deeper into the question. But never did he lose that charm, glamour—yes, he had that elusive thing so rare in a male, Glamour—or that complete beauty which made him so outstanding. That he succeeded as he did despite his tremendous physical beauty (it is the only word for it) is in itself a remarkable thing. There have been many extremely handsome men on the stage before and there will be again but in so many cases that beauty of appearance undid them, or it was blunted and dimmed by the passing years. Not so with Ivor. He triumphed over it and when he died at fifty-eight was handsomer and perhaps more attractive than ever. I have seen him with bad snuffling colds, with all sorts of drawbacks, but the charm and the glamour was always there because they were inherent.

He had great patience and, when he liked, great concentration. But he was not an erudite or well-read man. He read voraciously but he read novels, and I do not think he ever remembered what he read for any length of time. He knew little or nothing of the classics and quotations in his beloved crosswords nearly always bowled him over. But it did not matter. He was Ivor—the universal Ivor—and that was enough. What need had he for such things? He could create a new world and did so to the delight of thousands. It needed no classical knowledge to do that. There were no great depths to Ivor Novello. He found that out for himself as he attested in that document written in his cell. Yet he was in his own way a genius, and that very rare thing, a happy genius. Genius seldom confers that gift on its captives; but he conquered it and was happy. He was sufficient unto himself without any conceit, boast or pride. Pride—yes, he had that in his work and his achievement—but not in conceit. He was totally without " side " or swelled head; it never occurred to him that there was anything particularly clever in doing what he found he could do so well. It was a gift and he had it—so that was that: no occasion for waving flags. So many geniuses are dark and stormy. Ivor was not like that; but then his genius was not of the depths but of the light and on the surface, warm and shining. He adored light and he adored warmth. He did not need depth. He was like a fountain playing on a shallow pool. There is a little fountain in the Dutch Garden at Hampton Court which always reminds me of him. It plays perpetually and it sends out its fresh, cheery, gay music of splashing water; it reaches no height but it is like a silver flower amidst smooth green lawns and glowing beds of blossoms. Ivor was just like that—a fountain caught by the sun, his music warm and coloured as the flowers. The fountain playing always seemingly inexhaustible, and yet always right in the tune for its surroundings.

One of his greatest gifts was his truly astounding understanding of women, and of middle-aged women at that! It was almost uncanny. He wrote parts for them which were perfection. He knew how to treat them; he knew just what they would say; and he knew what they would like to hear in real life too. He not only did that himself but he always got it across the footlights. He was never selfish and he was quite without jealousy. He never, as do so many of his profession, exulted in the failures of others whilst professing to be sorry. He regretted failure. He was grateful of his own success; he never left that to chance; he never slacked off; he gave only the best and he took infinite pains.

Only once did I ever know him different. I had not seen him at a big first night and he was not playing at the time. Next day I met him and told him about the show. " I did not see you there, Ivor," I said. " No, duckie," he replied with one of those chuckles of his, " I'm going to-night—when they are all at their worst—and I'm going to catch them at it!" He did go and was unstinted in his applause and he sang the praises of that show in public places—and he meant it. But I thought I knew the reason for that second night visit. In fact I am sure I do. But that is another story. . . .

Another surprising thing about this model of handsomeness, this perfect profile was that he was as popular with men as with women. That is most unusual. But it was so with him.

His great secret was his understanding and his humanity. He was never out of touch with those people he had to amuse. He never lost them for a moment. He never got above himself. He never worried about social eminence. He was what he was and it was good enough for him. He could establish a contact with the humblest members of his immense following which was intimate and understanding. They felt he was one of themselves, and he felt it too. He was always in the audience himself—when he was on the stage—and he was always working with them not against them. He never got off-hand or careless. The best was only good enough for them, and for him.

That was what I admired most in him—that sense of Quality, only the best being good enough. That is the right way to live in the Theatre, the only way to really succeed.

He was everybody's friend and nobody's enemy. It was real joy to be with him. It does not seem possible to me now that I shall not wait for him in a dressing-room again, see him come quickly through the door with the entourage like a wake behind him, hear him say, " Popie " in that caressing voice, often accompanied by a hug and to feel that of all the people in the world I was the one he most wanted to see. He didn't, of course, but that was the impression. I liked to make him laugh, to hear that chuckle, to see that face wrinkle up and to see that direct gaze when he was really interested. Mine is and always has been a hard, harassing life, but he brought much pleasure into it. I knew him and he knew that I knew. Neither of us ever pretended, not that he ever did. He had a real sense of humour and he could laugh at himself. He loved a joke and he loved laughter. But his sense of humour never betrayed him into hurting people, as is so very often the case. His wit was a brand of his own, never trenchant, never acid or biting but often very much to the point. I have spoken of his gratitude. I do so again. It was so very real in his world of Illusion. He was grateful every time he succeeded. He never took it for granted that he would do so. Success so often breeds arrogance. That was not his case, there was not a particle of arrogance in him: he saw it in others and he loathed it. Nor was he bitter. Not even his imprisonment made him that, to outward appearances, although I am sure he had bitter thoughts about it in his heart. Coming when it did, it robbed him of the outward and visible honour which he surely could not have escaped. But what would have been the use of a title to him? Nobody would ever have called him " Sir Ivor ": he would have been Ivor to us, all the same. I think his friends resented his loss of it more than he.

I should like to put on record the extreme difficulty I find in making any sort of appraisement. I do not want to seem like a fan and I ask to be believed when I say that what I put down about him here is my actual belief. I have nothing to gain by doing otherwise. And even if I had, I should still write what I think. But I will aver, with all force possible, this thing: I have known, worked with and dealt with all the great people of my profession for the last half century (and that includes those ageing even at that time—a wonderful cavalcade of celebrity) but amongst them all there was never anybody like Ivor Novello. He was something unique, I cannot make comparisons. I can just say: he was Ivor doing things his way—complete in himself.

Who is to say what of him and his work will remain? The time for that to be judged is not yet. I was his critic as well as his friend and the man who told the world about him. I knew (as well as he did), what he could and could not do. And sometimes I really think I was able to help.

I have worked with him in big productions. I never saw him really tired or wilting. At the dress rehearsal of *King's Rhapsody* in Manchester when the heat was tropical and when the stage hands were lying exhausted out in the yard by the stage door, Ivor was as fresh and enthusiastic as a daisy. This was his life; this was what he enjoyed and he would not have missed a moment of it. He was oblivious of all else. But he sent those " boys " (stage hands, even if seventy, are always " boys ") out a drink. . . .

If one tries to assess him, it must be this: he was complete in himself. His plays were never so good when he was not in them. He was seldom so good in other people's plays as in his own (*The Happy Hypocrite* was the exception, but, he made it his own as actor-manager). Very few of his comedies will endure for long. Very few of his musical plays will live long, as such. Some of his music will do so: it will go into the national repertoire as companion to that of Sidney Jones, Paul Rubens, Leslie Stuart, Lionel Monckton, Edward German and Sullivan. His "Keep the Home Fires Burning" will be a classic British song, remembered for what it did in war. His sense of humour enabled him to burlesque his own work too—his own " We'll Gather Lilacs " and even " Keep the Homes Fires " in *Gay's the Word*. I do not think " Lilacs " will live as long as " Keep the Home Fires." I may be wrong but that is my impression; it is not so vital or exciting. "Rose of England" may last longer than "Lilacs." But Ivor's real greatness lay not in any one thing but in the Theatre itself: his complete mastery of it and his supreme ability to construct a complete show—words, music and acting. That he could do as nobody has done before him, and it remains to be seen who will do it after. He was The Theatre, and he could give the Theatre real Theatre, total and complete.

Will he himself be remembered? Yes, he will. But it will not be for any individual thing: it will not be for his acting, his authorship or even for his great gift of melody. He will be remembered because of what he did at Drury Lane and because he really formed an epoch of his own, an epoch of truly British shows when they were most needed, shows which stood up to and beat those flowing in from overseas. His place in the history of Drury Lane, in that heroic freize of great ones, is secure. He will be remembered as some are remembered, for the result of what they did, rather than how they did it. He created an epoch in his own sphere. Details will not matter: he will be a name which will last. Just as George Edwardes lives on in name though many people forget what he did and cherish only a connection of his with already departed playhouses like Daly's and the Gaiety, and as the memory of Cochran may be remembered for showmanship supreme, so they will remember Ivor Novello who was in himself an epoch of our Theatre. He will live on that way: he will become a Legend—the Novello legend—and in many ways indeed, that was what he was—a legendary figure in a world of legend, which he made himself by a whole lifetime of Achievement.

CHAPTER THIRTY

EXIT

AFTER weeks of grey skies and almost unceasing, pitiless downpour, the sun shone. There was a cold, blusterous wind from the east, a March wind which had swept the skies clear of cloud and left them high, blue and distant. It seemed as though spring, which had appeared unresponsive to its seasonal call, had suddenly stirred and was awakening. . . .

Outside the red-brick crematorium stood a crowd waiting. It was a truly British crowd and, as women predominated, it was used to waiting and did so patiently. Every moment brought fresh arrivals, every moment swelled the throng around the building and added to the line on either side of the approach route, a line three deep of waiting people, stretching farther than the eye could see, stretching, indeed, for some miles.

There were smart women in fur coats but they were in the minority. Most of this audience were middle-class and working-class people, just ordinary people, the ordinary women of London, of Britain, who were the true audience of the man to whom they had come to say good-bye. Most of them carried shopping baskets and bundles, most of them were in workaday clothes; but many of them carried little bunches of flowers in their hands, some even sprays of lilac, which must have made a hole in modest household budgets. But they had been bought willingly, and even lovingly, just in case—just in case there was a chance to lay them somewhere as a tribute to him who had given them such joy and pleasure.

It was perhaps the greatest tribute of all. Here was not a smart sophisticated West End gathering, though that type was represented and there were many waiting cars. No, here was that gathering of English, of British, ordinary folk who worked, who suffered, who carried on—the people who had braved the Blitz, fought two World Wars, who now faced hardship and poverty as they had faced death, the people to whom the man they mourned had opened the doors of a different life, had given them glimpses of that world they liked to see but could never enter, had cheered them and stirred them with his gift of music and song, had coloured their grey lives with his mastery of make-believe, and had given them, for a brief hour or two, the thing in which he himself so deeply and sincerely believed—Romance. This was the audience for whom he wrote his plays: the majority of the inhabitants of this island, not the exclusive few. For his appeal was to them; and he himself was of them and never forgot it. No glitter of success and riches had ever come between them and cut him off from the people from whom he had sprung and with whom he remained.

There was, of course, a little pushing, a little turmoil, but very little. Policemen, with that invariable patience which is part of the Force, told them to stand back, to keep the roadway clear. They would retreat an inch only to surge forward again. And many had little children with them, not brought to see a sight, a funeral, but there because the mother had nobody to whom she could entrust them whilst she came to bid adieu to the man who had given her the gold of another world.

There was one overpowering feeling, as one observed that crowd—a feeling of friendliness. These good people had not come to see the end of a great actor, composer or man of affairs. They had come to take farewell of a friend. That was how they all felt of the man who all of them called Ivor, never Novello.

And now the privileged few, his colleagues of the stage, his nearest and oldest friends began to arrive. Necks craned, there were rushes forward, there were mutters of names, cameras clicked, newsreels turned. Reporters scribbled names in notebooks, asked for details, how to spell this or that name for in the main the people sent on these occasions are unused to such gatherings, not familiar with the people they see. But the more experienced of them helped the others and the man who was in charge of that department gave lists, reeled off names, aided and assisted, answered questions four at a time. He was used to such affairs, but what struck him most was that on this occasion there was no desire for personal publicity at all, only once did he notice someone anxious to obtain it, who was not of the "Profession."

There was a greater urgency in the crowd now that the time was approaching. There was a stir, a noise, a surge and the roadway was blocked. Police pushed the front ranks back, dislodged those who had crowded into the doorway of the chapel. For a moment there was a swirl and there might have been a rush . . . but stealing over that spring air and mingling with the sunshine came the first notes of an organ. . . .

From inside that chapel the organ played and over the relaying loudspeaker the sound came to the ears of that crowd which was becoming restive and a little turbulent, over the spring air came the music of the man who was about to make his exit—the music of Ivor Novello.

And the crowd was still. It stood and listened as one by one the melodies once more exerted their magic and their sway. . . .

The great ones were arriving; Anna Neagle and Herbert Wilcox, Jack Buchanan, Vera Pearce, Leslie Henson, Irene Browne, Lea Seidl, Barry Sinclair, and his wife Nicolette Roeg (Old Novellians both), Lee Ephraim, Collie Knox (an old friend indeed), Christopher Hassall, who wrote magic words to that magic music, Sir Edward Marsh, a very dear and near friend, one of the oldest of them all, Alan Melville, Clement Butson, R. E. Gray of Theatre Royal, Drury Lane, representing the place of Ivor's triumphs and its chief, Prince Littler, Lizbeth Webb and Beryl Harrison, Emile Littler, Thorley Walters, Cicely Courtneidge herself and Jack Hulbert (*Gay's the Word* come to the last scene), Ethel Revnell, Mario from the Caprice (where Ivor loved so much to lunch, and an old friend of the Ivy days when Ivor sat at that table facing the door and who saw to it that the small but critical appetite was properly satisfied), Ralph Reader, W. A. Sutton, men and women from his shows, Dunstan Hart, Fred Hearne, chorus girls and boys, small parts and principals, and Lord Beaverbrook to represent the powers of the Press. Only a handful of those who wished to be there but the place was small and accommodation limited. In the gallery now and not in the stalls were the critics, the columnists, the men and women of the Press, with some of the profession amongst them too, Vivian Ellis from the sick bed, a brother composer and sincere admirer of the man who had gone. They had come to watch the man they had seen so often take his final curtain and to send the news of it all over the world. And still the music went on, Ivor's tunes, Mam's tunes, listened to by that enthralled mass of thousands of people who were now still, reverent and waiting.

A stir at the end—a mobile policeman on a motor bicycle—it was coming, he was coming, and the music of " We'll Gather Lilacs " swelled out. And then, slowly turning the corner and with cautious approach because of the dense mass of people, Ivor Novello appeared before his last audience, the biggest by far he had ever appeared before at one time. Under a great cross of white lilac he lay, with the cluster of red roses placed thereon, and a tiny bunch of violets in vivid contrast. In a coffin of lilac hue he passed before them . . . he passed the door and through the waiting aisles of humanity . . . he passed out of view again. After him came his Rolls, the car he loved, that black car with his initials I.N. in red, driven by the faithful Morgan, so long his chauffeur, and in the cars following were Olive Gilbert, Phyllis Monkman, Tom Arnold, Peter Graves, Fred W. Allen, Mrs. Edith Ellis (who looked after the flat, and the staff from " Redroofs " : John Crawford (butler), Tom Almond (chef), Mrs. Mabel Almond and Abel Street (gardener). Bill Wright, his dresser valet, William Newman (stage director) and Victor Mellanie (stage director of *King's Rhapsody*) helped as sidesmen. In the reserved seats were Mr. and Mrs. R. C. Macpherson, first cousins of Ivor Novello and the Misses Dadds, cousins also, his nearest relatives. There were other relations and friends from Cardiff. The Earl and Countess of Cromer were prevented from attendance by absence from this country or they would have been there.

The doors of the chapel were shut and inside the people waited, just as the crowd waited outside. They gazed on great bunches of white lilac flanking the altar and there was white lilac, too, along that little track which was to bear all that remained of Ivor Novello into the flames of eternity. A great bank of white lilac screened the chief mourners—it was white lilac everywhere to guide him home.

The chapel lights went up, but their glow was dimmed as the great door beside the altar opened and, as the last notes of " We'll Gather Lilacs " swelled out, he entered his last scene borne upon men's shoulders and was laid on that last little path which his mortal remains would travel, that handsome face still, those dark eyes closed and veiled, that slim, graceful, energetic body immovable for ever. . . .

The chief mourners filed to their places, the clergyman from Wales who was to speak the words of farewell over this great son of Wales, rose in his simple black gown and there was a silence of immortality over all.

But that door by the altar remained open and, as if in a frame, there stood still more of his last audience who had, so many of them, followed him all his life and now followed to his end. As far as one could see, there stretched that still, silent crowd of people with trees as their background in the distance. Small though the chapel was, this gesture, this open door allowed so many to actually see and hear and even more to feel close participation. And still the sun shone from that high Heaven of pale blue and there was the glitter of spring, of that Hope in which he who was leaving had always believed. The voice of the clergyman went out over the loudspeakers and those friends outside heard it all as Ivor would have wished. He who refused nothing, he who belonged to them, shared this last scene with them as with his nearest and dearest. Beauty, the thing he loved, was all around and shared by all. He passed in Beauty . . .

That song which had brought him fame had gone full circle. That message of Hope in " Keep the Home Fires Burning " had come true for him. . . . The sun had shone for Ivor, the dark clouds had turned themselves inside out, the silver lining showed, and the boy who had put the music to those words—Ivor—had gone home. . . .

INDEX OF NAMES

A

ABBOT, WILLIAM, 151
Abingdon, William, 240, 319, 334, 353, 358, 364
Addinsell, Richard, 356, 402, 404
Ainley, Henry, 77, 134, 202, 214, 281
Albanesi, Meggi, 284
Albery, Sir Bronson, 141, 276
Alexander, Sir George, 59, 78, 134, 140, 200, 208, 281, 468, 469
Allen, Adrienne, 117
  Frederick, W., 36, 56, 62, 63, 64, 141, 142-143, 204, 230, 231, 232, 238, 246, 247, 257-258, 259, 278, 287-289, 291, 293, 301, 357, 361, 364, 395, 423, 429, 441, 467, 472, 482-483, 490, 506, 531
  Hilary, 464
Almond, Mabel, 456, 531
  Tom, 456, 457, 531
Ambient, Mark, 136
Anderson, Percy, 138
Andrews, Maidie, 266, 300, 352, 364, 368, 406, 463, 478
  Robert ("Bobbie"), 117, 143, 153, 155-156, 162, 193, 213, 232, 264, 286, 301, 306, 307, 352, 378, 385, 410, 423, 455, 462, 463, 472, 481, 482, 487, 489, 490, 491, 492
Arlen, Michael, 213
Arne, Dr., 177
Arnold, Tom, 211, 237, 341, 371-372, 374, 375-377, 378, 379, 386, 392, 393, 396, 403, 405, 406, 409, 418, 420, 421, 423, 428, 431, 445, 446, 462, 464, 466, 471, 472, 478, 487, 489, 490, 491, 493, 501, 504, 516-517, 531
Arthur, Paul, 180
Arthurs, George, 144
Asche, Oscar, 80, 137-139
Ascherberg, Hopwood and Crew, Messrs., 95, 150, 151, 152, 289
Ashman, Ellen, 258
Ashton, Harry, 372
Ashwell, Lena, 59, 100
Asquith, Mrs. H. (Lady Oxford), 239
Austin, Alfred, 135
Ayer, Nat, D., 136
Aynesworth, Allan, 134

B

BACON, MAI, 68
Baddeley, Hermione, 214,
  Robert, 399
Baird, Ethel, 145, 213
Balcon, Michael, 219, 220
Balfe, Michael William, 175, 176, 177
Bankhead, Tallulah, 213
Banks, Leslie, 162
Bannerman, Margaret, 143
Barbour, Joyce, 129
Barnes, Winifred, 136, 144
Barnum, Phineas Taylor, 25
Barrett, Wilson, 208
Barrie, Sir James, 135
Barron, Muriel, 395, 451, 462, 463, 464
Barry, Joan, 215, 297
Barrymore, John, 213
Bascomb, A. W., 212
Bateman, Jessie, 204
Bates, Thorpe, 136, 160, 213
Batley, Dorothy, 187, 198
Battle, Carlos de, 167
Baxter, Beverley, 482
Bayley, Hilda, 175

Bayliss, Lilian, 107, 113
Beard, Seymour, 215
Beaumont, Hugh, 302, 303
  Roma, 44, 376, 377, 384, 385, 387, 388, 395, 402, 404, 449, 451, 463, 517
Beaverbrook, Lord, 482, 530
Beerbohm, Sir Max, 354, 355-356, 400, 401
Benham, Joan, 462
Benjamin, M. E., 275, 286-287
Benrimo, 165-166, 167
Benson, Sir Frank, 80, 137, 339
Berlin, Irving, 168
Bernhardt, Sarah, 134, 317
Berry, W. H., 75, 77, 125, 136, 157, 158-160, 213, 504
Bert, Hal, 145
Besier, Rudolf, 280
Best, Edna, 17, 44, 213, 214, 258, 306, 344
Betterton, Thomas, 78, 208
Blackden, Seton, 167
Blake, Wilson, 226
Blanche, Marie, 214
Bloom, Leslie, 185, 465
Blow, Sydney, 180
Boggetti, Victor, 187-188, 198, 268, 324, 464
Boosey's, Messrs., 95
  William, 157
Boote, Rosie, 68
Booth, H. S. J., 151
Bottome, Phyllis, 76
Boucicault, Dion, 134, 140
  Nina, 226
Bourchier, Arthur, 78, 134, 140, 205
Boxall, E., 320
Boyd, Dorothy, 297, 299
Braddell, Maurice, 198
Brady, Veronica, 300
Braham, Philip, 135, 139, 214
Braithwaite, Lilian, 16, 44, 86, 87, 117, 205, 244, 268, 272, 275, 276, 279, 286, 298, 351, 352, 373, 374, 514
Brandon-Thomas, Jevon, 167
Brayton, Lily, 80, 138, 139
Brewer, Sir Herbert, 40
Bridie, James, 280
Brighouse, Harold, 134
Broadbridge, Dollie, 501
Brookes, Olwen, 517
Brough, Jean Webster, 82, 175, 187, 194, 195, 198, 235-237, 397
Brown, Charles, 75, 225
  Louise, 306
  Marjorie, 356
Browne, Irene, 213, 299, 530
  W. Graham, 213, 244, 275-278
Browning, Robert, 360
Brummel, Beau, 125
Brunel, Adrian, 219
Bryant, J. V., 139
Bryen, Alderman T. F., 55
Buchanan, Jack, 160, 213, 530
Budd, Bill, 391
Bunn, Alfred, 176
Bunyan, John, 508
Burbage, Richard, 453
Burbidge, Douglas, 221
Burke, Billie, 17, 44, 71, 250, 251, 283
Burnaby, Davy, 129
Burrell, Ena, 368, 465
Bush, Douglas, 372
Butson, Clement, 530
Butt, Sir Alfred, 55, 131, 135, 140, 157, 215, 242
  Clara, 31, 39, 60
Byng, Douglas, 214, 216
Byrne, Cecily, 214, 374

C

CAHN-REIN, LESLIE, 102, 104, 105, 107, 109
Calthrop, Gladys, 404
Calvé, Emma, 60
Cameron, Audrey, 517
Campbell, J. L., 161
  Mrs. Patrick, 59, 78, 134, 268, 273, 373
Cannon, Esma, 462
Carey, Joyce, 306
Carl, Joseph, 385
Carney, George, 214

Carpenter, Constance, 258
Freddie, 385
Carroll, Lewis, 404
Carton, Sidney, 430
Caruso, Enrico, 60
Carver, Cherry, 162
Casalis, Jeanne (Jeanne de Casalis), 162, 164
Casson, Sir Lewis, 214, 378, 427, 429
Cavell, 333
Cecil, Sylvia, 464
Chaliapine, Feodor, 78
Chantry, Miss, 143, 204
Chapman, Hester, 465
Chappells, Messrs., 461
Charles, Guy, 226
Charlot, André, 131, 132, 140, 145, 160, 181
Chatterton, Ruth, 44, 262
Thomas, 346
Chekhov, Anton, 212
Cheshire, Harold, 297, 299
Chesney, Arthur, 181
Chevalier, Albert, 208
Chopin, Frederic, 35
Cibber, Colley, 335
Claire, Ina, 77
Clarence, O. B., 214
Clark, A. Gilbert, 400
Holman, 284
Clarke-Smith, D. A., 204
Clarkson, Joan, 204
Clifford, Miss, 48
Cochran, Sir Charles B., 135, 205, 210-211, 214, 229, 282, 317, 394, 527
Cochrane, Frank, 139, 352
Cohan, George, M., 144
Colbourne, Maurice, 324, 339, 354, 402, 512, 513
Collier, Constance, 17, 59, 71, 85-86, 117, 137, 175, 176, 181-186, 187, 188, 192, 193, 194, 195, 202, 203, 204, 213, 216, 218, 241, 242, 243, 250, 455, 496-497, 514
Collins, Arthur, 128, 140
José, 136, 146, 181, 213
Collyer, Beatrice, 186
Comber, Bobbie, 160, 214
Compton, Fay, 17, 44, 78, 117, 134, 139, 213, 221, 222, 255, 256, 297, 306, 517
Conrad, Conn, 212
Constable, Dora Grace (Grace Walton), 411-416, 420-422, 428
Cooper, Gladys, 17, 82, 117, 135, 139, 140, 175, 179, 180, 181, 193, 202, 203, 207, 214, 283, 467
Coulouris, George, 228
Courtneidge, Cicely, 24, 25, 44, 78, 136, 139, 213, 253, 254, 255, 310, 477, 478, 485, 504, 517, 530
Robert, 59
Coward, Noël, 117, 136, 140, 145, 164, 206-209, 211, 213, 214, 219, 223, 225, 226, 229-230, 243, 250, 264, 280-281, 306, 309, 455, 497
Coyne, Joe, 75, 77, 131, 132, 134, 144, 215
Crawford, Joan, 256, 269, 455
John, 260, 456, 531
Crisham, Walter, 18, 361, 366, 368, 369
Crocker, Henry, 297
Croft, Anne, 136
Cromer, Earl of, 341-342, 496, 531
Crossley, Ada, 70
Cruikshank, A. Stewart, 301-302
Stewart, Jnr., 302
Cummings, Peggy, 404
Currie, Finlay, 368, 391
Curzon, Frank, 59, 140, 179, 180, 201, 202, 203, 204, 205, 236
George, 214, 226
Cutts, Graham, 217

D

DADDS, MISSES, 531
Daly, Blyth, 228
Dana, Henry, 137, 138, 139

Dance, Sir George, 74-76, 128-129, 139, 141, 151, 164, 188, 189-190, 224, 226
Dane, Clemence (Winifred Ashton), 117, 122, 177, 354, 356, 400, 404
Danvers, Billy, 135, 214
Dare, Phyllis, 14, 16, 68, 392, 406, 472, 475, 504, 517
Zena, 14, 16, 44, 117, 269, 297-298, 299, 306, 361, 364, 366, 392, 404, 463, 472, 473, 475, 504, 514
Darewski, Herman, 139
Max, 213
Daubeny, Peter, 465
Davies, Clara Novello ("Mam"), 29, 31, 32, 33, 34, 36, 39-40, 41-42, 44-45, 46-47, 48, 51, 52, 54, 56, 62-63, 64, 65, 72, 76, 77, 79, 81, 83-86, 93-94, 95, 96, 105, 123, 141, 142, 143, 146, 147, 153, 155, 215, 220, 246-248, 257-258, 261, 286-194, 325, 330, 334, 335, 342, 367, 397-398, 403-404, 440, 460, 501, 505, 510 512, 514, 530
David (Ivor's father), 29, 42, 51, 81, 82-83, 95, 96, 123, 152, 153, 215, 259-260, 361, 397
Lilian, 214, 258
Rev. Meredith, 432, 435, 436, 437, 438, 439, 443, 453-454
Davis, Joan, 361
Day, Albert, 499
Edith, 215
Frances, 306
Mabel, 499
Dean, Basil, 122, 205, 220, 225, 226, 227, 228, 229, 377
De Bear, Archie, 214
Debenham, Cicely, 136, 160
De Courville, Albert, 135, 141, 214
De Frece, Lauri, 136
De Haes, Marcel, 160
D'Elaine, Cathryn, 162
Delany, Edward, 476
Delysia, Alice, 136, 214
Dempster, Carol, 178
Denis, Ernan Forbes, 76, 453
Dent, Alan, 176, 465
De Renzie, Leonard, 266, 319, 334, 391
De Reszke, Eduard, 56, 60
Desborough, Philip, 515
Deslys, Gaby, 125, 144
Dibdin, Charles, 177
Dickson, Dorothy, 18, 44, 117, 299, 300, 360, 362, 363, 364, 365, 366, 368, 369, 374, 377, 393, 399, 402, 465
Dietrich, Marlene, 367
Doble, Frances, 204, 228, 229
Drake, Fabia, 374, 517
Drayton, Alfred, 111
Duff, Lady Juliet, 431, 487, 509
Dukes, Ashley, 280
Du Maurier, Sir Gerald, 135, 140, 168, 203, 205, 208, 213, 242, 244, 251
Dunn, Leon, 506
Dupres, Paddy, 213
Duttson, Gordon, 464, 490

E

EADIE, DENNIS, 135, 140
Earle, Eileen, 180
Ediss, Connie, 59, 104
Edwardes, George, 25, 59, 60, 64-65, 66, 67, 75, 124, 125, 136, 157, 208, 210, 478, 527
Egan, Michael, 305
Elen, Gus, 208
Elgar, Sir Edward, 60, 93, 381, 516
Elliott, Gertrude, 213
Madge, 68, 258
Ellis, Anthony, 221
Edith, 531
Mary, 44, 153, 306, 317-318, 324, 325, 326, 327, 328, 332, 334-335, 337, 344, 349, 352, 377, 383, 384, 385, 387, 388, 394-395, 402-409, 516
Vivian, 68, 306, 530
Elliston, Daisy, 180

Elsie, Lily, 16, 44, 59, 64, 68, 75, 116, 117, 155, 238-241, 242, 244 245, 382, 455
Elton, George, 361-362
Emerald, Connie, 181
Emery, Winifred, 59
Emney, Joan, 145
England, Paul, 181
Ephraim, Lee, 530
Epstein, Jacob, 455
Esmond, H. V., 134
Evans, Rev, E. Gwyn, 30
(Ifan), William, 30
Evelyn, Fay, 153, 155
Evett, Robert, 136, 138, 141

F

FABER, LESLIE, 213
Fair, Adrah, 144
Fairbanks, Douglas (Jnr.), 256
Fairbrother, Sydney, 159
Farebrother, Violet, 221
Farjeon, J. Jefferson, 214
Farren, Fred, 186
Nellie, 68
Fauré, Gabriel, 322
Fearon, Jose, 214
Feldman, Bert, 92
Ferne, Fred, 372
Ferrers, Helen, 228
Feuvre, Guy le, 144, 145
Ffrangcon-Davies, Gwen, 212, 258, 378, 513
Field, Miss, 320
Fields, Gracie, 97, 309
Johnny, 144
Finck, Herman, 136, 139
Flagstadt, Kirsten, 23, 44
Flecker, James Elroy, 382
Floyd, Gwen, 117, 286
Fontanne, Lynn, 44
Foote, Samuel, 351
Forbes-Robertson, Jean, 213, 256, 351
Sir Johnston, 78, 281, 510
Ford, Lena Guilbert, 94, 95, 97, 98
Forwood, Anthony, 465
Foster, Frances, 501
Foyle, Christina, 68
Francis, Kay, 258
Frank, Julian, 196, 200, 204
Fraser, Alec, 213
Frederick, Pauline, 185
Freeman, Stella, 221
Friedlander, William B., 212
Frohman, Charles, 59, 141, 208, 225
Fry, Horace, 158

G

GABAIN, MARGERY, 228
Galli-Curci, Amelita, 52
Galsworthy, John, 214
Garbo, Greta, 22, 23, 44, 258-259, 457
Gardiner, Reginald, 204
Garrard, Gene, 214
Garrick, David, 179, 208, 330, 335, 346, 391
Doris, 228
Gattis, the, 141
Gaunt, William, 157-158
Gay, Gordon, 235
Maisie, 136
Gaynor, Gladys, 162
Geraldo, 395
German, Sir Edward, 516, 526
Gershwin, George, 215
Gielgud, John, 306, 322
Gilbert, Jean, 214
Olive, 35, 44, 117, 171, 233, 266, 324, 361, 362, 363, 364, 366, 368, 393, 395, 423, 438, 451, 453, 455, 462, 463, 472, 474, 475, 481, 482, 483, 484, 487, 489, 490, 491, 492, 514, 516-517
W. S., 269
Gill, Tom, 487
Glenville, Shaun, 136, 356
Godbold, Mrs., 503
Gomez, Arturo, 228
Gordon, Gavin, 356
John, 232
Gore, Walter, 204

Goring, Marius, 354
Goulding, Edmund, 258
Gounod, Charles, François, 54
Grace, Kathleen, 198
Grande, Joe, 129
Granville-Barker, Harley, 162
Gratton, Harry, 145
  Tiny, 145
Graves, George, 136
  Peter, 117, 260, 324, 361, 368, 369, 385, 391, 400, 406, 423, 453, 461, 465, 493, 517, 531
Gray, R. E., 242, 353, 399-400, 530
Greene, Evie, 385
Greet, Ben, 80
Grey, Clifford, 158
  Sylvia, 68
Griffith, D. W., 177, 178-179, 511-512
Grossmith, George (Jnr.), 59, 104, 124, 125, 127-129, 131, 141, 168, 215
  Weedon, 124
Groves, Fred, 286
Guitry, Sasha, 162
Gunning, Misses, 224
Guthrie, Tyrone, 281-283
Gwenn, Edmund, 135, 213

H

HACKETT, WALTER, 139, 249, 280, 284, 306
Haddon, Peter, 213
Hale, Binnie, 126, 136, 181, 215, 356
  Robert, 134
  Sonnie, 212
Hamilton, Hale, 78
  Henry, 368
Hammerstein, Oscar (II), 223, 310
Handl, Irene, 465
Hannen, Nicholas, 214
Harben, Hubert, 352
Harbord, Carl, 354
Harding, Lyn, 13-14, 30-31, 214, 324, 329, 338-339
Hardwicke, Clarice, 215
Hardy, Thomas, 212
Hare, Sir John, 59, 140
  Robertson, 111
Harris, E. Vincent, 143
  Gus, 346
Harrison, Beryl, 221, 530
  Frederic, 141
  Kathleen, 374
Harriss, R., 498
Hart, Dunstan, 385, 464, 530
Harvey, Sir John Martin, 80, 120, 121, 134, 140, 168, 205, 208, 468
  Muriel Martin, 120
Harwood, H. M., 161
Hassall, Christopher, 117, 272, 322-323, 325-326, 337, 352-353, 368, 376, 380-385, 387, 457-461, 472, 517, 530
  John, 368
Hawkins, Jack, 300
Hawthorne, David, 228
Hawtrey, Charles, 59, 78, 134, 140, 203, 283-284
Hay, Joan, 144
Haydn, Joseph, 54
Hazelton, George, 165
Hearn, Lew, 229
Hearne, Fred, 530
  Richard, 68, 391
Heatherley, Clifford, 324, 368, 369, 370
Hector, Frank, 129
Henson, Gladys, 117
  Leslie, 68, 103, 128, 129, 215, 268, 530
  Medora, 54
Herbert, A. P., 306
Heslop, Charles, 356
Hestor, George, 160
Hewlett, Maurice, 356, 501
Hichens, Robert, 156
Hicks, Seymour, 59, 70, 75, 136, 140, 168, 205, 303, 306, 405
Higson, Nell, 495
Hilliard, Stafford, 162, 164, 354
Hitchcock, Alfred, 219
  Raymond, 137
Hoare, C. Douglas, 180
Hoey, Iris, 78

Hollingshead, John, 208
Homfrey, Gladys, 129
Hope, Anthony, 62
Horniman, Miss, 80
Howell, John, 162, 164
Hubay, Jeno, 54
Hughes, Spike, 517
Hulbert, Jack, 135, 136, 139, 213, 253, 310, 478, 530
Hume, Benita, 207, 245, 268
Humphries, John, 135
Hunt, Martita, 286
Hunter, Ian, 214
Huntley, G. P., 136
  J. C., 77
Hurgon, Austen, 144
Huxley, Aldous, 49

I

IBBETSON, PETER, 250
Ifan, William, *see under* Evans
Inverni, Ethel, 54
Irving, Ethel, 78
  Sir Henry, 59, 106, 134, 468
  Laurence, 106

J

JACOB, NAOMI, 120, 480
Jacobson, Hilda, 68
James, Julia, 129
Janis, Elsie, 253-255
  Mother, 254-255
Jeans, Isabel, 187, 198, 217, 282, 283, 351, 352, 354
  Ronald, 160
Jefferies, Douglas, 221
Jeffreys, Ellis, 59, 110, 214, 243, 244, 250, 279, 286, 497
Jerrold, Mary, 465
Joel, Jack, 333, 340, 343-350, 352, 353, 367
Johns, Mervyn, 374
Johnson, Mr., 350
Johnstone, Alick, 319
Jones, Barry, 339, 374, 401, 402, 512-515, 517, 523
  Hannah, 198
  Henry Arthur, 272
  Sidney, 136, 139, 526
  Trefor, 324, 326
June, 212

K

KEAN, EDMUND, 120, 179, 208, 335, 346, 480
Keen, Malcolm, 214
Kelly, Sir Gerald, 68
  Renee, 135
Kemble, 208
Kendal, Dame Madge, 273
Kendall, Henry, 106, 107, 108-110, 111, 112, 117, 216, 267
  William, 221
Kennedy, Margaret, 220
Kent, Keneth, 107, 117, 295, 297, 298, 440, 441, 509-511
Kern, Jerome, 129, 136, 139, 310
Kerr, Fred, 284
King, Ada, 228
Kinkee, F. R., 54
Kirby, John, 214
Knox, Collie, 393, 530
Komisarjevsky, Theodore, 212, 221
Kosminski, Jessie, 54
Kubelik, Jan, 60
Kyd, Thomas, 427
Kynaston, Edward, 36

L

LAMBERT, LAWSON, 191
Lane, Grace, 339, 513
Lang, Matheson, 78, 80, 137, 140, 168, 175, 205, 208, 281
Lantz, Robert, 465
Lauder, Sir Harry, 54, 131, 135
Laughton, Charles, 221, 222
Laurier, Jay, 213
Laurillard, Edward, 125-128, 129, 131, 141, 144
Lawrence, Gertrude, 160, 213
Laye, Evelyn, 213

Lee, Vanessa, 376, 466-467, 472, 474, 475, 480, 517
Lehar, Franz, 213, 381
Lehmann, Beatrix, 213
Leigh, Gracie, 215
  Vivien, 354, 356, 466
Leister, Frederick, 213
Lennox, Vera, 145
Leonard, Augustus, 135
Leone, Henri, 129
Leotard, 96
Leslie, Sylvia, 160
Lessing, Madge, 134
Lester, Mark, 136
"L'Estrange, David," 187, 196, 204
L'Estrange, Julian, 187
Levergne, Antonin, 167
Leveson, Frank, 232
Levey, Thel, 134
Levy, Jose, G., 144
Lewis, Rev. H. T., 503
  Henry, 54
Lillie, Beatrice, 44, 117, 145, 213, 258, 455, 481
Lindo, Olga, 214
Lindsay, James, 187, 189, 198
Linnit and Dunfee, 377
Lion, Leon M., 136, 214
Liszt, Franz, 54
Littler, Emile, 530
  Prince, 302, 341, 530
Lloyd, Doris, 167
"Lloydy," *see under* Williams, Lloyd
Lohr, Marie, 17, 135, 139, 368
Lonsdale, Frederick, 136, 213, 214
Loraine, Robert, 162, 164
  Violet, 135, 395
Lorne, Marion, 284
Lovat, Nancy, 160
Lowe, Edmund, 257
Lowndes, Mrs. Belloc, 284
Lukas, Paul, 258
Lungo, Tony de, 228
Lunn, Kirkby, 60
Lupino, Stanley, 144, 145, 181
Lurgan, Lord, 326, 344
Lyle, Lyston, 134
Lynn, Olga, 56
  Ralph, 111, 213

M

McBEAN, ANGUS, 354, 370
McCormack, John, 54
McCrory, Suzanne, 32-33, 39
Macdonald, Murray, 374, 472
McFadyean, Barbara, 517
McGocklin, Barton, 54
Mackay, Barrie, 174
  Leonard, 144
McKinnel, Norman, 213
Macleod, Angus, 154
Macpherson, Mr. and Mrs. R. C., 531
Macready, William Charles, 208, 346
Macqueen-Pope, Moya, 367
Maitland, Lena, 297
Malone, J. A. E., 75, 147
"Mam," *see under* Davies, Clara Novello
Mannock, P. L., 211
March, Ethel, 54
Margetson, Arthur, 213, 226
Mariani, Mario, 228
Mario, 399, 530
Marlowe, Christopher, 427
Mars, Marjorie, 204, 221
Marsh, Sir Edward, 107, 109, 115, 116-117, 121, 123, 142, 143, 181, 187, 196, 264, 382, 423, 427, 441, 453, 459, 463, 465, 509, 530
  Mae, 178, 217
Marshall, Herbert, 258
Massine, Léonide, 214
Mather, Aubrey, 228
Matthews, A. E., 135, 212
Maturin, Eric, 213
Maude, Cyril, 17, 59, 78, 140, 400, 468, 469
Maugham, Somerset, 134, 214, 280, 465
Mayer, Daniel, 56, 141, 154, 156
  Rudolph, 141
Megone, Norfolk, 54
Meikle, John B., 502
Melandrinos, Andrea, 297
Melba, Nellie, 60

Mellanie, Victor, 531
Melnotte, Violet, 140, 222-224, 225, 227, 229
Melville, Alan, 477, 478, 481, 483, 487, 530
Mercanton, Louis, 156, 174
Merica, Harley, 162
Merriman, Seton, 62
Merson, Billy, 215
Mervyn, Edward, 162
Messel, Oliver, 318, 321
Meyer, Bertie A., 255
Michael, Ralph, 374
Michaelis, Robert, 160
Millar, Gertie (Countess of Dudley) 17, 59, 64, 68, 75, 77, 104, 124, 129, 136, 139
Miller, Gilbert, 141, 202, 203
  Ruby, 68, 135, 139
Mills, Henry, 52
  John, 306
  Watkin, 54
Milward, Dawson, 213
Minster, Jack, 464
Mitton, Whitworth, 54
Molnar, Ferenc, 221
Monckton, Lionel, 139, 385
Monkman, Phyllis, 44, 117, 135, 140, 204, 235, 299, 300, 465, 481, 484, 526, 531
Montgomery, Robert, 257
Moodie, Douglas, 517
Moore, Eva, 201
  Hilda, 213
  Mary, 59
  Murray, 144
Morgan, Arthur, 37, 121, 192-193, 413, 456, 531
Morley, Malcolm, 165, 166, 167
Morton, Charles, 27, 97
  Leon, 136
Moss, Stafford, 144
Moule, Ruby, *see under* Lee, Vanessa
Mundin, Herbert, 160, 213
Munns, Freddy, 319
Murray, D. L., 474
  Mrs., 291
Mussière, Lucien, 144
Myrio, 214

N

NAINBY, FRANK, 129
Nares, Owen, 168, 200, 213, 235, 258, 271, 284, 512
Nattova, 214
Neagle, Anna, 530
Neilson, Julia, 17, 59, 80, 140, 156, 157, 205
Neilson-Terry, Phyllis, 156, 308
Nelson, Billy, 356
Nesbitt, Cathleen, 214, 465
  Tom, 284
Newman, William, 392-393, 407, 431, 531
  Winnie, 38, 395
Newton, Pauline, 226
Nichol-Mirriam, Lt.-Col., 103
Nicols, Anthony, 385
Noble, Peter, 174, 207, 242, 294
Norfolk, Edgar, 374
Norman, Norman V., 214
Norton, Frederic, 138, 139
Novarro, Ramon, 178

O

O'BRIEN, BARRY, 239, 255, 377
O'Casey, Sean, 214
Odlum, Drelincourt, 180
Oldham, Derek, 215
Olivier, Laurence, 214
O'Neill, Colette, 162
O'Neill, Peggy, 213
Owen, F. V., 198

P

PACHMANN, VLADIMIR, 60
Paderewski, Ignace, 60
Page, Philip, 446, 452
Palmer, John, 477, 517
Palotta, Grace, 68
Parker, John, 306
Parsons, Alan, 113-114
Patti, Adelina, 39
Pawley, Nancy, 187, 198
Pawson, Hargrave, 297

Payne, Adney, 377
  Edmund, 59, 77, 104
  Walter, 377
Pearce, Vera, 530
Pearson, Lloyd, 266
Peel, Eileen, 286
Phelps, Norman G., 504
Picard, André, 180
Picasso, Pablo, 121
Pinero, Sir Arthur, 208, 279
Plançon, Pol, 60
Playfair, Nigel, 214
Pokorney, Leo de, 465
Polini, Marie (Mrs. Owen Nares), 284
Pollock, Elizabeth, 160
Porter, Cole, 168
Poulton, A. G., 144
Pounds, Courtice, 139
  Lorna and Toots, 215
Powell, Dilys, 40-41
  Sullivan, 190
Prentice, Charles, 324, 368, 386
Priestley, J. B., 280, 305, 309

R

RAINE, JACK, 180
Rains, Claude, 222
Raleigh, Cecil, 368
Rattigan, Terence, 280
Rawlins, W. H., 136
Ray, Gabrielle, 135
Rayner, Minnie, 45, 213, 245, 266, 273, 275, 276, 277, 279, 286, 324, 327, 361, 368, 385, 411, 521
Rea, Alec L., 205
Reader, Ralph, 97-98, 320, 370, 469, 470, 471, 495, 530
Redstone, Willy, 135, 139
Reed, Mrs., 504
Reinhardt, Max 319
Rejane, 174
Relph, George, 77, 226
Revnell, Ethel, 530
Reynolds, Tom, 126-127, 134
Ridgeway, Philip, 212, 221, 222
Ridley, Arnold, 213
Riego, Teresa del, 515
Ripley, Valerie L., 498, 507
Riscoe, Arthur, 306
Ritchard, Cyril, 68, 258, 406
Roberts, Dr., 47, 49
  Evelyn, 204
  Ralph, 129
Robeson, Paul, 213
Robey, George, 55, 135, 214, 395
Robson, Mary, 144
Rodgers, Richard, 168, 223
Roeg, Nicolette, 481, 530
Ronald, Sir Landon, 60
Rose, Richard, 300-301
Ross, Herbert, 160
Rowe, Frances, 461
Rubens, Paul, 136, 139, 385, 526
Rumford, Kennerly, 31
Rutherford, Margaret, 404-405, 462, 463

S

SACKS, J. L., 131-132, 135, 141
Sagan, Leontine, 319, 320-321, 331, 361, 368, 385, 388-389, 406
St. John, Christopher, 167
  Dorothy, 198
Samson, Ivan, 214, 361
Sands, Martin, 286
Santley, Maud, 54
Saunders, Madge, 129
Scott, W. J., 75
Sealby, Mabel, 136, 213
Secretan, Mrs., 467
Seidl, Lea, 530
Servais, Yvan, 144
Seymour, Madeline, 180, 214
Shakespeare, William, 208, 214, 281, 317, 342, 344, 346, 360, 377, 378, 379, 382, 427, 494
Shaw, G. Bernard, 206, 280, 298, 461
  Glen Byam, 204
  Sebastian, 268, 300
Shearer, Norma, 44, 262
Shepherd, Firth, 268
Sherbrooke, Michael, 162

Sheridan, Richard Brinsley, 208, 209, 241, 368
Sherwood, Robert E., 339, 513
Shillingford, Osmond, 221
Sibley, Dr. Churchill, 54
Siddons, Mrs. Sarah, 208, 346
Sieveking, Margot, 297
Simpson, Fraser, 136, 139
Sinclair, Barry, 117, 258, 410, 452, 466, 481, 483, 517, 530
  Edward, 465
Sitgreaves, Beverly, 162
Slater, George, 75
Smith, C. Aubrey, 136, 175, 205
  Dodie, 274, 280, 294, 306, 309
Snell, Madge, 297
Sokolova, Lydia, 18, 369
Soutar, Joe Farrers, 68
  Robert, 68
Spencer, Helen, 226
Squire, Ronald, 213, 214
Starr, Frank, 489
Stewart, Athole, 268, 279, 286, 297
Stockfield, Betty, 213
Stoll, Sir Oswald, 141
Strauss, Oscar, 213
Street, Abel, 531
Stuart, Leslie, 526
Sullivan, Sir Arthur, 54, 516, 526
Sutton, William Anthony, 98, 241, 320, 321, 330, 334, 340, 367, 370, 391, 469, 470, 495, 511, 530
Swaffer, Hannen, 89, 177, 211, 225, 254, 508, 511-512
Swete, Lyall, 214
Swinburne, Mercia, 129
  Nora, 214
Swinstead, Joan, 268, 300
Sydney, Ethel, 68

T

TALBOT, HOWARD, 136, 139, 157
Tashman, Lilyan, 257, 258
Tate, James, 136, 139, 249
Tauber, Richard, 307, 381, 466
Taylor, Bill, 372, 473
  Nellie, 136
Tearle, Godfrey, 205, 213
Tempest, Marie, 17, 59, 78, 203, 205, 213, 272-275, 276, 277, 278, 279, 306, 411, 499
Tennent, H. M., 297, 302-304, 307, 309, 310-315, 316, 319, 326, 328, 340, 344, 349, 352, 353, 367, 377
Terriss, Ellaline, 68, 405
Terry, Ellen, 59, 175
  Fred, 80, 140, 156, 205, 208
  Marion, 134
Tettrazini, Luisa, 60
Thalberg, Irving, 262
Thatcher, Heather, 44, 117, 215, 351, 352
Thomas, Jameson, 129
  Jane, 31
Thomson, Fred, 157, 160
Thorndike, Dame Sybil, 107-108, 206, 214, 404, 427, 429
Thorpe, Courtney, 213
Tich, Little, 135
Titheradge, Dion, 160, 181
  Madge, 17, 160, 161, 162, 164, 205, 213, 226, 276, 286
Toller, Rosalie, 79
Tomlin, Blanche, 134
Travers, Ben, 110-111, 213, 280, 349
Tree, Sir Herbert Beerbohm, 17, 59, 77, 85, 107, 113, 137, 138, 208, 281, 319, 355, 468
  Viola, 17, 44, 107-108, 113, 114, 115, 116, 117, 248, 250, 264, 241, 242, 244, 354, 381
Treloar, Sir William, 54
Tresmand, Ivy, 214
Trevelyan, Hilda, 135
Trevor, Austin, 213
  Spencer, 213
Trix, Helen, 160
Turner, Anna, 465
Tushingham, Ellen, 33-34, 36, 37 39
Twyford, J. H., 162

V

VACHELL, H. A., 134

Valentino, Rudolph, 178
Vanbrugh, Irene, 59, 134, 140, 205, 278-279
  Violet, 59, 205
Vane, Sybil, 95, 96, 506
Vanne, Marda, 214, 226, 258
Vaughan, Elizabeth, 228
  T. B., 179-180, 201-202
Vedrenne, J. E., 140
Venne, Lottie, 134
Vieu, Jane, 144

W

WADSWORTH, HILTON, 102
Wagner, Richard, 54, 60
Wakefield, Douglas, 356
Wallace, Edgar, 262-264, 377
  Nellie, 214
Waller, Lewis, 54, 59, 140, 168, 208, 271, 378, 468
Wallis, Bertram, 135
Walls, Tom, 75, 111, 134, 136, 213, 249
Walpole, Sir Hugh, 261
Walsh, Sheila, 137
Walters, Thorley, 478, 530
Walton, Grace, *see under* Constable, Dora Grace
Waring, Dorothy, 135
Watson, Henrietta, 226
  Margaret, 228, 297
Weaver, Wyn, 144
Webb, Alan, 374
  Lizbeth, 478, 530
  S. F., 353
Webster, Ben, 221
Weguelin, Thomas, 162, 164
Welch, Elizabeth, 324
  James, 77
Welchman, Harry, 78
Wells, Nancy, 500, 507
Wenman, Henry, 180
Weyman, Stanley, 62
White, Madge, 135
  Pearl, 214
Whitman, Walt, 385
Whitty, Dame May, 214, 262
Wilcox, Herbert, 530
Williams, Emlyn, 280
  Harcourt, 406
  Hugh, 167
  Lloyd ("Lloydy"), 36, 87, 117, 146-147, 171, 172, 178, 254, 297, 301, 324, 325, 330, 366, 381, 387, 395, 410, 423, 455, 464 467, 506
Wilson, W. Cronin, 198
Winn, Godfrey, 368
Winston, Bruce, 162, 164
Wodehouse, P. G., 160
Wontner, Arthur, 136, 214
Woodings, Pat, 297
Woods, Tom, 226
"Woody," 333
Wrather, Edgar, 361
Wray, T. C., 190
Wright, Bill, 37, 330, 445, 472, 474, 481, 483, 484, 487, 488, 490, 531
  Haidee, 214
Wyatt, Frank (Snr.), 224
  Frank, 224
Wylie, Julian, 212, 249, 307-308, 315, 316
Wyndham, Howard, 141
  Lady (Mary Moore), 141
  Sir Charles, 59, 140, 208, 468
Wynne, Wish, 77
Wynyard, Diana, 306, 462

Y

YORKE, ROBERT, 135
Youmans, Vincent, 215

INDEX OF PLAYS, FILMS AND SONGS

A

ALICE IN WONDERLAND, 404-405
Anatomist, The, 281
"Annie Laurie," 102
Antony and Cleopatra, 85
Arcadians, The, 74
Arc de Triomphe, 24, 61, 406-410, 431, 475
Argentine Widow, The, 239
Arlette, 131, 132, 144, 145
Autumn Crocus, 294
A to Z, 160

B

BALL AT THE SAVOY, 343, 345
Bamboula, The, 213
Banana Ridge, 111
Barrier, The, 78
Barton Mystery, The, 134
Basker, The, 134
Beauty Spot, The, 131
Beggars on Horseback, 212
Bella Donna, 134
Best of Luck, The, 134
Better Days, 212
Betty in Mayfair, 213
Bing Boys, The, 103, 123, 135, 139, 395
Birth of a Nation, The, 177
Bittersweet, 208, 280
Blue Kitten, The, 213
Bohemian Girl, The, 175, 176, 177
Bonnie Prince Charlie, 181, 185
Boodle, 213
Boomerang, 134, 135
Bow Bells, 322
Breakaway, 461
Bric-à-Brac, 135
Brief Encounter, 209
Business with America, 286
But the Flesh is Weak, 257
By the Way, 213

C

CARELESS RAPTURE, 24, 147, 269, 345, 353, 357-359, 360-368, 380, 383, 387, 391, 399, 470, 495, 521
Carnival, 157, 175
Caroline, 134
Carousel, 223
Cavalcade, 208, 280, 281, 309
Charles the King, 354, 356, 402
Charlot's Review, 213
Cherry Orchard, The 221
Children in Uniform, 319
Chu Chin Chow, 137-139, 140, 148, 352, 395, 410
Cinderella, 315
Cinderella Man, The, 284
" Clear the Road to Glory," 461
Cleopatra, 213
Clo-Clo, 213
Clowns in Clover, 253, 310
" Cobbler's Song," 352
Colonel Newcombe, 85
Comedienne, 86, 372, 373, 374
Come Over Here, 80
Constant Nymph, The, 206, 219, 220
Conversation Piece, 306, 309
Country Girl, The, 65
Crest of the Wave, 17, 24, 293, 345 368-376, 381, 383, 387, 391, 398, 400, 402, 411, 470, 521
Cuckoo in the Nest, The, 213

D

DADDY LONG LEGS, 134, 135, 141

LL

Daisy, The, 221
Dancing Mothers, 213
Dancing Years, The, 24, 61, 174, 176, 245, 266, 345, 375, 376, 377, 380, 382, 383-390, 392, 393, 396, 402-403, 407, 410, 412, 424, 427, 431, 440, 441, 442, 449, 452, 462, 466, 470, 471, 472, 479, 481, 499, 521
"Dartmoor Days," 160
Daughter of the Bear, The, 174
"Dear Eyes that Shine," 160
Dear Octopus, 274
Deburau, 162-163, 166
Disraeli, 135
Doctor's Dilemma, The, 298
Dollar Princess, The, 59
Dominant Sex, The, 305
Double Harness, 317
Down Hill, 202, 203, 204, 218, 219, 221, 232, 497
Durant and Durant, *see under* Theodore and Co.

E

EASY VIRTUE, 277
Eden End, 305
Emperor Jones, The, 213
Enter Kiki, 179-181, 185, 201, 283
Eternal City, The, 85
Ever Open Door, The, 78

F

FALLEN ANGELS, 213
Family Affairs, 305
Fickle Jade, The, 71, 72, 90
Firebrand, The, 202, 203, 221, 235, 236-237
Fishpingle, 134
Flies in the Sun, 283, 284, 296, 302
Flying Colours, 135
"Fold Your Wings," 325
Follow the Girls, 134
Frasquita, 213
Fresh Fields, 24, 269, 270, 272, 276, 278-280, 282, 283, 285, 286, 297, 298, 302, 400, 485
Full House, 268, 351-352, 392

G

GALLANT HUSSAR, THE, 220, 235
Gang Show, 320
Gate Crasher, The, 235
Gay's the Word, 24, 60, 136, 253, 280, 385, 477-479, 483, 484, 486, 504, 505, 526, 530
General John Regand, 78
Get Rich Quick Wallingford, 78
Ghost Train, 213
Girl from Ciro's, The, 134
Girl from Utah, The, 77
Girl on the Film, The, 78
Glamorous Night, 24, 61, 88, 144, 176, 296, 313, 315, 316, 320, Ch. XVIII, 343-354, 357, 358, 360, 361, 362, 366, 383, 385, 386, 394, 395, 402, 460, 469-470, 471, 475, 513, 514, 521
"God Save the King," 102
Going Up, 131, 132
Golden Moth, The, 157, 158, 160
Golden Toy, The, 305
Gondoliers, The, 224
Government Inspector, The, 221-222
Great Adventure, The, 77
Great Ruby, The, 364
Greeks Had a Word for It, The, 306
Green Hat, The, 213
Grounds for Divorce, 213

H

HAMLET, 78, 134, 213, 273, 306, 453
Hansel and Gretel, 506
Happy Day, The, 136
Happy Hypocrite, The, 354-356, 358, 378, 380, 400, 401, 402, 405, 494, 512, 515, 526
Hard Boiled Herman, 215
Harlequinade, 137
Hay Fever, 213, 277
Headmaster, The, 78
Henry V, 40, 134, 171, 356, 377-379, 385, 400, 412
Henry VIII, 214

Her Husband's Wife, 134
High Jinks, 136
His Home in Order, 279
Hobson's Choice, 134
Home Chat, 226-227, 229
Hope, The, 188, 366
Houpla, 136
House of Peril, The, 284
House that Jack Built, The, 253, 255
Hullo America! 135
Hullo Tango, 78
Hyde Park Corner, 306

I

" I CAN GIVE YOU THE STARLIGHT," 382, 387
" If You Were the Only Girl in the World," 135, 395
I Lived with You, 265-266, 267, 269, 271, 272, 277, 282, 294, 392, 393
Intolerance, 178
Iris, 201, 203, 221, 283
Ivan the Terrible, 78

J

JACK AND THE BEANSTALK, 356
Jill Darling, 306
Joseph and His Brethren, 77
Josephine, 317
Juno and the Paycock, 214

K

KATJA THE DANCER, 214
" Keep the Home Fires Burning," 26, 94-99, 100, 102, 103, 105, 108, 116, 123, 146, 147, 148, 149, 150, 152, 157, 159, 249, 393, 461, 463, 479, 498, 503, 506, 507, 526, 532
Keep the Home Fires Burning (Sheila Walsh), 137
King's Rhapsody, 16, 23, 24, 36, 60, 61, 118, 171, 173, 188, 200, 237, 241, 252, 269, 295, 296, 324, 382, 390, 407, 457, 460, 461, 472-476, 479, 480, 483-485, 510, 521, 526, 531
Kiss for Cinderella, A, 135
Kitty Mackay, 134
Knave and Queen, 317

L

LA BOHÈME, 104
" Laddie in Khaki, The," 99
Ladies into Action, 393
" Land of Hope and Glory," 93
" Land of Might Have Been, The," 181
Land of Smiles, The, 307
Last of Mrs. Cheyney, The, 213
Les Cathedrales, 134
Libel, 306
Light Blues, The, 136
Lilac Domino, The, 131
Liliom, 221, 222, 223, 229
Lily of the Valley, 479-480
Lionel and Clarissa, 214
" Little Damosel, The," 52
Living Dangerously, 306
Lodge, The, 294
Lodger, The, 219
London Calling, 206
London Review, The, 214
Love from a Stranger, 462
Lovers Courageous, 257
Lucky Break, 306

M

MACBETH, 137
Madame X, 185
Maid of the Mountains, The, 136-137, 145
Maitlands, The, 306
Man and Superman, 461
Man Without Desire, The, 178, 181
Marquise, The, 250

Marriage Market, The, 77
Marriages of Mayfair, The, 338
Mary Goes First, 78
Mary Read, 306
Mavouneen, 116
" Mayor of Perpignan, The," 407
Men in White, 306
Mercenary Mary, 212
Merrie England, 306
Merry Widow, The, 59, 136, 238
Merry Wives of Windsor, The, 85
Miarka, 157, 174
Milestones, 512
Misleading Lady, The, 135
Moon and Sixpence, The, 214
" Moon is on the Water, The," 150
Moon on the Yellow River, The, 306
Mr. George, 283
Mr. Manhattan, 137
Mr. Tod's Experiment, 284
Mr. Whittington, 306
Mr. Wu, 137
Murder in Mayfair, 301, 304, 306, 307, 321, 322
" Music in May," 366
Music in the Air, 306, 317
" My Dearest Dear," 382
My Lady Frayle, 136
" My Little Canoe," 251

N

NERO, 85
No. 17, 214
No, No, Nanette, 215

O

" O, FOR THE WINGS OF A DOVE," 51
" Oh Clementine," 369
" Oh God Our Help in Ages Past," 70
Oh I Say, 77
Oklahoma, 23, 215
Old Chelsea, 466
Old Heidelberg, 200-201, 221, 296
Once a Lady, 262, 294
One Night in Rome, 228
On Monday Next, 267
On With the Show, 214
Ordeal, 214
Orphans of the Storm, 178
Our Betters, 190, 191, 192 465
Our Nell, 181

P

PANTOMIME REHEARSAL, A, 267
" Paris Reminds Me of You," 406
Party, 265, 267, 268, 269, 270, 277, 373
Passing Show, The, 135
Pearl Girl, The, 78
Peg O' My Heart, 134
Pell Mell, 135
Perchance to Dream, 24, 35, 171, 251, 360, 458, 460, 462-467, 471, 479
Potash and Perlmutter, 128, 135
" Pray for Me," 522
" Primrose," 385
Proscenium, 81, 296-298, 299, 301, 302, 307
Punch Bowl, The, 214
Puppets, 181
Pygmalion and Galatea, 171

Q

QUEEN'S HUSBAND, THE, 339, 513
Queer Cattle, 317

R

RAFFLES, 190
Rain, 214
Rat, The, 86, 178, 185-195, 197-199, 200, 202, 203, 204, 217, 219, 223, 231, 238, 267, 320, 497, 500
Razzle Dazzle, 135
Return of the Rat, The, 220, 235

Reunion in Vienna, 306
Richard III, 120, 319
Rise and Shine, 357, 358, 360
Romeo and Juliet, 255, 281, 322, 344-346, 347
Rose Marie, 215, 309, 326
" Rose of England," 371, 381, 527

S

ST. HELENA, 511
St. Joan, 206
School for Scandal, The, 41
School Girl, The, 251
Sealed Orders, 78
Second Helping, 393
Second Mrs. Tanqueray, The, 78
See-Saw, 131, 135, 136, 143
Seventy Years of Song, 394
Shanghai, 131
" Shine Through My Dreams," 325-326, 381
Shining Hour, The, 306
Show, The, 214
Show Shop, The, 135
Sirocco, 223, 225, 227-230
Sky High, 214
Sleeping Car, 294
"Some Day My Heart Will Awake," 382, 472, 474
Son and Heir, The, 78
Southern Maid, The, 145
South Sea Bubble, The, 220, 235
Spanish Lovers, 167, 168, 179, 195
Sporting Love, 306
Spring Chicken, The, 113
Spring Cleaning, 214
" Spring of the Year," 51
Still Dancing, 214
Strange Interlude, 317
Streamline, 306
Strife, 78
Student Prince, The, 200
Sun Never Sets, The, 377, 400
Sunshine Sisters, The, 298, 299-300, 302, 465
Suzette, 144
Sweet Aloes, 306
Symphony in Two Flats, A, 245, 247, 248, 250, 251, 255, 256, 294, 512

T

TABS, 132, 145
Take a Chance, 321
Taken by Storm. *See under* Truth Game, The
Taming of the Shrew, The, 281, 282
" Tan Faced Prairie Boy, The," 385
" Tatters," 32-33
Tell Me More, 215
Tempest, The, 113
Tess of the D'Urbervilles, 212
Theatre Royal, 306
Theodore and Co. (Durant and Durant), 103, 104, 123, 129, 133, 139, 143, 152
Three Cheers, 135
"Three Hundred and Sixty-Five Days," 129
Three Sisters, The, 221, 307, 308, 310, 343, 345
" Till the Boys Come Home," 150, *See also under* " Keep the Home Fires Burning"
" Tipperary," 92
To-night's the Night, 103, 128, 129
Touch Wood, 306
Trelawney of the Wells, 267
Triumph of the Rat, The, 219
Truth Game, The (Taken by Storm) 238, 239, 241, 242-244, 246, 250, 251, 252, 256, 257, 275, 279, 497
Twelfth Night, 85, 107

U

ULYSSES, 85
Under Cover, 143

V

VANITY FAIR, 135
Vintage Wine, 306
Vortex, The, 206, 209

W

" WAIT FOR ME," 363
" Waltz of My Heart," 387, 402
Way Down East, 178
" We'll Gather Lilacs," 462, 463, 464, 479, 517, 526, 527, 531
" We'll Remember," 393
We Proudly Present, 465
" We're One Big Family," 368
" When the Great Day Comes," 99
Whip, The, 60, 188, 189
White Rose, The, 178, 181
Who's Hooper? 157
Who's the Lady? 78
" Who Were You with Last Night," 92
" Why Is It Ever Good-bye?" 366
Widow's Might, The, 110
Wild Violets, 343, 345
Willow Tree, The, 165
" Winnie Get Off the Colonel's Knee," 364
Winter's Tale, The, 282
Within the Law, 77

Y

YELLOW JACKET, THE, 78, 165, 166, 167, 168
Yes, Madam, 306